Sex and Gender

Sex and Gender

The Human Experience

James A. Doyle
Roane State Community College

wcb
Wm. C. Brown Publishers
Dubuque, Iowa

BOOK TEAM
James M. McNeil *Editor*
Sandra E. Schmidt *Assistant Editor*
Vickie Blosch *Production Editor*
Lisa Bogle *Designer*
Vicki Krug *Permissions Editor*
Shirley M. Charley *Photo Research Editor*

Wm. C. Brown *Chairman of the Board*
Mark C. Falb *President and Chief Executive Officer*

wcb

WM. C. BROWN PUBLISHERS, COLLEGE DIVISION
Lawrence E. Cremer *President*
James L. Romig *Vice-President, Product Development*
David A. Corona *Vice-President, Production and Design*
E. F. Jogerst *Vice-President, Cost Analyst*
Bob McLaughlin *National Sales Manager*
Marcia H. Stout *Marketing Manager*
Craig S. Marty *Director of Marketing Research*
Eugenia M. Collins *Production Editorial Manager*
Marilyn A. Phelps *Manager of Design*
Mary M. Heller *Photo Research Manager*

Cover image by Henri Matisse (detail). © Philadelphia
Museum of Art: purchased: John D. McIlhenny Fund.
Photo Credits—2.1: © Rose Skytta/Jeroboam, Inc.; 3.1: © Tim Jewett/EKM-Nepenthe; 4.1: © Tony
Esparza/CBS and Orion TV Productions, Inc. 1984; 4.2: © Donald Smetzer/Click, Chicago;
5.1: © Kent Reno/Jeroboam, Inc.; 7.1: © Emilio A. Mercado/Jeroboam, Inc.; 8.1: © David S. Strickler;
9.1: © AP/Wide World Photos; 9.2: top © AP/Wide World Photos, bottom © George T. Kruse/
Jeroboam, Inc.; 10.1: © Tom Ballard/EKM-Nepenthe; 13.1: © Bob Eckert/EKM-Nepenthe

Library of Congress Catalog Card Number: 84–72167

ISBN 0-697-00304-3

Printed in the United States of America
10 9 8 7 6 5 4 3 2 1

For Nan, the one person who is always there with total encouragement and
sage advice. The one who has taught me a most valuable lesson:
Life is not to be lived in solitary pursuit nor selfish endeavor.
This is your work as well as mine.

CONTENTS

3
THE PSYCHOLOGICAL PERSPECTIVE 51

8

EDUCATION AND WORK 201   NO 8

11
MENTAL HEALTH AND GENDER 298

12
SOCIAL MOVEMENTS AND GENDER   320

13
THE FUTURE OF SEX AND GENDER   352

PREFACE

Over breakfast, a few years ago, an editor-turned-friend asked "why not?" Why not describe the human experience in its full context—what it means to be born and labeled either female or male and live out one's life in so-called manly or womanly ways? At the time it presented a heady challenge, but I agreed to do it, and the project begun over eggs and coffee on a summer morning in Iowa is now complete. A few words, however, seem appropriate here to give the reader a sense of what goals guided this project since its inception and of how I tried to achieve them.

Overall, *Sex and Gender: The Human Experience* attempts to present a current, research-based, and comprehensive view of sex and gender. In addition, I have felt quite strongly for some time that an unbiased view of sex and gender was needed. Often I have been offended by texts that reflected their authors' biases too strongly. I've tried, and I believe I've been successful at, presenting many different views on sex and gender in a fairly unbiased way, letting readers draw their own conclusions.

I have also been disappointed with texts that rarely mention issues of concern to males or that have a single chapter dealing with "men's issues." I know quite well the argument that males have had more than their share of attention over the centuries and that it's the females' turn now. But one cannot grasp the whole idea of the human experience, especially in terms of the impact of one's sex and gender, by focusing only on one half of the human equation. To understand sex and gender, I believe both females and males must be considered; therefore, I've tried to present a balanced view by focusing on issues relevant to females and males alike.

Thus, my goals in writing *Sex and Gender: The Human Experience* have been to strive for a comprehensive and balanced, research-oriented text on both men and women. But how did I go about accomplishing these goals?

First, the topics dealing with sex and gender were broken down into manageable parts. Part I, "Perspectives," begins with the "overview" chapter that examines several general concerns. For example, we deal with the confusion between the terms sex and gender, the illusion of scientific objectivity, and the infusion of androcentric biases in studies of sex and gender (chapter 1). Then we move on to the "heart" of the perspectives section with a wide-ranging discussion of the various academic fields that have contributed to a better understanding of sex and gender. Chapters 2 through 5 cover the biological, the psychological, the sociological, and the anthropological perspectives. For each discipline, we examine the traditional theories and research and explore current findings, issues, and controversies.

Part II, "Issues," turns our attention to several social institutions that play a central role in any discussion of sex and gender. We begin by examining the issue of interpersonal power and the ways that different power bases affect male and female relationships (chapter 6). Although not normally thought of as an issue related to social institutions, I believe interpersonal power is basic to any discussion of social processes. Chapters 7 through 10 focus on those social institutions that have historically had the greatest impact on females and males in our society: language, educational and work settings, religion and politics, and the family. This section concludes by examining several gender-related issues that concern mental health professionals (chapter 11).

The last two chapters comprise part III, "Changes." This section begins with a discussion of the women's movement, continues with the emergent men's movement, and ends with the gay rights movement (chapter 12). Finally, we examine three topics that I believe will have an impact on the future lives of all of us: society's preference for male children and the medical technology used to determine a fetus's sex; androgyny and gender role transcendence; and the gender differences found in research on moral questions (chapter 13).

Sex and Gender: The Human Experience deals with the traditional topics one expects in any text on sex and gender, but it also examines several others not likely to be found in other texts. A sampling will serve to alert the reader to these more specialized topics: the on-going debate over sociobiology; the multicomponent approach to gender stereotypes; alternative gender role theories (i.e., Constantinople's and Pleck's work); the debate over comparable worth or pay equity; women's involvement in and treatment by formalized religion; eating disorders (i.e., anorexia nervosa and bulimia); the differences between analogue versus field studies of gender bias in therapy; consciousness-raising groups for men; institutional barriers to women in education, work, and politics; a historical analysis of both the women's and men's movements; and the gender differences in moral dilemmas.

Sex and Gender: The Human Experience covers a wide spectrum of issues and topics. However, some areas proved too specialized for an indepth analysis, such as the problems faced by minority women and men, women and men of lower socioeconomic status, and gay men and women. These special groups do not receive extensive treatment here because, while many of the general issues covered (e.g., sexism, interpersonal power, language, education, etc.) affect these groups as well, to focus on the specialized concerns of race, sexual life-styles, and socioeconomic status would have taken us too far afield from the topics of sex and gender. Further, these topics deserve more than a cursory examination. Still, minority women and men, gay people, and people living in lower socioeconomic groups are directly affected by the fact that they are labeled as either male or female at birth and are raised according to their society's prescriptions for both genders.

Several other features found in *Sex and Gender: The Human Experience* are worth noting. As most readers are aware, several topics have become rather controversial within the field of sex and gender. The Point/Counterpoint sections at the end of chapters 2–13 present two sides of a topical, current issue. The double standard of sexual behavior, women's supposed lack of mathematical ability, the evidence or lack of evidence for an ancient matriarchal social order, the advisability of male therapists for female clients, and the call for a "second stage" of the women's movement are just a few of the topics covered in these end-of-chapter sections. The purpose of these sections is to elicit the reader's critical thinking and to stimulate discussion of these issues.

Also, each chapter ends with a reading that provides an additional source for generating classroom discussions. Written by others, the readings present interesting and informative essays that relate to and supplement the chapter's material. Their inclusion may replace the need for supplemental readers for a course in sex and gender.

Each chapter also contains an end-of-chapter summary, a list of suggested readings, and boxes within the chapter that will stimulate the reader's involvement with the material.

Instructors who use *Sex and Gender: The Human Experience* for their classes may also wish to order the accompanying *Instructor's Manual* prepared by the author. Each chapter in the manual contains both multiple-choice and essay questions, as well as classroom discussions and activities composed of topical issues and/or exercises that can be used to generate classroom discussions. The manual also contains a list of current films on sex and gender that are suitable for use in the class.

Acknowledgments

No book dealing with the wide variety of research, topics, and issues covered in *Sex and Gender: The Human Experience* could be the sole production of the one individual whose name appears on the cover. The input of several talented and knowledgeable scholars proved immensely helpful in keeping me faithful to what the literature reported. For this service, I owe a special debt of gratitude to: Julia A. Ericksen, Temple University; Jane C. Hood, University of Wisconsin at Milwaukee; Arnold S. Kahn, American Psychological Association and Iowa State University; Letitia Anne Peplau, University of California at Los Angeles; Peter J. Stein, William Paterson College; Beverly Rankin-Ullock, Auburn University at Montgomery; Rhoda Kesler Unger, Montclair State College. Of course, any omission the reader may find in the following pages remains my responsibility.

Besides those just named, many dedicated and talented people at the Wm. C. Brown Publishers proved once again to this writer that a textbook is a collaborative process. While many people at Wm. C. Brown have been involved with this project, two stand out. First, special thanks to James L. Romig, a writer's ideal editor, whose initial support and guidance encouraged me to undertake this project. Second, I feel special kinship toward my developmental editor, Sandy Schmidt, whose expertise, guidance, and, yes, those seemingly endless prods all added immeasurably to the book you now hold. Closer to my home base, I cannot thank adequately the always-helpful library staff at Roane State Community College. Last and certainly not least, I wish to thank my partner, Nan Hope Doyle, who shared every aspect of this work. To all of these people and many others too numerous to mention, I can only say *thank you.*

Sex and Gender

Part I

PERSPECTIVES

Chapter 1

AN OVERVIEW

*T*he great enemy of truth is very often not the lie—deliberate, contrived and dishonest—but the myth—persistent, persuasive and
unrealistic. Too often we hold fast to the clichés of our forebears. We
subject all facts to a prefabricated set of interpretations. We enjoy the
comfort of opinion without the discomfort of thought.

John F. Kennedy

Bees, baboons, and birds are fascinating to watch, and with patience and
perseverance one can learn much about their activities and interactions.
Few living species, however, can match us humans for complexity of behaviors and entanglement of relations; it is far more difficult to observe
and analyze ourselves than to study bees, baboons, or birds. One problem
encountered when humans study other humans is that the observers may
delude themselves into believing they can be as objective when they analyze human action as when they observe bees, for example.

But, can total objectivity ever be had when humans observe their own
activities and antics? Can human observers ever completely set aside the
values, beliefs, and assumptions that are embedded in our social and cultural environment in order to study other humans objectively, totally objectively, that is? Would such an objective study require the same distance
that exists between humans and bees, for instance? For that matter, just
what would human actions look like to an outsider, that is, a social and
biological foreigner? With our penchant for sharing and stealing, poetry
and graffiti, and peace and war, what would we humans look like to aliens?
Would, for example, the aliens' final report include some of the following
observations?

Observations of the Human Species on the Planet Earth Located in a Distant Corner of the Milky Way Galaxy.

Observed the activities of approximately 4 billion similar creatures with moderately well-developed mental faculties. These creatures are collectively referred to as human beings. Human beings appear to have a preference for the number two, as seen by their insistence that their members can be categorized in terms of what they call a male or a female. For the sake of this report, we will adhere to this rather quaint distinction.

The male tends to be physically bigger and muscularly stronger than the female, although there are many exceptions to this physical difference. We did, in fact, observe many females who were bigger and stronger than some males. Males do seem to fight among themselves a great deal, and, according to human folklore, are thought to be the more aggressive species member. We witnessed, however, many incidents where females acted very aggressively and were capable of very violent acts.

Humans perform a variety of activities. Here again, we found the human penchant for the number two. For instance, most humans believe that the type of activity they call "work" is performed better if it is divided up between males and females. Humans call this their "division of labor" concept. There is great disparity in what kinds of work are assigned to either females or males. In some human groups, strenuous work is assigned to males, but, in other groups, such work is designated for females. The differences in work assignments usually depended on what part of the planet our observations were made. Nevertheless, one fairly consistent finding was recorded: In most parts of the planet, the female is assigned the work of rearing the species' young.

Besides categorizing work into two types, humans also dichotomize what they refer to as mental and social faculties. Among some human groups, females are thought to be more emotional and dependent, while males are viewed as more intellectual and independent. Other small human bands reverse this peculiar view and see the female as naturally the more independent and competent member of the species. It seems that what humans consider to be natural to their species depends to a large degree on what part of the planet they inhabit.

However, regardless of location, most humans believe that the male is somehow superior to the female. The reason for this is difficult to ascertain; we could find no reliable evidence of either one being superior over the other in any way except for some trifling instances of physical differences.

Thus, based on our observations of humans and their apparent lack of any real insight into their nature and, more significantly, their demeaning penchant to subjugate the female, we recommend that any further contact with them be dismissed as unwarranted at this time. Humans have been found to be such an inferior species that any contact with them would serve no useful purpose.

Sounds strange being reported on like that, doesn't it? Yet, the idea that an alien civilization would find us strange and our behaviors disconcerting is a common theme in popular science fiction literature (LeGuin, 1969). Our aliens' report, however, is fairly accurate, albeit not too flattering.

In trying to understand ourselves, we really don't have to go to such lengths as to enlist the aid of some alien research team. But we must be aware that looking at ourselves may not always be as easy as studying bees, baboons, or birds.

We will not examine every facet of human behavior, but only some of the features that touch us in significant ways. More specifically, we will focus on the issues of sex and gender, which are the most integral features of the human experience. Few aspects of our human experience touch us more deeply or shape our development more completely than does our biological sex and our social psychological gender. The human experience begins at conception when sex is determined as either *female* or *male*—a quaint distinction according to our alien visitors—and expands after birth to include one's gender, which arises from the experience of being raised to behave and think of oneself as either *feminine* or *masculine*. Inquiry into one's sex and gender is a most wondrous study but one that can be filled with misconceptions, prejudice, and, yes, even bias. To begin our discussion of sex and gender, we need to discuss these terms and some of the possible misconceptions that may exist about their meanings.

A BASIC DISTINCTION: SEX OR GENDER?

Sex and *gender* are often used interchangeably by laypeople and scientists alike; in the opinion of some, this synonymous usage can lead to more than a little confusion (Gould and Kern-Daniels, 1977; Lopata and Thorne, 1978). Thus, we need to begin our discussion with some basic definitions and related points worth considering.

The word *sex* has become a catchall term meaning many different things to many different people. In everyday usage, most people define *sex* as meaning one of two mutually exclusive and unchangeable biological categories—male or female—that most living species fit into, for example, a male *or* female dog, baboon, or human being. Sex can also designate an activity that creatures engage in for procreation or, in the case of humans, for the sake of pleasure. Sex, as used in the former sense, that of two dichotomous and unchangeable biologically based categories, can be both a deceiving and problematic concept.

Sex: The Dichotomy Inference

Among many living creatures, there is anatomical evidence of a basic *bisexuality* in their reproductive structures, at least during the early weeks of fetal development (Tobach and Rosoff, 1978). For example, during the first six weeks of uterine development, human fetuses of both genetic sexes (i.e., either XX or XY sex chromosomes' patterns) possess special sex tissues called anlagen, which have the potential to develop into either male or female sex structures. An extreme example of bisexuality can be found in the rare cases of true hermaphroditism when a person is born with both male and female reproductive and genital structures.

Compounding the confusion about sex even more are some common misconceptions about hormones. Most people talk as if males and females are dichotomous hormonally, as noted by the frequent references to the androgens as being "male hormones," while referring to estrogen and progestin as "female hormones." In fact, all three hormones are found in the bloodstreams of *all* individuals (Gadpaille, 1972). Thus, a person's sex is determined by the amounts of hormones, not by the kinds of hormones.

Even the supposedly dichotomous secondary sex characteristics have been shown to vary widely among individuals. Interestingly, most people determine a person's biological sex category (i.e., male or female) solely on the basis of visible and, we might add, highly variable secondary sex characteristics rather than on an examination of their genitals or hormonal mix, except at birth. However, not all males nor all females have the secondary sex characteristics thought typical for their sex. A biological male, for example, may possess a delicate body-build and soft facial features, and, consequently, he may be perceived by others as being more feminine than masculine (Darden, 1972). What all of this means is that when the word sex is used to mean one of two strictly separate biological categories, it is being used incorrectly. Rather, biological sex is better understood to mean a continuum whereon the reproductive structures, hormones, and physical features range somewhere between two extreme poles.

Sex: The Unchangeable Inference

Among several species of flora and aquatic life, sex is a rather *changeable* feature in an organism's life cycle. For example, the flower called a *jack-in-the-pulpit* and various fish like the *bluehead wrasse* and the *clown fish* are able to change their reproductive structures depending on various environmental factors. The growing evidence for sexual flexibility among several species of fish—what scientists call protogyny (female to male) and protandry (male to female)—suggests that this phenomenon may be more frequent in nature than was once thought (Warner, 1984).

Among humans, we now have the surgical ability to change a person's genital and secondary sex features from one sex to the other, as found among those who have opted for sex-reassignment surgery (Money, 1975a). The long-cherished idea that our biological sex at conception is immutably fixed forever is no longer credible given the evidence of plants, aquatic animals, and some humans also.

All this should suggest that sex is not simply a biological fact based on only two possible categories, nor is it immutable for life, at least not for all living species. In fact, some people have persuasively argued that sex is a social construct and not merely a biological given (Kessler and McKenna, 1978). It makes more sense to think of the word *sex* as referring to the reproductive structures, hormones, and physical characteristics that exist along a continuum ranging from extreme maleness to extreme femaleness, rather than as comprising a set of biological features of a strictly either-or and unchangeable kind. As we can see, the term *sex*, rather than being a straight-forward, unambiguous word, can be fraught with more than a little confusion.

Gender: A Needed Concept

Psychologist Rhoda Unger (1979a) has urged social scientists to use the word *sex* only when referring to specifically biological mechanisms (e.g., sex chromosomes or sex structures like the penis or vagina) and to use the term *gender* only when discussing the social, cultural, and psychological aspects that pertain to the traits, norms, stereotypes, and roles considered typical and desirable for those whom society has designated as male or female. In other words, Unger views sex as a biological construct; she defines gender in terms of its social, cultural, and psychological components. We must, however, again be cautious if we wish to avoid having the word gender take on an either-or meaning as does the word sex. Rather, gender and its components (gender stereotypes, gender norms, gender roles, and gender identities) can also vary along a continuum from extremely masculine on one end to extremely feminine on the other (Freimuth and Hornstein, 1982). Furthermore, gender should be thought of as *independent* of a person's biological sex (Green, 1974; Money, 1975a, 1975b). For example, a male may behave in ways usually considered unmanly in his society, but that, in and of itself, does not make him less of a male.

Like Unger, the late Carolyn Wood Sherif noted some of the inherent problems the word *sex* has brought to the study of gender. With special reference to the construct of *sex roles*, Sherif (1982) wrote that it "has become a boxcar carrying an assortment of sociological and psychological data along with an explosive mixture of myth and untested assumptions" (p. 392). One of the problems Sherif has with the term *sex roles* is that it

> uncritically couples a biological concept (sex) with a sociological concept (role). Thus, the concept suffers double jeopardy from myths about sex smuggled in uncritically and from denotative confusions in the sociological concept of roles. (p. 392)

Although a majority of researchers apparently still prefer the designation *sex roles* rather than *gender roles* (Baslow, 1980; Schaffer, 1981), we agree with Unger, Sherif, and others, and throughout our discussion will use the term *gender* rather than *sex* when referring to the nonbiological features flowing from a person's ascribed status of either male or female.

Many might suggest that preferring *gender* over *sex* or vice versa is a small point. However, we must be as precise as possible in our terminology in order to disentangle some of the confusion that often exists in this field.

BIAS: A FUNDAMENTAL ISSUE

All of us hold personal values, beliefs, attitudes, and assumptions, or what may be called biases, that influence our perception of the world around us. These *personal biases* cause us to focus our attention on certain features while avoiding others. In other words, our personal biases act like screens that distort our perception of the world we live in.

Few areas of inquiry are so fraught with personal biases as the study of males and females and their gender-related characteristics. A number of biases are especially noteworthy if we are to understand why so many people believe what they do about sex and gender, even in the face of contradictory evidence. In this section, we will cover four biases that influence our views: scientific bias, researcher bias, subject bias, and publication bias.

Scientific Bias: Value-Free vs. Value-Laden Research

People have always tried with varying degrees of success to learn about and understand the world they inhabit. Throughout most of history, religion provided many of the answers to most people's questions. About twenty-five hundred years ago, the study of orderly and logically consistent thought led to the development of philosophical inquiry, which became yet another means that people could use to arrive at truth. More recently, science arose and offered a new promise for understanding our world. This last approach, that of an empirically based science, assumed that knowledge could best be gained if one discounted doctrinaire authority or armchair philosophy and accepted systematic observations in their place. Thus, many consider science to be the superior way to acquire knowledge. Such a view contains the seeds of *scientific bias.*

One of the basic tenets of science and its scientific method is its insistence on *objectivity*. The objective scientist supposedly is detached from her or his subject and, through the scientific method, only observes, controls, measures, and analyzes external events as they happen, letting the accumulated evidence speak for itself. According to this view, a scientist is like an outsider (alien?) allowing the subject of study to unravel and show its orderly arrangements for all to see. A basic assumption inherent in science is that it is *value free.* That is, a scientist's personal biases supposedly are absent or removed from the study and are not allowed to interfere with the scientific process. Therefore, the perception of the world formulated by science is alleged to be a faithful and valid representation of reality.

But can science, or more precisely a scientist, ever be totally value free? Just because scientists say they approach their subject without personal biases does not make their scientific efforts truly value free. Saying that something is true doesn't automatically make it true.

In the past few years, several social scientists have argued persuasively that a value-free science is neither possible nor desirable (Koch, 1981; Sampson, 1978; Unger, 1983). Advocates of a value-free science, on the other hand, argue that only by removing one's personal bias can one be sure of a truthful rendition of the event(s) being studied. Such a view implies that a value-free observation is more valid than an observation made under the influence of a *value-laden* approach, or one where a scientist openly admits to holding certain biased viewpoints. However, those who believe that a value-laden approach distorts an observation of reality, whereas a value-free perspective reflects a truer version of reality, are themselves guilty of letting a particular bias influence their thinking. "The state of having no values," writes André Kukla (1982, p. 1016), "if it exists, is just another particular condition that observers may be in. It is continuous with and on the same epistemological level as the state of having any other particular value system." Thus, the belief that a value-free science affords a more valid account of reality is nothing more than another value-laden perspective for which there is no *a priori* guarantee to its claim of greater truthfulness of its findings.

We will note later how the study of gender may be better served with a value-laden approach rather than a purported value-free perspective.

Researcher Bias: Getting What One Looks For

As already noted, one of the more basic forms of bias may be the belief that simply by following certain scientific methods or procedures one is assured that all one's own biases have been thoroughly put to rest. In reality, there is little assurance that a researcher is not allowing some personal bias to creep into the research. For example, a researcher who is gathering data on nuturant behavior may systematically and precisely count the number of times a mother talks to or smiles at her baby while she is holding it. But why did the researcher study the baby's mother and not the father? Perchance did the culturally influenced belief that mothers are the best infant caregivers or that mothers and not fathers are normally expected to perform nurturant activities have any role in the selection of whom to study? Such culturally influenced assumptions on the researcher's part may actually affect the outcome and interpretation of such a study.

No matter how many degrees or years of study scientists have, they bring their own personal biases with them to their particular field of study. This fact is no less true and, in fact, may be more true in the field of gender-related topics than in other fields of study. Naomi Weisstein (1971), for one, makes a persuasive case that social scientists, especially male psychologists, have allowed their personal biases about women to color their research endeavors.

A researcher is just as likely to be influenced by his or her cultural beliefs, values, and expectations as is anyone else in society. Such bias is referred to as *experimenter bias*. Unwittingly, experimenter bias may cause a researcher to look at a problem in only one way, while avoiding other possibilities. For instance, the exclusion of fathers in parent-infant studies suggests a bias on the researcher's part. Experimenter bias may also show itself

Laugh Parade

By Bill Hoest

"I know it looks like an arrow, but you have all the symptoms of an ulcer."
By permission of William Hoest.

in the way a researcher words her or his questions. Even the types of questions a researcher asks may bias the results in favor of the researcher's hypothesis (Rosenthal, 1976). Too often, the questions we ask and the way we ask them can determine the answers we find. If our questions are embedded with our personal bias, we are more likely to find answers that support our bias.

Subject Bias: Giving Them What They Want

How many times have we all tried to outguess what another person wanted us to do in a particular situation? For that matter, how many times have we tried to make a favorable impression on someone we like or respect? Such common features of interpersonal relations may cause some research participants to try to outguess the purpose of the study or to give a researcher what the participants think the researcher is looking for. We are not suggesting that research participants intentionally try to interfere with a study. A study's design, however, may contain certain clues about what the research is all about and may have what social scientists call *demand characteristics* (Orne, 1962). Thus, even research participants may bias the results of the study simply because they try too hard to make a study come out as they think a researcher wishes. Moreover, a study may contain subtle hints about what outcome is being sought.

Publication Bias: Rejecting the Null

Almost everyone likes results. Even in science, it is disheartening to finish a study and find that the results confirm the null hypothesis (the statement that no difference exists other than that which could be expected by chance alone). One researcher has even suggested that science is prejudiced against finding support for the null hypothesis (Greenwald, 1975). For example, if a study finds no difference between women and men on a supposedly crucial variable, what can one say, except that women and men are similar? How boring! Also, how disappointing to the researcher, especially when the name of the game seems at times to be "differences" not "similarities." Even the popular press doesn't give equal coverage to studies finding women and men similiar but prefers those that report significant gender differences (Unger, 1983, pp. 19–20). Finding no difference in a study may even cause a researcher to file the study's results away in a file drawer because the researcher believes it has little chance for publication (Rosenthal, 1979). One possible reason that so many early studies reported many gender differences may have been that, all too often, studies finding no differences were unceremoniously put away and forgotten in researchers' file drawers.

We must keep in mind that sex and gender are topics laden with value judgments, assumptions, beliefs, and a basket full of other potentially biasing features. Rather than fall victim to the belief that one can or should discard personal biases in order to understand these issues, possibly a better approach would be to announce one's particular biases openly so that others may know right from the start what those biases are. Such an unscientific-sounding or tradition-breaking perspective will be our next issue for discussion.

THE STUDY OF GENDER: PUTTING ONE'S BIASES ON THE TABLE

When overhearing another criticizing something, one is tempted to say, "So, come up with something better." In the past several years, critical voices have been raised over the limitations of science's purported value-free orientation and its reliance solely on certain supposedly objective methods (Buss, 1975; Gadlin and Ingle, 1975). A major assertion is that science, rather than being value free as it professes, is really value laden. If science contains an unstated value system or biased viewpoint, it should state it openly so that others could judge its findings for what they are—a biased view of the world. Others may then choose to accept or reject its findings. If rejected, the critics then have a responsibility to come up with an alternative approach.

In this section we will first examine the unstated or implicit biases embedded in a strictly defined, empirically based, scientific study of gender. Next we will outline an alternative model, one with certain stated values and one that, in the words of Evelyn Fox Keller (1982, p. 589), may "carry a liberating potential for science."

Science: An Androcentric and Antifemale Institution

Science is embedded in a particular culturally influenced world view that often restrains and suppresses alternative or contrary world views (Kuhn, 1962). Science is no more immune from certain culturally influenced biases than any other social institution. Science is not simply a set of methods separate from the scientist. Rather, science is a dynamic process of inquiry growing out of the interaction between a culturally influenced scientist and the subject of his or her inquiry. Yet, many modern-day scientists believe their research is devoid of bias (value free) by virtue of their reliance solely on supposedly objective scientific methods. Even if science were value free—and it is not—there is *no* logical justification for believing knowledge acquired by its methods to be more valid than a value-laden approach (Kukla, 1982).

The question remains, what culturally influenced value system or set of biases can be singled out as infusing the so-called value-free science? Our contention is that science is deeply embedded with our culture's all-pervasive antifeminine and androcentric world views (Keller, 1978). Such an indictment is given credence when we note the following.

First, the stated goals of science are to understand or gain a knowledge of nature, to predict nature, and finally, to control nature. And with knowledge, prediction, and control of nature comes power over nature (Leiss, 1974). Implicit in this noble sounding ideal is the inference that *man* (the specific, not generic, sense) is separate from *nature*. Nature is the other, separate from man, and a force that must eventually bend to man's will. To this end, science is one means that can assist man in his conquest of and control over nature. Inevitably, man must separate himself from nature in order to achieve personal mastery and a fuller sense of selfhood (Keller, 1978).

Woman can also be thought of as one from whom *man* must separate if he is to develop a sense of his own personhood (Chodorow, 1978; Dinnerstein, 1976). Furthermore, woman has become a personification or embodiment of nature (e.g., mother nature) which man seeks to control. We may infer that to control nature is to control woman. Keller (1982) makes just this point.

> To see the emphasis on power and control so prevalent in the rhetoric of Western science as projection of a specifically male consciousness requires no great leap of the imagination. Indeed, that perception has become a commonplace. Above all, it is invited by the rhetoric that conjoins the domination of nature with the insistent image of nature as female, nowhere more familiar than in the writings of Francis Bacon. For Bacon, knowledge and power are one, and the promise of science is expressed as "leading to you Nature with all her children to bind her to your service and make her your slave," by means that do not "merely exert a gentle guidance over nature's course; they have the power to conquer and subdue her, to shake her to her foundations." (p. 598)

Thus, underneath science's goal of the ultimate domination of nature and its ("her"?) erratic forces lies the seeds of both an antifemale bias and a male-as-norm or androcentric world view.

Science's antifeminine bias is not only found in the rhetoric of early scientists like Bacon; it can be found in more recent views about women's and men's natures and in the way in which scientific findings have been used to justify the so-called natural order. For instance, Mary Brown Parlee (1975) charges the science of psychology with furnishing support for many of society's antifemale practices. She notes that "the body of 'knowledge' developed by academic psychologists happened (apparently) to support stereotyped beliefs about the abilities and psychological characteristics of women and men, and such beliefs happen to support existing political, legal, and economic inequalities between the sexes" (p. 124).

Second, science can be thought of as a nearly all-male club with a sign at its entrance that states boldly "Women not welcome." Although some may object, the fact remains that the number of women who have been allowed entrance into the various natural and social sciences is small compared to the percentage of women in the population. Throughout history, women who sought knowledge have been cast as evil incarnate (Eve's eating from the tree of knowledge) or as witches seeking alchemy's secrets (Allen and Hubbs, 1980; Garrett, 1977). In the last century, women stood on the periphery of science (Kohlstedt, 1978), and in this century, few have made it into science's august inner circle of influential policy makers (Aldrich, 1978; Bruer, 1983).

And last, science's androcentric bias finds still further expression with the omission of the female-as-subject from study. An analysis of early social psychological research finds few female participants in research (Schwabacher, 1972). Some topics apparently were better studied using only males or only females, but not both. Studies of aggression, for example, have usually focused on males, and females have been the natural choices for family dynamics and child-care studies (Frodi et al., 1977; McKenna and Kessler, 1977). Everyday experience, however, tells us that females can be very aggressive, while males can be very caring and nurturant. And yet, we would hardly think so if we read most of the early works on these topics.

Male researchers may have had many "logical" reasons for such a female exclusionary policy in human research, but finding that "virtually all of the animal-learning research on rats has been performed with male rats" (Keller, 1982, p. 591), seems ludicrous and more than a little telling of a male bias against female subjects that extends even to the animal kingdom. Such a selection bias favoring males can be explained by an implicit, if not explicit, bias that many male scientists have toward viewing the male-as-norm for all species. Within the biological sciences, such male bias may explain why biological constructs and theories have a peculiarly male slant (Haraway, 1978a and b, 1981; Longino and Doell, 1983).

Historically, males have controlled the social institutions that have defined what was real and what was not. Science is only one of the more recent social institutions that has influenced women's lives while prohibiting women's participation in the endeavor. Women's experiences have been disavowed, maligned, and distorted by science. We can suggest then that science is a male-centered social system that helps to perpetuate the power imbalance that exists between women and men.

A Feminist-Oriented Social Science: An Alternative

Several social scientists have called for a new value-laden approach—a *feminist orientation*—that will exorcise the androcentric and antifemale biases from the study of gender (Blau, 1981; Gould, 1980; Parlee, 1981; Sherif, 1979). Although this approach has not met with immediate or universal approval from established scientists, there is merit in looking at the topic of gender from a feminist perspective. Mary Brown Parlee (1979) outlines the case for such an approach:

> One hallmark of feminist research in any field seems to be the investigator's continual testing of the plausibility of the work against her own experience. The historian, for example, asks what it was like to be a woman and what were women doing at that place and time, and then proceeds to find out—using her own experience both as a guide to formulating questions and as a preliminary way of evaluating the completeness of the results. The usual scholarly principles of reliability, consistency, logical inference, and the like are also used to evaluate the results, but the additional criterion of how does it accord with my own experience does enter into the work process. And similarly in other disciplines, including psychology. Feminist psychologists thus have as a priority finding the best possible version of the truth about the subject matter rather than adhering strictly to a particular method. (p. 130)

Feminist research permits—no, insists—that the researcher become actively involved in the research process. It is not enough to simply administer more tests or introduce more controls; rather, the researcher must constantly ask him- or herself the question: "How does that which I propose to do reflect my own experiences in the real world, the world of my own experiences?" Such questions and attention to one's own experiences can lead to further refinements to the methods or design of the study. For example, before interacting with research participants, a feminist-oriented psychologist may ask her- or himself how she or he would feel on the other end of the investigation. What would I feel or experience if I were asked to do such and such? Furthermore, by asking questions of the research participants during and after the study, one can gain additional information that might have been missed. Above all, the feminist researcher is not detached from the investigation but rather becomes an integral part of the whole research procedure.

Rhoda Unger (1983) has outlined several specific points that when taken together provide a new and a more fruitful approach to the study of gender.

First, Unger notes that any particular methodology used to study human behavior must be analyzed for its unstated or implicit value system or ideology. The suggestion that truth can only be found through one specific method should act as a red flag that warns the researcher that the method is more important than the study's results. The fact is that knowledge may be acquired in many different ways, and each may have its own value.

Likewise, claims of universal truth should immediately alert the investigator to the possibility of an over simplistic view of reality. Unger argues that some elements of a social psychological relationship may only appear in a single context (e.g., in a laboratory) and not be found in the outside world. Such knowledge would have little or no generalizability to other areas of human experience. Possibly, the search for universal laws of human experience are little more than unwitting attempts to exert control over our subject matter and should be questioned by feminist researchers.

Also, rather than thinking of the research participant as separate from the research environment, it may be more fruitful to look for the reflexive or interactive dynamics inherent in the person–situation complex. In other words, the participant may affect the research situation just as much as the situation may affect the participant. The two—person and situation—form a dynamic dialectical interaction that must be taken into account for a fuller understanding of both. The very act of participating in research may cause a person to act in a certain way, a way entirely different from how she or he would act outside of the research situation. In the final analysis, research is a two-way street wherein the participant is every bit as influential to the outcome of the research as the manipulated variables that supposedly affect the participant's responses.

Unger also believes that both experimenter and subject biases are "inevitable accompaniments of research and not [simply] transient procedural contaminants" (p. 27). These biases should be examined and used to provide additional information about human relationships (Unger, 1981). Furthermore, because many participants can "size up" what is expected from them in the research, possibly the researcher could use the participant's views of the research procedure to give feedback to the participants and see how such information is then used by them.

Feminist research also emphasizes the ways that information gained from the research can be used to help the participants themselves. Overall, research should prove helpful, certainly not harmful, to those who share themselves with the researcher (Heide, 1979).

Even though Unger offers these features as tentative and not as some doctrinaire proposals that one must follow as if they were set in granite, they do provide the beginnings for an alternative approach to the study of human behavior. First and foremost, research is to be seen in its cultural context, never totally free from the concerns and values of the larger society (Eichler, 1977). We will have to wait and see just how the scientific establishment receives such proposals. One thing is clear, however; Unger and other feminist researchers have called attention to the problems posed by science and have proposed an alternative approach to rectify science's androcentric and antifemale biases.

A PREVIEW OF WHAT LIES AHEAD

A feminist perspective urges one to be wary of any viewpoint "that makes unwarranted claims to be the sole source of truth" (Unger, 1983, p. 26). Thus, we will begin our discussion by examining from several different perspectives the dynamic interweave between sex and gender.

We all began as just so much biological material. Egg, sperm, chromosomes, and hormones set the stage for what is to become our sex and the basis for what others will use to determine our appropriate gender-related characteristics (chapter 2). After birth, we begin to develop psychologically; one of the more important psychological features of our personality is our view of ourselves as either masculine or feminine (chapter 3). We are not born in isolation, nor do we develop without others' help. Parents and peers help to shape us in the ways that society believes essential (chapter 4). And last, the culture we are born into reinforces certain values and rules that also influence how males and females will live out their lives in terms of their gender roles (chapter 5).

After discussing the various perspectives and their views of sex and gender, we will discuss several social institutions that help to shape our views of what males and females should be like. We will start by examining the issue of power on the individual level (chapter 6). Next, we will cover several specific social institutions, such as language (chapter 7), education and work (chapter 8), religion and politics (chapter 9), the family (chapter 10), and the mental health field (chapter 11), to see their influence on gender.

We will end our work by detailing the women's and men's movements (chapter 12), and then in our last chapter we will discuss some of the more topical issues that many think will shape our thinking about gender in the near future (chapter 13).

Let's begin now by looking at what it means to be a biological female or male and some of the differences that our biology brings with it.

SUMMARY

Sex and gender are two of the most fascinating features of the human experience. As defined in this chapter, sex pertains to certain reproductive structures, hormones, and physical characteristics that exist along a continuum ranging from extreme maleness to extreme femaleness. Gender refers to those social psychological features associated with the status of either male or female. Many people have misconceptions about sex and gender. For example, they believe that sex and gender represent two mutually exclusive and unchangeable categories.

All of us have certain personal biases which can influence our view of the world around us. Personal biases are noteworthy when discussing sex and gender. Four types of bias are especially prominent: scientific, researcher, subject, and publication.

Traditional science is presented as being value free and thus a more valid way of studying our world. Traditional science, especially the social sciences, however, is not value free and, in fact, is influenced by certain androcentric and antifemale biases. Several researchers have called for a value-laden approach (feminist-oriented) to the study of gender, which challenges the male-dominated social sciences to look at the world in a new way, one that among many things incorporates the female's perspective.

SUGGESTED READINGS

Berger, P., & Luckmann, T. (1966). *The social construction of reality.* Garden City, New York: Anchor.

Buss, A. (1975). The emerging field of the sociology of psychological knowledge. *American Psychologist, 30,* 988–1002.

Hager, M. (1982). The myth of objectivity. *American Psychologist, 37,* 576–79.

Kuhn, T. (1962). *The structure of scientific revolutions.* Chicago: University of Chicago Press.

Payer, M. (1977). Is traditional scholarship value free? Toward a critical theory. Papers from the *Scholar and the Feminist IV: Connecting theory, practice, and values.* The Women's Center, Barnard College.

Roberts, H. (Ed.). (1981). *Doing feminist research.* Boston: Routledge & Kegan Paul.

Reading   *What If?*

How do boys and girls see each other? What kinds of problems do girls have that boys don't? What kinds of privileges do boys have that girls don't? The answers to these questions and others are somewhat surprising, especially when they come from young people asked to imagine themselves living the life of the other gender. The research conducted by Alice Baumgartner and reported here by social psychologist and author Carol Tavris makes for an interesting insight into how young people see each other's gender roles.

For ten years, public-school teachers and administrators have been trying to eliminate sex bias in the counseling they provide to children, in the books that children read, in the lessons they teach (by example as well as in content). To measure the effect of this effort, Dr. Alice I. Baumgartner and her colleagues at the Institute for Equality in Education, at the University of Colorado, came up with a startlingly simple method. They surveyed nearly 2,000 children throughout the state of Colorado: children in grades three through 12, from large metropolitan areas and from small rural communities. They simply asked one question: *If you woke up tomorrow and discovered that you were a (boy) (girl), how would your life be different?*

The answers were sad and shocking, for they show how little has in fact changed in children's attitudes in the recent years of social upheaval. What she found was a fundamental contempt for females—held by both sexes.

The elementary-school boys, for example, often titled their answers with little phrases such as "The Disaster," or "The Fatal Dream." Then they described how awful their lives would be if they were female: "If I woke up and I was a girl, I would hope it was a bad dream and go back to sleep" (sixth-grade boy). "If I were a girl, everybody would be better than me, because boys are better than girls" (third-grade boy). And this one, succinctly: "If I were a girl, I'd kill myself."

But the girls wrote repeatedly of how much better off they would be as boys. "People would take my decisions and beliefs more seriously" (11th-grade girl). "If I were a boy, my whole life would be easier" (sixth-grade girl). And this poignant response from a third-grade girl: "If I were a boy, my daddy might have loved me."

To probe the children's answers more carefully, Dr. Baumgartner compared their remarks in four categories: matters of appearance; how their activities would change; how they would be expected to behave; and how others would treat them.

Appearance

Boys and girls alike realize that girls, but not boys, are judged by their looks and therefore must pay a lot of attention to their appearance. One boy said with alarm: "I'd have to shave my whole body!" The girls, on the other hand, said that not having to attend to these matters was a definite advantage to being male. Noting the amount of time and energy that "proper" dress and makeup require, a tenth-grade girl said, "If I woke up and discovered I was a boy, I would go back to bed, since it would not take very long to get ready for school."

The boys' comments, however, show that being a girl is not just a matter of cleanliness and neatness; what really matters is *being attractive*. "The boys frequently said that if they had to be a female, they would want to be 'gorgeous' or look like a particular movie star," says Dr. Baumgartner, "but none of the girls made any reference to wanting to be handsome if they were male." As early as the third grade, boys are aware of the hazards faced by women who are "gorgeous": "If I were gorgeous, I would be jeered at and hear plenty of comments," said one little boy. By high school,

Source: "How would your life be different if you'd been born a boy?" by C. Tavris with A. Baumgartner, 1983, *Redbook*, February, pp. 92–94, 97. © 1983 by Carol Tavris. Originally appeared in *Redbook*. Reprinted by permission of Lescher and Lescher, Ltd.

when so many girls worry about being "gorgeous" to boys, the boys see the matter differently. "If I were a girl, I would use a lot of makeup and look good and beautiful to everyone," wrote one teen-aged boy, "knowing that few people would care for my personality."

Activities

Is women's work as valued and valuable as men's work? Don't you believe it, said these children. "Not one girl expressed a negative reaction to male activities," says Dr. Baumgartner, "but most of the boys had a critical or hostile reaction to female activities—no matter whether those activities involved school, play, home chores, marriage or eventual choice of occupation. Their general view is summed up in the words of a boy who said 'Girls can't do anything that's fun' and the depressing words of a girl who said her expectation as a female was 'to be nothing.'"

Girls continually pointed out that they would have more or different career choices if they were male: "I could run for President"; "I would consider work in math or science"; "I'd drop my typing class and start taking really hard classes, since my dad would let me go to college and he won't now." The boys felt they would *lose* choices if they were female: "I couldn't be a mechanic."

Behavior

Boys and girls learn early that girls may express their feelings but boys will be "sissies" if they do; boys are more belligerent than girls; and girls are weaker and more passive than boys, or at least are allowed to behave as if they were.

Many of the boys said that being female would restrain their active impulses: "Instead of wrestling with my friends, I'd be sitting around gossiping." "I," said one woebegone boy, "would have to hate snakes."

Indeed, when boys imagine themselves as girls, their language is filled with words of deprivation—what they would no longer be able to do: "I couldn't climb trees or jump the creek"; "I couldn't play football or basketball." But when girls imagine themselves as boys, their language is filled with images of what they would gain: "I could go hunting and fishing with my dad"; "I could run for President"; And: "Life on the home front would be a lot easier. I know that for a fact, since I've got a brother."

Many girls realized that one disadvantage of maleness is stoicism: "If I were a boy, I would have to stay calm and cool whenever something happened"; "I would not be allowed to express my true feelings." The girls often felt that as boys they would have to be "rowdy," "smart-alecky," "macho," and "show off more"—though a couple of them saw male aggressiveness as an alternative to female pacifism. "I'd *kill* my art teacher," said one girl, "instead of arguing with him as I do now."

Treatment by Others

Over and over, girls reported that if they were boys, they would be treated better than they are as girls: "I might be shown that someone cares how I do in school"; "I'd get called on to answer more questions"; "My father would be closer because I'd be the son he always wanted" (a sad and pervasive refrain).

Even the youngest boys and girls are aware of another disadvantage to being female: the prevalence of violence against women. Girls frequently mentioned that if they were boys, they would not have to worry about being raped or beaten up, and the boys feared for their safety if they became girls: "[If I were a girl], I'd have to know how to handle drunk guys and rapists" (eighth-grade boy). "I would have to be around other girls for safety" (sixth-grade boy). "I would always carry a gun for protection," said a fourth grader.

Chapter 2

THE BIOLOGICAL PERSPECTIVE

I gnorance of biological processes may doom efforts at social change to failure because we misidentify what the targets for change should be, and hence what our means should be to attain the change we desire.

Alice S. Rossi

Even the most casual observer can see that males and females differ. They look, move, and sometimes even act differently. Many people believe the differences make for a more interesting world, proclaiming *viva la difference!* It's not enough, however, to note that females and males differ. Rather by *how* much, in *what* areas, and more important, *why* do they differ? For centuries, sages and scholars alike have focused on the physical, or our biology, to account for the subtle and not-so-subtle differences between females and males. Looking at males and females from a biological perspective can afford us with much valuable information.

In this chapter we will begin our discussion of biology by briefly noting why the biological perspective remains so controversial even to this day. We then will focus on the prenatal period. Chromosomes and hormones play a large part in shaping our physical makeup, and we need be aware of their contributions. Next, we move to the postnatal period. Here we will examine some of the interesting features coming to light, such as the differences in brain functioning, the link between certain hormones and sexuality and aggression, and finally, the recent attention paid to menstruation and its more dramatic effects on some women. We will end our discussion of biology with one of the more controversial topics in this area, namely, sociobiology.

THE POLITICS OF BIOLOGY

Over the years, a debate over the hows, whats, and whys of sex and gender differences has taken on an almost circus-like atmosphere. Under science's "big tent," we find one group scurrying about their ring proclaiming the importance of biological factors, while in an adjacent ring, we see others

Reprinted by permission of Johnny Hart and News Group Chicago, Inc.

darting about charting the significant effects of social forces. All the while, the audience in the bleachers grows more confused with the claims and counterclaims coming from the rival rings. At times, it seems that if only the two competing shows could combine their efforts, the outcome would be so much more enjoyable, if not more instructive. One thing the competing groups have given rise to is the long-standing *nature vs. nurture debate.*

Why should there be such a struggle between those dedicated to explaining sex and gender differences? The debate over biology (nature) and social forces (nurture) seems to intensify when, according to Ann Oakley (1972), "the existing roles and statuses of male and female are changing." And certainly, men's and women's statuses and roles have been changing in the last several years. Thus, we shouldn't be too surprised that the nature-nurture debate seems to be at fever pitch nowadays.

Another reason for the continuing controversy is that, historically, biology has been used to defend the so-called natural order of certain social systems. For instance, during the Middle Ages, gross injustices and oppression were justified by what was called the divine right of kings. More recently, the institution of slavery was also defended on the basis of biological principles. Many proclaimed the naturalness of these systems with their inequities, stating that nature deemed that some had the right to oppress others. Today, we are becoming painfully aware that many in the past used biological differences to keep women in a subordinate and powerless position.

As a matter of record, during the last century and into the early part of this century, biological differences were used to rationalize women's unequal status in society. About one hundred years ago, it was commonly believed that a woman's "fragile" nature required her to be protected, that a woman's menses destined her to periodic bouts of uncontrolled emotions, and that her small brain limited her intellectual horizons. Consequently, women were prevented from pursuing certain professions such as medicine or law, were not allowed to vote, and were subjected to numerous other restrictions all by virtue of their "fragile" biology. Furthermore, because women gave birth, most believed they were forever destined for the chores of child raising as well as tending to household duties. Even when early researchers found females superior to males in certain abilities (e.g., verbal abilities), little was made of such talents. A more blatant (yet more scientific sounding) use of a biological principle employed against women was the *variability hypothesis* (Shields, 1975, 1982).

Stemming from Darwin's theory of evolution, the variability hypothesis stated that the more varied and widespread a species' behaviors, skills, and talents were, the more likely that species was to survive and develop. In other words, a species that possessed wide-ranging and adaptive abilities was more likely to survive and pass on its genes than a species whose abilities were more restricted or more rigidly expressed. Those who applied the variability hypothesis to humans thought that males, as a rule, showed more variability in their abilities than females showed. For example, one reason given for the greater number of male genuises throughout history was the male's greater intellectual variability. Men, according to this line of reasoning, were thought to be naturally predisposed to greater heights of intellectual achievements (and greater deficits also!) than women, whose achievements were limited—neither gifted nor retarded—to a more narrowly defined range of intellectual endeavors. If women were constrained by their lack of great intellectual achievements, there was little need or reason for more than a cursory or basic education for them. This is only one example of a supposed biological difference used to prevent women from gaining educational opportunities equal to those of men. It is not surprising, then, that biology and biological principles have taken on a controversial air in the discussion of sex and gender differences.

There is no question that women and men are biologically different. In some quarters, there is considerable interest in how some of these differences may predispose the sexes to act differently in some situations (Rossi, 1984). Thus, we need to explore some of the basic biological mechanisms and their effects on human development and behavior.

PRENATAL EVENTS AND SEX DIFFERENCES

For centuries, women have been viewed as something less than men. Men have been the norm, women the exception; men complete, women lacking. Even the tragic character Hamlet noted that, "Frailty, thy name is woman." Although Hamlet was no authority on biology, his analysis of the female's supposed frailty is more than a little misconceived. Contrary to Hamlet's view, others have noted that women are, in fact, biologically superior to men (Montagu, 1952).

A female's biological superiority is based on her having a type of genetic backup system in her chromosomal makeup. Specifically, females have two gene-packed sex chromosomes (XX), whereas males have one robust X and one rather smallish Y. The female's redundant sex chromosome pattern affords her with at least two advantages. The double-X pattern provides a more efficient immunization system that wards off infections better, thereby

TABLE 2.1   EIGHT STAGES OF SEX AND GENDER DEVELOPMENT

Stages	Male	Female
1. Chromosomal	XY	XX
2. Gonadal	Testes	Ovaries
3. Hormonal	Mostly androgens	Mostly estrogens and progestins
4. Internal organs	Prostate gland, vas deferens and seminal vesicles	Uterus and fallopian tubes
5. External organs	Penis and scrotum	Clitoris, labia and vagina
6. Assigned sex	"It's a boy!"	"It's a girl!"
7. Gender identity	"I'm a boy/man."	"I'm a girl/woman."
8. Gender roles	Expected masculine behaviors	Expected feminine behaviors

contributing, in all probability, to a female's greater longevity compared to the average male. Also, the second X apparently strengthens any trait or compensates for any weakness located on the first X. In terms of the female's basic genetic ingredients, she is anything but frail. If Hamlet were alive today, he might reword his comment to read something like, "Oh men, how fragile is thy beginning!"

To begin our discussion of biology's impact on human development, we need first review some basic biology that is related to the different stages of sexual development (see table 2.1). We will start by focusing on the first stage in sexual development.

The Sex Chromosomes

The human body contains billions of cells, and within most we find twenty-three *pairs* of chromosomes that look like threadlike strands of beads. Notice, we said most cells contain twenty-three pairs of chromosomes. The exceptions to this generalization are the specialized sex cells called *ova*, or *eggs*, in women and *sperm* in men; each of these sex cells has only twenty-three chromosomes. For conception to occur, one of the male's sex cells, or sperm, must impregnate a woman's egg, which allows the separate twenty-three chromosomes from each to combine to make the normal complement of forty-six chromosomes. The fertilized egg then contains forty-four chromosomes called *autosomes*, which are chiefly responsible for physical features such as hair texture, height, and eye color; the remaining two chromosomes, the *sex chromosomes*, determine the biological sex (stage 1). The female's egg always contributes an X sex chromosome and the male's sperm can either contribute an X or a Y sex chromosome. The biological sex of the embryo is therefore always determined by the father's contribution of an X or a Y. If the sperm contains an X sex chromosome, it is called a *gynosperm*, and if a Y, an *androsperm*.

The androsperm and gynosperm are physically different. The androsperm is lighter and has a sharper, spearlike head; the gynosperm is heavier with a rounded or blunted head. The androsperm also has a longer tail than the gynosperm, which allows the androsperm to move faster than the gynosperm (Goodall and Roberts, 1976). The androsperm's motility and lightness permit it to move more quickly through the cervical mucus, creating an advantage over the slower gynosperm and partially accounting for the greater number of male conceptions compared to female conceptions—estimates range anywhere from 145 to 160 male conceptions for every 100 female conceptions (Money and Tucker, 1975).

The sex chromosomes' contribution to fetal development has received considerable attention lately. To learn more about the effects sex chromosomes have on the physical structures, we will now turn our attention to three abnormal chromosome patterns: Turner's syndrome, Klinefelter's syndrome, and the double-Y syndrome.

Turner's Syndrome   In approximately one in every ten thousand female infants, an abnormal sex chromosome pattern is found in which the second female sex chromosome is either defective or missing (Hamerton et al., 1975). This condition is referred to as *Turner's syndrome*. Since it is the second sex chromosome that directs the development of the gonadal tissue into either functioning ovaries or testes, a female with Turner's syndrome always develops a female body with either underdeveloped ovaries or no ovaries whatsoever. Therefore, a Turner's female is unable to conceive a child.

A Turner's female usually has a short stature, a weblike configuration around the neck, eyelid folds, and a rather broad or shieldlike chest (Money and Granoff, 1965). Because her ovaries are absent or defective, she will need estrogen supplemental therapy during adolescence to stimulate the usual female secondary sex characteristics, such as normal breast development.

In one study comparing fifteen Turner females to similar but genetically normal females (i.e., 46,XX), the Turner females were found to be extremely interested in "feminine" activities, for example, playing with dolls and dressing up in feminine attire (Money and Erhardt, 1972). Most Turner females exhibit a strong desire to become biological mothers when they grow up, which, of course, is impossible (Polani, 1972). Also, Turner females show little or no impairment in intellectual ability, with some even showing significantly above-normal IQs (Money, 1964).

Klinefelter's Syndrome   A more common type of sex chromosomal abnormality occurs when there is a surplus of sex chromosomes. For example, there can be too many X or Y chromosomes. We will first discuss those males with a surplus of Xs (either 47,XXY or even 48,XXXY), who have what is called *Klinefelter's syndrome*. Approximately one or two out of every one thousand males have Klinefelter's syndrome (Hamerton et al., 1975).

A Klinefelter male is usually taller than the average male and appears rather gangling because of his long arms and legs. During adolescence, a Klinefelter male's breasts usually take on a female-like appearance by becoming larger than normal. His testes are infertile and produce abnormally small amounts of testosterone (Money and Erhardt, 1972).

A Klinefelter male usually has some impairment in intellectual functioning, and many are classified as mentally retarded. In prison populations, Klinefelter males have been found in greater numbers than expected by chance alone. However, finding more Klinefelters in prisons may be attributed to their lower IQs rather than to some genetic predilection for criminal activity (Witkin et al., 1976).

The Double-Y Syndrome   Approximately one out of every one thousand male infants has one or more extra Y chromosomes, which is designated as the *double-Y syndrome* (Hamerton et al., 1975). These males are taller than even Klinefelter males. Other than their above-average height, few other obvious physical features set these men off from normal (chromosomally speaking) males (Owen, 1972). A major psychological feature of the double-Y male, however, is a marked increase in his impulsivity and lack of tolerance for frustration (Nielsen and Christensen, 1974). Intellectually, he shows a slightly below-average overall ability (Witkin et al., 1976).

The issue that first caught the public's attention with respect to the double-Y syndrome was the much publicized research that found these men in greater numbers in prison populations than would be predicted by chance alone (Jacobs et al., 1965). The press highlighted this, and soon the public was convinced that the extra Y chromosome somehow predisposed such men to a life of violence and crime. However, the relationship between the extra Y and criminality has proved tenuous. In fact, male prisoners with an extra Y have less violent criminal histories than genetically normal male prisoners (Witkin et al., 1976). Rather than indicting the extra Y chromosome as the cause of violent and criminal behavior, it makes just as much sense to point to the fact that the XYY male's greater impulsivity and excitability, coupled with frequent emotional outbursts, may cause many of these men to run astray of the law. Their psychological profile, rather than their genetic abnormality, may be the culprit (Noel et al., 1974).

Implications of Chromosomal Abnormalities   We can see from the above that considerable information has been gained from studies of individuals who either have a sex chromosome deficit (Turner's syndrome) or surplus (Klinefelter's and the double-Y syndromes). For male development, at least two sex chromosomes are necessary, and one must be a Y. For female development, only one sex chromosome is needed, which must be an X, as found in the Turner female. However, a female with a single X chromosome will be infertile and physically different from a genetically normal (XX) female. Also, the presence of at least one X chromosome is essential for life. A single Y is never enough for development to occur.

Females with a surplus of Xs (47,XXX or 48,XXXX) are usually normal in physical appearance but may be infertile and slightly slower to develop (Tennes et al., 1975). When there is a surplus of Ys, we see a general tendency toward increased height. Males with an extra X show some feminine features, and males with an extra Y exhibit a tendency toward poor impulse control.

HORMONES AND SEXUAL DEVELOPMENT

For years, people have known that various chemicals could influence a person's behavior. Chemicals like LSD, amphetamines, and even the caffeine in coffee and cola have been found to alter a person's perception, behavior, and emotions. Yet, there are many naturally occurring chemicals produced in our bodies, known collectively as *sex hormones*, that have dramatic effects on our bodies from the earliest days of our development. We will, however, focus on only three such sex hormones—those produced by our testes, ovaries, and adrenal glands: testosterone, estrogen, and progesterone. Let's begin with the dramatic effects that testosterone has during the prenatal period.

Testosterone and the Adam Principle

During the first few weeks after conception, the growing male or female embryos possess a set of bisexual sex tissues known as *anlagen*, which can develop into either male or female sex structures. Sometime around a male embryo's sixth week, the Y chromosome somehow triggers the gonadal tissue to develop as testes rather than as ovaries (Stage 2). Although we do not know for sure what causes the development of testes rather than ovaries, scientists believe that a substance known as *H-Y antigen*, located on the Y chromosome, is responsible for testicular development (Jones et al., 1979). If the Y chromosome is absent, as in a normal female embryo, the gonadal tissue will develop as ovaries.

Male development is contingent first on the presence of the Y chromosome and second on the masculinizing effects of *testosterone*. If testosterone is lacking, the genetic male embryo will automatically develop in the female direction. Medical psychologist John Money has dubbed the presence of testosterone during the fetal period as the *Adam principle* (Money, 1973). It appears that nature prefers the female over the male because, for male development, something extra is needed—something that will masculinize the embryo in the male direction. Nothing extra (in the way of hormones) is needed for normal female development.

Once the gonadal tissue has been masculinized and testes develop, another series of developmental stages unfolds. First, the testes begin producing testosterone, which continues the masculinizing course (Stage 3). During the third month, testosterone causes the *Wolffian ducts* to differentiate as male internal sex structures, resulting in the development of the

Figure 2.1 Even to the casual observer, the physical differences between females and males are rather obvious. Physical endurance, upper body strength, and external sexual structures are some of the more obvious differences found between the sexes.

vas deferens, seminal vesicles, and prostate gland (Stage 4). During this stage, another testes-produced androgen called the Müllerian-inhibiting substance prevents the Müllerian ducts from differentiating in the female direction.

Sometime later, testosterone also causes the external sex structures to develop, namely, the penis and scrotum (Stage 5). Finally, at birth, the normal male genital structures prompt those present to announce that "It's a boy!" (Stage 6).

For the female embryo, the stages of sexual development proceed quite smoothly because, as we have already noted, nothing extra is needed for normal female development. With the combination of two X chromosomes (Stage 1), the embryo's sex tissues soon develop as ovaries (Stage 2). Later on, because of the relative absence of testosterone (Stage 3), the female fetus's Wolffian ducts degenerate and the *Müllerian ducts* develop as the fallopian tubes, uterus, and the upper part of the vagina (Stage 4). Next, the external sex structures develop, and the vagina, clitoris, and labia form (Stage 5). And last, at birth, the pronouncement, "It's a girl!" is heard (Stage 6).

Hormones and Abnormal Development

As stated earlier, sometimes the chromosome patterns can show abnormal configurations. Likewise, abnormal prenatal hormonal conditions can arise affecting the development of both the internal and external sex structures. First, we will focus on the hormonal abnormalities that arise when a normal male fetus's internal and external sex structures are insensitive to the androgens' masculinizing effects. Next we will describe the results of a female fetus being exposed to the masculinizing effects of androgens or androgen-like substances.

Androgen Insensitivity Syndrome   *Androgen insensitivity syndrome* is the most extreme case of an abnormal hormonal condition affecting a genetic male and is caused by an X-linked, recessive condition. Because the fetal gonads develop as testes, the Müllerian-inhibiting substance prevents the development of internal female sex structures. However, the androgens produced by the testes do little if anything to foster the development of a male's internal or external sex structures because these tissues, for some yet unknown reason, do not respond to the masculinizing effects of the androgens. But the small amounts of estrogen produced by the testes are able to stimulate female sex characteristics such as a vaginal opening. Consequently, at birth, most of these individuals have what appears to be external female sex structures.

If this condition is not noticed at birth or shortly thereafter, these infants will be designated as females, develop female gender identities, and, more than likely, accept the prescribed female gender role (stages 7 and 8 [Money and Ehrhardt, 1972]). Because they lack the normal internal sex structures of the female, however, they will not menstruate nor will they be able to conceive. Thus, the person who suffers from the androgen insensitivity syndrome is a genetic male who usually grows up as a female because the embryonic sex tissues did not respond to the masculinizing effects of the androgens.

Adrenogenital Syndrome   Recall that it is the male fetus that must have something added (testosterone) in order for complete masculinization to occur. The Y chromosome is not enough to insure proper male development, whereas for the female, nothing extra is required for normal development. However, if something extra is present, such as testosterone, a female fetus can develop serious problems. The most serious outcome is normally referred to as the *adrenogenital syndrome.*

The adrenogenital syndrome can have several causes. First, some women develop tumors on their ovaries or on their adrenal glands that in turn produce a surplus of androgens. If such a condition develops during pregnancy, some excessive androgen may reach a female fetus via the bloodstream. A second cause may be the fetus's own adrenal cortices. Normally, a fetus's adrenal glands produce a hormone called cortisol, which is similar to an androgen. Some female fetuses have a defective adrenal cortex that produces an abundance of cortisol, which can affect its body much like an androgen. And last, during the 1940s and 1950s, many women with histories of spontaneous abortions were prescribed a synthetic drug (progestin) that affected female fetuses much like androgen. Thus, some female fetuses have suffered the masculinizing consequences of being exposed either naturally or medically to an overdose of androgen or androgen-like chemicals during fetal development. The outcome and extent of adrenogenital syndrome depends on the amount of the androgen substance in the fetus's bloodstream and the time at which it occurs, leading to various degrees of masculinization of the external sex structures.

Psychologists Susan Baker and Anke Ehrhardt have conducted several studies on females with adrenogenital syndrome (Baker and Ehrhardt, 1978; Ehrhardt and Baker, 1978). The adrenogenital females observed in these studies were all treated soon after birth with cortisol, which prevented further masculinization of their bodies and allowed them to develop normal female secondary sex characteristics.

For the most part, these adrenogenital females displayed a higher than normal degree of *tomboyism*. In other words, when these girls were compared to their normal female siblings, they showed a preference for boys' toys over girls' toys and engaged in more energetic and outdoor sports than was commonly found among their female siblings. The adrenogenital females also showed a lack of interest in children or in babysitting activities. The adrenogenital females, however, did not have any difficulty in accepting their female gender identity, although some did show a preference for male gender-role behaviors.

Males can also be classified as adrenogenital when they are exposed to extremely high androgen levels before birth. The only difference between adrenogenital boys and their normal male siblings, however, is that the adrenogenital males show a greater interest in sports and outside activities (Ehrhardt and Baker, 1978).

These various hormonal abnormalities show the dramatic influence that the androgens have on either a male or female fetus. Without androgen and its masculinizing effect, or if the body's sex tissues are immune or insensitive to androgen, a male will develop in the female direction. If, somehow, excessive amounts of androgen or other androgen-like substances happen to occur during the female fetus's development, she will have varying degrees of masculinization of her sex tissues. The key issue in all of these conditions is that the androgens, especially testosterone, play a key role in the development of the internal and external sex structures. Now let's move our discussion to the effects that hormones have on the brain.

Hormones and the Brain

A majority of sex-hormone research has focused on the effects these hormones have on the sex structures and different behaviors of various animal species like rhesus monkeys, for example (Goy, 1978; Phoenix, 1978). For the moment, let's briefly highlight some of these findings.

Researcher Charles Phoenix (1978) has reported on the physical and behavioral effects of injecting pregnant rhesus monkeys with testosterone during certain critical periods of their pregnancies. Their female offspring were born *hermaphoditic,* meaning that they possessed both male and female sex stuctures, specifically, female internal sex structures (ovaries) and male external sex structures (a penis and an empty scrotal sac). The prenatal injections of testosterone masculinized these females' external sex structures but had little effect on their internal female sex organs. More impressive than the alterations in physical structures are some of the behaviors these hermaphroditic females displayed after birth.

Over a four-year period, Phoenix raised the hermaphroditic female monkeys with a group of normal male and female rhesus monkeys (i.e., these monkeys were not treated with testosterone *in utero.*) During play sessions, the hermaphroditic females resembled the normal males more than they did the normal females. The hermaphroditic monkeys engaged in rough-and-tumble activities, chasing, and threat displays, which are more characteristic of normal male, rather than female, play activities. The hermaphroditic females also engaged in more male-like sexual behaviors, such as initiating sexual activities and mounting activities. The hermaphroditic females' play and sexual activities, however, never reached the same levels as that displayed by the normal males. In other words, the hermaphroditic monkeys' behavior fell somewhere in between the behaviors displayed by normal male and female monkeys. Interestingly, the hermaphroditic females began to menstruate significantly later than the normal females (36.8 months vs. 29.2 months, respectively). Once the menstrual cycle became established, however, the hermaphroditic females showed a normal menstrual cycle, with the only difference being that bleeding occurred through their penises.

We must be cautious in our discussion of research based on rhesus monkeys, however, lest we fall victim to questionable generalizations from animals to humans. We do have a human condition, though, that resembles Phoenix's hermaphroditic monkeys, namely, the adrenogenital syndrome that we spoke about in the previous section.

The adrenogenital, or masculinized, human females were more likely to display rough-and-tumble play activities and be labeled as tomboys by their mothers and themselves. (Keep in mind, though, that most females think of themselves as tomboys at some period in their childhoods.) In keeping with their energetic play styles, adrenogenital females preferred "male" attire such as pants or slacks over "female" attire such as dresses. These young girls, however, did not object to getting dressed up if the occasion warranted it. Also, they were found less interested in maternal and nurturant activities. During their childhood years, these girls showed a marked interest in "male" toys—cars, trucks, and guns—and at the same time, they appeared indifferent or openly averse to playing with dolls. The masculinized girls old enough to be responsible for babysitting activities showed little interest in caring for little children. Most adrenogenital girls, although not rejecting the idea outright, did not show as much enthusiasm for eventually getting pregnant and raising children as did a comparison group of normal females. It seems that masculinized females show some of the behaviors and interests more akin to what is usually thought of as part of the male's gender stereotype.

Research into androgen's effects on females suggests that there are different female and male behavior patterns that apparently are influenced by specific hormones circulating through the brain. For example, adult male rhesus monkeys are quite hostile to infant monkeys and have been known to abuse and even kill them (Money and Tucker, 1975). Could the androgens somehow predispose males to show little interest or ability in parental behavior? Conversely, does the greater amount of estrogen or, more specifically, the relative lack of androgens predispose normal females toward an interest in nurturant and maternal behaviors?

The answers to these questions are complex. Among rhesus monkeys, for example, research finds adult males showing little interest in the young, but with prolonged exposure to the young, adult males do exhibit nurturant parental behaviors, albeit somewhat more roughly than most adult female monkeys normally exhibit. Research also shows that adrenogenital human females do not completely reject the notion of their getting pregnant and becoming mothers (Dewhurst and Gordon, 1984).

Although the evidence doesn't suggest that androgenized females disavow any future nurturant behavior, it does suggest that they are not as interested as nonandrogenized females are. Could it be that hormones somehow affect certain brain centers that are related to certain behaviors? We do not yet have a definitive answer to this question. What can be said, however, is that the presence or absence of the androgens appears to make certain behaviors easier to exhibit. Yet, the presence of androgens does not shut the door on a male or female exhibiting a whole range of what some may call masculine and feminine behaviors. John Money and Patricia Tucker (1975) sum up the findings about sex hormones and their effects on the brain in the following manner:

> The prenatal sex hormone mix apparently does not create any new brain pathways or eliminate any that would otherwise be there. The wiring for all the affected behavior is present in both sexes. What your prenatal mix did was to lower the threshold so that it takes less of a push to switch you on to some behavior and to raise the threshold so that it takes more of a push to switch you on to other kinds. More androgen prenatally means that it takes *less* stimulus to evoke your response as far as strenuous physical activity or challenging your peers is concerned, and *more* stimulus to evoke your response to the helpless young, than would otherwise be the case. *How* you respond once you're over the threshold depends on many things—your age, health, strength, physical development, cultural heritage, gender schemas, environment, training, and experience—but not simply on your prenatal sex hormone exposure.
>
> Prenatally determined differences in sensitivity to stimuli help to explain why dominance behavior and activities involving a high expenditure of physical energy are more characteristic of boys' play than of girls', and why parental behavior is more characteristic of girls' play than of boys'. When nativists of the "anatomy is destiny" school and sex chauvinists cite this

difference as evidence that men are predestined to be active and dominant, women to be passive and nurturant, however, they ignore the fact that all these behaviors are characteristic of both sexes and they discount the heavy cultural reinforcement that maximizes the original slight differences in the thresholds. (pp. 78–79)

Thus, the question about the influence of prenatal sex hormones on the brain revolves around the issue of differential thresholds for certain behaviors. Males seem disposed to roughhousing and energetic play, whereas females are more inclined to exhibit a concern for the young. This is not to say, however, that females cannot roughhouse or that males cannot show concern and care for the young. What the prenatal sex hormones may accomplish, besides directing the physical development of the reproductive structures, is to make certain behavioral options more likely to occur under certain circumstances (Baker, 1980). However, the influences of culture can easily override these hormonally induced options.

Some researchers believe that much of the research focusing on individuals who exhibit various hormonal abnormalities are flawed because they lack an awareness of the social and political biases supposedly inherent in their studies (Rogers and Walsh, 1982; Rogers, 1983). Specifically, much of the research conducted by John Money and his associates has been criticized for the relative lack of emphasis on social and cultural factors in determining the behavioral outcome of those displaying a hormonal abnormality. Although we need to be aware of the possibility of experimenter bias in research dealing with topics such as the possible hormonal influences on human behavior, it appears that Money and his associates have been extremely cognizant of such social influences as shown by the above quote and as pointed out by other researchers (DeBold and Luria, 1983). Few will question the influence of chemicals like aspirin or caffeine on a person's behavior, but some seem to overreact when it comes to the natural chemicals that flow through a person's bloodstream.

Let's now proceed with our discussion of some of the effects that our sex hormones have on postnatal events.

BIOLOGY'S POSTNATAL EFFECTS

The years between infancy and young adulthood are filled with many changes. Not only do our bodies grow bigger and more muscular, we also grow, in a manner of speaking, psychologically and socially. Few people would deny biology's influence on our physical makeup, but there is mounting interest in what part our biology plays in nonphysical areas, for example, certain emotional states.

In this section, we will begin at the top, with our brains. Recently, there has been much emphasis on the apparent differences between how male and female brains function. Next, we will focus on the role that sex hormones play in sexual activity and aggression. And last, we will examine the growing controversy over whether or not a woman's menstrual cycle may be linked to psychological problems or even to violent activities.

Some Differences in Grey Matter

From the outside, most adult brains look very much alike. Approximately three pounds in weight, our brains are packed with billions of nerve cells that allow us to perform countless operations, such as reading these words, writing a term paper, thinking about a favorite person, or even recognizing our favorite music. Before we examine some interesting differences between male and female brains, we should review a few basics: what the brain looks like and what different parts of the brain do.

Running right down the middle from front to back is a deep groove dividing the brain into two cerebral hemispheres, conveniently called the right and left hemispheres. Although the two hemispheres look amazingly alike, there are major differences between them. One of the biggest differences between them is that each has specific functions. For example, if you are right-handed—as most people are—your left hemisphere controls your right hand as well as the rest of the right side of your body. Your left hemisphere is called the *dominant hemisphere* because it controls most of your body's movements—the abilities to throw a ball, write a sentence, and speak out in class. When you want to speak, it is the "language centers" in your left hemisphere that command your tongue, lips, and vocal cords to move. Your right hemisphere understands language, but it usually is more involved with visual-spatial tasks and imagination (Gazzaniga, 1983). When you are thinking about going swimming, the pictures you conjure up of yourself in the water come from the "visual centers" located in the right hemisphere of your brain.

If, on the other hand (no pun intended), you are left-handed, then your right hemisphere controls the left side of your body. Your right hemisphere may be your dominant hemisphere, controlling your speaking and writing abilities, or possibly, it may be your left hemisphere that controls these functions. To make matters even more complicated, among some left-handers, both hemispheres share in the speaking and writing abilities. Why this is so is a puzzle for researchers. However, for most people, the two brain hemispheres control different parts of the body and execute certain verbal abilities (left hemisphere) as well as visual-spatial abilities (right hemisphere).

What does this short outline of a brain's structures and their functions have to do with males and females? For the answer, we must examine what happens to someone who suffers brain damage either in an accident or from a stroke. If a male suffers brain damage to his left hemisphere's language centers, he is apt to suffer a debilitating communication disorder called *aphasia.* Consequently, he may not be able to say what he wants to say in a logical order or even know what certain spoken words mean. If brain damage occurs in his right hemisphere, he is more apt to suffer a loss of visual-spatial abilities. When women suffer brain damage in either their left or right hemisphere, however, they usually do not show a specific loss of abilities associated with one or the other hemispheres (Inglis and Lawson,

1981). Finding that male brains are generally more apt to show greater activity or specialization on one side of the brain (left for communication and right for visual-spatial) has led some brain researchers to speculate that male brains are more *lateralized* than female brains. In other words, a male's hemispheres are more *asymmetrical,* meaning their two hemispheres are more apt to control certain functions independently, while a female's hemispheres apparently share different functions more equally between the two hemispheres (Levy, 1976, 1981; Levy and Reid, 1976).

What does finding males more lateralized in brain function mean? Actually, no one really knows what to make of it. Brain researchers are not even sure when lateralization occurs; some suggest that it is complete by age five (Carter and Kinsbourne, 1979), while others believe that lateralization of the brain is not complete until the onset of puberty (Waber, 1977). Further research into the causes and meanings of brain lateralization is necessary before any definite conclusion can be made regarding this interesting sex difference.

Hormones and Emotional Expressions

Most of us remember those early teen years—commonly referred to as puberty—when our bodies began doing some rather strange things. Causing these physical changes was the reemergence of our hormones. At puberty, a female's ovaries begin producing large amounts of estrogen, and a male's testes, androgen. The most dramatic effects of these hormones are the onset of the secondary sex characteristics and the beginning of reproductive capabilities. A young girl's breasts begin to develop and menstruation commences (indicating the production of eggs). A young male's voice deepens, the genitals enlarge, and the testes produce viable sperm. In both sexes, underarm and pubic hair appears.

But sex hormones have been linked to other features besides the physical ones. Many people believe they influence certain behaviors, such as sexual activities and aggression. Let's deal with these two areas now.

Sexuality For centuries, peoples from very different cultures have believed that a man's virility and sexual urges, or libido, were located in his testes. When a man lost interest in sex or lacked sexual ability (i.e., sexual impotence), numerous remedies could be found in the marketplace to remedy the situation. The Hindus believed that a man's libido could be restored if he drank the milk used to boil a ram's testicles. The Romans believed that a man's interest and his anatomy would rise if he ate a horse's testes (Bahr, 1976). Today, in the Western world, few practice such questionable treatments to stimulate a man's libido. However, testosterone has been used to treat castrated men and men with abnormally low levels of androgens to restore their sexual urges (Bermant and Davidson, 1974). Although the ancients may not have known about the specific mechanism related to sexual arousal, they were on the right path. Even today, when few would advocate eating animal testes, there are many mail-order products marketed that claim to increase a man's penis size and stimulate his sexual potency. We can see that popular knowledge has long included the notion that a man's testes or the chemicals emitted by them play a decisive part in sexual urges. But what is the relationship between sexual behavior and the testes, or, more accurately, the sex hormones produced by them?

One area of continuing interest has been the relationship between levels of testosterone in the bloodstream and the incidence of sexual activity. Researchers who studied one man's testosterone levels before, during, and after sexual activity (this man must have been very dedicated to scientific inquiry!) found his testosterone levels higher during and after sexual intercourse than before (Fox et al., 1972). Others, however, have found testosterone levels unrelated to the timing of sexual activity (Monti et al., 1977) or poorly related to such timing (Doering et al., 1978). The scant research on testosterone levels and men's sexual activity is equivocal.

Among females, on the other hand, androgen levels have been found to relate to sexual arousal. Consequently, some researchers have used testosterone as a method to increase sexual arousal in women (Sopchak and Sutherland, 1960).

Aggression   One of the most frequently mentioned gender differences is that males are more aggressive than females. Animal studies have found that the male of the species usually is the more aggressive (Moyer, 1978). From the weight of countless animal studies and more than fifty studies on human aggression, researchers Eleanor Maccoby and Carol Jacklin (1974) concluded that, "Aggression is related to levels of sex hormones, and can be changed by experimental administration of these hormones" (p. 243). Let's review some of the research on men and see the relationship between aggression and testosterone.

The first correlational study between aggression and testosterone levels using a sample of men was conducted by Harold Persky and several of his colleagues (Persky et al., 1971). Two groups of normal, healthy men were selected for the study. The first group consisted of eighteen college men between the ages of seventeen and twenty-eight, and the second contained fifteen men between the ages of thirty-three and sixty-six. Each of the men took a battery of tests, one of which was the *Buss-Durkee Hostility Inventory*, a paper-and-pencil test that asks the respondent to check off statements, such as the frequency of losing one's temper and getting into fights, that apply to himself. A significantly high correlation was found between high levels of testosterone and aggression scores among the younger men but not among the older ones. We could argue that aggression on a paper-and-pencil test is one thing, but what about the testosterone levels for those men who actually lose their tempers and get into fights?

Box 2.1

Testosterone Poisoning

Have you noticed that when males get together in all-male groups (for instance, in high-school hallways or on street corners), they often throw punches at each other (not body-throbbing punches, mind you, rather pulled-punches)? Then there are times when a group of males decides to break up into teams and shoot some baskets or throw a football around "just for the fun of it." Before you know it, these men are hell-bent, and each team can think only of one thing—winning. And what about all those husbands who get choked up when their spouses ask if they still love them after 11½ years of marriage? Rather than expose their sentimental feelings (which they consider unmanly), these husbands begin to recite a litany of all the things they've provided for their families, as if buying dishwashers for their wives or paying for their kids' braces eliminates the need to say "I love you."

More than a few women have been perplexed by these and other "male rituals." Some women have even given up trying to figure out males, thinking that their energies may be better directed at less enigmatic problems, like ending world hunger or working for a détente between the superpowers. But wait—finally, there may be an explanation for these male behaviors. Alan Alda (1975)—better known as "Hawkeye" Pierce of the television program MASH—may have come up with the reason for the troubling condition that plagues so many males. Alda believes that the condition underlying these baffling male behaviors can be nothing but an epidemic of what he calls *testosterone poisoning*.

Although Alda believes that testosterone poisoning is usually not fatal, he believes that if left unchecked, it can bring misery to untold millions of men and cause the women involved with them to waste years trying to cope with them. Alda has swept aside the veil of ignorance surrounding this condition and enumerated several warning signs that indicate that a male is suffering from a severe case of testosterone poisoning. All women and men over the age of eight should commit to memory these tell-tale warning signals.

First, testosterone poisoning causes its victims to become obsessed with winning. This symptom is especially prevalent when men gather in groups, either formally (in sales meetings) or informally (at their favorite bar). Before long, one of the men will speak reverently and say something like, "You know fellas, it's just like Vince Lombardi said, 'Winning isn't everything, it's the only thing.'" The others will nod

Source: "What every woman should know about men" by A. Alda, 1975, *Ms.*, October, pp. 15–16.

Box 2.1

Continued

their approval and respond with comments like "Right on." Simply put, males worship winning, the act of besting others; being numero uno means everything to the victims of this hormonal condition.

A second danger signal is an inordinate amount of violence among sufferers of this hyper-testosterone condition. Many of them use violence to cope with frustrating situations. A simple test is adequate to see if this symptom is present in your life. (Be honest now. There's no reason to keep your condition a secret, especially from yourself, is there?) When driving on the interstate, do you frequently feel like gunning the accelerator and sideswiping the car that passed you? Do you desire to smash your grocery cart into one that is blocking your passage through the aisle in the produce section? Do you ever feel like ripping the newspaper into shreds when it won't fold in half while you're reading it? Do you rate television shows according to how many people got "wasted" and how many cars got wrecked? If you answered "yes" to three of these questions, there's a good chance that too much testosterone is your problem.

Third, the victim of testosterone poisoning finds himself more interested in "things" than people. Again, stop and think about your daily life. Are you more interested in playing with your computer or tinkering with the car rather than in playing with your children or talking with your wife? If, after some thoughtful soul-searching, you admit that your real interest lie in dealing with mechanical "things" rather than with human beings, you're in big trouble.

Last, one of the surest signals of this dread condition is what can be called the "measurement syndrome." The male victim exhibits an ever-present need to quantify or measure everything in life. For instance, few males ever ask each other if they enjoy their work. No, when males talk to one another about work, there's only one burning question: "How much money do you make?" Males who suffer from a surplus of testosterone are constantly quantifying the things that are meaningful to them: their salaries, the number of cars in their garages, or the prices they paid for their houses in the suburbs. A number is all that matters.

Alda points out some other tell-tale signs of this condition, but you probably get the message by now. The question that you should be asking, if you're still with me on this subject, is "Can testosterone poisoning be cured?" Alda answers emphatically, yes. Only yes though, if the male sufferer is willing to reappraise his life and take some drastic steps to remedy his testosterone poisoning.

Box 2.1

First, don't think you're the only one with this condition. To some degree, every male suffers its malignant effects. Others who have the condition are at this moment working to rescue themselves from its hormonal clutches. The first step then: take hope; you're not alone.

Second, begin to appreciate life for what it is and stop trying to measure everything. Enjoy a sunset; listen to another (*really* listen); enjoy your children, and let them teach you things like the simply joy of sitting on the beach and running sand through your fingers. Don't worry that you look foolish playing in the sand; your kids won't tell anyone.

Last (and this is probably the most difficult for men with testosterone poisoning), admit that you can make a mistake or be wrong about something. A good exercise that helps is to admit to being wrong while in the company of women. (Alda never said it would be easy getting over this condition.)

According to Alda, women can help a male victim of testosterone poisoning. First, women should never show sympathy for the condition. Sympathy won't help. It is better for women to make it known that they expect—no, demand—that the men in their lives take an active part in curing themselves. Testosterone poisoning can be cured only when a male decides that he alone can cure it. There is one last thing a woman can do for the male sufferer in her life. When he is well on his way to relative health after experiencing a testosterone surplus, she should tell him that there is no such thing as testosterone poisoning.

In a study of prison inmates, Kreuze and Rose (1972) studied testosterone levels between those inmates who were classified as fighters and those classified as nonfighters. Interestingly, Kreuze and Rose found no difference between these two groups of men with respect to their testosterone levels, nor did they find a relationship between their testosterone levels and their scores on the *Buss-Durkee Hostility Inventory.* Others who have used different groups of men and different measures of aggression have found equivocal results, at best, between testosterone levels and male aggression (Doering et al., 1975; Persky et al., 1977; Tieger, 1980).

In an extensive review of the literature on aggression and testosterone levels, Joseph Pleck (1981) remarked that:

> Given the social importance of aggressive behavior, it is clear that research on its possible biological sources will continue to receive serious attention. At the present time, the evidence in animals for hormonal factors in male aggression is strong (albeit complex). But comparable evidence for human male aggression is much weaker and less consistent. (p. 170)

The Premenstrual Syndrome

A female's testosterone level remains relatively stable, but her estrogen and progesterone levels show considerable fluctuation during her monthly menstrual cycle. *Menstruation,* or the monthly flow of blood, occurs in most women between the ages of twelve and forty-five or fifty. Although menstruation is a normal and natural feature of a woman's life, many ancient peoples believed a menstruating woman was unclean. Others believed the menstruating woman unfit to handle food or even dangerous to others' safety and well-being (Delaney et al., 1977). Today, few people think of menstruation or menstruating women as dangerous, but many view menstruation as hindering women from taking on certain responsibilities and being treated fairly in many situations. Karen Paige (1973) noted as much when she wrote:

> Women, the old argument goes, are eternally subject to the whims and wherefores of their biological clocks. Their ranging hormonal cycles make them emotionally unstable and intellectually unreliable. If women have second-class status, we are told, it is because they cannot control the implacable demands of that bouncing estrogen. (p. 41)

Menstruation carries with it a heavy burden of cultural beliefs, misconceptions, and downright negative feelings by many men and some women (Koeske, 1976; Sherif, 1980). In the last several decades a new element has been added to the issue of the menstruating woman, namely, the *premenstrual syndrome,* or *PMS.*

First described by an American physician (Frank, 1931), the premenstrual syndrome, or tension, as it was originally called, is thought to occur during the preceding week or two before the onset of menstruation. PMS's symptoms vary among women, but there seems to be a fairly consistent pattern among most who report suffering from PMS. The prevalent psychological symptoms are tension, depression, anxiety attacks, irritability, and mental confusion. Physical symptoms include headaches, backaches, fatigue, water retention, and cold sores (Hopson and Rosenfeld, 1984).

In the last several years, PMS has become the center of much controversy. The controversy stems from the claims made by Dr. Katharina Dalton, an English physician, and others that PMS could be a factor in some women committing violent crimes and suicide and showing a greater likelihood of certain psychiatric illnesses (Dalton, 1959, 1980). In 1980 and again in 1981, two British women accused of murder had their charges reduced to manslaughter on the grounds that both suffered from PMS. The English courts in these cases accepted the defenses' contentions that PMS was cause for diminished responsibility in these crimes (Sommer, 1984). Setting aside the issue of extreme violence or psychiatric illness, we find that other researchers have reported that PMS sufferers are more likely to suffer debilitating and negative mood swings (Golub, 1976; Rossi and Rossi, 1977). The contention among these researchers is that PMS is a real biologically caused affliction that women need be aware of and seek medical and psychological help with.

However, other researchers disagree with Dalton and her characterization of the premenstrual period with its supposed link to aberrant behavior and extreme negative moods. Harold Persky (1978) tested a group of mentally and physically healthy young women and found their moods to be fairly consistent during the three phases of their menstrual cycle. But, other researchers who studied women with histories of anxiety and/or depression found a greater likelihood of PMS symptoms than for those women who suffer from anxiety or depression only occasionally (Schuckit et al., 1975; Wetzel et al., 1975).

The causes of PMS are not clear nor agreed upon by most researchers. Some point to fluid retention, brain changes, or a decrease in progesterone levels during the premenstrual period as possible factors in negative moods (Dalton, 1964; Janowsky et al., 1973). Others, however, point out that stress-producing social factors—being fired from one's job or getting a divorce—may play a decisive role in PMS symptoms (Parlee, 1973; Sherif, 1980). Whatever the causes for the premenstrual syndrome, few can deny that the negative social attitudes about menstruation can seriously influence a woman's perceptions of her own bodily states (Golub, 1983).

SOCIOBIOLOGY: A BREWING STORM IN THE SOCIAL SCIENCES

For some time now, there has been a battle over the issue of the relative importance of one's biology versus the impact of one's environment as determinants of human behavior. In the last several years, since the introduction of a new perspective on human social behavior called *sociobiology*, the debate has become especially heated.

Most will agree that our evolutionary heritage has played a significant role in the development of our human species. Some suggest that our early ancestors who were clad in animal skins, hunted for meat, picked berries and grubbed for edibles, and huddled around small fires in caves tens of thousands of years ago have more in common with us than many might think. Beatrix Hamburg (1978) suggested as much when she wrote:

> The evolution of human behavior and its relation to social organization are best understood in the context of early man in the period of hunting-and-gathering societies. The best available information indicates that out of the roughly 2 million years that hominids have existed, over 99% of this time has been spent in hunting-and-gathering societies. Agriculture as a major way of life was instituted only 5,000 to 6,000 years ago. The Industrial Revolution is a recent development of the last 100 years, and only the most minute fraction of humans have lived in an industrial or technological society. Our biological heritage chiefly derives from the era of man the hunter. The long period of man's existence in the challenge of a hunting-and-gathering way of life has afforded the opportunity for those adaptations to become firmly established in the gene pool. It has been postulated that our intelligence, interests, emotions, and species-specific patterns of social interaction are all the evolutionary residue of the success of *Homo sapiens* in the hunting-and-gathering adaptation. In effect, modern man carries essentially the same genetic heritage as early man. (p. 378)

Sociobiology is quickly becoming an established alternative view for explaining human social behavior. We will examine its tenets and then some of the major criticisms directed against it.

The Case for Sociobiology

Edward Wilson (1978), a major proponent of sociobiology, defines this new hybrid science as "the systematic study of the biological basis of all forms of social behavior" (p. 16). In their attempt to understand the biological principles underlying social behaviors, sociobiologists draw data from several different disciplines—genetics, anthropology, psychology, and sociology. Thus sociobiology can be considered a hybrid science.

Basically, sociobiologists believe that certain behaviors are inherited through one's genes, much like one inherits skin color or hair texture. The reason for certain behaviors having a genetic link is simply that these behaviors proved advantageous to the species' survival throughout the evolutionary period. For example, in an environment with many predators, an animal who was alert and fast stood a better chance of surviving than another who was lethargic and slow. The same reasoning is applied to humans and their complex social behaviors.

Sociobiologists, for example, believe that among early human groups, when males banded together and dominated women, there was a greater likelihood of the group's survival and development to higher levels (Tiger,

1969; Tiger and Fox, 1971). The key to sociobiology's view of social behavior is simply that certain social behaviors have "become genetically encoded in a species if they contribute to the fitness of those individuals that have them" (van den Berghe, 1978, p. 20).

With an eye to their genetic basis, several specific human social behaviors have been examined, such as altruism, aggression, homosexuality, and even ethics. One area that is especially interesting with respect to our preceding discussion of gender differences is that of maternal or nurturant behaviors. A common belief is that women are somehow predisposed to act more nurturant and have special feelings toward the young. Only the female can get pregnant and carry the fetus until birth, and only the female has the necessary mammary glands suitable for the infant's nourishment. In most societies we find that women also act as the primary, if the not the sole, caretaker of the newborn infants. But is there anything preventing the father from taking over after birth and performing many of the caretaking duties? Or are women directed by their genes or something called a maternal instinct after birth to continue their care of the young?

Sociologist Alice Rossi (1977) believes that biology plays a significant role in the development of a strong mother-infant bond. Rossi believes that, historically, women who have had a greater involvement with and in their children's growth are predisposed for such behaviors. Accordingly then, because men lack the biological bond with their offspring, they never develop the same attachment to the young. Rossi thinks that new mothers exhibit many responses toward their newborns that are not learned. For example, many mothers will automatically hold their infants in their left arms, which brings their infants close to their hearts where the infants can be comforted by the soothing and rhythmic sounds.

Although Rossi is an ardent and vocal feminist who favors equality between the sexes, she has argued that some behaviors are definitely under the influence of one's biology. Her views have caused some feminists to take exception to her views (Cerullo et al., 1977–1978; Chodorow, 1977–1978). Rossi, however, believes that biology is far too important a factor in the human experience to dismiss outright because of past misuses by sexists and racists who used biological constructs to oppress others.

The Case against Sociobiology

Sociobiology has been criticized by feminists as "opening the door to justifying the oppression of one group by another on the basis of biological inferiority" (Rogan, 1978, p. 85). Besides the concerns of many feminists about the possible misuses of sociobiology's tenets, there are several obvious flaws in its propositions.

First, the basis of sociobiology rests on the existence of some as yet unidentified genes. Wilson and others have outlined a whole realm of social behaviors ranging from altruism to xenophobia (i.e., fear of strangers) without so much as identifying even one possible gene that affects these behaviors. It seems somewhat unreasonable, then, to postulate that a set of social behaviors are caused by genetic material and then not be able to point to the material in order to study its effects.

The second and most telling indictment of sociobiology, however, is the extreme difference in terms of time when we compare biological evolution to cultural evolution. Several tens of thousands of years are only a drop in the bucket in terms of biological evolution. But a decade or two can witness preliterate societies whisked into a technological age and the social behaviors of those involved completely revamped. Social customs and rituals thought appropriate only ten, fifty, or a hundred years ago would today be seen as eccentricities at best, if not evidence of aberrant mental states.

Pointing to the contention that women by virtue of their biological makeup make better parents, researchers studied the fathers of first-borns and found evidence of a strong attachment or a bond between the fathers and their newborns that the researchers called *engrossment* (Greenberg and Morris, 1974). Others have found that fathers do, in fact, give considerable attention to and show affection for their newborn infants (Parke and O'Leary, 1975). Thus, research doesn't support the popular belief that women have some biological edge over men when it comes to nurturant social behaviors.

A major problem with sociobiology is that it relies too much on an overly simple or reductionistic explanation for some very complex issues. Also, sociobiology tends to dismiss alternative explanations for social behaviors as if it were the final authority on such topics (Gould, 1976). Maya Pines (1978) states the argument against sociobiology as follows:

> Sociobiology may give the illusion of offering new insights into the human condition. Yet its methods are still so gross, its notions of "fitness" so primitive (can fitness really be measured by the frequency of copulation or the number of offspring?), our information about animal behavior still so meager, and human culture so complex that sociobiology can provide very little enlightenment about the behavior of real people at this time. (p. 24)

Time will tell if sociobiology becomes an accepted part of mainstream social science. For the moment, there appear to be too many people—laypeople and scientist alike—who fear that its tenets could be more of a hindrance than a help in trying to make sense out of the issues that surround gender differences.

ONE LAST CONSIDERATION

We have covered many topics in this chapter and noted just how the sexes differ with respect to their sex chromosomes, hormones, and reproductive structures. However, one thing that is too often forgotten is that females and males have much in common. One example should suffice to bring this fact home. Although the genetic differences found among the sex chromosomes are often stressed—the robust X as opposed to the puny Y—we shouldn't lose sight of the other forty-four chromosomes (i.e., autosomes) that make up a human being. Thus, in sheer numbers alone (for chromosomes, that is) females and males have much more in common than they have differences. Some may suggest that we would be better off if we concentrated on our similarities rather than our differences.

SUMMARY

Biological principles have been used to justify all kinds of inequality and discrimination. However, it seems unwise to dismiss biology solely because of its misuse by unscrupulous persons.

Human development begins with our sex chromosomes and hormones. Several abnormal conditions exist that show the degree to which our biology influences later development, namely, Turner's, Klinefelter's, the double-Y, androgen insensitivity, and adrenogenital syndromes.

A male's brain generally shows greater lateralization than a female's, but the significance of this biological difference is not well understood. Researchers continue to look for biology's influence on behaviors such as sexuality and aggression. A continuing controversy has arisen over the effects that a female's menstruation has on her behavior. The premenstrual syndrome has caused some researchers to think that some women's violent behavior is linked to their monthly hormonal fluctuations, while other researchers believe such behavior is caused by social factors.

In the last decade, the study of sociobiology has caused a stir in the social sciences. Sociobiology has been hailed by some as a new approach to the study of human social behavior using biological constructs; others see it as little more than a scientific way of supporting the status quo.

SUGGESTED READINGS

Asso, D. (1984). *The real menstrual cycle.* New York: Wiley.

Bleier, R. (1984). *Science and gender: A critique of biology and its theories on women.* Elmsford, NY: Pergamon.

Hrdy, S. (1983). *The women that never evolved.* Cambridge: Harvard University Press.

Lewontin, R., Rose, S., & Kamin, L. (1984). *Not in our genes.* New York: Pantheon.

Lumsden, C., & Wilson, E. (1983). *Promethean fire.* Cambridge: Harvard University Press.

Money, J., & Tucker, P. (1975). *Sexual signatures.* Boston: Little, Brown.

Montagu, A. (1952). *The natural superiority of women.* New York: Collier Books.

Wilson, E. (1978). *On human nature.* Cambridge: Harvard University Press.

Point/Counterpoint

The Double Standard

Sexual activity among humans is essential for procreation. But just because sex is required in order to carry out the injunction to "increase and multiply" doesn't mean you have to enjoy it. For centuries now, many have believed that men and women and their desires for sexual activity were somewhat at odds. Since the nineteenth century, women were thought to be less enthusiastic about sex than men were. Not long ago, ministers and teachers alike taught that sex was a wifely duty, something wives had to submit to in order to oblige their husbands' desires for and needs of sexual pleasure. Men, on the other hand, were considered driven by strong sexual urges that, if not channeled into marriage, would lead them into a life of lust and depravity. Thus, many have thought of sexual activity in terms of a *double standard*. Women, according to the double standard, should refrain from sexual activity before marriage and enter marriage with their virginity intact. Men, although exhorted to strive for purity by church teachings and wise counsel, are expected to bring to their marriages a knowledge of sex. As the old saying goes, "Boys will be boys."

But where did this notion of the double standard originate? Morton Hunt (1959) traces the roots of the double standard back to the late Middle Ages when women were placed on pedestals and wrapped in the garment of purity, while men were thought of as little more than promiscuous brutes.

Recently, however, Donald Symons in *The Evolution of Human Sexuality* (1979) has attempted to link the double standard of human sexuality to our evolutionary history. Symons suggested that during the countless centuries that humans evolved in simple hunter-gatherer groups, males and females developed different and competitive reproductive strategies. Simply stated, it was to the male's advantage to have sex with as many females as possible in order to maximize his genetic contribution to succeeding generations. In contrast, the female was best served (biologically speaking) if she was choosier about with whom she had sex. That is, if a female wished her genetic contribution to be passed on, it was to her advantage to form a more permanent relationship with a male who could provide for her and her offspring. Thus, as Symons sees it, over the centuries that human evolution unfolded, the male developed a promiscuous sexual strategy, while the female took on a more restricted and selective sexual strategy. According to Symons, the double standard is a genetically determined difference between females and males.

Symons has been taken to task by many who suggest that his sociobiological view of male and female sexual activity is neither provable nor disprovable (Shapiro, 1980). One thing lacking in Symons's analysis of human sexual behaviors is the social and cultural contexts for such behavior. Sexual activity does serve a procreative end, but it also can have different meanings in a variety of different social and cultural situations. For one thing, Symons suggests that rape is primarily an act of desire or lust. The male who rapes a female, according to Symons, is showing just how powerful the male sexual urge is, even against the weight of social prohibitions. In other words, rape is just an extreme form, possibly even a pathological form, of a man's desire to have sex.

However, most believe rape to be an act of power and dominance, not lust or desire. Furthermore, Symons doesn't explain why women's sexual activities in some societies rival that of the men's. How can this be if women's sexual nature is supposedly more restricted by her genetic endowment? Symons's analysis of human sexual activity and the double standard may be interesting, but it is also very one-sided.

What do you think?

When Don Schollander swam the 400-meter freestyle in 4 minutes, 12.2 seconds at the 1964 Olympics, he set a world record and took home a gold medal. Had he clocked the same time against the women racing at the 1980 Moscow Games, he would have come in fifth. In the pool and on the track, women have closed to within 10 per cent or less of the best male times, and their impressive gains raise an intriguing question: will men and women ever compete as equals?

Athletics is one area of sex-difference research that generates little scientific controversy. Physiologists, coaches and trainers generally agree that while women will continue to improve their performances, they will never fully overcome inherent disadvantages in size and strength. In sports where power is a key ingredient of success, the best women will remain a stroke behind or a stride slower than the best men.

Muscle vs. Fat: A man's biggest advantage is his muscle mass. Puberty stokes male bodies with the hormone testosterone, which adds bulk to muscles. A girl's puberty brings her an increase in fat, which shapes her figure but makes for excess baggage on an athlete. When growing ends, an average man is 40 per cent muscle and 15 per cent fat; a woman, 23 per cent muscle, 25 per cent fat. Training reduces fat, but no amount of working out will give a woman the physique of a man. Male and female athletes sometimes try to build bigger muscles by taking anabolic steroids—artificial male hormones that stimulate muscle growth—even though physicians consider them dangerous and all major sports have outlawed them.

Bulging muscles alone can't make a woman as strong as a man. Men have larger hearts and lungs and more hemoglobin in their blood, which enables them to pump oxygen to their muscles more efficiently than women can. A man's wider shoulders and longer arms also increase his leverage, and his longer legs move him farther with each step. "A female gymnast who puts her hands on a balance beam and raises herself up is showing a lot of strength," says Barbara Drinkwater, a physiologist with the University of California at Santa Barbara, Calif. "But a woman won't throw a discus as far as a man." Although highly conditioned women can achieve pound-for-pound parity with men in leg strength, their upper-body power is usually only one-half to two-thirds that of an equally well-conditioned male athlete.

A few sports make a virtue of anatomy for women. Extra body fat gives a female English Channel swimmer better buoyancy and more insulation from the cold, and narrow shoulders reduce her resistance in the water. As a result, women have beaten the fastest male's round-trip Channel crossing by a full three hours. In long-distance running contests, women may also be on equal footing with men. Grete Waitz's time of 2 hours, 25 minutes and 41 seconds in last year's New York City Marathon was good enough to bring her in ahead of all but 73 of the 11,000 men who finished the race. "Women tend to do better relative to men the longer the distance gets," says Joan Ullyot, author of "Running Free." "On races 100 kilometers and up, it may turn out that women are more suited to endurance than men." Under the body-draining demands of extended exertion, a woman's fat may provide her with deeper energy reserves. Satisfied that women can take the strain, the International Olympic Committee has authorized a women's marathon for the 1984 Games. In previous years the longest Olympic race for females was 1,500 meters—less than a mile.

Tough: Women athletes have dispelled the myths about their susceptibility to injury. The uterus and ovaries are surrounded by shock-absorbing fluids—far better protected than a male's exposed reproductive equipment. And the bouncing of breasts doesn't make them more prone to cancer, or even to sagging. As for psychological toughness, Penn State physiologist and sports psychologist Dorothy Harris says that "if you give a woman a shot at a $100,000 prize, you discover that she can be every bit as aggressive as a man."

Going one-on-one with a man is not the goal of most women in sports. "It's like pitting lions against tigers," declares Ullyot. "Women's achievements should not be downgraded by comparing them to men's." But as organized women's sports grow up, they will have to face up to at least one serious masculine challenge. According to Ann Uhlir, executive director of the Association for Intercollegiate Athletics for Women, when a college starts taking its women's sports program seriously, it tends to put a man in charge.

Chapter 3

THE PSYCHOLOGICAL PERSPECTIVE

*M*an's world, woman's place remain, and our society continues to ascribe different psychological attributes to each sex, and to assign different duties and ways of living to men and women because it is assumed that they have differing capabilities, moral, social and intellectual as well as physical.

Elizabeth Janeway

After reading the last chapter, who can deny that males and females differ biologically? Many people have gone beyond these biological differences and suggested that females and males differ in other ways as well. For example, in Chinese cosmology the principles of *yang* and *yin* are thought of as opposite forces that complement each other. Yang manifests itself as an active masculine principle found in light and heat; yin is the passive female principle exhibited in cold and darkness. Although most don't turn to Chinese symbols to explain the world, many do associate different characteristics with males and with females and from these characteristics go on to see the world in terms of males being in control and females being controlled (Janeway, 1971).

In this chapter we will examine the many elements that comprise the issue of gender differences. We will, however, focus on the psychological differences at this time. Psychologists have long been interested in finding, measuring, and explaining psychological differences between the genders.

We will begin by looking at what is called gender identity or the subjective experience of being either male or female. We will also examine transsexualism, which is one of the most fascinating areas related to gender identity. Next, we will discuss the work of Eleanor Maccoby and Carol Jacklin and their encyclopedic study of gender differences. Afterward, we will turn our attention to what people consider to be typical behaviors for each gender in terms of gender stereotypes. Then we will examine how psychologists have conceived of the psychological constructs known as masculinity and femininity. Finally, we will outline several theories that attempt to explain the ways in which females and males come to learn their appropriate gender behaviors and roles.

Psychology is a rich science because it borrows so heavily from other disciplines like biology and sociology. Yet, the richness of the material can often lead to much debate over the basis of gender behaviors. Having our discussion of the psychology of gender differences sandwiched in between the biological and sociological perspectives gives us a clue to the different directions psychologists look toward for possible answers.

GENDER IDENTITY: A CORE INGREDIENT

What is *gender identity?* Gender identity, the seventh stage in sexual and gender development (see table 2.1 in chapter 2), is defined as the subjective feelings and perceptions of being one sex and not the other. There are few things people are more certain about than their being either male or female. Obviously, we didn't arrive at this awareness overnight. In fact, our gender identity developed over a period of time that began somewhere during our second year and probably was completed by our third or fourth birthday.

What influences the development of one's gender identity? John Money and several colleagues suggest that learning and social pressures play a dominant role in shaping one's awareness as either male or female (Money, 1980). Others believe that biological factors play the decisive role in gender identity formation (Gadpaille, 1980; Imperato-McGinley, 1974, 1976, 1979; MacLusky and Naftolin, 1981). Still others suggest that gender identity is a complex result of both biological and social factors (Diamond and Karlen, 1980). At this point in time, there is no general agreement among researchers regarding the development of gender identity. Furthermore, the debate is likely to continue into the near future as researchers learn more about this complex issue.

One of the most intriguing aspects of gender identity is found among people who exhibit extreme confusion over their gender identities and who display a condition called transsexualism.

Transsexualism

What would happen if tomorrow morning you woke up and discovered that your genitals somehow changed during the night? Last night you went to sleep as a female (or male), and this morning you found that you had the genitals of a male (or female). Chances are you would be very upset. Some people, however, find themselves in such a predicament every day when they awake and find themselves trapped in a body of the wrong sex. These people, commonly referred to as *transsexuals,* believe themselves to be the victims of a grotesque error in that their genitals do not match their gender identity (Blank, 1981; Braunthal, 1981). Estimates vary as to how many people experience this phenomenon, but most experts agree that approximately 1 out of every 100,000 males and 1 out of every 130,000 females fit the description (Pauly, 1974).

In 1953, the world suddenly became aware of the transsexual phenomenon when a former soldier went to Denmark and had his male genitals surgically removed; he then returned to the United States as a female (Feinbloom, 1976). Subsequently, newspapers and magazines headlined Christine Jorgensen's famous "sex change." During the early 1960s, British writer and mountain climber James Morris opted for sex reassignment surgery and later wrote of his transsexual experience in a book entitled *Conundrum* (1974). Since these two widely publicized transsexual changes, others have followed with varying degrees of notoriety. One of the most famous recent transsexuals is Dr. Richard Raskin, an eye surgeon, who changed his sex to become Renne Richards, the professional tennis player. Many people objected when Richards joined the women's professional tennis circuit because she was thought to have a distinct advantage over other women.

For transsexuals, a major goal is to change their body's sex organs to match their gender identity. Achieving this can be a prolonged and agonizing process that oftentimes ends up in self-mutilation or even worse. Attempts at changing a transsexual's gender identity through various psychotherapies has had only limited success (Katchadourian and Lunde, 1979; Tollison and Adams, 1979). Rather than live their lives as a lie, many transsexuals choose *sex reassignment surgery*, or the surgical removal of one set of sex organs and the construction of the opposite sex's sex organs.

Before undergoing sex reassignment surgery, a transsexual must be judged by a panel of qualified experts to be truly transsexual and not psychotic. The first step after a transsexual has been judged nonpsychotic requires that the transsexual live the life of the opposite gender (Money and Wiedeking, 1980). During this period, for instance, a male-to-female transsexual adopts the clothes, hairstyle, and mannerisms associated with females. Some even change their names to fit their new identity. In this way, the transsexual is given an opportunity to play out the new role as much as possible to make sure that he or she is prepared to live the rest of his or her life as the opposite gender.

During this time also, a male transsexual is given the hormone estrogen on a daily basis to stimulate female development, such as breast enlargement, reduction in muscularity, and a smoother skin texture. Estrogen treatment also causes the prostate gland and seminal vesicles to shrink. However, the pitch of the voice is not affected, and some must learn how to speak in a more "feminine" way. The female transsexual takes testosterone treatments to suppress menstruation and stimulate facial and body hair. Her breasts, however, require surgery to reduce their size. Thus, during this first period, lasting anywhere from one to two years, the transsexual lives the life of the opposite gender and receives frequent doses of the sex hormone associated with the opposite sex.

If all goes well and the transsexual is judged psychologically fit and able to adjust to a permanent physical change, sex reassignment surgery is the next step. For the male-to-female transsexual, the surgery requires that the penis and testes be removed. Next, the external female genitals are constructed, which results in rather normal-looking female genital structures. The more difficult female-to-male operation requires that a tube of abdominal skin be molded to form a penis. However, the new penis is not capable of erection nor able to experience tactile sensations. For some female-to-male transsexuals, then, a mechanical device that can be inflated is implanted within the new penis, thus mimicking an erect penis.

The outcome of sex reassignment surgery is mixed at best. One investigator who interviewed fifty male-to-female transsexuals found that over forty reported contentment and social acceptance of their new gender role, with only one totally dissatisfied with the results (Benjamin, 1966). Others who have done similar studies of postoperative male-to-female transsexuals found that the great majority were satisfied with the outcome of their surgery and their new life (Pauly, 1968). However, others have found that no significant psychological benefits accrued to the transsexuals who opted for such drastic surgical procedures (Meyer and Reter, 1979). Others have pointed out that one of the most pressing concerns facing those who help transsexuals is the number of mentally disturbed persons who seek sex reassignment surgery (Newman and Stoller, 1974). There is more than the usual need for strict controls and screening techniques to prevent those who really can suffer irreparable psychological harm from undergoing such drastic therapy (Lothstein, 1982). With the growing concern over the benefits versus the possible disasters associated with sex reassignment surgery, many hospitals that once performed this type of surgery have called a moratorium on this procedure for the time being.

As we can see, the transsexual phenomenon is filled with more than its share of controversy. And yet, we should extend every type of help possible to aid those who feel that their bodies don't match their subjective experience of who they are.

GENDER DIFFERENCES

In 1974, psychologists Eleanor Maccoby and Carol Jacklin published their now classic text *The Psychology of Sex Differences.* In this work, Maccoby and Jacklin examined over 1,400 published studies ranging over a broad spectrum of human activities, including cognitive functions, personality traits, and social behaviors. Their aim for such a massive undertaking was "to sift the evidence to determine which of the many beliefs about sex differences have a solid basis in fact and which do not" (p. vii). Their analyses revealed that many of the presumed gender differences were more myth than fact, whereas a few differences appeared to stand up. Let's begin by examining briefly some of their findings.

The Myths of Gender Differences

Myth 1: Girls are more social than boys. Maccoby and Jacklin could find no convincing evidence that girls are more social than boys. During early childhood, both boys and girls played with others with about equal frequency. Boys were no more apt to play with inanimate objects than girls were, and at certain times, boys actually played with their playmates more than girls did.

Myth 2: Girls are more suggestible than boys. Boys are just as likely as girls are to imitate others' behavior spontaneously. When there is pressure to conform to an ambiguous situation, both sexes are equally susceptible to persuasive face-to-face communication.

Myth 3: Girls have lower self-esteem than boys. Overall, girls and boys are similar in their personal views of self-confidence and self-satisfaction. They do, however, differ in the areas within which they feel self-confident. For example, boys are more likely to see themselves as powerful and dominant, whereas girls rate themselves higher in social competence. During most of their early school years, girls and boys believe they can influence their own fate. During the college years, however, young men are more likely to believe that they can control their destinies and are more optimistic about their futures than young, similarly-aged women are. We should not interpret this to mean that young women have lower self-esteem than young men. Maccoby and Jacklin suggest that young men are perhaps overconfident.

Myth 4: Girls lack motivation to achieve. Girls and boys can be equally motivated to achieve, but both are influenced by different factors that push their achievement levels. Girls are motivated to achieve in situations where there is less competition or social comparison. Boys, on the other hand, apparently require a sense of competition or ego-involvement in order for them to achieve the same levels of achievement as girls.

Myth 5: Girls are better at rote learning and simple tasks. Both boys and girls perform equally well on simple, repetitive tasks. Neither is more susceptible to simple conditioning on somewhat automatic processes.

Myth 6: Boys are more analytic than girls. To analyze, one must disregard unimportant aspects of a situation in favor of the important features of a task. Both males and females are as apt to pay attention to unimportant details as to the important ones.

Myth 7: Girls are more affected by heredity, boys more by environment. Both before and after birth, boys are more vulnerable to a variety of harmful agents. However, we cannot conclude from this that boys are more affected by their environments than girls are. Both males and females learn with equal facility in many different situations, and if learning is a measure of the effects of the environment, then both are equal in this regard.

Myth 8: Girls are auditory, boys are visual. Both female and male infants respond equally to sights and sounds in their environments.

However, some of the studies reviewed by Maccoby and Jacklin point to several areas where there seems to be some gender differences with respect to specific abilities and to one personality trait.

The Evidence of Gender Differences

Fact 1: Girls have greater verbal ability than boys. Girls' verbal abilities mature more quickly than boys'. During the early school years, girls' and boys' verbal abilities are similar, but beginning in high school and beyond, girls take the lead. Girls' greater verbal abilities include a better understanding and fluency of the complexities of language, better spelling and creative writing abilities, and better comprehension of analogies.

Fact 2: Boys excel in visual-spatial ability. Beginning in early adolescence, boys are better able to rotate an object in space. Boys also are better at picking out a simple design or figure that is embedded within a larger more complex design.

Fact 3: Boys excel in mathematical ability. Again, beginning in adolescence, boys show a greater facility with math than girls show. However, in those studies that use verbal processes in mathematical questions, girls do better than boys; on those that require visual-spatial abilities, boys do better than girls.

Fact 4: Males are more aggressive than females. Beginning in the early preschool years, boys are more physically aggressive than girls. Boys exhibit more mock-fighting and other forms of aggression than girls. Also, boys direct their aggression during these early years more toward other boys than toward girls. This difference continues throughout the school years and into adulthood.

Analyzing the Data

Some of Maccoby and Jacklin's conclusions have been challenged because, in many cases, they simply counted up the studies that found a gender difference (no matter which gender the results favored) from those that didn't. If there were more differences than similarities, Maccoby and Jacklin concluded a significant gender difference. Some have argued that such a procedure is questionable (Unger, 1979b). Others noted that many of the studies Maccoby and Jacklin reported contained relatively few participants, leading to the possibility of finding little or no gender differences with respect to the issue under study (Block, 1976). Julia Sherman (1978) re-reviewed many of Maccoby and Jacklin's studies and found that many times the magnitude of the differences were quite small. Along the same line, Janet Hyde (1981) re-analyzed Maccoby and Jacklin's verbal, quantitative, visual-spatial, and field articulation studies using a technique called meta-analysis. (Meta-analysis is a statistical technique whereby the data from several studies can be analyzed all together [Glass et al., 1981].) Maccoby and Jacklin had suggested that based on their analyses these abilities showed "well-established" gender differences. However, Hyde's analysis of these same studies prompted a note of caution for such a generalization. She concluded:

> The main conclusion that can be reached from this analysis is that the gender differences in verbal ability, quantitative ability, visual-spatial ability, and field articulation reported by Maccoby and Jacklin (1974) are small. Gender differences appear to account for no more than 1%–5% of the population variance. . . . Generally, it seems that gender differences in verbal ability are smaller and gender differences in spatial ability are larger, but even in the latter case, gender differences account for less than 5% of the population variance. (pp. 894, 896)

Other researchers have found that even though males are more likely to describe themselves as more aggressive, in real life situations, there is little actual gender difference in displays of aggression (Frodi et al., 1977). When provoked by insult or attack, women are just as likely to aggress as men are. However, women are less likely than men to instigate aggressive behaviors or act as third-party instigators of aggression (Gaebelein, 1977).

Psychologists have spent countless hours researching gender differences, as testified by the innumerable studies that have been published in the last fifty years. As found in reviews such as Maccoby and Jacklin's, Block's, and Hyde's, few genuine differences of any substantial nature can be found. When we do find differences, for example, that males dream more than females (Hall, 1984) or that females report they cry more often than males (Lombardo et al., 1983), we are tempted to say, "So what?"

For a long time, psychologists have mined the vein of individual differences but have not produced the highest grade of results for their efforts. Possibly, it's time to move to other fields where less emphasis is placed on static individual and group differences and more emphasis is placed on other more process-oriented approaches toward the study of gender (Deaux, 1984).

GENDER STEREOTYPES

What's oversimplistic in content, difficult to argue against, oftentimes both humorous and cruel, appeals to many people when not directed at them, and yet offends most who are the brunt of it? Why, *stereotypes*, of course! Stereotypes are everywhere. Comedians use them routinely, politicians orate against their opponents with them, and most of us fall prey to them at some time or other. Sadly, the real tragedy is that many people use stereotypes as their sole source of information about others.

But what is a stereotype, anyway? Simply defined, a stereotype is an oversimplified set of descriptive components about a visible group of people who are thought to share certain characteristics (Ashmore and Del Boca, 1979, 1981; McCauley et al., 1980). Nearly every group imaginable is designated by a set of stereotypes. What comes to your mind with respect to the traits, behaviors, and physical characteristics about groups like teachers,

Figure 3.1 What images come to mind when you think of the typical male and female? Do the two people above fit your images? They do if you accept the traditional gender stereotypes that our society perpetuates for the genders.

movie stars, students, police officers, or forest rangers? It should be obvious that every group has a set of stereotypes associated with it; some components of the stereotype may seem flattering, but others are less so. In this section we will concentrate on the specific stereotypes directed toward males and females—the gender stereotypes.

Mr. and Ms. Typical

What comes to mind when you think of a "typical" female? After a moment's pause, did words like gentle, talkative, passive, tactful, and of course, emotional cross your mind? Now, what about a "typical" male? This time did confident, aggressive, independent, dominant, worldly-wise, and the old standby, unemotional pop up? Don't be surprised if these personality traits came to mind when you thought about a typical male and female. The early research in *gender stereotypes* found that most people thought of the genders in such terms (Fernberger, 1948; McKee and Sherriffs, 1957, 1959). Each gender supposedly had its own set of components or clusters of traits; one for males and the other for females (Broverman et al., 1972; Rosenkrantz et al., 1968). Let's now examine the personality traits that we most generally associate with each gender stereotype. To do this we shall highlight the research of Paul Rosenkrantz (et al., 1968) and his colleagues.

Rosenkrantz asked a group of college males and females to examine a list of 122 bipolar items, such as *very aggressive* versus *not at all aggressive*

and *very dependent* versus *not at all dependent*, on a 7–point scale. The scale used in the study looked something like this:

1. Not at all aggressive   Very aggressive
   1 . . . . . 2 . . . . . 3 . . . . . 4 . . . . 5 . . . . . 6 . . . . . 7 . . . . .
2. Very dependent   Not at all dependent
   1 . . . . . 2 . . . . 3 . . . . . 4 . . . . 5 . . . . . 6 . . . . . 7 . . . . .

The students then were told to imagine that they were about to meet either an adult female or male for the first time and all they knew about this person was his or her gender. Using the scale, the students checked off the degree to which each of the bipolar items reflected what they thought characteristic of each gender. Overall, the students thought of an adult male as more typically aggressive, independent, dominant, ambitious, etc. An adult female was thought of as showing a *relative* absence of the characteristics associated with a male. These students saw a typical female as emotionally expressive, talkative, and concerned with security. Upon further study, the stereotypic characteristics for males and females fell into two broad categories or clusters: a competency cluster for males and a warmth-expressiveness cluster for females (see table 3.1). Others have found much the same with their measures of gender stereotypes (Spence et al., 1974).

Other more recent researchers, however, have taken the position that the gender stereotypes comprise more than only certain personality traits (Deaux and Lewis, 1983, 1984; Eagly, 1983; Eagly and Wood, 1982; Grant and Holmes, 1981, 1982; Locksley et al., 1980, 1982). Specifically, Kay Deaux and Laurie Lewis (1984) suggest that:

> a number of separate components of gender stereotypes can be identified: specifically, traits, role behaviors, occupations, and physical appearance, each of which has a masculine and feminine version. Although no component is seen as the exclusive province of one or the other sex, masculine and feminine components are significantly more strongly associated with males and females, respectively. The like-sex components (e.g., male role behaviors and masculine traits) bear some relationship to each other, but correlational analysis suggests that they are best viewed as separate factors that can vary independently. (p. 992)

TABLE 3.1   MALE-VALUED AND FEMALE-VALUED STEREOTYPIC ITEMS

Feminine Pole	Masculine Pole
Male-valued Items	
Not at all aggressive	Very aggressive
Not at all independent	Very independent
Very Emotional	Not at all emotional
Does not hide emotions at all	Almost always hides emotions
Very subjective	Very objective
Very easily influenced	Not at all easily influenced
Very submissive	Very dominant
Dislikes math and science very much	Likes math and science very much
Very excitable in a minor crisis	Not at all excitable in a minor crisis
Very passive	Very active
Not at all competitive	Very competitive
Very illogical	Very logical
Very home oriented	Very worldly
Not at all skilled in business	Very skilled in business
Very sneaky	Very direct
Does not know the way of the world	Knows the way of the world
Feelings easily hurt	Feelings not easily hurt
Not at all adventurous	Very adventurous
Has difficulty making decisions	Can make decisions easily
Cries very easily	Never cries
Almost never acts as a leader	Almost always acts as a leader
Not at all self-confident	Very self-confident
Very uncomfortable about being aggressive	Not at all uncomfortable about being aggressive
Not at all ambitious	Very ambitious
Unable to separate feelings from ideas	Easily able to separate feelings from ideas
Very dependent	Not at all dependent
Very conceited about appearance	Never conceited about appearance
Female-valued Items	
Very talkative	Not at all talkative
Very tactful	Very blunt
Very gentle	Very rough
Very aware of feelings of others	Not at all aware of feelings of others
Very religious	Not at all religious
Very interested in own appearance	Not at all interested in own appearance
Very neat in habits	Very sloppy in habits
Very quiet	Very loud
Very strong need for security	Very little need for security
Enjoys art and literature very much	Does not enjoy art and literature at all
Easily expresses tender feelings	Does not express tender feelings at all

Source: "Sex-role stereotypes and clinical judgments of mental health" by I. Broverman et al., 1970, *Journal of Consulting and Clinical Psychology, 34(1),* p. 3. Copyright 1970 by the American Psychological Association. Reprinted by permission of the author.

TABLE 3.2   STEREOTYPES OF MALES AND FEMALES: PROBABILITY JUDGMENTS

Characteristic	Judgment[a]	
	Men	Women
Trait		
Independent	.78	.58
Competitive	.82	.64
Warm	.66	.77
Emotional	.56	.84
Role Behaviors		
Financial provider	.83	.47
Takes initiative with opposite sex	.82	.54
Takes care of children	.50	.85
Cooks meals	.42	.83
Physical Characteristics		
Muscular	.64	.36
Deep voice	.73	.30
Graceful	.45	.68
Small-boned	.39	.62

a. Probability that the average person of either sex would possess a characteristic.

Source: "From individual differences to social categories: Analysis of a decade's research on gender" by K. Deaux, 1984, *American Psychologist, 39(2)*, p. 112. Copyright 1984 by the American Psychological Association. Reprinted by permission of the author.

An important feature of this new multicomponent approach to gender stereotypes is the emphasis on the relative versus absolute assignment of characteristics to males and females. For example, although one of the role components of the male's gender stereotype is that of financial provider for the family, many women also perform this role. Thus, people do not define the various gender stereotypic characteristics in terms of their being only associated with one gender and not the other. We can see this difference in people's perceptions of the relative differences in gender stereotypes by looking at some of the results found in Deaux and Lewis's study (see table 3.2).

Note that when people assign the role of financial provider to either males or females, there is a much higher degree of relatedness to males (.83) than to females (.47). However, even more interesting and germane to our discussion is the finding that although the difference in assignment is significantly different, "the pattern is clearly not one of the all-or-none variety" (Deaux, 1984, p. 112). No longer are men seen as the exclusive financial provider. Many of the characteristics once thought to be the sole feature of one gender or the other have been found to vary. Males can be thought of as, and are, graceful, caring for children, and warm. Likewise, many females can be thought of as, and are, competitive, sexually assertive, and muscular.

This new multicomponent approach to gender stereotypes with its emphasis on relative differences rather than absolutes appears more realistic and fruitful for researchers (Eagly and Stephan, 1984).

Learning the Gender Stereotypes

Two questions about gender stereotypes need to be addressed at this time. First, at what age do people begin to exhibit an awareness of the contents of gender stereotypes? And second, how can we explain why so many females and males behave in accordance with the gender stereotypes?

First of all, if researchers have presented a good case that most people perceive each gender in relatively stereotypic ways, how early do these perceptions begin? Most would agree that children live in a world where the genders are portrayed in different ways (see chapter 4). As for the basic biological distinctions between the genders, most children as early as two years of age know whether they are boys or girls. By age three, most can correctly apply gender labels to others; for instance, they know that adult males can be "daddies" and adult females can be "mommies" (Thompson, 1975).

However, we might expect that in these changing times with many women involved in occupations that not too long ago were considered "for-men-only" (e.g., engineers, lawyers, judges, and so on), children's perceptions of gender stereotypes would be significantly changed. In a rather straightforward study, Deanna Kuhn and her associates (Kuhn et al., 1978) observed a group of two- and three-year-old preschoolers. Interestingly, these children's parents were students and faculty members at Stanford University. We might expect then that these children would perceive males and females in less than traditionally gender stereotypic ways. However, even at this early age, these children (with their nontypical parents) already thought that girls were more likely to play with dolls, help their mothers, clean house, become nurses, and ask for help. Boys, on the other hand, were thought more likely to help their fathers, become bosses, and express aggression. Others have found that preschoolers typically stereotype each gender's actions in play activities by having boys go off to work, while girls stay home and cook (Garvey, 1977). By age five or six, children apparently have a thorough knowledge of the gender stereotypes (Brown, 1956, 1957). Thus, an awareness of the contents of gender stereotypes begins in the preschool years and is rather well-developed by the time a youngster goes off to first grade (Fagot, 1984 a and b).

That brings us to our second question. With so many social changes going on around us, many of which are contrary to the traditional gender stereotypes, how can we explain why so many people typically behave in accordance with them? In other words, just because children are aware of gender stereotypes at an early age doesn't mean they must act accordingly, or must they? A possible clue to this question may lie in the notion of *self-fulfilling prophecy* (Merton, 1968). According to Robert Merton, a self-fulfilling prophecy occurs when a person's expectations in and of themselves cause something to come true. The self-fulfilling prophecy may shed some light on why so many people behave as if gender stereotypes are actually the way typical females and males do act.

To explain how this could come about, let's focus on the process behind a self-fulfilling prophecy. Take two people, one we will call the *perceiver*, and the other, the *target*. When the perceiver has some expectation about the target, chances are that the perceiver will act toward the target in accordance with her or his expectation; the target, in turn, will respond in a manner consistent with the perceiver's expectations (Darley and Fazio, 1980). For example, a six-year-old boy who thinks stereotypically that all girls are fearful of bugs and squiggly creatures yells at his sister when she is startled at finding a worm in the backyard, "Scardy-cat, scardy-cat!" The little girl may begin to think that she should be fearful of crawly things even though she wasn't before. If others also treat the little girl as if she should be scared when confronted with insects, snakes, and other similar creatures, then possibly she will come to believe that she is, in fact, fearful in these situations. As a result, the little girl may grow up believing that all girls typically fear certain creatures, and she may act accordingly. Researchers, like Mark Snyder, have found that the power of the self-fulfilling prophecy explains to a great extent why so many males and females act in accordance with gender stereotypes (Skrypnek and Snyder, 1982; Snyder and Swann, 1978; Snyder et al., 1977).

Gender stereotypes are learned early in life through mechanisms like the self-fulfilling prophecy, rewards and punishments, and other social forces. The result is that most males and females come to behave as if the gender stereotypes, with their components of personality traits, role behaviors, and physical characteristics, are somehow valid representations of each gender.

Let's now move on to another issue of gender, those psychological features commonly referred to as masculinity and femininity.

MASCULINITY AND FEMININITY

If there is a basic motto that sums up the field of psychology, it may well be: "Everything that exists, exists in some quantity, and if it exists in some quantity, it can be measured." Psychologists have long been interested in measuring the purported psychological characteristics of *masculinity* and *femininity*. According to psychologist Anne Constantinople (1973, p. 390), the concepts of masculinity and femininity "have a long history in psychological discourse, but both theoretically and empirically they seem to be among the muddiest concepts in the psychologist's vocabulary."

How can masculinity or femininity—two concepts that are clearly understood by most people—be "the muddiest concepts in a psychologist's vocabulary?" The answer requires that we examine some of the history dealing with how psychologists have defined masculinity and femininity (M-F) over the years and what kinds of tests they have created that purportedly measure these psychological constructs (Lewin, 1984a and b).

Over the past fifty or so years, most psychologists interested in masculinity and/or femininity have focused their attention on scrutinizing the results of various tests developed to assess the personality characteristics or behaviors thought to define these psychological dimensions. However, a problem encountered in this research becomes apparent when we realize that over the years psychologists have developed three very different models of what constitutes masculinity and femininity. The three different approaches have been called the simple, the multilevel, and the androgynous conceptions of masculinity and femininity (Pleck, 1981, 1984). Let's discuss these different versions to see just how some of the present confusion came about.

The Simple Conception of Masculinity/Femininity

During the 1930s and 1940s, most psychologists accepted the then commonly held notion that the behaviors, attitudes, and interests generally associated with either masculinity or femininity (M-F) were exclusive features of males and females. In other words, males and females were not only thought to differ in terms of their basic personality characteristics, but also these characteristics were conceived of as opposite of each other. For example, masculinity was shown by a person's strong competitiveness, aggressiveness, and independence. The opposite of these would make up what would be called femininity. Therefore, a person would show the characteristics of femininity by the lack of competitiveness, aggressiveness, and independence. In terms of behavior, whatever a masculine person did, a feminine person didn't.

Much of the research during these years revolved around developing paper-and-pencil tests that would assess the degree of a person's masculinity or femininity. To accomplish this, large groups of males and females were given items to determine how they differed in their responses. For example, items like the following were found to differentiate between males and females. Females tended to give the answer noted in the brackets more frequently than males.

1. I do not like sports. [True]
2. Home chores do not appeal to me. [False]
3. I think I would like the work of a building contractor. [False]
4. I prefer a shower to a bathtub. [False]
5. I like mechanics magazines. [False]

(Items 1 and 2 come from the M-F scale taken from the *Minnesota Multiphasic Personality Inventory* and items 3–5 come from Gough's *Femininity Scale*.)

The more items a person answered in the "feminine" direction, the more feminine this person was supposed to be. Some of the more common M-F tests incorporating this "simple" conception of masculinity and femininity were Gough's *Femininity Scale* (1952), the M-F scale on the *Minnesota Multiphasic Personality Inventory* (Hathaway and McKinley, 1943), and the *Terman-Miles Attitude-Interest Test* (Terman and Miles, 1936).

The Multilevel Conception of Masculinity/Femininity

During the 1950s, the multilevel approach to masculinity and femininity came into vogue. Primarily because of the influence of Sigmund Freud's theory of the unconscious, researchers began to conceptualize masculinity and femininity as existing on two separate and independent levels within a person's personality—on both conscious and unconscious planes. It seems that many people still accept this multilevel model of gender characteristics if we listen to how they talk about others. For example, most of us have heard someone analyze a man's overt bravado and macho behavior as nothing but a cover-up for some deep seated insecurity over his masculinity. Such an analysis implicitly suggests that what a man is on the "outside" may not be the same as what he is on the "inside." According to this perspective, a person can exhibit either masculine or feminine characteristics at the conscious level (on the outside, so to speak) *and* masculine or feminine characteristics at the unconscious level (on the inside).

Using this multilevel model, a woman or a man may exhibit feminine or masculine characteristics consciously and feminine or masculine characteristics unconsciously. How would this be inferred? Take the example of a woman who consciously feels herself to be everything womanly or feminine. She likes what other women like, shows interest in womanly things, dresses in feminine fashions, and overall behaves according to traditional gender expectations. But while at work, this same woman does not defer to her boss's decisions. At work, she acts the way most people would expect a man to act in the presence of his boss. This woman just doesn't act deferential when in the presence of authority figures, which is what many people think women are supposed to do! Consequently, those who believe in the multilevel model suggest that this female displays feminine characteristics at the conscious level and masculine characteristics at the unconscious level, indicated by an assertive and independent quality when dealing with authority, which according to some is indicative of masculinity (Miller and Swanson, 1960). One of the better known masculinity/femininity tests incorporating a multilevel approach to assess this conscious and unconscious approach is the *Franck Drawing Completion Test* (Franck and Rosen, 1949).

The Androgynous Conception of Masculinity/Femininity

Finally, during the late 1960s and the 1970s, the third perspective on masculinity and femininity came about, namely, the androgynous model. From this perspective, unlike the simple version of M-F, masculinity was not thought of as being comprised of personality characteristics that were opposites of femininity. Nor was masculinity or femininity conceived as existing on different mental or conscious levels of personality, as presented by the multilevel model. Rather, the psychological characteristics of masculinity and femininity were viewed as being comprised of two independent dimensions that could be separate but could overlap as well (Gonen and Lansky, 1968).

Psychologist Sandra Bem (1974) developed a test called the *Bem Sex Role Inventory,* or the *BSRI,* that attempted to measure androgyny. Consisting of sixty socially desirable "masculine" (e.g., aggressive and self-reliant), "feminine" (e.g., shy and warm), and "neutral" (e.g., happy and sincere) adjectives, the person taking the test indicated the extent to which each item was true for themselves in terms of a 7–point scale ranging from 1 (i.e., never or almost never true) to 7 (i.e., always or almost always true). The test gives separate masculinity and femininity scores that can be combined into one of four types: (1) androgynous (high on both the masculine and feminine items); (2) masculine (high on the masculine items and low on the feminine ones); (3) feminine (low on the masculine items and high on the feminine ones); and (4) undifferentiated (low on both the masculine and feminine items). Others have also developed androgyny scales, such as Berzins, Welling, and Wetter's (1975) *PFO Andro Scale* and Spense, Helmreich, and Stapp's (1974) *Personal Attributes Questionnaire.*

Thus, in the past forty or so years, psychologists have conceptualized and measured masculinity, femininity, and androgyny in several different ways. However, most measures developed to tap masculinity and femininity have focused on what can be seen as merely different variations of instrumental (masculinity) and expressive (femininity) traits (Taylor and Hall, 1982). Such a limited view is thought of as less than useful to analyze the various features associated with gender (Deaux, 1984).

Much of the confusion surrounding masculinity and femininity is caused by the vastly different definitions presented. As long as researchers cannot agree on what they are measuring nor come up with a straightforward scale for its measurement, the future doesn't look bright for these constructs. Constantinople's contention that masculinity and femininity are some of the muddiest concepts in psychology appears to be not only a view of the past but of the future as well.

Psychologists have a problem with not being able to agree about their subject matter (Kimble, 1984). Part of the problem lies in the fact that not all psychologists accept the existence of personality features such as masculinity or femininity. Regardless of whether or not masculinity or femininity exists, they have been extremely important concepts. Maybe it's time, however, to shelve them and move on to other aspects of gender.

Let's now move on to a discussion of several psychological theories about how children develop their gender identities and learn their gender roles.

PSYCHOLOGICAL THEORIES OF GENDER DEVELOPMENT

As we noted earlier, social scientists do not always agree on what underlies the development of a person's gender identity. We will therefore present several theories, all of which have very different explanations for how gender identities and gender roles develop. We will detail three theories: the psychoanalytic-identification theory, the social-learning perspective, and the cognitive-developmental model. Let's begin with what is generally considered the most controversial theory of gender development, Sigmund Freud's.

The Psychoanalytic-Identification Theory of Gender Identity

Sigmund Freud (1927, 1959a, 1959b, 1965), the nineteenth century Viennese physician, turned the social scientific community upside-down with his theory of childhood sexuality and his view that the sexes differed physically and psychologically as well. Freud theorized that basic psychological gender differences (i.e., the characteristics of masculinity and femininity) were rooted in biology, and this thinking gave rise to his famous—some may suggest infamous—statement that "anatomy is destiny."

Freud theorized that a child's personality moves through five stages, namely, the *psychosexual stages*. Freud further speculated that depending on the interactions between the child and his or her parents, each stage could be fraught with problems.

The concept of *identification* is the basis for Freud's theory of gender development. By identification, Freud meant the child should acquire the personality traits, behaviors, attitudes, and roles of the same-sex parent. Little boys should, if they have properly identified with their fathers, develop masculine characteristics and learn the male gender role, whereas little girls (if all goes according to Freud's view) develop appropriate feminine characteristics and acquire the female gender role if they have identified with their mothers. The process of the child's identification with the same-sex parent is the crucial element in Freud's theory (Sears et al., 1957, 1965).

The Psychosexual Stages   During their first year or so, all infants form close attachments to their mothers and experience considerable pleasure from the stimulation of their mouths. Hence, Freud called this the *oral stage*. In the second year, boys and girls continue their close attachments with their mothers, and they experience pleasure from the expulsion or retention of feces, prompting Freud to label this second period, the *anal stage*. During these first two years or so, both boys and girls identify with their mothers as the primary love object.

During the critical third stage, the *phallic period*, the sexes diverge and begin to show personality differences. Freud theorized that in this stage the male's and female's identification process changed, causing each to develop their own respective masculine and feminine gender identities and roles. First, we'll discuss the boy's phallic period, then the girl's.

For the boy, the third stage is characterized by the development and the resolution of what Freud called the *Oedipus complex*. The Oedipus complex finds the boy experiencing a growing sexual attraction for his mother. Freud reasoned that, because the boy's mother had been the primary source of nurturance and love for him during his first years, the boy would develop a close attachment to his mother and, subsequently, wish to possess her for his own. However, at some time during the boy's third or fourth year, he discovers that girls have no penises. Consequently, the boy begins to fear that possibly the same physical calamity could befall him if his father were to discover his secret desires for his mother. To allay this fear, one that Freud called *castration anxiety*, the boy begins to identify with his father and to adopt his father's behaviors and, more important, his father's gender role. According to Freud, then, the boy's gender identity grows out of his identification with his father.

Freud's views on the female's phallic period is much more complex and more controversial than the male's. The little girl's phallic period contains what Freud called the *Electra complex*, which occurs when she discovers that she has no penis. Freud believed that before the girl made this discovery she had identified with her mother much like the male would. However, after the "painful" discovery that she does not have a penis, the girl supposedly becomes angry with her mother because it is she whom the little girl blames for her physical deficit. To compensate for her physical deficiency and allay what Freud called the girl's *penis envy*, the girl turns against her mother and directs her affections toward her father, the parent with a penis. After some time, however, the little girl comes to realize that wishing to possess her father will not, in and of itself, bring her a penis. She then, ever so begrudgingly, re-establishes her identification with her mother. The outcome finds the girl identifying with her mother and taking on the female identity and role.

The fourth psychosexual stage, the *latent stage*, finds both the young boy and girl consolidating their rather traumatic experiences from the previous stage. And finally, in the last stage, known as the *genital stage*, young boys and girls become attracted to the opposite sex and take on the adult responsibilities of starting their own families, where the whole psychosexual drama will be acted out again; this time, however, they will be the parents.

This brief description of Freud's theory shows Freud's distinct bias against women (Millett, 1972). Because of the female's purported anatomical deficiency in the guise of a missing penis, Freud believed that women were never able to fully develop their personalities to the fullest (Caplan, 1984; Horney, 1978). According to Freud, females did not develop as strong a superego as males did. Boys, on the other hand, because they only feared losing their penises but kept them all the same, developed a much more complete personality. Freud's own words show his rather male-biased views about the female. He wrote:

> I cannot evade the notion (though I hesitate to give it expression) that for women the level of what is ethically normal is different from what it is in men. Their super-ego is never so inexorable, so impersonal, so independent of its emotional origins as we require it to be in men. Character-traits which critics of every epoch have brought up against women—that they show less sense of justice than men, that they are less ready to submit to great exigencies of life, that they are more often influenced in their judgements by feelings of affection or hostility—all these would be amply accounted for by the modification in the formation of their super-ego which we have inferred above. (1927, pp. 141–42)

As noted above, Freud's views on the female's gender identity and gender role rests on his notion of penis envy. According to Freud, once females become aware of their anatomical loss they become obsessed with a narcissistic self-love and, later as adults, they seek out those who possess that which they do not have; that is, they seek men. Freud's idea of the female's penis envy seems, at best, specious reasoning, if not misogynous sentiment. If women envy men of anything, it certainly is not their penises but rather their more privileged male status and roles. The literature dealing with females and their feelings toward males seems to make this point quite emphatically (Sherman, 1971).

Modifying Freud's Views   Others who studied under Freud or who were influenced by his writings went on to modify his theories of gender identity, especially with respect to the formation of the female's gender identity. Several women made significant contributions to a greater understanding of female psychology and to a great extent rectified some of the male bias in Freud's theories.

Helene Deutsch (1944, 1945), for the most part, accepted most of Freud's ideas on female development and stressed the female's inclination toward passivity and narcissism. Deutsch stressed the role of motherhood as the most important feature in a woman's life. She did, however, downplay the importance of penis envy in a young girl's development.

Another female psychoanalyst, Karen Horney (1967), became an outspoken critic of Freud's theory. Horney emphasized the importance of social and cultural factors in the development of gender identity and gender roles. Horney was one of the first to stress the early mother-child relationship wherein the child thinks of the mother as an all-powerful and awesome figure. She was also one of the first to note that penis envy may exist in little girls, but it is the male's higher and more privileged status that girls envy, not his sex organ.

And last, Clara Thompson (1964) speculated that women were disadvantaged because too much emphasis was placed on their child-bearing and child-rearing functions, and not enough emphasis was placed on their creative abilities.

Whether seen as a boon to a greater understanding of personality development or villified as sexist ramblings, Freud's theories have nevertheless influenced both the scientific and literary communities. To dismiss Freud's ideas outright simply because of his unequal treatment of the female and his reliance on anatomical principles may be too extreme, given that his ideas did set the stage for a more careful analysis of gender identity development by those that followed. Others have built on Freud's ideas in developing their own views of gender identity development (Chodorow, 1971, 1976, 1978; Mitchell, 1974).

Let's now move on to the next theory of how the sexes acquire their gender roles, namely, the social-learning approach to gender development.

Social-Learning Theory of Gender Role Development

Rather than applying Freud's theory to explain how the young learn their gender roles, many psychologists have turned to a more behaviorally oriented model of learning called social-learning theory. Social-learning theory downplayed the earlier and more extreme forms of behaviorism, noting that each behavior need not be rewarded to be learned. An analysis of sex-typed or gender-related behaviors from the standpoint of social learning can be found in the writings of Albert Bandura and Richard Walters (1963) and Walter Mischel (1966, 1970).

The major constructs of social-learning theory are reinforcement, imitation, and modeling. The simplest mechanism for learning is that of a reward or reinforcement given to a person for performing a certain behavior. For example, when a mother praises (i.e., a powerful reward) her daughter for helping her with the dishes, according to social-learning theory, the daughter is likely to help her mother with the dishes in the future. On the other hand, if a father scolds (i.e., a form of punishment or the absence of a reward) his son for crying over a skinned knee, the boy may not cry the next time he hurts himself. Parents in this fashion teach their children gender-related behaviors (i.e., girls do dishes and boys don't cry) by simply reinforcing or punishing the children's gender-related behaviors.

Reinforcement and punishment alone, however, do not explain all the possible ways that people, especially the young, learn the gender-related behaviors that go into making up their gender roles. To broaden their explanation of how we learn gender roles, social-learning theorists suggest two further learning processes: *observational learning* and *imitation*.

A first step in learning a new behavior is simply observing how others perform a specific behavior. To watch another person (what social-learning theorists call a model) perform a specific behavior gives us a chance to see how to perform that behavior ourselves.

A second step in the learning process, imitation, simply refers to our copying or imitating the model's behavior that we have observed. Thus, we see that observation and imitation go hand in hand in learning all kinds of complex behaviors. For example, a little four-year-old girl who sits in the kitchen watching her mother make cookies is in a perfect situation for observational and imitational learning to take place. The little girl watches closely as her mother pours the flour into a bowl, adds the eggs and other ingredients, puts the mixture on a cookie sheet, and finally puts it into the oven. If the little girl has watched carefully her mother's sequence of behaviors, she may someday go into the kitchen alone and take out bowls and flour and begin to make her own cookies. Even if the little girl has never performed the complex sequence of baking cookies before, she is likely to imitate what she has seen her mother do in preparing cookies.

A crucial element in the social-learning perspective is that for children to learn their gender-related behaviors they need to imitate same-sex models more so than opposite-sex models. If little boys are to learn what is considered appropriate for little boys in terms of their gender role, they need to observe and imitate other males, especially fathers, older brothers, or other males that they may interact with or observe (e.g., on television). The same is true of little girls learning their appropriate female gender role; they need to observe and imitate other females rather than males. However, the research into the purported tendency for same-sex imitation to occur among young children does not stand up to the scrutiny of research (Maccoby and Jacklin, 1974; chapters 8 and 9). Other factors besides same-sex models appear to play a more important role in the child's choice of who to imitate. Research has shown that the perceived warmth, power, and dominance of the model, rather than the model's sex, plays an important role in who the child imitates (Bandura et al., 1963).

Now we will move to the last theory of gender role development, the cognitive-developmental approach.

Cognitive-Developmental Theory of Gender Roles

The cognitive-developmental theory owes its heritage to Jean Piaget, a gifted observer of children who suggested that a child's development does not occur in a vacuum. In other words, Piaget theorized that a child does not passively react to environmental conditioning, as proposed by the social-learning model, but rather the child actively interacts with his or her environment in the developmental process (Piaget, 1948). Although Piaget did not address the issues of gender roles directly, his theories led another psychologist, Lawrence Kohlberg, to apply Piaget's theory of *cognitive development* to gender roles.

Kohlberg (1966) suggested that a child moves through three stages in the process of learning appropriate gender-related behaviors that make up the child's gender role. During the first stage, beginning around two years of age, the child learns that there are two genders and comes to understand how to apply the labels "boy" and "girl." As the child develops during these preschool years, he or she learns to attach the appropriate gender label to himself (boy) or herself (girl). Thus, the first stage is for a child to become aware of his or her gender identity. Along with developing a gender identity and learning the appropriate gender labels as they apply to others, the child also learns to associate certain other gender-appropriate features, such as dress styles or hair lengths, with each gender (Conn and Kanner, 1947). For example, a three-year-old child learns to associate dresses with girls and short hair with boys. One feature that stands out during this first period is how rigid, or what Kohlberg calls concrete, a child's thinking is. By concrete, Kohlberg means that a child does not allow for exceptions to the things that he or she sees around them. A three-year-old boy who sees a Scottish gentleman clad in a kilt is apt to say that this person is a girl because only girls wear "dresses." As the child grows and develops through the next few years, the child's gender identity becomes more stable and extends out to include most of the expected gender-related behaviors that fall under the heading of gender role.

The second stage finds the older child (from five years to six or seven years) beginning to develop a system of values associated with its gender. That is, during this period, a child learns to value or find more desirable the behaviors associated with its own gender and begins to imitate other same-sex persons more so than opposite-sex persons. For instance, according to Kohlberg, the reason a six-year-old boy won't play with dolls is that he feels that playing with dolls is for girls and whatever girls do can't be as good (i.e., valued) as what boys do.

Finally, during the third stage, the child develops an emotional attachment to the same-sex parent, which reinforces that the child will learn the complex set of behaviors associated with his or her gender role. Notice that Kohlberg's notions of gender role development incorporate several features taken from the social-learning perspective. However, Kohlberg has rearranged the sequence of when imitation of same-sex models comes into play. Kohlberg notes that the differences between his cognitive theory of gender role development and the social-learning model can be summed up in the following syllogisms (adapted from Kohlberg, 1966, p. 89). The social-learning syllogism reads as follows:

I want rewards,
I am rewarded for doing boy things,
Therefore, I want to be a boy.

Whereas, the cognitive-developmental syllogism states:

I am a boy,
Therefore, I want to do boy things,
Therefore, the opportunity to do boy things (and to gain approval for doing
    them) is rewarding.

According to the social-learning perspective, the child enjoys being rewarded and finds that others (i.e., primarily his or her parents) reward him
or her for performing gender-related behaviors. Because the rewards are
desirable, the child continues performing the gender-related behaviors and
learning new ones (i.e., generalizing from already learned behaviors to
newer ones). On the other hand, the cognitive-developmental approach
stresses that the child first learns which gender he or she is; that is, the
child forms a gender identity and then begins to perform those gender-
related behaviors expected of his or her gender. Finally, the child accepts
that doing gender-appropriate behaviors is rewarding. From Kohlberg's
point of view, the development of the child's gender identity (i.e., "I'm a
boy" or "I'm a girl") is the first and most crucial step in the process of
learning the gender roles. The social-learning perspective, however, considers the formation of gender identity to be the last step in learning gender
roles.

A major criticism of the cognitive-developmental approach is that Kohlberg's analysis of gender role development was based on males only. Thus,
Kohlberg's theory is biased in the sense that it doesn't take into consideration that the female's cognitive development may differ from the male's.
Females do, in fact, appear to develop different cognitive structures, which
Kohlberg missed by his exclusion of them from his research (Gilligan, 1982),
and we will discuss these in chapter 13.

To better understand the three theories we have just discussed, we can
summarize their key concepts and their differences by examining box 3.1.

ALTERNATIVE MODELS OF GENDER ROLE DEVELOPMENT

Recently, two psychologists working independently have come up with
two very interesting proposals to explain gender roles and their development. The hypotheses generated by Anne Constantinople and Joseph
Pleck are extremely interesting and only wait the test of further research
to see just how well they explain gender role development.

Constantinople's Sex-Role-as-Rule Model

Anne Constantinople (1979) has proposed a working hypothesis to explain
gender-role development. In a thought-provoking article, Constantinople
outlined the major difficulties hindering the major psychological theories'
explanations of gender role acquisition and outlines what she calls the sex-
role-as-rule model. First of all, Constantinople notes that Freud's theory and

Box 3.1

Comparison of the Three Theoretical Positions of Sex-Role Development

Freudian-Identification	Social Learning	Cognitive-Development
Role of Innate Characteristics		
Large role: anatomy is destiny; body structure determines personality	No role	Small role: cognitive maturation; structuring of experience; development of gender identity.
Role of Child in Learning Process		
Active	Passive	Active
Motive		
Internal: reduce fear and anxiety	External: reinforcements Internal: expected reinforcements	Internal: desire for competence
Permanence of Learning		
Very permanent and irreversible	Permanent only if external reinforcements or self-reinforcements maintain behavior; difficulty in changing comes from internalized self-reinforcements and conditioned emotional responses.	Semi-permanent once schemata are stabilized; change depends on presentation of discrepant information and on the child's cognitive maturity.
Sources of Learning		
Parents or parent surrogates	Parents as well as the larger social system	Parents and the larger social system in interaction with the child's cognitive system.

Source: Reprinted from *Women and Sex Roles,* "A Social Psychological Perspective" by Irene H. Frieze, Jacquelynne E. Parsons, Paula B. Johnson, Diana N. Ruble, and Gail L. Zellman, by permission of W. W. Norton & Company, Inc. Copyright © 1978 by W. W. Norton & Company, Inc.

Box 3.1

Continued

Age of Learning Sex Identity

By 4 or 5	Throughout life, but early years are very important	Throughout life, but years between 3–20 are most important; years between 6–8 and 16–18 are crucial for change in stereotypic beliefs.

the social-learning and cognitive theories have little substantiating evidence to back up their claims to explain gender role acquisition.

Constantinople describes the acquisition of gender roles as being similar to the way in which rules or, better yet, rigidly adhered-to norms become the basis for how a child learns his or her gender role. First of all, she suggests that gender roles are not simply mental rules of gender-related behaviors divorced from a person's feelings or emotions. Gender roles, according to Constantinople, have both a cognitive and an emotional side to them. Blending both the cognitive and emotional elements in gender role acquisition is especially noteworthy in Constantinople's model. For example, when a father chastises his four-year-old son for putting on his sister's dress and looking like a girl, the father is not only providing information to the boy—boys shouldn't wear dresses—but he also is causing the boy some pain—pain in the sense that the boy feels bad as a result of his father's scolding. Thus the little boy learns what is expected of him in terms of the male gender role (i.e., boys don't wear dresses—a cognitive element) and also learns that if he is to avoid future pain (caused by his father's scolding), he must not wear dresses. Constantinople goes on to outline that her model makes certain "assumptions" about the nature of a young child.

Her first assumption is that children are motivated to avoid pain and maximize pleasure in their dealings with the world. This assumption follows the long-established hedonistic view that people in their dealings with others seek pleasure and avoid pain. Second, Constantinople suggests that a child's brain works in such a way as to allow it to create mental categories or schemata (plural form of schema) of all the incoming information or stimuli the child receives from the sensory world. Stated in another way, a child's brain is so designed as to prompt a child to process the information she or he receives through the senses into some meaningful (i.e., meaningful to the child) form of outline or category. And last, Constantinople believes that these early schemata or categories constantly expand to include additional information gained through experience. A child does not create a new category or schema for each new stimulus, but rather adds this to an already established schema for which the new stimulus seems best fit.

According to Constantinople, cognitive psychology is the most fruitful approach to take to understand gender roles, how they are learned, and how they become applied to a wide spectrum of people in addition to the child's family and close friends (e.g., the child's peer group). As a child learns the specific behaviors associated with each sex's gender role, the child shifts this new information to other situations or experiences that are important to the child. The information the child learns at home transfers to away-from-home situations (e.g., school situations).

As Constantinople sees it, *labeling* is the first step in the gender role acquisition process. As a child learns (beginning around eighteen months of age) different words or labels, some of the labels are more important to the child's gender and future gender role than other words are. The words *girl*, *boy*, *mommy*, and *daddy* are more important labels with respect to gender roles than words like *kitty* or *doggie*. What is especially important in terms of labeling is that as the child is learning to categorize objects, the child also is learning what label goes with what category. For example, a little boy may be given a toy truck and told to play with it. Eventually, the word *truck* and the object called a truck may be fitted into the schema made up of the word *boy*. Therefore, the original schema (i.e., boy) expands to include additional labels and objects (i.e., trucks).

Constantinople notes that the complex cognitive schemata that make up a youngster's view of him- or herself as one sex and not the other combines with observational learning and direct teachings from other significant people in the child's life. Reinforcement of both a positive and negative nature adds to a child's mastery of gender-role expectations. Constantinople further points out that the child's need for structure in his or her environment gives the acquisition process still another push. After admitting that her sex-roles-as-rules model is lacking in hard data to prove its tenets, she notes one of the thorniest issues that her views bring out for examination: why children are compelled or motivated to learn their gender roles. Can it be simply to avoid pain and gain rewards, or is it a basic need for certain cognitive structures to give meaning to one's experiences? Constantinople points out that a definitive study to answer this question may not be ethically possible. To do so would require that a child be raised without any social promptings or cues that relate to gender or gender roles other than those gained from anatomical differences. In other words, does having a penis or vagina, in and of itself, provide a schema for a young child that is sufficient to categorize other gender-related behaviors as more appropriate for males and for females?

Constantinople notes the difficulties inherent in proving her thesis, but she suggests that studies of other cultures with their different gender roles may be one way of providing further information to substantiate her ideas.

Pleck's Sex Role Strain Model

For over a decade, psychologist Joseph Pleck has been one of the most influential writers on the male's gender role (Pleck, 1974, 1975, 1976, 1981). In 1981, Pleck published *The Myth of Masculinity,* which quickly became recognized as one of the most insightful and extensively documented analyses of the male's gender role. In this book, Pleck outlines what he calls the *sex role strain* (SRS) model of gender roles, more specifically, the male's gender role. Pleck hypothesizes that gender-related behaviors and consequently the gender roles develop mainly out of a person's need for *social approval* or as a consequence of *situational adaptation.*

Pleck begins his analysis of the male's gender roles by suggesting that traditional views on gender role development have been dominated by what he calls the male sex role identity (MSRI) paradigm (Pleck, 1984). At the heart of the MSRI are the theoretical speculations of Freud's identification principles, as well as social learning and cognitive development constructs. Pleck notes that the MSRI is based on two themes that run throughout its principles. First, for a person to be considered psychologically mature and healthy, a person must act in accordance with his or her society's prescribed gender role. In other words, it is not sufficient that a person only knows that he or she is a boy or a girl; a person must also act in the ways that are prescribed by society for his or her gender: a boy should act, dress, and think in ways that society considers appropriate for all boys, and a girl should dress, act, and think in ways that society prescribes for all girls. According to the MSRI, someone like Boy George, who wears makeup and dresses in nonmasculine attire, can be considered as having an immature or inadequate gender role identity because he does not act like nor dress like a "typical" male. Second, according to the MSRI, development of gender role identity, especially for males, is a risky, failure-prone process. During the early years, many young males develop unhealthy gender role identities because of faulty socialization. Many things can go wrong that may cause a young male to develop an inadequate gender role identity. For example, a boy who grows up in a home with no father may, according to this view, develop "feminine" tendencies or become a homosexual. Thus, parents are especially important in the development of a young male's gender role identity. Signs of an inadequate male gender role identity may be found in certain unacceptable behaviors, such as extreme aggression, homosexuality, and delinquency, for example. After reviewing much of the research in the areas that supposedly support the MSRI, Pleck concludes that the evidence for such an approach to understanding gender role development is rather sketchy at best.

Pleck's theorectical perspective, the sex role strain (SRS) paradigm, is based on ten propositions.

1. Sex roles are operationally defined by sex role stereotypes and norms.
2. Sex roles are contradictory and inconsistent.
3. The proportion of individuals who violate sex roles is high.
4. Violating sex roles leads to social condemnation.
5. Violating sex roles leads to negative psychological consequences.
6. Actual or imagined violation of sex roles leads individuals to over-conform to them.
7. Violating sex roles has more severe consequences for males than females.
8. Certain characteristics prescribed by sex roles are psychologically dysfunctional.
9. Each sex experiences sex role strain in its work and family roles.
10. Historical changes cause sex role strain. (1981, p. 90)

In contrast to the MSRI perspective that states that a male's gender role identity is an innate feature of his psychological makeup, Pleck's SRS model states that a person's gender role identity is learned and is made up from the gender stereotypes and gender norms that society prescribes for each gender. In this new approach, sex or gender roles are "operationally defined by sex role stereotypes and norms." Thus, to understand gender role development, Pleck shifts the focus from the individual to society's prescriptions for males and females. Pleck goes on to assert that many of the prescriptions inherent in the traditional gender roles create problems for many people because many of the gender role components are overly rigid, allowing for little change, and because conformity to the gender roles are demanded for all. People oftentimes experience considerable personal strain and anguish because their society's gender roles are incompatible with their own personal values and interests. The consequences, however, for such violations may lead to serious personal and social problems for the individual, such as being labeled as a deviant or being ostracized by one's group. Pleck, with his social emphasis, places the blame for many people's problems with their gender roles squarely on society rather than on the person. Society, not the individual, is the culprit when we find a person deviating from the normal pattern of gender roles.

Pleck's analysis of gender role identity and gender role development and his suggestion that a new perspective, or paradigm, is called for is extremely interesting. For the moment, however, it lacks the critical examination and research support that will determine whether it can replace the tenets of the MSRI model.

Both Constantinople's and Pleck's analyses of gender role development provide new ways to look at gender roles. Given that the previous approaches to gender role development (Freud's, social learning, and cognitive development) have been found lacking in critical research support, it seems opportune to begin developing alternative approaches to these complex issues. Constantinople and Pleck have presented us with two alternative approaches that may provide the answers that social scientists are looking for.

SUMMARY

Over the past fifty years, psychology has proved a fertile ground for the study of gender at the individual level. Studies of gender identity, transsexualism, sex differences, gender stereotypes, masculinity, and femininity have been central concerns for many psychologists.

A person's awareness of his or her sex (gender identity) has been especially difficult to study because of the continuing debate over what factors—biological, social, or a combination of both—contribute to its development. Those individuals who form gender identities that are different from their biological sex (transsexuals) are especially baffling to social scientists, and the means of helping them are especially drastic (sex reassignment surgeries).

For centuries, scholars have assumed that males and females differ in countless social and psychological ways. The encyclopedic study made by psychologists Eleanor Maccoby and Carol Jacklin put most of these presumed differences to rest. However, several other psychologists have questioned even the few differences that Maccoby and Jacklin found.

Traditionally, gender stereotypes were thought to consist of two sets of relatively mutually exclusive personality characteristics, one set for males (instrumental-competency) and the other for females (emotional-expressive). More recent research has presented a multicomponent model of gender stereotypes where behaviors, personality characteristics, appearances, and roles are seen to be related and comprise the male and female gender stereotypes.

The psychological constructs of masculinity and femininity have proved to be some of the "muddiest concepts in all of psychology." Part of the problem lies in the fact that psychologists cannot agree on how to measure these supposed psychological features. Children as young as five years of age are aware of the definitions of masculinity and femininity, and concepts such as the self-fulfilling prophecy may help us to understand how young people come to act in accordance with what society deems apropriate for each gender.

Traditional psychological approaches to gender role development have been offered by Sigmund Freud's identification theory, Walter Mischel's social learning model, and Lawrence Kohlberg's cognitive development perspective. Alternative approaches to gender role development have recently been proposed by psychologists Anne Constantinople and Joseph Pleck.

SUGGESTED READINGS

Brooks-Gunn, J., & Matthews, W. (1979). *He and she: How children develop their sex-role identity.* Englewood Cliffs, NJ: Prentice-Hall.

Gilligan, C. (1982). *In a different voice—Psychological theory and women's development.* Cambridge: Harvard University Press.

Kaplan, A., & Sedney, M. (1980). *Psychology and sex roles: An androgynous perspective.* Boston: Little, Brown.

Maccoby, E. (Ed.). (1966). *The development of sex differences.* Stanford: Stanford University Press.

Maccoby, E., & Jacklin, C. (1974). *The psychology of sex differences.* Stanford: Stanford University Press.

Nicholson, J. (1984). *Men and women: How different are they?* New York: Oxford University Press.

Spence, J. (1981). Changing conceptions of men and women: A psychologist's perspective. *Soundings, 64(4),* 466–84.

Williams, J. (1977). *Psychology of women: Behavior in a biosocial context.* New York: Norton.

Point/Counterpoint

Women and Math

When it comes to numbers, women are supposedly just not as good at juggling them as men are. Throughout history, most of the great mathematicians have been males (Kolata, 1980). The question is, are men's brains "wired" for math? The controversy over whether men have an inherent math ability has increased in the last several years with the publication of the results of nearly 10,000 SAT math tests. The tests, taken by junior high-school boys and girls, show that twice as many boys scored over 500 (Benbow and Stanley, 1980, 1983). But not everyone is willing to concede that males somehow are better at math than females, at least, not because of some inherited quality.

Those who dispute the idea that males have superior math ability argue that, though Benbow and Stanley's results are rather dramatic, they only show that by junior high, males have developed a mathematical facility based on social factors. Before adolescence, girls do as well as or, in some cases, better than boys (Lewis, 1968). Others like Sheila Tobias and Carl Tomizuka (Tobias, 1978; Tomizuka and Tobias, 1981) argue that young mathematically gifted girls may not enter the talent searches, such as those from which much of Benbow and Stanley's data came from, for fear of social ostracism. Another possible reason young women may fall behind young men in math may be that females have less favorable attitudes toward math than males have (Fennema and Sherman, 1977). However, the tendency for young boys and girls to stereotype math as a male ability decreases during the high-school years (Fennema and Sherman, 1978; Sherman, 1982). Another factor may be that many young females experience a conflict as a result of being smart and deal with it by "playing dumb" (Sherman, 1983). Thus, many young women who have considerable mathematical ability may actually try to hide their abilities from others lest they be seen as unfeminine.

Some suggest that Benbow and Stanley's findings may be accounted for by other than genetic reasons. Factors such as motivation, attitudes toward math, and the ever-present pressures to conform to society's gender roles should not be taken lightly when looking at the evidence that fewer girls than boys score high on standardized math tests.

What do you think?

Reading *On Raising a Boy as a Girl*

What would you do if your infant son had an accident that destroyed his penis? Just such a case came to the attention of the medical staff of the Johns Hopkins Hospital in Baltimore. In the following excerpt we read about how a farm couple from Iowa dealt with this most unnerving situation. This case provides some evidence of just when a child's gender identity differentiates in either the male or the female direction. Cases like this one and others provide some evidence that the gender identity "gate" is open for some time after birth.

Dramatic proof that the gender identity option is open at birth for normal infants and that social forces can intervene decisively at least up to a year and a half after birth comes from a few cases such as one that occurred more than ten years ago.

A young farm couple took their sturdy, normal, identical twin boys to a physician in a nearby hospital to be circumcised when the boys were seven months old. The physician elected to use an electrical cauterizing needle instead of a scalpel to remove the foreskin of the twin who chanced to be brought into the operating room first. When this baby's foreskin didn't give on the first try, or on the second, the doctor stepped up the current. On the third try, the surge of heat from the electricity literally cooked the baby's penis. Unable to heal, the penis dried up, and in a few days sloughed off completely, like the stub of an umbilical cord.

When the parents saw what had happened they were stunned, and as soon as the baby could leave the hospital they took him home. They had no idea of where to turn for help, and they were so numbed by the catastrophe that they could hardly talk about it, even with each other. Eventually they recovered themselves enough to make inquiries, but the problem was beyond the experience of their local doctors. Finally they took the baby to a

famous medical center, but even there no help was forthcoming. They went back home without hope, their slender finances drained and they themselves almost paralyzed by the frustration of not knowing what to do. The father began having nightmares in which he attacked a doctor and shot him dead.

A plastic surgeon who knew of the Johns Hopkins program for helping hermaphroditic babies finally was called in as a consultant. He suggested the possibility of reassigning the baby as a girl. This was a new and frightening idea to the parents, and at first they shied away from it. Not long afterward, however, they happened to tune in on the last part of a television program about the work with transsexuals at Johns Hopkins. On the screen was an adult male-to-female transsexual who, they could see for themselves, looked and talked like a normal, attractive woman. After that they worked their way to the decision to reassign their son as a girl. They began using a girl's name, letting the child's hair grow, and choosing noncommittal clothes for this twin. A short time later, when the twins were seventeen months old, they made the trip to Johns Hopkins. They needed reassurance that the program they had undertaken was the right thing for the child, and they wanted the necessary treatment from a hospital that was far enough from home to minimize the risk that gossip would leak back to their community.

The professional resources of the Johns Hopkins Hospital and specialty clinics were promptly mobilized to assess the possible alternatives. The first thing to consider was the child's gender identity. From conception to the

Source: Sexual signatures: On being a man or a woman (pp. 91–95, 97–98) by J. Money and P. Tucker, 1975, Boston: Little, Brown. Copyright © 1975 by John Money and Patricia Tucker. By permission of Little, Brown and Company.

age of fifteen months, every force had consistently steered this child toward differentiation of a male gender identity, except that, from the age of seven months, there had been no penis to confirm the other sex determinants. However, since the child had only just begun to talk when the parents had decided on reassignment, there was an excellent chance that gender identity would not by then have differentiated very far in the male direction. That was encouraging, but there was also the question of the parents' expectations. For fifteen months, this child had been their son; could they make the difficult adjustment of accepting the same child as their daughter? It was a vital consideration, for any lingering doubts whatsoever in their minds would weaken the child's identification as a girl and woman.

The medical psychologist described the alternatives to the parents, using nontechnical words, diagrams, and photographs of children who had been reassigned. On the one hand, he explained, if the child grew up as a boy, a plastic surgeon could graft skin from the child's belly to fashion a penis. Female-to-male transsexuals had found, however, that after this kind of operation the tissues of the artificial penis often break down, allowing leakage during urination, and that the artificial urethral canal is not very good at resisting the inward advance of infection, which increases the danger of urinary and bladder infections. Another problem is that, since a skin graft penis has no touch or pain feelings, continuous care must be exercised to make sure that it does not become ulcerated by rubbing against clothing, or being bruised or squeezed. The most serious drawback, however, is that it has no sexual feeling and cannot erect. As a man, this child's testicles could generate the sperm to sire his own children, but it would be difficult to ejaculate them into the vagina, since he would have to

use an artificial penis support for sexual intercourse and would not experience the normal frictional sensations that produce orgasm.

On the other hand, if the parents stood by their decision to reassign the child as a girl, surgeons could remove the testicles and construct feminine external genitals immediately. When she was eleven or twelve years old, she could be given the female hormones that would normally feminize her body for the rest of her life. Later a vaginal canal could be surgically constructed so that her genitals would be adequate for sexual intercourse and for sexual pleasure, including orgasm. She could become as good a mother as any other woman, but only by adoption.

The medical psychologist stressed that there would be no turning back once gender identity had differentiated. The child was still young enough so that whichever assignment was made, erotic interest would almost certainly direct itself toward the opposite sex later on, but the time for reaching a final decision was already short. He explained that whichever way they decided, it was essential that they decide wholeheartedly; the child would need all their support in differentiating a gender identity, and any lingering doubts in their minds would undermine that support.

Though not highly educated, the twins' parents are intelligent and exceptionally sensible people. They quickly grasped the risk of delay and of mental reservations, however well concealed, about the child's sex. With the alternatives thus spelled out, they reconfirmed their decision on sex reassignment: The child would be a girl. They had reached the conclusion of an agonizing decision in favor of castration. The girl's subsequent history proves how well all three of them succeeded in adjusting to that decision.

At the age of twenty-one months, the little girl was brought back to Johns Hopkins for the first stage of surgical feminization, removal of testicles and feminization of external genitals. When her body reaches adult size, she can decide when to schedule construction of the vaginal canal. If she waits until shortly before she is ready to begin her sex life, sexual intercourse will help to keep the canal elastic and unconstricted. Meanwhile, there's nothing about her genital appearance to make her feel self-conscious, even if she gets into the bathtub with her twin brother.

The twins and their parents come back to Johns Hopkins once a year for general psychological counseling and a checkup. Although the girl had been the dominant twin in infancy, by the time the children were four years old there was no mistaking which twin was the girl and which the boy. At five, the little girl already preferred dresses to pants, enjoyed wearing her hair ribbons, bracelets and frilly blouses, and loved being her daddy's little sweetheart.

Throughout childhood, her stubbornness and the abundant physical energy she shares with her twin brother and expends freely have made her a tomboyish girl, but nonetheless a girl. Her dominance behavior has expressed itself in fussing over her brother, according to their parents, "like a mother hen," while he, in turn, takes up for his sister if he thinks anyone is threatening her. Their mother reported that dolls and a doll carriage headed her Christmas list when she was five and that, quite unlike her brother, the girl was neat and dainty, experimented happily with styles for her long hair, and often tried to help in the kitchen.

Although this girl is not yet a woman, her record to date offers convincing evidence that the gender identity gate is open at birth for a normal child no less than for one born with unfinished sex organs or one who was prenatally over- or underexposed to androgen, and that it stays open at least for something over a year after birth.

Chapter 4

THE SOCIOLOGICAL PERSPECTIVE

*A ll the world's a stage, and all the men and women merely players.
They have their exits and their entrances; and one man in his time
plays many parts.*

Shakespeare

We are social creatures who from our first days until our last interact with others—others who have a significant impact on what and how we think, feel, and behave. With its focus on the patterns of human interaction among various groups, the field of sociology has much to offer to a discussion on gender. Nineteenth century sociologists like William Graham Sumner and Lester Ward saw women's and men's gender-related behaviors as extensions of their biology. These early sociologists perceived women as being destined to care for infants by virtue of their "maternal instinct"; men were seen as more aggressive because of their belligerent impulses. Early sociology contained strains of sexism as well as an androcentric focus (Gould, 1980).

The reemergent women's movement of the late 1960s and early 1970s caused many feminist-oriented sociologists to focus their attention on the stratification of and discrimination against women and other related issues that were seen as integral parts of Western society's social structures (Huber, 1976a; Lopata, 1976). During this period, sociologists focused considerable attention on the socialization process and the important socializing agents (e.g., parents and peers) that taught the individual what was expected of him or her in terms of gender. Sociologists also examined the social institutions (e.g., education and politics) that perpetuated the inequality of status, prestige, and power found between females and males. In the past decade or so, sociologists have played a large role in analyzing gender from the perspectives of how we learn about what is expected of us and how society through its powerful institutions reinforces and supports a basic inequality between females and males.

In this chapter we will examine how people come to learn what is expected of them in terms of their gender label as either female or male. First, we will discuss several sociological constructs that make up the basis of social interaction, namely, status, roles, and norms. Next, we will focus on the female and male gender norms that underlie society's definitions of gender roles. Then we will discuss the socialization process and several socializing agents like parents and peers that act as major social forces shaping our gender roles. And finally, we will examine three mainstream sociological theories, focusing on how they explain certain aspects of our gender roles. We will save our discussion of those social institutions (e.g., education, religion, and politics) that perpetuate unequal status for males and females for later chapters where we can devote more attention to them.

STATUS, ROLES, AND NORMS:
THE BUILDING BLOCKS OF GENDER

All human groups are made up of people who occupy a position or rank within the group. A person's position in a group is called a *status*. Some common examples of statuses are woman, husband, daughter, soldier, physician, minister, TV celebrity, and senior citizen. A status serves to inform others where a person "fits" in a group. In other words, a status is a social label that *identifies* a person's position in a particular group.

A status not only serves as a social label, it also allows people to be *ranked* in terms of other peoples' statuses. For example, the status of mother has a higher rank in a family group than, say, a daughter. Thus a status not only identifies or labels a person's position in a group, it also carries with it a certain evaluative ranking with respect to others. Some statuses are more highly valued or ranked in our society than others: teachers have more status than students, managers more than employees, physicians more than nurses, and males more than females.

Sociologists distinguish two types of statuses: ascribed and achieved. *Ascribed status* refers to a person's position in a group that he or she has little or no control over. Some common examples of ascribed statuses are a person's biological sex, a person's color or race, and a person's age as in the ascribed age-related statuses of adolescent or senior citizen. In other words, you had nothing to do with your sex, skin color, or your present age. The status that comes from being female or male, black or white, young or old is an ascribed status.

Achieved status refers to those social positions that a person generally has more control over. The statuses of student, husband, quarterback, scientist, and rabbi are all achieved statuses because they are social positions or statuses that a person earns or chooses to become through personal effort.

What should be obvious from our discussion thus far is that everyone has several ascribed and achieved statuses. Sociologists refer to the number of individual statuses held by one person as a *status-set* (Merton, 1968). A typical college student probably could list a number of ascribed and achieved statuses like female, white, young adult, daughter, sister, Jewish, sociology major, girl friend, class president, and so on. All of these statuses give others who relate to this person some indication of how they should interact with her, and they give others an indication of the rank she holds in a particular group. For example, a daughter knows that she should defer to her mother's judgment about her coming home at a particular hour on the weekend.

Every status carries with it a set of *norms* or prescribed behaviors that combine to make up a *role*. (Actually, a status may have several sets of prescriptive norms, which means a status may have several roles associated with it.) A person who occupies a certain status is usually expected to act in certain ways, perform certain obligatory behaviors, and, quite often, enjoy special privileges related to a particular status. For instance, the achieved status of father carries with it certain normative obligations like contributing to the support of his children, teaching them how to behave as members of society, being available to help them when they have problems, and if necessary, getting them out of difficulties. By the same token, a father has certain privileges like getting cards and ties on Father's Day and basking in the joy of his children's accomplishments. The norms a society prescribes for a particular role usually provide a type of blueprint of how a person should act.

One question sociologists are particularly interested in is how we learn the norms that make up our various roles. Sociologists generally believe that role behaviors are learned from the people around us (our parents, peers, teachers, and other influential people in our lives), as well as from various media (television, books, and magazines). Although most norms and their consequent roles associated with various statuses are not normally written down, some statuses are so important to a particular society that certain prescribed role behaviors may be entered into the basic documents of a country. The Constitution of the Republic of Ireland, for example, prescribes that mothers should not work outside of the home.

> In particular, the State recognises that by her life within the home, woman gives to the state a support without which the common good cannot be achieved. The State shall, therefore, endeavour to ensure that mothers shall not be obliged by economic necessity to engage in labour to the neglect of their duties in the home. (Article 41, Section 2, Subsections 1 and 2)

The ascribed statuses of female and male and their accompanying roles are to many people the most important social structures that each of us must contend with. These specific social structures literally give definition to each person's daily life.

GENDER NORMS

All societies prescribe certain behaviors, beliefs, and attitudes (i.e., the shoulds and the should nots) for each gender. These prescriptions make up the *gender norms*. The gender norms taken together comprise the *gender roles*. In other words, gender norms are the prescriptive guidelines that form the gender roles. But what does our society prescribe for females and males in terms of their gender norms? We should state at the outset that society's gender norms are somewhat generalized in their prescriptive weights, and there will be exceptions to them, but we can outline what is generally prescribed for both genders. Let's begin with the female's gender norms.

The Female Gender Norms

The female's primary gender norm is what Nancy Russo (1976) calls the *motherhood mandate*. Little girls are encouraged—encouraged may be too gentle a term for how little girls are dealt with in this respect—to play with dolls. Why is this so? In most peoples' minds, doll play and all that goes along with it is an important way for little girls to learn appropriate nurturant behaviors that will supposedly be necessary later on. Later on, young girls are somehow considered to be more capable of handling babysitting activities and responsibilities than are boys of a similar age. Finally, one of the first questions asked of the newly married woman is when she is going to have a baby. Thus, having a baby and becoming a mother can be seen as the central feature or gender norm of a woman's life and the very core of a woman's identity as a person. According to Nancy Russo (1976),

> Characterizing motherhood as prescribed, however, does not adequately communicate the centrality of this behavior to the definition of the adult female. "Being pretty" is also prescribed, but one can compensate for not being pretty (by being a "good mother," for example). Motherhood is on a qualitatively different plane. It is a woman's *raison d'etre*. It is mandatory. The mandate requires that one have at least two children (historically as many as possible and preferably sons) and that one raise them "well." As long as this situation exists for the vast majority of women in Western society and the world in general, prohibitions may be eliminated and options widened, but change will occur only insofar as women are first able to fulfill their mandate of motherhood. (p. 144)

Others besides Russo see a female's primary gender norm as revolving around a woman's biological capability to become a mother (Bernard, 1974; Hardin, 1974; Peck and Senderowitz, 1974). The motherhood mandate also includes the injunction that a woman should strive to be a "good" mother— good in the sense that she devote a majority of her time and energy to caring for the children (Contratto, 1984). For females then, becoming a mother is the central gender norm.

Although most females are influenced by the motherhood mandate, there are several problems associated with it. Sociologist Jessie Bernard (1981a) describes some of these problems.

> Even if the young woman is in sync with the institutional timing for entrance into the world of mothers—early twenties—she may not be prepared. Although it has been taken for granted from her birth, by the girl herself as well as others, that she will become a mother and although she has been surrounded by books, pamphlets, articles, old wives' tales and lore, she is, as Alice Rossi pointed out some time ago (1968), quite unprepared for it. She can prepare her body for childbirth, but how can she prepare it for the sleepless nights, the fatigue, the anxieties, the feelings of helplessness in the face of a crying infant that cannot communicate its pain? for the nameless fears? the unlimited responsibilities? the endless duties and obligations? the pervasive guilt? (p. 166)

Second only to the motherhood mandate in prime importance is what may be called the *marriage mandate.* Marriage is for many women a *rite de passage,* an entrance into the world of adults, freedom from parental control, and a means for fulfilling a basic tenet of womanhood. In marriage a woman takes on the role that many see as one of her primary responsibilities, that is, becoming a homemaker. As with the motherhood mandate, the marriage mandate does not fully prepare most females for many of the less than ennobling activities prescribed for the woman-homemaker: the cleaning, caretaking, and countless other tasks that fill a homemaker's day (Lopata, 1971). Generally speaking, a female finds herself faced with two major mandates or socially prescribed gender norms, those of becoming a mother and a married woman. More and more women are challenging these two gender norms and seeking other alternatives to fulfilling their place in society. Time will tell whether the gender norms of motherhood and marriage will somehow become the less-than-the-ideal goals for most women.

The Male Gender Norms

The male's gender norms do not focus on the elements of parenting and marriage as they do for the female. We may even suggest that fathering does not carry the same impact for the male's identity as mothering does for the female's. We should be careful here not to give the impression that being a father is not something most men find personally satisfying nor a significant feature in their lives (Feldman and Nash, 1984; Gilbert, 1975). (In a recent national poll, "more than 90 percent of the men said being a husband/father is the most satisfying role in their lives" [Findlay, 1984, p. 3D].) What is suggested, however, is that most men's sense of identity is not as totally focused on parenting as is the case for most women. When it comes to specific male gender norms, we find a series of loose-knit prescriptive elements or themes that males should evidence in their lives.

Robert Brannon (1976) has intuitively grouped the male's gender norms into four categories:

1. No Sissy Stuff: The stigma of all stereotyped feminine characteristics and qualities, including openness and vulnerability.
2. The Big Wheel: Success, status, and the need to be looked up to.
3. The Sturdy Oak: A manly air of toughness, confidence, and self-reliance.
4. Give 'Em Hell!: The aura of aggression, violence, and daring. (p. 12)

Recently, Doyle (1983) added a fifth, the sexual element, to Brannon's normative categories. According to Doyle, the five male gender norms are the antifeminine element, the success element, the aggressive element, the sexual element, and the self-reliant element. Let's examine each in turn.

Males are admonished never to act in any way that may be interpreted as feminine. The *antifeminine element* is basic to the male's gender norm. If women are thought of as too emotional, dependent, or nonassertive, men must be the opposite to prove themselves manly or masculine in the ideal sense. The antifeminine bias in most men's attitudes and behaviors has been pointed out by several authors who have written extensively about men's lives (Farrell, 1974; Jourard, 1974).

Being number one or the best is another male prescription and is referred to as the *success element.* Here we find the injunction that males should prove their manhood by doing better than others at work, sports, or whatever else men do. Men seemingly strive in countless ways to outdo others and by doing so prove themselves more manly than others. There are many ways a man can show himself to be a success, for example, by having a bigger office, a bigger car, a prettier woman on his arm, or even by being able to outdrink another. It is not surprising that many men measure their success in terms of the size of their paychecks (Gould, 1974). Money or, better yet, the amount of money a man earns seems a convenient and easily quantifiable measure of both his success and his manhood.

Males are expected—no, enjoined—to fight for what they consider right. Down through the centuries, males have been pictured as naturally more aggressive than females. The *aggressive element* is the third male norm prescribed in varying degrees for men. Research has found that most males prefer to use force as a way of dealing with public disturbances rather than nonviolent, or what many men think of as "feminine," means (Blumethal et al., 1972).

The *sexual element* is the fourth norm prescribed for men. Sexual conquest is for many males one of the strongest proofs of manhood (Gross, 1978). Many men see themselves as the initiators of sex, whereas most females define themselves in terms of being objects of sexual advances (Phelps, 1979). For both sexes, sexual knowledge, sexual attitudes, and sexual activities play an integral part in their self-concepts. However, the male-as-sexual initiator/controller is a most important norm for males to live up to.

The last male gender norm is the *self-reliant element*. Males must be cool, unflappable, in control, and tough, in other words, self-reliant in most situations (Fasteau, 1974). Although this last element is difficult to grasp, every male feels the pressures to be, or rather, to act as if he is in control of himself and of whatever situation he finds himself in. Obviously, this last injunction is rather difficult to exhibit at all times. Nevertheless, many males feel the pressure to act out the self-reliant norm in their everyday lives.

Thus, we see that in our society both females and males have very explicit gender norms. Not all females and males continuously fulfill all the prescriptive gender norms placed on them, but that in and of itself does not deny the presence of such gender norms. We now need to ask how we learn the specific gender norms that constitute our gender roles.

THE SOCIAL MOLD: SHAPING THE GENDER ROLES

Passing by a hospital nursery, one can observe just how similar most newborn babies really are in their appearance and, more important, in their behaviors. If it weren't for the pink and blue blankets scattered among the bassinets, one would not know a female from a male! (As with most generalizations, the claim that newborn babies of each sex are strikingly similar needs some qualifying. An average male neonate tends to be slightly longer and heavier than a female [Vulliamy, 1973]. Male neonates are more prone to breathing, reflex, and heart problems [Singer et al., 1968], and they are more likely to be affected by other sex-linked characteristics like color blindness and hemophilia [Barfield, 1976].) Even to the casual observer, it is apparent that most infants spend most of their first few weeks sleeping, with only short periods of wakefulness (Gibson, 1978). Then why is it that so many people earnestly see male infants as being so different from female infants? An answer may be simply that most parents see their children through "gender-colored" glasses that focus on presumed gender differences where few exist. Because parents see their infants differently, there may be a tendency to treat each gender differently. Treating male and female infants differently is just the first step in the long process called socialization which, among many things, leads to the creation of two very different gender roles.

But what do we actually mean by the term socialization? *Socialization* is the process by which all people (i.e., children, adolescents, adults, and senior citizens alike) learn what is expected of them through their interactions with others. Socialization can be thought of as a social mold that shapes each person to fit into a group. A child, for example, learns certain basic feeding skills, including which utensil to use with which type of food. Depending on the society, a child may be taught to use a spoon and fork or a set of chopsticks. Children and others must learn the ways, traditions, norms, and rules of getting along with others, and socialization is the process by which everyone learns the lessons that others deem necessary for them to fit into their group.

SOCIALIZING AGENTS

When a mother tells her daughter to pick up the dishes on the kitchen table, when a little girl sees a picture in the Christmas catalog of little girls playing with a miniature stove, or when a young boy recites the Boy Scout oath that he should be "physically strong, mentally awake, and morally straight," we can see different *socializing agents* at work. Any person or social institution that shapes a person's values, beliefs, or behaviors is a socializing agent. Socializing agents are especially effective during a person's early years, when one is most impressionable. An effective socializing agent usually is respected by the person being socialized.

Some of the most important lessons a child learns and those that are reinforced throughout a child's early years and beyond are her or his gender roles. Let's examine some of the different socializing agents (i.e., parents, different media, teachers, and peers) that combine to shape a child's gender role.

Parents as Socializers

Parents are one of the more important socializing agents. But just how early in their children's lives do parents begin to teach their children what is expected of them in terms of their gender label?

In a fascinating study, Jeffrey Rubin (1974, pp. 516–17) and his associates found that first-time parents saw their one-day-old infants in terms of gender differences. Typically, fathers saw their newborn sons "as firmer, larger featured, better coordinated, more alert, stronger, and hardier," while other fathers saw their daughters "as softer, finer featured, more awkward, more inattentive, weaker, and more delicate." These fathers saw gender-related differences when actually none were obvious. More than likely, these fathers' notions of gender stereotypes played an important role in why they saw their newborn infants so differently. Other researchers have found similar patterns where parents see their children in terms of gender stereotypes rather than their children's actual behaviors (Lamb et al., 1979). As infants grow older, their parents' notions about gender stereotypes continue to influence how parents treat their children. Various studies have reported that parents treat each gender differently (Lewis, 1972).

Parents know their infant's sex, and some may suggest that they are reacting to real gender differences and not to something they have preconceived in their minds. What about adults who don't have first-hand knowledge of an infant's sex (i.e., they have not examined the infant's genitals)? Do they also treat male and female infants differently? The answer is most emphatically yes. Research shows that one of the more important factors influencing how an adult interacts with an infant is the infant's gender label (Seavy et al., 1975; Sidorowicz and Lunney, 1980). For instance, a helpful toy salesperson (a stranger) will select toys for a child according to a child's gender (Kutner and Levinson, 1978). To highlight just how important a child's gender is for an adult, let's examine one study to see how adults use gender to guide their play with an infant.

Jerrie Will, Patricia Self, and Nancy Datan (1976) asked eleven mothers to play with a six-month-old infant. Five of the mothers played with the infant who was dressed in blue pants and named "Adam." Later, the other six mothers played with the same infant who was then wearing a pink dress and being called "Beth." (Actually, the infant was a six-month-old male.) Placed in a room with the infant, the mothers were given several toys to entertain the child with, specifically, a plastic fish, a doll, and a train. When asked to play with either "Beth" or "Adam," the respective mothers generally offered Adam the train and Beth the doll. Not only did these mothers offer different toys on the basis of the "perceived" gender of the infant, they even interacted differently with the infant. The mothers who thought they had Beth smiled more and held her closer to themselves than did the mothers who had Adam. After the observations were completed, the mothers were interviewed, and all stated that mothers should not treat male and female infants differently. However, as found here, and in other studies, parents and nonparents alike do interact with and treat infants differently on the basis of the perceived gender of the infant, and this differential treatment continues as children grow older.

Besides providing gender-related toys for their children, parents also play with boys and girls differently. Parents are more likely to interact and talk more with their daughters, while parents with sons are more apt to "roughhouse" and play more actively with them (Tauber, 1979). Female infants are usually seen as more fragile by both mothers and fathers alike (Minton et al., 1971). There are many reasons for this differential treatment, but we can suggest that parents want their sons to be rough and tough, or "masculine," and daughters are encouraged to be neat and orderly, or "feminine," in their behaviors (Fagot, 1978).

Even a child's bedroom doesn't escape the parents' concern over what is expected of little boys and girls. When the decors of preschoolers' bedrooms are examined, obvious touches of "masculine" and "feminine" motifs are likely to be found. In boys' bedrooms, the prevalence of sports' equipment, trucks, and military paraphernalia is common; in girls' rooms, dolls, and household items are more often included in the decors parents furnish (Rheingold and Cook, 1975).

Parents also continue shaping their children's gender roles through the kinds of jobs they assign them around the house. In a state-wide sample (Nebraska) of 669 boys and girls between the ages of two and seventeen, researchers Lynn White and David Brinnerhoff (1981) found distinctive gender differences in the kinds of jobs young people did. Basically, boys did "men's work": mowing the lawns, shoveling snow, taking out the garbage, and other general yard-work chores. Girls, on the other hand, did "women's work": cleaning up around the house, doing the dishes, cooking, and as we might expect, babysitting for younger siblings. Others have also found similar divisions of labor along gender lines in their studies of task assignments (Baker, 1984; Goldstein and Oldham, 1979).

Social Class, Race, and Gender Socialization   Undoubtably, parents are a most important socializing agent during the early childhood years. For most parents, the goal of socialization is to prepare the child for future life. To accomplish this, most parents pass on a value system that they believe will serve the child well and permit her or him to fit into society. In a series of international studies dealing with socialization and parental values, Melvin Kohn (1977) found that the parents' social class determined to a large degree the contents of the value system that parents passed on to their children. Kohn found that, for the most part, lower-class parents stressed obedience to authority. Staying out of trouble was an important concern of these parents, and thus they fostered within their children a sense of conformity to others' standards, whether these others be the child's parents, teachers, or the police. Middle-class parents tended to teach their children the value of self-control and consideration of others. Both lower- and middle-class parents believe in teaching their children to conform to society's rules, but their orientations differ somewhat in how the children conform. The lower-class child learns to comply with authority for authority's sake, whereas the middle-class child conforms because the values of society are considered right and just. The middle-class child's obedience is more lasting because the child has internalized society's rules (Gecas and Nye, 1974).

Among lower-class white children, we find a greater degree of traditional gender stereotypic behaviors than either among middle- or upper-class white children (Nadelman, 1974). However, males of all classes tend to exhibit more traditional gender-related behaviors and attitudes than females (Doyle and Moore, 1978). Black males seem more accepting of nontraditional female roles (such as working women) than white males do (Axelson, 1970), and black females appear to hold less gender stereotypic attitudes toward gender roles in general than white females do (Gold and St. Ange, 1974).

Besides the influence of parents' socioeconomic and racial statuses on what is taught to children, the gender label, as we have noted, determines to a great extent what kinds of values parents wish their children to learn. We can see this gender-related difference in the emphasis placed on the value of independence. Boys are often encouraged by their parents to exhibit independent behaviors, but girls are expected to show more dependent behaviors. Parents teach either independence or dependence to a child in many ways, but there are clear differences in what is taught to each gender. For example, young boys are more often permitted to leave their yards and play with others than young girls are (Hoffman, 1975; Saeger and Hart, 1976). Boys, it seems, are subtly encouraged to roam away from parental supervision, but girls are discouraged from such independence-producing behavior. Some research even suggests that how a father relates to his daughter may play a role in the development of dependency. It has been suggested that among father-daughter relationships where there is a warm and affectionate bond, the daughter tends to do less well academically, possibly, because her father does not stress the values of independence and achievement enough (Radin, 1981). In the final analysis, it seems that parents are more likely to value a budding sense of independence and autonomy in their sons but are more likely to value dependency and conformity to authority for their daughters.

Obviously, parents are not the only socializing force in a child's life. There are also other forces present in the child's early life that shape the content of the gender role.

Media as Socializers

The mass media—books, magazines, comics, radio, television, films, and records—play a significant role in people's lives. The hours of entertainment they provide are beyond calculation. But mass media provide more than mere entertainment; they teach, persuade, and shape people's lives. A recurrent theme in much of the media is how the genders should live. When we see an advertisement in a magazine, listen to popular songs, read a romance novel, or watch a soap-opera, the message is often decidedly traditional in content—males should act "masculine," and females "feminine" (Freudiger and Almquist, 1978; Modleski, 1980). Let's examine some of the more important media and focus on just what messages they emphasize in terms of gender roles.

The Printed Word   Children's books with their stories of human-like animals and real people provide both countless hours of enjoyment and a powerful vehicle for the socialization of gender roles. Sociologist Lenore Weitzman (1979) writes:

> Through books, children learn about the world outside their immediate environment: they learn what other boys and girls do, say, and feel, and they learn what is expected of children their age. Picture books are especially important to the preschool child because they are often looked at over and over again at a time when children are in the process of developing their own sex role identities. In addition, they are read to children before other socialization influences (such as school, teachers, and peers) become important in their lives. (p. 7)

The gender roles presented in children's books often offer a biased and narrow portrayal of the female's role. To learn more about the not-so-subtle gender messages contained in these early primers, we need to examine how the genders and their roles are portrayed. Lenore Weitzman (1972), along with several of her colleagues, conducted a content analysis of several prize-winning children's books (i.e., the Caldecott Medal winners between 1967–1971). A majority of the books told stories about males, but a few females were present in the stories. The gender-bias in these books becomes striking when we note that human male characters outnumbered human female characters by eleven to one. The bias becomes even more obvious when animal characters (e.g., rabbits, horses, puppies) are added. The ratio of male to female animals is a whopping 95 to 1. As for the stories themselves, males performed a variety of different and exciting activities and roles that portrayed them as acting competently and in charge of the stories' action. When females did enter the stories, they usually did so in a rather limited and, for the most part, quite passive way. The message in these primers is rather clear: Boys live exciting and independent lives, whereas girls are primarily auxiliaries to boys. (To put it more bluntly: It's a man's world, kids!)

In a more recent study of the Caldecott winners (i.e., those published between 1972-1979), Kolbe and LaVoie (1981) found a marked improvement in the stories' gender ratio. Human males outnumbered human females by only 1.8 to 1. However, if we again include the animal characters, males outnumber females by 2.66 to 1. Obviously, recent authors of children's books have tried to improve the representation of female characters in their children's stories. Although the gender ratio has improved, the fact of the matter is that females *outnumber* males in the real world—a fact apparently forgotten by most authors of children's literature.

Besides the distorted gender ratios portrayed in these books, just what kinds of activities are the books' characters doing? In Weitzman's study, a majority of the male characters engaged in "masculine" activities, and the few female characters primarily worked around the home doing traditional "feminine" jobs. In Kolbe and LaVoie's study, seventeen out of the nineteen books contained traditional gender roles for their characters. Most astonishing is that in all the Caldecott winners studied—both in Weitzman's and in Kolbe and LaVoie's samples—no female character was portrayed working outside of the home. Surely, many of the children reading these books can't help but notice that their mothers work outside of the home, while the mothers in their story books stay home all day.

Although there has been a trend among some children's books to present the gender roles in nonsexist ways (Davis, 1984), most children's books portray the genders and their gender roles in a way that is highly gender biased and nonreality oriented. Mary Key (1975a) sums up the prevalent gender role messages in most children's books as:

> In general, children's books show that boys: climb, dig, build, fight, fall down, get dirty, ride bikes, and have many adventures, while girls sit quietly and watch. Boys are taught to express themselves; girls to please. (p. 56)

Television Without a doubt, television plays a significant role in the socialization process for young and old alike. When it comes to children's television and its commercials, we find considerable gender biases and sexism in its content (Mayes and Valentine, 1979; Welch et al., 1979). An early study of the highly acclaimed "Sesame Street" even found its presentation of the gender roles relatively biased in traditional ways (Gardner, 1970).

TABLE 4.1   GENDER ROLES IN 300 TELEVISION COMMERCIALS

Role or Occupation	Percentage Male	Percentage Female	N
Baby and infant care	—	100	12
Inmate in nursing home	—	100	7
House cleaning	3	97	35
Washing clothes and dishes	3	97	32
Shopping	3	97	32
Cooking and serving food	6	94	80
Store owner	50	50	8
Salesperson	71	29	14
Product expert	74	26	82
Builder	80	20	25
Riding motorcycle	88	12	8
Farmer	90	10	10
Engaging in sports	93	7	72
Driving a vehicle	94	6	32
Office worker (not secretary)	100	—	15
Soldier	100	—	25
Service station worker	100	—	11
Miscellaneous occupations (secretary, nurse, doctor, etc.)	51	49	57

Notes: N is the total number of people participating in that particular role. People not performing a particular task (those standing or walking, for instance) were not counted. The only overlapping role was "product expert"; those people sometimes had another role.

Source: The question of sex differences: Psychological, cultural, and biological issues (p. 216) by Katharine Blick Hoyenga and Kermit T. Hoyenga, 1979, Boston: Little, Brown. Copyright © 1979 by Katharine Blick Hoyenga and Kermit T. Hoyenga. Reprinted by permission of Little, Brown and Company.

But children do not limit their viewing habits to children's fare only. It's prime-time television that draws the largest numbers of every age group. Let's begin with those TV segments that pay for the shows, the commercials. Katharine and Kermit Hoyenga (1979) studied some 300 prime-time television commercials with an eye to how the gender roles were presented (see table 4.1). Overall, their research found:

> There are more exclusively male than exclusively female occupations. . . . In only three cases was the product expert a female when a man also appeared in the commercial, and two of these commercials were for medical products. Overall, females are more often pictured using medical products (64 percent were females) and products designed to enhance the user's appearance or smell (75 percent). Only a few commercials included any type of sexual interaction (kissing, caressing), but the male was always the aggressor. If commercials were the only basis for inferring behavior and role assignments, the person watching them would conclude that women must stay at home, that they are allowed out of the house only in the company of men, and, rarely, of children, and that they are rarely allowed to drive cars. (p. 215)

In general, TV commercials portray women almost soley in the helping role, waiting on others and living out their lives in service to others, never really taking charge of their own lives (Dominick and Rauch, 1972; Walstedt, 1977). Such a view perpetuates traditional views of women's role in society.

Recently, however, a few television sponsors have made an effort to introduce counterstereotypic gender presentations. For example, we occasionally see Josephine the Plumber tackling a stopped up drain and showing a man what needs to be done. But do such commercials have an effect other than being novel? Joyce Jennings (Walstedt) and several colleagues (1980) found that women who watched counterstereotypic TV commercials were more self-confident and less likely to conform to group pressure in other situations. Portraying women in counterstereotypic ways may have positive effects for women in the TV audience in terms of their building self-confidence as self-determining and achievement-oriented individuals (Geis et al., 1984).

For the most part, however, advertisers present the genders in traditional and stereotypic ways. Males celebrate the end of another day at the office or plant by stopping at a local bar with the gang to throw down a few beers. If not in a bar, a man is out in a distant woods or by a remote stream all because he chose the right kind of four-wheel drive vehicle. In contrast, women in most commercials seem interested only in stemming the telltale signs of age, marveling over the softness of bathroom tissue, bemoaning the waxy buildup on their kitchen floors, or standing seductively by some car as a male describes the power under the hood. As Lucy Komisar (1971) sees the treatment of women in advertising:

> Advertising . . . legitimizes the idealized, stereotyped roles of woman as temptress, wife, mother, and sex object, and portrays women as less intelligent and more dependent than men. It makes women believe that their chief role is to please men and that their fulfillment will be as wives, mothers, and homemakers. It makes women feel unfeminine if they are not pretty enough and guilty if they do not spend most of their time in desperate attempts to imitate gourmet cooks and eighteenth-century scullery maids. It makes women believe that their own lives, talents, and interests ought to be secondary to the needs of their husbands and families, and that they are almost totally defined by these relationships. (p. 310)

In the television shows packaged in between the commercials, we find women generally excluded or portrayed in very narrow and traditional roles (Butler and Paisley, 1980; Hashell, 1979; Tuchman, 1978). Two rather exhaustive government sponsored studies of television programming (U.S. Commission on Civil Rights, 1977, 1979) concluded that television portrayed most women as having no definable occupation or means of support. Of those women employed outside the home, a majority held occupations associated with traditional "women's work" like nurses and household workers (Kalisch and Kalisch, 1984). Besides showing women performing traditional female tasks, the studies also found that women, for the most part, were portrayed as being dependent on men for their livelihood; men were generally portrayed as being more independent and in charge of a variety of situations (Dominick, 1979). Male TV characters are shown in ambitious, adventuresome, strong, and dominant roles, whereas females are more often cast in dependent, submissive, and weak or auxiliary roles (Busby, 1974). In the most general sense, male TV characters play either heroes or villains, and females appear as either adulterers or victims of men's actions (Goff et al., 1980). Although males occasionally are portrayed in less than flattering ways, they are usually shown as the "important ones" in the drama (Jennings [Walstedt] et al., 1980). *Dallas*'s J.R. may not be a likeable character nor one most men may wish to emulate, but the drama focuses on him, a characteristic of TV drama that most female characters do not share, except for the few shrewish females on the prime-time soaps. For a woman to be the central figure in a TV drama, she must be a calculating libertine who will do anything to get her way (Cantor and Pingree, 1983). Night after night and show after show, television portrays men as independent, aggressive, and in charge of their lives but portrays women as, by and large, mere appendages to men's lives and the drama that swirls about them.

Television affects the value system of those that watch it. The messages beamed into the living rooms of millions of people every day shape their attitudes, beliefs, and gender roles. With regard to television's influence on gender roles, the research of Terry Fruch and Paul McGhee (1975) is most revealing. Basically, these researchers found children who were "heavy" television viewers (i.e., twenty-five or more hours a week) held more traditional gender stereotypes and values than those who were "light" viewers (i.e., ten or less hours a week). Others have also found that "heavy" television viewing, as well as how television portrays the gender roles, has an effect on the viewers' conceptions about gender stereotypes among preschoolers (Gross and Jeffries-Fox, 1978) and young adults (Eisenstock, 1984). A cautionary word is noteworthy here about these studies, however. To date there has been no experimental data presented to show a causal connection between heavy television viewing per se and watchers' gender stereotyped attitudes. Viewing television may influence a person's gender stereotype attitudes, or people who hold traditional gender stereotypes may watch more television, or a third possibility is that both variables are influenced by some other factor.

The television characters that entertain us each week present us with very definite pictures of how we should act. In the main, female characters are the bystanders watching men overcome all kinds of problems. There are far too few dramas where a female character is presented in a competent and self-determining way. Granted, we do find an occasional female character like Joyce Davenport, the public defender in "Hill Street Blues," who plays a highly competent, assertive, and decent human being, or the new breed of female detectives like the two portrayed on the TV series "Cagney & Lacey." However, in most of the highly rated TV shows, women are either auxiliary to the action and seemingly there only to add some "sugar and spice" and fulfill the sexual needs of the male characters, or they are powerful matriarchs who are evil and manipulative. Shows like

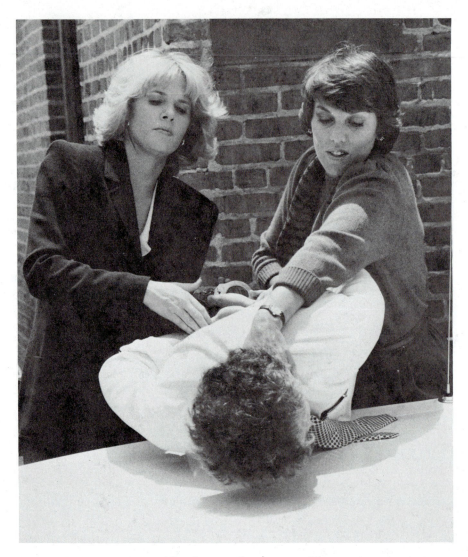

Figure 4.1 For several decades, television has portrayed women in stereotypic roles. However, television is beginning to feature women in nontraditional roles, like those seen on the police program "Cagney and Lacey."

"Dukes of Hazzard," "Dallas," "Magnum," "The A-Team," and "Love Boat" place male characters at center stage with females portrayed as enticing examples of male fantasies.

Other media forms besides television influence our views of how we should behave and how we should play out our gender roles. In popular magazines (Franzwa, 1975) and music (Reinartz, 1975), for example, men and women are usually portrayed in traditional gender-stereotypic ways, with men portrayed as aggressive and in control and women dependent on their menfolk for support.

Teachers as Socializers

The stated purpose of formal education is to teach the young the basics: "readin', writin', and arithmetic." However, the educational system teaches far more than the basics. Social values like conformity, competition, achievement, discipline, cooperation with others, and orderliness are only a few of the values taught and reinforced in school. The teacher is a key element in the educational system. What and how students learn and also how the students see themselves and define their roles are influenced by the teacher's expectations and behavior and by the effects of the teacher being a role model for them. The impact of a teacher's expectations shouldn't be taken lightly. In one study, a teacher was told that the class was divided between bright students and average students on the basis of some test results (Rosenthal and Jacobson, 1968). Later in the school year, the "bright" students actually did better on standardized tests than those who had been labeled average. Surprisingly, the only difference between these two groups was the teacher's knowledge of the earlier purported test results which the researchers had actually made up. Although not every teacher is susceptible to biased information about students (Babad, 1979), many teachers hold traditional gender stereotypes about their students that can affect their students' views of what is expected of them (Zimet and Zimet, 1977).

Teachers treat the genders differently. Psychologist Lisa Serbin (1973) and several of her colleagues studied how teachers treat preschool children and how this treatment influenced the children in learning their gender roles. In the classroom, Serbin found that preschool boys generally acted more aggressively, whereas girls behaved more dependently. Clearly, these behaviors mirror the commonly accepted gender stereotypes for each gender. Serbin also found that the teachers' behaviors toward their students helped reinforce these gender-specific behaviors. Specifically, when boys acted aggressively, their teachers were more likely to reprimand them than they were to reprimand girls who acted in a similar manner. Research has shown that reprimanding a child for a particular behavior may have the same effect as reinforcing that behavior and, consequently, that behavior is more likely to continue (Brown and Elliott, 1965). Thus, the teachers' reprimands may have reinforced the boys' aggressive behaviors. When girls behaved dependently, the teachers' interactions with them can be seen as a type of reinforcement for their dependent behaviors. When girls needed assistance, their teachers often required that the girls come to them for help, which reinforced the girls' dependency on an adult. Boys, however, weren't required to come to their teachers for assistance. In summary, Serbin found that teachers play a decisive role in their students' acquisition of behaviors associated with traditional gender stereotypes.

Through the early grade school years, girls generally do better scholastically than boys. However, somewhere near the end of high school, many girls' academic performance declines even below that of those boys whose grades were lower than the girls' just a few years earlier. How can we explain this turnabout in girls' academic performance?

During the 1970s, Carol Dweck and several colleagues conducted a series of studies looking into the effects of what they termed *learned helplessness* (Dweck, 1975; Dweck et al., 1978). Learned helplessness occurs when people reduce their effort because they assume that failure is inevitable. If, for example, a child perceives that failure at some task is more likely than success because of lack of ability, then the child may concede that he or she can do little to avoid failure.

But what would make a person feel that he or she must inevitably fail? If a person fails and believes the failure was due to a lack of personal effort, then failure is not inevitable but could be avoided in the future by redoubling one's effort. But what about a person who fails and assumes the failure was due to a lack of ability? For this person, redoubling of effort will do little to insure future success. Failure in the latter case is assumed to be due to one's lack of ability, which can't be changed, and in the former case, failure is assumed to be caused by lack of effort, which can be changed. Dweck's research found that girls are more likely to attribute their academic failures to a lack of ability, and boys attribute their academic failures to a lack of effort. In Dweck's analysis, girls can fall victim to a sense of learned helplessness. But why is this so?

Dweck suggested that boys generally receive much more negative feedback about their behaviors and academic performance from parents and teachers alike. Eventually, boys learn to dismiss much of this negative feedback as irrelevant, almost as if they learned to "turn a deaf ear to it." Girls, on the other hand, receive much less negative feedback from adults about their behaviors and academic performance, and thus when they do receive it, they tend to take it "more to heart." In other words, boys become oblivious to criticism because there is so much of it, whereas girls become oversensitive to it because of the relatively little amount they deal with. Dweck also found that boys receive relatively less negative feedback about their academic performance than girls do (Dweck et al., 1978). From their observations, boys were more heavily criticized for their conduct or for breaking rules than girls were. Thus, although girls receive less negative feedback than boys do, the negative feedback they do receive is more likely directed at their poor academic performance. Consequently, girls come to believe that poor academic performance is attributable to lack of ability, something over which they have little control. What all of this means is that girls tend to believe that they are less likely to succeed because they have been taught to think of themselves as less capable intellectually than boys.

As already suggested, boys generally do not do well in school during the early grades, at least not as well as most girls. The boys' lack of early success may be due to their supposedly greater inclination toward rebelliousness toward authority, rather than to any inherent intellectual dificiency. As boys proceed through the school years, they begin to achieve better grades. This academic turnaround may be explained by the increase in pressures to achieve as boys get closer to the college years, or it may be explained by the lack of the debilitating effects of learned helplessness. There is always pressure on young males to work harder once they come to believe they will soon take on the "breadwinner" role.

Besides the young male's increasing scholastic demands, there is the additional pressure to succeed at sports and to show themselves as accomplished athletes. In fact, sometimes it seems that sports play a greater role in most boys' lives than their school work (Coleman, 1976). Although most young boys and men would argue that athletics teach important basic skills needed in today's world (especially those highly prized masculine values of competition, loyalty to one's own group, toughness, discipline, and self-reliance) not all boys find athletics a positive nor personally rewarding experience (see box 4.1).

As we can see, students learn more than the three R's from their teachers. Besides being a place where students learn the basics, school is also a place where students interact with others of their own age, or what most people refer to as a peer group. However, the time the young spend in school does not equal the amount of time they spend with their friends just hanging out at the local fast-food place or driving around together.

Peers as Socializers

By definition a *peer group* is made up of those individuals with whom we share a similar status as well as many similar values and behaviors. One of the main functions of a peer group is to be a sounding-board where a person can try on new behaviors and perfect those already learned. During adolescence, the peer group is probably the most powerful socializing agent in a young person's life. During the transition from childhood to early adulthood, or that period called adolescence, most teen-aged boys and girls strive more for the approval and acceptance of their peers than they do for that of their own families. The importance of the peer group is summarized best in the following statement:

> The peer group provides an opportunity to learn how to interact with age-mates, how to deal with hostility and dominance, how to relate to a leader, and how to lead others. It also performs a psychotherapeutic function for the child in helping him deal with social problems. Through discussions with peers the child may learn that others share his problems, conflicts, and complex feelings, and this may be reassuring. . . . Finally, the peer group helps the child develop a concept of himself. The ways in which peers react to the child and the bases upon which he is accepted or rejected give him a clearer, and perhaps more realistic, picture of his assets and liabilities. (Mussen et al., 1974, p. 515)

The next time you are strolling around a shopping mall or walking down a crowded street, notice the groups of young people who are interacting together. What do you notice about the groups? Probably one of the first impressions that will strike you is the similarity in dress and behavior. One

Box 4.1

Out in Right Field

Throughout my entire school career, the time of day I dreaded most was Gym class. Whereas other kids seemed to look forward to Gym as some sort of relief from sitting at a desk and listening to a teacher, I dreaded the thought of sports.

The curse followed me throughout my entire life. In elementary school, part of the year we played baseball outdoors. The two best players (never me) were captains and they chose—one by one—players for their teams. The choosing went on and on, the better players getting picked first and me and my type last.

During the game I always played the outfield. Right field. Far right field. And there I would stand in the hot sun wishing I was anyplace else in the world. Every so often a ball looked like it was coming in my direction and I prayed to god that it wouldn't happen. If it did come, I promised god to be good for the next thirty-seven years if he let me catch it—especially if it was a flyball. The same thing occurred when it was my turn to bat. It was bad enough, but if there were any runners on base—or any outs—and it all depended on me—I knew we were lost.

The rest of the year in elementary school consisted of indoor Gym class, some of which were coed. The coed Gym classes consisted of things like dance lessons. The teachers would teach us essential dances like the fox trot, the mambo and the merengue. These were always a chore because it was you and your girl partner—usually matched by height—and I of course was the shortest—and matched up with the shortest girl—who towered over me anyway. Dances like the Virginia Reel and square dancing which were a group thing, I usually enjoyed a lot. A lot, that is, until it became clear from the actions of the rest of the guys in dance class that I was the only one having a good time. After that even that type of dancing was awful.

Junior high school was equally awful. For it was in junior high that real Gym classes started—Gym class with lockers and smelly locker rooms and gym uniforms and showers with eight million other guys.

I hated the sight of my gym uniform. The locker room stench almost knocked me out. And during Gym class I tried my best not to exert myself, so I wouldn't sweat too much so I wouldn't have to take a shower with eight million other guys.

In junior high we still did things like play baseball. But things started to get rougher and rougher. We did things like wrestling. And gymnastics. To this day I can't climb a pole or a rope. Calisthenics were and are a bore.

Source: Unbecoming men: A men's consciousness-raising group writes on oppression and themselves, published in 1971, by Times Change Press, Box 187, Albion, CA 95410. Reprinted by permission.

Box 4.1

High school was the same old stuff. However, in high school, sports started taking on new dimensions because the most highly prized girls looked to the best athletes. The football and basketball players. I was out of the competition from the beginning, but that didn't make it any less awful.

There was absolutely no relief from sports in the early part of my life, for it happened not only in school, but also at home. My older brother was a good athlete. He went to ballgames and even tried out for and made some teams. He plastered our room with hateful pictures of the Dodgers at bat. Sports consumed his entire life, and he would get home from school, change his clothes and run out to play.

My father related to my brother completely in this way. They had a fine sports relationship, and would go off to ballgames together—or talk at the dinner table of the day's ballgames or the latest standings which they both knew by heart. I was completely left out of this. After a while I grew resentful and wanted no part of it. Yet, every so often my father would try. He would take me out back for a while with a ball, bat and glove and try to make a man out of me. Patiently he would throw a ball in my direction and I swung and missed it. After he quickly grew tired of that he would once again explain to me how to use the fielding glove he stuck on my hand and I would try my hand at catching. I soon grew tired of this—mainly because I missed so often and had to go chasing down the block after the ball. These sessions never lasted very long. Even Sundays were no relief—the television was usually on and blasting a ballgame. I grew to hate the sound of Mel Allen's voice.

My father and brother seemed to have a great relationship. I didn't. Never with my father, nor with my brother. I guess I was left to my mother. We seemed to get along fine.

area where peers influence their members is that of appearance. Young people generally dress to impress their friends. Much of the interaction that takes place between adolescent peers helps to reinforce their conceptions of gender roles. Young boys show off their "masculine" behaviors for girls, and girls act as if they find the boys' "masculine" behaviors quite appealing. Girls coach each other on the "ways" of boys, and vice versa.

One question many people ask about peer groups, especially adolescent peer groups, is in what ways do peers influence the young as opposed to the family's influence? Research suggests that peer groups are more likely to influence their members in terms of dress, lifestyle, and sexual activities, whereas the family appears to influence basic values and life-long goals for the young (Troll and Bengtson, 1979).

SOCIOLOGICAL PERSPECTIVES ON GENDER ROLES

In this section we will examine three sociological perspectives. We will describe in turn the functionalist, the conflict, and finally the symbolic interactionist approaches. Each has their proponents and their critics. One thing is certain, however; the field of sociology is much richer because of each.

The Functionalist Perspective

To understand how the *functionalist perspective* explains gender roles, let's first describe three basic features that underlie its approach to group dynamics. To do this we will turn to the foremost functionalist spokesperson, Talcott Parsons (1971).

According to Parsons, the first principle underlying all groups is the *interdependency* of their members. For example, in a "traditional family" the wife depends on her husband for economic support, and the husband depends on his wife for caring for the children. The children naturally depend on their parents for their support and sustenance. Thus every family member depends on the others for some sort of support.

The second feature that underlies all groups is that groups are held together by a set of common *social values*. Social values are those desirable or worthwhile qualities or ideals that people support. Our traditional family may hold strong feelings about relatives, parental authority, respect for elders, or even having and raising children. All of these values and many others help bond the family members together.

The third element among groups is a need for *stability* and *equilibrium*. If a group is to last or continue to be a cohesive social unit, it must avoid conflict or at least avoid as much conflict as possible between its members. If conflict should arise, it must be resolved if the group is to remain stable. To ensure a group's stability, certain social patterns or roles are needed whereby all the group members know what is expected of them. In other words, conflict can be avoided between group members if they adhere to their prescribed roles. If in a family a problem arises between the children, for example, one or both of the parents may intervene and try to smooth the ruffled feelings of the disputing parties; at least that's how it's supposed to work.

Thus, according to Parsons, all groups, if they are going to last, exhibit a set of basic characteristics that include interdependency, a common set of social values, and a degree of equilibrium or stability brought about by prescribed roles that reduce intra-group conflict.

Parsons and his colleague Robert Bales (1955) further elaborated that a group generally requires two kinds of leaders for the group's smooth functioning. The first type, an *instrumental leader,* is one who oversees the group members to ensure that all are performing their assigned tasks. Such a leader is responsible for maintaining the relationships between the group and all outside groups. A second type, an *expressive leader*, emerges within the group and is responsible for the group's emotional needs. Primarily, the expressive leader tries to prevent the day-to-day conflict that may arise within the group. Keeping the lines of communication open between members, making sure that group members' feelings are not hurt, and in general, acting like a counselor who listens to members' complaints and who works out solutions for the group's problems are just a few of the expressive leader's chief responsibilities. A group, according to Greer Litton Fox (1983), "needs a 'head' and a 'heart'." With this brief outline of group characteristics and types of leaders, we can focus on the gender roles specifically.

According to Parsons and Bales, the family and its division of labor evolved over the centuries due mainly to the basic biological differences found between the early males and females. They reason that among the earliest human social groups—going back before 10,000 B.C.—the major problem was survival. The female, however, was limited in her travel because she was required to stay close to her infant. Thus the female best served the group's survival needs by searching for food near the campsite. The male was not restricted by the infant's needs and was therefore free to roam far distances from the campsite. Parsons and Bales speculate that the biological differences between males and females and their consequent strategies for food gathering shaped the division of labor pattern. Over a period of time, males took on the instrumental role of meeting with outsiders and tending to the business of the family, and females adopted the expressive role of caring for infants and staying close to the home base. These two leadership roles evolved into what today we call the traditional gender roles.

Let's now focus on the family and see how the age-old gender roles built upon the division of labor supposedly fulfill the three functionalist requirements of all groups. Recall that the first element was that all members of a group are interdependent. In the traditional family unit, the husband is expected to be the primary provider, or breadwinner, for the family's sustenance. At the same time, the wife is expected to provide emotional support and act as the primary caretaker for spouse and children. The husband's and wife's roles are seen as complementary and interdependent. In their roles as parental authorities and teachers, both parents interact with their children, whose roles as obedient and respectful youngsters complete the interdependency expected between parent and child.

The second element that supposedly holds the family together, common social values, can be exemplified by respect for parents' wishes, acceptance of the father's authority, reverence for the mother, and the value placed on the children's welfare. All of these values and others supposedly are taught to the children through the socialization process. The outcome of such socialization, if all comes out as it should, is that the children will learn their expected gender roles and grow up to be socially fit adult men and women in terms of their gender roles. If the children learn their prescribed gender roles, it is hoped that they will come to value these same gender roles for themselves and pass them on when it comes time for them to take on the parent roles.

The last element, that of stability or lack of conflict, is thought to come about by all family members adhering to their prescribed roles. For example, if the husband does not fulfill his instrumental role, the family will suffer, and the group's equilibrium will become disrupted. If the husband-father does not provide for his family's financial well-being, it may become necessary for the wife to take outside employment, leaving her little time or energy to fulfill her expressive functions for the family. Phyllis Schlafly (1981) argues that the increasing numbers of women who work full-time jobs outside of the home are actually taking jobs away from male bread-winners, thus disrupting the families of these unemployed men and undermining the role of motherhood in the long run.

While the functionalist perspective has added to our understanding of why traditional gender roles may have developed, some believe that it is too conservative and not adequate in explaining the recent changes in gender roles (Peplau, 1983). Sociologist Gerald Marwell (1975) believes that traditional gender roles based on a division of labor may have been suitable in times past. But today, with the complex and rapid social changes, the functionalist view of gender roles is of little help. Marwell believes that modern-day societies are best served if people are treated on the basis of ability rather than on some outmoded idea of instrumental and expressive roles. The real contribution of the functionalist perspective may not be in its analysis of present-day gender roles, but rather that it was an early attempt by sociologists to explain how gender roles developed.

The Conflict Perspective

During the 1960s, certain groups (i.e., blacks, students, and women) became outspoken in their dissatisfaction with society's *status quo*. Along with the street demonstrations, protests, and revolutionary rhetoric, another sociological perspective made its presence felt as it focused attention on the inherent conflict that existed between competing groups. The *conflict perspective* drew its theoretical roots from the seminal ideas of Karl Marx, Friedrich Engels (1942), and Georg Simmel (1955). Marx's theory of class conflict provided the basis for conflict theory. According to Jonathan Turner and Leonard Beeghley (1981), conflict theory is grounded in the following assumptions.

1. All social systems distribute scarce and valuable resources unequally.
2. The resulting inequalities create conflict of interest among various strata and classes in the system.
3. These conflicts of interest eventually generate overt conflicts between those who control valuable resources and those who do not.
4. In the long run, these conflicts result in the reorganization of social systems. In the past, new patterns of inequality always brought about further conflict and change. (p. 545)

Although there are many variations to conflict theory, most adherents subscribe to the notion that society is made up of competing groups that continually struggle for scarce resources (Dahrendorf, 1959).

If the functionalist perspective gives a view of *how* the gender roles came about, the conflict perspective provides the *why* by which gender roles remain intact even when there is no justification for unequal status arrangements between women and men. To see how the conflict perspective explains gender discrimination, let us examine a recent example of job discrimination in which women lost out in the workplace.

World War II found millions of men in uniform and plants and factories in need of able-bodied workers. To fill the worker-gap, tens of thousands of women ("Rosie the Riveter") entered the labor force. These women proved themselves capable of performing "men's work" and assisted greatly in the war effort (Anderson, 1981). After the war, however, the returning servicemen found themselves competing with women for scarce jobs. Conflict between them was inevitable because both groups wanted the same scarce resource—jobs. The problem was how to make women return to the home as full-time homemakers and leave the jobs for men. But how could society justify the need for women's return to the home after what women accomplished in the name of the war effort? The solution was for the reemergence of traditional gender roles with its implicit sexist ideology that women were not capable of doing "men's work." The message went out that women should stay at home and tend to their housework and children and do what nature had intended them to do. Thus when men found themselves in competition with women for scarce jobs, the gender role ideology that women were inferior to men was used to keep women from gaining greater access to jobs and the resultant economic freedom that having a paycheck would bring. Here we see an example of the conflict that erupts when two groups (females and males) want the same scarce resource (jobs) and how gender roles are used to prevent women from gaining access to more power, prestige, and wealth. Conflict theory notes that gender roles serve men by promoting the ideology that women are inferior to men and should remain under men's economic domination.

Conflict-oriented theorists have argued that traditional gender roles are one of the most powerful social mechanisms by which one group (men) dominates another group (women) (Collins, 1971, 1975; Sokoloff, 1980). The traditional pattern of gender roles reinforces men's dominance over women. Men maintain their superiority over women by controlling society's valued resources (e.g., jobs, money) and the powerful social institutions (e.g., government and religion). Presently, there is little reason or motivation for most men to change this system of inequality because of the prevalent view that they will lose more than they gain in a truly egalitarian society. The conflict perspective also notes that many of the characteristics found in the battle between women and men are similar to those found between whites and blacks (Hacker, 1951).

Another way of analyzing the gender roles from a conflict perspective has focused on men's need to exploit women for their work and for the children they bear (Hartmann, 1981). This line of reasoning suggests that, historically, men needed workers to farm the land and do the chores. Women provided such a supply of workers, but they could also provide additional workers, namely, children. But a man needed to know who his children were so that he could pass on his land and wealth to his own children and not to some other man's. One way to know one's own children was to isolate a woman so that a man could be sure that the children she bore were truly his. Thus the traditional gender roles have persisted long beyond any need for them because they provide the means of keeping women isolated from the world where they could gain power.

Symbolic Interactionism

George Herbert Mead's (1934) theoretical speculations on the concept of the self lead to the sociological perspective known as *symbolic interactionism*. Symbolic interactionism focuses on the *symbols* used by people for social interaction and the meanings a society imposes on these symbols. As used here, symbols are either physical gestures (e.g., smiles, frowns, nodding) or verbal gestures (e.g., language) that are understood by both a sender and a receiver.

Generally speaking, symbolic interactionism rests on three assumptions (Lauer and Handel, 1983). First, humans inhabit a world of meaning. People do not simply respond to objects or events in their environment, but rather to the meanings they attribute to the events or objects they encounter. Second, the meanings we have of events or objects are flexible, or changeable. Today's best friend can be tomorrow's worst enemy. A raised fist may mean nothing today but may mean revolution or "power to the people" tomorrow. The objects and events that populate a person's world do not necessarily have the same meaning forever. And third, although a person has great flexibility in determining the meaning of the environment she or he lives in, there are certain aspects that a person cannot wish away. A person, for example, may not wish to see danger in a situation like going for a hike in the desert, but danger may be there regardless of what the person thinks or wishes.

Symbolic interactionists like Erving Goffman (1959) and Harold Garfinkel (1967) argue that social actions between people cannot be understood simply by analyzing individual personalities nor in terms of the situations people find themselves in. Rather, symbolic interactionism stresses that social behavior can be understood better by analyzing the symbols people use and the meanings people place on them. For example, what does a stare or prolonged gaze mean? If you find yourself being stared at, do you interpret the stare as interest or anger? According to symbolic interactionism, the interpretation of the physical gesture, the stare, is the important key to understanding the social interaction that may take place between you and the other person. If you are a female and the one staring at you is male, you may think of the stare as meaning interest. But if you are a male and the other is a male also, you may think the stare means anger. The meaning of the stare depends to a great extent on what society has taught us about the appropriate gestures for interest and anger between the genders.

In this section we will focus on two features commonly associated with gender roles and analyze them from a symbolic interactionist perspective, namely, the meanings of occupations and the judgment of "friendliness."

The Gender Meanings of Occupations   According to symbolic interactionism, the persistence of gender roles in any society can be explained by the tendency for most people to conform to long-established social expectations and the meanings attached to gender categories rather than to the few biological differences found between women and men. For example, there is no justifiable reason that a female cannot be a truck driver, nor a male a nurse. A female may possess the requisite skills to drive a truck, and a male may have the knowledge to perform nursing duties. But in several studies with children as young as five, we find children expressing very definite ideas about what kinds of jobs are appropriate for men and women. The children's selection of jobs and who should perform them fall mainly along traditional gender role lines—males are truck drivers and females are nurses, and that's that (Archer, 1984; Franken, 1983). In most children's minds, the occupation of truck driver is associated with men and nursing with women. It is as if trucks took on a symbolic representation of manliness and a nurse's uniform that of womanliness. Consequently, many young boys aspire to be truck drivers, and many young girls think in terms of their being nurses one day. According to a symbolic interactionist approach, the reason for this is that most young children have learned their society's prescribed meaning of these occupations. Truck driving means one thing and nursing another. The boy who wants to be a nurse or the girl who wants to be a truck driver is showing that he or she has a different interpretation—different from their society—of these gender-related occupations. Once learned, most children conform by stating that these occupations are associated with one gender and not the other.

The Meaning of a Smile   When a female smiles at a male, what does the smile mean? Friendliness or sexual interest? Jessie Bernard (1968) suggests that cultural beliefs may often lead to confusion on the part of women and men as to what certain gestures mean. A woman may smile at a man and mean for the smile to communicate friendliness or civility in a social situation. A man, on the other hand, may interpret a woman's smile as a sign of the woman's sexual interest in him (Abbey, 1982). Women interpret a smile as having one meaning, but many men interpret a woman's smile

Figure 4.2 Girl meets boy.
According to symbolic interactionism, social interactions like "first-meetings" are based on one's expressions and how others' interpret them. The young girl's (shown above) posture, facial expressions, gestures, and words are meaningful features of how she feels toward the young boy. His responses toward her are based to a large degree on his interpretations of how she reacts toward him. Do you think she is interested or not? Your answer depends on your interpretation of her expressions.

to mean something quite different. Again, according to symbolic interactionism, the gesture *per se* is not the focus of attention but rather the meaning placed on the smile by a person in terms of expected gender role behavior.

The symbolic interactionist perspective suggests that we learn our gender roles in much the same way that we learn all our social roles, through interaction with others. Symbolic interactionism has been extremely valuable in directing our attention to the subtle and not-so-subtle meanings attached to certain symbols that support our society's gender roles. For instance, look at the many magazine advertisements showing a woman and a man together. What do you see? Quite often, you'll see a man touching a woman, gazing directly at a woman, or standing or sitting in such a way that he appears taller than the woman. Notice how few ads show a woman touching a man, gazing directly at a man, or appearing taller than a man. Can we infer anything from these differences in the expressive ways that males and females interact? Yes we can, and most of us do. Researchers have suggested, for example, that a man touching or gazing at a woman and his appearing taller than a woman carry the meaning of a man's dominance and a woman's submissiveness. (Goffman, 1979; Leffler et al., 1982). The symbolic interactionist perspective with its focus on the commonly shared meanings of gestures and expressions between males and females has made us all more aware of the subtle ways that traditional gender role patterns are conveyed and perpetuated in society.

SUMMARY

Neither born in isolation nor raised in seclusion, we all need others to become fully human. Sociology studies the relationships among and between people. Sociologists are especially interested in the positions or statuses that people occupy within various groups. Each person has numerous statuses; some we have no control over (ascribed status), while others we must do something to earn (achieved status). Each status carries with it a set of prescriptive behaviors, called norms, that make up a particular role. Our gender norms and roles are some of the most important features of our lives.

The norms associated with being female encompass the prescriptions that a female should have children and marry in order to fulfill herself as a female. The norms for males usually prescribe that a male should shun acting feminine, be a success, be aggressive when the occasion warrants it, be the initiator in sexual relations, and be self-reliant and tough.

Most sociologists emphasize the importance of socialization as the primary means a group uses to teach the young what is expected of them. Parents, media, teachers, and peers are important socializing agents for teaching the young their gender roles.

Over the years, several sociological theories have been developed to explain gender roles, namely, the functionalist, the conflict, and the symbolic interactionist perspectives. Each has a different view of the gender roles.

SUGGESTED READINGS

Doyle, J. (1983). *The male experience.* Dubuque, IA: Wm. C. Brown Publishers.

Epstein, C. (1981). Women in sociological analysis: New scholarship versus old paradigms. *Soundings, 64(4),* 485–98.

Farrel, M., & Rosenberg, S. (1981). *Men at midlife.* Boston: Auburn House.

Gould, M. (1980). The new sociology. *Signs, 5(3),* 459–67.

Lott, B. (1981). *Becoming a woman: The socialization of gender.* Springfield, IL: Thomas.

Luepton, L. (1984). Adolescent sex roles and social change. New York: Columbia University Press.

Tuchman, G., Daniels, A., & Benet, J. (Eds.). (1978). *Hearth and home: Images of women in the mass media.* New York: Oxford University Press.

Weitzman, L. (1979). *Sex role socialization.* Palo Alto, CA: Mayfield.

Williams, F., LaRose, R., & Frost, F. (1981). *Children, television, and sex role stereotyping.* New York: Praeger.

Point/Counterpoint

A Cost-Benefit Analysis of the Superwoman's Gender Roles

Over the last decade or so, more and more women have been struggling with a new version of their gender role. Evidence of this new role appeared on a recent TV commercial where we heard about those women who can "bring home the bacon, fry it up in a pan, and still make her man feel like a man." The commercial went on to say that such a Herculean accomplishment was due mainly to a special fragrance that the women dabbed behind their ears. Setting aside the value of one perfume over another, today's women are encouraged to pursue careers, be involved in all kinds of social activities, be a supportive and nurturant wife and mother, *and* be successful in all of these roles. The new image of the *superwoman* has finally burst on the scene. She is all things to all people: competent worker at the office, perfect hostess and social director, loving mother, and caring wife. Supposedly, she is more complete as a person, happier in her marriage, more patient with her children, and viewed as competent by others.

One thing left out in the description of the superwoman, however, is that she is also exhausted (Shaevitz, 1984). She may find personal fulfillment in her achievements at work and experience an increase of self-esteem because she receives a paycheck, but she still must come home and tackle the housework. Her evenings and weekends are filled with endless chores: preparing dinner, doing dishes, separating the laundry, and many other jobs that are necessary to keep the family going. Can the average woman accomplish all of this? Sylvia Rabiner (1976), for one, thinks that "the superwoman who knits marriage, career, and motherhood into a satisfying life without dropping a stitch is as oppressive a role model as the air-brushed bunny in the *Playboy* Centerfold or 'That Cosmopolitan Girl' " (p. 11). Can any person, female or male, be expected to be all things to all people?

What do you think?

Reading — *The Story of X*

What would you think of a couple who was raising their child with absolutely no reference to the child's biological sex? Does it sound preposterous? Maybe it's not. In the following, Lois Gould recounts just such a family in the classic children's story about a child named X.

Once upon a time, a Baby named X was born. It was named X so that nobody could tell whether it was a boy or a girl.

Its parents could tell, of course, but they couldn't tell anybody else. They couldn't even tell Baby X—at least not until much, much later.

You see, it was all part of a very important Secret Scientific Xperiment, known officially as Project Baby X.

This Xperiment was going to cost Xactly 23 billion dollars and 72 cents. Which might seem like a lot for one Baby, even if it was an important Secret Scientific Xperimental Baby.

But when you remember the cost of strained carrots, stuffed bunnies, booster shots, 28 shiny quarters from the tooth fairy . . . you begin to see how it adds up.

Long before Baby X was born, the smartest scientists had to work out the secret details of the Xperiment, and to write the *Official Instruction Manual*, in secret code, for Baby X's parents, whoever they were.

These parents had to be selected very carefully. Thousands of people volunteered to take thousands of tests, with thousands of tricky questions.

Almost everybody failed because, it turned out, almost everybody wanted a boy or a girl, and not a Baby X at all.

Also, almost everybody thought a Baby X would be more trouble than a boy or a girl. (They were right, too.)

There were families with grandparents named Milton and Agatha, who wanted the baby named Milton or Agatha instead of X, even if it *was* an X.

There were aunts who wanted to knit tiny dresses and uncles who wanted to send tiny baseball mitts.

Worst of all, there were families with other children who couldn't be trusted to keep a Secret. Not if they knew the Secret was worth 23 billion dollars and 72 cents—and all you had to do was take one little peek at Baby X in the bathtub to know what it was.

Finally, the scientists found the Joneses, who really wanted to raise an X more than any other kind of baby—no matter how much trouble it was.

The Joneses promised to take turns holding X, feeding X, and singing X to sleep.

And they promised never to hire any babysitters. The scientists knew that a baby-sitter would probably peek at X in the bathtub, too.

The day the Joneses brought their baby home, lots of friends and relatives came to see it. And the first thing they asked was what kind of a baby X was.

When the Joneses said, "It's an X!" nobody knew what to say.

They couldn't say, "Look at her cute little dimples!"

On the other hand, they couldn't say "Look at his husky little biceps!"

And they didn't feel right about saying just plain "kitchy-coo."

The relatives all felt embarrassed about having an X in the family.

"People will think there's something wrong with it!" they whispered.

"Nonsense!" the Joneses said cheerfully. "What could possibly be wrong with this perfectly adorable X?"

Clearly, nothing at all was wrong. Nevertheless, the cousins who had sent a tiny football helmet would not come and visit anymore.

Source: " 'X' A fabulous child's story" by Lois Gould. Copyright © 1978 text by Lois Gould—only. Reprinted by permission of Brandt & Brandt Literary Agents Inc.

And the neighbors who sent a pink-flowered romper suit pulled their shades down when the Joneses passed their house.

The *Official Instruction Manual* had warned the new parents that this would happen, so they didn't fret about it. Besides, they were too busy learning how to bring up Baby X.

Ms. and Mr. Jones had to be Xtra careful. If they kept bouncing it up in the air and saying how *strong* and *active* it was, they'd be treating it more like a boy than an X. But if all they did was cuddle it and kiss it and tell it how *sweet* and *dainty* it was, they'd be treating it more like a girl than an X.

On page 1654 of the *Official Instruction Manual*, the scientists prescribed: "plenty of bouncing and plenty of cuddling, *both*. X ought to be strong and sweet and active. Forget about *dainty* altogether."

There were other problems, too. Toys, for instance. And clothes. On his first shopping trip, Mr. Jones told the store clerk, "I need some things for a new baby." The clerk smiled and said, "Well, now, is it a boy or a girl?" "It's an X," Mr. Jones said, smiling back. But the clerk got all red in the face and said huffily, "In *that* case, I'm afraid I can't help you sir."

Mr. Jones wandered the aisles trying to find what X needed. But everything was in sections marked BOYS or GIRLS: "Boys' Pajamas" and "Girls' Underwear" and "Boys' Fire Engines" and "Girls' Housekeeping Sets." Mr. Jones went home without buying anything for X.

That night he and Ms. Jones consulted page 2326 of the *Official Instruction Manual*. It said firmly: "Buy plenty of everything!"

So they bought all kinds of toys. A boy doll that made pee-pee and cried "Pa-Pa." And a girl doll that talked in three languages and said, "I am the Pres-i-dent of Gen-er-al Mo-tors."

They bought a storybook about a brave princess who rescued a handsome prince from his tower, and another one about a sister and brother who grew up to be a baseball star and a ballet star, and you had to guess which.

The head scientists of Project Baby X checked all their purchases and told them to keep up the good work. They also reminded the Joneses to see page 4629 of the *Manual*, where it said, "Never make Baby X feel *embarrassed* or *ashamed* about what it wants to play with. And if X gets dirty climbing rocks, never say, 'Nice little Xes don't get dirty climbing rocks.' "

Likewise, it said, "If X falls down and cries, never say, 'Brave little Xes don't cry.' Because, of course, nice little Xes *do* get dirty, and brave little Xes *do* cry. No matter how dirty X gets, or how hard it cries, don't worry. It's all part of the Xperiment."

Whenever the Joneses pushed Baby X's stroller in the park, smiling strangers would come over and coo: "Is that a boy or a girl?" The Joneses would smile back and say, "It's an X." The strangers would stop smiling then and often snarl something nasty—as if the Joneses had said something nasty to *them*.

Once a little girl grabbed X's shovel in the sandbox, and zonked X on the head with it. "Now, now, Tracy," the mother began to scold, "little girls mustn't hit little—" and she turned to ask X, "Are you a little boy or a little girl, dear?"

Mr. Jones, who was sitting near the sandbox, held his breath and crossed his fingers.

X smiled politely, even though X's head had never been zonked so hard in its life. "I'm a little X," said X.

"You're a *what*?" the lady exclaimed angrily. "You're a little b-r-a-t, you mean!"

"But little girls mustn't hit little Xes, either!" said X, retrieving the shovel with another polite smile. "What good's hitting, anyway?"

X's father finally X-haled, uncrossed his fingers, and grinned.

Reading _Continued_

And at their next secret Project Baby X meeting, the scientists grinned, too. Baby X was doing fine.

But then it was time for X to start school. The Joneses were really worried about this, because school was even more full of rules for boys and girls, and there were no rules for Xes.

Teachers would tell boys to form a line, and girls to form another line.

There would be boys' games and girls' games, and boys' secrets and girls' secrets.

The school library would have a list of recommended books for girls, and a different list for boys.

There would even be a bathroom marked BOYS and another one marked GIRLS.

Pretty soon boys and girls would hardly talk to each other. What would happen to poor little X?

The Joneses spent weeks consulting their _Instruction Manual_.

There were 249 and one-half pages of advice under "First Day of School." Then they were all summoned to an Urgent Xtra Special Conference with the smart scientists of Project Baby X.

The scientists had to make sure that X's mother had taught X how to throw and catch a ball properly, and that X's father had been sure to teach X what to serve at a doll's tea party.

X had to know how to shoot marbles and jump rope and, most of all, what to say when the Other Children asked whether X was a Boy or a Girl.

Finally, X was ready.

X's teacher had promised that the class could line up alphabetically, instead of forming separate lines for boys and girls. And X had permission to use the principal's bathroom, because it wasn't marked anything except BATHROOM. But nobody could help X with the biggest problem of all—Other Children.

Nobody in X's class had ever known an X. Nobody had even heard grown-ups say, "Some of my best friends are Xes."

What would other children think? Would they make Xist jokes? Or would they make friends?

You couldn't tell what X was by its clothes. Overalls don't even button right to left, like girls' clothes, or left to right, like boys' clothes.

And did X have a girl's short haircut or a boy's long haircut?

As for the games X liked, either X played ball very well for a girl, or else played house very well for a boy.

The children tried to find out by asking X tricky questions, like, "Who's your favorite sports star?" X had two favorite sports stars: a girl jockey named Robyn Smith and a boy archery champion named Robin Hood.

Then they asked, "What's your favorite TV show?" And X said: "Lassie," which stars a girl dog played by a boy dog.

When X said its favorite toy was a doll, everyone decided that X must be a girl. But then X said the doll was really a robot, and that X had computerized it, and that it was programmed to bake fudge and then clean up the kitchen.

After X told them that, they gave up guessing what X was. All they knew was they'd sure like to see X's doll.

After school, X wanted to play with the other children. "How about shooting baskets in the gym?" X asked the girls. But all they did was make faces and giggle behind X's back.

"Boy, is _he_ weird," whispered Jim to Joe.

"How about weaving some baskets in the arts and crafts room?" X asked the boys. But they all made faces and giggled behind X's back, too.

"Boy, is _she_ weird," whispered Susie to Peggy.

That night, Ms. and Mr. Jones asked X how things had gone at school. X tried to smile, but there were two big tears in its eyes. "The lessons are okay," X began, "but . . ."

"But?" said Ms. Jones.

"The Other Children hate me," X whispered.

"Hate you?" said Mr. Jones.

X nodded, which made the two big tears roll down and splash on its overalls.

Once more, the Joneses reached for their *Instruction Manual.* Under "Other Children," it said:

"What did you Xpect? Other Children have to obey silly boy-girl rules, because their parents taught them to. Lucky X—you don't have rules at all! All you have to do is be yourself.

"P.S. We're not saying it'll be easy."

X liked being itself. But X cried a lot that night. So X's father held X tight, and cried a little, too. X's mother cheered them up with an Xciting story about an enchanted prince called Sleeping Handsome, who woke up when Princess Charming kissed him.

The next morning, they all felt much better, and little X went back to school with a brave smile and a clean pair of red and white checked overalls.

There was a seven-letter-word spelling bee in class that day. And a seven-lap boys' relay race in the gym. And a seven-layer-cake baking contest in the girls' kitchen corner.

X won the spelling bee. X also won the relay race.

And X almost won the baking contest, Xcept it forgot to light the oven. (Remember, nobody's perfect.)

One of the Other Children noticed something else, too. He said: "X doesn't care about winning. X just thinks it's fun playing boys' stuff *and* girls' stuff."

"Come to think of it," said another one of the Other Children, "X is having twice as much fun as we are!"

After school that day, the girl who beat X in the baking contest gave X a big slice of her winning cake.

And the boy X beat in the relay race asked X to race him home.

From then on, some really funny things began to happen.

Susie, who sat next to X, refused to wear pink dresses to school any more. She wanted red and white checked overalls—just like X's.

Overalls, she told her parents, were better for climbing monkey bars.

Then Jim, the class football nut, started wheeling his little sister's doll carriage around the football field.

He'd put on his entire football uniform, except for the helmet.

Then he'd put the helmet *in* the carriage, lovingly tucked under an old set of shoulder pads.

Then he'd jog around the field, pushing the carriage and singing "Rockabye Baby" to his helmet.

He said X did the same thing, so it must be okay. After all, X was now the team's star quarterback.

Susie's parents were horrified by her behavior, and Jim's parents were worried sick about his.

But the worst came when the twins, Joe and Peggy, decided to share everything with each other.

Peggy used Joe's hockey skates, and his microscope, and took half his newspaper route.

Joe used Peggy's needlepoint kit, and her cookbooks, and took two of her three baby-sitting jobs.

Peggy ran the lawn mower, and Joe ran the vacuum cleaner.

Their parents weren't one bit pleased with Peggy's science experiments, or with Joe's terrific needlepoint pillows.

They didn't care that Peggy mowed the lawn better, and that Joe vacuumed the carpet better.

In fact, they were furious. It's all that little X's fault, they agreed. X doesn't know what it is, or what it's supposed to be! So X wants to mix everybody *else* up, too!

Peggy and Joe were forbidden to play with X any more. So was Susie, and then Jim, and then *all* the Other Children.

But it was too late: the Other Children stayed mixed-up and happy and free, and refused to go back to the way they'd been before X.

Finally, the parents held an emergency meeting to discuss "The X Problem."

They sent a report to the principal stating that X was a "bad influence," and demanding immediate action.

The Joneses, they said, should be *forced* to tell whether X was a boy or a girl. And X should be *forced* to behave like whichever it was.

If the Joneses refused to tell, the parents said, then X must take an Xamination. An Impartial Team of Xperts would Xtract the secret. Then X would start obeying all the old rules. Or else.

And if X turned out to be some kind of mixed-up misfit, then X must be Xpelled from school. Immediately! So that no little Xes would ever come to school again.

The principal was very upset. X, a bad influence? A mixed-up misfit? But X was a Xcellent student! X set a fine Xample! X was Xtraordinary!

X was president of the student council. X had won first prize in the art show, honorable mention in the science fair, and six events on field day, including the potato race.

Nevertheless, insisted the parents, X is a Problem Child. X is the Biggest Problem Child we have ever seen!

So the principal reluctantly notified X's parents and the Joneses reported this to the Project X scientists, who referred them to page 85769 of the *Instruction Manual*. "Sooner or later," it said "X will have to be Xamined by an Impartial Team of Xperts.

"This may be the only way any of us will know for sure whether X is mixed up—or everyone else is."

At Xactly 9 o'clock the next day, X reported to the school health office. The principal, along with a committee from the Parents' Association, X's teacher, X's classmates, and Ms. and Mr. Jones, waited in the hall outside.

Inside, the Xperts had set up their famous testing machine: the Superpsychiamedicosocioculturometer.

Nobody knew Xactly how the machine worked, but everybody knew that this examination would reveal Xactly what everyone wanted to know about X, but were afraid to ask.

It was terribly quiet in the hall. Almost spooky. They could hear very strange noises from the room.

There were buzzes.

And a beep or two.

And several bells.

An occasional light flashed under the door. Was it an X ray?

Through it all, you could hear the Xperts' voices, asking questions, and X's voice, answering answers.

I wouldn't like to be in X's overalls right now, the children thought.

At last, the door opened. Everyone crowded around to hear the results. X didn't look any different, in fact, X was smiling. But the Impartial Team of Xperts looked terrible. They looked as if they were crying!

"What happened?" everyone began shouting.

"*Sssh*," ssshed the principal. "The Xperts are trying to speak."

Wiping his eyes and clearing his throat, one Xpert began: "In our opinion," he whispered—you could tell he must be very upset—"in our opinion, young X here—"

"Yes? Yes?" shouted a parent.

"Young X," said the other Xpert, frowning, "is just about the *least* mixed-up child we've ever Xamined!" Xclaimed the two Xperts, together. Behind the closed door, the Superpsychiamedicosocioculturometer made a noise like a contented hum.

"Yay for X!" yelled one of the children. And then the others began yelling, too. Clapping and cheering and jumping up and down.

"*SSSH!*" SSShed the principal, but nobody did.

The Parents' Committee was angry and bewildered. How *could* X have passed the whole Xamination?

Didn't X have an *identity* problem? Wasn't X mixed up at *all*? Wasn't X *any* kind of a misfit?

How could it *not* be, when it didn't even *know* what it was?

"Don't you see?" asked the Xperts. "X isn't one bit mixed up! As for being a misfit—ridiculous! X knows perfectly well what it is! Don't you, X?" The Xperts winked. X winked back.

"But what *is* X?" shrieked Peggy and Joe's parents. "*We* still want to know what it is!"

"Ah, yes," said the Xperts, winking again. "Well, don't worry. You'll all know one of these days. And you won't need us to tell you."

"What? What do they mean?" Jim's parents grumbled suspiciously.

Susie and Peggy and Joe all answered at once. "They mean that by the time it matters which sex X is, it won't be a secret any more!"

With that, the Xperts reached out to hug Ms. and Mr. Jones. "If we ever have an X of our own," they whispered, "we sure hope you'll lend us your instruction manual."

Needless to say, the Joneses were very happy. The Project Baby X scientists were rather pleased, too. So were Susie, Jim, Peggy, Joe, and all the Other Children. Even the parents promised not to make any trouble.

Later that day, all X's friends put on their red and white checked overalls and went over to see X.

They found X in the backyard, playing with a very tiny baby that none of them had ever seen before.

The baby was wearing very tiny red and white checked overalls.

"How do you like our new baby?" X asked the Other Children proudly.

"It's got cute dimples," said Jim. "It's got husky biceps, too," said Susie.

"What kind of baby is it?" asked Joe and Peggy.

X frowned at them. "Can't you tell?" Then X broke into a big, mischievous grin. "*It's a Y!*"

Chapter 5

THE ANTHROPOLOGICAL PERSPECTIVE

A nthropologists engaged in women's studies often note that their approach is not merely additive, but rather calls for a basic rethinking of the relationship between the sexes. Their immediate contributions, however, have tended to be concerned fairly exclusively with women. This may have been a fruitful short-term strategy, but in the long run could become self-defeating, since it perpetuates the marked status of women. . . . Women are seen as a problem requiring some kind of special attention, while men are more or less taken for granted, or at least not focused upon in a comparably explicit way. But would it not be better to view men as being just as problematic as women? To insist that we need more studies of men as men—that is, studies based not on an uncritical assumption that what men do is more interesting or important than what women do, but studies carried out with a particular focus on gender?

Judith Shapiro

Just off the coast of Ireland lies the isolated island of Inis Beag, where little more than 350 people live. The inhabitants of Inis Beag may live in "one of the most sexually naive of the world's societies" (Messenger, 1971). On Inis Beag, sexual activity is forbidden to all but the married. For these people, sexual activity is only for procreation. Consequently, the married women expect little from sex in the way of pleasure. Although the men believe themselves to have strong sexual urges, they seldom initiate sexual activity with their wives because they think too much sex would drain them of their limited energy. On those rare occasions when a married couple does have sex, they do so in the most perfunctory manner. On Inis Beag, a couple's intimacies occur infrequently, at night, under the covers, and fast.

On the other side of the globe, in the South Pacific, lies an island that many would consider a paradise: the tiny Polynesian island of Mangaia at the southern end of the Cook Island chain. Under the tropical sun and next to the blue Pacific waters, we find a people about as different from those on Inis Beag as you can find anywhere (Marshall, 1971). The young of Mangaia begin to explore their bodies at an early age. Masturbation is common among the young and not discouraged by their elders. Soon after puberty, when the young males have gone through a painful circumcision rite, boys and girls meet at night on the beach or in one-room huts for what can be called vigorous sexual activities. The men of Mangaia believe themselves more manly if they can withhold their own orgasm until their partner has experienced three, four, or more orgasms.

How can we explain the vastly different attitudes and behaviors of these two island peoples? Surely, they both have similar anatomical structures with the requisite chromosomes, hormones, and reproductive structures. What can account for the different uses they find for their sex organs? In a word, the cultures of Inis Beag and Mangaia play a decisive role in shaping these two groups' sexual practices.

In this chapter we are going to investigate the impact of culture on the behavior of females and males. We will begin by examining some of the basic concepts about culture. We then will note the different gender roles found among the inhabitants of a remote area of New Guinea. Next, we will explore some of the cultural universals related to gender roles around the globe. And last, we will explore some recent social experiments in which traditional gender roles have been reshaped into what some claim is a more egalitarian social structure. The anthropological perspective is essential if we are to better understand the flexibility of human behavior. Also, it forces us to remedy our narrow-minded views of how others experience their gender roles.

CULTURE

A group of youths playing basketball at their local Boy's Club, four women playing bridge at the Senior Citizens Center, several gay couples strolling down Christopher Street in New York City, a raucous group clapping to the country music coming from a stage in Nashville, and a newlywed couple enjoying the sights at Niagara Falls all have something in common. They all have *culture*. Culture is an integral part of all of our daily lives; it helps us to adapt to our environment and gives us continuity with our past. But what is culture? Many people mistakenly think that culture is something that only a few have that sets them apart from the "common folk." But, in fact, everyone has a culture and is immersed in it from birth to death. Without culture we would not be truly human (Geertz, 1968, 1973).

The idea that culture is something that a select few have has its roots in nineteenth century anthropology. When Charles Darwin published *On the Origin of Species* (1859/1967), he speculated that living organisms evolved from simple structures to more complex ones. Soon after, Darwin's theory of evolution influenced many nineteenth century arm-chair anthropologists who applied his theory to the development of societies. According to the view of social evolution, human groups could be described as evolving from savages, at the bottom of the human scale, to the civilized, or "cultured," at the top. Consequently, the idea of "low" and "high" culture became a commonly accepted notion (Levin, 1984). Today, however, the common view among anthropologists is that all humans (regardless of their life-style) have a culture, and their culture is what sets them apart from other animal species.

The Contents of Culture

Culture is best understood as being comprised of everything that engenders a way of life. Thus, we can say that culture consists of the accumulated knowledge, the values, and the symbolic expressions of a particular group of people.

Knowledge refers to all the information we share about our world. Knowledge can be either *empirical* or *existential* in form. *Empirical knowledge* consists of information that is gained and passed on from one generation to the next; it is based on scientific inquiry, common sense understandings, religious teachings, and oral and literary sources. Such knowledge is taught in schools, in churches, and around campfires. *Existential knowledge* pertains to more abstract issues and is more likely to deal, for instance, with such questions as "Why are we here?" and "Where did we come from?" Usually, this kind of knowledge is considered the domain of philosophy and religion.

Values consist of socially shared beliefs about what is good or desirable. In the American culture, for example, freedom, individuality, achievement and success, and material comfort are a few of the commonly accepted values (Williams, 1970). The norms or rules that govern our everyday lives are other examples of some values that help to shape our lives.

Culture's *symbolic expressions* range from the music of Michael Jackson to the music of Bach, from the paintings in an art gallery to the spray-can murals on the side of a building, and from breakdancing in Harlem to the ballet performed in an auditorium in Los Angeles. All of these cultural expressions reflect the personal experiences of their creators.

As we can see, then, culture takes many forms. Essentially, culture expresses the many sides of a people's way of experiencing their world and of the way they effectively deal with their environment.

The Characteristics of Culture

If we examine the cultures of the pygmies of the African Ituri Forest or the Appalachian people in West Virginia, certain common characteristics can be found.

First, the contents of a particular culture are *learned*. Culture is not passed down from one generation to the next in the genes. A person learns his or her culture from others—sometimes from family members, from peers, or from television.

Next, culture is *broadly shared* among the members of a group. The ideas, the behaviors, and the symbols that comprise a culture are agreed on as to their meanings by the various members of a group. Among small groups, such as the African pygmies, the traditions and common knowledge are generally uniformly shared and agreed upon by all members of the group. In a larger and more complex group, such as American society (where many different ethnic groups, religions, and races come into contact with each other), we are apt to find various *subcultures* and *countercultures*. A subculture shares many of the same cultural contents of the larger culture but also has its own distinct values, norms, and life-style. Such is the case in a distinct ethnic minority concentrated in one location, for example, San Francisco's Chinatown. A counterculture is a subculture that is opposed to certain basic features of the larger dominant culture. For instance, the Hell's Angels (a motorcycle gang) are opposed to many of the basic values of American society (Yinger, 1982).

Lastly, although we may be fascinated by the Ituri Forest pygmies' hunting spears or the personal computers used by New York stock brokers, a culture's material artifacts (e.g., spears, computers, music, paintings, and the like) are not the most important feature of a culture. Rather, the important feature of a culture is the underlying *meaning* these objects have for the people involved. A pygmy's spear and a stock broker's computer may both be seen by their owners as tools for survival. A spear differs from a computer in many ways; however, they also share similar meanings for their owners.

Ethnocentrism and Cultural Relativism

Culture allows us to make sense out of our world and organize its elements. Culture also may blind us by disposing us to think that our ways are the *only* ways of understanding and organizing our world. Many of us have a tendency to see our culture as the one way and the right way of viewing the world. The belief that our way is the only way and the best way of perceiving the world is called *ethnocentrism*. When we judge another group by our cultural standards, we fall victim to ethnocentrism. If, on the other hand, we look at other groups with their different values, beliefs, and life-styles and note that these are just their ways of adapting to their lives' circumstances, albeit strange from our own, we have what is called a *cultural relativistic perspective* (Benedict, 1961; Hall, 1981).

With this brief overview of the concept of culture, we are now ready to examine its impact on the gender roles as seen in different societies. Females and males have interacted for countless centuries, and we can learn much about present-day gender roles by trying to understand that our ways are not the only nor the "right" ways for such interactions to transpire. We can learn much by opening our minds to how others deal with this most important aspect of the human condition.

GENDER ROLES IN NEW GUINEA: NOT EVERYONE SEES IT THE WAY WE DO

In any discussion of gender roles in other cultures, the pioneering work of anthropologist Margaret Mead ranks at the top. During the early 1930s, Margaret Mead set off to explore the ways that gender roles were defined among several preliterate societies in northeastern New Guinea. There Mead found the material for what was to become the basis for the now classic study of gender roles entitled *Sex and Temperament in Three Primitive Societies* (1935/1963). Each of the three societies that Mead studied—the gentle Arapesh, the cannibalistic Mundugumor, and the head-hunting Tchambuli—had very different conceptions of what was expected of their male and female members. Let's examine each of these three societies in turn to see just how differently they defined gender roles.

The Arapesh

Mead first encountered the mountain-dwelling Arapesh in the area bounded by the sea to the north and extending back into the coastal mountains and grassy plains to the south. Life among the Arapesh, as described by Mead, was "organized . . . in a common adventure that is primarily maternal, cherishing, and oriented away from the self toward the needs of the next generation" (p. 15). To describe Arapesh men and women, terms like cooperative, unassertive, and gentle seemed best. Whether caring for the crops or for the children, both males and females worked cooperatively for the good of all. Aggressive behaviors were strictly prohibited in Arapesh society. An Arapesh male who displayed aggressive behavior—a major element of the male role in virtually every other society—was ostracized from the group or at least shunned for any such display of "deviant" behavior. Competition in any form—an integral part of the American male's gender role—caused the participants to be regarded with shame and disgust. In Arapesh society then, status and prestige were conferred on those who shared and cooperated within the group. Mead described the Arapesh male and female in terms that Western people have come to associate with the female's role. She wrote:

> To the Arapesh, the world is a garden that must be tilled, not for one's self, not in pride and boasting, not for hoarding and usury, but that the yams and the dogs and the pigs and most of all the children may grow. From this whole attitude flow many of the other Arapesh traits, the lack of conflict between old and young, the lack of any expectation of jealousy or envy, the emphasis

upon cooperation. Cooperation is easy when all are whole-heartedly committed to a common project from which no one of the participators will himself benefit. Their dominant conception of men and women may be said to be that of regarding men, even as we regard women, as gently, carefully parental in their aims. (p. 135)

The traits most admired among the Arapesh were epitomized in the caring, cooperative, gentle, loving, nurturant, sharing, and selfless person.

The Mundugumor

Traveling up the Sepik river, Mead encountered the Mundugumor people, who were then known especially for their cannibalistic practices and for their penchant for warfare. Speaking of the Mundugumor male, Mead described life as a constant battle:

The Mundugumor man-child is born into a hostile world, a world in which most of the members of his own sex will be his enemies, in which his major equipment for success must be a capacity for violence, for seeing and avenging insult, for holding his own safety very lightly and the lives of others even more lightly. From his birth, the stage is set to produce in him this kind of behavior. (p. 189)

Because the Mundugumor mother viewed her maternal duties as burdensome and unrewarding, the child quickly learned to fend for him- or herself. The child's early experiences of maternal neglect and rejection fostered a degree of self-reliance that promoted the personal traits that the Mundugumor cherished most, namely, competition and aggression. Any show of tenderness or kindness toward another was strictly frowned upon by the Mundugumor. Consequently, the submissive, withdrawn, or gentle Mundugumor was viewed as a misfit and shunned by others. Life among the Mundugumors was a trial, and only the most fit—the aggressive and unyielding ones—held the positions that brought one honor and respect.

Thus, Mead found a fundamental similiarity in both the Arapesh and the Mundugumor societies: males *and* females were both molded toward identical trait patterns. The Mundugumor emphasized a harsh self-centeredness, while the Arapesh promoted a gentle other-centeredness. Personality differences between males and females in these two societies were therefore discouraged. To find a society in which female and male personalities were considered different and were encouraged, Mead had to travel west of the Mundugumor to a people called the Tchambuli.

The Tchambuli

Living around Lake Aibom, the Tchambuli were a head-hunting society in which the usual gender roles were reversed from what we know in the West. Tchambuli women, for example, were responsible for the village's business. The village women earned the money used by the family, were responsible for the farming, fishing, and manufacturing required by the village, and even made the decisions that affected the village (e.g., giving their approval of who marries who). Tchambuli women were easygoing, hard-working, and reliable. Generally, an air of affability existed among the village women. Tchambuli men, on the other hand, were considered the weaker sex. Men seemed only interested in their own adornment and in self-aggrandizing pursuits. They spent their days in other men's company, fretting over their costumes and other body adornments. Relationships among the constantly preening men could only be described as catty and suspicious. Around women, Tchambuli men became timid, and they appeared in awe of the opposite sex:

> [T]he Tchambuli [man] may be said to live principally for art. Every man is an artist and most men are skilled not in some one art alone, but in many: in dancing, carving, plaiting, and so on. Each man is chiefly concerned with his role upon the stage of his society, with the elaboration of his costume, the beauty of the masks he owns, the skill of his own flute-playing, the finish and *elan* of his ceremonies, and upon other people's recognition and valuation of his performance. (p. 245)

Mead's work among the Arapesh, the Mundugumor, and the Tchambuli gave us a richer appreciation of the variety of gender roles practiced among other societies. Not everyone sees the gender roles as we do, and this is a most important lesson for all to learn—one that anthropologists, such as Margaret Mead, have been teaching in order to eliminate any vestiges of ethnocentrism we may have about gender roles.

CULTURAL UNIVERSALS AND GENDER ROLES

Thus far, we have emphasized the variety and differences in various cultures with respect to the gender roles. However, are there certain gender-related features that are likely to be found among all, or nearly all, groups with vastly different cultural traditions? In other words, are there what anthropologists call *cultural universals* (Murdock, 1945) when it comes to gender-specific behaviors or features of the gender roles? The answer to this question is yes. We will now turn our attention to several areas where there appears to be some unanimity among different human groups about expectations of male and female behavior.

We will begin our discussion by examining the well established behavioral patterns in which males perform certain jobs and women perform others. This pattern is usually referred to as the division of labor. Next, we will focus on the pattern of male dominance over the female in vastly different cultural settings. And last, we will examine exceptions to the universal feature of having only two relatively exclusive gender roles—several cultures where there are more than two gender roles.

TABLE 5.1 CROSS-CULTURAL DATA FROM 224 SOCIETIES ON SUBSISTENCE ACTIVITIES AND DIVISION OF LABOR BY SEX

Activity	Number of Societies in Which Activity Is Performed by				
	Men Always	Men Usually	Either Sex	Women Usually	Women Always
Pursuit of sea mammals	34	1	0	0	0
Hunting	166	13	0	0	0
Trapping small animals	128	13	4	1	2
Herding	38	8	4	0	5
Fishing	98	34	19	3	4
Clearing land for agriculture	73	22	17	5	13
Dairy operations	17	4	3	1	13
Preparing and planting soil	31	23	33	20	37
Erecting and dismantling shelter	14	2	5	6	22
Tending fowl and small animals	21	4	8	1	39
Tending and harvesting crops	10	15	35	39	44
Gathering shellfish	9	4	8	7	25
Making and tending fires	18	6	25	22	62
Bearing burdens	12	6	35	20	57
Preparing drinks and narcotics	20	1	13	8	57
Gathering fruits, berries, nuts	12	3	15	13	63
Gathering fuel	22	1	10	19	89
Preservation of meat and fish	8	2	10	14	74
Gatherings herbs, roots, seeds	8	1	11	7	74
Cooking	5	1	9	28	158
Carrying water	7	0	5	7	119
Grinding grain	2	4	5	13	114

Source: "Comparative data on the division of labor by sex" by G. Murdock, 1935, *Social Forces*, 15, pp. 551–53. Copyright © 1935 University of North Carolina Press. Reprinted by permission.

Division of Labor

Most of us at one time or another have heard someone mention that such-and-such a job was "men's work" or "women's work." The notion that certain tasks are best accomplished by men rather than women or vice versa is one that appears throughout most societies (Afonja, 1981; Bell, 1981; Wong, 1981). Anthropologists have long studied what is termed the *division of labor* along gender lines (Kelly, 1981). One of the most extensive studies to focus on the division of labor among preliterate groups was conducted by George Murdock (1937). Murdock studied 224 societies and found strong evidence for a gender-based division of labor (see table 5.1). In general,

Murdock found that predominately male activities were generally those that required strength, long periods of travel away from the campsite, and a high degree of cooperation. The activities performed by females, on the other hand, were usually those that required less strength and less travel and that could be performed alone. Biological differences such as a male's greater physical strength and a female's greater involvement in child-bearing and child-rearing may have played a significant role in the differences found by Murdock.

However, when we examine the division of labor dealing with the manufacture of certain items, we find that biological differences play a small role in determining who does what. As shown in table 5.2, men in nearly every society made weapons, for example. Women, on the other hand, were chiefly responsible for making and repairing clothing. Yet, weapon making requires neither great strength, mobility, nor group cooperation. And making clothes is not easier than making weapons, nor does it require one to work alone or to be less mobile. Why, then, is weapon making an almost totally male activity and the manufacture of apparel nearly always a female task? Murdock suggests that not only has the division of labor arisen by virtue of some obvious physical differences, but also has included those tasks that are somehow related to physical differences, even if only indirectly. Therefore, because weapons were generally used by men on the hunt, weapon making probably was assumed to be a labor that men should be responsible for.

We must keep in mind, however, that among the groups studied by Murdock there was considerable overlap of activities among males and females. Although there is evidence that a division of labor along gender lines existed among many early subsistence groups, there also was a great amount of cooperation among the genders for the work that needed to be accomplished. Both females and males contributed to the groups's sustenance, and according to some, the females did more than their share (Dahlberg, 1981). Furthermore, in today's society, strength and mobility are usually not required for most jobs, so there really is no need to regard jobs as either men's work or women's work.

The Dominant Male

In nearly every society studied by anthropologists, we find that usually males dominate and control females (Friedl, 1978; Leavitt, 1971; Nash, 1978; Rosaldo and Lamphere, 1974). In spite of that, females are not entirely powerless (Mueller, 1977).

We should be clear from the outset that we differentiate power from authority. The female often wields considerable *power*, or influence, in decisions of social importance, but *authority* is usually vested in the male. Anthropologists Kay Martin and Barbara Voorhies (1975) see the distinction between power and authority as follows.

TABLE 5.2 CROSS-CULTURAL DATA ON THE MANUFACTURE OF OBJECTS AND DIVISION OF LABOR BY SEX

Activity	Number of Societies in Which Activity Is Performed by				
	Men Always	Men Usually	Either Sex	Women Usually	Women Always
Metalworking	78	0	0	0	0
Weapon making	121	1	0	0	0
Boat building	91	4	4	0	1
Manufacture of musical instruments	45	2	0	0	1
Work in wood and bark	113	9	5	1	1
Work in stone	68	3	2	0	2
Work in bone, horn, shell	67	4	3	0	3
Manufacture of ceremonial objects	37	1	13	0	1
House building	86	32	25	3	14
Net making	44	6	4	2	11
Manufacture of ornaments	24	3	40	6	18
Manufacture of leather products	29	3	9	3	32
Hide preparation	31	2	4	4	49
Manufacture of nontextile fabrics	14	0	9	2	32
Manufacture of thread and cordage	23	2	11	10	73
Basket making	25	3	10	6	82
Mat making	16	2	6	4	61
Weaving	19	2	2	6	67
Pottery making	13	2	6	8	77
Manufacture and repair of clothing	12	3	8	9	95

Source: "Comparative data on the division of labor by sex" by G. Murdock, 1935, *Social Forces, 15,* pp. 551–53. Copyright © 1935 University of North Carolina Press. Reprinted by permission.

Power refers to the ability to coerce others toward desired ends, whereas authority refers to legitimate or legal power. A survey of human societies shows that positions of authority are almost always occupied by males. Technically speaking, there is no evidence for matriarchy, or rule by women, Amazonian or otherwise. Of even greater significance, however, is that the assignment of power and authority may vary independently. Leadership positions are generally occupied by males, but power may attach itself to either sex. This is especially well illustrated by matrilineal societies, in which senior women assign public offices to males, but may reserve the actual decision-making for themselves. (p. 10)

As a rule, males have the more privileged, more valued, and higher status positions in most societies (Blumberg, 1978). As suggested by many researchers, males have a definite edge in almost every group. Although females may have various amounts of power within their groups, they usually are dominated by males. We need to examine some of the various ways that males dominate females in other cultures.

The Traditional World of Male Dominance

Few cultures are as totally male dominant as those in the Middle East, where the male (and the male's gender role) is preeminent over the female (Wadley, 1977). We need only turn to the age-old Hindu code and read that "In childhood a woman must be subject to her father; in youth, to her husband; when her husband is dead, to her sons. A woman must never be free of subjugation." The social structures of most Muslim societies reinforce male dominance and female subservience (Beck and Keddie, 1978).

In India, one historic means of reinforcing the female's inferior status was by performing the now-prohibited practice of *suttee,* or the act of burning or burying women alive with their deceased husbands (Mazumdar, 1978). On the surface, suttee, outlawed by the British in the early nineteenth century, kept the widow from dishonoring her deceased husband, but it was also a social ritual testifying to the status of the female in comparison to the male. Dorothy Stein (1978) explains the rationale behind suttee:

> The orthodox Hindu belief was that the widow was responsible for her husband's predeceasing her, by sin in a previous life if not in the present, for in the normal course of events the wife was expected to die first. A lifetime of austerity was considered scarcely enough to expiate her survival. Suttee, then, was primarily based on the belief that women are by nature sexually unreliable and incapable of leading chaste lives without a husband to control them. (p. 255)

Scenes of bazaars with veiled women moving through the crowds seem intriguing and somewhat mysterious to Western eyes. *Purdah*, the social practice of secluding women from the public world, is still found in many Middle Eastern countries (Fernea and Fernea, 1979; Lindholm and Lindholm, 1980). The degree to which a woman is secluded from the public's eye varies from class to class. For example, in some societies, a woman may leave her home but must wear the *chador*, the head-to-toe garment; in other societies, she must not leave the home at all (Papanek, 1973; Sharma, 1978). Regardless of the extent of purdah, the intent is always the same: to protect a woman's chastity by keeping her secluded from men (Mernissi, 1975). Women in the Middle East are thought to possess powerful sexual urges that, if allowed to be expressed outside of marriage, would bring shame on the women's families. Although several Middle Eastern observers do not view purdah as oppressive or demeaning to women (Abu-Lughod, 1983; El Guindi, 1981), many Western social scientists see it as a powerful means to reinforce male dominance and keep women inferior and subservient (Paige, 1983; Sharma, 1978).

Besides the institution of purdah, the Islamic religion also condones polygyny, or the taking of more than one wife. The sacred book of Islam, the Koran, enjoins men not to take a second wife unless he can provide for her well-being. However, among many Islamic cultures taking a second wife is one way that a man can get back at his first wife for her lack of wifely

respect. If a Muslim man is too poor to take a second wife but has grown tired of his first wife, he may simply repudiate her, which in effect is the same as divorcing her; he then takes a second wife. Thus the practice of serial monogamy has become quite frequent among less wealthy Muslim men (Leavitt, 1971, p. 401).

Women in Islamic countries have little legitimate authority over their own lives, but that does not mean they have little or no power over their own lives or the lives of their children. Many ways can be found to circumvent the restrictions placed on women. A common story is told of the Islamic mother who wished to have her daughters vaccinated by a local physician. Because the physician was male, the woman's husband refused to let her take their children to see the doctor or for him to give the necessary shots, which would have required that the daughters expose their arms to an unrelated male. Through messages, the woman contacted the physician and arranged for him to come to her home; she then had her daughters stick their arms out through one of the windows where the physician inoculated each.

Not all Moslem societies are unaffected by the recent social changes brought about by the infusion of petro-dollars. Countries that only a decade or two ago were pre-industrial in nature have been pushed into the twentieth century, with all the accompaniments of modern cities, government bureaucracies, and changes in people's lives. A sociologist and specialist in Muslim societies, Fatima Mernissi (1975), sees that in most newly developing Muslim countries there is considerable tension between the ancient traditions that separate the sexes and exclude women from anything other than their roles as outlined by purdah and the modern social forces that push for change and modernization. Mernissi believes that until women gain a greater measure of personal freedom, many of the changes brought about by the wealth from oil will have little lasting value in the lives of the common folk (see box 5.1).

Box 5.1

Kuwaiti Women: The Exception to the Rule

KUWAIT (AP)—She dresses in the latest Western fashions, drives her own car, shops in exclusive boutiques and goes out to lunch with friends. She is the modern Kuwaiti woman—far ahead of her demure cousins in the other Arab states on the Persian Gulf.

In Saudi Arabia, Qatar and the United Arab Emirates, women generally are obliged to stay at home except for visits to relatives or to the doctor. And when these women do go out, they must be veiled.

In Kuwait, one of the oldest oil-producing states on the gulf, the veil was abandoned long ago. Women here now take education, careers and relatively independent lifestyles for granted.

Also unlike their Gulf cousins, Kuwaiti women are not restricted to certain "female" careers, such as teaching and nursing.

Kuwait has a woman undersecretary of education. The chairman of the contract adjucation committee at the Planning Ministry is a woman, as is a dean of the law school at the state-run university. Countless other women hold degrees from prestigious foreign universities.

Whereas Saudi Arabia bans women drivers and the employment of women in male-run offices, Kuwaiti women drive to jobs as secretaries, clerks and assembly-line workers. Even Bedouin women in their traditional tribal dress are seen behind the wheels of new American or Japanese cars.

Now that Kuwait's royal rulers are considering restoring parlimentary democracy after nearly a four-year suspension, women may be given the right to vote as well.

"Now it can really begin," said Mrs. Lulwa Kataami, a long-time advocate of women's rights here.

For years, Mrs. Kataami and her colleagues in the Kuwaiti Women's Association have been discreetly pushing for greater equality. Their campaign has been conducted in the form of carefully worded memorandums submitted to Sheik Jaber al-Ahmad, Kuwait's emir, or ruler.

They are aided by constitutional guarantees of equal treatment for women.

Having won the right to be educated and work, the women now are focusing on the sensitive problems of women's rights in marriage and divorce.

The feminist campaign comes at a time of resurgent Islamic fundamentalism in the Arab world.

Kuwait, which is just across the Persian Gulf from Iran, naturally has felt the winds of Ayatollah Ruhollah Khomeini's brand of Islam. On Fridays, the mosques here are fuller than ever, a Moslem religious faction

Source: Courtesy of The Associated Press.

Box 5.1

now dominates the student council at the university and Kuwait television carries more religious programs.

A move is afoot to make sexual relations between unmarried, consenting adults a crime. Running off with a lover can still land a married woman in jail for several years.

Mrs. Kataami emphasizes that women do not seek to change the Islamic foundation of the marriage and divorce laws in Kuwait—"only a more 'correct' interpretation of them."

The Women's Association is asking the emir to appoint a woman to the Justice Ministry's committee that handles divorce applications.

"At the moment, the woman's point of view is rarely heard," Mrs. Kataami said.

The association also is tackling the sensitive question of polygamous marriages. Under Islamic law, men can take as many as four wives. However, Mrs. Kataami said, "the Koran [the Islamic holy book] only allows a husband to take a second wife if he can guarantee equal treatment between them. We interpret that as covering emotionally equal treatment as well, and that we think is impossible."

Another cause being championed is the right of a woman to marry the man of her choice. At the moment, if a Kuwaiti woman commits the "social sin" of marrying a non-Kuwaiti (who are the bulk of the 1.1 million population of the state) she stands to lose all the privileges of citizenship.

"This must be changed, because it does not apply to a Kuwaiti man marrying a foreigner," said Mrs. Kataami.

She added that she also wants to see women undertake a form of obligatory social service as an equivalent to military conscription, which was recently introduced in Kuwait.

"We want every educated Kuwaiti woman to do a period of service before she starts work. In this I mean teaching or social work."

This, she maintains, would help eradicate illiteracy among women in five years. About 68 percent of Kuwaiti women still are illiterate.

Predicting more personal freedom for Kuwaiti women, a local psychiatrist commented, "If you allow a woman to become a doctor or a lawyer or whatever, then the next step is logical. How do you contain it?"

Figure 5.1 Although found in nearly every society, signs of male dominance are more obvious in Asiatic societies.

Another example of the ways women are suspect for their supposedly sexual powers in many Islamic countries is the ritual of *female excision*. In the simplest and least drastic form, female excision consists of nicking the clitoris with a sharp instrument, causing a small incision. In this form, female excision is much like the common ritual of male circumcision, which is sanctioned in most Western societies for male infants. However, in some Middle Eastern countries, a more radical form of female excision is practiced. Here, an infant's entire clitoris and labia are surgically removed for the purpose of "protecting" her chastity in adulthood (Morgan and Steinem, 1980). The thinking behind this extreme form of female excision is that with the removal of the sensual parts of the female's genitalia, the female will remain faithful to her husband rather than be tempted toward other male lovers. Somewhat surprising to many Western femininist groups is that many Middle Eastern women's associations do not reject the practice of female excision as an unacceptable cultural practice (Cullen, 1982).

If we move farther to the east toward China and Japan, we continue to find a long-standing tradition of male dominance in almost every society.

(We will examine the post-revolutionary Chinese People's Republic in the next section.) The role played out by the female in traditional Chinese and Japanese societies was one of total subjugation and dependence on the male in the guise of father, brother, husband, and sons, much the same as we saw in the Middle East (Kristeva, 1975). Anthropologist Margery Wolf (1980) points out the basic inequalities in the lives of Chinese males and females by describing what she sees as the distinctly different worlds each lives in. She writes:

> Few women in [prerevolutionary] China experience the continuity that is typical of the lives of the menfolk. A woman can and, if she is ever to have any economic security, must provide the links in the male chain of descent, but she will never appear in anyone's genealogy as that all-important name connecting the past to the future. If she dies before she is married, her tablet will not appear on her father's altar; although she was a temporary member of his household, she was not a member of his family. A man is born into his family and remains a member of it throughout his life and even after his death. He is identified with the family from birth, and every action concerning him, up to and including his death, is in the context of that group. Whatever other uncertainties may trouble his life, his place in the line of ancestors provides a permanent setting. There is no such secure setting for a woman. She will abruptly leave the household into which she is born, either as an infant or as an adult bride, and enter another whose members treat her with suspicion or even hostility. (p. 177)

We need only read Maxine Hong Kingston's *The Woman Warrior* (1976) to get a personal glimpse into the "uterine" world of the female in the China of old. Her description of the suicide of her paternal aunt—the "no name woman"—is especially revealing about the treatment of women in a totally patriarchal society.

Only Two Roles?

Normally in most societies we find two gender roles, one prescribed for males and the other for females. The presence of only two gender roles, then, can be considered a universal cultural feature. But as in all generalities, we find some exceptions, which often prove more interesting to examine (Blackwood, 1984). Here we want to examine four exceptions to the rule of two gender roles, namely, the berdache, the nadle, the alyha, and the hwame.

The Berdache   Among the North American Indians there was a special category of people known as the *berdache* (Forgey, 1975; Jacobs, 1968). According to anthropologists Charles Callender and Lee Kochems (1983), a berdache was

> a person, usually male, who was anatomically normal but assumed the dress, occupations, and behavior of the other sex to effect a change in gender status. This shift was not complete; rather, it was a movement toward a somewhat intermediate status that combined social attributes of males and females. The

terminology for berdaches defined them as a distinct gender status, designated by special terms rather than by the words "man" or "woman." Literal translations of these terms often indicate its intermediate nature: halfman-halfwoman, man-woman, would-be woman. (p. 443)

The berdache suffered neither scorn nor shame for his or her new gender role. Berdaches generally assumed the occupations of the gender whose attire they wore. For example, male berdaches usually became extremely skilled in sewing and cooking. Generally, the man who took a male berdache as his wife was rewarded by having a well-run household.

A common misconception about the male berdache is that he turned to the life of a berdache to avoid warfare. From their analysis of different Indian nations where berdaches were found, Callender and Kochems could find no evidence to substantiate such a claim of cowardice. In the final analysis, the berdache was simply a separate gender role.

The Nadle Among the Navajo and the Mohave Indian tribes, infants born with ambiguous genitals were assigned to the gender role of a *nadle* (Olien, 1978). The nadle was treated with extreme deference. Accordingly, the nadle wore women's clothing when engaged in women's work, and men's clothing when involved with men's activities. Hunting and warfare were the only two activities prohibited the nadle.

The Alyha and the Hwame Among the Mohave Indians, two other gender roles were recognized: the *alyha* and the *hwame*. A Mohave male who chose to live the life of a woman was called an alyha. In nearly every respect, the male-turned-alyha dressed and acted like a woman; the alyha even mimicked a woman's menstrual flow by cutting his upper thigh (Olien, 1978). The female who wished to live as a man was ceremoniously ushered into her new status as a hwame. The hwame dressed and acted out the male gender role, with the exception of not being permitted to go into battle nor serve in a leadership role.

Thus, we can see with the berdache, nadle, alyha, and hwame that among some groups of North American Indians there were more than two gender roles that a person could live out.

THE SOCIALIST EXPERIMENTS

The nineteenth century social philosopher Karl Marx condemned the male-dominated capitalistic system for its tyranny over the lives of the working person. The writings of Marx and his collaborator Frederick Engels spawned one of the most elaborate social experiments ever to be conceived, that of a society where all—women and men alike—were truly equal. Both Marx and Engels believed that as long as women remained restricted to housework, with its lack of remuneration, and prevented from gainful employment, they would never be men's equal (Sanday, 1973). In this section, we will focus on four societies where the dream of gender equality has been, to greater or lesser degrees, implemented.

First, we will examine the Communist countries of the USSR and the People's Republic of China, where Marx's ideas were translated most ambitiously (Croll, 1981a and b). Then we will note the social changes brought about in the decidedly socialistic expressions seen in the country of Sweden and those found in the Israeli community called a kibbutz. Let's begin with the much-promised utopian existence ushered into Russian culture with the overthrow of the Czar and the workers' revolution that promised a true egalitarian life-style for all citizens regardless of gender.

Mother Russia and Soviet Motherhood

Few modern-day countries have the constitutional guarantees providing for the total equality of all its citizenry—male and female alike—that the Soviet Socialist Union does (Sedugin, 1973). In 1918, Lenin, one of the founding fathers of Communist Russia, decreed that women were to be men's equal. More recently, the Soviet Union's Constitution guaranteed all Soviets total equality under the law, ensuring them equal pay for equal work and access to and promotion within any job regardless of sex, as well as equal political status before the Soviet Union Supreme Communist party. Some might suggest that with Lenin's blessing and the Constitutional guarantees, the USSR must surely be a feminist utopia. However, Soviet women have found themselves in a type of double-duty bind. Granted, Soviet women find greater occupational opportunities than most other European women or, for that matter, even most women in the United States (Geiger, 1968). However, the Soviet woman still carries the main responsibilities for most of the household chores along with her daily job outside of the home. Even Lenin seemed aware of the inequalities foisted on Soviet women for carrying what must be considered two full-time jobs, while for the most part, Soviet men pay little attention to assisting with family responsibilities. With respect to this problem, Lenin wrote: "So few men— even among the proletariat—realize how much effort and trouble they could save women, even quite do away with, if they were to lend a hand in 'women's work.' But no. . . . They want their peace and comfort" (quoted in Scanzoni and Scanzoni, 1981, p. 61).

Since Lenin and the Communist revolution, no Soviet need fear that she or he will not be treated equally when it comes to the guarantee of the right to work. To work in the Soviet Union is a prerequisite to eat. To work in almost any type of job from construction to the professions is a right and a duty of the good Soviet. However, the pictures of Soviet women serving as physicians as proof of their equality is a distortion. World War II, which resulted in the loss of millions of Soviet men, had more to do with the number of female physicians we find in the USSR today than did the Communist rhetoric of gender-role equality (Dodge, 1966). Well over half of all Soviet physicians are female, but female doctors predominate in the lower-status specialities (e.g., pediatrics), while the higher-status positions (e.g., surgery) are generally considered male specialities. As in medicine, the trend in other professions has also been for women to occupy the lower-status positions, leaving the higher ones for men (Lapidus, 1978). The fact that women make up over half of the labor force in the USSR only assures them of what we mentioned above—the tiring double-duty work of running the household along with their job-related responsibilities. As if Soviet women did not have enough to occupy their time, they also spend countless hours every week going from one line to yet another waiting to purchase the needed family goods and groceries. Soviet women have been liberated in terms of the law, but their freedom to work has only added duties to those that they already have as primary housekeepers as well.

The Communist party is quick to point out that the woman who does not shoulder her work duties is a parasite upon whom all others may heap shame and scorn. According to the party, there are four types of Soviet woman. The first type is called a *Comrade Positive*. The Comrade Positive is one who takes her rightful place among the workers and happily contributes her fair share to the goals of the Communist party. The second, the *Comrade Willing*, is the woman who wants to work but is unable to because of her maternal or domestic responsibilities, such as caring for young children. Next, the label *Comrade Reluctant* is given those women who are slovenly or lazy in carrying out their work and family duties and yet feel a sense of remorse or guilt about their lack of enthusiasm. Last, the title *Comrade Parasite* is reserved for women who neglect their duties and feel no remorse or shame for such un-Communistic behavior (Field and Flynn, 1970).

The problem in evaluating the gender roles in the modern day is that, setting aside all the legislation and political talk, the Soviet woman still suffers under the age-old role of being chiefly responsible for the home, while the man is free to pursue and advance himself in the world outside of the home. This social division of labor is given credence when we consider that membership in the Communist party, the only avenue open to advancement within the Soviet system, is held mainly by males—of the nearly seventeen and one-half million Communist party members, women make up just over 25 percent of the party's membership. Even the officials within the Communist party recognize that reality does not mirror the facts when it comes to women in the USSR and point to the problem of Soviet women being required to carry the double burden of outside employment along with the duties of the household, whereas males need only work outside the home. Ludmilla Zemlyannikova, secretary of Soviet trade unions, examines the plight of Soviet women in such terms. She believes that "It would be wrong to paint the life of our women in general in rosy colors. Society has created every possibility for their cultural growth. Socialism has emancipated women socially, politically and economically, but it cannot relieve them of household care in one stroke" (quoted in Daniloff, 1982, p. 54).

Let's now move to the most populous nation on earth and examine how women have fared under communism as practiced in the People's Republic of China.

Lotus Blossoms and Women's Equality

In mainland China the female's status has historically been lower than that of the male's. For centuries, the teachings of the fifth century B.C. Chinese philosopher Confucius were employed to condone all kinds of practices testifying to women's inferior status, such as foot-binding, legal concubinage, female infanticide, and the selling of female infants by those families too poor to afford a daughter's wedding. All this changed with the 1949 Revolution and the leadership provided by Chairman Mao. The total subjugation of the female to her father and then to her husband gave way to an emphasis on the woman's economic freedom and the institution of egalitarian marital relationships (Curtin, 1975; Stacy, 1975; Walstedt, 1978).

However, the rhetoric of equal pay for equal work has not yet been fully implemented into the factory system, which is supposedly the backbone of the new social system of the People's Republic. For example, in many of China's factories, men hold the majority of supervisory positions, technical positions, and semiskilled laborer positions, which earn for these men approximately $47 to $60 a month. In these same factories, women are more often found in the lower-paying jobs, such as assembly work, where the pay is likely to be from 15 to 20 percent lower than those of their male colleagues (Wallace, 1982). Women have definitely benefitted from the changes brought about by the revolutionary changes that swept China in the late 1940s, but we must be careful that we differentiate between what is propaganda and what is really taking place in the rural areas where many of the patriarchal traditions still govern peoples' lives.

Thus, in the two Marxist countries we see that old patriarchal traditions of male supremacy are not totally uprooted even when the sanctions of these socialist governments push for the reformation of the female's status and roles. Next we need move to the west to examine what has taken place in the roles that men and women are expected to play out in the progressive socialist country of Sweden.

Reluctant Fathers and Paternity Leave

Few countries have made as much effort to change the traditional roles of the male as provider and the female as housekeeper as has the socialist country of Sweden. Although other socialist countries have moved to eradicate patriarchal privileges and higher male status, only Sweden has emphasized that changes in the male role are necessary if the changes in the female role are to have any permanent effect. Noting the need for a change in men's roles, Alva Myrdal (1971) writes:

> In Sweden, the debate has progressed beyond the conventional focus of discussions of family problems, i.e., the conflict between women's two roles—family and work. Its scope has been enlarged to encompass the two roles of men. Men are no longer regarded as 'innocents abroad' in family affairs. Instead, it is becoming increasingly recognized even outside sociological circles that their role in the family must be radically enlarged. No longer can they be allowed to confine themselves to the role of 'provider', they must begin more fully to integrate the family into their life plans. (p. 9)

Unlike most Western societies, Sweden has not waited until the last few decades to begin to question the roles played by men and women in the family and in the workplace. The Swedish people have debated the issues of the male's double standard of morality and the "bondage" of women within the institution of marriage since the late nineteenth century (Myrdal and Klein, 1956). Sweden, in fact, had been in the forefront of change in gender roles long before American women won the right to vote (Dahlstrom, 1971).

The single biggest social area attesting to Sweden's commitment to changing the gender roles' *status quo* is that of family policy. The Swedish government has instituted generous benefits for either the mother *or* the father who stays home with children. Some of these inducements come in the form of generous tax breaks for multiple-child families and, of greater consequence when it comes to changing the traditional gender roles, parental-leave benefits for the parent (be it the mother or the father) who stays home to care for the child. These progressive practices have not been instituted simply to eradicate outmoded gender roles, but rather to encourage parents to have children. Furthermore, the Swedish government has taken the stand that Swedish women will gain equality in the workplace only if Swedish men take an equal share of the duties related to the home and to the raising of the children (Baude, 1979).

Beginning in 1974, the Swedish government adopted a policy to encourage fathers to take paternity leaves during the first months of their infants' lives. However, even with a massive advertising campaign picturing fathers taking care of their children, only about 5 percent of the fathers who are eligible for such paternity leave have availed themselves of this nontraditional life-style (Lamb, 1982). The reasons that so few Swedish fathers take paternity leave are somewhat disconcerting when we remember that the government is publicly behind such a role reversal. Many of the Swedish fathers point out that they fear retribution from their employers—an action prohibited by the government—if they take paternity leave. Other fathers point out that if they did in fact take an extended leave of absence, their jobs and advancement in their work would suffer more so than would their wives' work were the wives to take an extended leave. And still others point out that they believe that a child benefits more from the mother's presence than from the father's.

Thus, in Sweden, where the government has made a concerted effort to bring about real equality between the sexes, patriarchal attitudes seem to die hard. May-Britt Carlsson (1977), Organizing Secretary of the Swedish Central Organization of Salaried Employees, describes the problem:

> The majority of men in Sweden still follow traditional roles. Men still dominate the labor market and do not assume the dual role that working women do in taking responsibility for home and child care. What is needed, then, is an analysis of the male role leading to change and adaptation in both the traditional male and female roles. . . . This is no easy task and no one . . . has offered a blueprint for success. . . . For true equality between the sexes, the traditional masculine role must not become the pattern for women to follow. The roles of both men and women must be transformed. (p. 270)

The bottom line in the country-wide experiment to change the traditional gender roles of Swedish males and females, at least when it comes to reinforcing greater participation of fathers in the raising of their children, seems to be somewhat of a disappointment if not a downright failure (Haavio-Mannila, 1975).

For our last look at where a concerted effort has been made to change traditional gender roles we will move to Israel, where we find a social experiment of dramatic proportions with the agricultural communities known as the kibbutzim.

Changes Down on the Farm

During the late 1940s, a small group of European immigrants began a bold social experiment in Israel. Initially, the kibbutz (the singular form for *kibbutzim*) was an agriculturally based social commune where gender equality was paramount in the group's ideology (Maimon, 1962; Weithorn, 1975). To accomplish this, the mothers on the kibbutz were "freed" from being the sole caretakers of their children. Rather, the children of the kibbutz's members were raised in a communal children's house, or *creche*, where a caretaker, or *metapelet* (usually a woman), was responsible for the children's socialization (Rabin, 1970). The goal of raising the children in this manner was to ensure that all kibbutz members—females and males alike—could fully participate in the kibbutz's farming, managing, and marketing activities on an equal basis (Mednick, 1975). However, the goal for full equality of females and males on the kibbutz was more an ideal than a reality, as attested to by many observers (Gerson, 1971; Talmon, 1972; Tiger and Shepher, 1975; Blumberg, 1976). Melford Spiro (1971) wrote of the undermining of the kibbutz's goal for female emancipation in the following way:

> In view of its emphasis on the economic equality of the sexes, how is it that the women have not become "rooted" in the economic life of the kibbutz? It has already been noted that when the vattikim first settled on the land, there was no sexual division of labor. Women, like men, worked in the fields and drove tractors; men, like women, worked in the kitchen and the laundry. Men

and women, it was assumed, were equal and could perform their jobs equally well. It was soon discovered, however, that men and women were not equal. For obvious biological reasons women were compelled at times to take temporary leave from that physical labor of which they were capable. A pregnant woman, for example, could not work too long, even in the vegetable garden, and a nursing mother had to work near the Infant's House in order to be able to feed her child. Hence, as the kibbutz grew older and the birth rate increased, more and more women were forced to leave the "productive" branches of the economy and enter its service branches. But as they left the productive branches it was necessary that their places be filled, and they were filled by men. The result was that the women found themselves in the same jobs from which they were supposed to have been emancipated—cooking, cleaning, laundering, teaching, caring for children, etc. In short, they have not been freed from the "yoke" of domestic responsibilities. (p. 225)

Gender equality on a broader scale, encompassing the whole of Israeli society, also appears to be more illusory than fact (Aloni, 1973, 1974; Izraeli et al., 1982; Tabory, 1984). Although Israeli women must serve in the armed forces, and most people recall the strong political presence of Golda Meir, Israeli society finds women unequal to men. Sharon Brandow (1980, p. 403) writes that "the mass of the [Israeli] female population exists in a subordinate 'second sex' position which differs little from that of women in other parts of the world." Others do not agree with this perception of Israeli society, noting that although total equality is not yet a reality, it is moving in that direction (Bar-Yosef and Lieblich, 1983).

In each of the social attempts presented above, the heart of the problem of bringing full gender equality has not been one of not trying. In the Soviet Union, the People's Republic of China, Sweden, and Israel's kibbutzim, the leaders have attempted to change age-old traditions and roles that favor males and prejudice females. The issue is not so much in attempting to change the female's traditional role of maternal responsibility, but rather in not doing enough to change male attitudes and behaviors (Hacker, 1975). Anthropologist Michelle Rosaldo (1974) succinctly states the underlying problem in unfulfilled attempts to bring about true gender equality:

[T]he most egalitarian societies are not those in which male and female are opposed or are even competitors, but those in which men value and participate in the domestic life of the home. Correspondingly, they are societies in which women can readily participate in important public events. (p. 41)

SUMMARY

Culture, or everything that makes up a way of life, plays a large part in what we become. Although we have a tendency to think that male and female relationships are similar the world over, anthropologists like Margaret Mead have found that gender roles vary considerably in different parts of the world.

Although there is great diversity among various cultures, most cultures find certain universal patterns of male-female relations, such as a division of labor and varying degrees of male dominance. However, among some American Indian tribes, we find evidence of more than two gender roles.

During this century, several countries (i.e., the Soviet Union, the Republic of China, Sweden, and Israel) have attempted to eliminate the unequal statuses found between females and males. Their attempts, however, have not been entirely successful.

SUGGESTED READINGS

Adams, C., & Winston, K. (1980). *Mothers at work: Public policies in the United States, Sweden and China.* New York: Longman.

Andors, P. (1983). *The unfinished liberation of Chinese women, 1949–1980.* Bloomington: Indiana University Press.

Greenberg, B. (1981). *On women and Judaism.* Philadelphia: Jewish Publication Society of America.

Hussain, F. (Ed.). (1984). *Muslim women.* New York: St. Martin's Press.

Mamonova, T. (Ed.). (1984). *Women and Russia.* Boston: Beacon Press.

Martin, K., & Voorhies, B. (1975). *Female of the species.* New York: Columbia University Press.

Sanday, P. (1981). *Female power and male dominance: On the origins of sexual inequality.* New York: Cambridge University Press.

Shapiro, J. (1981). Anthropology and the study of gender. *Soundings, 64(4),* 446–65.

Point/Counterpoint

Matriarchy: Fact or Fiction

Elizabeth Gould Davis (1972) has published a new account of human history. Davis suggests that some 10,000 years ago the "golden age of matriarchy" existed. During this age, women ruled the civilized world. Their reign was noted for its justice for all creatures. Fertility was controlled by women using natural and harmless methods. The female sex was honored for its beauty and sensual qualities, and worship centered on the Great Mother Goddess.

Somehow (Davis is rather unclear on this point) a small band of discontented and rebellious men seized power from the female rulers and set out to destroy all vestiges of the once powerful matriarchal system. Men took control of women's lives and prevented them from using contraceptives. The religion of the Great Mother Goddess was replaced by a male-oriented religion with a stern and unforgiving father figure substituted for the loving mother figure. Peace, harmony, and justice were soon replaced by warfare, discontent, and inequality. Furthermore, Davis suggests that the golden age of matriarchy has been keep secret until only recently because historians—mostly male—purposely rewrote the historical records in order to exclude any mention of the once glorious time when women ruled the world.

Most anthropologists can find little evidence for the purported golden age of matriarchy (Binford, 1979). The few artifacts of female goddesses and the many legends of Amazonian women are not sufficient proof of such a historical epoch. There is no evidence of any society known to us in which women had authority over men's lives, as in the different forms of government or various religions practiced by humans through the ages.

Although the world and human history may have been better off if matriarchy was the rule, it seems to be more fiction than fact.

What do you think?

Reading   *The Boys' Dormitory*

Anthropologist Margaret Read observed the Ngoni people of Southeastern Africa for several years. One of the most interesting aspects found among the Ngoni tribes was their method of teaching young males their place in Ngoni society. One such means was by separating the youthful Ngoni male from his home and raising him in a "boys' dormitory." However, the Ngoni boys' dormitory is like nothing young males in the Western world have ever experienced.

The hut known as the boys' dormitory and the whole system of living which it represented was a traditional feature of Ngoni village life. In their culture it had three main purposes. Formerly, when as they said "war was our school," it was the place where boys slept and lived together, and where they learned to defend themselves and to obey authority. It was in a sense the preparatory school for the regiment, and the herding of cattle was the basis of the curriculum. Once a boy went to sleep in a dormitory he never left it until he married, unless he was seriously ill. In the days of warfare, he learned in the dormitory and out herding the cattle a knowledge of the bush and its wild life and of his fellows, and the qualities required in self-defense and in mutual aid which he would need when, at the age of eighteen or so, he was called up into the new regiment formed by the Paramount. Dormitory life was therefore rooted in the Ngoni past and though its original purpose and outcome had disappeared with the suppression of tribal wars, it was still part of the organization for herding cattle and was regarded as a necessary training ground for young manhood. . . .

The first of these purposes was to remove boys, once they had their second teeth, from the influence of the women. Ngoni men were outspoken in condemning the effects of all women's influence on boys. They made a slight exception in favor of the mothers and grandmothers of high-ranking Ngoni clans. Non-Ngoni women they always suspected, and often rightly, of introducing youths and girls to ideas and practices which were contrary to Ngoni custom, particularly in connection with sex and magic. It was partly a belief that dormitory life would "Ngoni-ize" the boys and counteract non-Ngoni influences from whatever source that made them so unyielding about boys leaving the women's supervision at what they considered a crucial stage.

There was no doubt that this abrupt transition, like the sudden weaning, was a shock for many boys between six-and-a-half and seven-and-a-half. From having been impudent, well fed, self-confident, and spoiled youngsters among the women many of them quickly became skinny, scruffy, subdued and had a hunted expression. The subdued and hunted looks passed off as they adjusted themselves to their new environment and there were boys, generally those exceptionally well grown and physically strong, who showed no apparent signs of shock. They all, however, showed the effects of irregular and inadequate feeding. The younger boys were chronically hungry, and their hair, skin, and bony knees and ribs were eloquent of calory, protein, and vitamin shortages.

The other main purpose of dormitory life in Ngoni culture was to mix up all the boys in the village and let the common life together teach them how to get on with their age-mates and knuckle under to their superiors in age. Age

Source: Children of their fathers: Growing up among the Ngoni of Malawi (pp. 48–50) by M. Read, 1968, New York: Holt, Rinehart and Winston. Copyright © 1968 Holt, Rinehart and Winston, Inc. Reprinted by permission of CBS College Publishing.

and strength were the only criteria for authority. Older brothers might try to protect and intercede for younger brothers but it was not encouraged. All the young ones had to take their chance equally, without regard for their family name or their father's position.

The dormitory was primarily a sleeping place, but through the group of boys who slept there the herding of cattle was organized and the off-duty amusements and occupations of the older boys were planned. The young ones had to "fag" for the rest—fetching wood and water, keeping fires going, sweeping the hut, taking messages, huddling in a corner at night when the oldest boys brought girls in, and submitting to beating both as a warning and as a punishment. They were usually beaten once or twice soon after their arrival and then threatened with much worse if they ever divulged what went on in the dormitory.

Part II

Issues

Chapter 6

Interpersonal Power

*P*ower tends to corrupt and absolute power corrupts absolutely.

Lord John Acton

Why should power corrupt its possessor? The answer or answers are more difficult to come by than simply posing the question. Part of the problem or the confusion over power and its effects on an individual lies in the fact that "in the entire lexicon of social concepts, none is more troublesome than the concept of power" (Bierstedt, 1950, p. 7). Scholars over the years have focused on the power found in specific social institutions (i.e., religion, business, education, government, etc.), while little attention was paid to studying powerful individuals. And yet power is first and foremost an interpersonal issue. For too long, power at the interpersonal level has been a topic too little studied (Cartwright, 1959). Before we can discuss power from an institutional perspective (chapters 7, 8, 9, 10), we need to understand just what power is, how it influences the person who holds it, how it affects the relationships between people, and finally, how it rests in the hands of some, specifically men, more so than with others, specifically women (Kahn, 1984).

In this chapter we will focus on the interpersonal aspects of power and suggest that power is a central feature underlying nearly every aspect of female-male relations. We will begin our discussion by outlining the different types of power an individual may possess. Next we will note the different ways males and females use their power. Then we will examine the issues of feeling powerful and the effects that having power has on the individual. Finally, we will focus on power in heterosexual relationships and one of the most hostile expressions of power, sexual assault.

TABLE 6.1 DIFFERENT POWER TYPES, POWER BASES, AND SOME POWER MESSAGES

Suppose that several people want John Jones to have a physical examination. How can they go about getting him to make an appointment?

Power Types	Power Bases	Power Messages
Reward	Ability to reward	If you have your physical, I'll cook your favorite dinner. (Wife)
Coercion	Ability to punish	John, if you don't get a physical, your breakfast will be "well-done." (Wife)
Referent	Similarity to the other and the other's liking for you	Honey, you'd make me very happy if you'd get a physical. (Wife)
Expert	Possession of skills and knowledge not possessed by another	John, you haven't been to see me for several years, and it's time for your physical. (John's physician)
Legitimate	Social position	John, if you want that additional life insurance, you'll have to have a physical. (John's insurance agent)
Informational	Ability to explain why another should change	Dad, I was reading in my health book that men over forty should have a physical every year. (John's daughter)

Source: "Social influence and power" by B. Raven, 1965. In I. Steiner and M. Fishbein (Eds.), *Current studies in social psychology*, New York: Holt, Rinehart & Winston.

INTERPERSONAL POWER

What is the essence of power at the interpersonal level? *"Power*, specifically social or interpersonal power, refers to the ability to achieve ends through influence" (Huston, 1983, p. 170). In other words, power enters into a relationship when people (i.e., *powerholders*) have the ability to achieve ends by influencing others (i.e., *target persons*).

But how do people get others to achieve certain ends? One of the first indepth analyses of this issue was conducted by John French and Bertram Raven (1959; Raven, 1965). French and Raven listed six different types of power that people use in their interpersonal relations: *reward, coercive, referent, legitimate, expert,* and *informational* (see table 6.1). French and Raven also studied the consequences stemming from the use of the various power types with respect to the degree of liking the target person would have for the powerholder and the target person's willingness to comply with the powerholder's wishes over a period of time. When considering the issues of the target person's liking for the powerholder and length of time of the target person's compliance, several facts must be kept in mind. For example, a person holding a gun on another can exert tremendous influence or power over that person, but for how long? How does such power leave the target person feeling about the powerholder? As French and Raven noted, some power bases are more likely to increase the target person's liking for the powerholder and ensure the target person's compliance with the powerholder's wishes or requests for a considerable period of time even in the powerholder's absence. Still other types of power can cause the target person to feel extreme dislike for the powerholder and can bring about a change in the target person only when the powerholder is present, as in the case of the person with a gun. According to French and Raven, the power types differ with respect to the degree of liking they create in the target person for the powerholder as well as the length of time the target person will comply with the powerholder's wishes.

Let's begin our discussion of power by first examining each of the six power types and their bases and noting some of their consequences on relationships between target persons and powerholders.

The Power Types and Their Bases

A person possesses *reward* power when that person has something of value for which another person is willing to do something. Usually, a person with reward power possesses any one of several kinds of resources, or things of value, that others perceive as worthwhile or desirable. Resources come in one of two types: *concrete* and *personal resources*. Concrete resources are comprised of those valued things that are tangible (e.g., money or gifts). Personal resources are less tangible (e.g., a person's friendship, affection, or even pleasant words that cause another to comply to the powerholder's bidding). More often than not, the target person will feel positive toward a powerholder who uses reward power. Although the target person's compliance with the powerholder's wishes will be assured in the short run, long-term compliance is less certain, especially if the powerholder withholds the desired resources.

The second power type, *coercive power*, is held by one who threatens to withdraw a reward or threatens to punish the target person unless that person complies with the powerholder's wishes. Obviously, coercive power is one of the strongest forms of power one person can have over another. The use of coercive power, however, is likely to instill in the target person a strong dislike or even hatred for the powerholder. Furthermore, the use of coercive power generally does not assure long-term compliance with the powerholder's wishes once she or he is gone.

A person who is admired or liked by others has what is called *referent power*. In other words, if I like you or admire you, I am more likely to comply with your wishes than if I don't like or respect you. According to French and Raven, people with referent power oftentimes don't even know they exercise such power over others. One with referent power normally enjoys a positive relationship with the target person, and the target person's compliance with the powerholder's wishes may last for a considerable time even in the absence of the powerholder.

© 1975 United Feature Syndicate, Inc.

Legitimate power comes to the person who holds a social position in society that confers authority over others. The basis of legitimate power, or what can also be called *authority,* is found in society's social positions or roles (i.e., doctors, judges, police officers, etc.) wherein one person has certain rights over another's behavior—in our society a police officer has authority, or legitimate power, over monitoring the driving habits of motorists. In most instances, according to French and Raven, the target person feels indifferent toward a person with legitimate power. Also, compliance with the wishes of one with legitimate power is usually quite complete. Legitimate power is one of the more complicated forms of power because it entails a knowledge of a society's social structures and the roles played out by its members in their different social statuses.

Expert power is possessed by one who has superior knowledge or ability in a specific subject area. For example, most people will defer to an auto mechanic's decision about how to fix or maintain their cars because they consider the mechanic to be more knowledgeable than they are about a car's engine and its functioning. The target person of expert power generally feels somewhat indifferent toward the person holding expert power and will, in most cases, comply with the powerholder's wishes in the long run.

A person who has access to some information that others may want or would find valuable is one who has *informational power.* Informational power should not be confused with expert power. One need not be knowledgeable or skilled to have informational power, but simply be the possessor of some information that others think is important or valuable or information that others want. A major difference between informational power and the other five power bases is that informational power isn't based on the relationship between the powerholder and the target person. The essential feature of informational power is that one person holds information that others will be influenced by. The powerholder's personality and other attributes are of little importance. Thus the question of liking the powerholder holds little value for this power type.

Gender Differences in the Use of Various Power Bases

It is not surprising that people attribute different power bases to males and females. Traditionally, males have been viewed as having and using both reward and coercive power more than females have (Johnson, 1976; 1978). In fact, males have usually had greater access to various concrete rewards (e.g., money) and could therefore get others to comply with their wishes. On the other hand, women throughout the ages have had fewer concrete resources at their disposal with which to cause others to do their bidding.

For centuries, men have used coercive power—threats and punishment—to get their way. Stories abound about how males have commonly used their strength and force as a means to get others to do their bidding. One of the most extreme examples of coercive power can be found in marital abuse and sexual assault cases where spouses exert power and domination over their mates. We will have more to say about sexual assault in a later section.

Recall that a person with referent power is one who is liked or respected by others. Nearly everyone has admired someone in their lives, someone for whom they were willing to do almost anything. A distinctive feature of referent power is the absence of an aggressive element in the relationship between the powerholder (i.e., the one liked or respected) and the target person (i.e., the person who likes or respects the other). We might suggest that women would be more likely to use referent power than men would be because women are traditionally viewed as being more sensitive to others, more concerned with harmony in the group, and thought of as less aggressive than men. Indeed, Paula Johnson (1978) suggests that in general most people associate the use of referent power with women more than with men. However, males are taught early that they should not identify with women and to view women in negative ways (Doyle, 1983). Thus women's use of referent power with men may not be as pervasive as some may think.

The use of legitimate power depends on the powerholder having a socially sanctioned position or role that confers authority over others. In most societies men have an abundance of legitimate power because of their access to a variety of positions that sanction their authority over others, especially women and children. In the traditional family, for example, the mother has legitimate authority over the children, but the father still has ultimate authority over all the family members, including the mother.

Males are often found in positions that bring with them an amount of expertise or superior knowledge or ability and therefore expert power. Until the latter part of this century, most people felt little need for anything more than a basic education for their female children, although male children were sent to school to gain all the education and knowledge they could. Consequently, professional men in our society outnumber professional women in almost every high-status category (see chapter 8). In professions such as engineering and medicine, the disparity between men and women is especially obvious. Men, with their generally superior training and skills, are more apt to have more access to expert power than women are. Even when females do evidence expert power, they are more likely to be seen by others as less likeable and less feminine than are males who use this form of power (Falbo et al., 1982).

Somewhat related to the gender difference found in expert power is that found in informational power. Again, in most situations, males have greater access to information desired by others than women have. Thus we can say that men have greater informational power than women have.

Overall, it appears that males have a greater number of power bases or, more precisely, are viewed as using a greater number of power bases than women are. In all but referent power, there is a clear gender difference favoring males over females in the use of reward, coercive, legitimate, expertise, and informational power bases.

Strategies of Power Use

Although a general disparity exists with the numbers of power bases that women and men have, women still are able to influence others to comply with their wishes. Women are not powerless, but they do lack authority in many areas. The ways that women and men influence others to achieve their goals do appear to differ. Paula Johnson (1976) finds that the *power strategies* used by females and males appear to fall along three separate dimensions. She outlined the gender differences in power strategies in the following manner: the *directness* a person uses to get others to comply, the *resources* a person uses, and the degree of *competence* a person shows in influencing others (see table 6.2).

Direct Versus Indirect Power When a person says, "Shut the door!", that person is using a direct form of power. When a person tries to influence another without that person being aware that he or she is being influenced, that would be an indirect form of power. For example, if I want you to shut the door, I may say, "Gee, it sure is cold in here," hoping that you will offer to close the door. Manipulation is another name for an indirect use of power. Generally speaking, those with little status or power and with few concrete resources are more apt to use an indirect power strategy to get others to comply with their wishes. Those with high status and many resources need not try to manipulate others to do their bidding; they can rely on the more direct form of power.

Thus males with their usually greater number of resources and their usually higher status are more likely to use more direct forms of gaining others' compliance. Many women, on the other hand, have little or no legitimate authority outside of the home; therefore, in most situations with others outside of their families, women must rely on more indirect forms of power. Many people become very skillful at using indirect power, as

TABLE 6.2 JOHNSON'S THREE DIMENSIONS OF POWER

Typically Masculine Power Strategies	Typically Feminine Power Strategies	Short-Run Advantages of Feminine Power Strategies	Long-Run Disadvantages of Feminine Power Strategies
Direct	Indirect	The person influenced may believe it was her/his own idea.	If effective in the short run, this strategy has concealed your power.
Concrete rewards	Personal rewards	People who like you may be easily influenced by your affection and attention.	Your span of influence is very narrow—dependent upon the goodwill and affection of others.
Competence	Helplessness	Tends to work very well for women, who may be seen as legitimately helpless in many situations.	May leave you feeling helpless. Others may come to see you as weak and incompetent.

Source: The new partnerships: Women and men in organizations (p. 98). by Nina L. Colwill, 1982, Palo Alto, CA: Mayfield. Reprinted by permission of Mayfield Publishing Co. Copyright 1982 by Mayfield Publishing Company.

can be seen by those spouses and secretaries who can successfully lead their mates and employers to believe that the ideas they offer are actually the mates' and employers' own ideas.

Although the use of an indirect form of power may prove beneficial in the short run because one can influence another to comply with one's wishes, in the long run, it may prove disadvantageous. The secretary who relies on indirectly influencing the boss may never receive any credit for the ideas he or she so skillfully managed to get the boss to carry out. The boss ends up with the credit for all the changes that the secretary covertly initiated, leaving the secretary as the only one who knows that he or she is the one who should receive the credit.

Personal Versus Concrete Resources   In every transaction wherein one person tries to influence another, there is some resource or resources that enter into the process. Johnson lists two main types of resources: personal resources such as friendship, affection, or approval and concrete resources such as money, knowledge, or strength. In most instances, males have more concrete resources at their disposal than females do. Males often have more money and more education, which leads to greater knowledge and expertise, and of course, the average male is usually physically stronger than the average female. Males gain these advantages, except for the physical one, through their socialization. Females are more likely to have more personal resources such as openness and friendliness toward others by virtue of their socialization to be emotionally supportive toward others.

In the short run, having and using personal resources may be useful in getting people with whom you have a positive relationship to comply with your wishes. With personal resources, the relationship is central. With concrete resources, the relationship is less essential as a prime ingredient to assure that one gets one's way. A person with money need not be liked nor friendly in order to have others do his or her bidding.

Competence Versus Helplessness   Regarding the issue of competence versus helplessness as a power strategy, few beliefs are as strong as the notion that males are more competent than females in most areas, except those traditionally identified as "feminine." Such a grandiose belief is not hard to explain given the fact that the male stereotype contains traits like independent, active, and dominant, which, taken together with other socially-desirable male traits, add up to a successful and competent person by our society's definition (Broverman et al., 1972). The generalized belief that males are more competent than females is so pervasive that it ranges across all types of activities from writing essays (Paludi and Bauer, 1983), to painting (Pheterson et al., 1971), to the belief in a male's superior ability in numerous jobs and occupations (Dipboye et al., 1975; Feather and Simon, 1975). However, some research has found a recent shift in public sentiment about female competence, suggesting that people are beginning to see women as being competent in some situations (Shinar, 1978). But most people still hold on to the belief that males are more competent in general than females (Lott, 1983; Ruble, 1983).

The notion that females are generally less competent than males is supported by the stereotype of the female as being "the weaker sex." By this token, many men feel more inclined to assist a "helpless" female than a "helpless" male (Pomazal and Clore, 1973; West et al., 1975).

A major problem in using a helpless strategy to influence others is that in the long run the person using such a technique can suffer a loss of self-esteem. Furthermore, feigning helplessness can make one dependent on another, which can have serious consequences if the relationship between the helpless one and the helper dissolves. Overall, although females have been portrayed as more helpless than males, women have shown that this portrayal is far from accurate. Women are as competent in their personal and work lives as men are.

FEELING POWERFUL

Thus far we have noted that males in general have more power bases than women have and that males are more likely to use a more direct and, some may argue, a more effective means of influencing others than women use. But power over others is only one facet of the power issue. Besides having power over others, we also need to look at the issue of having a sense of control or power over one's own life. A person who believes that he or she controls his or her own life can be said to possess a sense of *autonomy*.

Do females and males have equal or nearly equal amounts of personal autonomy? To answer this question we need first refer to our previous discussion about the gender stereotypes (chapter 3). Recall how the gender stereotypes can be conceived as being made up of two distinct clusters: one associated with masculinity and called the "competency cluster," and the other associated with femininity and referred to as the "warmth-expressiveness cluster" (Broverman et al., 1972). For each stereotypic cluster there is a male side and a female side. On the male side, or pole, of the competency cluster such traits as independent, dominant, and not easily influenced are normally found; on the female pole we find such traits as dependent, submissive, passive, and easily influenced. Masculinity appears more likely to be associated with high power, dominance, and control, whereas femininity appears related to low power and lack of control.

We might suggest that such stereotypic views of masculinity and femininity are likely to affect how individual females and males think of themselves in terms of their control over the events that shape their lives. A masculine person might be more inclined to attribute personal accomplishments to skill or ability—self-determinism. A feminine person might attribute personal achievements more to fate or luck—environmental determinism.

Locus of Control

One way to focus on the element of personal control or feeling powerful is by noting the construct called *locus of control*. Locus of control is the generalized belief or expectancy a person has about the degree of influence or control she or he has over the events encountered in her or his life (Lefcourt, 1976). People who believe that they control to a large degree the events in their lives possess an *internal locus of control*. Those who believe that they have little or no control over their lives or actions have an *external locus of control*. Much of the research about how males and females perceive themselves in terms of locus of control is credited to the work of Julian Rotter (1966), who developed a scale to measure the locus of control construct.

Based on a series of studies, Rotter concluded that in general there were no significant gender differences in a person's perception of her or his own locus of control. However, other researchers have found a fairly consistent pattern whereby females tend to score higher in external and males higher in internal locus of control (Maccoby and Jacklin, 1974). In one study males were asked to fill out Rotter's scale the way they thought an extremely masculine male would, and females the way an extremely feminine female would. The results showed masculinity positively related to internal scores on the locus of control scale and femininity to external scores (Hochreich, 1975). Thus it seems that females or those who score high in femininity are more likely to be "externals," whereas males or those who score high in masculinity are more likely to be "internals." We should note that other researchers have failed to find such a clear-cut difference between gender stereotypes and internal and external locus of control scores (Johnson and Black, 1981). We should also note that there are some cultural variations with respect to locus of control. Specifically, females from the United States and New Zealand show a lesser degree of external orientation than females from Sweden and Japan (McGinnies et al., 1974).

But how do we explain such a gender difference on locus of control scores? One possible explanation is that a person's prior experience or socialization can foster such a gender difference. Research has shown that females are more likely to attribute their success to luck, and males are more likely to attribute their success to ability or skill (Deaux and Emswiller, 1974; Deaux et al., 1975). When people attribute their achievements to luck, they tend to believe that they personally have little or no control over their lives; they believe that fate or luck (not skill or ability) is behind their achievements. Interestingly, people who are judged to be externals are more likely to judge their achievements on the basis of luck, whereas internals more on skill (Phares, 1976). Thus prior experience may play a role in the gender difference found on Rotter's scale of locus of control.

Prior experience may be only one factor that contributes to the difference in the ways women and men explain their achievements. Another more specific explanation is provided by psychologist Carol Dweck and her associates (Dweck et al., 1978, 1980). Dweck noted that teachers are more likely to tell young girls they failed because of lack of ability, while they tell young boys they failed because of lack of effort. Thus girls may come to believe they lack ability in many areas, and therefore feel that they have little or no control over their environment and consequently their own lives, causing them to develop an external locus-of-control orientation. Others have noted that such experiences may lead to what is called "learned helplessness," which is one of the power strategies that females more than males are likely to use to get another to comply with their wishes (Seligman, 1975). A woman who feels that her actions mean little in terms of their outcomes may in fact give up and feel personally helpless and the victim of external forces.

In the sense of feeling personally powerful or in control of one's own life, women appear to be at a disadvantage when compared to men in general.

THE EFFECTS OF HOLDING POWER

Having power over others can change a person in many ways. One of the more obvious changes that power can bring is that it can make a power-holder happy. At least, many people say that the reason they want power is to gain greater personal satisfaction and pleasure in their lives. Thus one of the first effects of having power is a heightened sense of pleasure. As one social critic noted:

> To lord it over others is a means of security, freedom, goods, and so on. But it is also a good in itself. A good which can overwhelm every other good dictated by reason and conscience alike. It is strangely gratifying to make people come and go at our bidding, to overrule their minds and their wills, to take away their power, and virtually annihilate them. . . . There is a soul fulfillment in mastery over human beings. There is no pleasure quite like it, and for its sake men have risked every good and done every conceivable evil. It is well to remember these facts and take them seriously. (Haroutunian, 1949, p. 9)

But having power over others may not only bring a sense of pleasure with it; it may also change the powerholder in other ways, some of which have dramatic effects on the powerholder as well as on those who are the target of power. David Kipnis, in his book *The Powerholders* (1976), suggested as much when he noted that the successful use of power not only changes a person's perception of him- or herself, but it also affects the powerholder's views of others over which that power is wielded. Kipnis refers to these changes in a person with power as the *metamorphic effects* of power.

Metamorphic Effects of Power

As already noted, males as a rule have more power bases than females have. It therefore stands to reason that the metamorphic effects of power would be more prominent among men than among women. But just what are the metamorphic effects of power of which Kipnis speaks?

According to Kipnis, one of the first metamorphic effects of having power is an exalted or vain view of oneself. People who have power over others think of themselves as superior to the targets of their power. How such a perception of one's own superiority develops is an open question, but it probably comes about gradually from the interactions between the powerholder and the target. For example, the target does the powerholder's bidding: comes when requested, goes when asked, and so on. The powerholder is much like a puppeteer who holds the strings and causes others to move. Such control over another cannot help but produce an exaggerated or aggrandized self-perception of importance and superiority within the powerholder. Of course, such power and its consequent self-aggrandizement for the powerholder can foster resentment or worse within the target for the powerholder. "The effects of power," wrote the nineteenth century American historian Henry Adams, "on all men is the aggravation of self, a sort of tumor that ends by killing the victim's sympathies." Kipnis noted that even the ancients were keenly aware of the self-puffery brought on by power.

The Greek dramatists were particularly sensitive to the fate of persons who were at the high tide of their power and status. In the plays of Sophocles, for instance, the viewer is confronted with the image of great and powerful rulers transformed by their prior successes so that they are filled with a sense of their own worth and importance—with "hubris"—impatient of the advice of others and unwilling to listen to opinions that disagree with their own. Yet, in the end they are destroyed by events, which they discover, to their anguish, that they cannot control. (p. 169)

Power also leads the powerholder to think that he or she is in control of his or her life rather than controlled by external forces. Having power may be yet another life experience that prompts the development of an internal locus of control. Recall, in our discussion of Rotter's locus of control, the finding that men are more likely to be "internals" and women "externals." In Rotter's terms then, men who normally have more power than women have are more likely to view themselves as being in charge of their own lives and the lives of others, especially women. Women, on the other hand, often perceive themselves as targets of men's power and are more apt to define their lives as being controlled by others. Thus power and its imbalance between females and males may be yet another factor contributing to men perceiving themselves as being in charge and women seeing themselves as being controlled rather than controlling.

Another metamorphic effect of power is the increase in the powerholder's self-esteem. People with power usually have the needed resources to satisfy their desires. Besides having desires fulfilled by others, powerholders are also more apt to be praised and flattered by the targets of their power. Those with little power are not as likely to have their wishes and desires met, nor are they apt to be on the receiving end of praise and flattery. Powerless people may learn to rely on techniques such as helplessness to gain their desires. But acting helpless rather than powerful does not appear to increase one's level of self-esteem. As we noted earlier, researchers have found evidence that women are more likely to use a helpless strategy to gain or exert power over others, and as a consequence many women may suffer a loss of self-esteem in the process (Johnson, 1978; Kanter, 1984).

Yet another metamorphic effect occurring in the powerholder is the sometimes subtle (or even not so subtle) change in morality. A powerholder may feel that he or she is above the common rules that govern others and choose to live by a code of his or her own making. According to Kipnis, power can lead to ". . . the fact that commonly held norms and values are ignored by powerholders when such norms and values appear to threaten or restrict the powerholder's use of his resources" (p. 175).

And last, power may cause the powerholder to feel contempt for the target person. The powerholder may view the target person, at worst, as a nonperson, and, at best, with a kindly paternalistic air. "[T]he less powerful," according to Kipnis, "become objects of manipulation with a lesser claim on human rights than is claimed by the powerholder. In Martin Buber's terms, it is the transformation of one person's perception of another from 'thou' to 'it,' from individual to object" (p. 176).

As we can see, power over others can have substantial effects on the one who possesses it. Not only do powerholders see themselves as exalted and in charge of their world, they are also more than likely to come to think of those with little or no power as something less than fully human. The idea that power can have a corrupting effect on an individual is not an idle observation, but one that gives support to the proposition that only when human beings, female and male alike, have equal access to various power bases can humans form genuine and mutually rewarding human relationships.

HETEROSEXUAL RELATIONSHIPS AND POWER

We have already noted that the various types of power appear to be unevenly distributed between females and males. Also, the gender stereotypes and their associated traits of masculinity and femininity show a difference with respect to power or powerlessness; the masculine traits of dominance and aggression add to one's sense of power, whereas the feminine traits of submission and passivity reinforce one's feelings of powerlessness. Furthermore, we noted that females tend to use less direct and more subtle types of power strategies to influence others than males do. We should note also that researchers have found that when females do use what can be considered a masculine type of power, for example, coercion, they are more likely to be seen as less likeable and more hostile and aggressive than males who use such "masculine" power types (Buss, 1981; Jago and Vroom, 1982).

Until now, we have talked about power and the differences found among females and males in a rather general way. But what about those females and males who know each other intimately and have a personal investment in each other, for example, dating or married couples? Does power have anything to do with couples who are romantically involved? Or does the issue of power become less important when we look at intimate relationships? Although many lovers may feel that power is something totally unrelated to their special relationship, researchers have found that even in the most intimate of relationships, power and its use or misuse is every bit as pervasive a phenomenon as love.

The question of power and which partner has the bulk of it was put to a test when psychologist Anne Peplau (et al., 1976) along with several of her colleagues asked over 200 dating couples "who has more to say in your relationship?" Having the last word about which movie to go to or to have or not have sexual relations are just a few of the ways that power can be expressed in an intimate relationship. About half of the couples reported they had what can be called an egalitarian relationship. An *egalitarian relationship* is one where power is supposedly shared fairly equally between the partners. Most of the remaining couples noted that the man had the final say in the relationship. Those few couples where the female reportedly was more powerful expressed the most dissatisfaction in the relationship compared to those couples who shared power or where the male had the most power. In a review of the literature, this time with married couples, researchers found that where the wife had the bulk of the power there was also greater dissatisfaction expressed than in those egalitarian marriages or traditional husband-dominant marriages (Gray-Little and Burks, 1983). We might conclude that in those intimate male-female relationships where the woman is dominant, there is less satisfaction expressed than in more equal or somewhat traditional male-dominant relationships. Why a relationship that finds the female in the dominant position proves less satisfying has not yet been explained satisfactorily. Possibly, the male in such a relationship feels threatened by the reversal of traditional roles, and the greater perceived status of the female in power may contribute to a greater degree of discontent or worse on the part of the male, which may undermine the relationship (Hornung et al., 1981).

Power in Courtship

Nearly everyone at one time or another has been involved in the *courtship game,* or what can be referred to as "the institutional way that men and women become acquainted before marriage" (McCormick and Jesser, 1983, p. 65). Although many involved in courtship and its rituals may deny any aspect of power, preferring to see it in more romantic and idealized terms, power certainly plays a decisive role in any courtship.

Take, for example, the element of having or not having sexual relations. If one dating partner wishes to have sexual relations and the other doesn't, we have a classic case of how power comes into play in the relationship. In general, among dating couples, women have the last say when it comes to "how far to go" in terms of sexual expressions (Peplau et al., 1977). Traditionally, women were expected to act passively toward men's sexual advances or to somehow curtail or outrightly refuse their sexual advances (Gagnon and Simon, 1973; Komarovsky, 1976). Thus the issue of power becomes especially revealing in the area of sexual relationships.

Traditionally, males were the aggressors or initiators, and females were expected to act in more reserved ways in sexual relationships. However, the "double standard"—that the male should be sexually experienced and the female should reserve herself for her husband—has been changing in the past several decades. We are more likely today than in previous generations to find females more involved sexually at a younger age and with several men before marriage (Zelnick and Kanter, 1980). Today's single females and males may be less influenced by traditional role-playing strategies to influence another regarding sexual experiences before marriage. However, in general, the stereotype of the average male is still very much tied up with the aggressor role, in which he is expected to use every possible strategy to have sex; the stereotype of the average female still sees her as trying to avoid having sex (LaPlante et al., 1980; McCormick, 1979). Equating sex with power may seem foreign to some, but in cases of sexual assault, we see the merger of both most clearly.

RAPE AND SEXUAL ASSAULT

Few words strike as much terror in a person's heart as rape. Few human acts are so fraught with misinformation and misconception as rape. Few other acts so degrade a human being as rape. And few other acts show the imbalance of power between men and women and men's quest for domination over women as rape does.

Rape is first and foremost an act of *violence,* an attempted or completed sexual assault instigated by one or more persons against another human being. The historical roots of rape run deep in the patriarchal tradition of male violence toward women (Brownmiller, 1975; Chappell et al., 1977; Russell, 1975). Rape, to be understood, must not be seen as simply a violent sexual act of a few lunatics or pathologically disordered persons, but rather a violent sexual act performed by many and reinforced by the dominant patriarchal values coming to the fore in their most twisted and disturbing forms in our culture (Burt, 1980; Dworkin, 1974). A few cultures may be less prone to violent sexual acts between males and females, but ours and most others are definitely "rape-prone" cultures (Benderly, 1982; Schwendinger and Schwendinger, 1983). No discussion of power and its imbalance between women and men would be complete without a discussion of rape.

In this section we will first take up the issue of rape as an act of dominance (not sex) and of power (not pathology) that is ingrained in the very fiber of the male's gender role. Next we will attempt to put the statistics of rape in perspective by trying to give some scope to the enormity of the act of rape in the everyday lives of many women and some men. And then, we will note the rising concern and some of the actions taken among feminists and nonfeminists alike over the issue of rape as a social phenomenon of epidemic proportions and not merely an isolated criminal act affecting a few.

Rape and Power

Throughout most of this century those who influenced what others thought about rape saw it as a "victim-precipitated phenomenon" (Albin, 1977). Sigmund Freud (1927), in his study of the female personality, theorized that the female was more "masochistic" than the male and that rape—either in fantasy or in fact—was the one sexual act wherein the female acted out her masochism to the utmost. However, such nonsense was soon dismissed by the psychiatric and psychological communities who began to speculate that rape was the result of a disordered or aberrant sexual impulse within a certain small group of men (Bowman, 1951). Today, however, rape—whether the victim is female or male—is seen as an act of power or dominance of one person over another. Recently, some social scientists have noted that rape is one of the most terrifying means used by men to dominate other men inside and outside of prison (Flanagan et al., 1980; Groth and Burgess, 1980; Kaufman et al., 1980). To focus on rape as a power or dominance act we need only analyze how rape is used in prison:

> Rape in prison is rarely a sexual act, but one of violence, politics and an acting out of power roles. "Most of your homosexual rapes is a macho thing," says Col. Walter Pence, the Chief of Security here at the Louisiana State Penitentiary at Angola. "It's basically one guy saying to another: 'I'm a better man than you and I'm gonna turn you out ["turn you out" is prison slang for rape] to prove it.' I've investigated about a hundred cases personally, and I've not seen one that's just an act of passion. It's definitely a macho/power thing among the inmates." (Rideau and Sinclair, 1982, pp. 4–5)

A prime ingredient in rape is the element of aggression that is so deeply embedded in the male's gender role (Cherry, 1983). For many men, aggression is one of the major ways of proving their masculinity and manhood, especially among those men who feel some sense of powerlessness in their lives. The male-as-dominant or male-as-aggressor is a theme so central to many men's self-concept that it literally carries over into their sexual lives. Sex, in fact, may be the one area where the average man can still prove his masculinity when few other areas can be found for him to prove himself manly or in control, or the dominant one in a relationship. Diana Russell (1973) addresses this issue when she declares that rape is not the act of a disturbed male, but rather an act of an over-conforming male. She writes:

> Rape is not so much a deviant act as an over-conforming act. Rape may be understood as an extreme acting-out of qualities that are regarded as super masculine in this and many other societies: aggression, force, power, strength, toughness, dominance, competitiveness. To win, to be superior, to be successful, to conquer—all demonstrate masculinity to those who subscribe to common cultural notions of masculinity, i.e., the *masculine mystique*. And it would be surprising if these notions of masculinity did not find expression in men's sexual behavior. Indeed, sex may be the arena where these notions of masculinity are most intensely played out, particularly by men who feel powerless in the rest of their lives, and hence, whose masculinity is threatened by this sense of powerlessness. (p. 1)

The fusion of aggression and sexuality for many men can be seen when we examine the area of sexual arousal as stimulated by graphic scenes of rape. Initially, researchers found that convicted rapists were more sexually aroused by depictions of violent sexuality than were men who had not raped (Abel et al., 1978). Thus it was thought that rapists must have a very low threshold for sexual arousal, and that the least little provocation would set off a male rapist (e.g., a woman who would assertively say "no" to sexual advances or even put up a fight was enough to trigger off a rapist, or so it was thought). In more recent studies, however, when men who had never raped were exposed to depictions of sexual assault, they reported a heightened sexual arousal from such scenes and an increase in their rape fantasies (Malamuth and Check, 1981a). Another disquieting note is that when nonrapist males were shown depictions of sexual assault, they reported the possibility that they would even consider using force themselves in their sexual relations (Malamuth and Check, 1981b; Malamuth et al., 1980).The research appears to suggest that most men (i.e., rapists and nonrapists) find violence a stimulant to heighten or arouse their sexual feelings. There is evidence that seems to indicate that males in general find sexuality related at some level to an expression of aggression, and in turn aggression heightens their sexual fantasies or actual sexual behaviors (Friday, 1980).

In summary, we can say that sexual assault or rape is first and foremost an act of sexual violence that to some degree draws upon the sexual fantasies of the rapist; it is linked to the rapist's need to show superiority and dominance over another.

The Problem of Numbers

Rape is one of the most underreported of all serious crimes in the United States and in other countries as well. When we try to get a true picture of the enormity of its incidence, we find the issue complicated by the lack of reliable rape statistics. The crime of rape presents some uniquely confounding problems.

One problem we encounter is the simple fact that many, if not most, rape victims simply refuse to come forward and report to the authorities incidents of sexual violence. For many rape victims, a sense of shame or guilt or self-blame about their role in the rape assaults may be enough to prevent them from coming forward and pressing charges. Those who do press charges, however, are apt to meet with questions, accusations, and other degrading and humiliating experiences by the very authorities that are sworn to uphold the laws of society that make the rape of a person a serious felony.

Another problem is that when rape victims do press charges against their assailants, their life histories, especially sexual activities, are dragged before the public. In many instances, the public seems willing to blame the victim for the asault rather than the rapist (see box 6.1). The reason for such an attribution of guilt to the victim rather than to the assailant seems to lie in the fact that many people have a tendency to blame others for their misfortunes, as if the world we live in was and is a "just world" where bad things happen only to those who somehow bring on or somehow deserve the consequences of their acts (Krulewitz and Payne, 1978). Consequently, a likely result of such a "just world" orientation is that more often than not, the defenders of rapists will try to show that the rape victims acted in such a manner as to infer their complicity in the sexual assaults or that they "had it coming" because of their actions. We find such a courtroom tactic used by many defense attorneys, and it was one that apparently did not work in the much publicized 1984 New Bedford, Massachusetts, gang-rape case. There the rape-victim's motives for stopping at a bar were questioned and inferences were made impugning her behavior while in the bar. For example, during the trial, it was pointed out that the rape victim had talked with several of the accused rapists before the gang rape occurred. (If the mere act of talking is sufficient cause in some people's minds for a group of men to rape a woman, then we indeed have a twisted view of the causes of rape.) Thus, with all the barriers preventing the victims of sexual assault from coming forward, it is no wonder that rape continues to be one of the most underreported crimes. Even so, the Federal Bureau of Investigation (1977) reported that in the decade between 1967 and 1977 the number of reported rapes doubled in the United States. Doyle (1983) noted that:

> During 1977 alone, over 63,000 cases of rape were reported by the FBI. The most shocking feature of these statistics is that rape is considered by many experts in crime statistics to be one of the *least* reported violent crimes. The best available estimates suggest that for every one reported rape case there are anywhere from three to ten unreported cases. The conservative estimate of three means that over a quarter of a million women were forcibly raped in the United States in 1977! (p. 189)

While we have no absolute statistics for the total number of completed or attempted rapes committed annually in North America, we can estimate the probability of a woman being the victim of sexual assault during her lifetime. Allan Johnson (1980) estimated that "Nationally, a *conservative* estimate is that, under current conditions, 20–30 percent of girls now twelve years old will suffer a violent sexual attack during the remainder of their lives" (p. 145). Even with this estimate, however, we should keep in mind that this percentage excludes females under twelve, married women, and male rape victims. The enormity of the incidence of rape becomes even more staggering when we note that untold numbers of children under twelve are often the victims of sexual assault (Rush, 1980; Russell, 1984), as well as the many cases of male rape both inside and outside of prison (Scacco, 1982).

Rape As a Social Concern

Due to the mounting concern over women's rights heralded by the re-emergent women's movement, sexual assaults and their debilitating consequences for the victims have become one of the more pressing central issues of the 1970s and 1980s. Consequently, many social scientists have turned their attention toward understanding the dynamics of rapists and their motives, the institutional and cultural factors promoting rape, and of course, the various factors affecting the assault on rape victims and their reactions (Jacobson and Popovich, 1983; Towson and Zanna, 1983).

Box 6.1

Did He Have It Coming?

John Jones walks 6 blocks from his office to the subway after work. Occasionally he has given some coins to some of the beggars who solicit money along his route.

One evening, he stayed at work later than usual because he had been invited to a dinner party. Since there wouldn't be time for him to go home and change, he brought clothes with him and changed in the restroom. It was getting dark as he left the office and stepped out into the rainy evening. Most of the office workers had left for home over an hour ago, and the street was deserted. About halfway to the subway John noticed one of the beggars to whom he had occasionally given money approaching him. The man held out his hand, but John smiled at him and said, "Sorry, but I'm afraid I don't have any extra today," and continued on his way. He had the feeling that the beggar was following him, so with a slight sense of apprehension, he began walking more quickly. The next thing he knew, he'd been tackled to the ground, and the beggar told him to give him his wallet or "I'll cut you up good." Since it had gotten quite dark, John couldn't see if the man had a knife or some other weapon, and so he decided that maybe it would be best if he just gave up the wallet. The beggar grabbed it and ran off.

John picked himself up and decided to go home to call the police. When he got home, he still felt upset, so he fixed himself a drink, took a shower and changed into dry clothes to try to calm down before phoning the police. He was told to come down to the station to file a report.

Throughout his dealings with the police, and later, in court, John was continuously exposed to statements and questioning which suggested that he hadn't really had the money stolen or that he had provoked the beggar into the assault:

1. Since it is 6 blocks between your office and the subway, why don't you take a cab? Aren't you asking for it when you parade the street every night?
2. Have you ever given away money to anyone before?
3. Did you ever give money to the person you *claim* mugged you?
4. What were you doing walking through the neighborhood at that time of night?
5. You don't look like you've been hurt, how do we even know the assault occurred?
6. Can you prove your wallet was taken?
7. Why were you so dressed up; wasn't that just inviting the assault?

Source: Sexual interactions (p. 568) by Elizabeth R. Allgeier and Albert R. Allgeier, 1984, Lexington, MA: D.C. Heath. Copyright © 1984 by D. C. Heath and Company. Reprinted by permission of the publisher.

Box 6.1

8. You've given him a dollar or two before and you now claim he took your wallet containing $50.00, but in giving him some money, weren't you in effect consenting to give him all your money?
9. You didn't resist the mugger; therefore, you must have really wanted to give him your money.
10. You say that he threatened you, but you also say that you didn't see the knife, and in fact, you handed over your wallet to him, so it doesn't sound like a mugging at all.
11. If an assault really occurred, why didn't you call immediately? Why did you wait two hours before calling? Maybe you really wanted to give the man your money at the time, but then changed your mind later.

To combat the growing number of rapes, more and more people are beginning to think in terms of prevention and not only of ways to deal with the debilitating aftermath of sexual assault. Many different ways have been suggested to stop the growing wave of sexual assaults in our society.

Two such preventive approaches commonly thought of are, first, a "restrictive approach" that focuses on women changing their life-styles (e.g., not going out alone or not talking to strangers), and second, an "assertive approach" that suggests that women learn martial arts in order to fight back if assaulted (Riger and Gordon, 1979). Both of these approaches have, however, some drawbacks. The restrictive approach, asking women to change their pattern of living, is an affront to women. Do we ask merchants to stop keeping money in their cash registers to prevent robberies? Why then should women change, for example, their dress or their social habits? The assertive approach has one possible value: the demise of the myth of the "defenseless woman" (Connell and Wilsen, 1974). However, one problem with this approach is that many times in order to coerce a victim a rapist uses a deadly weapon, which totally nullifies any preventive action or force a victim may take to ward off an assailant.

Along with teaching young children and women to skillfully defend themselves, it seems that a broader based attack against sexual assaults should be taken against the social and institutional factors that promote sexual violence in our society. Two additional areas should be addressed if we are to see a reduction and, hopefully, an elimination in sexual assaults in our society. First, we need to examine the male's gender role with its prescriptive aggressive element, especially aggression against women (Krulewitz and Kahn, 1983). Aggression and violence are still seen by many as an integral part of the male's gender role (Dittes, 1984; Doyle, 1983). One way to reduce sexual assault in our society would be to redefine the male gender role, incorporating nonaggressive or nonviolent elements rather than aggressiveness. Of course, many people would object to such a major change in the male role, fearing that our country would fall prey to its national enemies who may wish to attack a nation of nonaggressive men.

Another controversial change that would reduce the number of sexual assaults is an open attack on hard-core and violence-oriented pornography and the multi-million dollar business that supports it. First of all, we should dismiss the notion that only males find sexually explicit materials arousing. Research has found that men *as well as* women find various kinds of erotic material sexually stimulating (Fisher and Byrne, 1978). However, the pornography industry has mainly directed its sales to a male audience. Although some erotic material does not focus on violent sexual aggression, a large proportion of the male-oriented pornography that is sold in stores across our country portrays the female as the victim of physical and sexual assault (Dworkin, 1981; Lederer, 1980).

Researchers Neil Malamuth and Edward Donnerstein have found that exposure to violent pornography generally increases sexual arousal as well as negative attitudes toward women and favorable attitudes toward sexual assault (Donnerstein, 1980, 1983; Donnerstein and Hallam, 1978; Malamuth and Donnerstein, 1982; Malamuth and Spinner, 1980). Thus one possible way to reduce the sexual violence in our society against women would be to eliminate such material. However, those who oppose such a plan immediately bring up the issue of a person's First Amendment rights, which guarantee freedom of speech; such opposition, however, misinterprets the Constitution and its intent (Kaminer, 1980).

Would society be as accepting if various media presented graphic anti-Semitic portrayals of Jews being shoved into gas chambers or American Indians being shot for sport for their land? And yet many people support the multi-million dollar industry that shows women assaulted and maimed for the sake of sexual stimulation.

If our society is to rectify the age-old problem of unequal power between females and males, we need to challenge many of our behaviors, our attitudes, and our social institutions that continue to cast women in an inferior role. Until that day, the problem of inequality between the genders is everyone's concern.

SUMMARY

Interpersonal power entails the ability to achieve one's own goals by influencing others. In general, males tend to have a larger number of power bases—reward, coercive, expert, legitimate, and informational—than females have; females have greater referent power. Several differences have been found in how each gender influences others in terms of power strategies.

As a rule, males perceive themselves as having greater control over their lives than females do. This difference is borne out by finding males displaying an internal locus of control, whereas females are more likely to show an external locus of control pattern. As might be expected, having power affects a person in several ways, all of which come under the heading of the metamorphic effects of power. Power is also an integral feature of intimate relations. Studies generally find males holding more power in intimate relations than females hold.

Rape and sexual assault are extreme manifestations of power and domination of one person over another. There is considerable debate as to how best to end the increasing number of rapes in our society. The victimization of women in explicit pornography has been shown to increase sexual aggression among most men.

SUGGESTED READINGS

Holmstrom, L., & Burgess, A. (1983). *The victim of rape: Institutional reactions*. New Brunswick, NJ: Transaction Books.

Huston, T. (1983). Power. In H. Kelley et al. (Eds.), *Close relationships*. New York: W.H. Freeman, 169–219.

Kempe, R., & Kempe, C. (1984). *The common secret: Sexual abuse of children and adolescents*. San Francisco: W. H. Freeman.

Kipnis, D. (1976). *The powerholders*. Chicago: University of Chicago Press.

Lipman-Blumen, J. (1984). *Gender roles and power*. Englewood Cliffs, NJ: Prentice-Hall.

Lips, H. (1983). *Women, men and the psychology of power*. Englewood Cliffs, NJ: Prentice-Hall.

Russell, D. (1984). Sexual exploitation. Beverly Hills, CA: Sage.

Yaffe, M., & Nelson, E. (Eds.). (1982). *The influence of pornography on behavior*. New York: Academic Press.

Point/Counterpoint

The Continuing Debate over Power

Not everyone is willing to concede that males have more power than women. Some even agree with author George Gilder (1975, p. 13), who says that "Women, in fact, possess enormous power over men." Gilder doesn't deny that men usually have greater concrete resources, such as money; nevertheless, he believes that women have other more important power bases that overshadow and outweigh men's power bases. Gilder primarily argues that women's "enormous power" comes from their sexual superiority. Women not men, Gilder points out, have almost total control over the sexual and the erotic activities that define so much of human interplay. Gilder notes that in primitive societies men had their physical strength to counterbalance women's greater sexual powers. But today, when physical strength is almost meaningless, women have gained the upper hand in the power game. According to Gilder, if women were to gain equality with men in matters of social and personal power, women and men would not be equal; instead, women would be totally dominant, and society would suffer a type of "sexual suicide."

Of course, many disagree with Gilder's analysis of the power balance. An interesting perspective on this question can be found in Arnold Kahn's (1984) analysis of why so many men resist so strongly any notion of equality with women in the area of power. Kahn believes that control, or power, over women is an integral part of many men's self-definitions. Men, through the ages, have controlled women's lives, and this control has become part of their male role. Consequently, many men believe that their power over women makes them "real men"; if equality were to be realized, these men would lose their feeling of superiority over women and children (Mayes, 1979).

What do you think?

Reading

Author Lindsy Van Gelder interviewed some of the most powerful women in our country to gain some insight into what power means and how they use it. Clearly these women are "shakers and movers," and they know firsthand what power can do for an individual's self-concept.

Joan Ganz Cooney: President, Children's Television Workshop, New York; developer of "Sesame Street."

"I've been a boss, and I've also been bossed, and I'd be dishonest if I said that being the boss isn't better. I'll give you an example. A few years ago, I wanted to do a science show for children. There were people at CTW who wanted to abandon the project, but *I* was the one who was in the position to stand there and say, 'Are you telling me that the Children's Television Workshop *cannot* do this kind of show? I will *never* accept that!" ["3–2–1 Contact" went into its second-season production this fall.]

Ninfa Laurenzo: Tacos a la Ninfa's, Houston. She owns thirteen restaurants in three cities ($28 million in sales), served on the Houston MTA board, and was named "National Hispanic Businesswoman of the Year" by the U.S. Hispanic Chamber of Commerce.

"I suppose I do have power. There's a recognition that you have the ability to come up the ladder and put your business on a multi-million-dollar level, and you have the ability to talk to people and have them listen. But you have to carry it graciously, so graciously that you stay humble. My biggest thrill? Recently a theater group [Theater Under the Stars] here in Houston put on a play based on various events in my life: being a widow of mixed extraction, having my business burn down, struggling, being aggressive in a kind of way. Before the play, I had never perceived myself as *important*. On opening night I couldn't contain myself."

Donna Shalala: President of Hunter College of the City of New York. Also a member of the governing board of the American Stock Exchange, trustee of the Committee for Economic Development, and member of the New York Partnership.

"The way that I realized that I was 'powerful' was that in this job, I suddenly began to have *access* to powerful people. Before, when I was in Washington [as special assistant to the Secretary of Housing and Urban Develpment], I was *prominent*, but now *everybody* returns my phone calls. And I get invited to all the mainframe dinner parties in town. Of course, I take all this with a bit of a giggle. And I'm having the best time of my life. Don't let anybody tell you that power is just 'motivating' people—I 'motivated' people when I was a teacher. Power is having the mayor, city council president, and Secretary of Education show up at your inauguration."

Justice Joan Dempsey Klein: Administrative presiding justice, California Court of Appeal, Second Appellate District, and cofounder and past president of the National Association of Women Judges.

"Sometimes you do feel ambivalent about power. In a criminal case, it's profoundly humbling to realize that you're calling the shots on someone's freedom, their life. But after you become seasoned, you accept that. You can't possibly second-guess yourself, or you'd go mad, truly—you couldn't stay on the bench. You just judge each case and move on to the next.

Source: "Okay, you're in power; now what do you do?" by L. Van Gelder, 1982, December, *Ms*, pp. 41–42, 45–46, 76. Reprinted by permission of Lindsy Van Gelder.

"I think I've been helped to be confident about using power by the fact that I've been an athlete all my life—tennis, swimming, basketball, track, and other sports. It helps balance out that thing that people throw at you about being second best because you're a woman. I just never believed it."

Pat Russell: Los Angeles City Council member and president of the Southern California Association of Governments (SCAG).

"I don't think power is a dirty word. Politics *is* power. As head of SCAG—which does regional planning for the six southern California counties—I'm governing an area which, if it were a separate nation, would rank fifteenth in the world in gross national product. I mean, that's power.

"Part of exercising power is knowing when something is ready to happen. Sometimes you have to create the readiness. For example, when I was a city councilwoman in late 1969, the area I represented around our airport—LAX—was in terrible trouble. The airport was encroaching on the community, particularly in the case of one runway. People couldn't stay because of the noise, but they couldn't move away and get anything for their homes. The attitude of the city administrator and most of the city's business community was essentially 'you can't balk progress.'

"I had to go down in flames on this issue in the council several times—I just didn't have the support. So I started doing media interviews. What I learned, in the words of one of my colleagues, was that you can't just talk, you've got to get down in the trenches and *fight*. What I did was create a psychological climate in which the other members of the council found it more of a squeeze to be pro-airport than anti-airport. I got their support on a crucial vote to close the runway. The council didn't have the power to close the runway, but that vote in turn pushed the airport administration, which did have the power.

"It was pretty exciting!"

Patricia ("Tish") Nettleship: Cofounder, president, and chief executive officer of the

North Pacific Construction Company, Los Angeles—a $100 million business. She is vice-chair of the Industry Policy Advisory Committee on Trade Policy, and chair of a Commerce Department international trade policy task force.

"Yes, I do have power. The word used to have negative connotations for me, but I now perceive power as an extremely useful device to bring civilization forward. I'm not embarrassed by it. I feel that power is something people are born with. Some people walk into a room when they're five years old, and they have tremendous presence. It's an ability to make things happen, to create achievement.

"How does it feel to exercise power? There are two kinds of power that I can think of offhand. One is when you have the power to make yourself feel wonderful about what you're accomplishing. Tomorrow I'm going to Europe for three weeks [under the aegis of the Department of Commerce], doing a sort of whistle-stop tour of various cities where there may be general ill-feeling about the world market among our trading partners. I feel pretty confident that I have the power to change a few people's minds—and the net result will ultimately be major changes in the world economy.

"Another kind of experience is when you can use power to stop someone or something from frustrating you. I had an example of this today. My office had filled out a form somewhat incorrectly, and some bureaucrats were using this as an excuse to spin our wheels. They said it would take eight weeks to reprocess our application, which would mean that we wouldn't even be able to participate in the project. To make a long story short, I called the governor of the state involved, and asked him to help cut the red tape. It was *very* satisfying.

"My code of business ethics is this: you should never use power to get someone to do something illegal or wrong. But if you can use it to get someone to do their job faster and better . . . go ahead!"

Chapter 7

LANGUAGE AND COMMUNICATION

> *The feminist thinker who wishes to tackle the puzzles of power and take up the questions of meaning must consider the nature of language itself.*
>
> Jean B. Elshtain

Human language with its words and gestures has helped create a veritable split in the human family, a division between females and males. At one moment our communications smooth relations between the genders and the next they create an imbalance or asymmetry that shows in no uncertain terms the difference in power between women and men. Although language is essential for human interaction, it remains one of the most powerful forces buttressing the age-old inequalities between the genders and has helped to keep women and men separate and unequal.

In this chapter we will examine language and its role in the way the genders relate. We will begin by looking at how language generally favors the male while disparaging the female. We will then look at some of the ways males and females use language differently. And finally, we will focus on nonverbal communication to see how females and males communicate subtle gender differences with respect to dominance and status.

THE SPOKEN WORD

Human language is one of the most distinctive features of the human race. With its subtle variations, language allows us to express our deepest feelings as well as our loftiest thoughts. With language, two people can become more intimate or can separate forever. Language is not, however, gender-neutral. Language divides, separates, and differentiates women from men. Language reinforces sexist gender stereotypes by elevating men and denigrating women.

In our analysis of language, we will discover that many of the commonly accepted gender stereotypes are baseless. For example, who has not heard one of the many variations of the story of the husband sitting quietly at a table while his wife talks on endlessly? As we will see, the image of the ceaselessly talking wife henpecking her silent mate is more myth than fact. Although these gender stereotypes are unfounded and should be put to rest (Hilpert et al., 1975), the real importance of looking at gender and language is in finding just how power or, better, the imbalance of power affects the words we use as well as how each gender communicates (Elshtain, 1982). Women "work" harder at communication than men do, but their payoff is less. Such an imbalance can be attributed in part to the differences in power that males and females have in their relationships (Henley, 1977).

One of the many benefits of having power is not needing to "work" as hard in carrying on a conversation with someone who is less powerful. A powerful person may interrupt a less powerful person with little or no thought about showing poor manners. Also, a powerful person need not pay as much attention to the conversation of one with little power, but the one with little power had better pay attention to what the powerful person has to say. The more powerful person in a two-person relationship determines to a large extent when an interaction will occur, how long it will last, and what topics will be discussed.

Pamela Fishman's (1978) research shows that in situations between women and men, women generally exert more effort to carry on conversations than men do. Fishman studied the everyday give-and-take conversations of three married couples who tape-recorded their daily conversations over a four- to fourteen-day period. Basically, Fishman found the wives had to "work harder" to initiate and carry on a simple conversation with their husbands. The wives initiated significantly more conversations than their husbands did. (If you've ever tried to get others to talk while they seemed preoccupied, you can appreciate the notion of "working at" making a conversation succeed.) For the most part, the husbands gave only perfunctory replies in response to their wives' attempts at initiating conversations. On those rare occasions when the husbands initiated conversations, their wives responded more fully, and generally conversations ensued. Husbands, it seemed, had more attentive listeners than wives did! Another area where the wives and husbands in Fishman's study differed was in the numbers of questions asked or statements made. Fishman found that wives asked significantly more questions, whereas husbands made almost twice as many statements. What does "question asking" and "statement making" have to do with power? For one thing, when you ask a question, you are somewhat assured that your conversational partner will respond in some fashion, if only to give a one-word answer. But if you make a statement, your conversational partner need not say anything or may only give a perfunctory reply such as "So?" Fishman concluded that wives, at least those in her study, had to ask significantly more questions to assure a flow of communication, whereas the husbands relied on statements in the majority of cases, which the wives responded to in ways that assured a continued conversation. Columnist John Leo (1984, p. 98) succinctly summed up women's and men's conversational patterns by noting, "For the average woman, having a civil conversation with a male is like playing tennis with a partner who is asleep."

When it comes to communicating, we can suggest that a powerful person can use statements to a great extent, reflecting a command of the conversational flow; the less powerful person must rely on questions as a means to get a conversation started. Thus, the research of Fishman and others finds that men and not women usually display communication strategies that suggest that men direct the flow, timing, and even the topics of most male-female conversations (Spender, 1980; Zimmerman and West, 1975). It seems that men show their power even in the simple discourse that takes place between them and the women with whom they are involved.

Before we deal with some of the different ways that males and females communicate verbally, let's take up the crucial issue of sexism in language and learn just how our language sometimes pictures the female as the invisible and often less noteworthy portion of the human race.

Linguistic Sexism

Recently, I overheard a couple having a rather heated conversation at a nearby table in a restaurant. The man was asking the woman why she was so insistent on being addressed as "Ms." at the office rather than "Miss." The woman took pains to explain that she didn't like having a title that defined her in terms of her relationship or lack of relationship with a man and that the distinction did not amount to a trivial matter (Feather et al., 1979; Heilman, 1975). But the woman's arguments fell on deaf ears; when I left they still were locked in a debate over the merits of "Ms." as opposed to "Miss" or "Mrs." But what's in a word anyway? Why the big deal over what you call or don't call a person as long as it isn't abusive or obscene?

But words are important! Words, those written scribbles on paper and spoken utterances emanating from people's mouths, are some of the most powerful and richly endowed creations of the human spirit. Surely, everyone recalls Edward Bulwer-Lytton's famous statement that "The pen is mightier than the sword." Lytton's statement is no mere rhetoric, not when we consider how powerful language is and the ways that powerful people use language. Those who have power know this fact well. For as historian Sheila Rowbotham (1973) points out, language "is carefully guarded by the superior people because it is one of the means through which they conserve their supremacy" (p. 32). Words are extremely important. Words give definition and meaning to reality. How we see the world and the things in it are to a great extent structured by the types and numbers of words we use. Our world is populated by both females and males, and yet the English language not only favors the male but affords males greater power over females. Males, by their control of language, can name, and by naming they make valid their existence. Again, Rowbotham (1973) states the case for language being a potent vehicle of men's power: "Language conveys a certain power. It is one of the instruments of domination. . . . The language of theory—removed language—only expresses a reality experienced by the oppressors. It speaks only for their world, for their point of view" (p. 32). Consequently, males exert an even greater degree of power over females because of language. To make the point that our language and the way we speak it contains sexist elements, we will discuss a special form of sexism known as **linguistic sexism,** or the fact that sexist ideology is perpetuated and reinforced through the content of a language (Nilsen et al., 1977). Linguistic sexism in the English language takes one of three distinct forms, namely, how the English language *ignores* the female, how it *defines* the female, and last, how it *deprecates* the female.

Ignoring the Female   Although females make up almost 52 percent of the human race, they are systematically left out in our daily speech. In fact, when we talk about our species as a whole, we talk about "man" or "mankind" and not "woman" or "womankind." However, since females are the majority, it would be perfectly logical to use "womankind" rather than "mankind" as the generic word meaning human race. Furthermore, we are taught that when we read the word "he," it supposedly is a pronoun robust enough to include females as well as males in its definition. The English language takes what psychologist Wendy Martyna (1980) calls a "he/man" approach.

> The "he/man" approach to language involves the use of male terms to refer both specifically to males and generically to human beings (*A Man for All Seasons* is specific; "No man is an island" is generic). The he/man approach has received most attention in current debates on sexist language, not only because of its ubiquity but also because of its status as one of the least subtle of sexist forms. In linguistic terms, some have characterized the male as an unmarked, the female as a marked, category. The unmarked category represents both maleness and femaleness, while the marked represents femaleness only. Thus the male in Lionel Tiger's *Men in Groups* excludes the female in Phyllis Chesler's *Women and Madness*, while the male in Thomas Paine's *Rights of Man* is supposed to encompass the female of Mary Wollstonecraft's *Vindication of the Rights of Woman*. (p. 483)

But the "he/man" generics don't always live up to their name. When generic pronouns (e.g., he, his, him) are used in spoken or printed forms, more often than not, the listener or reader conjures up a picture of a male, not an image of *both* a male and a female (Cole et al., 1983; Key, 1975b; Stericker, 1981). For example, what comes to your mind when you read, "Every student in the classroom did his best on the test." Does your mind really conjure up a scene of little boys *and* little girls all working feverishly away on a test? Or, do you unconsciously imagine a room full of boys at some all-male prep school bent over their desks with pencils in hand staring at their test papers? In several studies investigating the impact of the generic pronoun "he" in textbooks, it was found that most of the antecedents in the texts referred to males, and not males and females (Bertilson et al., 1982). In yet another study, students thought of males rather than males *and* females when they read the purported generic "he," "him," or "his" (Schneider and Hacker, 1973). The use of the generic pronouns can, in fact, misrepresent reality. An example of such linguistic doublethink is provided by sociologist Joan Huber (1976b) when she notes that in one sociology text she found the statement: "The more education an individual attains, the better his occupation is likely to be, and the more money he is likely to earn." The use of the generic pronouns in this statement (i.e., "his" and "he") is misleading. In fact, this statement sometimes holds true *only* for males.

Watching our words may seem like a small concession and one requiring little effort. Rather than "mankind," why not "humanity," "human beings," or just plain "people?" Rather than something being described as "man-made," why not "artificial," or "synthetic?" As we have already noted, words are powerful symbols, and ignoring over half the human race is not only sexist but totally unrealistic of the world we live in (Burr et al., 1972; Fillmer and Haswell, 1977). For too long, women have existed as the "other" in a second-class position, and language has contributed greatly to this perception (de Beauvoir, 1952).

Defining the Female   How many times have you heard a woman referred to as "Bill's wife/daughter/widow?" Defining the female in terms of her relationship to a man is one of those commonly accepted customs that most people rarely question. And yet more and more women today are keeping their maiden names after marriage. But in the first place, why should a woman give up her surname once she marries, outside of keeping up with the ancient patriarchal tradition of the woman being seen as yet another possession or property of her husband?

What does this change in name signify? If a name is part of one's identity, then changing one's name implies (if not requires) that the person change or lose some aspect of his or her identity to some degree. When a woman marries and takes on her husband's name, she loses a powerful symbolic tie to her past identity: her name. Leo Kanowitz (1969) sees the change in a woman's name upon marriage as thus:

> The probable effects of this unilateral name change upon the relations between the sexes, though subtle in character, are profound. In a very real sense, the loss of a woman's surname represents the destruction of an important part of her personality and its submersion in that of her husband. . . . This name change is consistent with the characterization of coverture as "the old common-law fiction that the husband and wife are one . . . [which] has worked out in reality to mean that the one is the husband." (p. 41)

Men, of course, do not change their names, and thus they continue to have a degree of continuity with their pre-marriage identity. By taking her husband's name, the married woman to a large extent changes her self-identity as well as her social status to include, in the words of sociologist Talcott Parsons, "[t]he woman's fundamental status [as] that of her husband's wife, the mother of his children." She now becomes, to many people's way of thinking, "Mrs. James Smith," dropping even her given female name in the process. For all those who think this is "making mountains out of mole hills," ask them if changing the groom's name to that of the bride's would be an acceptable practice? Chances are that most would think the groom changing his name to that of the bride's would be different somehow. Different yes, but it would also indicate that he was no longer considered the first in the relationship, the one whose name the couple takes as their identity. But isn't that what happens to most married women? They become subsumed under their husbands, and their name change signifies as much. As we have said, a person's name is part of her or his very identity. And tradition holds that a woman's identity must be submerged into that of her husband's. Some married couples, however, refuse to comply with this patriarchal convention (see box 7.1).

Deprecating the Female   Throughout history the female has been deprecated and abused by the pronouncements of men. Listen to just a small sampling of some of the deprecations heaped on women by some men.

> There is a good principle which created order, light, and man, and an evil principle which created chaos, darkness, and woman.   Pythagoras

> The five worst infirmities that afflict the female are indocility, discontent, slander, jealousy, and silliness. . . . Such is the stupidity of woman's character, that it is incumbent upon her, in every particular, to distrust herself and to obey her husband.   *Confucian Marriage Manual*

> Most women have no character at all.   Alexander Pope

> My secretary is a lovable slave.   Morris Ernest

The list could go on and on, but these few samples should give a fair example of the kinds of words used in conjunction with the female. Words such as "evil," "chaos," "darkness," "stupidity," and "slave" are anything but flattering. Even when we examine some parallel terms, we find a less than subtle deprecation of the female, for example, "mister-mistress" or "bachelor-spinster." When we note the numbers of words indicative of sexual promiscuity, we find well over 200 such words to describe a sexually licentious female (e.g., whore, prostitute, harlot, slut, courtesan, concubine, tramp, etc.), but we only find just over 20 words to describe lustful men (satyr, dirty old man, etc.) (Stanley, 1977). Can it be that men somehow are more moral than women as the word-count would have us believe?

Box 7.1

Taking Your Own Name

Women and men who opt today for marriage have a wealth of choices before them in the matter of choosing and changing last names. They can both keep their original names (and leave the suspicion in their landlord's mind that they really didn't get married), but if they decide to have children, they will find that the problem of deciding on a last name has only been postponed, not resolved. When that time comes, they could give the baby his last name (and leave her a minority in the family) or they could give the baby her last name (permanently alienating his parents and leaving the suspicion in the minds of the hospital staff that the baby is out-of-wedlock). Choosing between two names is not easy. Because of these considerations, the option of using hyphenated last names is becoming increasingly popular.

Here's how it generally works today. When Mary Smith marries Jon Jones, she can begin to use the name Smith-Jones as her surname and she thereby maintains a portion of her original identity. This is the most frequent way that hyphenated names are used. But her action alone is really not much of an improvement over our present system. If Jon does not also change his name, then when she is out with Mr. Jones, people, will keep calling her Mrs. Jones or Mary Jones, and their children will undoubtably end up being named Jones. The situation where Jon and Mary both use the hyphenated name Smith-Jones after marriage has much to recommend it, being both equitable and fairly simple, but looking forward to the future, one can easily see that real problems loom for the next generation. When Judy Smith-Jones, Mary and Jon's daughter, gets ready to marry Darryl Thomas-Black, the son of equally liberated parents, what will be their family name? Will their daughter be named Cathy Thomas-Black-Smith-Jones? And her daughter? The apparently simple solution of hyphenated last names, which solves the problem for Mary Smith and Jon Jones, can become a real headache for their children and grandchildren.

The Solution

There is a simple way of transmitting last names which avoids these problems. It has the advantage of being easy to start using, easy to continue and completely non-sexist, in that the direct male and female lines of descent carry equal weight. Here's how it works. When Mary Smith and Jon Jones marry, they adopt either Smith-Jones, or Jones-Smith as their family name. The choice could be aesthetic, alphabetical, or by the flip of a coin. They give this name to their children, Brian Smith-Jones

Source "Taking your own name" by Catherine Lilly, 1984, *New Directions for Women, 13*, No. 6, p. 11. Reprinted by permission of Catherine Lilly.

Box 7.1

Continued

and Judy Smith-Jones. The children are instructed to remember which name is their female surname (Smith, from their Mother) and which is their male surname (Jones, from their Father). When Judy marries, she will take her female surname, Smith, and join it to the male surname of her husband (or to his only surname, if his parents had not yet gotten around to hyphenating) to make a new family name. Judy's daughters will pass on Smith to their children and her sons will pass on their Father's name. On the other hand, Judy's brother Brian Smith-Jones will use Jones, his male surname, to create a new family name with his wife when he marries and his sons will pass on Jones while his daughters pass on the name they have inherited from their Mother. Following this system, the family name created by a couple for themselves and their children combines the most important surnames from each parent, the Mother's female surname and the Father's male surname.

What makes this new system less sexist than our present system is this: Under the present system a man—say Jon Jones—carries a family name that is the same as that of his forefathers and which identifies them as a family. For example we have Jon Jones, son of Steve Jones, grandson of Arnold Jones, great-grandson of Edward Jones, etc. But in the present system a woman does not share a name with her fore-mothers. Mary Smith may be the daughter of Dianne Smith, who is the daughter of Julia Collins, who was the daughter of Anna Hamilton, etc. How many women today know the maiden name of their maternal great-grand-mother? But every man knows the surname of his paternal great-grand-father—it's the same as his! Under our present system, the female line of descent has been erased and women today only carry the name of father or husband.

This new system of passing on hyphenated last names equalizes the male and female lines of descent. Using it, Mary Smith-Jones' daughter would be, for example, Judy Smith-Brown, and her grand-daughter would be Eileen Smith-Golsalves, and her great-grand-daughter would be Norma Smith-Lehman. In each generation, the female surname Smith is passed on and an ancestral line of women with a common family name is created. Of course, exactly the same thing happens to Jon Jones' male descendants, who will all carry the name Jones. Can't you imagine the eager anticipation with which a mother and grand-mother might await the birth of a daughter who would carry on their family name? Imagine the pride of a daughter carrying a name which has been distinguished by the women whose genes she carries!

Box 7.1

How to Get Started

Unmarried woman: If your name is Mary Smith, you have two options. The simplest way is that you can use the name Smith as your female surname, combine it with your husband's name to make a hyphenated family surname when and if you get married and instruct your daughters to pass on the name Smith to their children and your sons to pass on their Father's name. On the other hand, together with your Mother, sisters, maternal grandmother and other female relatives, you can create a new female surname (since Smith belongs actually to your Father). If the new name is, say, Flower, change your name to Mary Flower-Smith and use Flower to form a family name when you marry.

Married woman with no children: Suppose Mary Smith has already married Jon Jones and changed her name to Mary Jones. You need not change your name again, but when your children are born, name them Smith-Jones (or Flower-Jones) and instruct your daughters to pass on Smith or Flower and your sons to pass on Jones.

Married woman with children: If you are a married woman who in the traditional manner carries her husband's last name (say Mary Jones, wife of Jon Jones) and your children are also named Jones, it's still not too late to begin the process. Here is your strategy. Decide, together with your daughters (and sisters and mother, if possible) on a female surname. If you decide to create a new name, say Flower, you and your daughters should begin to use Flower-Jones as your surname and Flower should be passed on as a female surname. Or, your daughters can begin the process, using either Jones or some newly created female surname, as described above in the situation for unmarried women.

Men: Since men already carry a male surname, which they would pass on to their children both under our present system and the new system, there is no need for them to change their names. When they marry, they should consider forming a new hypenated family name by joining their family name, which is a male surname, to their wife's female surname.

Whatever your stage in life, as a woman today you have the unique opportunity to create new female surnames and to teach your daughters how to pass them on. These will be the female family names that could survive for hundreds of years. Choose well!

We find the female deprecated even when people are asked to judge the merit of some production (e.g., a painting or piece of writing); people perceive the quality or value of an object as less if the author or creator is female. For example, researchers have found that a production bearing a female's name is generally seen as being of lesser merit than the *same* piece bearing a male's signature (Paludi and Bauer, 1983; Pheterson et al., 1971). Also, such supposedly innocuous female euphemisms as "girl" or "gal" have been found to cause people to look unfavorably at the woman being described (Dayhoff, 1983; Lipton and Hershaft, 1984).

Thus many of the words used to describe women are highly negative and deprecatory (Allen, 1984). When a young girl reads of what men think of her gender, what must she learn from such invectives? In the final analysis, women are the victims of an age-old system of verbal deprecation that forces many to think little of themselves and their abilities.

It seems clear that the English language treats women in less than an equitable fashion. And yet this should come as no surprise when we note that language, like most other features of our society, is but one ". . . symbolic system closely tied to a patriarchal social structure" (Kramer et al., 1978). Males have played the largest role in creating language, and their views of women have been translated far more faithfully than many may wish to acknowledge. We live in a sexist and patriarchal society, and our language portrays these ideologies well. Learning to watch our language is a cliché most of us were taught as children. If avoiding offensive language is something we value, why then can we not watch our language even more closely lest it offend over half of the human race?

Verbal Outputs

Do women and men talk differently? To many people's way of thinking, the answer is yes (Leo, 1984). Many would argue that speech patterns as well as topics can be divided into "feminine and masculine speech" (see box 7.2).

Those who study language patterns have noted that, in general, masculine speech seems direct and powerful while feminine speech appears indirect and powerless (Lakoff, 1973, 1975). Robin Lakoff, for one, has noted that women's speech patterns contain significantly more tag questions, qualifiers, and longer request phrases, all of which convey a sense of powerlessness in their conversations with others. Various empirical studies have confirmed Lakoff's intuitive analysis of the differences between women's and men's speech patterns (Crosby et al., 1982; Kemper, 1984). Several studies have found that people who use "feminine speech patterns" are perceived as less competent and less convincing than those who don't use such speech patterns, regardless of whether the speaker is male or female (Erickson et al., 1978; Newcombe and Arnoff, 1979). Those speech patterns

Box 7.2

Masculine and Feminine Speech

Examine the answers to the following questions and compare those on the left to those on the right. Which do you think is more likely to be spoken by a man? by a woman? (Erickson, Lind, Johnson, & O'Barr, 1978.)

Then you went next door?

And then I went   Yes.
immediately next door,
yes.

Approximately how long did you stay before the ambulance arrived?

Oh, it seems like it was   *Twenty minutes. Long*
about, uh, twenty minutes.   *enough to help get Mrs.*
Just long enough to help   *Davis straightened out.*
my friend Mrs. Davis,
you know, get
straightened out.

How long have you lived in Durham?

All my life, really.   *All my life.*

You're familiar with the streets?

Oh yes.   *Yes.*

You know your way around?

Yes, I guess I do.   *Yes.*

If you thought the responses on the left were more likely to come from a woman and that the responses on the right were more likely to come from a man, then your judgments agree with those of many others who have suggested gender-related differences in language use (e.g., Lakoff, 1975). Following are some examples of the more frequently suggested differences between men's and women's language.

Women fuss and   Men show anger and
complain: rage:

"Dear me, I shut the   *"Damn! I shut the*
window on my finger."   *window on my finger."*

Women use tag   Men avoid tag
questions: questions:

"It's a good day for   *"It's a good day for*
swimming, isn't it?"   *swimming."*

Women use more   Men use fewer
intensifiers: intensifiers:

"This lecture is so very   *"This lecture is*
confusing."   *confusing."*

Women soften   Men do not soften
commands: commands:

"Would you please shut   *"Shut the door!"*
the door?"

"Al, you're a sweetheart. Listen, gotta
run. Call me Friday for a quick bite.
Beautiful! Love to Fern and the kids.
Ciao!

Bill Basso/*Esquire Magazine.*

commonly associated with females are generally perceived by others to be
the speech of a powerless and incompetent person; the purported male
speech patterns more often convey a sense of power and competence.

Let's move on now from our discussion of perceived power and masculine and feminine speech and focus on some of the areas where we find
evidence to suggest that some differences do, in fact, exist between the ways
females and males talk. Yet before we begin, we should be mindful of a
cautionary note with respect to the following discussion. "There has been
a tendency in this field," writes Cheris Kramer, Barrie Thorne, and Nancy
Henley (1978), ". . . to emphasize findings of difference between the sexes
more than findings of no difference." These authors go on to say that

> Some researchers who initially hypothesized sex differences did not find
> them, but such research is less often reported and circulated than studies
> which point to differences, regarded as more "significant." Researchers may
> tend to presume and overreport differences rather than similarities between
> the sexes because our culture is infused with stereotypes which polarize
> females and males. . . . What is notable is how few expected sex differences
> have been firmly substantiated by empirical studies of actual speech. (p. 640)

Before we accept too quickly those few verbal differences reported in the literature as universal findings, we would do well to remember that they may be the exception more than the rule. We should bear in mind also that even when men and women use identical words with the same pronunciation and converse with similar speech patterns, those listening may still perceive and evaluate what they hear in very different ways (Addington, 1970; Condry and Condry, 1976). Most people hold certain assumptions about what women and men do and what they should say. Again, as Cheris Kramer and her colleagues (1978) note, "Women's speech is conceptually and socially, if not in fact, separate from men's speech" (p. 647).

Talk, Talk, Talk   Few stereotypes are as pervasive about men and women in our culture as those that portray women engaged in endless chatter while men sit by in painful silence. According to many men, they must surely suffer from some exotic auditory disorder because they so often find themselves victims of their wives' seemingly constant verbal output. Contrary to popular belief and all those morning-after tales spread by some men, the fact is that men, not women, talk more. In study after study, the evidence is rather conclusive: men are the more talkative members of the human species (Aries, 1976; Edelsky, 1981; Smith, 1979).

In one of the earliest studies of husbands and wives and their communication patterns, Fred Strodtbeck (1951) found that husbands out-talked their wives and not vice versa. Using both married and unmarried couples, other researchers found similar evidence that showed that men are more "gabby" than women (Hilpert et al., 1975). In one of the most frequently cited studies of verbal output, Marjorie Swacker (1975) asked women and men to tape record their impressions of different paintings. The participants were told to take as much time as they needed to describe the paintings they saw. Females talked for an average of just over three minutes; males rattled on for an average of over thirteen minutes. In fact, three of the men in Swacker's study talked on until the tape ran out (i.e., a thirty-minute tape). Finally, Swacker had to bring these three "art critics" tactfully to a halt. When researchers Barbara and Gene Eakins (1978) tape-recorded a college faculty meeting, they also found the male faculty surpassing their female colleagues for verbal output. Not every study, however, has found men more talkative than women. Some have found that women talk as much (Piliavin and Martin, 1978)! Overall, we suggest that when it comes to verbal output, males win the "gabby" award hands down. Even when women do get a chance to get a word in edgewise, they are more apt to be interrupted by men than vice versa, attesting to the power difference between males and females in general (Zimmerman and West, 1975). Again, the rules of conversation allow the powerful person to interrupt the powerless person as we see between mothers and children, the one conversational relation where women are seen in a more powerful position (West and Zimmerman, 1977).

Figure 7.1 Many people believe that females talk more than males, but research shows the opposite to be true.

Talking about Ourselves   We often hear that most people's favorite topic is themselves. In everyday life, it seems that no matter what people talk about, school, work, family, and so on, they more often than not get the discussion to center on their personal experiences. Talking about oneself may be extremely pleasing and even healthy (Jourard, 1964), but social scientists have found that males and females differ in the amount of personal information they share with others, as well as with whom they share this information.

The late Sidney Jourard suggested the term *self-disclosure* to indicate when people share personal or intimate information about themselves with others. Jourard, along with several colleagues, found that males usually disclosed less about their personal feelings than females did (Jourard, 1971). Sociologist Mirra Komarovsky (1964) found that male blue-collar workers, for example, had special difficulty in disclosing personal information about themselves and were also uncomfortable in listening to others' self-disclosures. Komarovsky (1976) later studied male college students and found them to be more self-disclosing than her blue-collar sample, but the college students still limited their self-disclosures primarily to women—girl friends and mothers—and not to other men.

The pattern of male resistance to self-disclosure has been found in laboratory studies as well (Axel, 1979; Gerdes et al., 1981). It is interesting that women, who generally exhibit more self-disclosing information to a wider range of people than men do, report that they like others who self-disclose to them, whereas men do not (Petty and Mirels, 1981). Thus there seems to be some empirical evidence to support the constant request of many women that the men in their lives open up more and share their feelings with them. Women, so the research suggests, would actually like the self-disclosing man more than one who keeps everything to himself. Men, however, appear to be somewhat uncomfortable when another discloses too much. Among many men, especially those who hold traditional attitudes about gender roles, the act of disclosing personal material is interpreted as a sign of weakness, and men shun any sign of weakness for fear of appearing effeminate (Lombardo and Lavine, 1981). Even though men talk more than women, they talk less about those intimate and personal matters that for reasons unknown they believe better left unsaid. However, males may exceed females in disclosing personal information in opposite-sex relationships in order to control the development of the relationships (Derlega et al., 1984). Some males, it seems, use self-disclosure as a strategy to influence the way females feel about them.

Communication Strategies

If women have less power than men in most situations, we should not be surprised to find that women's speech patterns are often filled with words that weaken their messages. A person with power may speak directly, make commands, state a direct request, and avoid excessive words. In nearly every instance, this describes the verbal or communication strategies of the male. Let's highlight just four different communication strategies to see some common differences in how women and men speak and the effects these different strategies have on the perception of the speaker's power.

Tag Questions A *tag question* is a very special hybrid verbal creature. A tag question is partly a statement and partly a question. For example, if I were to say, "Jimmy Carter was a fine president, wasn't he?" Here we have a statement, "Jimmy Carter was a fine president," and a tag-along question, "wasn't he?" When someone tags a question onto a statement, we might infer that they are just being polite by asking for our opinion on the subject addressed in the statement. And many times, a tag question does just that: it shows a degree of politeness and consideration for another's idea on the subject of the initial statement. But on the other hand, the tag-along question at the end of a statement may make the statement seem weaker, less assertive, and less commanding. For example, if I were to say, "I think arms control would be good for world peace, don't you?" Here you may think that I am somewhat less sure of my idea of how to attain world peace because I appear to be asking for your approval of my statement by asking "don't you." If I believe strongly enough in my idea about world peace, I probably will not need to ask for your support or approval.

Thus in some situations, tag questions may be seen as showing that the people who use them are unsure or even afraid to assert their own opinions or to stand up for their own ideas in the face of possible rejection. One young, perceptive woman analyzed her own use of tag questions in the following way.

> I often say to my boyfriend, "That's a pretty good album, isn't it?" I suppose I put it that way because I don't want to put my tastes on the line and commit myself like I would if I announced, "That's a good album." Then he could contradict me and say, "No, I don't think the arrangements are good." By tailing a question to my statement, I don't come on so strong and I'm putting part of the judgment on his shoulders. Since I don't stick my neck out, I don't lose much. In fact, if he violently dislikes the album I can always say, "Oh, I didn't think so anyway. That's why I asked." (quoted in Eakins and Eakins, 1978, p. 41)

Although there is very little empirical research on the use of tag questions in mixed-sex relationships, Robin Lakoff (1973) suggests on the basis of her intuitive analysis of tag questions that females are more likely to use them when discussing their personal feelings. For example, "I don't feel like going to the movies tonight, do you?" is the kind of tag question that Lakoff suggests is more common in women's speech than in men's. If Lakoff's hypothesis is correct, and there has been some supportive research for it (Crosby et al., 1982), we may infer that the female's greater tentativeness in strongly expressing her opinions or beliefs may be partially the result of the power difference between women and men. This is one area of verbal output that needs further study to determine just how prevalent tag questions are in women's speech as compared to men's speech.

Qualifiers A *qualifier* is a word or words that blunt or soften a statement. Take, for example, the direct statement, "Jones is a dead-beat!" No question about it, the person who makes such a statement is putting forth his or her idea in no uncertain terms. But what of the statement, "Well, ah, I think Jones is a dead-beat," or "I may be wrong about it but I think Jones is a dead-beat." What we have in these last two statements are watered-down statements about Jones. In the first we hear "Well, ah," and the statement about Jones. Using such qualifiers reveals tentativeness and uncertainty. Even more tentative is the second statement, which has a disclaimer preceding the statement: "I may be wrong about it but . . ." In general, the scant research findings on the use of qualifiers finds women slightly more likely to use them in their speech than men (Eakins and Eakins, 1978; Pearson, 1985).

Lengthening of Requests As we all know, you can make a request of someone in several different ways. A drill instructor may simply say "Attention!" Another person may say "Will you please pay attention?" Which one of these two requests seems to be more direct, more forceful, and more in command? Of course, the one-word request, "Attention," does the job in the most direct and powerful way. Adding more words—"will you please pay"—reduces the impact of the request. Again the research is slight and mostly based on poorly controlled observations, but it shows that women tend to use longer requests in their speech than men do (Eakins and Eakins, 1978).

Fillers   *Fillers* are those words or phrases like *you know, ah, uhm, let me see, well,* and *oh.* Again, little research has been done on fillers, but according to the research that is available, females are more apt to use fillers in their conversations than males are (Eakins and Eakins, 1978; Pearson, 1985). Females use fewer fillers in female-female conversations than in female-male conversations. This may suggest that women are more comfortable in conversing with other women than with men.

Females may be somewhat more likely to use tag questions, qualifiers, longer requests, and fillers because they are aware of the power imbalance in gender relationships with men, which contributes to their use of communications strategies that weaken or dilute their messages.

NONVERBAL COMMUNICATIONS

Obviously, people differ in their verbal abilities and skills. Some speak eloquently while others stumble and grope through their everyday speech. In some areas women and men differ in their verbal patterns. It should not, therefore, come as a surprise to find that men and women also differ in some of their nonverbal communications as well. In this section, we will first look at the research evidence that males and females differ in the way in which and the frequency with which they express their emotions. We shall note also that females are generally better at expressing or sending nonverbal messages as well as receiving others' nonverbal messages. Then we will look at several specific areas of nonverbal patterns where the genders differ, namely eye contact, touch, and body posture. As we will see, the areas of nonverbal communication provide yet another fascinating study of how females and males differ with respect to communication styles.

Emotions and Gender

Most men can remember their boyhood days when one of the worst insults one could hurl at another little boy was to call him a "cry baby." Little boys aren't supposed to cry, aren't supposed to show fears, aren't supposed to act like, like "little girls," of course (Doyle, 1983). Little boys grow up to be big boys, and for most, the lessons of childhood seem to take root. In everyday life, one isn't shocked to see a woman cry when she feels pain, anger, or is upset. But what do we see when men are upset or in pain? Most men will not cry; that would be "feminine." Men are more apt to show anger rather than tears when they get upset (Pleck, 1976). Men who cry or show some sign of hurt and pain are apt to be branded as weak or effeminate.

There is no concrete evidence that females and males experience different emotions, but there is considerable experiential evidence in all of our lives to suggest that women and men differ, more often than not, in how they express their emotions and what emotions they feel free enough to express in public.

Senders and Receivers

Have you ever known a person who seemed to know what you were feeling even before you mentioned a word? A person who seemed to know your feelings and possibly made you a bit uncomfortable with such insight into your personal life? Chances are that person was a female, and you may have said that she possessed something many people call "female intuition." The idea that women possess a sixth sense may strike some as merely so much hokum, but there is growing evidence that females are more adept in some aspects of nonverbal communications than males (Hall, 1978, 1979; Mayo and Henley, 1981). In fact, females seem more able to express their emotions or feelings nonverbally than men (Sabatelli et al., 1980, 1982). *Encoding* is the term used to refer to this ability. Also, there is evidence that females are more proficient at evaluating or judging others' nonverbal messages, or what is referred to as *decoding* (Buck, 1976).

But how can we explain the female's purported better skills in such matters? As we noted in a previous chapter, the gender stereotypes for males and females differ in several areas that are related to nonverbal skills. The male stereotype contains elements such as instrumentality and control; the female stereotype involves elements such as expressivity, supportiveness, and interpersonal sensitivity (Broverman et al., 1972; Spence and Helmreich, 1978). Because these gender-related stereotypic differences have become part of our cultural norms, there is a strong possibility that parents and other significant socializing agents encourage female and male children differentially with respect to these traits' expressions. For example, little girls may be reinforced to be more emotionally expressive than little boys are. In fact, there is some evidence showing that differential parental treatment may affect a child's nonverbal ability (LaFrance and Carmen, 1980). Thus it may not be that females possess anything as mysterious as a sixth sense at all, but rather that their upbringing may influence them to develop a slightly better ability in certain nonverbal skills.

The idea that early socialization of children plays a role in the female's generally more skillful use and interpretation of nonverbal cues has received some empirical support. In a series of studies conducted by psychologist Miron Zuckerman and several colleagues (et al., 1981, 1982), it was found that females or males who score high on so-called feminine traits are better at sending nonverbal messages than males or females who score high on so-called masculine traits. Specifically, these researchers found that femininity scores positively correlated with one's ability at sending both auditory and facial cues. We must keep in mind that these results did not find females *per se* better at sending nonverbal messages, but those who scored high in feminine traits (i.e., androgynous and feminine females and androgynous and feminine males). Males who are sensitive and emotionally expressive are just as good at sending nonverbal messages as sensitive and emotionally expressive females are. In yet another study, males who scored androgynous were found to be more expressive of their feelings than those males who scored very high only in masculine traits (Narus and Fischer, 1982). These studies indicate that females don't possess a sixth sense by virtue of their biological sex, but rather because of upbringing that encourages certain traits.

The evidence is fairly clear that women in general or those with feminine traits appear better at sending nonverbal messages, but the research is somewhat ambiguous about which gender has the edge in interpreting nonverbal messages (Schneider and Schneider-Düker, 1984).

Eye Contact

When two people look at each other, there can be several messages that can be inferred from such nonverbal behavior. If the "eyes are the mirror of the soul" as one adage suggests, then we might expect that *eye contact* can be a very powerful nonverbal message. When researchers videotaped women and men in conversations and then timed the amount of eye contact between the participants, the results are fairly straightforward. Females generally show more social eye contact than males, meaning that in conversations between same-sex and opposite-sex pairs, females will look at the other more than males will (Aiello, 1972; Mehrabian, 1971). Eye contact may be linked to a person's expression of affection or just wanting to develop a relationship with another. According to the research, women tend to show greater eye contact and display longer gazes at others than men do (Russo, 1975).

Another form of eye contact, however, can imply aggression and is usually known as *staring*. Most women tend to look away when they notice they are the target of someone else's stare. The reason for such avoidance may be linked to the idea that staring is often interpreted as an aggressive or even sexual nonverbal message (Exline, 1971).

Touch

Touching another person has been thought to be one of the most powerful means of suggesting status or dominance in a dyad. For example, most people would find it acceptable for a manager to touch the shoulder of a subordinate, but for a subordinate to touch the shoulder of a manager is another situation altogether. Touching another is one way to express power or dominance over another (Henley, 1973, 1977). In general, males or those with more power and dominance in most situations are more apt to touch a female and not vice versa. However, the research on the power implications of touch must be carefully interpreted because of some inconsistencies (Stier and Hall, 1984).

Touching may be interpreted to mean power, but it also may have an affectional or sexual connotation to it (Pearson, 1985). Thus if a woman was to touch the arm or shoulder of a man, it may be interpreted as being sexual—many men do just that. But women are supposed to know that when a male manager puts a hand on the shoulder of his female secretary, it is nothing more than a simple friendly gesture, or is it?

Although the research on touching is rather scanty, two studies stand out. In the first, both male and female librarians either touched or did not touch those to whom they gave a library card. Those people who were touched by the librarian had more positive opinions of the library and the librarian than those who were not touched during the transaction (Fisher et al., 1976). It seems that in a public situation, another's touch can be interpreted in a positive and friendly way. This would suggest that touching is a most important way of forming friendships and one that most people find desirable. In another study, this one conducted by Carie Forden (1981), students watched a videotape of a male and female conversing. One group of students saw a female touch a male on the shoulder; another group saw a male touch a female on the shoulder. Forden found that when the students saw a female touch a male she was thought quite dominant, and a male who was touched was seen as passive. Forden concluded that touching does carry a dominance message and that touching seems more appropriate for males to do than for females.

Body Position and Posture

Researchers have begun to systematically catalog how body positions and posture (which are as revealing as verbal cues) convey different messages about relationships (Goffman, 1979; Hall, 1966; Pearson, 1985). Consequently, we are learning some rather interesting differences in the ways females and males position their bodies and what these positions mean in terms of a person's status and dominance (Frieze and Ramsey, 1976). For example, males are more likely to occupy or control more *personal space* around their bodies than females occupy. From this specific nonverbal message, we can infer that males are more dominant and have a higher status than females. The rationale here is that the person who controls more physical space is more powerful, more dominant, and has a higher status than the person who controls less space.

With respect to body position, males tend to sit in a more relaxed way than females. In general, females tend to display a more restricted body posture than males, who seem to have a wider range of possible body positions. Traditionally, little girls are encouraged to sit in "ladylike" ways.

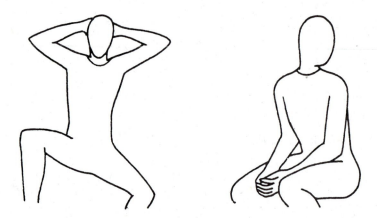

Figure 7.2 Although there are no obvious biological cues to either of these figures' physical sex, most people can tell which is more likely a man and which is a woman from their seated postures.

Source: Women and sex roles, A social psychological perspective by Irene H. Frieze, Jacquelynne E. Parsons, Paula B. Johnson, Diana N. Ruble, and Gail L. Zellman, by permission of W. W. Norton & Company, Inc. Copyright © 1978 by W. W. Norton & Company, Inc.

Specifically, females are taught to sit with their legs close together or crossed at the ankles and their hands placed on their lap. Males, on the other hand, are more apt to sit with their legs crossed by putting the ankle of one leg over the knee of the other leg or sitting with the legs apart. The male's body posture usually appears more relaxed than the female's. These generalized sitting postures and their nearly universal association with either males or females can be seen even when a drawing is "sexless" (see figure 7.2). With no other cues besides body position, few people would have any difficulty in pointing to which drawing best represents a male posture and which represents a female posture.

Most of our information pertaining to body posture and gender differences is of the anecdotal type rather than from controlled studies. Many people have had, for instance, personal experiences in which they were reprimanded for standing or sitting in ways not deemed appropriate for their gender. Two such examples can serve to make this point:

> When I was a kid I was sitting on the sofa reading and my legs were crossed, right knee draped over left. My father said, "You're sitting like a girl!" and demonstrated the right way: He placed his left ankle on his right knee so that his thighs were separated at the immodest masculine angle. For a couple years after that I thought men were supposed to cross legs left over right, while women crossed them right over left. Or was it the other way? I could never remember which. So rather than make a mistake and do it like a girl, I preferred not to cross my legs at all.

And another man recounts:

> I was out by the mailboxes talking with my nextdoor neighbor, a football coach, whom I respected enormously. We were standing there talking. I had my hands on my hips. He said jokingly that I was standing a woman's way, with my thumbs forward. I was 27 years old and I had never really thought about the best way to stand with my arms akimbo. But now, whenever I find myself standing with thumbs forward I feel an effeminate flash, even when I'm alone, and I quickly turn my hands around the other way. (both quotes taken from Wagenvoord and Bailey, 1978, p. 44)

Overall, there do seem to be several areas where females and males differ in their communication. What is most revealing about many of these differences is that many of them reinforce the power differences that exist between the genders. As we have seen, power and status need not be openly flaunted but can be rather subtle in their nonverbal presentation.

SUMMARY

Language is one of the most powerful features of culture. The English language has a strong undercurrent of linguistic sexism, exemplified by the ways the female is ignored, defined, and deprecated in our language.

Several differences are found in the verbal output of females and of males. For example, males generally talk more than females, but males disclose less about their personal lives than females do. Also, some slight differences have been speculated about in the use of certain verbal patterns; females are found to use more tag questions, qualifiers, longer requests, and fillers.

When it comes to communication's nonverbal features, several differences between males and females are found in terms of emotional, expressions, sending and receiving nonverbal messages, eye contact, touching, body positions and postures.

SUGGESTED READINGS

Eakins, B., & Eakins, R. (1978). *Sex differences in human communication.* Boston: Houghton Mifflin.

Elshtain, J. (1982). Feminist discourse and its discontents: Language, power, and meaning. *Signs, 7(3),* 603–21.

Henley, N. (1977). *Body politics: Power, sex and nonverbal communication.* Englewood Cliffs, NJ: Prentice-Hall.

Pearson, J. (1985). *Gender and communication.* Dubuque, IA: Wm. C. Brown Publishers.

Wiemann, J., & Harrison, R. (Eds.). (1983). *Nonverbal interaction.* Beverly Hills, CA: Sage.

Point/Counterpoint

The Battle of the Pronouns

Grammarians have long taught that the pronoun "he" used in the generic sense refers to both male and female. The pronoun "she," however, can only mean a female. All those who wish to change tradition and grammatical standards are simply going too far when they begin to tamper with the unmarked status of the male pronoun "he."

But what would we say if pronouns were based on some other human quality rather than sex? If, for example, borrowing from Virginia Valian and Jerrold Katz (1971), we found that "In culture R the language is such that the pronouns are different according to the color of the people involved, rather than their sex . . . the unmarked pronoun just happens to be the one used for white people. In addition, the nonwhite people just happen to constitute an oppressed group. Now imagine that this oppressed group begins complaining about the use of the 'white' pronoun to refer to all people."

Such an example may seem extreme, but the point is rather clear. Females do suffer from sexism in our society. Furthermore, they must accept that their status is devalued even more so by their own language. Would nonwhite people accept the convention of being referred to as white? Most would argue that such a linguistic convention would smack of pure racism. Then why does the generic pronoun "he" continue to be defended when it is every bit as demeaning to females as "white" would be to describe nonwhites?

What do you think?

Reading   The Game

Most people at one time or another have had to watch their words least they be misunderstood. One of the most precarious of communication strategies can be found in those dialogues where a less powerful person must communicate with a more powerful person. A less powerful person must know how to structure the communication to maximize the chances of getting what he or she wants without offending the more powerful person. Such is the case described by Leonard Stein who outlines "the game" that a nurse must often play with a doctor.

One rarely hears a nurse say, "Doctor, I would recommend that you order a retention enema for Mrs. Brown." A physician, upon hearing a recommendation of that nature, would gape in amazement at the effrontery of the nurse. The nurse, upon hearing the statement, would look over her shoulder to see who said it, hardly believing the words actually came from her own mouth. Nevertheless, if one observes closely, nurses make recommendations of more import every hour and physicians willingly and respectfully consider them. If the nurse is to make a suggestion without appearing insolent and the doctor is to seriously consider that suggestion, their interaction must not violate the rules of the game.

Object of the game. The object of the game is as follows: the nurse is to be bold, have initiative, and be responsible for making significant recommendations, while at the same time she must appear passive. This must be done in such a manner so as to make her recommendations appear to be initiated by the physician.

Both participants must be acutely sensitive to each other's nonverbal and cryptic verbal communications. A slight lowering of the head, a minor shifting of position in the chair, or a seemingly nonrelevant comment concerning an event which occurred eight months ago must be interpreted as a powerful message. The game requires the nimbleness of a high wire acrobat, and if either participant slips the game can be shattered; the penalties for frequent failure are apt to be severe.

Rules of the game. The cardinal rule of the game is that open disagreement between the players must be avoided at all costs. Thus, the nurse must communicate her recommendations without appearing to be making a recommendation statement. The physician, in requesting a recommendation from a nurse, must do so without appearing to be asking for it. Utilization of this technique keeps anyone from committing themselves to a position before a sub rosa agreement on that position has already been established. In that way open disagreement is avoided. The greater the significance of the recommendation, the more subtly the game must be played.

To convey a subtle example of the game with all its nuances would require the talents of a literary artist. Lacking these talents, let me give you the following example which is unsubtle, but happens frequently. The medical resident on hospital call is awakened by telephone at 1:00 A.M. because a patient on a ward, not his

Source: "The game" by Dr. Leonard I. Stein. In *Archives of General Psychiatry,* June 1967. Copyright 1967, American Medical Association. Reprinted by permission.

own, has not been able to fall asleep. Dr. Jones answers the telephone and the dialogue goes like this:

This is Dr. Jones.
(An open and direct communication.)

Dr. Jones, this is Miss Smith on 2W—Mrs. Brown, who learned today of her father's death, is unable to fall asleep.
(This message has two levels. Openly, it describes a set of circumstances, a woman who is unable to sleep and who that morning received word of her father's death. Less openly, but just as directly, it is a diagnostic and recommendation statement; i.e., Mrs. Brown is unable to sleep because of her grief, and she should be given a sedative. Dr. Jones, accepting the diagnostic statement and replying to the recommendation statement, answers.)

What sleeping medication has been helpful to Mrs. Brown in the past?
(Dr. Jones, not knowing the patient, is asking for a recommendation from the nurse, who does know the patient, about what sleeping medication should be

prescribed. Note, however, his question does not appear to be asking her for a recommendation. Miss Smith replies.)

Pentobarbital mg 100 was quite effective night before last.
(A disguised recommendation statement. Dr. Jones replies with a note of authority in his voice.)

Pentobarbital mg 100 before bedtime as needed for sleep; got it?
(Miss Smith ends the conversation with the tone of a grateful supplicant.)

Yes, I have, and thank you very much, doctor.

The above is an example of a successfully played doctor-nurse game. The nurse made appropriate recommendations which were accepted by the physician and were helpful to the patient. The game was successful because the cardinal rule was not violated. The nurse was able to make her recommendation without appearing to, and the physician was able to ask for recommendations without conspicuously asking for them.

Chapter 8

EDUCATION AND WORK

> *The education that you get generally leads males towards a wider and better choice of careers than females. Young men are more likely to leave school with the qualifications necessary for a skilled job, but this is not the end of the story. It is the training you get, either immediately before or during the early years of work, that determines your progress—your chances of promotion and higher earnings.*
>
> *Carol Adams and Rae Laurikietis*

The educational system is one social institution that leaves a lasting impact on most people's lives. From preschool to graduate school, males and females are taught the necessary skills to become "productive" citizens. Yet the educational system treats males and females differently to a considerable degree. Many of these differences flow from the gender-based expectations found in our society.

A great many people march off every day to offices or factories where they put in a "day's work for a day's pay." Work not only provides people with incomes, it also furnishes a social environment where people interact and play out the many role behaviors learned at earlier ages. For many men and women, work is an essential source of their self-identity as well as a means to prove themselves competent and capable.

In this chapter we will look at both the educational system and the workplace and see the importance of gender in determining how individuals are treated by these social institutions.

THE EDUCATIONAL SYSTEM AND GENDER

Our complex and technological society demands that its citizenry master certain skills thought necessary for the orderly functioning of its social structures. Abilities such as reading, writing, and arithmetic are essential skills that are necessary for most people to adequately deal with the demands of everyday life. For the most part, school is where we learn these basic skills. Schools, however, teach other things too. Socially approved values, attitudes, and beliefs are as much a part of the school's curriculum as reading and writing are (Hyman and Wright, 1979). The so-called *hidden curriculum* of our educational system stresses such socially desirable traits as orderliness, conformity, respect for authority, competency, and discipline, all of which are thought necessary for students whether they become doctors, salespersons, or secretaries (Jackson, 1968). All too often, though, the goals of education are translated very differently, leaving lasting effects for each gender (Best, 1983). Even among first- and second-graders, we find evidence of gender bias in the kinds of jobs children think about in terms of their future employment (Archer, 1984; Franken, 1983). We can get a sense of the impact of the early grades on children's perceptions of their world and the gender differences they learn in the following poem.

WHAT DID YOU LEARN IN SCHOOL TODAY,
DEAR LITTLE GIRL OF MINE?
I learned how to cook and sew,
I learned that's all girls need to know.
I learned that men go up in space,
That man is the word for the human race.
That's what I learned in school today,
That's what I learned in school. (quoted in Adams and Laurikietis, 1977,
    p. 30)*

Such a gender-biased view of the world reinforces many of the common gender stereotypes and is a factor in prompting young boys' interest in more than twice as many occupations as young girls. Consequently, when young girls reach high school, they tend to restrict their occupational aspirations. Many females focus on jobs that bring less status and less money than the jobs that boys think about (Wirtenberg and Nakamura, 1976). The charge of sexism, or the view that females and/or their activities are less important than males and/or their activities, can be leveled at the educational system (Association of American Colleges, 1982).

How do we account for the wide disparity between boys' and girls' occupational goals? Practically speaking, there are many socializing forces in school that shape the outcome of a student's life. Recall that in chapter 4 we discussed the effects that teachers can have on shaping gender role behaviors along traditional lines. However, teachers are only part of the gender bias we find in the educational system.

Many school systems literally direct males and females into different courses by what can be called a differential *tracking system*, whereby boys are taught to think about becoming doctors and engineers while girls are encouraged to think in terms of becoming nurses and secretaries (Alexander and Cook, 1982). We need to examine the educational system's academic programs, hiring practices, and athletic activities as examples of some of the ways in which the educational system wittingly or unwittingly treats females and males differently.

*From Adams, C. and R. Laurikietis, *The gender trap.* © 1977 Academy Chicago Ltd. Reprinted by permission.

Programs

Gender bias in our school systems has a long and rather dismal history. It was not until 1833 that the first woman was even allowed admission to an institution of higher learning, namely, Oberlin College in Ohio. But even at Oberlin, a highly progressive and liberal institution for its day, early female coeds primarily learned the arts and home economics, which were "intended to prepare them for homemaking or teaching" (Deckard, 1983, p. 245). Nineteenth century Oberlin College coeds were discouraged from pursuing academic programs thought too strenuous for females such as science and commerce, which were areas of study considered suitable "for men only" (Flexner, 1971). Besides their course work, these pioneering young women were also required to engage in other nonacademic duties: "Washing the men's clothes, caring for their rooms, serving them at table, listening to their orations, but themselves remaining respectfully silent in public assemblages, the Oberlin 'coeds' were being prepared for intelligent motherhood and a properly subservient wifehood" (Flexner, 1971, p. 30).

Today, college women no longer wash men's clothes or listen quietly to their orations as part of their educational experience at Oberlin College or any other college or university. Still, gender bias in its more subtle forms can still be found in most modern-day schools, ranging from the early grades all the way up through the professional and graduate levels. For example, with the explosive development in computers and their related technology in the last several years, students today must have a grasp of basic mathematical principles and reasoning (Fiske, 1982). And yet, remedial programs to assist students who have difficulty with these academic skills are sorely lacking in many school systems. This problem becomes a gender-oriented issue when we note that many female students have problems with math and science-related areas; without some remedial help, many will go into the work-world unprepared for the technology that awaits them. In contrast, remedial programs directed at helping students with reading difficulties—a problem more frequently encountered among males than females—have been set up in most school systems for years. On the surface, it seems that within our educational system, programs directed at eliminating academic deficiencies among males are given a higher priority than programs that could assist females.

Furthermore, there is growing concern that females are losing out to males in the important area of "hands-on" experience at computer terminals (*Girls losing their turns at the terminals*, 1984). This, along with the lack of gender-specific remedial programs, can be taken as more than circumstantial evidence that gender bias exists to some degree in many school systems.

Another area where gender bias creeps into educational programs is the practice (somewhat in decline today) of encouraging male and female students to take different academic programs that lead to different skills, many of which are gender-oriented. Many programs taken in the junior-high years funnel females into traditionally feminine courses (e.g., home economics and typing) and encourage males to take traditionally masculine courses (e.g., wood working and shop). However, recent efforts by educators have attempted to change the gender bias in these gender-oriented courses. One such educational system studied the effects of mixing both males and females in courses that were once gender-oriented, and the results proved rather positive for both. Commenting on a recent attempt in the Los Angeles school system for coed courses, Henrietta Wexler (1980) pointed out that

> Students in the coed classes saw fewer differences in male and female personalities than did their counterparts in the traditional school . . . [they] saw men and women as being more nearly alike in assertiveness, kindness, inventiveness, and adventurousness. The girls saw themselves as being not only good at cooking and sewing but also at building things and working with tools and machines. Boys saw themselves not only as active and forceful but also as domestic and gentle. (p. 32)

In spite of the fact that gender bias is found in many schools and that male and female students are covertly, if not overtly, treated differently by the educational system, women have many of the same academic goals as men have (Adams, 1984; Goldberg and Shiflett, 1981; Regan and Roland, 1982). More and more women want to learn academic skills that will better prepare them to be self-sufficient and skilled in abilities that would lead to high-paying positions in the labor market, although the fact remains that fewer women than men pursue advanced programs that will lead them into the higher status and better-paying occupations such as medicine and law (Baird et al., 1973; Epstein, 1981).

As we have already noted, it was only within the last century and a half that women have been able to pursue a higher education. The number of women who pursue a college education has steadily grown over the years. For example, in 1960 only 17.8 percent of high school female graduates went on to college, compared with 30.3 percent of male high school graduates. By 1981, the percentage of female high school graduates entering college rose to 30.4 percent, while 34.7 percent of the male high school graduates went off to college. By 1981, women made up just over half of all college students in the United States and almost 45 percent of all graduate students (U.S. Bureau of the Census, 1982).

Sexism in the Classroom　The more blatant forms of gender bias in academic programs have decreased somewhat in recent years. Any school that would deny a female admission to a particular program would probably face a lawsuit. But what about the more subtle forms of sexism, those embedded in our culture that influence both administrators and teachers alike and that can have serious consequences for women in educational settings (Association of American College, 1982)? Sexist attitudes and beliefs can not be eliminated as easily as sexist admission policies and course offerings.

One area that is receiving greater attention is sexual harassment of females by male professors. It is estimated that approximately 20 to 30 percent of all college women experience some form of sexual harassment during their college careers (Benson and Thompson, 1982). Sexual harassment need not only mean sexual overtures to a female student by a male teacher, but it may also include such practices as sexist humor or snide comments about women's intelligence.

Other less obvious forms of sexism in the classroom have been noted in the recent report compiled by the Association of American College's Project on the Status and Education of Women (1982). The committee reported that several variations of subtle sexism found in many of today's college classrooms can have negative effects on female students. For example, a male teacher might interrupt a female student but not a male, or a teacher may use sexist language (e.g., "he" or "mankind"), or a teacher may reflect gender stereotypes in discussing certain professions (e.g., using "he" when talking about doctors but "she" when discussing nurses). Although some may argue that such subtle forms of sexism do little in the way of harming females in the college classroom, Alexander Astin (1977) sees it differently.

> [E]ven though men and women are presumably exposed to a common liberal arts curriculum and other educational programs during the undergraduate years, it would seem that these programs serve more to preserve, rather than to reduce, stereotypic differences between men and women in behavior, personality, aspirations, and achievement. (p. 216)

Thus, according to Astin, one of the main features of most education is that it preserves society's views of what is expected of women and men. At times, the whole educational system seems bent on socializing men and women toward different ends, men for the marketplace and women for the home place. But things are changing.

Medical School: An Example of Institutional Socialization   Over the past century the medical profession has become a powerful influence controlling nearly every facet of our society's health care system (Starr, 1983). The job of physician is one of the most prestigious and high-status occupations in our society. Historically, females were prohibited from earning a medical degree in this country (Mandelbaum, 1978). In 1849, Elizabeth Blackwell became the first woman to become a doctor. She had been turned down by twenty-nine medical schools before she gained admission. But women are making significant inroads into medical schools and the medical profession: the percentage of women in medical schools rose from 11 percent to 26 percent between 1972 and 1980; and the percentage of female physicians rose from 6.8 percent in 1960 to 13.4 percent in 1980. However, we should not think that, because of the increase of females in medical schools, discrimination against females has ended (Clayton, et al., 1984).

What happens to these women who enter medical schools (male-oriented institutions)? What does going through one of the most intense learning experiences do to the attitudes and values of women and men alike? Jane Leserman (1981) surveyed 264 males and 89 females as freshmen (1975) and 258 males and 83 females as seniors (1978) in three North Carolina medical schools to discover the impact of medical school on students' value systems.

Overall, entering females were more liberal or humanitarian than males were. Female students were more likely than male students to support equalizing doctor-patient relations, to support pushing for economic and political changes in delivery of health care, and to support setting up practice in inner-cities rather than in rural areas. By their senior year, however, Leserman noted that all students (women and men alike, but men more so than women), developed more conservative attitudes and values. Leserman concluded that although the numbers of women and other minorities had an impact on the medical school, the medical school, through the influence of its medical faculty, had a greater impact on the students. One of the more obvious changes was that the number of students who felt that there was a need for more female physicians decreased after the freshman year. Also, there was a lessening of humanitarian values and attitudes with a shift toward a more conservative orientation. Merely increasing the number of women in medical schools will not in itself change the male-oriented value system unless more liberal and humanitarian women and men can achieve positions of leadership and authority within the medical school system. And that day is still in the future.

Employment in Education

Few areas in education show the prevalence of gender bias as much as the area of teacher employment. (Occupational roles in general will be discussed more fully in the next section.) Historically, the teaching profession enjoyed a position of high status and considerable respect in our country. During the eighteenth century and into the nineteenth century, teachers were considered pillars of their communities right alongside other high-status professionals such as ministers and physicians. At that time, teaching was almost totally an all-male profession. As women began entering the teaching profession in greater numbers (circa 1830s–1850s), they were restricted primarily to teaching the early grades, where the goal was not so much to educate children as to civilize them (Kaufman, 1984; Katz, 1975). As the years went by, women took over more of the classrooms. However, the position of principal—a position of greater status than that of teacher—in most grade schools remained in the hands of males (Estler, 1975; Strober and Tyack, 1980; Tyack, 1976).

During this century, the teaching profession became more dominated by women, especially among the primary grades. However, women teachers found their career paths blocked at higher levels of the educational system (Szafran and Austin, 1984). At the college or university level, for example, it seems that male professors were and are preferred over females. In 1982, women comprised 71 percent of all grade school teaching positions, while they made up only 24 percent of all college and university teachers. But even among the 24 percent who were teaching in higher education, they mainly filled the lower ranks (i.e., instructor and assistant professor) where the salaries were not as high nor the job security as great as among the higher ranks (i.e., associate professor and full professor); women represented less than 10 percent of the higher ranks (*Chronicle of Higher Education*, 1982; Department of Labor, 1980). This pattern of discrimination is not limited to the United States; it can also be found in the colleges and universities of Canada, the United Kingdom, and Australia (Blackstone and Fulton, 1975; Jones and Lovejoy, 1980; Vickers and Adam, 1977).

A Question of Salaries   A rather simple way to document the charge that women are discriminated against in colleges and universities is to compare the salaries of male and female teachers at the different teaching ranks or levels. The degree of salary inequity and the best method for detecting it have spawned a lively debate in the past few years, but the bottom line is that women are paid less than men at every rank (Gollob, 1984). The National Center for Educational Statistics surveyed 2,748 institutions of higher learning for the academic year 1982–1983 and found the following averages for college faculties:

Rank	Men	Women	Difference
Professor	$35,557	$31,703	$3,854
Associate	27,006	25,400	1,606
Assistant	22,428	20,928	1,500
Instructor	18,164	17,064	1,100
Lecturer	20,980	18,347	2,633
No academic rank	26,358	23,721	2,637
AVERAGE	$28,394	$23,020	$5,374

If salary is one measure of a person's worth in the marketplace, then we can conclude from the above salary discrepancies that female faculty are less valuable in the academic marketplace.

Sociology: A Case in Point   Over the past decade, several sociologists have studied the extent to which women are represented on sociology faculties at both the undergraduate and graduate levels (Jackson, 1972; Nigg and Axelrod, 1981; Williams, 1982). In a recent survey (i.e., 1982–1983 academic year) covering the southern region of the United States, Nancy Kutner and William Lacy (1984) found that "of the 2,333 full- and part-time members teaching sociology in the SSS [Southern Sociological Society] region for whom data were obtained 29% (678) were women" (p. 21). Of those schools reporting graduate programs in sociology, 25 percent of the faculty were women. In general, female sociologists were more often found in small institutions (i.e., student enrollment under 2,000) than in larger institutions, 35 percent as opposed to 27 percent respectively.

Kutner and Lacy also found a wide disparity between the academic ranks held by male and female sociologists in their sample of the southern United States. Only 13 percent of the women, but 28.6 percent of the men, held a full professorship. However, women made up 26.8 percent and men 12.2 percent at the instructor/lecturer level. Thus men held over twice as many full professor positions, and women held over twice as many instructor/lecturer positions.

The chairperson of a department is the one assigned with the task of policy making and leadership of an academic discipline. For the most part, based on Kutner and Lacy's data, we can say that women are virtually excluded from such positions in sociology departments across the South. In their sample, only 3 percent of the schools offering a graduate program in sociology had female chairpersons. However, in schools without a graduate program but with a formal sociology department, the percentage of female chairpersons rose to almost 16 percent. In schools where sociology was included with other social science disciplines, 10.5 percent reported a female chairperson. (A similar pattern of gender discrimination can be found among psychology faculties in the Southeast as well [Kimmel, 1974, 1984] as well as among professional historians [Phillips and Hogan, 1984].)

Overall, not only have women found themselves receiving lower pay in every teaching rank, they have been excluded from those higher ranks where security and prestige are part of the benefits. Women have been held to the lower ranks where the teaching responsibilities and committee assignments are most demanding; men have achieved higher positions in both teaching and administrative levels, where the benefits in terms of money and prestige are greater. Although teaching may be considered a female occupation, that stereotype is only true at the lower ranks in higher education and among the primary grades. Rather than a reversal of this pattern of gender discrimination, some believe that the trend is actually moving toward even more discrimination in academic pay and positions favoring men over women. Noting such dire possibilities, Marion Kilson (1976) states that, "Despite raised consciousnesses, affirmative-action guidelines, day-care centers, and women's studies programs, the status of women in higher education promises to decline" (p. 935). We must work against such a future. The best minds and talent know no gender, but this message doesn't seem to have registered among those that inhabit the halls of academia.

Athletic Programs

On nearly any Friday evening during the fall, one is apt to find cheering crowds rallying the local high school's football team on to another victory. On a crisp autumn Saturday afternoon on most large college or university campuses, one finds college football and tens of thousands of fanatical alumni and students all rooting for their team. In many ways these athletic spectacles mirror the traditional gender roles of our society. Fighting to win another victory, the football players—all male—are out on the field actively engaged in battle with the opposition's team, while the short-skirted female cheerleaders dance along the sidelines cheering on the men. The helmeted men—the doers—and the vaguely sexual women—the supporters—play out their male and female roles on the gridiron (Eitzen and Sage, 1978).

During the late 1960s and early 1970s, gender bias, or what was commonly referred to as sex discrimination in education, came under increasing fire from many different segments of society. Many believed that women were not being treated fairly in the educational system. Finally, Congress passed the Educational Act of 1972, which contained a series of legislative measures that are commonly known as the *Title IX provisions*. The intent of the Title IX was to eliminate all gender bias in schools; if a school failed to follow its guidelines, the school risked losing its federal funding.

The basic requirements set out by Title IX for a school to end gender bias are rather straightforward. First of all, schools must comply with the provisions that guarantee that the sex of an applicant will not enter into the decision to hire or promote a faculty member. Single-sex classes or programs were also forbidden, as was any discrimination on the part of financial-aid programs. Probably the most controversial feature of Title IX was its requirements related to athletic programs. Title IX simply stated that schools must provide equal athletic facilities and programs for both female and male students. Thus the colleges and universities across the country that received any federal monies had to provide female students with the same athletic programs that were provided the male student or, if they didn't, the school lost its federal funding. Title IX's intent is not the eradication of the "separatism" found in men's and women's athletic programs but rather the elimination of the unequal allotment of physical and financial support for the separate athletic programs. In fact, as the history of female athletic and physical education programs has shown, separatism proved to have many hidden benefits for women collegians (Kennard, 1977).

Predictably, Title IX and many of its provisions have come under increasing attack from those who believe that the federal government has gone too far by encroaching upon the educational system. The critics seem especially perturbed by the incursion of the government's heavy handedness in athletic programs. Title IX's opponents seem more concerned about Title IX's impact on athletic programs than almost any other segment of higher education. (Some might infer from such a one-sided attack that many of Title IX's opponents are more concerned with football and basketball than with any other part of higher education.) Some of the most outspoken criticisms of Title IX have come from conservative politicians and amateur sporting organizations such as the National Collegiate Athletic Association

Figure 8.1 On campuses across the nation, increasing numbers of female students are participating in sports programs. Much of the credit goes to the implementation and enforcement of Title IX.

(NCAA), which has lobbied extensively against Title IX's provisions mandating equal athletic programs for female and male college athletes.

Collegiate sporting associations (e.g., the NCAA) are not the only ones opposed to Title IX's implementation. Several high-ranking government officials seem just as determined to take the "teeth" out of Title IX. For one, the Reagan administration has worked to eliminate the impact of Title IX. In early 1984, the Supreme Court ruled that federal funding was to be forfeited only by those specific departments or programs where there was a clear violation of Title IX. This was seen by many as a victory for the Reagan administration to curtail government intervention in the school system. Specifically, the Supreme Court ruled that when a Title IX violation was proven, only the offending department or program (not the entire institution) would lose federal funding. For example, if the athletic department failed to meet Title IX provisions, it would lose federal monies, but the school's admission department would not. The problem with such a ruling is that most of the athletic departments affiliated with major colleges and universities do not need federal monies to continue operation. The revenues generated from their sporting events often run into the millions of dollars, and alumni often contribute huge sums for athletics. Thus many opponents to the Supreme Court's ruling fear that Title IX's impact will be substantially undermined by such a change and that women's athletic programs will suffer.

Obviously, from the controversy brewing over the implementation of Title IX and the efforts of national organizations such as the NCAA and conservative politicians, the gains made over the past decade in eliminating the educational systems' gender-biased practices are far from guaranteed. Without protections such as Title IX, many feel that the educational system will drift back to its unfair and unequal treatment of female employees, students, and athletes (Lichtenstein, 1981; Sandler, 1981).

Another area that has seen significant change because of the implementation of Title IX is the increasing number of women in athletic department positions. It is not at all uncommon today to find a female as the head coach for a women's varsity team. Women like Pat Head Summit, head coach of the nationally acclaimed University of Tennessee's women's basketball team, have proven their skills in a predominantly male world. Testifying to Summit's ability is the fact that she was chosen as head coach for the 1984 Olympic Games' women basketball team that won a gold medal. However, nationally, women have not made the inroads that many would expect into leadership positions within athletic departments (Hoferek, 1980). Even when men's and women's athletic programs have merged, we find few women in top management positions (Beck-Rex, 1979). Why there is such a discrepancy between women and men in top positions is still a problem to be reckoned with. Women neither lack the capability for such positions nor the personality traits that would assist them in such positions (Williams and Miller, 1983). It seems that gender bias may still be lurking in the offices and locker rooms of education's athletic departments.

Leading institutions of higher learning (e.g., Stanford and the University of Chicago) have been committed to affording equal facilities and equal advantages to both men and women since the turn of the century (Gelpi, 1982). However, as we have seen, in academic programs, in employment opportunities, and in athletic programs serving female students and staff, females have been oppressed by the educational institution as a whole. The preachments of equality for all who pass through academia's arches sound rather hollow when noting the extent of discrimination and sexist policies that are found in the large or small, great or average, public or private academic institutions. For those females who withstand and persevere beyond the bias set against them, their struggle to achieve prominence in academia is still beset by yet another problem. In the words of Mary Daly (1978), the aspiring female/scholar needs be wary of academia because:

> In universities . . . the omnipresent gases gradually stifle women's minds and spirits. Those who carry out the necessary expeditions run the risk of shrinking into the mold of the mystified Athena. . . . Reborn of Zeus, she becomes Daddy's Girl, the mutant who serves the master's purposes. The token woman, who in reality is enchained, possessed. (p. 8)

WORK, THE WORKPLACE, AND GENDER

"What do you want to be when you grow up?" Such is the question put to many young children by either their parents, relatives, or even by some of their friends. The mid-fifties' occupational favorites of "cowboy" or "fireman" have been replaced by the mid-eighties, high-tech career options of "computer specialist" or "astrophysicist." Times are certainly changing!

Having a job or, if you prefer, a career, is an important part of most people's lives. It provides for the basic and not-so-basic essentials of living. A paycheck not only provides the means for financial security, it also gives a sense of self-worth and self-respect as well. Many young people get their first taste of work or paid employment by working part time while still in school, for example, at a fast-food chain cooking up fries and burgers or at a discount store stocking shelves and waiting on customers. These first jobs are a valuable learning experience for the young, teaching them responsibility and dependability. Also, these first jobs appear to be harbingers of things to come. That is, adolescent females usually find jobs in which they receive lower pay than males "with the biggest discrepancies in manual labor and skilled trades, where boys dominate the scene; and in babysitting and clerical work, where girls prevail" (Greenberger and Steinberg, 1983, p. 470). Others have also found similar patterns among adolescents whereby boys obtain higher paying jobs than girls (Greenberger and Steinberg, 1981; Lewin-Epstein, 1981; Marini and Greenberger, 1978). But the important job, the one after graduation, is the job or occupation that most young people plan on and their parents fret over. After graduation, many young people think about getting that first "real job" or maybe beginning a career where they will make "real money" and have everything they ever wished for— a car, clothes, and an apartment of their own.

But what kinds of jobs or careers await the young person? Will little Debbie, for instance, grow up and be a physicist, and will Debbie's little brother, Todd, grow up to be a nurse? Possibly, but even in our technologically-oriented society where talent, ability, and motivation are valuable assets to an almost limitless range of occupational choices, Debbie's and Todd's future work roles may be more predictable than many people may think.

Even before these two little future workers arrive in first grade, they may have already made up their minds about what they want to be when they grow up. In fact, they've already had several possible jobs recommended for them when they grow up. Todd might have read that little boys can be

A *fireman* who squirts water on the flames, and
a *baseball player* who wins lots of games.
A *bus driver* who helps people travel far, or
a *policeman* with a siren in his car.
A *cowboy* who goes on cattle drives, and
a *doctor* who helps to save people's lives.
A *sailor* on a ship that takes you everywhere, and
a *pilot* who goes flying through the air.
A *clown* with silly tricks to do, and
a pet tiger owner who *runs the zoo.*
A *farmer* who drives a big red tractor, and
on TV shows, if I become an *actor.*
An *astronaut* who lives in a space station, and
someday grow up to be *president* of the nation.

And another children's book suggests that Debbie could be

A *nurse* with white uniforms to wear, or
a *stewardess* who flies everywhere.
A *ballerina* who dances and twirls around, or
a *candy shop owner*, the best in town.
A *model* who wears lots of pretty clothes,
a *big star* in the movies and on special TV shows.
A *secretary* who'll type without mistakes, or
an *artist*, painting trees and clouds and lakes.
A *teacher* in nursery school some day, or
a *singer* and make records people play.
A *designer of dresses* in the very latest style, or
a *bride* who comes walking down the aisle.
A *housewife* someday when I am grown, and
a *mother* with some children of my own. (Quoted by
Weitzman et al., 1972, p. 1145)*

If we take the above messages to heart, it seems that young boys' and girls' future occupational roles are fairly well structured in ways such as to portray men's work as being more exciting and more active, and with higher status than most of the jobs designated for women.

In this section we are going to cover the area where work, the workplace, and gender all intersect. We will focus primarily on women and work, not because men are not important in a discussion of work and the workplace, but because the impact of gender on jobs, salaries, and other related issues is more telling when focused on the female side of the work issue. [Although males have few occupational barriers to overcome, there is pressure to succeed at whatever job they take on because part of their male identity is riding on it (Doyle, 1983). Being a success is one of the more important elements in the male's gender role.] Thus we will discuss the issues of women's participation in the labor force and their earnings. We will also examine work ghettos where we find certain jobs primarily occupied by women rather than by equal numbers of women and men. Next

*From Weitzman, Lenore et al., "Sex-role socialization in picture books for preschool children," in *American Journal of Sociology*, Vol. 77, p. 1145. © 1972 The University of Chicago Press. Reprinted by permission.

we will note some of the contributing factors that promote segregation in the work force, leaving women at a greater disadvantage than men in general. Then we will discuss what is fast becoming one of the most controversial issues of the 1980s: the disparity in salaries that exists in job categories that require comparable skills, training, and effort. The better we understand the problems that women and other minorities have in job-related areas, the sooner we can do something to end the pervasiveness of discrimination and segregation in the workplace.

Some Common Myths about Gender and the Workplace

Several myths have evolved regarding the workplace and workers. These myths act as barriers keeping some groups out of certain jobs while favoring others. Janet Saltzman Chafetz (1974) and Judith Long Laws (1976) have enumerated several of these myths and their impact on women. In this section we will only detail three of the more important myths related to women and the workplace: the myths of *pin money,* home-bound women, and women's lack of motivation.

Some of the most popular TV shows in the late 1950s and early 1960s were shows that featured families. "Ozzie and Harriet," "Life with Father," "Father Knows Best," and "Leave It to Beaver" were just a few that millions tuned in to every week to see the latest trials and tribulations of family life in America. Looking back on those early family shows, one finds many similarities: husbands who worked outside of the home, wives who stayed home full time and never were seen in anything but dresses, and two kids who caused many of the problems that their loving parents had to solve in the space of twenty-three minutes. Gone are the days, however, when in the majority of households we found the husband as sole provider and the wife as full-time homemaker. Also gone are the days when mothers with children in school took on part-time jobs simply to fill vacant daytime hours when their children were in school and to earn what was commonly called "pin money." Pin money was the euphemism for that small amount of money that a woman earned to be used for little extras for her family or, if she was frivolous enough, for herself. In the minds of many, pin money was nonessential money because it was the husband's salary that supposedly provided for the family's needs and wants. The idea of pin money came to be one way to devalue a woman's financial contribution to the family's economic well-being, as well as a way to soothe a husband's pride that rested to a large degree in the knowledge that his salary was the family's primary income.

But did most American families really resemble those shown on the early TV shows? Did most wives and mothers really stay home waiting expectantly with cookies and milk for their young charges and with the evening's paper and slippers for their work-harried husbands? A few statistics compiled by the U.S. Bureau of the Census (1982) may put to rest this common myth about married women.

In 1940, just over 27 percent of the total civilian work force was female, while in 1981 that figure jumped to 43 percent. We find, however, that more men than women are employed in the civilian labor force for any given year. In 1960, approximately 83 percent of all men (i.e., 16 years and older) were employed in the civilian work force. But in 1981, only 77 percent of all men were employed in the civilian labor force. Thus there was a drop of about 6 percent in men's participation in the work force in a little over twenty years. The employment picture for women (i.e., 16 years and older) during this same period, however, shows just the opposite trend. In 1960, just over 37 percent of all women 16 years and older were employed in the civilian work force. By 1981 that number increased to over 52 percent, which is a 15 percent hike in a little over twenty years. With respect to all working women 16 years and older, we find different numbers of working women depending on their marital status. The single largest category of working women has been and still is the single female; in 1981 a full 62 percent of that category was employed outside of the home. Other categories of women are not far behind. Forty-two percent of all separated, divorced, or widowed females in 1981 were employed outside of the home. Also in 1981, we find that 51 percent of all married women whose husbands were present in the home were employed. Even women with children are entering the paid labor force in ever increasing numbers. In 1981, over 62 percent of all women with children between the ages of six and seventeen and with husbands present in the home worked in the civilian labor force. In the same year, almost 48 percent of all women with children under six and with husbands present in the home were in the paid labor force. More recently, in 1983, 45 percent of those mothers with children under one year of age were employed. As we can see then, women, whether single or married, with or without children, divorced or widowed, make up a large proportion of the work force. The days when a woman's place was thought to be in the home have changed, and American attitudes toward working women have changed as well. For example, in 1978, nearly 75 percent of all Americans approved of women working outside of the home even if their husbands' salaries were sufficient for the family (Cherlin and Walters, 1981). Not only have more men become more accepting of women working outside of the home, but more and more women have come to resist the idea that they should give up their jobs even during their children's early years. The idealized version of the home-bound mother and wife has dimmed considerably since the days of "Ozzie and Harriet." Married women with families are becoming a major part of the work force for many of the same reasons that men go off to work every day, namely, financial needs (Blau, 1975).

The last myth, that of the unambitious female, is probably the most difficult one to dislodge from many people's minds. Sharon Sutherland (1978) states the issue as follows:

> Although the objective barriers to the full participation of women in society have been lowered, women remain grossly underrepresented at the higher levels of virtually every occupation. Indeed, as employment pressures and changing task definitions channel men into fields traditionally dominated by women—primarily school teaching or librarianship, for example—the pattern of male chiefs and female Indians establishes itself in even these preserves. It is sometimes said, however, that the ghetto exists primarily in our own minds, that *women will invariably refuse or subvert the success they work so hard to earn.* (p. 774; italics added)

The doggedness with which this myth hangs on is due, at least in part, to the popularity of the *fear of success* construct (Horner, 1972; Tresemer, 1976). In 1964, Matina Horner, a graduate student at the University of Michigan, performed a study in which she asked students to respond to the following cue: "At the end of first term finals, Anne finds herself at the top of her medical school class." Based on the responses gathered from a majority of the females in the study, Horner postulated that many females had a fear of success. Two typical responses given by the females in this study were:

Anne feels guilty. . . . She will finally have a nervous breakdown
   and quit medical school and marry a successful young doctor.
It was *luck* that Anne came out on top because she didn't want to go to
   medical school anyway.

The popular media ran with the idea that women feared success whereas men did not, and many people felt they had "scientific" justification for thinking that women lacked the motivation to become successful in the business or professional world. The problems with this research, however, and the many studies it spawned, seem almost endless: a lack of replication of the findings, a confounding of "fear of success" with "fear of failure," and other methodological problems (Shaver, 1976). One thing is certain after the more than twenty years that women's motivation or commitment to work has been questioned; the institutional and social barriers are much greater than any possible "fear" that some women may have at succeeding in the workplace.

The idea that women work only for pin money, or for those little extras too small to bother their husbands about, is more myth than fact. As we already noted, in 1981, 42 percent of all women who were separated, divorced, or widowed worked in the labor force. This group surely wasn't working for pin money. For these women and most others as well, the salaries they bring home is anything but so-called pin money. These women work to survive and to support their children.

The idea that nearly all women spend their adult years at home waiting for their Ozzies to come in after a hard day's labor is clearly more myth than fact. The notion that women spend their days baking cookies for their children while their husbands are off at work may be a stereotype of women as presented on early television, but it surely doesn't reflect life on the other side of the television screen.

And finally, the notion that somehow women fear success and will subvert their own progress is, like the other notions, simple fancy. If given a chance, women will perform as well as men in the labor force, but many institutional barriers must first fall by the wayside.

A Fair Day's Pay

A couple of years ago a friend stopped me and asked about a button I was wearing on my jacket. "What does the '59' stand for?" he inquired. I explained that "59" stood for the amount of money the average, full-time female worker earned in comparison to every dollar earned by the average, full-time male worker. My friend didn't seem too impressed by either my explanation or my involvement in the issue of salary inequities suffered by females. I suspect the question of salaries and their unequal distribution for female and male workers just didn't seem to be one of the more pressing concerns at the moment for this person.

Salaries not only provide for one's needs, they are also a tangible means to show someone her or his worth in the job market. As we noted before, increasing numbers of women are employed today, more than ever before, and a large proportion of these women are the sole breadwinners for their families. When it comes to the salaries these women earn, one fact stands out. As a group, women earn significantly less than men (Davis and Hubbard, 1979; P. Wallace, 1982). Ironically, many women who accept that women in general are discriminated against deny that they themselves are the victims of wage discrimination (Crosby, 1984). In fact, the problem has gotten worse rather than better in the last twenty-five years or so. In 1960, for example, the average income for a full-time female worker was approximately 61 percent of that earned by a full-time male worker. However, in 1980, the average had slipped to 60 percent. In other words, full-time working women earned 60 cents for every dollar earned by a full-time working man (U.S. Bureau of the Census, 1982). To highlight the wage disparity, we should note that the average working woman must work nearly eight and a half days to earn as much as the average working man earns in five!

But wait, many will say that the income disparity between women and men results from women, on the average, working in jobs that pay less than men. You can't expect a female secretary to earn as much as her male manager, can you? These people point out that surely when women and men have the same kinds of jobs, the same amount of skills, the same educational backgrounds, and the same levels of experience, women will make the same amount of money as men make. That's why, they argue, that on the average *all* working women earn only 60 cents for every dollar earned

TABLE 8.1   MEDIAN INCOME OF MALES AND FEMALES BY OCCUPATIONAL CATEGORY (in dollars)[a]

	1975 Male	1975 Female	Difference	1980 Male	1980 Female	Difference
Total	$12,758	$ 7,394	$5,254	$18,612	$11,197	$ 7,415
Percent[b]		58.8			60.2	
Professional, technical and kindred workers	16,133	10,639	5,494	23,026	15,285	7,741
		65.9			66.4	
Managers and administrators, except farm	16,093	9,125	6,968	23,558	12,936	10,622
		56.7			54.9	
Sales	14,025	5,460	8,565	19,910	9,748	10,162
		39.8			49.0	
Clerical and kindred workers	12,152	7,562	4,590	18,247	10,997	7,250
		62.2			60.3	
Crafts and kindred workers	12,789	7,268	5,521	18,671	11,701	6,970
		56.8			62.7	
Operatives, including transport workers	11,142	6,251	4,891	15,702	9,440	6,262
		56.1			60.1	
Laborers, except farm	9,057	6,937	2,120	13,097	7,892	5,115
		76.6			60.9	
Service workers, except private household	9,488	5,414	4,074	12,757	9,747	3,010
		57.1			76.4	

a. Data are for persons 14 years old and over working full time, at longest job during year, 1975; 15 years and older, 1980.
b. Female income as a percentage of male income.
Sources: Current Population Reports, Series P-60, No. 105 and No. 127. U.S. Bureau of the Census

by a man. As a rule, women are the secretaries and men are the bosses. However, the facts belie this old argument supporting the basis for unequal salaries. Even when we compare working men with working women who have comparable educational status and occupational credentials, and who have pursued their careers full time throughout most of their working years, we still find great disparity between the women's and men's incomes (Lyon et al., 1982). The bottom line is that when job category, education, and experience are all taken into account, there still is a wide disparity between the salaries of women and men, suggesting that women suffer from a very costly form of discrimination (see table 8.1). Part of this salary disparity is due to the cultural belief that men should earn more than women because men supposedly are the primary "breadwinners" of the family.

Several weeks later I passed that friend of mine who had asked about my "59 cent" button and inquired, "Did you see the news on TV this morning?" "Nope, anything going on I should know about?" he asked. "Remember that button I was wearing the other week? Well, this morning one of the newscasters mentioned that the potential life-time earnings of a man with a bachelor's degree was $329,000 and only $142,000 for a woman with a bachelor's degree." "So," my friend said, "it's only money." Some people never see the light!

Work Ghettos

Setting aside for the moment the question of equivalent jobs and unequal salaries for men and women, one of the major reasons that women receive, on the average, only 60 cents for every dollar earned by men is that for the most part women hold very different kinds of jobs than men hold (Miller and Garrison, 1982; Scott, 1982). When we look at various job categories, one striking fact that stands out is the proportion of jobs that have a disproportionate number of either females or males in them. It is as if there existed *work ghettos* in the labor market (see table 8.2). In 1981, for example, over 99 percent of all secretaries were female whereas 99 percent of all plumbers and pipe fitters were male. Generally speaking, the occupations that are categorized as "women's work" (e.g., secretaries, child-care workers, and librarians) (Panek et al., 1977) usually carry with them extremely low salary ranges, low prestige and status, and little chance for advancement or promotion. Some occupations that have historically been male dominated (e.g., the legal profession) have seen an infusion of females in the last several decades. Just over 1 percent of all lawyers in 1910 were women; by 1980 that number had grown to just over 12 percent (Epstein, 1981). Some professions that once were mostly male dominated have in fact become nearly female-dominated professions, for example, real-estate agents (Prial, 1982).

How do we account, then, for the work ghettos that we find so prevalent in the business sectors? And why do the jobs that women generally occupy pay so much less than those that men occupy? To answer these and other related gender-work questions we need to explore the issue of job segregation.

Job Segregation   Segregation in communities, schools, and jobs has been a fact of life throughout most of this country's history. For example, blacks were segregated as to where they could live, go to school, work, and even where they ate in public restaurants or which restrooms they used in public facilities. In the past several decades, most forms of racial segregation have been abolished, if not in practice, at least in principle. But *job segregation* still exists to a large extent for women (Beck et al., 1980; England, 1984). Some jobs are *de facto* segregated simply because women make up nearly the entire work force. Occupations such as secretary-stenographer, household worker, waitress, elementary schoolteacher, and bookkeeper are nearly totally female-dominated occupations. These five occupations account for almost 25 percent of all working women. Thus these five occupations represent a kind of occupational ghetto for females and are sometimes referred to as the "pink-collar" ghetto. Compounding the problem of job segregation is the fact that the jobs dominated by women generally have lower pay scales than those dominated by men (England and McLaughlin, 1979; England et al., 1982).

One explanation for female workers' lower pay is the economic principle of "supply and demand" brought on by job segregation (Blau, 1975).

TABLE 8.2 PERSONS EMPLOYED IN SELECTED OCCUPATIONS, PERCENTAGE FEMALE, 1981

Occupation	Percentage Female
Secretaries	99.1
Child-care workers, except private household	95.5
Bank tellers	93.5
Telephone operators	92.9
Registered nurses, dietitians, and therapists	92.6
Waiters	89.3
Billing clerks	88.2
Cashiers	86.2
File clerks	83.8
Elementary school teachers	83.6
Librarians, archivists, and curators	82.8
Sales clerks, retail trade	71.2
Social and recreation workers	62.4
Secondary school teachers	51.3
Real-estate agents and brokers	49.8
Writers, artists, and entertainers	39.8
Bank officers and financial managers	37.5
College and university teachers	35.2
Computer specialists	27.1
Sales managers	26.5
Life and physical scientists	21.9
Stock and bond sales agents	17.0
Post-office mail carriers	15.7
Lawyers and judges	14.1
Physicians, medical and osteopathic	13.7
Precision machine operatives	12.8
Police and detectives	5.7
Dentists	4.6
Engineers	4.4
Truck drivers	2.7
Construction laborers, including carpenters' helpers	2.2
Carpenters	1.9
Electricians	1.6
Automobile mechanics	0.6
Plumbers and pipe fitters	0.4

Source: U.S. Bureau of the Census, *Statistical Abstract of the United States, 1982–83.* Washington, D.C.: U.S. Government Printing Office, 1982, pp. 388–90.

Generally speaking, there are more trained female workers (i.e., large supply) than there are jobs available (i.e., low demand), especially in segregated female occupations. Economist Barbara Bergmann (1974) was one of the first to use the term *overcrowding* to explain the relationship between job segregation and lower wages. Economists Francine Blau and Carol Jusenius (1976) explain overcrowding in these terms:

> Put simply, overcrowding is the interplay of a relatively low demand for a particular type of worker with a relatively large supply of that same type of worker. Thus, overcrowding can result from an excessive number of individuals trained (in a broad sense) for a given occupation or set of occupations and/or it can result from an excessive number of limitations being placed on the total set of occupations open to an identifiable group of workers. (p. 183)

Studies have found a basis for Bergmann's notion of overcrowding as affecting women's salaries. Evelyn Glen and Roslyn Feldberg (1977) found that during the last century, clerical work was primarily a male-dominated occupation that brought the male worker relatively high status and good wages. However, during this century, women became the dominant group in clerical work, and the status accruing from such work has fallen, as have the wages relative to male-dominated jobs that require similar skills.

Causes of Job Segregation

Job segregation appears to be one of the dominant causes for women's lower wages in the work force. But what factors normally contribute to women being segregated in so few jobs? Here we will look at three different explanations: the belief that a woman's biology prevents her from competing in the work force for high paying jobs; the socialization of young girls to avoid higher status positions; and, last, the various social or institutional forces that build barriers to prevent women from entering high-paying and high-status positions.

Anatomy Is Occupational Destiny   Recently, I heard a man say that his daughter wasn't going out for football because girls weren't meant for such a rough-and-tumble sport. Most women couldn't compete for a position on the defensive line of the Dallas Cowboys or Washington Redskins, but few other jobs demand such brute physical strength. By the same token, few men could make it into professional football either. When women are kept out of occupations for reasons of their biology, it is usually because of discrimination and not because women are actually restricted by their physical makeup. In the last several years, even in occupations where men have historically dominated (e.g., in coal mines and in heavy construction), women have shown they can do the work as well as men (Dukes, 1984).

Socializing Women Out of the Marketplace   We noted in a previous chapter that males and females are socialized differently. As a result, boys and girls learn to become more comfortable with certain types of jobs. For example, many fathers will work with their sons on the family cars, which may give young boys a basic knowledge of the workings of combustible engines. These young boys may grow up to be auto mechanics, race car drivers, or even car salesmen. Young girls washing the dishes and doing the laundry may grow up to be household workers or maids. The difference in pay between an auto mechanic and a household worker is considerable.

Socialization may even influence the attitudes females and males have toward work and the possibility of rewards and success contingent on work. Joan Crowley, along with several of her colleagues (et al., 1973), reported on the differences between the attitudes of male and female workers as a possible factor contributing to women's lower wages. Basically, these researchers found the male worker more concerned about his promotions, whereas the female worker was more concerned about a job's social aspects and the number of hours demanded by the job. From this we might suspect that women are less ambitious than men and that this may be partially to blame for women's lower pay. However, Rosabeth Kanter (1984) and others (Helmreich and Spence, 1977) suggest that women are no less ambitious or motivated for success than men are, but many women may give up because they realize that they are in "dead-end" jobs.

Personality characteristics is another area where socialization may play a role in the future jobs that women and men hold. We have noted on several previous occasions that the stereotypic view of masculinity is one of instrumentality, independence, assertiveness, and emotional constraint (Broverman et al., 1972). Such characteristics lend themselves to success in the business world. On the other hand, the belief in women's purported greater emotionality, supportiveness, and concern for social cohesiveness may not be as helpful in the marketplace, especially in jobs that demand independent action and confidence in one's own ability.

However, although socialization probably plays a role in job segregation, we should not focus only on this important feature to explain the difference found between the genders in their occupations and the resultant disparities. If we do, we may fall victim to seeing job segregation solely in terms of a person's past and forget that other forces outside the individual also conspire to discriminate against women.

Social and Institutional Barriers   A prerequisite for discrimination is that the target of discrimination be visible and belong to a group that is characterized by society as having undesirable or less-valued traits or characteristics (Baron and Bryne, 1984). Females are highly visible and distinct from males, and more often than not the characteristics and traits commonly associated with females are viewed as less desirable than those attributed to males (Broverman et al., 1970). Even those jobs customarily thought of as "women's work" are thought of by many as less worthwhile or desirable than jobs associated with men (Touhey, 1974).

However, it is not likely that most males will be blatantly antifemale in their attitudes toward females, but there are still innumerable ways in which antifeminine sentiment is demonstrated among males (Doyle, 1983). The area of job segregation is but one of the more formidable ways of discriminating against females; there are also several social and institutional outlets for such discrimination.

Prejudice. One thing that prevents women from gaining a foothold in the male-dominant job market is simple and blatant *prejudice* against women. Some men simply cannot accept women entering a "man's working world."

Box 8.1

The Difference between a Businessman and a Businesswoman

A BUSINESSMAN is aggressive; a BUSINESSWOMAN is pushy.

He's good on details; she's picky.

He loses his temper because he's so involved in his job; she's bitchy.

When he's depressed (or hungover), everyone tiptoes past his office; she's moody, so it must be her time of the month.

He follows through; she doesn't know when to quit.

He stands firm; she's hard.

His judgments are her prejudices.

He is a man of the world; she's been around.

He drinks because of the excessive job pressures; she's a lush.

He isn't afraid to say what he thinks; she's mouthy.

He's close-mouthed; she's secretive.

He exercises authority diligently; she's power mad.

He climbed the ladder of success; she slept her way to the top.

He's a stern taskmaster; she's hard to work for.

and NOW you know—the difference between a businessman and businesswoman!

Source: Anonymous.

Or when women do, there is a conscious attempt to belittle them and their work in comparison to men's (see box 8.1). According to a recent Gallup Opinion Poll (1976), a full two-thirds of the men questioned said they would not want to work for a female boss. Even for those women who have made it in a male-dominant profession, the insidious nature of prejudice against women remains a constant threat. One female lawyer pointed out that:

> If you're a woman, you have to make fewer mistakes. . . . A woman must put greater effort into her work . . . because if you make a fool of yourself, you're a damn fool woman instead of just a damn fool. (Epstein, 1981, p. 278)

Gatekeepers. Another way that job segregation is perpetuated is by the presence of *gatekeepers*, especially in high-status professions such as law, medicine, and engineering. A gatekeeper is one who keeps women out of various careers or limits their advancement. Graduate school professors who believe that women have no place in their particular profession can be especially powerful gatekeepers. Gatekeepers often don't see themselves as prejudiced against women *per se.* They rationalize that their resistance to females entering the profession is based on "facts." To their way of thinking, women can never be as serious about a career as a man; even if women do enter the field, they'll leave once they start their families. Jo Freeman (1975a) describes the problem of gatekeepers as encountered by female graduate students in the following way:

> "Any girl who gets this far has got to be a kook" one distinguished (male) member of the University of Chicago faculty told a female graduate student who had come to see him about being on her dissertation committee.
>
> This was just one of many such statements collected by women students at the University in the spring of 1969 to illustrate their contention that "some of our professors have different expectations about our performance than about the performance of male graduate students—expectations based not on our ability as individuals but on the fact that we are women." There were many others. They included:
>
> "The admissions committee didn't do their job. There is not one goodlooking girl in the entering class." . . .
>
> And most telling of all: "I know you're competent and your thesis advisor knows you're competent. The question in our minds is are you *really serious* about what you're doing." This was said to a young woman who had already spent five years and over $10,000 getting to that point in her Ph.D. program. (pp. 194–95)

Although most male gatekeepers would deny their prejudice toward women, research has found evidence that highly gifted women may escape a gatekeeper's preventive attention, but women of average talent certainly do not (Supplitt, 1979).

Another serious problem many females face with men who have power over them in graduate school is that of sexual harassment. For example, in a nation-wide poll of recently graduated female psychologists, nearly 25 percent reported they had had sexual intimacies with a male professor at some time during their student years (Pope et al., 1979). Of course, not all of these contacts constituted sexual harassment. But we must bear in mind that men with positions of power over women, as in the case of male professors and female students, exert tremendous influence and leverage. Not all male professors use their power to intimidate their female students either in sexual areas or as gatekeepers, but we must be vigilant in such unequal interpersonal situations.

Lack of Informal Groups. Women who have acquired sufficient training, education, and experience, and who have attained a career, may still experience a subtle form of discrimination. As most successful men in a profession will attest to, who you know is often more important than what you know. Many a businessman or professional man had his career immeasurably helped by the aid of a mentor, a sponsor, or some other person who knows where there is a job opening or who even has a possible solution to a job-related problem (Speizer, 1981). The men's professional network, or what is sometimes referred to as the "old boys' club," has helped many men advance their careers. But for women it is very different. The lack of *informal groups* for many women professionals can be very debilitating to their careers (Forisha, 1981). As Judith Lorber (1984) sees it:

Those who are excluded from informal work groups are at a disadvantage in filling the true requirements of their jobs, since important aspects of the work experience are not shared with them. Additionally, they are not sponsored for promotion and, should they gain a formal position of power, they discover it is extremely difficult to find loyal subordinates or exert their authority. Therefore, they rarely rise to truly high levels of power and prestige within their work organizations. As a result, they have fewer resources to offer their colleagues, which further perpetuates their exclusion from the colleague peer group. (p. 371)

Of course, many men might say that being shunned by professional colleagues should not dissuade a truly talented and highly motivated person; if a woman wants to "play with the big boys," she had better be prepared to take up the challenge of possibly having to "go it alone." Most highly successful men, however, did not "go it alone." The idea of the successful loner is quite unrealistic given the interpersonal nature of most professions today (White, 1975).

Conflict between Roles. Most men who are highly successful feel little conflict between their work role and their family role. Having a wife who takes care of the pressing problems of raising the children and tending to the everyday chores of running a household can be a blessing that most busy men who are scrambling up the career ladder often forget. More than one professional woman has thought about what the benefits of having a full-time "wife" would do for her career. One of the problems married professional women with children have is that they cannot devote full time to their careers during that period when full-time involvement may be essential for later advancement. According to economist Lester Thurow (1981),

The decade between 25 and 35 is when men either succeed or fail. It is the decade when lawyers become partners in the good firms, when business managers make it onto the "fast track," when academics get tenure at good universities, and when blue-collar workers find the job opportunities and the skills that will generate high earnings. . . .

But the decade between 25 and 35 is precisely the decade when women are most apt to leave the labor force or become part-time workers to have children. When they do, the current system of promotion and skill acquisition will extract an enormous lifetime price. (p. F2)

And yet many women professionals try to interweave their professional and family roles into some blend where neither suffers. One female attorney combined her law practice with her responsibilities as a mother in the following fashion:

None of my children was going to be raised by a baby-sitter. So I make it my business to be home by three, unless something extraordinary happens. And I try not to go out at night. Of course, if I have to, like with small claims where you just can't fit it all into the day, I work at night. But I try to make it a practice that I work just as a teacher would: between nine and three. (quoted in Epstein, 1981, p. 365)

When one considers the scope of the different forms of discrimination against women, added to the socialization that prevents many young women from venturing into "male-only" occupations, it is a wonder that the number of women who succeed in business or professional careers is as large as it is. Women must cope with their socialization, which for many gave them little encouragement to seek achievement in nonfeminine pursuits. Women who did pursue professional careers have had to contend with male prejudice, gatekeepers who wittingly or unwittingly made their pursuits more difficult, the lack of informal groups where peer contacts could prove helpful, and, finally, the struggle between their responsibilities to families and the demands of their careers. There is more truth than many men might think in the saying that "A woman has to do twice as much as a man to be considered half as good." However, women may take some consolation in noting the phrase that follows the above quote, "Fortunately, it isn't difficult."

The Dilemma of Comparable Worth

The name Helen Castrilli may not mean much to most people, but she is a central figure in one of the most controversial social and economic issues of the 1980s. Castrilli works at a state-run mental hospital in the state of Washington. She is a secretary and earns approximately $1,300 a month. A consulting firm, hired by the state, recently reviewed Castrilli's and other state workers' jobs and found that employees doing comparable work were being paid different wages; the difference amounted to as much as $350 a month. The major difference between these comparable jobs appeared to be that those jobs that paid less were generally held by females, and the higher paying jobs were usually held by males. It seemed to be a likely case of job discrimination on the basis of sex. Castrilli and several other co-workers went to court and sued the state, claiming sex-discrimination as the basis for their lower salaries. In December 1983, Judge Jack Tanner, a federal district judge, ruled in Castrilli's favor and ordered the state to increase the wages of and give four years' back pay to over 15,000 workers. The cost to the state to carry out the judge's ruling is estimated at somewhere between 500 and 800 million dollars.

The issue of job discrimination based on sex goes back to 1963 when the federal government passed the Equal Pay Act, which required equal salaries for men and women doing identical work. Thus the notion of "equal pay for equal work" took on the force of law. Few people today question the fairness of this doctrine, stating that if one person does the same work as another, they both should receive the same pay. But what about those jobs that are not identical but demand a comparable or equivalent amount of knowledge, skill, accountability, and other similar working conditions from their workers? In other words, should two comparable jobs, say a

TABLE 8.3 AS SOME EXPERTS SEE THE "WAGE GAP" —

Studies by "job evaluators" in Washington State, Minnesota and Illinois found these disparities in monthly salaries in male-dominated and female-dominated state-government jobs ranked of roughly "comparable worth":

Predominantly Male Job		Comparable Predominantly Female Job	
Washington			
Carpenter	$1,654	Social-service worker	$ 961
Security officer	$1,114	Telephone operator	$ 808
Mechanic	$1,462	Medical-record analyst	$ 892
Highway engineer	$1,654	Registered nurse	$1,392
Illinois			
Accountant	$2,470	Nurse	$1,794
Electrician	$2,826	Secretary	$1,486
Highway worker	$1,816	Clerk-typist	$1,075
Minnesota			
Delivery driver	$1,382	Pharmacy assistant	$1,202
Auto-parts handler	$1,505	Dining-hall director	$1,202
Game warden	$1,808	Behavior analyst	$1,590

Source: U.S. News and World Report, Basic data: Washington State, Illinois Commission on the Status of Women, Minnesota Commission on the Status of Women.

highway engineer and registered nurse, pay the same wage? Or should these jobs and other comparable jobs pay what the market will bear? That's the heart of the issue called *comparable worth* (Remick, 1984; Taylor, 1984).

The issue of comparable worth actually broke into the news some years before the Castrilli case made headlines. In 1981, again in Washington State, a court ruled that prison matrons must be paid the same as prison guards. Prior to 1981, Washington state prison guards earned more per month than the prison matrons. Those who argued against equal pay for the matrons noted that the matrons received less because their job was not as demanding nor as dangerous as the guards'. However, others argued that the only reason the matrons received less was that they were women, and women's work has, throughout history, been underevaluated compared to men's work.

As we have noted in previous sections, jobs traditionally held by women (e.g., secretaries and nurses) tend to pay less than jobs traditionally held by men (e.g., truck drivers and accountants). When these jobs are evaluated and points assigned on the basis of certain occupational factors, they appear comparable in their requirements or demands on the worker, if not strictly identical in duties. Thus on the basis of a point system, carpenters and social-service workers, accountants and nurses, and auto-parts handlers and dining-hall directors have all been judged to be of comparable worth; nevertheless, the average monthly salaries for these jobs differ significantly in various states (see table 8.3).

"And just why do we always call my income the second income?"
Drawing by Vietor; © 1981 The New Yorker Magazine, Inc.

A major assumption in any discussion of comparable worth is that the value or worth of various jobs can be quantified in some objective fashion. Social scientists, especially those involved in industrial organizations, have been working on the development of valid and reliable measures for evaluating jobs and their component factors since the 1930s and 1940s (Bales, 1984). And yet not all experts in job evaluation agree on the means of evaluation. The type of measurement for such evaluation, as well as the findings, can be disputed as being biased.

The real opposition to evaluating different job categories in terms of comparable worth seems to be coming from certain government agencies and corporations that stand to lose literally billions of dollars if comparable worth standards are applied to the hundreds of jobs that traditionally have paid less than other jobs (*U.S. News & World Report*, 1984). Many people argue that rectifying the problem of salary inequities between females and males should not come about by enacting new laws nor through the courts nor, for that matter, through the use of complicated formulas that compare the worth of one job against another. They argue that allowing the marketplace to determine the worth or value of someone's work is still the best way to solve the problem of wage disparity. Economist Jane Bryant Quinn (1984) sees another way for women to receive higher salaries. She writes:

If not by law, how else can underpaid women win a decent wage? One way is to quit practical nursing and learn to operate an offset press [both jobs were evaluated as "comparable"]. Another way is to organize. Nurses in Denver lost their comparable-worth case in court but won higher pay by going out on strike. . . .

Many women are wary of unions and with reason; most unions never did much for them. But the same techniques that worked for male blue-collar workers will work again. (p. 66)

Going on strike, however, is not always the answer, as many unemployed workers who went out on strike and lost their jobs have found out.

The issue of the comparable worth of traditionally female-dominated jobs as opposed to traditionally male-dominated jobs is growing. The vast number of women who work in the secretarial pools and on the hospital wards are certainly underpaid for the work demanded of them. Many are the sole breadwinners for their families. If the marketplace rules the day, the age-old discriminatory practices against women will continue. Flooding the court rooms with endless cases of job discrimination may not be the most desirable answer, but for the moment it may be one of the best alternatives to wake up our society and begin to bring down those institutional forces that view women as second-class citizens and pay them accordingly.

SUMMARY

In a modern society like ours, formal education is essential for providing a person with the skills to become a fully-participating member of society. Traditionally, the educational system has favored males over females. Although there has been a serious attempt to remedy sexism in education, there still are signs of sexism in various academic programs, in employment opportunities at the university or college level, and in athletic programs.

The workplace not only provides a means of making a living, it also gives the employed a sense of identity and self-worth. Several myths have evolved over the years about women workers. The ideas that women work only for some extra pin money and that they lack the motivation to succeed in the workplace have been shown to be false. Females find discrimination to be common in the workplace. For example, the average female worker earns only sixty cents compared to the average male worker's one dollar. Also, a large proportion of female workers are forced into certain job categories, creating a type of low-paying and low-status job ghetto. Several social barriers—prejudice against female workers, the presence of gatekeepers, lack of informal groups, and conflict between women's work roles and mother roles—continue to keep women in low-paying and low-status jobs.

The issue of comparable worth promises to be one of the most controversial social concerns for this decade. Businesses and the federal government appear to be blocking moves to implement equalizing salaries on the basis of a person's contributions rather than setting salaries according to job titles. Studies have found that when jobs have similar duties and responsibilities, but unequal pay, the higher-paying jobs are more likely to be held by males, while the lower-paying jobs employ more females.

SUGGESTED READINGS

Best, R. (1983). *We've all got scars: What boys and girls learn in elementary school.* Bloomington: Indiana University Press.

Farley, J. (Ed.). (1981). *Sex discrimination in higher education.* Ithaca, NY: ILR Publications.

Forisha, B., & Goldman, B. (Eds.). (1981). *Outside on the inside: Women and organizations.* Englewood Cliffs, NJ: Prentice-Hall.

Frazier, N., & Sadker, M. (1973). *Sexism in school and society.* New York: Harper & Row.

Howe, F. (1984). *Myths of coeducation.* Bloomington: Indiana University Press.

Kanter, R. (1984). *Men and women of the corporation* (2d ed.). New York: Basic Books.

Leghorn, L., & Parker, K. (1981). *Women's worth.* Boston: Routledge and Kegan Paul.

Perum, P. (Ed.). (1982). *The undergraduate woman: Issues in educational equity.* Lexington, MA: Lexington Books.

Remick, H. (Ed.). (1984). *Comparable worth and wage discrimination.* Philadelphia: Temple University Press.

Szafran, R., & Austin, S. (1984). *Universities and women faculty.* New York: Praeger.

Point/Counterpoint

Are Boys Discriminated against in School?

Much has been said in recent years about the many ways females have been and are discriminated against by our educational system with its sexist treatments in textbooks, the "tracking" system built into some curricula, and the counseling procedures that direct females into lower paying occupations. But could it be that boys, more so than girls, are really the little noted victims of a not-so-subtle discrimination pattern within our school systems?

The most influential proponent of the male student-as-victim is Patricia Sexton. Sexton's most direct statement on this matter came with her book, *The Feminized Male* (1969), wherein she contended that school, especially elementary school, is a "feminized" environment populated by dominating female teachers who are prejudiced against "real" boys. Female teachers, asserted Sexton, reinforce the behaviors of females and effeminate boys who seem more in line with the educational goals of a tightly controlled environment where discipline, routine, and order prevail. Sexton argued that to help "real" boys attain a masculine identity they should be exposed, during their elementary years, to more male teachers who could act as suitable masculine role models. Although Sexton's ideas are rather extreme, others have presented similar ideas about the negative effects of female teachers on young boys (Biller, 1974).

More recently, Stanford University psychologist Diane McGuinness (1979) noted that with society's push for equality, our school systems have tried to eradicate any and all individual differences, some of which she believes have a biological basis (McGuinness and Pribram, 1979). McGuinness believes that boys are biologically more active and that they learn in ways that differ from same-aged girls. Too often, the outcome in the push for a homogenized learning environment is that males are seen as not fitting into the educational regime and thus end up being victimized by having negative labels (e.g., "hyperactive") attributed to them. One dire consequence of such negative labels is that boys are more likely to be treated with drugs that affect their moods, personality, and learning potentials. The basic fault of our educational system, as McGuinness sees it, is that our school system, "fail[s] to develop all of girls' abilities and misuse[s] some of the abilities of boys" (p. 88).

In a rather extensive review of the literature, Joseph Pleck (1981) noted that Sexton's thesis that female teachers adversely affect a young boy's sense of masculinity is unfounded. If Sexton were correct, why then do we not find most boys, if not a large proportion of them, leaving school or ending up as psychological cripples because of their years of learning under "de-masculinizing female teachers." Pleck contends that if school is such a trauma for males, why do we find so many who go on to college, professional schools, and graduate schools and succeed? If Sexton's thesis is correct, we should expect to find the upper grades and beyond populated mainly by females, who with their superior education would end up in the highest paying jobs. As we know by looking around us, no such female-advantage is readily obvious in the real world.

The case that McGuinness brings up about young boys being more likely to be labelled as deviant and disruptive in early school is quite sound. But to attribute this to the push for equality for all students is, in the minds of many, unfounded.

What do you think?

_____

Reading   *The Issue of the 80s*

In 1984, the American Psychological Association asked Congresswoman Geraldine A. Ferraro (D-NY) to discuss the issues of pay equity and job evaluations. In the following excerpt, Ferraro describes some of the concerns surrounding pay equity and what it means for the future of female employment.

There has been a great deal of discussion over just what the terms *pay equity* and *comparable worth* mean. We are all familiar with the phrase "equal pay for equal work," which was mandated by the Equal Pay Act. Although this concept has gained almost universal acceptance, it does not go far enough. Since the passage of the Equal Pay Act in 1963, employers have found creative ways to circumvent its mandate, such as altering job duties slightly for women and thereby keeping them outside the scope of the law. The concept of pay equity emerged in response to the recognition that, because most women and men do not perform equal work, the Equal Pay Act was of limited utility in closing the wage gap.

Pay equity simply takes the logical next step to equal pay for equal work: It calls for equal pay for work of comparable value. Men and women should receive comparable salaries for jobs that are not the same but that require equivalent overall effort, skill, responsibility, and working conditions. Most of the controversy, it seems, swirls around the word *worth* in the phrase *comparable worth.* How do we know what a job is worth? Most of us have always accepted that a job is worth what it is paid. But when we see that the jobs women perform have artificially depressed wages, it becomes difficult to accept this measure of job worth. The real issue is sex-based wage discrimination. According to attorney Newman (1984),

> It really doesn't matter what a job is "worth," or what an employer chooses to pay. What does matter is that an employer may not discriminate against its female employees who

perform work of equal skill, effort and responsibility by paying them less than it chooses to pay the occupants of traditional male jobs.

Does this mean revolutionizing the workplace, as critics of pay equity contend? Will we be legislating the wages to be paid for specific jobs and imposing uniform job evaluation techniques on all employers? Not at all. First of all, pay equity advocates are not suggesting that nurses in Peoria be paid the same as electricians in Buffalo, even if the work they do is comparable. Rather, the effort is directed at individual employers to pay their own nurses, electricians, carpenters, and secretaries on a fair and comparable basis.

Second, the hue and cry over instituting job evaluations is unjustified. Job evaluations have been a basic tool in developing pay plans in the public and private sectors for more than 40 years, long before pay equity became the issue it is today. In fact, many employers used their job evaluation systems in defense of Equal Pay Act claims to show that the jobs women were performing were not equal to men's.

In 1981, the Supreme Court handed down a landmark decision on pay equity in the case of *Gunther v. County of Washington.* The Court declared that women were no longer confined to bringing claims of sex-based wage discrimination under the Equal Pay Act, but could pursue such claims under Title VII of the Civil Rights Act, which prohibits sex discrimination in employment practices, including compensation. In that case, female jail matrons charged that the county paid them disproportionately less than it paid male prison guards. The women did not assert that their jobs were equal

Source: "Bridging the wage gap: Pay equity and job evaluation" by Geraldine Ferraro, 1984, *American Psychologist, 39,* No. 10, 1169–70. Copyright 1984 by the American Psychological Association. Reprinted by permission of the publisher and author.

to the men's; they agreed that the men spent most of their time guarding prisoners whereas the women guarded fewer prisoners and spent a large portion of their time doing clerical work. However, they presented as evidence a county-conducted evaluation of male and female jobs that, although it ranked the matron (female) and guard (male) jobs differently, showed that the county paid the women only 70% of the evaluated worth of the female jobs whereas the men were paid 100% of the evaluated worth of the male jobs.

This case raised two important points. The first is that the Court did not impose a job evaluation scheme on the county nor did it make an independent judgment as to the worth of the female matrons' jobs compared to the male guards' jobs. Rather, it simply took as evidence an existing job evaluation that showed the county to be artificially depressing the wages of female jail matrons 30% below what the county itself had determined such jobs to be worth.

The second point is that job evaluations probably offer women the best hope of achieving pay equity in the workplace. If employers are unwilling to institute them (as they may be now for fear of implicating themselves in lawsuits), female employees and their unions may increasingly seek outside consultants to study their employers' wage-setting practices, using job evaluation techniques. However, it is important that industrial/organizational psychologists, personnel specialists, and others involved with designing job evaluations keep in mind that job evaluations will further the cause of pay equity only to the extent that they themselves are free of sex bias.

The National Academy of Sciences report (Hartmann & Treiman, 1981) identified several major problems with many job evaluation plans, particularly those designed before antidiscrimination laws were enacted. Many existing plans simply incorporated the sex bias that was already present in an employers' pay structure. For example, many employers developed their job evaluation systems by analyzing what attributes of jobs best predicted prevailing pay rates. Using this method, one knows in advance that the highest paid job will receive the highest score, and the existing wage differentials will be perpetuated.

Another problem occurs when job evaluators bring outdated, stereotyped assumptions into their analysis. For example, the job evaluator for the Government Printing Office awarded no points to female bindery workers for training or experience in hand sewing "because the sewing was of the variety most women know how to perform," thereby undervaluing the female compared to the male bookbinder jobs.

In addition, the way a job factor is measured may also affect substantially the outcome of an analysis. For example, if "effort" is measured by the degree of physical strength required in a job, many male-dominated jobs will receive higher scores than female-dominated jobs that are equally demanding, but whose effort is better measured by concentration, manual dexterity, and eye or back strain.

Another potential source of bias is the use of multiple job evaluation plans by an employer. Many organizations use one system for white-collar, executive jobs, another for clerical jobs, another for blue-collar jobs, and so on. This lack of uniformity makes it difficult to compare jobs across different occupational sectors. Because the segregation of women into different job sectors from men is a major source of the wage gap, the inability to compare jobs across sectors renders such job evaluations useless in analyzing and eliminating wage discrimination.

There are, I am sure, other potential sources of discrimination to be found in the design and implementation of job evaluations. Most are not intentional, but are the result of outmoded assumptions and practices that have failed to be adapted to social and legal change. Instead of waiting for these practices to be challenged in a pay equity lawsuit, it would be far better for job evaluation professionals, sensitized to the concept of pay equity, to instigate change from within.

The issue of pay equity holds great promise and challenge for the working women of our country. It promises women fair and decent wages based not on their sex but on the value of their work. But the challenge of pay equity is that remedying it is a slow and expensive process.

However, we do not need major new federal legislation on the scale of the Equal Pay Act to achieve pay equity. What we do need is vigorous enforcement of the laws, such as Title VII, that provide for the elimination of discrimination in employment. Unfortunately, in the Reagan administration, the very agency charged with securing equality in employment for women and minorities—the Equal Employment Opportunity Commission (EEOC)—has turned a deaf ear to women's appeals for pay equity. Proponents for pay equity in Congress have introduced several initiatives to require the government to reassume a leadership role in the pay equity movement.

Fortunately, the lack of support on the part of the Equal Employment Opportunity Commission has not stopped the drive for pay equity from going forward. Thanks to the commitment of individual women and supportive unions, major strides have been made in remedying wage discrimination through negotiation, collective bargaining, and litigation. The use of job evaluation studies has figured prominently in these pay equity success stories. I hope that there will be increased activity and research to perfect this pay equity tool so that we may move closer to bridging the wage gap—and ultimately the poverty gap—between men and women.

Chapter 9

RELIGION AND POLITICS

T he debate on women and religion is the single most important and radical question for our time and the foreseeable future precisely because it concerns religion and because it affects all possible people and peoples.

Patricia Martin Doyle

American politics is still a predominantly masculine exercise. But today, as their lives have opened into new careers and broader avenues of participation in American life, women are acquiring political power to a degree that they never have before.

Lance Morrow

Religion and politics are two areas where discussions between two usually rational people holding different views quite often take on an adversarial air. Consequently, what starts out as an ecumenical or a bipartisan dialogue breaks down leaving both sides more firmly entrenched in their own particular viewpoint. Few social institutions, however, have as much influence on each and every one of us as do religion and politics, even for those who do not attend church nor vote in elections.

In this chapter, we will begin by examining the institution of religion. We will note how the Judeo-Christian tradition has affected our thinking about gender, with special attention given to how religion has defined and treated women. Next, we will focus on politics. Here again, we will concentrate on how women, who only a little over sixty years ago won the right to vote, are now being seen as one of the most powerful voting blocks in our political system.

We shall try to present the ideas in a nondogmatic fashion. Little is gained by simply attacking either institution—religion or politics—as a major source of sexist ideology. It is hoped that the reader will come to see that religion, which claims to support the highest of human and spiritual values, has more often than not treated half the human race in shockingly shameful and degrading ways; the same indictment can be leveled at the body politic. However, those who wish to rectify such oppression can better do so by first understanding the extent of these institutions' injustices against women and then setting out to change these institutions by working to eliminate sexism within, rather than merely railing against them. For all their faults, and there are many, we are not about to get rid of either religion or politics. But we can change how they both treat and view women.

RELIGION AND GENDER

When people question why their lives take certain turns and not others, when people mourn another's death and seek solace in the belief of an afterlife, or when people simply look for guidance to some of life's imponderable questions, they may turn to religion for these and other answers. Thus, religion offers an emotionally satisfying explanation for many of life's problems, such as suffering and death (Berger, 1967).

What is *religion*? Sociologist Emile Durkheim (1965/1912) defined religion as that organized system of beliefs and rituals that focuses on the "sacred." By sacred, Durkheim meant those aspects of reality beyond simple human comprehension, consisting of special categories that stand apart and have special meanings. Durkheim contrasted the sacred with that of the "profane," which consists of the ordinary and everyday aspects of life.

But what does religion with its focus on the sacred have to do with gender roles, which concern some of the more mundane aspects of everyday life? To answer this, we should note that Durkheim believed that one of religion's main functions was to support a society's existing social arrangements by legitimizing the relationships between people. In other words, Durkheim thought that religion was a powerful social institution that reinforced society's traditional definitions of what was prescribed and expected of people in terms of their various social roles. Looking at religion from this perspective has caused several authors to point out that religion both advocates a *status quo* view of gender roles and provides support for society's patriarchal views of gender differences and thus endorses various forms of gender discrimination (Daly, 1968, 1973; Neal, 1979; Ruether, 1974a). Without question, religion does play a role in shaping a society's views of traditional gender roles. Some even suggest that, "Religion is probably the single most important shaper of sex roles" (Wilson, 1978, p. 264).

Social philosopher Karl Marx (1964/1844) offered another view of religion, one very different from Durkheim's. Marx believed that the dominant religion of a society, for example, the Judeo-Christian tradition for Western civilization, primarily reflected the interests and values of the powerful and privileged within that society. Marx's rather unabashed disdain of organized religion centered on his belief that religion was little more than a drug used to narcotize the general public into complacency and compliance. Marx's statement that religion was an "opium of the people" reflects his negative view of religion most succinctly. For Marx, organized religion was simply a mind-deadening social institution that was used to keep the public passive by focusing the oppressed citizenry's attention on some afterlife spiritual kingdom where their earthly miseries would end. Marx saw religion as one of the main institutional pillars supporting capitalist societies in which the poor and powerless were promised future rewards (heaven), thus diverting their attention from the true cause of their miseries: the economic inequities fostered by the rich and powerful members of society. We may infer from Marx's analysis that religion serves the interests of men—the powerholders—to the detriment of women—the target of men's power.

As we have seen, religion is viewed in a variety of ways. Some people see religion as a social force supporting the *status quo* of society and the traditional gender roles (Durkheim). Others see religion as an institution oppressing the powerless for the benefit of the powerful (Marx). Still others view religion as a radical movement pushing for social reform (as in Central and South America where "Liberation Theology" works to remedy the conditions of the poor and destitute). But regardless of how religion is seen, it has been and continues to be a force that has helped shape past and current thinking about the relationships between women and men and what is expected from both.

In this section, we will begin by examining the ways that women are presented in the Old Testament, with its many different and often contradictory messages. We then will move our discussion to the issue of early Christianity and examine how the liberating words and deeds of Jesus Christ soon faded into a misogynous treatment of women. And finally, we will examine some of the recent theological and social forces that are pushing for full female participation in church rituals and leadership positions.

Women in the Old Testament

To a large extent, Western civilization owes its cultural and social heritage to Judeo-Christian traditions and values. Our way of life, with its peculiar world view, extends back at least three thousand years to the language, laws, myths, and poetry of the Old Testament portion of the Bible. Regardless of whether or not one is a believer, the Bible has had an impact on each and every one of us. The complexities of the writings and the span of time that the Bible covers prevents both easy analysis and single-minded interpretation. Condemned by some as being sexist and praised by others as being liberating, the Bible is one of the most, if not the most, important historical documents of our culture. To gain a better understanding of the relationships between women and men, we need to examine what the Bible has to say about both sexes, but particularly about women.

A study of the Old Testament is made especially difficult by the fact that it was written by several different authors during a period of time that spanned well over a thousand years (approximately 1200 to 300 B.C.). Yet, some generalizations can be made. The most important fact is that the authors of the Old Testament did not see the exposition of women's roles as a major feature of their writings. The Old Testament was, first and foremost, a book written about and for men. In the words of scripture scholar Phyllis Bird (1974), the Old Testament was a "man's book."

> For most of us the image of woman in the Old Testament is the image of Eve, augmented perhaps by a handful of Bible-story "heroines," or villainesses, as the case may be (Sarah, Deborah, Ruth, Esther, Jezebel, Delilah). Some may also perceive in the background the indistinct shapes of a host of unnamed mothers, who, silent and unacknowledged, bear all the endless genealogies of males. But it is the named women, by and large, the exceptional women, who supply the primary images for the usual portrait of the Old Testament woman. These few great women together with the first woman (curiously incompatible figures in most interpretations) fill the void that looms when we consider the image of woman in the Old Testament. For the Old Testament is a man's "book," where women appear for the most part simply as adjuncts of men, significant only in the context of men's activities. (p. 41)

Besides being a man's book, the Old Testament has been charged with being antifeminine or antiwoman. However, to say that the Old Testament is this or that is difficult to prove given the number of authors who contributed to it, the span of time represented in the various books, and the social, political, and religious changes that took place over the time span of its writings. We must keep in mind that the Old Testament represents the writings of more than a thousand years, beginning when the Jews were little more than a loosely-knit group of seminomadic tribes and ending when they were a rather settled and somewhat unified peasant agricultural and pastoral society. Within the Old Testament, we read of women being placed in positions of honor and respect right alongside men; in other places, we read of women being used in degrading and dehumanizing ways. To prove this point, we need only read the following quotes:

> I brought you up from the land of Egypt, and redeemed you from the house of bondage; and I sent before you Moses, Aaron, and Miriam. (Micah 6:4)

> Everyone who curses his father or his mother shall be put to death. (Leviticus 20:9)

> So God created man in his own image, in the image of God he created him; male and female he created them. (Genesis 1:27)

> [T]he men of the city, base fellows, beset the house about, beating on the door; and they said to the old man, the master of the house, "Bring out the man who came into your house, that we may know him." And the man, the master of the house, went out to them and said to them, "No, my brethren, do not act so wickedly . . . here are my virgin daughter and his concubine; let me bring them out now. Ravish them and do with them what seems good to you; but against this man do not do so vile a thing." (Judges 19:22–24)

> If a woman conceives and bears a male child, then she shall be unclean seven days. . . . But if she bears a female child, then she shall be unclean two weeks. (Leviticus 12:2,5)

We see in just these few passages that all of the Old Testament writers do not regard women in the same way. At times, a woman holds a place of honor; at other times, she is seen merely as someone for men's sexual use or in terms of her inherent uncleanness. To better understand women's position in the Old Testament, we need first discuss the controversy surrounding the two accounts of creation and then move on to a discussion of women's roles in the Old Testament.

The Creation Stories   Much of the controversy over women's status in the Old Testament stems from the two views of creation as described in Genesis. In Genesis 1:27, we read: "And God created man to his own image; to the image of God he created him. Male and female he created them." Yet, in Genesis 2:22, we read: "And the Lord God built the rib which he took from Adam into a woman; and brought her to Adam."

Thus, there are two versions of creation. Some contemporary writers have noted that the account of woman being made from Adam's rib and created second implies a degree of inferiority and subordination of women's status with respect to men's. Some authors have used this version to justify the idea of a husband's dominance over his wife (Sapp, 1977). Others, however, have noted a different interpretation of this passage, pointing out that being created second need not imply woman's inferior status (Swidel, 1976).

> In the early myth, woman is created as help and succor to man's loneliness. Far from denoting the idea of service in a subordinated position, the word "help" ('ezer) is generally applied to God, who is *par excellence* the succor of those in need and in despair. Woman is not a mere tool of physiological or psychological delight. She fulfills a function of creative complementariness. Without her, man is created incomplete. It is the woman who brings man to completion. Woman is presented as the completion of man's creation. She is not a secondary being inferior to man because, as some exegetes have thought in the past, she is created after him and out of him. The order of creation goes from the imperfect to the perfect. Woman constitutes the crowning of creation. (Terrien, 1976, p. 18)

Although we could debate the interpretations given to either one of the creation stories, the fact remains that in chapter 3 of Genesis, the female is tempted by the serpent and is described as being chiefly responsible for man's and woman's expulsion from paradise. God curses Eve because of her act and foretells her sufferings and her subjugation to man. "Unto the woman he said, I will greatly multiply thy sorrow and thy conception; in sorrow thou shalt bring forth children; and thy desire shall be to thy husband, and he shall rule over thee" (Genesis, 3:16). Unfortunately, many people have used Genesis with its stories of creation and expulsion to support a misogynous view of woman.

The Two Periods in Jewish History   Setting aside the debate over the meaning of the two versions of creation, what can we make of the different views of women in various parts of the Old Testament? One possible explanation lies in the extreme social changes that took place for the Jewish people during the sixth century B.C. Prior to the fall of Jerusalem (587 B.C.), Jewish women held a *relatively* high status within the Jewish community. Women were viewed in a rather positive fashion, as can be seen in the portrayal of them and the feminine presence in the Song of Songs, for example. During this period, women were primarily extolled for their wifely and motherly virtues. A Jewish man found his place in the world outside of the home, while a Jewish woman found her niche within the home. The dutiful and resourceful wife became the ideal for all Jewish women to emulate (Proverbs 31:10–31).

The Jewish woman was to make her home her life's center and her family her focus of attention. Granted, there were the few exceptional matriarchal women (e.g., Sarah, Rachel, and Rebeccah) mentioned in different places in the Old Testament, but it is highly unlikely that these few and their extraordinary deeds were typical of the women of pre-exile Israel. In fact, the women of Israel during the pre-exile period were not treated as well as nor did they attain the status of many of their female contemporaries in other lands. For example, a wife in Egypt was often the head of the family, with the rights and obligations that such a position entailed. And in Babylon, a wife could acquire property and be party to contractual agreements. Yet, the status of the women of Israel was higher than other women in the region, such as those living in Assyria. During the pre-exile period, we can say that Jewish women's roles were sometimes valued less and sometimes valued more than were women's roles in other areas. But, given what is said of Jewish women in books written before the fall of Jerusalem, it does not seem warranted to suggest that Jewish women of this period were generally despised.

After the fall of Jerusalem (587 B.C.), however, and the rise and rigidification of Jewish laws, Jewish women's status did most assuredly fall. During these years, there was a change in how the Jewish nation viewed women in general. The Jewish nation became obsessed with an awareness of sin and ritual cleanliness. The prophet Ezekiel spoke of sex and sexuality in terms of ritual uncleanness, not in terms of love. Ritual uncleanness became associated with physical contact with corpses, foreigners, and *women*.

In summary, we can say that the Old Testament portrays a masculine and patriarchal world where women, before the fall of Jerusalem, are valued in their roles as dutiful wives and concerned mothers. After Jerusalem's fall, women are seen as the embodiment of sin and evil. This latter view remained in force through custom and ritual until a young rabbi from Galilee broke with it in ways never before imagined.

Women in the New Testament

Christianity's roots spread out to several sources. The religious rituals of Judaism, the culture of the Hellenized Roman world, and of course, the teachings of the young rabbi known as Jesus of Nazareth all played a role in Christianity's early development. If Jesus' teachings about a future kingdom far greater than the glories of Rome troubled the Roman leadership, his teachings about and behaviors toward women proved more than a little unsettling to many of his Jewish male contemporaries. Jesus' views about women and his interactions with them showed in no uncertain terms that he broke with established Jewish traditions regarding women's place in society (Ketter, 1952).

Many of Jesus' contemporaries considered his relationships with women to be nothing less than scandalous, for it was Jesus who broke with Judaic tradition and law and conversed openly with women as equals. Jesus compounded his tradition-breaking behavior not only because he openly spoke with women, but because he openly spoke with women who were despised by the Jewish community. Many of the women Jesus conversed with were foreigners and/or public sinners. For example, there was the woman—a Canaanite woman no less—who asked Jesus to help her daughter who was afflicted with devils; Jesus performed a miracle and cured her daughter (Matthew 15:21–28). There was the Samaritan woman whom Jesus told that he was the Messiah, and she believed and went and proclaimed the good news to the surrounding townsfolk (John 4:7–30). And, there was the prostitute who washed Jesus' feet with her tears and was forgiven her many sins (Luke 7:36–50). In fact, Jesus traveled with many women, many like the former prostitute Mary Magdalene, whose reputation made her an outcast and the brunt of "righteous" men's scorn and hatred. Nevertheless, women of all types traveled with Jesus; they took his message to heart and ministered to his needs (Luke 8:1–3). Jesus may have been what people today would call the first feminist (Swidler, 1971).

Yet, the early Christian church soon fell into a misogynous pattern, and many people have pointed to St. Paul's writings as being the basis for the antifemale approach taken by the Church ever since that time. In this section we will concentrate first on Jesus and note how he redefined women's roles; we will then move to St. Paul to see just how he dealt with the question of women's place in the early Church.

Jesus Redefines Women's Roles   The exclusion of women from all but domestic duties was by Jesus' time a well-established norm within Jewish society. Women did, however, fare much better in Roman society, with many attaining a classical education and some even reaching positions of influence. In the pagan religions of the day, women held a prominent place and served as vestal virgins in many cults. In fact, many pagan religions were organized around female goddesses such as Isis and Astarte. But such was not the case in Judaism, which was organized around the monotheistic male figure Jahweh. By Jesus' time, Jewish women were seen strictly as obedient servants to their menfolk, and their primary duties were confined to the home. Yet, Jesus brought forth an entirely different view of womanhood, one which caused much consternation among not only the Pharisees, who tried to trick Jesus in legal games, but also his male followers, who evidenced the prevalent antifemale Jewish sentiment of the day. No account so graphically points to Jesus' radically different view of woman's place than does his encounter with the two sisters Mary and Martha.

> In the course of their journey he came to a village, and a woman named Martha welcomed him into her house. She had a sister called Mary, who sat down at the Lord's feet and listened to him speaking. Now Martha who was distracted with all the serving said, "Lord, do you not care that my sister is leaving me to do the serving all by myself? Please tell her to help me." But the Lord answered: "Martha, Martha," he said "you worry and fret about so many things, and yet few are needed, indeed only one. It is Mary who has chosen the better part; it is not to be taken from her." (Luke 10:38–42)

It is this passage, above all others, in the New Testament that points out the extent to which Jesus chose to break with tradition over women's place in society. In this encounter, Jesus established a view of woman heretofore unacceptable in Jewish society. In describing this passage, scripture scholar Constance Parvey (1974) noted:

> The inclusion of this story about Jesus, unique to Luke's gospel, is the keystone of the changed status of women that it reflects. While previously the learning of scriptures was limited to men, now it is opened to women. The story of Mary and Martha enabled women to choose. Mary departed from her ascribed role and was commended by Jesus for so doing. This meant that other women were encouraged to choose this new alternative: to be allowed, as were the young men, to learn the scriptures at the feet of a rabbi. (p. 141)

Jesus' message and his actions are clear with respect to women: they are the equal of men in that most important aspect of Jewish life, that of learning. Women are to learn the message of the New Gospel and spread it just as Jesus commanded of his male followers. They are not men's servants, nor are they to defer to men.

The men around Jesus were not as accepting of women as he was. Let's now discuss one of the most influential followers of Jesus and one who many believe set the stage for the later antifemale sentiment and attitudes that swept the early Christian church: St. Paul.

St. Paul and Women Probably no other early Christian leader has been so frequently vilified as the source of present-day antifemale sentiment as Saul of Tarsus, whose persecution of Christians led him down a road where, after a thunderbolt conversion, he became the one called Paul. Yet, St. Paul may be the one who tried harder than most other early disciples to deal with the social and religious complexities of the chaotic first years after Jesus' resurrection. It was, for example, Paul who argued with Peter for the right of gentiles to be baptized. It was also Paul who saw the need to eliminate all social distinctions between the free and the slave, between male and female (Galatians 3:28).

The basis for many people's thinking that Paul was responsible for much of the antifemale sentiment in the early Christian church stems, for the most part, from his dealings with and preachings to the Christian congregation located in Corinth. At Corinth, Paul found tension and divisiveness among the Christian congregation, and much of it was attributed to the members who had been influenced by gnostic teachings. Speculation has it that many of these "troublesome" members spoke out and openly prophesized in the worship services, causing a rift in the congregation (Parvey, 1974). Jewish tradition specifically prescribed that women were to be silent and segregated in religious services, and at Corinth many women were acting in peculiarly non-Jewish ways. Thus, Paul, probably frustrated by the errant ways of some of the congregation, took it upon himself to admonish the congregation.

> Any man who prays or prophesies with his head covered dishonors his head, but any woman who prays or prophesies with her head unveiled dishonors her head—it is the same as if her head were shaven. (I Corinthians 11:4–5)

> As in all the churches of the saints, the women should keep silence in the churches. For they are not permitted to speak, but should be subordinate, as even the law says. (I Corinthians 14:34–35)

Rather than an attack against the female members of the Corinthian congregation *per se*, we may consider that Paul was rebuking the congregation's members, both female and male, for their disorderly and indecent conduct in religious services. In the second quote, Paul forbids women to speak in the service, suggesting that he is following with Jewish tradition, but later on he states: "So, my brethren, earnestly desire to prophesy, and do not forbid speaking in tongues; but all things should be done decently and in order" (I Corinthians 14:39–40). No mention here that women should remain silent and restrained as many would think an antifemale stance would dictate. No, Paul's apparent flip-flop suggests that his real concern is the growing gnostic influence and its effects on the congregation's unity and practices rather than simply squelching women's public utterances in religious ritual.

Yet, if we accept that Paul may not have been as misogynous as many believe him to have been, how then can we account for all those who have pointed to his writings as the basis for the later Church's antifemale practices and sentiments? Constance Parvey (1974) goes straight to this issue.

> The subordinated role of women in the Christian tradition is not so much a problem caused by Paul as it is a problem of how the Christian tradition has since chosen to interpret Paul. By using his dicta against women as a justification for maintaining the status quo, the Church has overlooked the new theology of men and women in Christ that was envisioned, and neglected these uniquely new theological formulations of I Cor. 11:11–12 and Gal. 3:28. With this neglect it lost its meaning for the continual transformation of itself from the old to the new creation. (p. 137)

Paul, the fiery disciple, may not have been misogynous, but others that followed surely used his words to further their misogynous beliefs and acts.

Women in the Early Church

During Christianity's first century, it seemed that women were drawn to the teachings of Jesus more than men were. We infer this because women are mentioned so prominently by the early commentators. Yet, because of the Jewish custom of the day, men's, not women's, activities should have received most of the attention of the early Christian writers. Thus, women must surely have played a larger role in the growth of the new church than many present-day Christians may think. Women are frequently mentioned in the Acts of the Apostles (e.g., Acts 13:50, 17:4, 12), for example, the woman called Lydia who lived in the town of Thyatira and was a dealer in purple dye (Act 16:14–15). Lydia was a woman of no small means nor influence; she was an established person in her own right and probably had a household of slaves and servants. It is recorded that after she was converted by Paul, Lydia's entire household became baptized.

Also, a number of women who are mentioned in Acts broke with Judaic tradition and behaved in characteristically nontraditional female ways. In fact, we read about several who chose the way of Mary and not of Martha by studying the scriptures alongside men. Other women broke with the traditional role of the subservient wife who remains silent and deferential in her husband's company. Many wives joined their husbands to spread the Good News and became active in the public ministry. One of the more prominent husband-and-wife teams was Aquila and Priscilla, who worked with Paul (Acts 18:18,26; I Cor. 16:19). If we wish to have further proof of just how influential women were to the early Christian church, we need only note the miraculous account surrounding the death of the woman called Tabitha. Constance Parvey (1974) believes Tabitha to have been one of the most important of all among the early Christians, namely, a disciple. She writes:

> There were also other women with special status, including one who was referred to as a "disciple"—a Jewish woman of independent means, a seamstress living in the Jewish city of Joppa, who was called Tabitha (also referred to as Dorcas) (Acts 9:36–43). Tabitha was evidently well known and admired for her charitable work, her fine craftsmanship as a seamstress and her graceful manner (Tabitha means "gazelle"). Like Paul and Barnabas, she was never named with "the Twelve." Unlike them, her designation as "disciple" has been minimized by the Church. Contrary to popular belief, there is no agreement in the New Testament itself as to how many disciples there actually were, or who they were. The term can imply one who is merely a follower, or it may refer to one who is under the instruction of a specific rabbi or teacher and part of a small elite group of his adherents. Whatever the specific significance of the title "disciple" as applied to Tabitha, she was felt to be so valuable to the Christian community in Joppa that many widows wept at her death and Peter rushed to her side from a neighboring town to raise her from the dead—the first such miracle performed by an apostle. To be recorded as raised from the dead, and to be the focus of the first such miracle by a fellow disciple, she must have been considered indispensable to the congregation. Her exact status remains unknown, but that she was much more than merely one of the many followers is clear from the story about her. (pp. 144–45)

Yet, the early Christian community, with its concern over the immediacy of the Lord's return, soon gave way to the struggle between different versions and interpretations of the scriptures. As we mentioned above, the influence of gnosticism proved most troublesome to many of the early Church leaders. Probably one of the more serious rifts in the early Church was over the image of God as female or male or both (Pagels, 1976). In fact, many of the early "heretical" gospels, for example, the *Gospel of Thomas* and the *Secret Book of John*, which were not accepted as "orthodox," mention a female presence in reference to the Deity. Many of the early Christians influenced by the gnostic traditions offered prayers that included both a male and a female presence. "From Thee, Father, and through Thee, Mother, the two immortal names, Parents of the divine being, and thou, dweller in heaven, mankind of the mighty name" (quoted in Pagels, 1976, p. 294).

The Early Church Fathers and Women   The growing conflict between Christian and gnostic teachings led many of the early Church Fathers to focus on the question of the natures of women and men. By the third and fourth centuries, the common Christian view of woman's nature was that she was not made in the image of God. Woman was incarnate evil and the cause of man's downfall. Woman could only be complete when she was united with a man in marriage. Augustine, one of the most influential of the early Church Fathers, noted as much when he wrote:

> How then did the apostle tell us that the man is the image of God and therefore he is forbidden to cover his head, but that the woman is not so, and therefore she is commanded to cover hers? Unless forsooth according to that which I have said already, when I was treating of the nature of the human mind, that the woman, together with her own husband, is the image of God, so that the whole substance may be one image, but when she is referred to separately in her quality as a helpmeet, which regards the woman alone, then she is not the image of God, but, as regards the man alone, he is the image of God as fully and completely as when the woman too is joined with him in one. (quoted in Ruether, 1974b, p. 156)

Others were even more misogynous in their preachings. Tertullian, for example, a Church Father of the second century, laid the blame for the fall of humankind entirely on the shoulders of Eve and all of her daughters. It was woman and woman alone who was to blame for sin and evil. Tertullian felt no compunction in preaching his antifemale beliefs, thus setting the stage for others to follow in one long litany of misogynous sentiment.

> *You* are the Devil's gateway. *You* are the unsealer of that forbidden tree. *You* are the first deserter of the divine Law. *You* are she who persuaded him whom the Devil was not valiant enough to attack. *You* destroyed so easily God's image man. On account of *your* desert, that is death, even the Son of God had to die. (quoted in Ruether, 1974b, p. 157)

By the fourth century B.C., misogyny already had become a staple feature of Church doctrine. The liberating teachings of Jesus toward women were, for all intents and purposes, swept out of the Church and replaced by a patriarchal Church structure that raised man to the level of the near-divine, while casting women in the role of adulteress and sin incarnate (Prusak, 1974). However, during the fourth through tenth centuries, many women became involved to a large degree in the growing monastic movement. Some women even attained the position of abbess, which suggests that even though a patriarchal spirit was becoming entrenched in the Church, some women still achieved high status within its hierarchal structures (McLaughlin, 1974).

Medieval and Reformational Times and Women   Over the centuries, Christian tradition and teachings became more and more misogynous. We find, for example, the great Dominican scholar Thomas Aquinas stating that woman is a misbegotten male (McLaughlin, 1974; Winslow, 1976). According to Thomas, woman's inferiority to man is justified by the Genesis account of creation—the one relating that Eve was created after Adam and out of his rib. Eleanor McLaughlin (1974), a scholar in medieval history, interprets Thomas's view of women's subordinate nature in the following manner:

> Finally, as the Church takes her origin from Christ, so sacramentally it is proper that woman be formed of man. Her creation from the side rather than his head is a reminder that she is not to be despised. The subordination and inferiority of Eve—and therefore of all womankind—to the male are thus established before the Fall in the order of God's original creation: first, by reason of the primacy of Adam's creation, who was not only first in time and the founder of the human race but also the material source of the first woman; and second, by reason of finality, for Adam displays the peculiar end and essence of human nature, intellectual activity, whereas Eve's finality is purely auxiliary and summed up in her bodily, generative function. (pp. 217–18)

One of the problems faced in the medieval Church was the proliferation of female convents. As their numbers grew, so did resentment toward religious women. By the end of the thirteenth century, the resentment toward religious women had grown to such proportions that men sought to justify their efforts to prevent women from flocking into the monastic life. The extent of misogynist sentiment toward aspiring nuns and sisters can be seen in the following late thirteenth century Church statement.

> [T]he iniquity of women surpasses all iniquities which are in the world, and that there is no wrath greater than the wrath of a woman, that the poisons of vipers and dragons are healthier and less harmful for men than familiarity with women . . . wanting to provide our descendants with things necessary for the well-being of their souls as well as their bodies, we shall receive under no condition any more sisters for the increase of our perdition, but rather we shall avoid accepting them as if poisonous beasts. (quoted in McLaughlin, 1974, pp. 242–43)

Finally, the pecuniary excesses of the Roman Catholic church caused a sixteenth century Augustinian monk to revolt against the Church hierarchy. Martin Luther protested not only the exclusion of God's people from religious ritual, but the Church's stance on human sexuality and, indirectly, on the degradation of womankind. Rather than seeing celibacy as the perfect state, Luther championed marriage as the chosen state for the blessed. Luther, along with the other Protestant patriarchs like Knox and Calvin, believed that the institution of marriage was sacred but preached that women should remain submissive to men in all matters (Douglass, 1974; McLaughlin, 1976; Williams, 1978). A wife's duty to remain obedient and submissive to her husband was paramount in the Reformation's view of marriage. Even if a wife was mistreated and abused, she was to bear her sufferings in patience and silence, ever prayerful that her husband would desist from his brutalities by observing her example of humility and resignation. When a woman sought counsel from John Calvin, for example, with the complaint of her husband's abuse, Calvin replied:

We have a special sympathy for poor women who are evilly and roughly treated by their husbands, because of the roughness and cruelty of the tyranny and captivity which is their lot. We do not find ourselves permitted by the Word of God, however, to advise a woman to leave her husband, except by force of necessity; and we do not understand this force to be operative when a husband behaves roughly and uses threats to his wife, nor even when he beats her, but when there is imminent peril to her life, whether from persecution by the husband or by his conspiring with the enemies of the truth, or from some other source . . . we exhort her . . . to bear with patience the cross which God has seen fit to place upon her; and meanwhile not to deviate from the duty which she has before God to please her husband, but to be faithful whatever happens. (quoted in Douglass, 1974, pp. 300–301)

However, John Knox became increasingly vexed over the way some women of his day were usurping men's authority in marriage. He countered this trend with the opinion that women's nature was: "weake, fraile, impacient, feble, and foolishe; and experience hath declared them to be unconstant, variable, cruell, and lacking the spirit of counsel and regiment" (quoted in Douglass, 1974, p. 301).

Setting aside the debate over the benefits gained from the break with Rome by these early reformers, we can see that the reformationists' views on the nature of women seem to have been every bit as misogynous as their Roman predecessors. However, not all the reform churches held such antifemale beliefs. The sixteenth century Anabaptists, for example, placed many women in high positions of authority within the church structure (Williams, 1978).

Thus, we see that in the formative centuries of Christianity, up until just a few centuries ago, women's status waxed and waned. Women went from a position of importance in early Christianity to a position of vilification during the patristic period, and finally to a position of some status accorded women as wives and mothers during the reformation period. Women's treatment by religion has been less than laudatory, and overall, religion's legacy to women has been one of extreme misogny. George Albee (1984) sums up the treatment of women by religion over the centuries as follows.

In the name of religion, five hundred thousand women were burned alive as witches over the centuries. The world's major religions have perpetuated the most terrible barbarisms on women, [as well as] other forms of inequality and exploitation. (p. 83)

Women and Religion Today

The movement to eliminate the centuries-long misogynous treatment of women by the Church did not just spring up in the past several decades with the increased awareness of women's second-class religious citizenship. In fact, one of the more controversial aspects of the nineteenth century feminist movement was the debate over the inherent sexist treatment of women by established patriarchal religions. To draw attention to the inequities and injustices suffered by women, Elizabeth Cady Stanton, along with twenty-three scholars, produced *The Woman's Bible* in two parts at the end of the last century. Many of Stanton's feminist allies disavowed Stanton's work, with its reinterpretation of the Bible and the issue of sexism in religion, however, because they feared that it would surely cause controversy and take away from the organized attempt to win women their right to vote. But even today, scholars are still taking up with renewed vigor the work begun by Stanton to eliminate sexism from the Bible (Russell, 1976).

Others have pushed the issues surrounding religion and women's roles in the church. Today, the question of ordination seems to be one of the most pressing theological concerns for many Christian denominations (Christ and Plaskow, 1979; Swidler and Swidler, 1977). In the last several years, some churches have ordained women as ministers and as priests, for example, in the United Methodist and Episcopalian congregations. However, of the over 750 females ordained by the United Methodist church, none have been given a pastorate of a church with over 300 members, nor have any been charged with a multiple staff, nor have any been elected as bishop (Lyles, 1979). As for the Episcopal church, fewer than 800 women worldwide have been ordained. The question of female ordination, however, has split the Episcopal church's hierarchy. For instance, the Archbishop of Canterbury, the Most Reverend Robert Runcie, is opposed to any further female ordinations because he thinks it would damage the possibility of religious rapprochement with the Roman Catholic church (Apple, 1984). Among Jews, only a handful of women have taken up the Mary-role by becoming rabbis in their own right. All of the female rabbis—fewer than 100—have come from the Reform group; among Orthodox and Conservative Jewish synagogues, no female has ever achieved the position of rabbi. In the Roman Catholic church, the question of female ordination remains one of the most contentious issues (Elizondo and Greenacher, 1980; Gardiner, 1976; Ruether and McLaughlin, 1979). The possibility that the Roman Catholic church will ordain females to the priesthood seems very distant at the present time given the stance against such a change taken by the recent popes. However, as more women venture into this male-dominant profession, research into their backgrounds and motivations will provide important insights into the role of women as ministers (Steward et al., 1983).

In addition to theological issues, other issues of importance to women are also becoming concerns for many theological scholars, issues such as abortion and relationships between women and men in general (Harrison, 1983; Ruether and Bianchi, 1976; Russell, 1974; Schaef, 1981). The recent controversy over Sonia Johnson's stand on the ERA is a case in point. Johnson, a Mormon, openly supported the ERA and was censured by the Mormon church for her position (Weathers and Lord, 1979). Research has shown that religious denominations that are more traditional in their theological teachings (e.g., the Baptist and Mormon churches) are more likely

Figure 9.1 Above we see the Reverend Mary Schron, an Episcopal priest, celebrating a Eucharist service. Such scenes would have been impossible up until a few years ago. Although the number of female clergy is small, many believe that female clergy will become commonplace in the future.

to discriminate against women's achievements in the workplace and support traditional roles for women (Rhodes, 1983).

In summary, we can conclude that religion, which is one of the more powerful social institutions, has looked generally upon women as the "other" or as a second-class participant in religious ritual. The exception to this pattern of female discrimination may be found in the dissident religious-healing cults where many women have gained considerable power and influence (Finkler, 1981). But overall, even though women make up the majority of most churches' memberships, women continue to find themselves sitting in the churches' back pews listening to men, who for centuries have enjoyed the privilege of being up-front, nearer the sanctuary.

POLITICS AND GENDER

If men approach religion as if they and they alone were divinely charged with an androcentric mission, then men approach politics as if it were their very own game whose rules specifically exclude women from playing. In many ways politics is a game, albeit a game with very high stakes, wherein the winner walks away with varying amounts of power. To a large extent, politics is power and power is politics (Zellman, 1978). As we saw in chapter 6, the use of direct power is a practice more often attributed to men than to women (Johnson, 1978). The same can be said of politics, which until very recently has been kept as one of the social arenas that men have reserved mainly for themselves.

In this section, we will concentrate on politics and see how women, for the most part, have been systematically denied access to political power. We will begin by reviewing the history of women in political movements ranging from women's involvement in the Revolutionary War up to the current debate over the impact of women's preferences in political matters, known as the gender gap. Next we will discuss some of the important barriers erected to hinder women's full participation in politics.

Women in Politics

Although politics has primarily been a male domain, over the centuries some women have taken an active part in politics and political intrigues. Women like the English monarchs Mary I and Elizabeth I played their parts to the hilt, so to speak, in the political drama of the sixteenth century. Yet, even these great queens found themselves counseled by men, not women, behind the throne.

In American politics, women have traditionally been onlookers watching men make decisions and pass laws that to a great extent took little notice of or had little concern for women's plight. However, women's presence has been felt at various times in the early political arenas.

The Revolutionary Period and Women's Involvement   During the stormy years immediately preceding the American Revolution, colonial men argued and debated the issue of America's ties with England. As the early patriots' resistance toward England's control of the colonies grew, colonial women became increasingly involved in the resistance movement. A good example of women's involvement is that colonial women banded together to form the *Daughters of Liberty* (Kerber, 1980). The Daughters of Liberty met in public to spin cloth and to encourage other women to make their own cloth, thus ending America's dependence on imported English cloth (Deckard, 1983). The public statements and actions of the Daughters of Liberty served as an example to encourage others to stand up against English domination.

Colonial women not only made their own cloth as a patriotic and political gesture against England's interference, they also "lobbied" against the consumption of tea. Women from all over the colonies met in small groups to pledge an end to the use of English tea. One way that many colonial women used to discourage tea drinking was the trading of recipes for tea-substitutes, such as the new drink for which many colonists had to acquire a taste, namely, coffee. One of the better-known colonial protest groups came from North Carolina and became known as the *Edenton Ladies Tea Party*. Ironically, these women met not to discuss tea, but rather to discuss various ways they could break England's grip over the colonies (Norton, 1980).

After war finally broke out, many colonial men spent long periods away from their homes. Consequently, their wives took over the duties of running the homes and farms. Before the war, what was expected of women and men was usually defined in traditional terms: women were to keep the home and children, while men were to tend to the "outdoor affairs." The war placed a great strain on family relations because of the long separations of married couples, and it also began to erode the traditional separation of gender-related activites. Abigail Adams was one woman whose life was dramatically changed by the war.

At the war's outbreak, Abigail Adams (wife of a future president of the United States) found herself, like so many other colonial women, responsible not only for the care of her four children, but also for running the household and farm. One lesson soon learned by many of these women-turned-heads-of-households was that they could perform the duties once thought of as male jobs. Adams's "raised consciousness" of the inferior status of colonial women prompted her to speak out about the injustice perpetrated on women. She desired that the "revolution against tyranny" would lead to a new social and political order where the rights of all free people— women as well as men—would be guaranteed. In the early spring of 1776, she wrote to her husband of her concerns:

> In the new codes of laws which I suppose it will be necessary for you to make I desire you would remember the ladies, and be more generous and favorable to them than your ancestors. Do not put such unlimited power into the hands of husbands. Remember all men would be tyrants if they could. If particular care and attention is not paid to the ladies we are determined to foment a rebellion, and will not hold ourselves bound by any laws in which we have no voice, or representation. (quoted in Bartlett, 1980, p. 392)

After the war, Americans had a new definition of what was appropriate for women's roles. Never again could people assert with such assuredness that a woman could not handle the day-to-day tasks of running a farm or the many other duties of keeping a house without the assistance of a man. The question of women's rights, however, did not spawn a "rebellion" as promised in Abigail Adams's letter to her husband some years earlier.

Ironically, when the New Jersey state constitution was drawn up in 1776, it loosely defined the category of voter to include "all free inhabitants" who met specific property qualifications. Thus, for some years, property-holding single women and widows had the right to vote in New Jersey's elections. However, in 1807 the state legislature saw fit to rescind the woman's vote. The reason given by the all-male assembly was that they feared that women were too easily manipulated!

Thus, the Revolutionary War set the stage, so to speak, for a new definition of the gender roles in America. After the war, it was abundantly clear that the gender roles were not inextricably fixed by nature but could change if the situation warranted it. Although few dramatic changes with respect to gender roles occurred in the everyday lives of those of the new republic, the grip of popular wisdom on what constituted women's behavior was broken, and in the not-to-distant future, women were to once again champion their cause in the political arena.

The Rise of Feminism   Although we will examine the history of the feminist movement in greater detail in chapter 12, we need to point out here that beginning in the 1830s and 1840s, many women had their first taste of political involvement. Ironically, the path leading to women's political involvement came by way of religion. Around the early 1800s, a religious movement called the *Second Great Awakening* swept the country. From the distant mountains of Kentucky and Tennessee to the urban settings of New England, large numbers of people flocked to revivals and camp meetings to find salvation. The religious fervor of this movement was based on an emotional outpouring of one's belief, rather than on a serious study of doctrine. The religious experience known as conversion came about through an emotional release prompted by the group's support. Revivals were noted for their "loud ejaculations of prayer, . . . some struck with terror, . . . others, trembling, weeping and crying out . . . fainting and swooning away, . . . others surrounding them with melodious songs, or fervent prayers for their happy resurrection, in the love of Christ" (quoted in Norton et al., 1982, p. 186).

The religious fervor of the Second Great Awakening found special favor among women (Cott, 1975; Douglas, 1977; Welter, 1974). Women, who were thought more emotional than men by conventional wisdom, dominated the religious services. In the name of salvation, they began to speak out in public and to organize among themselves. Consequently, women learned valuable techniques that would serve them well later on in their struggle for their own rights. Before these women took up the issue of women's rights, however, many turned their attention to the crusade to end slavery. Large numbers of women publicly supported the antislavery cause and advocated an end to the misery and injustice suffered by black people. Two of the more outspoken female abolitionists were Angelina and Sarah Grimke. The Grimke sisters traveled extensively, speaking against slavery. When these two "firebrands" from North Carolina met severe criticism because they "dared" speak before mixed groups of women and men, the Grimke sisters noted that the criticism was not, for the most part, directed at their abolitionist message, but rather at what many considered their impudence—women who were so reckless as to speak out in public before men. The idea that women should be silent and subordinate before men left these two crusaders angered at the unfair treatment accorded to women.

In 1838, Sarah Grimke wrote a powerful tract that was included in the now famous *Letters on the Condition of Women and the Equality of the Sexes* that called specifically for women's rights (Lerner, 1975).

A turning point in women's political involvement with respect to their own rights came in 1840 when the World Anti-Slavery Convention met in London. Abolitionists from around the British empire and the United States met to support a world-wide ban on slavery. Among the convention's participants were some of the most active and well-known female abolitionists of the day: Lydia Maria Child, Maria Weston Chapman, Lucretia Mott, and others. When the female delegates sought seating in the main auditorium, they were refused. The convention ruled that it would be unseemly for such "delicate" women to sit with men; therefore, women were relegated to sit "behind a bar and curtain, where they could observe the proceedings without being viewed by the participants" (Wagner, 1984, p. 35). Consequently, many of the females in attendance returned to the United States determined that women needed to fight for their own cause.

Thus, the battle for women's rights began when women abolitionists found themselves attacked by friend and foe alike for the cause of anti-slavery. In 1848, the first convention to deal specifically with the women's issue was held in Seneca Falls, New York. Over the next seventy years, women fought ceaselessly to win their American right to vote. The battle took many forms, and women soon learned that a simple appeal for justice was not sufficient to sway others' opinions of the righteousness of their cause. American feminists took lessons from their English sisters and used unconventional tactics such as public marches and open protests to get their message—the injustices suffered by women at the hands of men—across to the public (Hurwitz, 1978).

Women did not win the vote until 1920 with the passage of the Nineteenth Amendment to the Constitution, but there were some small gains during the previous decades of struggle. For example, in 1869 the state of Wyoming granted women the right to vote. However, Wyoming did not accord women their right as citizens for any but the most selfish of reasons. Specifically, Wyoming in the 1860s was in dire need of women, and those in charge of state politics thought suffrage would attract more women to their state (Deckard, 1983; Flexner, 1971). Although the years from 1850 to 1920 found feminist-oriented women concentrating on winning the vote, many women got directly involved with other political and social issues ranging from unionism to socialism (Buhle, 1980; Dye, 1980).

During the years spanning the decades from 1830 to 1920, women had learned much about how politics worked. From those early years when women stood up at religious revivals and publicly proclaimed their conversions, to some sixty years later when they organized, marched, picketed, and attacked the male-dominated institutions in order to win a better life for all women, women found that the game of politics could be played by women as well as by men (Kraditor, 1971).

The decades after the passage of the Nineteenth Amendment found the feminist movement without a cause. With so much energy expended on the single issue of the vote, after the battle was won, many within the suffrage movement lost interest in continuing the fight for other women's issues. The promise of many of the early feminist pioneers that politics would become more humane and responsive to the country's well-being by including women's votes proved rather baseless (Scharf, 1980; Ware, 1981).

During the immediate years following passage of the suffrage amendment, some women found themselves in high political positions. Some even attained the governor's seat of their respective states. Women like Miriam "Ma" Ferguson of Texas (elected in 1924 and 1932), Nellie Taylor Ross of Wyoming (elected in 1925), and Lurleen Wallace of Alabama (elected in 1966), all served as their states' highest elected political officials. However, these women's accomplishments are somewhat muted when we note that Ferguson served because of the popularity of her husband, who was impeached as governor of Texas, Ross served out the unexpired term of her dead husband, and Wallace served because Alabama's state constitution prohibited her husband from seeking re-election. Thus each of these three women came to the office through marriage. It was 1974 when Ella Grasso of Connecticut finally won a governor's seat on her own merit without first being married to a governor. Soon after, Dixie Lee Ray of Washington (elected in 1976), Martha Layne Collins of Kentucky (elected in 1983), and Madeleine Kunin of Vermont (elected in 1984), won their respective state mansions on their own without the aid of a husband/governor.

Two recent examples also attest to women's emergence into the political sphere. In 1981, Sandra Day O'Connor became the first female Supreme Court Justice. Ironically, O'Connor, who graduated in the top 10 percent of her law class at Stanford University in the early 1950s, could not find a position in any of the law firms in San Francisco or Los Angeles after her graduation because of the long-standing tradition of not hiring female lawyers. She was, however, offered a job as a legal secretary! And in 1984, Geraldine Ferraro, a congresswoman from New York, became the first woman nominated by a major political party for the office of Vice-President.

The reemergence of the women's movement in the 1960s focused many women's attention on politics (Freeman, 1975b). In the past several years, in fact, we have heard about the emergent political clout of women in terms of the gender gap. Let us now take a look at this political phenomenon and see to just what extent women are changing the rules of the political game.

The Gender Gap   Soon after the 1980 elections, political analysts quickly pointed out the emergence of what has become known as the *gender gap*. At the heart of the gender gap phenomenon is the fact that since the early 1980s, women have in increasing numbers registered as Democrats rather than as Republicans. Furthermore, women were found more critical of President Reagan's policies than men were (see table 9.1).

Figure 9.2 Women like Geraldine Ferraro and Dianne Feinstein are changing the picture of politics. Politics, at least at the national level, can no longer be seen as a "male-only" club.

TABLE 9.1   GENDER DIFFERENCES IN VIEWS ON MAJOR ISSUES, 1982

Respondents' Views	Percentage				
	Women, Age 18–44	Men, Age 18–44	All Women	All Men	Both Sexes
Those approving Reagan's job performance	44	54	41	50	45
Those fearing Reagan will get United States into war	57	42	52	38	46
Those who would vote for Reagan backer for House	39	50	37	47	42
Those who would vote for advocate of different policies	51	38	48	40	44
Those who would permit women to have abortions in first three months	56	59	48	53	50
Those favoring proposed Equal Rights Amendment	62	64	53	55	54
Those considering Reagan's life-style extravagant	55	40	52	39	46
Which party is best on unemployment:					
Republicans	21	30	19	26	22
Democrats	51	46	54	50	51
Which party is best on inflation:					
Republicans	32	44	29	42	35
Democrats	39	29	37	31	34
Which party is best on Social Security:					
Republicans	21	35	22	31	26
Democrats	55	46	54	49	52
Which party is best on defense:					
Republicans	32	46	29	41	35
Democrats	41	29	37	30	33

Source: Copyright © 1982 by The New York Times Company. Reprinted by permission.

Specifically, in a May 1982, *New York Times*/CBS Poll, 55 percent of the women surveyed identified themselves with the Democratic party and only 34 percent with the Republican party. The same poll found that 49 percent of the men who were questioned identified themselves as Democrats and 37 percent as Republicans (Lynn, 1984). Regarding policy issues, women more so than men took a more critical view of Reagan's job performance. Only 41 percent of all women approved of Reagan's presidential performance, while 50 percent of all men approved (Lynn, 1984). Women's more pronounced dissatisfaction over Reagan and their disenchantment with the Republican party, coupled with the fact that women under age forty-five tend to vote more heavily than do similar-aged men, indicates a possible problem for the Republican party and a potential boon for the Democratic party in future elections. This precarious state of affairs has not gone un-noticed by the Reagan administration (Mann, 1984). Commenting on this trend, pollster Louis Harris noted:

> For the Democrats, this means that just on the basis of sex difference, their entire margin today is dependent on the vote of women. One can only conclude that a major area of concentration for the Democrats must be to nurture and sustain those positions and causes that hold special relevance for women. For President Reagan and the Republicans, the single and most formidable obstacle to their becoming a majority party in the 1980s is the vote of women. (quoted in Mann, 1981, p. 1)

However, finding women differing from men on various political issues is not something that just sprung up in the 1980s. Women's disenchant-ment with the Republican party may be a new phenomenon, but American women's political views have differed from men's for some years. Ever since the 1950s, as a matter of fact, larger numbers of women than men have registered their displeasure over such issues as political corruption, the Vietnam War, military expansionism, and the misuse of the environment (Baxter and Lansing, 1980; Lynn, 1975; Rossi, 1982, 1983a).

The political future of the major political parties and their candidates appears to be in the hands of women if women will vote in the numbers they represent (Smeal, 1984). Beginning with the 1984 elections and con-tinuing with those to come, women will have the numbers to decide who will govern and who will not (Abzug and Kelber, 1984).

The gender gap, however, did not carry the Democratic party to victory in 1984 as many predicted. Although more women voted than men as ex-pected (53% vs. 47%, respectively), a majority of women voted for Reagan rather than Mondale (57% vs. 42%, respectively) (*The New York Times*/CBS Poll, 1984). Why women did not support the Mondale-Ferraro ticket in greater numbers is an open question. Speculating on women's support for Reagan, Ann Lewis, political director of the Democratic National com-mittee, noted that women are affected by an expanding economy every bit as much as are men and that it appears a majority of voting females sup-ported the status quo and were influenced by pocketbook issues rather than any so-called women's issues (Women voters, winners and losers, 1984). All that can be said for the moment is that we will have to wait for future elections to see if the gender gap proves as potent a political force as many have thought.

Political Barriers and Women Politicians

Several recent surveys of Americans' willingness to vote for a qualified female presidential candidate have found that approximately eight out of every ten women and men would do so (Cherlin and Walters, 1981; Schreiber, 1978). Yet, the question is not so much whether Americans will vote for females, but rather, whether there will be sufficient numbers of qualified women candidates for public office. If being a woman *per se* does not cause a problem or a liability in seeking a public office (Lynn, 1984), then why are there so few qualified females in the political process?

The answer lies in the simple fact that, historically, women have found significantly more social and institutional barriers preventing them from seeking public office than men have. In this section we will note some of the more common and significant barriers preventing women from moving into the political arena in larger numbers.

Socialization and Political-Oriented Traits   We have noted in previous discussions that women and men are socialized toward different goals. Politics is generally not seen as a career goal for most women (nor for most men, for that matter). Could there be certain personality traits that men, more so than women, are socialized to exhibit that would increase men's chances of entering politics? One such trait that seems a likely candidate for a gender difference is ambition.

Jeane Kirkpatrick (1976) in her classic study of the 1972 participants in the national political conventions noted that, "in both parties, in all candidate groups, and in all age cohorts women had significantly lower levels of ambition for public office than men" (p. 411). Other researchers have noted a similar gender difference with respect to female and male politicians (Farah, 1976; Jennings and Farah, 1978). To put up with the demands of running for political office requires that the candidate truly wants to be victorious. In other words, a political candidate must be ambitious and desirous of victory if she or he is to win political office nowadays. In contrast, other more recent research has not found any evidence that female politicians, as a group, are less ambitious than male politicians (Merritt, 1982).

One critical difference, however, has been found between male and female politicians. As a group, female politicians tend to be more public-minded or public-spirited in their approach to political involvement than male politicians are. Male politicians appear more self-serving in their style and approach to politics (Kirkpatrick, 1974; Lynn and Flora, 1977; Merritt, 1982). Finding female politicians more public-minded than male politicians may have far-reaching consequences for the future of our political system. We might suspect that just on an intuitive basis, the public-minded politician may be a more conscientious politician, putting the good of all before self-serving and narrow-minded interest groups' needs. Perhaps someday politicians may have a better public image if more women enter political office.

Structural Barriers to Female Politicians   Most politicians come from groups like the business community and certain professions like law. Geraldine Ferraro, for example, went to law school at night while she was a school teacher and earned a law degree. Consequently, she obtained a position in a large city's prosecutor's office, a position that is often a spring-board into politics. Thus, part of the reason that so few female political candidates have emerged is the limited numbers of women found in what can be described as "political pools" (Welch, 1978). As more women enter the business world and various politically oriented professions (e.g., law), we should see the numbers of female political candidates increase.

Another barrier that prevents a woman from entering politics is the "gatekeeper" phenomenon. As we discussed in the employment section (chapter 8), gatekeepers are individuals who have the position and power to keep certain groups out of their professions. Over the years, political party leaders, the *de facto* gatekeepers of the political arena, have prevented many well-qualified women from entering politics (Darcy and Schramm, 1977). On the other hand, a powerful gatekeeper can help launch a political newcomer. Such was the case when Congressman and House Speaker Thomas "Tip" O'Neill helped persuade Walter Mondale to choose Geraldine Ferraro as his vice-presidential running mate in 1984.

Still another barrier facing many young women who may be interested in politics is the lack of female politicians as role models. The limited number of women, especially married women with families, who have successfully blended a political career with family life may prove a handicap for prospective women politicos (Lamson, 1968). As the lives of political women like Geraldine Ferraro, Dianne Feinstein, Elizabeth Holtzman, Juanita Kreps, Elaine Noble, Elizabeth Dole, and Rose Bird become better known, and as people become aware of how these and other women have woven politics and family life together, it is hoped that more women will step forward and throw their hats into the political ring (Lamson, 1979).

Situational Barriers to Female Politicians   The motherhood role is still one of the most important elements of female identity. Naomi Lynn and Cornelia Flora (1977) found that motherhood was an especially difficult barrier preventing many women from pursuing political office. The odd hours and constant demands on time that are required of the politician create special problems, especially for women with children (Lee, 1976).

Another problem faced by many female politicians is their relationships with their husbands. One's spouse can either help or hinder one's progress in pursuit of one's goals. The media's concern over Geraldine Ferraro's husband's (John Zaccaro) finances proved just this point. At times during the early months of the 1984 campaign, Ferraro's campaign took a back seat to questions of her husband's business dealings. One irate columnist wrote: "Most married women who will run for office in the future will have husbands involved in a business or a profession, a government job or another political office. Will the husband's work and his other interests forever dominate and take precedence over a female candidate's own background and qualifications?" (Kassell, 1984). The answer was definitely yes in Ferraro's unsuccessful bid for political office.

There are no valid reasons that women cannot enter politics, nor are there any reasons that once they have entered they cannot pursue a prolonged career of service to their community and to their country, a career that is every bit as distinguished as any man's. The problem is, however, that prescriptive gender roles, various structural barriers, and some potent situational barriers all conspire to keep the numbers of dedicated political women low. When people, regardless of gender, let others who are possibly less qualified serve in the political arena, our society suffers not only in the short run, but in the long run as well. As many of these barriers weaken and give way, it is hoped that more women will move into the political ranks, where their presence may make a discernible difference in the quality of our lives.

SUMMARY

Our views of how males and females should relate have been shaped to a large degree by the Old and New Testaments. Generally speaking, early Judaic traditions glorified the female in her wifely and motherly roles. However, this view was supplanted around the fifth century B.C., after which women were portrayed as unclean and were to be kept separate from men.

The rabbi Jesus shocked many people by openly associating with women who were shunned by Jewish society. Jesus added a new dimension to women's roles by supporting their involvement with learning. The writings of Paul were used by many later Christian leaders to support their antifemale stance. Although the leaders of the Reformation took a more positive view of marriage, they still supported a strict interpretation of women's subordination to men, especially in marriage. Today, controversy continues about women's place in religious matters, and more women than ever before are pushing for total equality in religious matters.

Politics has usually been a male-only pursuit. However, women have been involved in various political actions since colonial revolutionary times. During the nineteenth century, women played a significant role in the abolitionist movement, which ultimately led women to work for their own suffrage.

Today, women are a powerful force in politics as the recent attention to the gender gap shows. Still, many structural and situational barriers exist that keep women from exercising their full involvement in politics.

SUGGESTED READINGS

Fiorenza, E. (1983). *In memory of her: A feminist theological reconstruction of Christian origins.* New York: Crossroad Publishing.

Flammang, J. (Ed.). (1983) *Political women.* Beverly Hills, CA: Sage.

Keohane, N. (1981). Speaking from silence: Women and the science of politics. *Soundings, 64(4),* 422–36.

Rossi, A. (1982). *Feminists in politics.* New York: Academic Press.

Ruether, R. (1981). The feminist critique in religious studies. *Soundings, 64(4),* 388–402.

————. (1983). *Sexism and God-talk.* Boston: Beacon Press.

Siltanen, J., & Stanworth, M. (Ed.). (1984). *Women and the public sphere.* New York: St. Martin Press.

Point/Counterpoint

Women against Women

On June 30, 1982, the deadline for the Equal Rights Amendment (ERA) found the amendment three states short of the mandatory thirty-eight states needed for ratification. How could a constitutional amendment that clearly was supported by a majority of Americans fail in its bid for ratification (Daniels et al., 1982)? One possible answer lies in the fact that the passage of the ERA quickly became a battle that pitted women against women. In fact, more women than men opposed the ERA (Lear, 1976).

On the one side, women like Phyllis Schlafly, Marabel Morgan, and Anita Bryant crisscrossed the country speaking against the ERA's ratification. Groups with names like HOT DOG (Humanitarians Opposed to Degrading Our Girls), POW (Protect Our Women), and STOP-ERA all made headlines in their push to defeat passage of the ERA. The anti-ERA groups and the conservative writings of Phyllis Schlafly (1977), Anita Bryant (1976), and Marabel Morgan (1975) pointed out that ERA's passage would do irreparable harm to women and to their families. Such nonissues as unisex bathrooms, women in combat, and an end to alimony all helped to sway some women's opinions against the ERA. By and large, three main issues were constantly brought up to dissuade women from supporting the ERA (Marshall, 1984).

First, the passage of the ERA would defy the natural order of gender differences. These purported gender differences were assumed to be part of the natures of women and of men. The ERA would, in the minds of many opponents, undermine these basic differences. Second, the family unit with the husband-as-breadwinner and the wife-as-homemaker was doomed by the ERA. No longer would husbands be expected to provide for their families; under the ERA, wives would have to leave their little children and go off to work. Third, our country's vitality would be sapped by the ERA. Opponents were quick to assert that supporters of the ERA were not only wild-eyed, radical feminists, they also were pro-homosexuality, pro-abortion, and pro-socialism; therefore, our country would certainly fall into moral decay with the ERA in place. The fears of many people were played on and the specter of such emotion-laden issues as homosexuality, abortion, and communism all helped to sway state legislatures to withhold support of the amendment's ratification.

ERA's proponents were anything but wild-eyed, radical, men-hating communists. Women like Betty Ford and Rosalyn Carter—anything but misfits, militants, or freaks—supported the passage of the ERA. Rational arguments were presented that effectively cancelled out each and every one of the opponents' arguments against the ERA (Eisler, 1978). But in spite of that, those in favor of the ERA were unable to get beyond the scare tactics of the opposition, and the ERA went down in defeat.

Part of the problem was that the opposition proved more effective and more savvy at using nonissues than many proponents were prepared for. The rise of conservatism during the 1970s also may have helped the opposition's cause (Dworkin, 1983). Probably the single biggest reason for the ERA's defeat was that the pro-ERA forces never seemed able to muster the support of the working-class woman; rather, they relied too much on the support of the college-educated and professional women as their support base (Arrington and Kyle, 1978). Without a doubt, the ERA will be once again introduced before the national and state legislatures. Then we'll see which group wins the next round in the battle for Equal Rights.

What do you think?

Reading — *The Coming of Lilith*

In early mythology, the woman Lilith was presented as Adam's first wife. When Lilith refused to be subservient to Adam, she was expelled from Paradise and sent to live with demons (Walker, 1983). During the Middle Ages, children were told of Lilith as an example of what happens to errant women. Below is a different version of the Lilith myth, one that tells of Lilith's meetings with Eve and the development of sisterhood.

In the beginning the Lord God formed Adam and Lilith from the dust of the ground and breathed into their nostrils the breath of life. Created from the same source, both having been formed from the ground, they were equal in all ways. Adam, man that he was, said, "I'll have my figs now Lilith," ordering her to wait on him, and he tried to leave to her the daily tasks of life in the garden. But Lilith wasn't one to take any nonsense; she picked herself up, uttered God's holy name, and flew away. "Well, now Lord," complained Adam, "that uppity woman you sent me has gone and deserted me." The Lord, inclined to be sympathetic, sent his messengers after Lilith, telling her to shape up and return to Adam or face dire punishment. She, however, preferring anything to living with Adam, decided to stay right where she was. And so God, after more careful consideration this time, caused a deep sleep to fall upon Adam, and out of one of his ribs created for him a second companion, Eve.

For a time Eve and Adam had quite a good thing going. Adam was happy now, and Eve, though she occasionally sensed capacities within herself that remained underdeveloped, was basically satisfied with the role of Adam's wife and helper. The only thing that really disturbed her was the excluding closeness of the relationship between Adam and God. Adam and God just seemed to have more in common, being both men, and Adam came to identify with God more and more. After a while that made God a bit uncomfortable too, and he started going over in his mind whether he might not have made a mistake in letting Adam talk him into banishing Lilith and creating Eve, in light of the power that [he] had given Adam.

Meanwhile Lilith, all alone, attempted from time to time to rejoin the human community in the garden. After her first fruitless attempt

Source: Epilogue: The coming of Lilith (pp. 341–43) by J. Goldenberg, 1974. In R. Radford Ruether (Ed.), *Religion and sexism.* New York: Simon and Schuster. Copyright © 1974 by Rosemary Radford Ruether. Reprinted by permission of Simon & Schuster, Inc.

to breach its walls, Adam worked hard to build them stronger, even getting Eve to help him. He told her fearsome stories of the demon Lilith who threatens women in childbirth and steals children from their cradles in the middle of the night. The second time Lilith came she stormed the garden's main gate, and a great battle between her and Adam ensued, in which she was finally defeated. This time, however, before Lilith got away, Eve got a glimpse of her and saw she was a woman like herself.

After this encounter, seeds of curiosity and doubt began to grow in Eve's mind. Was Lilith indeed just another woman? Adam had said she was a demon. Another woman! The very idea attracted Eve. She had never seen another creature like herself before. And how beautiful and strong Lilith had looked! How bravely she had fought! Slowly, slowly, Eve began to think about the limits of her own life within the garden.

One day, after many months of strange and disturbing thoughts, Eve, wandering around the edge of the garden, noticed a young apple tree she and Adam had planted, and saw that one of its branches stretched over the garden wall. Spontaneously she tried to climb it, and struggling to the top, swung herself over the wall.

She had not wandered long on the other side before she met the one she had come to find, for Lilith was waiting. At first sight of her, Eve remembered the tales of Adam and was frightened, but Lilith understood and greeted her kindly. "Who are you?" they asked each other, "What is your story?" And they sat and spoke together, of the past and then of the future. They talked not once, but many times, and for many hours. They taught each other many things, and told each other stories, and laughed together, and cried, over and over, till the bond of sisterhood grew between them.

Meanwhile, back in the garden, Adam was puzzled by Eve's comings and goings, and disturbed by what he sensed to be her new attitude toward him. He talked to God about it, and God, having his own problems with Adam and a somewhat broader perspective, was able to help him out a little—but he, too, was confused. Something had failed to go according to plan. As in the days of Abraham, he needed counsel from his children. "I am who I am," thought God, "but I must become who I will become."

And God and Adam were expectant and afraid the day Eve and Lilith returned to the garden, bursting with possibilities, ready to rebuild it together.

Chapter 10

THE FAMILY

We generally take the family in which we grow up for granted. It is part of the natural backdrop of our lives. At various times, we may like or dislike our parents or siblings, fight with them, love them, ignore them; but the roles they play in our lives are generally invisible. We are usually not aware of them.

Bryan Strong, Christine DeVault, Murray Suid, and Rebecca Reynolds

Families provide many things for their members, not the least of which are a base of security and support and an interpersonal web of often needed and helpful relationships. In the Old Testament we read about the benefits of family relations.

> Two are better than one, because they have a good reward for their toil. For if they fall, one will lift up his fellow; but woe to him who is alone when he falls and has not another to lift him up. Again if two lie together, they are warm; but how can one be warm alone? And though a man might prevail against one, two will withstand him. A three-fold cord is not quickly broken. (Ecclesiastes 4:9–12)

In this chapter we are going to examine the family. After briefly outlining the origins of the family, we will focus on the traditional family roles of the husband/father and the wife/mother. First, we will examine the husband's work role and then take a look at the concern over the husband's involvement or lack thereof in the family role, including household work and childcare. Next, we will look at the traditional role of the wife/mother as the guardian of the home and at the impact of the motherhood mandate. Then we will note how the institution of marriage affects men and women quite differently, suggesting that generally husbands fare much better than wives. Next, we will describe some of the nontraditional roles that we are seeing in families today: househusbands, child-free couples, wives who earn more than their husbands, and single parents. We will end our discussion by examining the issue of family violence.

THE ORIGINS OF THE FAMILY

When did the first family come into existence? Did its members feel commitment or love for each other? And why did females and males stay together? These and many other questions that we could ask are all difficult to answer because no one really knows with certainty when or where the family originated. No recorded evidence exists that outlines when that fateful event took place and under what circumstances. Somewhere between 100,000 to 2,000,000 years ago seems to be a good estimate of when our hominid ancestors initially banded together in the first familylike social units. To better understand the family as we know it today, we should at least try to imagine how and under what circumstances the family developed. Anthropologist Kathleen Gough (1984) provides one possible scenario for the origin of the family. (Keep in mind that these views and others about the origins of the family are purely speculative. The genesis of family relations and other social behaviors are continually being questioned [Eckholm, 1984]).

Gough suggests that the first evidence of family life can be traced to the time when apelike creatures in Africa began to walk upright. Over a period of time, the upright hominids cautiously descended from their tree-top domains to the ground, where lush vegetation was more plentiful. With their front limbs free and with the use of an opposable thumb, the hominids could better grasp and hold objects, such as vegetation, weapons, and of course, their infants. As the edible vegetation grew more scarce, the hominids were forced to seek other food sources. The next step was most likely the development of hunting skills. Rather than scavenging dead or near-dead animals for food, the swift-running hominids probably banned together in groups and began to hunt healthy animals. However, to hunt successfully demanded cooperation between group members, and cooperation for the hunt required a more elaborate communication system. According to Gough, language and humanness are linked. The question of whether or not the family unit was in place at this time of human development is hard to answer. Gough notes:

> It is not known whether some kind of embryonic family came before, with, or after the origin of language. Since language is the accepted criterion of humanness, this means that we do not even know whether our ancestors acquired the basics of family life before or after they were human. The chances are that language and the family developed together over a long period. But the evidence is sketchy. (1984, p. 83)

With hunting came the beginnings of a division of labor between group members (Lee and Devore, 1968). By its very nature, hunting required stamina and the freedom to travel great distances over a wide range of territory. Male hominids were especially adept at hunting because of their great physical strength, stamina, and, of course, their expendability. Females, however, were needed to care for their young and were able to forage for food closer to the campsite. One advantage accruing from this division of labor was that the food provided by females was a more reliable source for the group than that provided by males from the hunt (Tanner, 1981). The greater contribution made by females to the group's survival has become a more widely accepted observation recently (Dahlberg, 1981).

A change in mating behavior also led to the development of the family as we know it today. Among primates in general, the female is sexually receptive only at certain times or when she is "in heat." Among our hominid ancestors, however, the female became sexually responsive year-round. This change in mating behavior permitted the development of a bond connecting the male and the mother and their offspring. With the development of year-round sexual activity, the hominids took another step toward becoming a family unit (Pfieffer, 1969).

Thus several features combined to foster the development of the family: an upright walking posture and opposable thumb; the development of the hunting-gathering social pattern and year-round mating; and the large hominid brain with its expandable cortex, which prolonged the dependency of the young and made possible the acquisition of language. As already noted, it is difficult to date with any certainty when all of this came about. And yet each of these elements apparently played a part in the development of the family unit.

THE FAMILY AND GENDER ROLES

The family and gender roles go together like the proverbial "horse and carriage." As Jean Lipman-Blumen (1984, p. 99) states, "The family is the cradle of gender roles." As noted above, the early division of labor—women as gatherers and child-caretakers and men as hunters—became a pervasive social pattern for most women and men throughout most of human history. Whether today's gender roles are direct by-products of our biology (Wilson, 1978) or simply a set of social constructions that have developed over the centuries and magnified a few biological differences (Thorne, 1982) continues to be a highly debatable issue. What is certain, however, is that we learn many of the elements of our gender roles very early in life. As described in chapter 4, the family plays a large part in teaching the young what is expected of them in terms of their gender roles, primarily through the socialization process.

In this section we will concentrate on the gender roles assigned to adult males and females in the family. We will first concentrate on the husband/father and wife/mother and note some of the expected behaviors assigned to each. Before we begin, however, you may want to look over the checklist in table 10.1 to see just what behaviors you believe husbands are more likely to perform than wives in today's families. After you finish, think about your responses to who does what in a family in terms of their connection to the hunting and gathering patterns of old. In other words, what does

TABLE 10.1 GENDER ROLES IN THE HOME: A QUIZ

	He	She
1. When you go out together, who drives?	0	0
2. Who fills out the income tax forms?	0	0
3. When you go to the movies, who buys the tickets?	0	0
4. When you're overdrawn at the bank, who calls?	0	0
5. When you have dinner at a friend's house, who helps clear the dishes?	0	0
6. Who will be called first when your child gets sick at school?	0	0
7. Who writes the "Thank you" notes for the gifts you receive as a couple?	0	0
8. Who is more likely to ask, "Where are my socks/stockings?"	0	0
9. When the car needs repair, who takes it to the garage?	0	0
10. Who does the laundry?	0	0
11. Who dusts and vacuums?	0	0
12. Who knows where to find the thermometer?	0	0
13. Who knows where to find the pipe wrench?	0	0
14. Who knows where to find the kids' summer clothes?	0	0
15. When you have guests for dinner, who makes the drinks?	0	0
16. When you have guests for dinner, who makes the coffee?	0	0
17. Who waters the house plants?	0	0
18. Who waters the lawn?	0	0
19. When you go on a trip, who packs the suitcases?	0	0
20. When you go on a trip, who packs the car?	0	0

hunting or gathering have to do with who drives the car when a couple goes out, or who buys the movie tickets, or who writes a "Thank you" note for the gifts a couple receives?

Husbands and Fathers

Quite often, people think that males can be husbands and fathers with little thought or effort. Yet, being a husband and father in today's society has its fair share of problems and joys. Enoch Bennett believed that "Being a husband is a whole-time job," and Wilhelm Busch noted that "Becoming a father is easy enough, but being one can be rough." Thus, we want to look at husbands and fathers and their roles, attending to what it is that makes these two roles both difficult and desirable. Although most boys grow up to be husbands and fathers, a majority have little or no preparation for the demands that accompany such roles. Ask most little boys what they want to be when they grow up and few will say "I want to be a husband and a daddy." Rather, most will say they want to be something else, such as a doctor, a truck driver, or possibly even an astronaut. Taking the role of worker is the destiny for most boys. As boys grow older, they begin to see their futures in terms of their being workers/providers for their families.

In this section we will first look at the male's traditional provider role in the family and then at his involvement in the family as a father. In the past several years, the topic of men's roles as providers and fathers has spawned considerable research and theoretical speculation (Emihovich et al., 1984; Lamb, 1981; Lopata and Pleck, 1983). Let's begin with the provider, or breadwinner, role, which is thought by many to be the central feature of the man's role in the family.

Bringing Home the Bacon   Ask almost any person what is expected of a man in a family and most will respond with terms that describe the husband/father in the *provider role*. Most people think of the husband/father as being the family's primary economic source or breadwinner. The issue of men's "breadwinning responsibilities" has recently received considerable attention in the social science literature (Rodman and Safilios-Rothschild, 1983).

It appears that a majority of men work not for self-fulfillment but rather because they believe that being a provider is expected of them. Most men and women, in fact, believe that men should be the primary breadwinners, for their families (Slocum and Nye, 1976). In other words, a "real man" is one who can be a good provider for his family (Bernard, 1981b). For a large proportion of working married men, being the economic support of their families is a primary reason for putting up with jobs that bring little in the way of personal satisfaction or self-fulfillment. In one survey, pollster Daniel Yankelovich (1974) estimated that close to 80 percent of all working married men believe their breadwinner roles give them their primary purpose in life. Yankelovich describes these men in the following manner.

> Their half-hearted satisfaction with their jobs reflects a precarious social bargain. The attitude of many of them can be summed up this way: "I put up with a lot of crap on the job but it's a living; I do the best I can, and besides I'm willing to make some personal sacrifice to see that my family is well provided for." Many men learn to accept the frustrations of boring work and lack of involvement in the decisions that make work meaningful precisely because they accept the necessity of making sacrifices for their family. . . . In other words, the typical adult American man readily accepts the need to make some sacrifices for his family, in particular the sacrifices demanded by the frustration of the workplace. Accepting these hardships reaffirms his role as the family provider and hence as a true man. (pp. 44–45)

And yet, the married male has not always been assigned the sole bread-winner role in the family. During the countless centuries that humans have lived in families, both women and men have shared in the various activities that provided for the family's needs. Beginning with the hunter-gatherer society and continuing through the agricultural period, the entire family was an economic unit in which all members cooperated for the economic well-being of the family. Not until the recent emergence of industrialization do we find the husband/father taking over the role of primary or sole breadwinner for the family unit. However, the early stages of industrialization still found men, women, and children working together.

The split between the worlds of work (men) and family (women), by and large, came after industrialization was firmly planted in the social structure of society (E. Pleck, 1976). As industrialization spread and became the norm, women and children were excluded from the workplace, leaving the husbands/fathers/workers to become the family's primary breadwinners. As time went by, the wife/mother was relegated more to the home, where her life revolved around housework and family needs. Thus the role of men as the family's primary breadwinners is a rather recent social creation.

However, with the dramatic increases in the cost of living in the last decade or so, fewer husbands/fathers could earn sufficient incomes to provide single-handedly for their families' needs. Since 1950, more women than ever before have entered the job market to help provide additional incomes for their families' needs. Today, the average married couple are apt to be co-breadwinners, with husband and wife sharing in the economic duties of the family (Barrett, 1984; Blumstein and Schwartz, 1983; Staines and Pleck, 1983).

To attest to how deeply entrenched the male-as-breadwinner ethic has become in our culture and in men's minds, we need only look to the consequences that many men suffer when they find themselves unemployed and thus no longer able to fulfill the cultural mandate of being the primary breadwinners. The plight of the unemployed husband/father was analyzed by sociologist Mirra Komarovsky in the late 1930s in her now classic study entitled, *The Unemployed Man and His Family* (1940). For the majority of the fifty-seven unemployed men in her study, Komarovsky found that the single biggest consequence of unemployment for these men was a perception of lost status and personal humiliation for not fulfilling the prescribed breadwinner roles in their families. Komarovsky went to the heart of men's identification as family breadwinners when she noted:

> [I]n addition to sheer economic anxiety the [unemployed] man suffers from deep humiliation. He experiences a sense of deep frustration because in his own estimation he fails to fulfill what is the central duty of his life, the very touchstone of his manhood—the role of family provider. The man appears bewildered and humiliated. It is as if the ground had gone out from under his feet. (p. 74)

Work, providing for one's family, and bringing home a paycheck all intertwine to prove and validate a man's manhood (Gould, 1974). And yet, times are changing, and few men today can prove their worth totally by being their families' sole providers in such an economy as ours.

Housework and Childcare　"In our society," writes Heidi Hartmann (1981), ". . . the sexual division of labor by gender makes men primarily responsible for wage labor and women primarily responsible for household production" (p. 373). However, the husband/father can no longer divest himself from his responsibilities to his family in terms of his *family role*. In the view of current research on men's roles, modern-day husbands/fathers

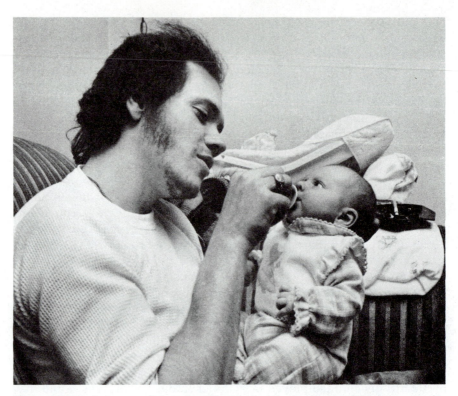

Figure 10.1 Today, many fathers are discovering the joys and fulfillment, as well as the responsibilities, associated with child care.

have two separate but interdependent roles. Today's husband/father must face up to the responsibility of being not only a provider but of being more fully involved with his family as well (Pleck, 1983; Pleck et al., 1980). Such a conclusion is noted by Alva Myrdal (1971):

> Men are no longer regarded as 'innocents abroad' in family affairs. Instead, it is becoming increasingly recognized even outside sociological circles that their role in the family must be radically enlarged. No longer can they be allowed to confine themselves to the role of 'provider', they must begin more fully to integrate the family into their life plans. (p. 9)

But to what extent are a majority of husbands/fathers involved in their families with respect to housework and childcare? With more wives entering the work force, there is greater pressure on husbands to "help out" around the house today than there was, say, fifty years ago. Generally speaking, numerous researchers using a variety of research methods find today's husbands/fathers participating in housework chores and childcare to a relatively greater degree than their fathers and grandfathers did (Ericksen et al., 1979; Model, 1982; Robinson, 1980). Although husbands/fathers are engaged in more housework than previous generations of men, we should not think that wives/mothers have been freed from the burdens of housework or that their husbands do anywhere near their "fair share" of the work involved in keeping the households running (Cunningham, 1983; Herbert and Greenberg, 1983).

Just how much work do husbands/fathers do around the house anyway? In one of the most extensive studies of husbands' involvement with household chores, Joseph Pleck (1983) analyzed the diary entries kept by both husbands and wives in a national sample consisting of 887 couples. These couples were asked to record all of their activities involving housework and childcare in four different twenty-four–hour periods over the course of one year. Excluding the diaries that were not filled out properly and also excluding the husbands who were not employed on the days the diaries were filled out, the final sample included 249 husbands and 298 wives. The results of Pleck's analysis can be seen in table 10.2.

Comparing the time spent in childcare and housework by husbands and wives, Pleck (1983) notes:

> Aggregating across all subgroups, employed husbands spend nearly two hours a day on all family work compared to four hours for employed wives and six and three-quarters hours for nonemployed wives. Husbands perform about 32 percent of the couple's total family work if the wife is employed, and 21 percent if the wife is not employed. Husbands perform somewhat lower proportions of the couple's total family work when there are preschool children in the family (27 percent and 19 percent in couples with employed and nonemployed wives respectively), and somewhat higher proportions when there are no children (36 percent and 22 percent). (p. 256)

One finding that deserves special attention in table 10.2 is the relatively small difference in family chores between the husbands of employed and of nonemployed wives. As many have pointed out, it seems that the employed wife has what can be considered two full-time jobs, one at home and the other in the paid labor force (Tilly and Scott, 1978). However, several studies have found that relative to husbands of nonemployed wives, husbands of employed wives perform a greater share of family chores (Duncan and Duncan, 1978; Perrucci et al., 1978). These studies' findings can be somewhat misleading, however, because employed married women are likely to do less housework than unemployed married women. Thus, although married men with employed wives are doing a larger proportion of the housework, the basis for this may be that their working wives are doing less also, and therefore their husbands do a greater proportion of the total housework.

Let us now move our discussion to the wife/mother and see what changes have occurred in the female's role in the family over the past several decades.

TABLE 10.2 TIME USE (HOURS/DAY) OF EMPLOYED HUSBANDS AND OF WIVES IN HOUSEWORK, CHILDCARE, AND ALL FAMILY WORK, BY WIVES' EMPLOYMENT STATUS AND PARENTAL STATUS: 1975/76 STUDY OF TIME USE

Group	Housework		Childcare		All Family Work		N	
	Husband	Wife	Husband	Wife	Husband	Wife	Husband	Wife
All Couples	1.61	4.52	.24	.91	1.85	5.43	249	298
Wife employed[a]	1.63	3.37	.24	.64	1.87	4.00	129	143
Wife not employed[a]	1.59	5.60	.25	1.16	1.83	6.76	120	155
Youngest Child 0-5	1.35	4.68	.44	1.86	1.79	6.51	81	94
Wife employed	1.38	3.48	.43	1.20	1.81	4.69	29	30
Wife not employed	1.34	5.25	.44	2.16	1.78	7.40	52	64
Youngest Child 6-17	1.75	4.73	.28	.81	2.03	5.55	80	105
Wife employed	1.74	3.71	.26	.52	2.00	4.24	44	58
Wife not employed	1.77	5.97	.29	1.16	2.06	7.14	36	48
No Children in Household	1.72	4.14	.03[b]	.12[b]	1.75	4.26	88	99
Wife employed	1.76	3.02	.03[b]	.11[b]	1.79	3.12	56	56
Wife not employed	1.64	5.62	.02[b]	.14[b]	1.66	5.76	32	43

[a]Means for the subgroup according to wives' employment status are adjusted by MCA for differences in subgroup distributions on parental status.
[b]Includes care to children outside the household.

Source: "Husband's paid work and family roles: Current research issues" by J. Pleck, 1983. In H. Lopata and J. Pleck (Eds.), *Research in the interweave of social roles, Vol. 3: Families and Jobs,* p. 256. Greenwich, CT: JAI Press Inc.

Wives and Mothers

In his nineteenth century play *A Doll's House*, Henrik Ibsen (1958) wrote about a married couple who became strangers in their own home. The wife, Nora, believes she must leave her husband, Helmer, and her children in order to "find herself." The following exchange between Helmer and Nora points to the dilemma faced by many wives in trying to subscribe to their "sacred duties" as wives and mothers.

> Nora. To-morrow I shall go home—I mean, to my old home. It will be easier for me to find something to do there.
> Helmer. You blind, foolish woman!
> Nora. I must try and get some sense, Torvald.
> Helmer. To desert your home, your husband and your children! And you don't consider what people will say!
> Nora. I cannot consider that at all. I only know that it is necessary for me.
> Helmer. It's shocking. This is how you would neglect your most sacred duties.
> Nora. What do you consider my most sacred duties?
> Helmer. Do I need to tell you that? Are they not your duties to your husband and your children?

Nora. I have other duties just as sacred.

Helmer. That you have not. What duties could those be?

Nora. Duties to myself.

Helmer. Before all else, you are a wife and a mother.

Nora. I don't believe that any longer. I believe that before all else I am a reasonable human being, just as you are—or, at all events, that I must try and become one. (pp. 64–65)

By mid-nineteenth century, most middle-class women were for all intents and purposes relegated to *Kinder, Kuche,* and *Kirche* (i.e., children, kitchen, and church). Even today, many people still believe that women should focus their energies solely on their families and homes. Somehow women are thought better adept at making a house into a home and caring for children's needs. Although more and more married women and mothers find themselves working outside of the home nowadays, the home is still thought of by many people to be a woman's natural place. In this section we will first look back through history and trace women's role as revolving around domestic and maternal duties. Then we will examine the conflicts that arise for many women because of the emphasis placed on mothering and on motherhood.

Guardians of the Hearth   As noted earlier, over the centuries women have been as instrumental in the sustenance of their families as men have been (Dahlberg, 1981). However, in the last century or so, women and men have found themselves separated as if both belonged in two different worlds. The world of men consisted primarily of the world of business and commerce, while the women's world centered around the more narrowly defined boundaries of the home. Such a separation was dubbed the "doctrine of the spheres" during the middle nineteenth century (Cott, 1977). The separate worlds of women and men were evident even to a foreign visitor to our shores. In 1831 and 1832, Alexis de Tocqueville visited each of the states and marveled at the equality he found in people's lives. However, he also noted that the lives of men and women were for all intents and purposes two separate worlds. In 1840, Tocqueville wrote:

> In no country has such constant care been taken as in America to train two clearly distinct lines of action for the two sexes, and to make them keep pace one with the other, but in the two pathways which are always different. American women never manage the outward concerns of the family, or conduct business, or take a part in political life; nor are they, on the other hand, ever compelled to perform the rough labor of the fields, or to make any of those laborious exertions which demand the exertion of physical strength. No families are so poor as to form an exception to this rule. (p. 225)

Although all women in mid-nineteenth century America were not exempt from "the rough labor of the fields, or to make any of those laborious exertions which demand the exertion of physical strength" as described by Tocqueville (Faragher, 1979), he was correct in his observation of the existence of two worlds.

Supporting the separate worlds of women and men was the belief in the inherent differences between them. Such purported differences encouraged the popular belief that women were better suited for domestic work and men for worldly activities. Women were not expected to do well in the world of business or commerce because of their purported limited mental faculties. But women were thought to be emotionally and physically better suited for domestic and maternal duties, which prompted women to be thought of as the "hearts" and "guardians" of the families, those most capable of providing the emotional bonds to keep families intact (Contratto, 1984). If men labored in the harsh outer world, they could return each evening to the protective security of their homes (made so by their wives). Historian Barbara Harris (1984) summed up the view of the home-as-refuge as follows:

> The function of the home was to provide a haven from the materialistic, competitive, and ruthless environment of early industrial capitalism. In an enclosed world free of vice and conflict, virtuous women would heal the physical and spiritual wounds their husbands sustained in the marketplace. (p. 17)

Along with providing suitable and secure homes for their families, women also were thought to be imbued with natural moral superiority. The belief in women's moral nature acted as a catalyst for many women to venture to distant lands to bring the message of religion and civilization to the "heathen" (Hunter, 1984). Women who were less adventurous or disinclined to missionary work stayed home and were expected to act as guardians of their families' morality, especially for the male members. Women were expected to counsel their sons not to lose their virginity before marriage, and they were also expected to control their husbands' boundless sexual passion (Perry, 1979). Husbands were admonished to save their sexual energies only for their wives; wives were encouraged to curtail their husbands' sexual expressions lest they drain themselves of the needed energy to do "battle" in the outside world and provide for their families (Barker-Benfield, 1972).

The separate spheres of men and women collapsed after World War I. Since the 1920s, the ideal has been that women and men should take on reciprocal companionate roles (Pleck and Pleck, 1980). Although the separate worlds have diminished during this century, women, until the 1950s, were still thought of as "queens" of their households; men were seen as kings returning nightly to their castles. As we have pointed out in a previous chapter (chapter 8), beginning in the 1950s, women entered the paid work force in ever-increasing numbers, thus helping to erode even further the belief that women should restrict themselves solely to the house.

The Motherhood Mandate   Ask almost anyone "who is best suited to care for a child?" and chances are you will hear a chorus of responses all exclaiming "Mothers." In most peoples' minds, mothers win hands-down in any contest for who can best fulfill children's physical, emotional, and psychological needs. In fact, most women believe that the most important function any woman could perform in her lifetime is becoming a mother. The notion that becoming a mother is an ultimate achievement is not as ancient as many may believe. Such a child-centered existence extends back only one or two hundred years in history. The ideal of woman's selfless dedication to her children even at the cost of her own well-being is only lightly rooted in our recent American history. Alexis de Tocqueville (1840) describes the total dedication of America's pioneer woman with the following portrait:

> Around this woman crowd half naked children, shining with health, careless of the woman, veritable sons of the wilderness. From time to time their mother throws on them a look of melancholy and joy. To see their strength and her weakness one would say that she had exhausted herself, giving them life, and that she does not regret what they have cost her.

If some think that Tocqueville's description is little more than an overly romantic portrayal of motherhood, we can find other more current analyses of mid-nineteenth century women. Barbara Harris (1979) describes a mother's role in the following terms:

> The most important function of the morally superior nineteenth-century woman was bearing and raising children. In the Victorian period motherhood came to have the emotional and semisacred connotations that tempt one to write it with a capital "M." The mother's task was to care for her children physically, preserve their moral innocence, protect them from evil influences, and inspire them to pursue the highest spiritual values. If a woman failed in this duty, she jeopardized the whole progress of civilization, an awesome responsibility indeed. . . . This glorification of motherhood and exaggeration of its responsibilities was as new an element in Anglo-American culture as the opinion that females were particularly virtuous. Indeed, the two ideas evolved together and reinforced one another in eighteenth and nineteenth century thought. (p. 71)

The "sacralization" of motherhood is not, then, an ancient element in the female's role. However, much of the pressure on women in the last century or so and which is especially evident today has inspired numerous social scientists to focus their attention and research on the question of motherhood and mothering (Gerson et al., 1984; Hare-Mustin and Broderick, 1979; Russo, 1976, 1979).

In the past century a cult of motherhood has developed and spawned what may be called the *motherhood mystique*. Psychologist Michele Hoffnung (1984) describes the motherhood mystique as consisting of four elements.

First, a woman's ultimate achievement and meaning in life is realized by her becoming a mother. Following from this, then, a childless woman is thought to never really actualize her full potential as a woman. Only by having a child can a woman experience fulfillment. Second, in the traditional sense, being a mother generally brings into play several other different roles, such as wife and homemaker. These additional roles are thought not to conflict with the role of mother. In other words, motherhood should not cause any problems or conflicts with the duties and responsibilities of the other role expectations required of the wife/homemaker. Thus, many people believe that motherhood never interferes with the relationship between the wife and husband and that it actually makes a marriage a better relationship than it was before the birth of a child. Third, a mother, if she is to be considered a "good" mother, should never feel anything but the most positive feelings about her motherhood experience and about her child. A good mother is therefore seen as one who is ever patient, content, and consistent in her dealings with her child. Anything less (e.g., if feelings of resentment toward her child should creep into her awareness) suggests that the mother is possibly a bad mother. And fourth, the mother's continual attention (some may suggest the word doting) is good for the child. The good mother should be on twenty-four-hour call if she is to be a good mother. This last element is especially disquieting for mothers who must work because of the fear they have that their time away from their children may somehow portend a bad outcome for the children's development.

Because of various features of the mystique surrounding motherhood, many of today's working mothers feel guilty about the time they must spend away from their children. Although our society praises motherhood with its "Mother's Day" and proclamations of "Mother of the Year," motherhood and mother-work bring little in the way of high prestige or other rewards that are normally thought of as desirable in our society, such as additional power or money (Heckinger, 1981). In many ways, such as by providing day-care centers, maternity and child-care leaves, and flexible work schedules, European countries are far more advanced in coming to terms with women as both mothers and paid employees (Lamb and Levine, 1982; Norgren, 1984). But providing day-care centers and flexible work schedules is not enough. Women must be allowed to control their own reproductive destinies, and women's worth as human beings must not be equated solely in terms of their having children; not until that time will women be seen as individuals first, just as much as men are.

TWO MARRIAGES: HIS AND HERS

Marriage, the social and oftentimes religious institution that formalizes the intimate relationship between two people, is considered to be a union where two become one. And yet the idea of two becoming one, as well as the belief that marriage affects both spouses similarly, is not held by most authorities on the subject. No less an authority than Jessie Bernard (1971, 1973) sees marriage not as one institution but two—his and hers. She writes:

> A substantial body of research shores up Emile Durkheim's conclusion that the "regulations imposed on the woman by marriage are always more stringent [than those imposed on men]. Thus she loses more and gains less from the institution." Considerable well-authenticated data show that there

are actually two marriages in every marital union—his and hers—which do not always coincide. Thus, for example, when researchers ask husbands and wives identical questions about their marriages, they often get quite different replies even on fairly simple factual questions. Although in nonclinical populations roughly the same proportion of men and women say they are happy, by and large when husbands and wives are asked about specific items in their relationships, the wives' marriages look less happy than their husbands'. For as Durkheim found, marriage is not the same for women as for men; it is not nearly as good. (1971, pp. 146–47)

Why is it that marriage is thought of as "not nearly as good" for women as for men? The answer lies, at least partially, in the unequal status and the power imbalance that marriage accords a husband and a wife. Historically, wives were thought of as little more than a husband's property (Scanzoni, 1972). We need to go back only about a hundred years to find a time when a wife was not allowed to control property, even the property she inherited from her premarriage family. According to English common law, the husband had total control over his wife. For example, a husband controlled his wife's wages, had the last say in their children's education and religion, and even had the right to physically beat his wife if she displeased him (Chapman and Gates, 1977; Kanowitz, 1969). Today we hear more about marriages that seem more like corporations in which one spouse (husband) plays the role of chief executive, while the other (wife) acts like a junior partner. And there is a growing number of marriages in which both spouses have full-time careers and both share in all decisions as equal partners (Scanzoni and Scanzoni, 1981). A marriage where there is relative equality between the spouses' rights and privileges is called an *egalitarian* marriage. The difference between these two modern-day types of marriage seems to be in the amount of power a wife has in the marriage. To examine why many wives may not "have it as good in marriage" as their spouses, we need to examine the issue of power in marriage.

Marital Power and Happiness

One of the more often reported studies of the so-called new marriage relationships was conducted in Detroit just over twenty-five years ago (Blood and Wolfe, 1960). Over 900 wives were questioned about who in their marriages had the final say in matters like "what job the husband should take," "what car to buy," "what doctor to call when someone in the family was sick," and "how much to spend on the weekly groceries." By and large, the study found that husbands generally made decisions about their jobs and about buying new cars, while wives decided on which doctors to call in cases of illness and how much to spend on the weekly groceries. In tabulating their results, Robert Blood and Donald Wolfe assumed that all decisions were relatively equal in importance; thus they noted that many of the families in their study appeared to have an egalitarian marriage. However, we could question the assumption that deciding to buy a new car is equivalent to deciding about how much to spend on groceries. Most people would have to say that these decisions are not equivalent, and families that distribute the decision-making process along these issues are anything but egalitarian (Gillespie, 1971; Steil, 1984).

Other researchers have explored the degree of marital satisfaction or happiness in terms of who has the more power in the marriage. Using many of the same decision-making categories found in Blood and Wolfe's study and in others, researchers found that marriages in which either the husband is dominant or where the couple shares in decisions (the egalitarian marital arrangement) appear to have greater marital satisfaction than marriages where the wife is dominant (Gray-Little, 1982).

In an exhaustive study of the literature on power among married couples and marital happiness and satisfaction, Bernadette Gray-Little and Nancy Burks (1983) note that "The most prevalent finding . . . is that marriages in which the wife is the dominant partner, whether in decision making or some other aspect of control, are more likely to be unhappy than any other type of marriage" (p. 531). Why should a marriage in which the wife dominates be less happy than those in which either the husband dominates or the couple shares power jointly?

One explanation for this is that wife-dominant marriages are at odds with cultural norms. In other words, the traditional marriage pattern (husband-dominant) and the more modern one (egalitarian) both have cultural approval or social support, and thus couples living in either type would sense that their marital arrangement is accepted and approved by society. Chances are, then, that such couples would feel more positive about their relationships and report greater satisfaction. However, in a wife-dominant marriage, there is a lack of cultural approval, and the participants may feel less satisfied living in a relationship that others see as a departure from the norm. Consequently, the couple may be more apt to report dissatisfaction in their personal and marital lives (Buric and Zecevic, 1967).

Another possibility is that husbands in wife-dominant marriages either can not or will not assume the husbandly duties prescribed by social norms. Therefore, the wife, the husband, or both may be more likely to report greater dissatisfaction in the relationship than those in other marital arrangements. According to this view, in the wife-dominant relationship the wife is unfairly burdened with some aspects of her husband's role in addition to her responsibilities as a wife, leaving her in an unhappy state of affairs.

As of yet, there does not appear to be any simple explanation for why wife-dominant marriages are less happy than husband-dominant or egalitarian marriages. In fact, some confusion exists with respect to the terms used in this area of study. For example, in speaking of an egalitarian marriage, researchers are now more apt to define two types of egalitarian marriages: *syncratic* and *autonomic* (Gray-Little and Burks, 1983). The syncratic relation describes a marital pattern in which both the wife and the husband wield power and make decisions jointly in all areas. The autonomic pattern refers to an egalitarian relationship in which husband and wife each exercise power and control over separate areas. Thus, we can see that even egalitarian marriages are not all identical.

Nevertheless, one thing is certain: marital power, decision-making, happiness, satisfaction, and marital patterns are complex issues that cannot be separated from the perceptions of those involved in the relationships. To understand marriage, we need first to look at how the participants think and feel about the relationship (Kelley, 1979).

NONTRADITIONAL FAMILIES

In this section we will look at several recent changes in the ever-changing mosaic of the family. First we will take note of husbands who exchange their work role for the domestic role. Next we will examine some features associated with married women who remain child-free. Our third issue is the growing number of dual-earner couples where the wife earns more than her husband. And finally, we will discuss single-parent families.

Househusbands

During the last century and most of this century, husbands have been expected to be the primary provider for their families' economic needs. And yet in this changing world, some husbands have opted out of the nine-to-five work world and have taken over the responsibilities of full-time housework and childcare (Lefkowitz, 1979). Dubbed *househusbands*, the media has featured the "trials and tribulations" of these men in newspapers and books alike (*Knoxville News-Sentinel*, 1984; McGrady, 1975).

No one knows for sure just how many "househusbands" there are in the United States, but a conservative estimate would be somewhere between 1 and 2 million men. Little is known about the causes underlying this dramatic change in married men's lives. Some are unemployed. Some may just be tired of the "rat race" and opt for an extended leave of absence, swapping roles with their wives who work full time in the labor force. Others, probably the majority, have jobs that can be done in the home (e.g., writers or artists). The rapid growth of the personal computer may also be a factor allowing many to stay at home and yet still be employed. The "electronic cottage" of the 1980s allows a person to stay at home full time and yet, by means of a personal computer with a telephone hook-up or modem, still be able to bring in a paycheck.

Few studies have been conducted on househusbands. William Beer (1982), for one, interviewed fifty-six purported househusbands to gauge their reactions to their novel marital arrangements. Although Beer's study suffers from several methodological flaws, his study at least addresses the issue that more men are beginning to take over some of the responsibilities of household chores and childcare while their wives are off at work. Most of the househusbands in Beer's sample reported a positive feeling toward their marital arrangements.

Are househusbands merely a fad, or are they a sign of changing times? At the present time we cannot answer this question. We can say, however, that many of these nontraditional men are showing all of us that men can run a house and care for children very well.

Child-free Couples

In the past several years, a growing number of married couples have chosen to be childless or, as many wish to call it, *child-free couples*. Traditionally, one of the first questions asked of a newly married couple is, "So when do you expect to start your family?" Nowadays, many couples either purposely decide to remain child-free for a period of time or decide to remain child-free for their entire marriages. Such couples are not as likely to be viewed with suspicion as they might have been just a few decades ago. Attesting to the recent interest in child-free couples, several researchers have looked at how child-free couples differ from those with children (Gerson, 1983, 1984; Houseknecht, 1979).

Susan Bram (1984) undertook one of the first studies to focus solely on the differences in terms of the attitudes and behaviors found among child-free couples, couples who delayed having a child, and couples with a child under two years old. Bram reported only on the females in her study, leaving the results gathered from the males for a later report. Overall, Bram found child-free women to be less traditional in their behaviors, attitudes, and self-images than the other women in her study. For example, the child-free women were more likely to have attained more education in terms of professional or graduate degrees than the other two groups. Also, the child-free women were more likely to mention the importance of companionship in their marriages ("being together at home," "being alone together") and express themes of egalitarianism in their marriages than were the other two groups. And last, the child-free women were more likely to identify with and support the goals of the women's movement than the other women were—a difference found in other research (Gerson, 1984). Bram sees the emergence of the child-free couple as yet another step in the ever-changing gender role structures taking place in our society. She writes:

> The woman who has chosen to enter the traditional institution of marriage, albeit in a nontraditional manner, has opted to combine affiliative and achievement needs in a new, but not completely unique, manner. In fact, each childless woman could be understood as an experiment in new combinations of affiliative and achievement motives. (p. 204)

The impact that child-free couples will have on society is yet unknown. What is certain, however, is that as the number of child-free couples grows, social institutions will have to change to adapt to an emergent life-style specific to child-free couples.

Wives Who Earn More

In the traditional marriage, the husband brought home the paycheck and the wife ran the household. The modern marriage finds both husbands and wives earning an income, but the wife is still primarily responsible for the household chores. On the average, working wives earn approximately 40 percent as much as their husbands (Bianchi and Spain, 1983). And yet, there is another possible marital arrangement in terms of employment and pay, and that is the marriage in which the wife is the primary earner in the family. In 1981, approximately 12 percent of the married couples in the civilian population (5.9 million out of 49 million) found the wives earning more than their husbands. In this group, approximately 4 percent (1.9 million) were couples in which the wives were the sole breadwinners and 8 percent (4 million) were couples in which the wives earned more than their working husbands (Bianchi and Spain, 1983). The effects on the marriage of the working wife who earns more than her husband have been debated. Some believe that a wife earning more than her husband has a detrimental effect on the marriage (Rubenstein, 1982; Rubin, 1983). Others argue that marital satisfaction for both partners is not lessened by the wife's higher earnings (Simpson and England, 1982). And others point out that working wives' personal satisfaction improves, but their husbands suffer additional stresses (Kessler and McRae, 1982).

A common misconception about wives who earn more than their husbands is that these women make up a new breed of "superwomen," superwomen to the extent that they are the top-level managers and professional women whose achievement levels and career aspirations are greater than their husbands' (Forman, 1984). However, in their study of wives who earn more than their husbands, Suzanne Bianchi and Daphne Spain (1983) concluded that

> If one merely compares wives who are primary earners with those who are secondary earners in dual-earner couples, one finds that primary earners are a more elite group than secondary earners in terms of educational attainment, occupational placement, and earnings. However, the majority of primary-earner wives are not college educated and are not in professional or managerial jobs. "Superstar wives" with higher achievements than their husbands may be an interesting group, but this analysis shows they probably do not represent the majority of couples in which the wife was the major contributor to earnings in 1981. (p. 24)

We will have to await further study to determine conclusively the effects on a marriage in which a wife out-earns her husband. As for now, all we can say about the 12 percent of the married couples that fit this marital pattern is that they are a minority group whose life-styles and marital roles are well worth studying.

Single-Parent Households

Single-parent households are the fastest growing segment of the various household arrangements today, accounting for nearly 22 percent of all families with children (Household and family characteristics, 1983). Between 1970 and 1979, the number of single-parent households increased by nearly 90 percent in the United States. In spite of that, the single-parent household still carries a stigma because it deviates from what most consider the norm for a family structure, which is both parents living together (Strong and De Vault, 1983).

Most single-parent households tend to be created by divorce rather than by death of a spouse or by birth outside of marriage (Thompson and Gongla, 1983). However, being a widowed single parent has some advantages over being a divorced single parent. For example, a divorced single-parent mother tends to receive less support from her relatives or in-laws than a widowed mother does. Thus, the problems faced by the divorced single mother are much greater than other single-parent mothers. Because a majority of single-parent households are headed by females (Sheils, 1983) and because of the prominence of job discrimination faced by women in general, many single-parent women live below the poverty line (Payton, 1982). Moreover, the nearly three quarters of a million single-parent fathers have many unique problems of their own (Findlay, 1984).

Most single-parent women wish to remarry because of the added stresses of raising children alone and the considerable role-overload faced in trying to be "all things" to their children. The presence of children may or may not hamper the chances of a woman's prospects for remarriage (Koo and Suchindran, 1980).

The number of single-parent households appears to be on the increase in our society. As divorce becomes more socially acceptable, there seems no likelihood that this segment of our population will decrease in the years to come. However, we should not think that all features of single-parent status are bleak. Many single-parent women and men, for example, have adjusted to their new status and have made new and productive lives for themselves (Findlay, 1984; Miller, 1982).

DOMESTIC VIOLENCE

Open almost any daily newspaper or switch on any local news program and gruesome scenes of violence are common topics. Yet many of the stories of personal injury or even death are not about people who are strangers to each other. Rather, they focus on one of the most devastating and least understood types of violence, *domestic violence*. Even though there is so much publicity about domestic, or family, violence, most family violence remains a family's best kept secret. Attesting to the privatization of family violence, the first book to examine family violence was entitled *Scream Quietly or the Neighbors Will Hear* (Pizzey, 1974). Still, the public is becoming more aware of the seriousness and magnitude of domestic violence due in large measure to the efforts of the women's movement.

In the past decade or so, several researchers have turned their attention to reaching a fuller understanding of the issues and dynamics surrounding domestic violence (Finkelhor et al., 1983; Gelles, 1980; Straus et al., 1980; Wiggins, 1983; Yllo and Straus, 1980). In this section we will first take up the question of the magnitude and degree of marital violence. Next we will look at several different views about the probable causes for marital violence. Then we will examine domestic violence, especially wife-beating, in terms of institutional forms that support power inequities between women and men.

The Growing Phenomenon of Domestic Violence

Family violence is neither a rare nor a recent phenomenon (E. Pleck, 1979). History is filled with espisodes of family and marital violence. In the Old Testament a husband could have his wife put to death for her unfaithfulness and his children beaten or even killed for breaking the injunction to "honor thy father and mother" (Steinmetz, 1978). Through the centuries, attitudes toward domestic violence suggest a type of benign acceptance rather than disgust. This is due in large part to our society's patriarchal social order, which regards men as absolute rulers in their homes (see box 10.1).

In the past couple of decades, the women's movement has focused public attention on the plight of the battered wife and has forced the public to become aware of the magnitude of family violence. But how prevalent is domestic violence in modern-day marriages? This question is difficult to answer because of the usually private nature of its commission and the hesitancy on the part of many of the victims to seek outside help. Although asking a national sample of married couples "Have you hit or threatened to hit your spouse in the past week, month, or year?" may seem like a perfectly straightforward way of determining the extent of marital violence in our country, few people would answer the question truthfully. The problem is that for many people, family and marital violence are taboo topics and not readily admitted to. And yet, we have some evidence of the magnitude of the problem with estimates of families that harbor violence in their midst. For example, in studies of couples seeking divorces, physical abuse is often cited as reason for divorce or a frequent complaint lodged by one or the other spouse during the divorce proceedings (O'Brient, 1971). However, marriages that end in divorce do not truly represent the "average" marriage, and we should be careful about our interpretation of such findings.

Police records of family disputes involving physical violence are not the answer either, simply because the majority of violent episodes among family members are thought to go unreported. Nevertheless, in nearly 85 percent

Box 10.1

Wife Beating: The Legacy of Patriarchy

The patriarchal family has prevailed throughout the history of western civilization. Much of the ideology and many of the institutional arrangements that supported patriarchy are still reflected in our culture and our social institutions. Let's look at this legacy of patriarchy.

In ancient Rome the law first proclaimed by Romulus in 753 B.C. stated that married women were to conform entirely to the wishes of their husbands and that husbands were to rule their wives as possessions. All property was owned by the husband. The husband was given the legal right to punish his wife for any misbehavior such as adultery, drinking wine, attending public games without his permission or appearing unveiled in public. The husband was given full power to judge and punish her. Speaking about the appropriate response to marital fidelity Cato said in the fifth century B.C.: "If you catch your wife in adultery, you could put her to death with impunity, she, on her part, would not dare to touch you with her finger; and it is not right that she should."

Christianity embraced the hierarchical family structure and celebrated the subordination of wives to their husbands. Although the teachings did not advocate force, they did demand the obedience of the wife to her husband.

During the Middle Ages in Europe there were many laws of chastisement. The French code of chivalry specified that the husband of a scolding wife could knock her to the earth, strike her in the face with his fist and break her nose so that she would always be blemished and ashamed. Women in Spain, Italy, France and England could be flogged through the city streets, exiled for years, or killed if they committed adultery or numerous "lesser" offenses.

Under English Common Law a married woman lost all of her civil rights, had no separate legal status and became the chattel of her husband. The right of the husband to chastise his wife was considered a natural part of his responsibilities. When the old common law was changed to the new civil law a husband was still allowed "for some misdemeanors to give his wife a severe beating with whips and clubs; for others, only to apply moderate correction."

All of the legal systems of Europe, England and early America supported a husband's rights to beat his wife and so did the community norms. Men were to rule their wives because "the man who is not master of his wife is not worthy of being a man." By this time, though, husbands were expected to show some restraint, at least in their public beatings of wives. The beatings were to conform to the rules of legitimate punishment (i.e., to not be too severe). Upon observing a man severely

Source: "Wives the 'appropriate' victims of marital violence" by R. Dobash and R. Dobash, 1977–1978, *Victimology 2(3–4)*, pp. 426–43. Reprinted by permission from *Victimology: An International Journal.* © 1978 Victimology Inc. All rights reserved.

Box 10.1

attacking his wife a neighbor exclaimed, "Oh, that's a bit much. We all know that wives need beating but you must be reasonable all the same."

In America various states legally gave husbands the right to chastise their wives physically. In 1824 the Supreme Court of Mississippi upheld this right. In 1865 a court in North Carolina ruled that the State could not interfere in cases of domestic chastisement unless permanent injury or excessive violence was involved. To not interfere, while seemingly a neutral statement, meant of course that husbands were to be allowed to continue to beat their wives.

Finally, in the last of the nineteenth century the laws in America and England allowing husband abuse were abolished. By 1878 in England women were allowed to use cruelty as a grounds for divorce. The rejection of the legal rights for husbands to physically assault their wives was complete in America in 1891 when the courts declared that "the moral sense of the community revolts at the idea that the husband may inflict personal chastisement upon his wife, even for the most outrageous conduct." Many groups objected to this change, and community norms often allowed it to continue in private. So little was done to bring about any meaningful change in the daily lives of women that by 1910 the Suffragettes made assaults on wives one of their platforms.

of the cases in which a woman is killed by her husband or lover, the police had previously been called to quell domestic violence (McGrath, 1979).

In a national sample of over two thousand families, Murray Straus, Richard Gelles, and Suzanne Steinmetz (Straus et al., 1980) found that one out of every six couples engage in at least one violent act each year. Richard Gelles (1979) notes that over the course of a marriage, the chance that a couple will experience marital violence is just over one-quarter. Overall, we can conclude (as have those who have studied large national samples) that: "The American family and the American home are perhaps as or more violent than any other American institution or setting (with the exception of the military, and only then in time of war)" (Straus et al., 1980, p. 4).

Recently, attention has been drawn to the fact that men as well as women can be on the receiving end in domestic violence (Steinmetz, 1977–1978). The methods of violence used by men and women, however, are usually different: men usually use physical force, such as hitting or choking; women are more apt to throw objects or use kitchen utensils, like knives, to inflict injury (Steinmetz, 1977). Some have suggested that focusing on the issue of battered men and equating its occurrence with battered women somehow makes light of the whole matter of domestic violence (E. Pleck et al., 1977–1978; Fields and Kirchner, 1978). We should be mindful that even though wife-beating is more pervasive and, in all likelihood, more serious, battered husbands deserve our concern also.

Although a precise figure cannot be arrived at from police records, divorce cases, or even the extrapolations from national surveys, we can conclude that millions of families each year are embroiled in domestic crises that end up with one or the other spouse physically injured or worse. Because we are talking about millions of victims and not just a handful, domestic violence warrants our serious attention and should be labeled as one of the most serious social problems today.

Tracking Down the Elusive Causes of Domestic Violence

"How could he (or she) have done that to his (her) wife (husband)?" is frequently asked when people hear about an incident of domestic violence. Many people are puzzled by violence between people who supposedly love and care for each other. If we are to stem the terrible tide of domestic violence, researchers must continue to search for its cause or causes.

Initially, researchers believed that psychologically disordered individuals were chiefly responsible for domestic violence (Galdston, 1965; Snell et al., 1964). After countless psychological studies, however, most researchers today can find no evidence to warrant the belief that family violence is caused by disordered thinking or that perpetrators of domestic violence are any more likely to exhibit psychological disorders than is any other segment of society (Gelles, 1983; Straus, 1980). Thus we need to look for other possible causes to explain this baffling social problem.

In looking for the cause or causes of domestic violence, we should not lose sight of the fact that America is a violence-prone society, one with an ambivalent view of the role that violence plays in our society (Doyle, 1983). On the one hand, Americans decry the violence found in many of America's urban settings and, on the other, many relish watching violent activities such as sporting events.

Although much of the current research into domestic violence dismisses individual pathology as accounting for domestic violence, many researchers accept the idea that something about the victim may precipitate the violence. In other words, they believe that somehow the victims of domestic violence, especially women, are "to blame" for the violence perpetrated upon them. For example, many suggest that a battered wife is somehow complicit, either knowingly or unknowingly, in the act of wife-beating. There are four major dimensions that allude to the notion that women somehow act in ways that can lead them to become the victims of violence (Wardell et al., 1983): the "traditional sex-role socialization" view

(Pagelow, 1981), the "provocative wife" perspective (Gayford, 1978), the "learned helplessness" notion (Walker, 1977–1978), and the "personal resource" theory (Rounsaville, 1978). To understand these different views of wifely complicity, we need to examine each in some detail.

A Matter of Gender Roles   Some suggest that a battered woman stays in a violent relationship because she believes the situation is inescapable or is part of her lot in life. But this suggestion also attributes family violence at least partially to the victim, who has accepted her victim-status as part of the gender role system. The idea is that traditionally oriented women are more likely to be victims of domestic violence because of their acceptance of traditional gender roles in which men are supposed to dominate and control women by force if need be. However, there is no evidence that battered women are any more traditional in their views of gender roles than women who are not battered. Consequently, the idea that gender roles and socialization contribute to creating family violence seems unwarranted (Wardell et al., 1983).

The Provocative Woman   Another theory is that battered women have somehow provoked violence by all kinds of unacceptable behaviors—unacceptable to the batterers that is. Behaviors like nagging or being silent, appearing unkempt or dressing too stylishly, being obsessed over cleanliness or the lack of cleanliness, or even showing a lack of interest or too much interest in having sex have all been suggested as provocative behaviors. The point of this approach is simply that whatever the woman does can be thought of as provocative by the man and thus can cause him to react in a violent way (Gayford, 1978). In other words, whatever the woman does or doesn't do can be seen as instigating the violence that is directed toward her. The victim is blamed for the violence, and the batterer is relieved of any responsibility for the aggression. Such an explanation seems too absurd for words.

Learned Helplessness   Some have painted the picture of the battered wife as one who possesses poor self-esteem and as one who is more likely to accept that her own actions and responses have little to do with outcomes. Such a woman believes that she has no direct control over the circumstances of her life (Walker, 1979). In a sense then, this approach blames the woman for believing that she is helpless in the face of the abuse she suffers. But oftentimes a battered woman does not simply believe she has little or no control over her actions; she, in fact, has no control over a ruthless person who is bent on battering, dominating, and controlling her every action. It seems highly unlikely that all a battered woman needs to do to stop the abuse is to think more positively about herself.

Superior Women Get What's Coming   The last explanation suggests that women are culpable in their own violence and implies that violence is more likely to occur in those situations where wives outshine their husbands in some presumably important way, and thus to gain back a measure of self-respect, these husbands must batter their resourceful wives. Such an explanation can be seen in the following analysis of family violence:

> One should find that violence is most common in those families where the classically dominant member (male-adult-husband) fails to possess the superior skills, talents or resources on which his preferred superior status is supposed to be legitimately based. Hence it was expected that violent behavior would be disproportionately prevalent in families where the husband-father was deficient relative to his wife-mother in achieved status characteristics. (O'Brient, 1971, p. 698)

The problem with this perspective is that women, as a rule, do not have more resources than men have in income, education, or nearly any other valued resource imaginable that would account for the significant number of battered women. In families where wives do make higher salaries than their husbands, there is no evidence that family violence is any greater than in families where the husbands earn more than the wives.

All of these perspectives have in common the tacit assumption that the woman is somehow to blame for the violence that is directed toward her. Instead of looking at domestic violence from the viewpoint of the individual, we might be well served to look at it from the view of the imbalance of power that is normally found between women and men.

The Issue of Power   In several preceding areas, we have noted the imbalance in power between men and women. Our society and its many institutions are decidedly sexist and misogynous. Although much of the recent literature on domestic violence reflects a sincere wish to change the pattern of violence against women, many of the notions expressed continue to reinforce the belief that somehow women are to blame for the violence heaped on them.

A more realistic view of domestic violence can be found in the imbalance in power and the idea that men have a right to dominate women in nearly every social situation. Domestic violence is actually a symptom of a social system wherein males believe that their will is law and that belief is supported by the social structures. Women are the outsiders, the others, the second-class citizens in a land where the insiders control all of the most influential power bases. To eliminate domestic violence, we should not simply concentrate on the individual—either the battered or the batterer—but rather on the social, political, and economic forces that perpetuate the bias against females. When males no longer believe they have the right to control women's lives, and when they stop thinking in terms of aggression as part of their manly mandate, we will see a reduction of domestic violence. The elimination of domestic violence is not well served by concentrating on the victims; rather, we should be concentrating on the social forces that perpetuate the unequal status of women and the sexist ideology that permeates our social fabric.

SUMMARY

The family is an integral social institution in most societies. Although the origins of the family are difficult to know with certainty, several experts believe that the early division of labor and year-round sexual activity laid the basis for the family as we know it today.

The traditional roles of husband/father generally involved protecting and supporting the other family members. Husbands/fathers usually spend little time in home or child-care activities. Recent studies, for the most part, show that today's husbands/fathers spend less time than wives/mothers in housework and child-care activities, but they spend more time in these activities than their fathers or grandfathers did. The traditional roles of wife/mother encompassed housework and the care of children. Generally speaking, the institution of marriage appears to favor husbands more than wives. In recent years, several nontraditional roles have emerged in the family, for example, househusbands, child-free couples, wives who earn more than their husbands, and single parents.

Today, there is a growing concern among researchers over the extent of domestic violence. The experts do not all agree on the causes of domestic violence, and several possible causes have been presented. The imbalance in power between most husbands and wives remains one of the most plausible causes for domestic violence.

SUGGESTED READINGS

Aldous, J. (Ed.). (1982). *Two paychecks: Life in dual-earner families*. Beverly Hills, CA: Sage.

Bernard, J. (1972). *The future of marriage*. New York: Bantam Books.

Blumstein, P., and Schwartz, P. (1983). *American couples*. New York: Morrow.

Brehm, S. (1985). *Intimate relationships*. New York: Random House.

Dobash, R., and Dobash, R. (1979). *Violence against wives*. New York: Free Press.

Faux, M. (1984). *Childless by choice*. New York: Doubleday.

Klinman, D., and Kohl, R. (1984). *Fatherhood U.S.A.* New York: Garland Publishing.

Staines, G., and Pleck, J. (1983). *The impact of work schedules on the family*. Ann Arbor, MI: Institute for Social Research, University of Michigan.

Straus, M., and Hotaling, G. (1980). *Social causes of husband-wife violence*. Minneapolis: University of Minnesota Press.

Point/Counterpoint

Are Women the Better Parent?

Only women can give birth. But after birth, which parent—mother or father—can give the better care? Most layfolk will immediately opt for the mother; among their many reasons for siding with the "mothers-are-best" contingent is their belief in the so-called maternal instinct. And yet, in discussing childcare, most social scientists deny any such natural preference of mothers over fathers. Rather, most social investigators point to the influence of culture or the strong influence of one's social environment to explain why women spend more time and energy with the young.

In 1977, an eminent social scientist and feminist, Dr. Alice Rossi of the University of Massachusetts, published a short article entitled "A biosocial perspective on parenting." Therein, Rossi outlined her "radical" views that women possessed "a biologically based potential for heightened maternal investment in the child . . . that exceeds the potential for investment by men in fatherhood" (p. 24). Essentially, Rossi argued that modern-day social sciences had overtly denied or avoided any mention of the potential influence of a woman's body (i.e., biological features such as hormones) in influencing her responsiveness to and care for her child. Rossi suggested that to understand the "bond" between a mother and child, scientists (especially social scientists) needed to examine more closely the interaction between a woman's biological makeup as well as her environmental upbringing. Furthermore, Rossi went on to argue that because males lack certain hormonal substances excreted during pregnancy, they were not as well equipped in their care-giving potential as an infant's mother. Rossi believed, however, that fathers could acquire equal facility in infant caregiving if they availed themselves of "compensatory education," which would allow the development of an array of desirable parenting skills. Thus, Rossi suggested that women by virtue of their biology were inherently better parents than men were, but that men could be educated to become more involved parents. Rossi has since extended her earlier arguments that point to the interaction of biology and culture (Rossi, 1984).

To say the least, many within the social scientific community took Rossi's remarks to be borderline, if not outright, heresy and an attack against feminist theory. We should keep in mind that Rossi herself had been and still is a champion of feminist causes, not only in her academic work but in her private life as well [Rossi, 1983b]. Her feminist credentials made her remarks about a biosocial basis to parenting more difficult for her colleagues to accept. [e.g., Rossi, 1964; Rossi and Calderwood, 1973]. A measure of the impact that Rossi's article had on the social scientific community came quickly with several "big-name" social scientists lining up either "for" or "against" Rossi's modest proposal for a biosocial approach to parenting (Gross et al., 1979). Several noted the naivete and lack of logic in Rossi's article. One opponent took the strong position that Rossi's ideas were, at best, only harmful and, at worst, "dangerous to women and to others outside the circles of power, as a rationale for accepting 'as is' " (Gross et al., 1979, p. 700). For many individuals, any discussion of possible biological elements in parenting leads to issues of women's oppression and the justification of male dominance over women. Apparently, in a topic as central to human life as parenting, we cannot avoid the concern over exploitation and oppression of women in discussions of biology's potential influences on parenting.

What do you think?

Reading
Parley Explores the Father's Role

Almost any weekend somewhere across the country, conferences are being held to explore the role of fathers and their effect on child development. Experts mingle with "average" dads to discuss the changing landscapes of fatherhood. Below is a report by Glenn Collins for The New York Times *on a recent conference devoted to fathers and their relations with children.*

Boston—"I treat my children completely equally—oh, I say that to people all the time," said Ron Fox, sitting to the right of his son and the left of his daughter. "But there is a certain part of me that may have felt more *protective* toward my daughter. And I guess that's a form of discrimination."

"It's true, Steven gets to go out later than I did when I was his age," said 19-year-old Lesley Fox of her 17-year-old brother. "Protecting your daughters like that becomes a problem, I suppose, when it gets in the way of their independence."

They spoke at "Fathers and Daughters, Fathers and Sons," a conference devoted to exploring the differences in fathers' relationships with their male and female offspring. More than 120 people, many of them parents and their children, gathered in the auditorium of Wheelock College on a recent rainy morning. There, they listened to family panel discussions, participated in workshop sessions and learned about recent fatherhood research concerning the questions of sex roles.

"Fathers have enormous influence on the sex-role identification of their children," said Dr. Ron Levant, clinical associate professor of counseling psychology at Boston University, who organized the conference. "Fathers are major instigators where children's gender concepts are concerned."

For example, in-home observations of parents in studies by Michael E. Lamb, a developmental psychologist at the University of Utah Medical Center, have shown that by the time their children are 13 months old, many fathers "radically decrease the time and attention they give to their daughters and increase the time given to their sons," said Dr. Levant, director of the Fatherhood Project, a counseling and educational service at Boston University for men and their families.

"Fathers seem to become a more salient role model to sons," added Dr. Levant, "while the mothers, for the most part, continue to give equal attention to children of both genders."

Other research has shown that fathers are more likely to express approval of their children when sons and daughters play with toys traditionally considered to be appropriate, such as trucks for boys or dolls for girls. One such study, by Dr. Judith Langlois, a developmental psychologist at the University of Texas at Austin, showed that "the kids who got the least approval from fathers were the boys who played with dolls or pots and pans," said Dr. Levant.

"It appears that father acts as the gatekeeper of sex-role appropriate behaviors," said Dr. Levant. "Men have emphasized traditional masculine roles for their sons. It's ingrained in us as men in very basic ways."

However, the last two decades have signaled significant changes in the images of both mothers and fathers, said Fran Litman, director of the Center for Parenting Studies at Wheelock College, which sponsored the conference.

"With 45 percent of mothers with children under the age of 3 employed out of the home," she said, "the question is how expectations of fathers and mothers are changing."

Dr. Levant said some fathers are trying "to reconsider how we're socializing our children." As increasing numbers of women enter the work force, he added, "are we preparing girls to be good little girls, or are we preparing them to be ready for the rough-and-tumble world of work?"

The conference audience listened while four fathers sat on stage with their children and talked of the way fathers relate to daughters and sons in the areas of discipline, support, friendship and expectation.

Then those in the audience gathered in groups of 20 to speak openly to each other of their feelings about their own fathers' warmth, distance and competitiveness, and shared their hopes about their own children.

The conference served to raise the consciousness of some of the fathers. "I wasn't really aware that fathers might treat their daughters so differently," said Michael Brzoza, who attended the conference with his daughters, 7 and 4, and their 3-year-old neighbor, Julie Ann Wrens. "Being here, I've also realized that there are a lot of fathers in the same boat—trying to be different kinds of parents than the ones we had."

Some of the parents present said that they wanted to raise their daughters in a nonsexist way. "But it can drive you crazy, constantly worrying about nonsexist toys and nonsexist behavior," said Evan Longin, a psychologist. "I think that far more important is the expression of a whole attitude, a whole style of life."

Power of External Stimuli "I remember trying so hard to buy nonsexist toys and to be a nonsexist parent," said Joan Fox, mother of Steven and Lesley, who joined a workshop session with the rest of her family. "I remember trying so hard to do that, and suddenly one day reflecting that, despite all our efforts, my son was doing little-boy things and my daughter was doing little-girl things. I don't think we can ignore the power of the external stimuli on our children, that are so important in shaping their attitudes. And the whole issue of heredity and environment is very hard to sort out."

Some of the daughters present in the workshop discussions reported pressure from their fathers to conform to traditional feminine stereotypes. However, others said that, in some middle-class milieus, the pressures on both daughters and sons may be different than in previous generations. "Both of my parents have pushed me," said Miss Fox, a sophomore at Brandeis University. "Half of Brandeis is prelaw or premed and if you don't want to be a doctor or a lawyer, you ask yourself, 'What else is there?' "

Some daughters felt secure that their parents would accept them no matter what they did. "I'm sure if my sister were thinking of being a wrestler or a car mechanic, I think my parents would be supportive," said 15-year-old Sabrina Putnam, a ninth-grade student at Noble and Greenough School in Dedham.

"My father's really understanding," said 11-year-old Melissa Longin, of her father, Evan. "He treats us equally," she said, glancing at the other Longin offspring, 7-year-old Todd.

"But I think I'm pretty sheltered," said Melissa, "and I think that's too bad because some day I'm going to grow up."

Not every father in the previous generation fit the distant, uncaring stereotype. "My father was very affectionate," said Richard Bourne, a Northeastern University professor who was a conference panelist along with his sons Michael, 11, and Steven, 14. "It was extraordinary," he said. "He was like a contemporary father."

'Glad I Had a Daughter' Not all of the fathers at the conference expressed traditional attitudes, either. "I've always been glad I had a daughter," said a father in one of the afternoon workshop sessions. "I've never understood why men were supposed to want sons more. I get a lot from my daughter and that's the truth."

"I had a tough time hugging my sons, though hugging my daughters came naturally," said a father next to him.

But for both daughters and sons attending the conference, perhaps 15-year-old Miss Putnam expressed best what a good father should be. "I hope my father will be there when I need him," she said, as her father, Eliot, looked on. "To be there and to care."

Chapter 11

MENTAL HEALTH AND GENDER

*S ince clinicians and researchers, as well as their patients and sub-
jects, adhere to a masculine standard of mental health, women by
definition, are viewed as psychiatrically impaired—simply because they
are women.*

Phyllis Chesler

In general, people seem apprehensive, anxious, and emotionally upset when
a society's status quo is challenged or disrupted. In the past decade or so,
many men and women have experienced considerable personal strain because society's traditional gender roles have been challenged from many
sides. Consequently, we need to discuss the issues of mental health and
mental illness as they relate to both genders.

In this chapter we will begin by examining the differences found in the
absolute numbers of men and women who are diagnosed and treated for
various personal or emotional problems. Next we will examine four specific behavioral or emotional disorders in which there is an appreciable
gender difference, namely, anorexia nervosa and bulimia, depression, and
antisocial personality. Then we will take up the charge that therapy and
counseling are biased against women. And last, we will explore some of
the alternative therapies used with men and with women as well as nonsexist or feminist counseling or therapy.

A QUESTION OF NUMBERS

The current literature on mental illness is rather clear on one point: women
are diagnosed and treated for mental illness at a much higher rate than
men (Chesler, 1972; Dohrenwend and Dohrenwend, 1976; Gove, 1979; Gove
and Tudor, 1973, Rohrbaugh, 1979). However, the finding that more women
than men are diagnosed and treated for mental and emotional problems
must be viewed cautiously. As a matter of record, from the turn of the century until the early 1960s, men outnumbered women in mental health

treatment facilities (Al-Issa, 1982; Bohn et al., 1966; Dorn, 1938). Thus the gender differences in the rates of mental illness at different periods in time continues to be a puzzle (Dohrenwend et al., 1980).

Why should more women than men be diagnosed and treated for various mental disorders nowadays? Several possible reasons have been suggested. One possibility is that women are not more mentally or emotionally ill than men, but that women are simply more likely to exhibit behaviors that others are apt to define as signs of mental illness. Women, for example, have been taught that they should be emotional, while men have been taught the opposite. A person who is too emotionally expressive may be thought of as disturbed or troubled. If women are encouraged to express their emotions and they express feelings of sorrow or sadness, for example, some may quickly come to the conclusion that women are more readily predisposed to emotional disorders. Men, on the other hand, are taught from their early years to suppress their emotional expressions. According to this perspective, then, it is little wonder that women may be seen as displaying more emotional problems than men simply because women have been taught to express themselves in this way. The difference, then, in the rates of emotional illness could be related to the possibility that men disguise or will not admit their emotional problems, whereas women wear their emotional problems on their sleeves, so to speak. However, several studies have found little support for this particular view (Gove and Geerken, 1977).

Another possibility is that women are, in fact, more mentally ill than men are. Although this explanation may seem extreme, the rationale for such a view is rather straightforward. In our society, women suffer greater discrimination and inequality because of our culture's embedded sexism. Consequently, many women are more likely to experience certain trauma-producing events (e.g., rape and marital abuse) to a greater degree than men (Carmen et al., 1981). Thus, women's unequal social position and the subsequent abuse many women experience may precipitate many women's emotional problems. Furthermore, many working mothers not only have to deal with the discrimination in their workplaces, but they also must contend with the workload of keeping up their homes. Many women find themselves doing "double-duty" in the workplace and at home, which can cause some to experience greater personal strain than, say, their husbands (Gove, 1980; Rendley et al., 1984; Shehan, 1984).

These two views, however, do not fully explain why more women then men are diagnosed and treated for mental illness. In fact, when the data are examined more closely, only some categories of women are more likely to be diagnosed and treated for mental illnesses. For example, married women have a higher rate of mental illness than married men, but single men have a higher rate of mental illness than single women (Gove, 1979). It is difficult to determine why married women may suffer more emotional problems than single women. However, several authorities have noted various reasons for such a state of affairs. Jeanne Marecek (1978) explains this difference by noting that many married women experience a loss of status and autonomy as well as difficulties associated with being a mother, all of which can create severe stress and lead to emotional problems. Jessie Bernard (1975) suggests that women in general are taught from childhood to be more dependent on others. Consequently, many women have a large part of their self-identities tied to their ability to successfully establish intimate relationships. If for some reason the intimate relationship sours, a woman may experience emotional problems as a consequence of thinking herself a failure as a woman. Men, on the other hand, are not as likely to define themselves in terms of their relationships with others. If relational problems develop, males may blame others rather than themselves for the relational breakups. However, research suggests that when long-term, intimate relationships like marriage break up, the males suffer more. For example, widowers experience more distress than widows (Stroebe and Stroebe, 1983).

Another possible explanation for women's greater incidence of mental illness is proposed by Phyllis Chesler (1972). Chesler suggests that women in our society are in a "no win" or "Catch-22" situation when it comes to their mental health. According to Chesler, women can be labeled as emotionally disturbed for either overconforming or underconforming to the female's gender stereotypes. In other words, a woman who is overdependent, too emotional, and less rational is overconforming to the traditional female gender stereotype. On the other hand, a woman who is independent, puts her career ahead of family interests, doesn't express emotions, and acts in a worldly and self-confident manner is one who is underconforming to the female gender stereotype. In either case, the woman may be thought disturbed.

One last possibility and one that has recently created some controversy among the mental health profession is offered by Marcie Kaplan (1983a, 1983b). Kaplan claims that the various categories of mental illnesses listed in the American Psychiatric Association's (1980) *Diagnostic and Statistical Manual of Mental Disorders* (DSM-III), the manual used by mental health professionals to categorize the various symptoms associated with mental or emotional illnesses, contains "masculine-biased assumptions about what behaviors are healthy and what behaviors are crazy" (p. 788). The basis for Kaplan's argument is that the same behavior that is thought of as indicative of emotional disturbance in a female goes unnoticed or is not thought of as indicative of mental illness if seen in a male. The categories for different emotional and mental problems are thus arbitrarily defined by the psychiatric establishment to the detriment of women. A man, Kaplan asserts, would not be thought emotionally disturbed if he put career ahead of family, was unable to express his emotions, and felt little concern over others' feelings. No, this man is acting in ways expected of most men. But women who act according to their social expectations can be thought of as disturbed. It seems, then, that simply being too "feminine" or not "feminine" enough is grounds for being considered disturbed (Herbert, 1983). In many ways, Kaplan's assertion of masculine bias in the DSM-III parallels the thinking of Chesler.

Not surprisingly, those who helped in the development of the DSM-III believe that Kaplan has overstated her case by charging male bias in the diagnostic categories of disturbed behaviors (Kass et al., 1983; Williams and Spitzer, 1983). These authors assert that "strenuous efforts were made to avoid the introduction of male-biased assumptions" (Williams and Spitzer, 1983, p. 797). However, given our society's attitudes toward women and the underlying sexist ideology that permeates our social institutions that when men and women behave in ways that don't fit their prescribed gender roles, they may still be looked at very differently. In questioning the potential male bias of DSM-III's categories, Marjorie McC. Dachowski (1984) noted that,

> We are more likely to label women who cannot adapt as *sick* and men who cannot adapt as *criminal*, but in fact both groups are out of step with our social system and are being pressured, one way or another, to make significant behavioral changes if they wish to be a functioning part of our society. (p. 703)

The issue of whether or not gender bias exists in the official diagnostic categories of emotional or mental disorders remains a perplexing problem. Can we ever be sure that our views of what mental illness is or, for that matter, that our definition of mental health will ever be free from the pervasive gender biases that are part of our culture?

There is no one simple answer for why more women than men are now diagnosed and treated for emotional and mental problems. As we can see, the area of mental health and mental illness is fraught with several problems, not the least of which is the question of whether females and society's expectations of them can ever be judged without the influence of antifemale bias.

GENDER-RELATED PROBLEMS

Several emotional disorders are more likely to be found among women than among men. For example, extreme emotional problems like hysteria and depression, severe anxieties like simple phobia and agoraphobia, and eating disorders like anorexia nervosa and bulimia are just a few of the disorders more commonly found among women than men (Chambless and Goldstein, 1980; Wooley and Wooley, 1980). On the other hand, antisocial personality, substance abuse disorders, and paranoid personality disorders are more frequently found among men than women (Kaplan, 1983a). The exact reason for this gender difference is unknown. However, when we examine several of the emotional disorders more commonly found either among women or men, we discover an interesting feature. In many of the so-called "female disorders" (e.g., depression, anxieties, and eating disorders), the person's negative feelings, anxiety, or personal conflict are directed "inward" against the self. In general, these persons exhibit behaviors that are self-critical, self-deprecating, and self-destructive. As for the so-called "male disorders" (e.g., antisocial personality), the person's conflict is more likely to be directed "outward" against others rather than inward. These persons are more likely to strike out at others rather than harm themselves. Thus, borrowing Gordon Allport's (1958) terminology, many of the emotional illnesses associated with women can be described as *intrapunitive*, or inward-punishing, whereas many of men's emotional illnesses can be thought of as *extrapunitive*, or outward-punishing.

In this section we will look at three types of emotional problems in which there is an obvious gender difference. We will first examine eating disorders and depression, both of which are more frequently found among women. Then we will focus on the antisocial personality disorder, which is found more frequently among men.

Eating Disorders

Every society has its definition of what is beautiful or attractive. Social psychologist Karen Dion (Dion et al., 1972) and several of her colleagues have documented that attractive or beautiful children and adults are thought of by others as more interesting, more exciting, more sensitive than less attractive individuals, and as possessing many other positive characteristics. Being beautiful or being thought of as beautiful brings with it certain advantages.

Women have usually been more willing than men to harm themselves mentally and physically to achieve the elusive status of being beautiful (Tolmach and Scherr, 1984). A major feature of what is thought of as beautiful in the Western world today is a thin body. If we believe many of the commercials on TV ("You can't pinch an inch"), thin is in and fat is out. With beauty so prized and rewarded in our society, it is little wonder that many women seem so concerned with keeping their bodies youthful and beautiful, and one way to do that is to keep thin. Consequently, some women are on a never-ending cycle of dieting, weekly visits to health and fitness centers, and generally working for the "fashion model" look that almost borders on emaciation. For many women, especially younger women, the concern over weight is taken to extremes. We will discuss two different eating disorders in which the victims show extreme fear of being fat: anorexia nervosa and bulimia.

Anorexia Nervosa   Once a rarity, *anorexia nervosa* has recently taken on near epidemic proportions. Estimates suggest that approximately 1 percent of all women between the ages of twelve and twenty-five—approximately 260,000 women—suffer from this severe eating disorder (Coleman et al.,

1984). The tragic death of the popular singer Karen Carpenter in 1983 brought nationwide attention to the plight of the anorexic. Female anorexics far outnumber males, with estimates suggesting a 20 to 1 ratio (Crisp, 1977; Sterling, 1984). The onset of anorexia generally occurs before age twenty-five and generally is characterized by three common symptoms: self-induced severe weight loss, persistent amenorrhea (i.e., abnormal absence of or suppression of menstrual discharge), and an intense fear of losing control over eating and becoming fat (Garfinkel and Garner, 1982; Levenkron, 1982; O'Neill, 1982; Russell, 1979). The anorexic is not one who goes through the "normal" ritual of dieting to lose a pound or two but one who voluntarily induces a dramatic loss of body weight (i.e., 25 percent of original body weight) that can damage body organs and threaten his/her life. Such is thought to be the case with Karen Carpenter, for example. Officially, Carpenter died of cardiac arrest, but her serious anorexic condition is thought to have been a contributing factor.

Although several psychosocial characteristics have been suggested as contributing to anorexia, such as a distorted body image and an extreme concern with pleasing others (Bemis, 1978; Minuchin et al., 1978), there is no universally accepted theory about its onset. Our society's obsession with the "fashion model" look for women may lead some young women to develop an intense fear of gaining weight because they may associate gaining weight with rejection by others. Even mental health professionals and therapists stress losing weight for a better self-image, and many women may take the message to the extreme (Hare-Mustin, 1983).

Bulimia   *Bulimia*, or the "binge-purge" syndrome, has received considerable attention in the past several years (Cauwels, 1983; Schlesier-Stropp, 1984). Initially, several researchers believed that bulimia was a subcategory of anorexia nervosa (Casper et al., 1980; Garfinkle et al., 1980). However, in the latest edition of the DSM-III, bulimia was classified as a separate eating disorder (American Psychiatric Association, 1980).

Bulimia is characterized by episodes of inconspicuous gross overeating ("food binges") that usually last for an hour or two. The food binge stops when the bulimic experiences severe abdominal pain, goes to sleep, is interrupted, or engages in self-induced vomiting. Although the bulimic, like the anorexic, has an abnormal concern with becoming fat, the bulimic differs from the anorexic in several ways. Generally, a bulimic is only slightly underweight or even of normal weight (Fairburn, 1981). Also, amenorrhea is not a usual feature among bulimics (Schlesier-Stropp, 1984). Although both anorexics and bulimics have a morbid fear of becoming fat, the bulimic's weight fluctuates between weight loss and weight gain, whereas the anorexic loses weight to an extreme degree.

The exact extent of bulimia is unknown, but authorities consider it a fairly common problem (Pyle et al., 1981). One of the reasons why a reliable estimate of the number of bulimics is difficult to make is that extreme secrecy surrounds the bulimic's behavior. The bulimic's food binges and vomiting usually occur in private. Adding to the problem is the bulimic's normal appearance in terms of body weight. Also, his or her eating habits in social situations appear quite normal (Fairburn and Cooper, 1982). Although many authorities believe only females engage in bulimic behaviors (Pyle et al., 1981), others have found that some males also exhibit this eating disorder (Herzog, 1982).

Both anorexia nervosa and bulimia are growing problems in our society. It seems that as long as our society stresses thinness as a major criterion of beauty, we will have many young people (especially young women) jeopardizing their physical well-being.

Depression

Nearly everyone at one time or another has had a bout with the "blues." But there is a sizable portion of the population, with estimates ranging from 15 to 25 percent, who at some time in their lives will suffer from extreme sadness and despair that is serious enough to interfere with their work, social, and family lives. Serious or *clinical depression* is usually signaled by two prominent symptoms: *dysphoria* and *loss of interest*. Dysphoria refers to a state of extreme sadness and worry and feelings of hopelessness. Also, depressed persons usually show little interest in activities that once gave them pleasure and happiness.

Evidence suggests that women are more likely than men to experience serious bouts of depression (Chino and Funabiki, 1984; Silverman, 1968) and to be diagnosed as depressive both in psychiatric centers and in the community at large (Weissman and Klerman, 1977). Married, divorced, or separated women exhibit more depressive symptoms than comparable men. Single men and widowers, however, show more signs of depression than single women or widows (Radloff, 1975). Generally, estimates suggest that depression occurs about twice as often in females as in males (Seiden, 1976). Several different theories have been suggested to account for the greater incidence of depression among women than among men (Weissman, 1980).

One general view is that women are no more likely to experience depression than men are, but that women are more likely to admit to depressive symptoms than men (Weissman and Klerman, 1977). However, the evidence for this view is somewhat equivocal (King and Buchwald, 1982).

Others suggest that because women suffer greater discrimination in society than men suffer, the consequence is "legal and economic helplessness, dependency on others, chronically low self-esteem, low aspirations, and ultimately, clinical depression" (Weissman and Klerman, 1977 p. 106). Another view suggests that women are more susceptible to depression by virtue of the learned helplessness that is acquired through the socialization process (Seligman, 1973, 1975) and the acceptance of the female gender role (Tinsley et al., 1984). Still others believe that because women are socialized to be less assertive, they are less likely to obtain as many rewards from their environment than men, and this may cause in some women a tendency toward depression (Kelly, 1983). Thus, there are any number of social factors that may prompt women to show signs of depression (Guttentag et al., 1980; Robbins and Tanck, 1984).

Another possibility that may explain why women are more likely than men to exhibit depression is that they are less likely to be rejected by others for behaving in depressed ways. However, this has not been found by all researchers (Yamamoto and Dizney, 1967).

Depression is one of the most serious emotional disorders and afflicts millions of people. The fact that more women than men suffer from depression should prompt investigators to explore every possible lead to find the basis for this debilitating emotional illness. In an attempt to suppress or eliminate their feelings of isolation, abandonment, and depression, some women may even turn to promiscuous behavior (Scarf, 1980). For men, depression may lead to alcohol abuse (Seixas and Cadoret, 1974; Weissman et al., 1977).

Antisocial Personality

Although we have noted that women are more likely than men to be diagnosed as mentally or emotionally ill, the rate of mental illness among young boys is greater than among young girls (Gove and Herb, 1974). One of the problems more frequently found among young boys and men is that of antisocial personality (Rosenfield, 1980). The *antisocial personality* is signaled by a lack of ethical or moral development and by behavior that is contrary to socially acceptable guidelines. The terms *sociopathic personality* and *psychopathic personality* are other designations frequently used to refer to this disorder. More males fit this description than females, with estimates suggesting that the ratio is approximately 3 to 1 (American Psychiatric Association, 1980).

People who are diagnosed as antisocial personality types generally exhibit several of the following characteristics (Coleman et al., 1984). First, antisocial personalities lack what most would call a conscience, or a sense of personal ethics. Also, they don't appear to feel any guilt or anxiety about hurting others' feelings. Quite often, they act impulsively and do not stop to think how their actions may affect others. Also, they frequently put on a front or a good show and display a general disregard for authority. And last, antisocial personalities have difficulty establishing good interpersonal relationships. Overall, antisocial personality types prove to be manipulative and exploitative people who use others to further their own ends.

What causes such a callous type of personality? Researchers have ventured several possibilities that range from possible abnormal brain functioning (Hare, 1970), to a lack of emotional arousal of anxiety (Chesno and Kilmann, 1975), to the possibility of being a rejected and loveless child (Wolkind, 1974).

Another cause may be the social expectations placed on males. For example, our society encourages boys more than girls to become aggressive, competitive, and success-driven, to win at all costs if need be (Doyle, 1983). Such an orientation may lead to the development of features associated with the antisocial personality characteristics later on in the early adult years (Smith, 1978). Young boys are also encouraged to hide their feelings, especially their tender feelings of love and concern for others, which, if taken to the extreme, can become fertile ground for acting in what may be considered as antisocial ways (Doyle, 1983). Whatever the cause, the antisocial personality is an irresponsible and callous person who treats others with little or no concern for their feelings.

THERAPY AND COUNSELING: THE CONCERN OVER SEX BIAS

Earlier we noted that some believe that women are ill-served because of the purported masculine bias of the psychiatric categories of emotional and mental illnesses. In this section we will examine the charge that sex bias also infiltrates therapy and counseling.

Most think of therapy and counseling as effective ways of helping a mentally or emotionally distressed person. And yet, for well over a decade, several feminist-oriented social scientists have voiced severe criticism of traditional therapy and counseling and have sounded a warning that therapy may be hazardous to women's mental and emotional well-being (Chesler, 1972, 1973; Fields, 1975; Mowbray et al., 1984; Tennov, 1975). Concern over the possible "dangers" inherent in therapists' and counselors' treatment of women, to a great extent, grew out of the findings of the now classic study conducted by Inge Broverman (et al., 1970) and colleagues. We need to examine Broverman's study if we are to understand better just what much of the concern over sex bias in therapy and counseling is all about.

Broverman asked a group of seventy-nine mental health specialists or experienced clinicians (forty-six male and thirty-three female psychologists, psychiatrists, and social workers) to describe the traits that characterized a mature, healthy, and socially competent adult woman, adult man, or an adult whose gender was not designated. They were asked to check off a series of descriptive bipolar characteristics that best described each person. The descriptive categories contained bipolar items such as those listed below:

Very subjective	Very objective
Very submissive	Very dominant
Not at all ambitious	Very ambitious
Very passive	Very active
Feelings easily hurt	Feelings not easily hurt

To say the least, Broverman's data proved rather interesting. First, there was considerable agreement in the way the clinicians described the stereotyped characteristics of adult men and adults in general, which differed from the stereotyped characteristics assigned to adult women. Second, there was considerable agreement among the female and male clinicians in the way they described the different persons. Overall, Broverman found that the clinicians in her study—both male and female—had what could be called a "double standard" for mental health. In other words, the criteria of mental health these clinicians applied to an adult also applied to an adult man but not to an adult female. Broverman noted that "the general standard of health is actually applied only to men, while healthy women are perceived as significantly less healthy by adult standards" (p. 5). Specifically, adult females were thought of as

[B]eing more submissive, less independent, less adventurous, more easily influenced, less aggressive, less competitive, more excitable in minor crises, having their feelings more easily hurt, being more emotional, more conceited about their appearance, less objective, and disliking math and science. (pp. 4–5)

Soon after Broverman's study, Phyllis Chesler published her scathing indictment against the predominantly male professions of psychiatry and clinical psychology in her book *Women and Madness* (1972). Chesler charged the mental health profession with a conspiracy against women, carried out mainly by the male psychiatric and psychological establishments. She wrote:

The ethic of mental health is masculine in our culture. This double standard of sexual mental health, which exists side by side with a single and masculine standard of *human* mental health, is enforced by both society and clinicians. Although the limited "ego resources," and unlimited "dependence," and fearfulness of most women is pitied, disliked, and "diagnosed," by society and its agent-clinicians, any other kind of behavior is unacceptable in women! (p. 69)

Others were quick to provide support for the existence of a double standard of mental health wherein the standards set for women differed greatly from those set for men (Wise and Rafferty, 1982). Therapists were not the only ones who were accused of discriminating against women. Career and vocational counselors also were found to evidence gender bias toward women's career aspirations (Donahue and Costar, 1977). In the minds of many, the culprit behind the "double standard" for mental health as well as career opportunities was society's prevalent sexist ideology. Such sentiments were forcefully stated by Gardner (1971) who minced no words in suggesting that the helping professions actually were more harmful to women than helpful.

This research supplies empirical support for what feminists have long suspected: that therapy is bad for women. Right now, in our excessively sexist society, it is unlikely than *anyone*, without special training in feminism, can create conditions which would encourage females to exercise their right to select goals if the goals are at variance with the goals of the counselor. . . . Today, it is probably not a serious misrepresentation to say that all counselors are sexist. (pp. 713–14)

As Broverman's and Chesler's work became better known, there was some evidence that the problem of sexism, or gender bias, lessened somewhat among the helping professions. In her review of ten studies of counselors' and therapists' attitudes toward women, Julia Sherman (1980) found that, for the most part, clinicians hadn't changed much over the decade since Broverman's classical study. However, she did find that female clinicians were less biased than male clinicians. Recall in Broverman's study that there was little difference between the female and male clinicians. Also, Sherman noted that older professionals and those with a Freudian orientation were more likely to be biased against women than were younger and non-Freudian-oriented counselors and therapists.

In contrast, during the 1970s, several researchers found little evidence for gender bias in therapy and counseling (Billingsley, 1977; Johnson, 1978). Other reviewers stressed that a clinical judgment was rarely based solely on a client's gender label (Abramowitz and Dokecki, 1977; Davidson and Abramowitz, 1980; Smith, 1980). Moreover, Mary Smith (1980) reviewed over thirty published and nonpublished (doctoral dissertations) studies of gender bias in counseling and therapy and found some rather surprising results. Using the statistic called meta-analysis in which several studies' results are pooled and analyzed together, she found there was "no evidence for the existence of counselor sex bias when the research results are taken as a whole" (p. 404). Smith found several other interesting features in the data she analyzed. There was greater bias found in earlier studies than in the later ones, suggesting that professionals apparently had become more aware of or sensitive to the issue of gender bias over the decade. The studies published in professional journals were more likely to report gender bias than nonpublished studies. And, studies with the poorest controls or those with confounding variables were more likely to find evidence of gender bias than were better controlled studies. Smith concluded that

Empirical evidence for the contention that counseling and psychotherapy are sexist and bad for women is extremely weak. . . . Motivation to conduct research of this type was frequently ideological; that is, investigators seemed intent on establishing counselor sexism (a foregone conclusion in many minds). (p. 406)

So how are we to interpret the conflicting data over whether or not therapy and counseling are bad for women? On the one hand, several studies point out the presence of a double standard that if applied can be considered harmful to female clients. On the other hand, considerable research suggests that gender bias is minimal or not as pervasive as some may think.

The solution to the dilemma of whether gender bias exists in therapy or counseling may be settled if we note a methodological difference among many of the studies involved. A large portion of the studies finding a lack of gender bias among therapists are *analogue studies*. Analogue studies are those in which a therapist or counselor is presented with a "contrived" situation where the patient's gender is the independent variable in the study. For example, a counselor may be presented with a written case study—involving either a female or male client—and asked to make a clinical judgment based on the material in the case. The important feature to keep in mind is that reading an analogue study is not the same as sitting across from a "flesh-and-blood" client in a "real" therapy session. The analogue is a substitute for the real thing and, many argue, a poor substitute for the study of potential therapist bias.

Yet, when naturalistic data of what transpires in actual therapy or counseling sessions are examined or when records from real therapy sessions between clients and therapists are analyzed, there appears to be substantial evidence for therapist bias against women. For example, women are seen for longer periods of time in therapy and given stronger prescriptive medications than men are (Fidell, 1980; Stephenson and Walker, 1979). Thus the conflicting results may be due to the type of studies examined. Analogue studies provide little evidence of gender bias, but in naturalistic studies, gender bias appears to be a real problem. In summarizing the issue, Rachel Hare-Mustin (1983) concludes that

> Clinical analogues have failed to produce impressive evidence of sex bias, whereas naturalistic studies have produced supporting data. It may be that analogue studies have become too transparent and subject to responses in the socially desirable direction. More sophisticated research designs are needed to deal with the complex factors in evaluating therapy. (p. 595)

Is therapy and counseling harmful to women? It depends on where you look and on what kind of data you look at. As Hare-Mustin sees it, we are in need of a more sophisticated approach to study the issue. The problem is serious enough for all interested parties to put forth the effort to determine the extent to which sexism exists in the helping professions.

NONTRADITIONAL THERAPIES

A person who is distressed or emotionally distraught with his or her life may turn to a counselor or a therapist for help. But we need to ask what the goals are that the therapist may have in mind in order to best help the client. For instance, should a therapist help clients adjust to their life situation by gaining insight into why they feel the way they do? Or should a therapist encourage and assist clients to break free of what they perceive to be constrictions or limitations in their life? We have a quandary of sorts in defining the goals of therapy and counseling: Is counseling and therapy "adjustment oriented" or "change oriented" (Gove, 1980)? The man who feels his work is meaningless and becomes upset or depressed with his life or the woman who feels overdependent on others and wishes she could be more independent may both seek professional help. But what kind of help do they need? And what are the goals a therapist may bring into the counseling sessions? Should the woman be helped to adjust to her dependency and learn to accept others' support? Should the man be encouraged to "tough it out" at work because it is only a few more years until retirement? Do these two people need intensive counseling to help them adjust to the status quo called for by their traditional gender stereotypes and roles? Or should both be helped to break free from the restrictions of their past conditioning, to take charge of their own lives, and to seek personal fulfillment by examining other options and choices which may be contrary to their past experiences (Gilbert, 1980; Hare-Mustin, 1978; Toomer, 1978)? Concern over the question of how best to deal with men's and women's unique problems as related to gender roles has led the helping professions to an intense study of both sexes (*The Counseling Psychologist*, 1978, 1979).

Several feminists have noted that traditional therapies and counseling strategies are political in nature because they serve the needs of society's dominant group and do little more than support society's status quo (Halleck, 1971; Levin et al., 1974). Thus, several nontraditional approaches to counseling and therapy have been instituted in the past several years to help both women and men find alternatives and options that are free of outmoded and potentially harmful gender stereotypes and roles (Robbins and Siegel, 1983). Let's examine three nontraditional strategies that are used to help people break free of traditional gender stereotypes and roles: consciousness-raising groups, assertiveness training, and feminist therapy.

Consciousness-raising Groups

Several feminists maintain that *consciousness-raising* or *CR groups* are a powerful alternative or adjunct to traditional therapies (Brodsky, 1977; Reed and Garvin, 1983; Wong, 1978). CR groups differ from other more traditional forms of therapy. Usually, in a CR group, several people meet in a group member's home. Also, CR groups usually are leaderless, or the members take turns being responsible for getting the session started; this assures that no single member can take over and monopolize the discussion or act as an authority figure within the group. Normally, the main focus for the CR group centers on the group members' feelings and self-perceptions.

Barbara Kirsh (1974) maintains that many of the personal problems that women experience are a direct result of their socialization process. For example, females are taught at an early age to belittle their achievements and their value as human beings. Rather than seeking help from male therapists, who may represent just another male authority ignoring the value of women, women meet in a CR group to define their own experiences in terms of their own criteria. Thus for many women, the CR group becomes a form of resocialization.

In the past several years, some men have followed the lead of women and have formed all-male CR groups where men can deal with their feelings of what it means to be men in our society (Brannon and Creane, 1984; Farrell, 1974; Wong, 1978). The benefits accruing to the male members of unstructured and leaderless CR groups are many. For example, males can learn how to deal with little or no structure in a group, which for many men is seen as an arena where they can show off for others. Personal issues such as emotional constraints and concerns over expressing positive feelings toward other men and fear of homosexuality (De Cecco, 1984; Lehne, 1976) are just a few of the issues that all-male CR groups can deal with. CR groups have become one of the most powerful resocialization techniques, and literally tens of thousands of women and men have been helped by them.

Assertiveness Training

A common problem that many females have is standing up for their own rights. Many women have been taught that they should defer their own interests and needs in favor of others' needs. Because of this, one of the most common forms of self-help in the 1970s was the popular *assertiveness training programs*. Assertiveness training is one means by which a person learns to stand up for her or his rights without violating the rights of another person during an interaction (Jakubowski, 1977, 1978; Dunham and Brower, 1984).

Many people are confused about the meanings of the terms nonassertiveness, assertiveness, and aggressiveness. For example, if someone asked to borrow one of your textbooks, there are several different responses you could give. "Ah, well, ah, let me see, I guess I shouldn't make a big deal over it, so you can borrow my book." Such a reply suggests that you don't really want to lend out your book but you don't seem to know how to say no. This would be an example of a nonassertive response. But if you were to say "What are you, some kind of nut? I don't lend my books to anyone." This reply makes it plain that you don't lend your books out, but it also would probably hurt the other's feelings in the process and is an example of an aggressive response. An assertive reply, however, may go something like this: "I'd really like to help you out, but I don't feel comfortable lending my books out. I hope you understand my view." Here you have stated your right to decide not to lend your books, but you have done it in a way that doesn't hurt the other's feelings in the process.

One way that many women learn assertiveness is from interacting with other women. Too often, women have learned they should be obsequious to men, and they may therefore have difficulty standing up for their rights in situations that involve men. Hence, an assertiveness group is a safe situation in which women can practice asserting personal needs and feelings.

Feminist Therapy

Many people think the terms *feminist therapy* and *nonsexist therapy* mean the same thing. However, some feminists wish to differentiate between the two because each is based on different assumptions (Rawlings and Cater, 1977). Feminist therapy is usually based on a philosophical critique of society wherein women are seen as having less political and economic power than men have. Another assumption is that the bases for women's emotional or personal problems are social, not personal. A major goal of feminist therapy is for women to learn to strive for and acquire economic and psychological independence. And finally, feminist therapy generally accepts the idea that society's definitions of gender roles and the complementariness expected between men's and women's behaviors must end.

Nonsexist therapy usually means that the therapist has become aware of and has overcome, for the most part, his or her own sexist attitudes and values. For example, a nonsexist therapist would look at an independent woman or a dependent man as not necessarily evidencing emotional or personal problems by acting in counterstereotypic ways. Another assumption that nonsexist therapists make is that marriage is not thought to be any better for women than for men. And last, both women and men are encouraged to act in androgynous ways rather than in stereotypic masculine or feminine ways. In summarizing the differences between these two alternative approaches to therapy, Marilyn Johnson (1980) notes:

> The primary distinction between the nonsexist and feminist therapist is that the feminist incorporates feminist theory and practice into therapy and the nonsexist does not. Both believe in egalitarianism between the sexes; this belief springs from a humanistic philosophy among nonsexists and from feminist ideology in feminists. Proponents of each approach offer their own messages to the client. *Nonsexist:* Some of your problems arise from the way the world is. If you had been socialized differently, you would not have to work through these many issues. *Feminist:* Some of your problems arise from the way the world is. Remember that the power differential between women and men is an often ignored contributor to your problem. You can work to change your life and you will have the support of many others like yourself. (p. 366)

As we can see, there are certain basic differences between feminist therapy and nonsexist therapy. However, both take a "change oriented" approach in assisting the client to work out the problems in her or his life. Also, these two approaches take into account that women's and men's lives are not complementary, and that both must have the freedom to work out their own definitions for healthy and fulfilling life-styles.

SUMMARY

Much attention has been given to the fact that women are more likely than men to be diagnosed as suffering from debilitating mental or emotional disorders. Gender differences do appear among some psychological disorders. For example, women are more likely to exhibit certain eating disorders such as anorexia nervosa and bulimia and specific emotional disorders such as depression. However, a personality pattern known as an antisocial personality is more commonly found among men.

A growing concern among many mental health professionals is the presence of gender bias in therapy and counseling. Researchers have contended that the mental health profession holds a double standard of mental health that penalizes women for acting in "nonfeminine" ways. To eliminate the constricting effects of gender roles, several new approaches to therapy have recently been introduced: consciousness-raising groups, assertiveness training, and feminist therapy.

SUGGESTED READINGS

Brodsky, A., & Hare-Mustin, T. (Eds.). (1980). *Women and psychotherapy: An assessment of research and practice.* New York: Guilford.

The Counseling Psychologist. (1978). [Special issue on counseling men]. *7*, 1–72.

The Counseling Psychologist. (1979). [Special issue on counseling women]. *8*, 1–75.

Davidson, C., & Abramowitz, S. (Eds.). (1980). Women as patients. *Psychology of Women Quarterly, 4(3),* 309–423. [Special issue].

Gomberg, E., & Franks, V. (Eds.). (1979). *Gender and disordered behavior: Sex differences in psychopathology.* New York: Brunner/Mazel.

Hare-Mustin, R. (1983). An appraisal of the relationship between women and psychotherapy. *American Psychologist, 38(5),* 593–601.

Kinroy, B., Miller, E., & Atchley, J. (Eds.). (1984). *When will we laugh again? Living and dealing with anorexia nervosa and bulimia.* New York: Columbia University Press.

Mowbray, C., Lanir, S., & Hulce, M. (Eds.). (1984). *Women and mental health: New directions for change.* New York: Haworth Press.

Schaffer, K. (1980). *Sex-role issues in mental health.* Reading, MA: Addison-Wesley.

Solomon, K., & Levy, N. (1982). *Men in transition: Theory and therapy.* New York: Plenum Press.

Walker, L. (Ed.). (1984). *Women and mental health policy.* Beverly Hills, CA: Sage.

Point/Counterpoint

Male Therapists for Female Clients—Help or Hindrance?

Given that most therapists are male and most clients are female, it is not surprising to find that most female clients end up going to male therapists or counselors for help with their emotional problems. In the last decade or so, however, the question of whether or not females should go to male therapists or counselors has become a controversial issue. Some feminists respond with a definite NO—females should avoid male therapists and counselors at all costs (Chesler, 1972).

The reasons for a female boycott of male therapists seem convincing on the surface. First of all, many female therapists and clients attest to the restrictive gender biases that permeate many counseling sessions (APA, 1975). Although these findings can be contested on methodological grounds (Stricker, 1977), the American Psychological Association felt the need to publish a set of guidelines for the treatment of women in therapy (APA, 1978).

Also, in the emotionally charged setting of therapy, we must be wary of the possibility that a sexual element may infiltrate the therapy or counseling session. There is always a possibility that a female client may become overdependent on her male therapist or counselor, which may lead to feelings of physical attraction. It goes without saying that the male therapist must be careful not to take advantage of an emotionally vulnerable female client. Needless to say, manipulating a client into a sexual relationship can be extremely harmful for the client. Just because therapists are professionals doesn't mean that such an occurrence is impossible. One study found that male psychology interns gave more sexually stimulating psychological tests to their female clients than to their male clients (Masling and Harris, 1969). Even more upsetting is the finding that male therapists are much more likely to have sexual relations with their female clients than are female therapists with their male clients. Based on self reports, just over 5 percent of male therapists reported having sex with their female clients, whereas only .6 percent of female therapists reported such behavior (Holroyd and Brodsky, 1977).

Another issue is that males, no matter how well-intentioned and trained, may not understand the experiences of women. Phyllis Chesler (1971), one of the most outspoken critics of male therapists for women clients, puts the issue squarely in terms of the imbalance of power in therapy as potentially harmful for women. She writes:

> Male psychologists, psychiatrists, and social workers must realize that as scientists they know nothing about women; their expertise, their diagnoses, even their sympathy is damaging and oppressive to women. Male clinicians should stop treating women altogether, however much this may hurt their wallets and/or sense of benevolent authority. For most women the

psychotherapeutic encounter is just one more power relationship in which they submit to a dominant authority figure. I wonder how well such a structure can encourage independence—or healthy dependence—in a woman. I wonder what a woman can learn from a male therapist (however well-intentioned) whose own values are sexist? How free from the dictates of a sexist society can a female as patient be with a male therapist? How much can a male therapist empathize with a female patient? (pp. 384–85)

However therapy is a very complex process and the gender of the therapist and client is only one variable that may affect the outcome (Orlinsky and Howard, 1976). As therapist Annette Brodsky (1980) sees it, instead of an absolute "No" in all cases,

there are more likely to be two answers: (a) 'no' for young single women uncertain as to their direction in life, or in their relationship with men, or both; and (b) 'yes' if the client is older, or married. We do not, however, know what other factors, yet to be studied, may also have a bearing on the answer. (p. 335)

As for the purported prevalence of gender bias in therapy, we can teach male interns and trainees to be more sensitive to and aware of women's unique problems and to become aware of their own hidden gender biases. Gender bias on the part of male therapists may not, in fact, be a major problem, but it may reveal ignorance about women's unique problems (Sherman et al., 1978). Ignorance can be cured. Thus the issue of whether or not male therapists and counselors should treat female clients is not simply a cut-and-dried issue but one with many sides.

What do you think?

A society's views of mental health never develop in a vacuum, but rather are tied to the values and folkways of the group. In the following excerpt, we find that our modern day views of women's mental health and the views of appropriate treatments for women can be traced back at least through three distinct historical phases.

There seem to have been three major phases in the development of psychotherapy for women. The first emerged from what Hugh Trevor Roper called the appalling "witchcraft craze" of the 16th and 17th centuries. This was the crowning misfortune of an age of war, schism and pestilence. Because of this craze, large numbers of men, women and children were put to death, often after suffering dreadful tortures. In theory, there was the clear distinction between the witch and the bewitched; the bewitched were the victims of the malice of witches expressed through witchcraft, while witches were those who had made a pact with the devil, selling their immortal souls for immediate advantages. The religious practitioners of the day believed that bewitchment should be treated by exorcism, which included rigorous activities of various kinds not always clearly distinguishable from torture. Those who became witches were in principle excommunicated until they repented but, even after repentance, they were liable to be executed, often by burning, in order to save their souls even at the expense of their mortal bodies. The Inquisitors and their colleagues did not hesitate to employ the most extreme measures for mortifying the offending flesh and terrifying the minds of those who had strayed. Their aim was to ensure sincere repentance, no matter what the cost in pain and suffering, so as to save the immortal souls of those who had been duped by Satan.

The witch craze became inextricably muddled with the religious quarrels of the day and, for reasons which are still not wholly clear, most witches were women. Consequently, the furor of the Inquisitors was expended in torturing and burning tens of thousands of these unfortunates. There can be little doubt that many of those who were bewitched and those who were held to be witches suffered from mental illnesses. In 1563, at the height of the witch craze, the enormously courageous Johann Weir published his famous book, *De praestigiis daemonum*, in which he opposed the belief in demons and witches and suggested that many of the witches were mentally ill. His action made it likely that he himself would be accused of witchcraft and so suffer extreme penalties. Although this did not happen, it was more than a century and a half before Weir's humane point of view became gradually accepted. By the mid-eighteenth century, it became unfashionable to burn mad people at the stake. Nevertheless, their condition was not particularly happy. It was not until the end of the 18th and the beginning of the 19th century that reformers like the Tukes, the great Quaker reformers who founded the retreat at York in the 1790's, and their counterparts in North America developed retreats or asylums for those afflicted by madness. It was in this setting that medical attention became focused upon the problem of mental illness in women. Whatever the limitations of diagnosis and treatment during those times, at least the afflicted people were seen as patients and treated medically.

The second series of events which has had such an enormous bearing on women's affairs and which has totally changed their lives has been so successful that, on the whole, we hardly ever think about it. These events had

Source: "Changing views of women and therapeutic approaches: Some historical considerations" (pp. 3–6) by H. Osmond, V. Franks, and V. Burtle, 1974. In V. Franks and V. Burtle (Eds.), *Women in therapy.* New York: Brunner/Mazel. © 1974 Brunner/Mazel, Publishers. Reprinted by permission.

their beginnings with doctors like James Gordon, Thomas Watson, Oliver Wendell Holmes, and the great Semmelweiss; they culminated in Pasteur and Lister with the development of antisepsis and later asepsis. One consequence of this was the rise of the science of bacteriology which has had a great bearing on the health of mothers and children alike. At the same time, the introduction of anesthesia not only wholly altered the scope but, due to Queen Victoria's prescience and her inspired notion of using her position as Defensor Fidii and head of the Church of England, it became proper for women to have anesthetics in childbirth. Bishops and others had been uncertain about this and quoted biblical texts justifying women's suffering in childbed. Victoria as monarch and mother used her great authority to announce that it was proper for women to have anesthetics to help them bear children without pain and celebrated this by inhaling chloroform at the birth of Prince Leopold.

It is difficult to overestimate the effects of these developments not only upon the physical health of women, but also upon their psychological outlook. At this time, childbearing was a risky business for both mother and child. Many mothers lost a high proportion of those children whom they had conceived and carried with such peril to themselves. In such circumstances, women did not have to be particularly prudish or especially preoccupied with Victorian respectability to be rather less than wholly enthused about sexual relations. For many women it had been the obvious cause of death of their mothers, sisters, and daughters; school friends expected many of their peers to die in childbed. Every pregnancy involved grave dangers. Most of these obstetrical dramas occurred not in the hygienic seclusion of well-run hospitals, but in homes, thus spreading gloom and terror throughout whole families and often communities. So successful

has medicine been regarding these matters that it is difficult if not impossible to evoke the atmosphere in which many women approached pregnancy during the pre-bacteriological era. The imaginative can guess what it was like; the unimaginative should look at the record. . . .

A third great influence on women during the 1860's was the establishment of a profession for women by that extraordinary social reformer, Florence Nightingale. Before this, for most women, the opportunity for acquiring professional and administrative skills was very limited indeed. . . .

Recognizing both the need for nursing and the need for women to have an appropriate profession, Florence Nightingale provided a slightly sheltered, but absolutely vital field in which women would be able to acquire techniques of management and governing from which for a variety of reasons they had usually been excluded. The occurrence of two World Wars in the first part of the twentieth century made it clear to even the most misogynistic that healthy and capable women raised from generations who did not expect to die in childbed and had not lost many children early in their lives were very different creatures from the stereotype of women who had lived in those early eras when sex, death and procreation went hand in hand—often to the grave. It is against this background of social and medical progress, which made the lives of millions of women less perilous and so more hopeful, that the need for adequate contraception and family limitation, pioneered so courageously by Margaret Sanger, Marie Stopes and others, became self-evident.

This then is the unseen context or, perhaps more accurately, the behind-the-scene context against which we believe women's liberation and the interest in that old rag-bag of activities which we now call psychotherapy for women can best be viewed.

Part III

CHANGES

Chapter 12

SOCIAL MOVEMENTS AND GENDER

If there's nothing more powerful than an idea whose time has come, there is nothing more ubiquitously pervasive than an idea whose time won't go. The division of the world by sexes, challenged a century and more ago by the militants of the first wave of Feminism, still endures and, what's more, still prevails, in spite of new attacks upon it. "Man's world" and "woman's place" have confronted each other since Scylla first faced Charybdis. If the passage between is stormier today than it has ever been, the two old saws still rear above the flood, leaning together in logical intimacy, dividing the world in order to encompass it. For if women have only a place, clearly the rest of the world must belong to someone else and, therefore, in default of God, to men.

Elizabeth Janeway

"Nothing endures but change" wrote Heraclitus. And yet change is often resisted. Over the centuries, social movements have provided a powerful impetus for social change. Although the American Revolution, the suffrage movement, the 1960s' civil rights marches, and the antinuclear movement show wide differences in their means and ends, they all share several elements: "a commotion, a stirring among the people, an unrest, a collective attempt to reach a visualized goal" (Herberle, 1951, p. 6). Thus a social movement is a group of people organized and led to some extent to promote or resist social change. Social scientists have analyzed social movements in terms of their types (Aberle, 1967; Blumer, 1961) and the stages they pass through from inception to demise (Mauss, 1975).

Society's definitions of gender roles have also changed throughout history (Doyle, 1983). Today, the gender roles are once again being challenged by certain social movements, and there is growing evidence that these social movements will continue into the near future.

In this chapter we will concentrate on the social movements that have pushed and are still pushing for new definitions of society's gender roles. First we will examine the social conditions that have created the women's movement. We will trace the roots of the modern-day women's movement back to the early strivings for economic independence in the late Middle Ages by the women who challenged many powerful patriarchal social structures. We will continue by exploring the rise of feminism in the nineteenth century, and we will end by discussing the reemergence of the women's movement of the 1970s and 1980s. Next we will focus on the small groups of men, separated by ideological differences, who are calling for changes in men's lives. And last, we will examine the gay rights movement, which is linked to both the women's and men's movements.

One thing that should be kept in mind in the following discussion is that people don't change in a vacuum; rather, the social forces that surround them either prompt change or restrain it. Although individuals affect the times they live in, the social forces that arise from various social institutions play a decisive role in creating the situations wherein individuals may choose to act or idly sit by the sidelines.

THE WOMEN'S MOVEMENT

Many people believe that what is presently called the *women's movement* is a rather recent social phenomenon. In fact, the history of the present-day women's movement extends back several centuries. Whenever there has been an upheaval in society and in its social institutions, we are apt to find the prevalent gender roles challenged and to some extent modified or changed. We will concentrate here on three separate periods in history, each of which has had an effect on women's gender roles: the late Middle Ages (from the eleventh century to the fifteenth century), the latter half of the nineteenth century, and from the mid-1960s to the present. In each of these periods we find significant changes in the social structures of society; therefore, it is not surprising that the female's traditional gender role has been challenged and changed during each of these periods.

Feminism in the Late Middle Ages

During medieval times, the image of womanhood was limited to that of childbearer or sexual seductress (Ferrante, 1975). A common picture of the medieval woman is that of an unschooled and illiterate person whose life was totally dominated by men. During her early years, a young woman was ruled by her father and brothers; after marriage she was ruled by her husband in all secular matters. In all spiritual affairs, the church's clergy ruled over a woman. Thus, in medieval drama, medieval women were merely shadowy figures in the background while men were on center stage.

Recently, scholars have begun to challenge the nearly universal view that men dominated women in the Middle Ages. For example, some women, like Hildegard von Bingen (1098–1179) and Isotta Nogarola (1418–1466), to name just two, gained considerable prestige and status for their scholarly works (Grant, 1980; King, 1978). Less visible but just as important were the female "ambassadors of culture" who owned books, for they "substantially influenced the development of lay piety and vernacular literature in the later Middle Ages" (Bell, 1982, p. 743). There were other women (usually less educated than von Bingen and Nogarola), who also broke the tradition of women's total dependency on and subservience to men. There were some women who avoided marriage altogether and lived in all-female religious or secular communities. Those who joined female religious groups, however, usually found themselves under the rule of existing male religious communities (Bolton, 1975). We will focus our attention on the women who joined secular communities where direct male domination was remarkably absent. Although not constituting a majority, the medieval women who charted a new life-style—either of scholarship or without men and men's domination—laid the pattern, in a manner of speaking, that other women would follow several centuries later.

The Beguines   During the medieval era, the once powerful Roman Catholic church found itself under increasing attack from heretical groups. Groups such as the Albigensians and Waldensians openly attacked the Church and the institution of marriage, which the Church had sacramentalized. The Albigensians believed marriage to be an abomination: "physical marriage has always been a mortal sin, and that in the future life no one will be punished more severely because of adultery or incest than for legitimate matrimony" (Herlihy, 1973, p. 134). The Waldensians believed that both men and women should eschew marriage and seek spiritual perfection in the single life. These anti-Church groups attracted many women who despised the "lecherous" ways of the Church's clergy. Furthermore, many families turned their daughters over to these groups for an education, something they would not have gotten from the Church (Herlihy, 1975).

Many orthodox Catholic women who wished to join a religious convent were actually prevented from doing so by the Church. Although some religious orders welcomed women, the majority did not and declared that they had justification for excluding female aspirants: "women inevitably contributed to indiscipline. . . . Women were also considered to be receptive to all forms of religious prophecy and to be completely unrestrained in relationships with their leaders or patrons" (Bolton, 1976, p. 143).

Thus large numbers of women during this period sought the single life. This self-imposed celibacy was due to many factors: the popularity of heretical groups with their prohibitions against marriage, the churchmen who would not allow women into the religious life, and the fact that there were more marriageable women than men in the population (Guttentag and Secord, 1983). To survive economically, many of these single women found it necessary to pursue alternative life-styles.

Many single women joined communities known as the *Beguines*. During the twelfth century in Northern Europe, the Beguine movement attracted mainly unmarried and widowed women (McConnell, 1969). Unlike the unmarried women who entered religious convents, the Beguines did not take vows of chastity nor practice an ascetic life-style. The Beguines did not have a single founder nor rule of life, unlike the norm for the religious communities of women. The Beguine communities supported themselves through various occupations that could be practiced within their local communities. The Church took a rather dim view of the Beguine communities and decreed them to be an "abominable sect of women."

By the fourteenth century, many unmarried women, either individually or in groups such as the Beguines sought nontraditional means of self-support. One means of self-support was to enter the various trades or guilds that represented different occupations. Initially, entrance into a guild was strictly forbidden to all women. Over a period of time, however, women found their way into the labor force in such occupations as weaving and sewing. Finally, near the end of the Middle Ages, some guilds were comprised of all female members; the members of these guilds became widely accepted by their communities as skilled craftswomen (Guttentag and Secord, 1983).

Although a majority of women of the latter Middle Ages did not enter all-female secular groups (e.g., the Beguines) nor solely provide for their economic sustenance outside of marriage, a small but decidedly independent number did. What is most important about the Beguines and other independent women during this period is that these women broke away from tradition and lived on their own without the supervision and support of men. Today's women's movement can be thought of as a continuation of the efforts of these medieval women who challenged and changed the traditional male-dominated gender role of women.

The Women's Movement in the Nineteenth Century and Early Twentieth Century

The nineteenth century found social change the rule in England and in the United States. One thing that should be pointed out here is that in the United States there was no single American life-style during the nineteenth century. During this period, at least three different areas in the United States could be delineated as having distinct life-styles: the established industrial New England states, the antebellum agrarian South, and the ever-expanding frontier stretching westward from the Ohio Valley. The conditions of life for women were vastly different in each of these geographical areas. One thing most nineteenth century women had in common, however, was their experience of hard and ceaseless work.

In the New England states, women found themselves involved in the daily routines of working to help support their families. Large numbers found work in the textile factories of New England. Those not working in textile mills helped support themselves and their families by weaving and sewing in their homes. The change in the meaning of the term "spinster" helps show how the textile industry affected women's lives. Originally the term simply meant a female spinner. But eventually the term came to mean an unmarried woman (Cott, 1977).

The South has been romanticized as the portion of the United States where women were placed on pedestals and men were the epitome of gentlemanly ways. In fact, the women of the antebellum South, even those who lived in a grand way, were not strangers to work. Historian Anne Scott (1970) describes the daily life of a Southern lady and mistress of a plantation as one of work from sunrise to sunset. Scott writes:

> No matter how large or wealthy the establishment, the mistress was expected to understand not only the skills of spinning, weaving, and sewing, but also gardening, care of poultry, care of the sick, and all aspects of food preparation from the sowing of seed to the appearance of the final product on the table. Fine ladies thought nothing of supervising hog butchering on the first cold days in fall, or of drying fruits and vegetables for the winter. They made their own yeast, lard, and soap, set their own hens, and were expected to be able to make with equal skill a rough dress for a slave or a ball gown for themselves. It was customary for the mistress to rise at five or six, and to be in the kitchen when the cook arrived to "overlook" all the arrangements for the day. A Virginia gentleman's bland assertion that "a considerable portion of her life must be spent in the nursery and the sickroom" was a simple description of reality. (p. 31)

The few women who ventured West to the ever-receding frontier found life even more harsh and unforgiving than did the women in the South and East. Frontier wives worked alongside their husbands in fields and woods. The lack of even the most common amenities proved to be one of the harsher realities of life. To tame the land and make a home, women's work was every bit as essential as men's work. To say the least, the traditional ideal of the genteel and frail woman had no place on the frontier.

Thus, during the nineteenth century, most women's lot was that of nearly continuous work. Women had few rights, and, for the most part, they were considered inferior to men.

Before the nineteenth century, few voices were raised to protest women's subordinate role and inferior status. One exception was Mary Wollstonecraft, who wrote a powerful treatise, *A Vindication of the Rights of Women* (1792), which called for an end to women's "slavish obedience" to men. Although Wollstonecraft's book set the stage for a women's movement to develop, most women resisted because they believed that such a movement was opposed to all that was natural. In 1838, Caroline Norton, who had worked to secure a mother's rights over her children, wrote: "The wild and stupid theories advanced by a few women of 'equal rights' and 'equal intelligence' are not in the opinion of their sex. I, for one (I, with millions more), believe in the natural superiority of man, as I do in the existence of God. The natural position of woman is inferiority to man" (quoted in Klein, 1984, p. 531).

However, the women's movement of today actually has its roots in the early antislavery or abolition movement that began in the early part of the nineteenth century. Sarah and Angeline Grimke, the daughters of a South Carolina slave holder, were two notable female abolitionists who also became involved with the "women's issue" during their fight against slavery.

Sarah Grimke blamed men for women's subjugation, a point of view not readily admitted to by most men and women of that period. In 1837 she wrote:

> All history attests that man has subjugated woman to his will, used her as a means to promote his selfish gratification, to minister to his sensual pleasure, to be instrumental in promoting his comfort; but never has he desired to elevate her to that rank she was created to fill. He has done all he could to debase and enslave her mind; and now he looks triumphantly on the ruin he has wrought, and says, the being he thus deeply injured is his inferior. . . . But I ask no favors for my sex. . . . All I ask of our brethren is, that they will take their feet from off our necks and permit us to stand upright on that ground which God designed us to occupy. (quoted in Hole and Levine, 1984, p. 534)

Surprisingly, the majority of male abolitionists (although they championed the freedom and the rights of the slave) did not support women's rights. The female abolitionists were looked upon by their male confederates only as willing workers for the cause of antislavery—willing workers in the sense of handing out leaflets and ministering to males. Even the most dedicated female abolitionists were not allowed to occupy official positions within the abolitionist movement.

The demeaning second-class status of female abolitionists became obvious in 1840 at the World Anti-Slavery Convention held in London, England. The female delegates were prohibited from engaging in any of the proceedings and relegated to sit in the galleries away from the official events. Among the women snubbed by these "righteous" male abolitionists were Lucretia Mott and Elizabeth Cady Stanton, who vowed to press for women's rights as well as an end to slavery when they returned to the United States. However, it was a full eight years after their return from England that the first Women's Rights Convention was held in Seneca Falls, New York, on July 19 and 20, 1848. The Seneca Falls Convention is generally regarded as the birth of the modern-day women's movement.

The only resolution at the Seneca Falls Convention that was not passed by unanimous agreement was the one dealing with women's suffrage. However, two years later at a women's convention held in Salem, Ohio, the question of women's suffrage was a prominent issue, and for the first time, men were prohibited from participating in the convention's activities. The fact that men were barred from participation signaled a new fervor among the new feminists' consciousness.

> [The Salem Convention] had one peculiar characteristic. It was officered by women; not a man was allowed to sit on the platform, to speak, or vote. *Never did men so suffer.* They implored just to say a word; but no; the President was inflexible—no man should be heard. If one meekly arose to make a suggestion he was at once ruled out of order. For the first time in the world's history, men learned how it felt to sit in silence when questions in which they were interested were under discussion. (quoted in Hole and Levine, 1984, p. 537)

One of the most moving stories of this period is the confrontation between a group of antifeminist clergymen and an ex-slave by the name of Sojourner Truth. The incident occurred at the second National Woman's Suffrage Convention, held in Akron, Ohio in 1852, when a group of clergymen took the floor and spoke at length about women's "inferior nature" and their "proper place in God's plan." They went on and on about women's delicate nature and their need for men's benevolent protection. No longer able to tolerate these men's harangues, Sojourner Truth took the floor and recounted her days as a slave. She told how she had endured the whip, suffered physical privations, and watched helplessly as her children were sold to other plantation owners. And when it came to the issue of women's fragile and delicate nature, Sojourner Truth held up her strong arms and said, "I have plowed and planted and gathered into barns, and no man could head me! And ain't I a woman?" (quoted in Brawley, 1921). Her epochal statement, "And ain't I a woman?" stands as a testament to all women who have been exploited, mistreated, and abused by insensitive, uncaring, and powerful men.

The Turbulent Years (1865–1920)   During the Civil War years, the women's movement receded into the background of social concerns. Most of the women who worked for women's rights during the 1850s believed that once the war ended, the rights of both blacks *and* women would be assured. Such was not to be the case. After the Civil War, the abolitionist movement and women's movement parted company. The abolitionist and women's rights alliance that had worked for decades to win a measure of human dignity for blacks was soon shattered because the newly won freedom was to be for the black man only, not the white woman, and surely not for the black woman. Sadly, many of the white male abolitionists were merely interested in putting an end to slavery for business reasons. With slavery abolished, these "high-minded" men saw no need for women's emancipation. Thus, after years of being linked to the cause for black freedom, the women's movement finally came into its own (DuBois, 1978).

The emergent women's movement was not, however, to be a monolithic social force with a single voice or with an organization where all worked for the same goals and supported similar tactics. On the contrary, the newly formed women's movement that began in the late 1860s was to witness several turbulent decades, during which women from many different organizations fought the battle for women's suffrage from many different perspectives. During the latter half of the nineteenth century and during the early twentieth century, the women's movement included many groups with many different ideologies and strategies.

In 1869, Elizabeth Cady Stanton and Susan B. Anthony formed the militant National Woman Suffrage Association (NWSA), which worked for women's suffrage, lobbied against the exploitation of women, and lobbied for better working conditions for women. Also in 1869, the American Woman Suffrage Association (AWSA) was founded; the AWSA was more moderate and restricted its efforts solely to winning women's right to vote. Thus, almost immediately the women's movement had two organizations with very different views of what needed to be accomplished, as well as how to accomplish them.

The fight for federal suffrage began almost immediately after the war's end. An amendment for women's suffrage was introduced in Congress in 1868 and every year thereafter. Wyoming was the first territory to grant women's suffrage, thanks to the ceaseless work of Esther Morris. (However, Wyoming's legislators' support of women's suffrage was motivated less by their concern for women's rights than by their desire to encourage Eastern women to move west and reverse the chronic shortage of women in the territory.) When Wyoming sought statehood in 1889, many Southern congressmen fought its admission because of its passage of women's suffrage. When confronted by the powerful Southern block, a Wyoming delegate telegraphed the legislature back home and asked if they wished to repeal women's suffrage. The reply from Wyoming was succinct and defiant: "We will remain out of the Union a hundred years rather than come in without the women" (quoted in Deckard, 1983, p. 262). Wyoming won statehood in 1890.

In the same year, the National and American organizations merged to become the National American Woman Suffrage Association (NAWSA). Since its inception in 1869, the National organization had grown more conservative and focused primarily on the suffrage issue, setting aside its original concerns for better working conditions and an end to female exploitation by industry. The new organization consisted mainly of middle- and upper-class women who worked for women's suffrage but forgot about the plight of millions of working-class women whose lives were pure misery and exploitation in the factories and sweat shops of urban areas. "As the movement became more respectable," writes Barbara Deckard (1983), "the typical member was no longer a nonconformist and iconoclast. . . . Antiimmigrant and antiblack feeling and rhetoric were very strong at the time, and both were reflected in the new, prosuffrage rhetoric" (p. 265). The NAWSA's antiblack sentiment was as much a ploy to curry favor with Southern congressmen as it was an indication of just how far the women's movement had come in less than thirty years from the time when it was in the forefront for the struggle for black rights. However, Southern congressmen were never persuaded to support women's suffrage.

While many middle- and upper-class women were busy working to win the right to vote, other women were working in factories and textile plants, on farms, in stores, and in domestic service to others. The number of employed women steadily grew during this period: 4 million in 1890 to 5.3 million in 1900 to 7.4 million in 1910. In 1900, the International Ladies Garment Workers Union formed to rectify the countless injustices so widespread in the textile and garment industries. The National Women's Trade Union League was formed in 1903. The first thing on their agenda was to lobby Congress to study the intolerable working conditions of most working women. For the most part, women union members were suspicious of the women who fought only for women's suffrage. In the eyes of many union-oriented women, suffrage had become a middle-class and elitist women's issue. The union worker Mother Jones remarked "you don't need a vote to raise hell!" (quoted in O'Neill, 1969, p. 54).

Another social force making its contribution to women's rights was the Socialist party, which went on record at its 1901 convention to support "equal civil and political rights for men and women" (Buhle, 1971). In 1904, a Woman's National Socialist Union was formed. Josephine Kaneko founded the newspaper *Socialist Woman* in 1907; this newspaper advocated socialism and women's rights. In the main, however, socialist men expected their wives to remain in the background and fight for socialist goals rather than women's rights, believing that "women, like blacks, needed no special demands or special organizations but should just join the party; the victory of socialism would solve all problems" (quoted in Deckard, 1983, p. 270).

During the early years of the twentieth century, the "NAWSA did little and accomplished almost nothing" (Deckard, 1983, p. 272). After a trip to England, where women's rights were being championed by militant women who used radical means such as public demonstrations, marches, and imprisonment to win women's rights, Harriot Blatch returned to the United States and founded the Women's Political Union in 1907. By 1914, certain factions within the NAWSA became committed to more militant actions and were expelled from NAWSA. These women joined forces with the Women's Political Union, and the Women's party was born. The Women's party was militant in its women's rights activities and pacifistic with respect to the United States' entry into World War I. Among women who fought for women's suffrage during the years leading up to the war, another serious split developed between those in favor of war (NAWSA) and those opposed to war (the Women's party).

After the war's end, there was considerable public sentiment in support of women's suffrage. Many women had worked tirelessly in the war movement. Finally, in May and June of 1919, both houses of Congress passed the Nineteenth Amendment, giving women the right to vote. The next step was to gain the necessary two-thirds ratification from the states. By the summer of 1920, thirty-five states had ratified the Nineteenth Amendment, but one more state was needed. The South was committed to fight against its passage, so the only state left to gain the needed two-thirds was the border state of Tennessee. In August, Tennessee was flooded with both proponents and opponents of the amendment. The amendment passed by only two votes, but those two were enough to make the Nineteenth Amendment part of the Constitution of the United States. The day was August 26, 1920, and the Nineteenth Amendment was part of the Constitution. To achieve this goal, Carrie Chapman Catt, NAWSA's president, calculated that it took:

. . . fifty-two years of pauseless campaign . . . fifty-six campaigns of referenda to male voters; 480 campaigns to get Legislatures to submit suffrage amendments to votes; 47 campaigns to get State constitutional conventions to write woman suffrage into state constitutions; 277 campaigns to get State party conventions to include woman suffrage planks; 30 campaigns to get presidential party conventions to adopt woman suffrage planks in party platforms, and 19 campaigns with 19 successive Congresses. (quoted in Hole and Levine, 1984, p. 541)

What is lost in Catt's enumeration is the visceral element: the fact that millions of women from vastly different backgrounds and ideologies—working women, socialites, socialists, populists, temperance leaguers, union members, pacifists, and militants worked together and separately to gain for all women a measure of the human dignity and respect that had been denied them for centuries. Not only did these women gain the right to vote, they won a sense of accomplishment and achievement in winning a battle against the centuries-old sexist doctrines that had prevented women from exercising their rights as citizens of the United States.

The Modern-Day Women's Movement

Once women had gained the right to vote, many expected that they would turn out *en masse* at the polls. However, it is estimated that only 43 percent of all eligible women voted in the fall of 1920 (Gruberg, 1968). Even so, most male politicians were ever so ready to accommodate women. Both the Republican and Democratic parties included most of the organized women's demands in their party platforms in 1920 (Chafe, 1972; Lemons, 1973). A number of bills passed Congress in the early 1920s, all of which had the support of various women's groups. For example, there were bills to fund programs to help teach mothers to better care for their babies, to regulate meat inspection, to standardize and equalize men's and women's citizenship requirements, and to extend the civil service's merit system to include women (Deckard, 1983, p. 283). In 1923 and every year thereafter, the Equal Rights Amendment was introduced into Congress until it finally passed in 1972.

But the liberal forces of the women's movement soon weakened and were replaced by a nationwide surge of conservatism. According to Barbara Deckard (1983), several factors contributed to this untimely end to what was expected to be a new era for women and for the political system as a whole.

The conservative swing [in the country] reflected the economic upswing in the 1920s . . . and the fact that a large, native-born industrial labor movement was still nascent and weak. The women's confused response to the all-out attack on them was also conditioned by the narrow, legalistic ideology of the suffragists that propagandized suffrage as the single goal—neglecting basic social and economic equality. As a result, the women's liberation movement disappeared almost completely after 1923 and, for other reasons as well, remained dormant for 40 years (from about 1923 to 1963). (p. 286)

The war years (1941–1945) saw women entering into the work force in numbers never before seen (Trey, 1972). "Frail and genteel" women did everything from operating cranes to working in the lumber industry as lumberjacks (jills?) to showing their machine skills as precision tool-makers. However, the war years saw little progress in terms of women's issues and women's rights. After the war, industries fired women in order to give their jobs to the returning soldiers. Four million women were fired between 1945 and 1947. The country fell back into the sexist pattern of insisting that men remain in the work force and women in the kitchen.

The Reemergent Women's Movement   Three events occurred in the early 1960s that revitalized the women's movement. First, in December 1961, President John F. Kennedy, at the urging of Esther Peterson, then director of the U.S. Women's Bureau, appointed a commission to examine the status of women in America. Subsequently, commissions on the status of women were formed in all fifty states. Second, Betty Friedan's *The Feminine Mystique* (1963) articulated the problems many women were facing in their everyday lives. And third, Congressman Howard W. Smith (D., VA.) miscalculated on a crucial vote in the Congress. Smith, an arch-conservative and chairman of the powerful House Rules Committee, planned to scuttle a civil rights bill that was to be voted on in 1964. Against the bill because it would have prohibited job discrimination against black men, and fearing that many liberal congressmen would vote for it, Smith decided to sabotage the bill by adding an amendment. Smith's amendment included "sex" as another category. He reasoned that with the inclusion of sex, the bill would be so radical that moderates and even a few liberals would vote against it. But, to Smith's astonishment, the bill, along with the amendment, passed. Thus, when the 1964 Civil Rights Act was passed, it prohibited employers, labor unions, and employment agencies from discriminating on the basis of race, color, religion, national origin, and *sex*. Many of the early feminists privately said, "Good job, Howard, we couldn't have done it without you!" A liberal president, a homemaker turned feminist/author, and a conservative Southern congressman were all instrumental in the reemergence of the women's movement.

However, the Civil Rights Act of 1964 was only as good as the enforcement behind it. Although the Equal Employment Opportunity Commission (EEOC) was responsible for the enforcement of such laws, the Commission seemed more concerned about protecting the rights of black men than about protecting women's rights. In June 1966, several women met with Betty Friedan while attending the Third National Conference of the President's Commission on the Status of Women. From this informal meeting the National Organization for Women (NOW) was born. In October, a press conference was called announcing the existence of NOW and presenting its goal: "To take action to bring women into full participation in the mainstream of American society *now*, exercising all the privileges and responsibilities thereof in truly equal partnership with men" (quoted in Deckard, 1983, p. 324).

As the newly reemergent women's movement gained momentum, it soon became evident that it actually had two distinct branches, both of which had very different orientations, memberships, and organizational tactics.

The Traditionals   The first group, one that we can call the traditional camp or wing of the modern-day women's movement, began with the founding of NOW. Over the years, NOW grew into an organization comprised of a national governing board and well over 800 local chapters. The membership has been primarily middle-class, white, college-educated women who initiated legal suits, lobbied, staged boycotts, and used other traditional strategies to achieve social change.

At the second national NOW conference, held in November 1967, a women's Bill of Rights was drawn up. Looking back now, the demands set forth in this document may not be thought of as extreme nor radical in content. Bear in mind though that the year was 1967 and the women's movement was neither a household word nor a powerful social force. The public's attention was focused more on the growing Vietnam conflict, and few were aware of women's plight as second-class citizens. At the top of the list of demands was the call for an Equal Right's Amendment to the Constitution. The delegates further demanded that the federal government should place greater emphasis on enforcing the 1964 Civil Rights Law which banned discrimination against women in employment. Other demands dealt with instituting maternity leave as a benefit in the employment sector, an increase in child-care facilities, equal opportunities in both the educational and employment sectors, and finally, that women should have the last word in terms of their bodies, especially in terms of reproduction.

Two of the demands proved too radical for some of the members in attendance, namely, the equal rights amendment and the abortion proposal. The women from the United Auto Workers argued against the call for an Equal Rights Amendment because their union officials opposed such an amendment. And many others argued against the abortion proposal, saying it was not an issue of women's rights. However, NOW continued to grow and become one of the more visible organizations championing women's rights during the 1970s.

Other traditional feminist's organizations were also founded during this time that more or less focused on very specific goals. For example, the Women's Equity Action League (WEAL) was formed for the purpose of securing less gender-stereotypic legislation; the National Women's Political Caucus (NWPC) was formed, which promoted women seeking political office. The infra-structure governing NOW and other professional women's organizations have been rather formal, with elected officers, boards of directors, by-laws, and a national membership. The traditional branch of the modern-day women's movement has opted to use political, economic, and social tactics that most people in positions of power can understand.

The Radicals   A second group of the women's movement was a less structured and, some would say, more radical branch advocating changes in women's lives. During the late 1960s, thousands of women (mostly young and college-educated) began to see that many of the social movements of that time (e.g., the student movement and the anti-Vietnam movement) relegated their female members to little more than "manning typewriters and mimeograph machines, bringing coffee, and serving as 'chicks' to be 'balled' for sport and relaxation" (Sherif, 1976, p. 375). Angered with such patronizing male attitudes and behaviors, many young, leftist-oriented women across the country began to develop their own women's movement. In detailing the meteroic rise of this radical branch of the women's movement, Jo Freeman (1984) writes:

> This expansion was more amoebic than organized, because the younger branch of the movement prides itself on its lack of organization. Eschewing structure and damning leadership, it has carried the concept of "everyone doing her own thing" almost to its logical extreme. The thousands of sister chapters around the country are virtually independent of each other, linked only by journals, newsletters, and cross-country travelers. Some cities have a coordinating committee that tries to maintain communication among local groups and to channel newcomers into appropriate ones, but none of these committees has any power over the activities, let alone the ideas, of any of the groups it serves. One result of this style is a very broadly based, creative movement, to which individuals can relate as they desire, with no concern for orthodoxy or doctrine. (p. 545)

The radical branch of the women's movement has spawned several groups that have all added their own distinctive ideologies and approaches to women's issues. Groups like the New York Radical Women, the Redstockings, the Stanton-Anthony Brigade, and the Feminist approached women's issues with varying degrees of militancy. One result of the radical approach to women's liberation was the conciousness-raising group. The conciousness-raising, or CR, group was a resocializing technique whereby women met in small groups to exchange thoughts and share feelings about what it meant to be women in a sexist society. The CR groups that spread across the country in large and small cities and towns did more to make the women's movement a truly grass-roots social phenomenon than all the legislation passed during this period (Steiger, 1981).

Although there was a limited connection between the traditional and radical women's groups, many saw a value in both approaches.

> On both sides there was considerable ambivalence. Betty Friedan warned NOW that the basic support for the women's movement would come from young women, however alien their style might be. Some radical women felt that both types of organizations were necessary and valuable. "The more we talk about test-tube babies, the more NOW can demand child-care centers and abortion repeal." Others were ambivalent. They knew that organizations like NOW appealed to women who would never join the more radical groups and they believed that much of the work the moderate groups did was valuable. Yet, they feared that, under the influence of these groups, the women's

movement might make the same mistake as the suffragists—that of "creating a bourgeois femininist movement that never quite dared enough, never questioned enough, never really reached beyond its own class and race. (Deckard, 1983, p. 336)

One thing that all the different factions could agree on, however, was the passage of the *Equal Rights Amendment (ERA)*. Setting aside all the rhetoric, slander, and myth-making accusations about the ERA, it is a rather simple and straightforward proposition. It reads:

Section 1. Equality of rights under the law shall not be denied or abridged by the United States or by any State on account of sex.
Section 2. The Congress shall have the power to enforce, by appropriate legislation, the provisions of this article.
Section 3. This amendment shall take effect two years after the date of ratification. (SJ RES 10)

Unfortunately, the ERA passed its legal ratification period on June 30, 1982, and failed to gain an additional three states to secure a total of thirty-eight states for ratification. The reasons for the defeat of ERA are complex, but some of the possible factors are the skillful anti-ERA campaigns run by such groups as *STOPERA*, the *Moral Majority*, and other right-wing, conservative groups (Dworkin, 1983; Eisenstein, 1982). Also, some people just didn't know what the ERA stated, which led them to have all kinds of misconceptions about it (Jacobson, 1983). President Ronald Reagan's opposition to ERA certainly did not help. His opposition broke the presidential tradition that was set by his six predecessors, who had all supported ERA's passage.

The campaigns against ERA in various state legislatures were earmarked by half-truths and deceptive issues conjured up to play on people's fears—unisex bathrooms, young female soldiers dodging enemy bullets in some forlorn foxhole, and the end of heterosexual relations in favor of homosexual ones. All of these false issues and others kept many Americans in a state of confusion and helped to defeat a constitutional amendment that would have made it illegal to discriminate against a person on the basis of her or his sex. Probably the single biggest mistake made by ERA's proponents was that they miscalculated the political savvy of their enemy. Even with the defeat of ERA, the women's movement is not dead. The concern over the gender gap in politics and the lessons learned by the defeat of ERA will probably haunt all future presidential candidates. Feminist women and men have learned a hard lesson; they most surely will be better prepared the next time that the ERA is again introduced in the U.S. Senate and the House of Representatives.

Setting aside the debate over how far women have come since that first women's convention in 1848, we find that in the last several years women have made considerable progress in their struggle for full equality in several social sectors. (We should mention the fact that a flourishing women's movement has been taking place for some years in several European countries. The interested reader will find a wealth of material in works pertaining to the women's movement in Germany [Altbach, 1984; Harrigan, 1982; Jenssen-Jurreit, 1982] and in France [Burke, 1978; Kaufman-McCall, 1983; Stewart, 1980].)

During the 1980s, some have suggested that the women's movement has peaked or has served its purpose and is once again moving toward its demise. In March 1984, *Ms.* magazine commissioned Louis Harris and Associates to poll a national sample of women and men to examine several issues crucial to women in the 1980s, such as the gender gap and gender equality in the workplace. Regarding the results, Gloria Steinem (1984) reports:

> Perhaps more important for the future than any other single result of this Harris poll, a full 57 percent of American women nationwide now believe that the Women's Movement "has just begun." Only 24 percent believe it "has peaked and will be less important in the future"; 13 percent believe it "has now reached its full size and impact"; and 6 percent are "not sure." (p. 54)

Thus a majority of the women of the United States believe that the women's movement is "alive and well." What will be accomplished in the years to come from the efforts of millions of women is anyone's guess. But one thing is certain; the women's movement has been the single most influential social movement in the past several decades, and it doesn't look as if it is about to be quietly pushed into the background.

Now let's consider the social movements involving issues of concern to men and analyze the so-called fledgling men's movement of the 1970s and 1980s.

THE MEN'S MOVEMENT

Why is a *men's movement* needed? Surely, men don't need liberation in the same way that women do? Or do they? Most women would argue that men already have it all—the "it" being the three "Ps": power, position, and privilege. Few people deny that men have the advantage when it comes to many of the elements that women have been working so fervently for during the past hundred years or more. So what can males gain from a men's movement? In fact, hasn't nearly every movement over the centuries—political, religious, military, and economic—been a men's movement of sorts in that at least some men have benefitted? However, as the term men's movement is used here, we mean the very recent and still somewhat embryonic social movement that has called attention to the limiting features of the male gender role and the social institutions that have supported sexist ideology. Men are every bit as affected by certain psychological and emotional constraints as women are (Brannon, 1982). Many authors have noted, for example, that some features of the male gender role are rather damaging for men in general (David and Brannon, 1976; Doyle, 1983; *Ms.*, 1984; Pleck, 1976; Pleck and Sawyer, 1974; Sawyer, 1970).

The prescriptive norms of the male gender role have changed over the centuries with various social institutions upholding different norms for males to prove their manhood (Brandes, 1983; Filene, 1974; Macleod, 1983; Pleck and Pleck, 1980; Stearns, 1979). But overall, we can suggest that the male gender role has stressed dominance and control of the environment. It is these and other aspects of the male gender role that are presently being challenged by some men and by many women.

Are most men really aware of the costs and consequences of their male gender role? Are men, even a few, willing to admit that their strivings toward masculinity or the macho image in the guise of power, success, and control over others often leads not only to the rape of women's bodies and minds, but also to the rape of the land and its resources and the extinction of other living species—themselves included? Are men even dimly aware that their obsession with power and conquest may lead to war and destruction (Etheredge, 1978; Fasteau, 1974)? Are men, even those who claim to be feminists, likely to notice the pressures and drains they place on women by their short-sighted view of what needs to be changed to make this world and their relationships with women truly equal (see box 12.1)? Or, are even the few men who have stepped forward to examine their male gender role and its limitations doing little more than whining about how isolated and lonely they are (Geng, 1976)? It's hard to say just how ready men really are for a genuine attempt to bring down the stereotypes, attitudes, behavior patterns, and the countless other ingredients of the male gender role, let alone the patriarchal social structures that have for centuries oppressed various minority groups, including women. In the past decade what has been called a men's movement has taken two rather different courses, each of which looks at the issues related to masculinity, patriarchy, and sexism from different perspectives. Let's examine each movement to understand what it is that some men are seeking to change in terms of their role in society.

Box 12.1

He's A Feminist, But . . .

I was shocked to learn that the first stage of this wave of feminism is over. Men are rumored to have changed. Everywhere I look—newspaper headlines, conference reports, coffee-break gossip—evidence piles up: a Bell Telephone employee not only asked for paternity leave last year, but he actually used it; the chair of a men's conference on the East Coast enthusiastically announced that women don't need to be angry any more—men are allies now—and declared the beginning of "no-fault liberation"; on the West Coast, groups of men are attending classes with their toddlers and are learning to speak in little tongues; and a friend wrote recently that her physician/husband has even "learned to pick up some of his things."

But here I am, still standing on the sidelines at halftime, still holding my unopened bag of confetti in my hand. My mind is preoccupied with the problem of Fred, the Feminist Man. While Fred has made considerable progress on issues like violence against women and equal pay and child care, I cannot see that he has yet developed any real empathy. I dread what the next 10 years might mean for women if men continue to labor under this handicap.

"Hit the ball and drag Fred, "my friend sighed, summarizing our discussion of a "nice guy" who didn't quite "get it." She was referring to the punch line about a golfer who returned home two hours late from his golf game and explained to his wife that his companion, Fred, had a case of sunstroke and collapsed on the ninth hole.

"It was awful," he shook his head sadly. For the next nine holes, it was 'hit the ball and drag Fred, hit the ball and drag Fred.' "

Fred is the generous, likable man who genuinely wants the approval of the women he admires and takes pride in the label "feminist." Much of his behavior has changed, it's true. He no longer calls the women he works with "honey" or "toots." He makes his own coffee. Pampers do not frighten him. But when these changes spring solely from his desire to please, there's no guarantee that actual comprehension has happened. Fred understands feminism only as a set of rules: Don't call women "girls." Let them open their own doors (sometimes). Let them have their own names and credit cards. Don't beat them. Don't rape them.

But where Fred has managed to grasp some of the particulars of the Women's Movement, the whole picture still eludes him. In other words, he has learned something, but still understands very little. It's a failure of empathy.

Source: "He's a feminist, but . . ." by M. Blakely, 1982, *Ms.,* October, pp. 44, 86. © 1982 by Mary Kay Blakely, as originally appeared in *Ms.* magazine.

Box 12.1

As a result, every new issue comes as a surprise. ("I can understand equal pay, but why do you need your own checking account? Don't you trust me?") Every time the allied front moves forward an inch, Fred has apoplexy and expires from the game. A "time out" must be called, to revive him and explain.

This Fredness is a serious drain on energy. I remember once, after a long public discussion of rape (What *is* rape, really, and do women like it at all, and aren't women ever responsible for it?), there was a strong feeling of mutuality among the women and men who worked so hard to understand one another. Shortly afterward, I published a column that destroyed the equanimity. It was on sexual harassment. Friends reported that confusion broke out in private conversation with the significant men in their lives. These men, some of whom were in consciousness-raising groups, or belonged to organizations with names like Men Against Violence Against Women, took serious exception to my objections to men's commonplace behavior.

The discussions, as it turned out, proved to be fruitful. The women reported that lights had dawned, comprehensions were reached. It was another good "learning experience."

At first, I readied my bag of confetti. Here, five good men had traveled through surprise and affront and hurt and moved, bumpily, and unsteadily, toward recognition. Another victory, another hurdle surmounted, another issue set to rest. Yes, harrassment offended women. Yes, it was a male power play.

But why did it take five separate women five separate hours to convince these men of the same truth they had argued the year before? The truth was cast in a different environment—from the devastating landscape of rape to the common fields of harrassment—but the truth was the same.

The whole experience left me in despair, wishing to move on to new truths—pressing, urgent truths we need to discover about war and the earth and our places in it. Instead, we are still wallowing around arguing the same truths over and over and over. These men are naming the cost of liberation: few men can learn and accept equality without exhausting some women in the process. These are the terms of change.

So I'm keeping my confetti bagged until I see that sign of self-learning, that glimmer of independent thought. Rather than teaching men "things"—details, items, facts—one simple clue should suffice: "Imagine that you are me." Let all assumptions about women be filtered through that phrase. Think of your masculinity, sexuality, your livelihood, your education, your relationships, through the light of that idea. Imagine

Box 12.1

yourself as your wife/mother/daughter/sister/lover/secretary/waitress. This is the method that women have used to survive for centuries, the uncanny ability to divine and imagine and recognize men's needs—from protecting their egos to memorizing their underwear size.

I'd like to think that men might learn to think like a woman. My "liberation" depends on it.

Imagine what life would be like if men developed that ability. Suppose the visible, external changes were to evolve into an invisible, internal consciousness. Fred would be able to see how every detail contributes to the whole: how harrassment is a dangerous tentacle of rape; how language is an expression of the oppression we bear; how the way he thinks of his mother has everything to do with the way he thinks of me; how unquestioned manhood and fatherhood loyalties will lead inevitably to war.

In the meantime, Fredness threatens to overwhelm us.

A friend of mine has been changing diapers for years without applause, but she was recently complimented on her husband's ability to do the same. Yes, it was wonderful, she agreed. "And next week," she said, in a voice tellingly drained of enthusiasm, "we're going to learn how to call the baby-sitter." Hit the ball and drag Fred.

The Early Years and the Women's Movement

Most of the men who formed the early nucleus of the present-day men's movements came to a heightened awareness of their gender role and its effects on themselves and others by way of the women's movement. Many of these men had previously been involved in other liberal causes and social movements, such as the civil rights movement, the student movement, and the anti-war movement, that rocked the United States during the 1960s. The move from concern over Vietnam or free speech on campus to an awareness of gender-related issues was, for most of these men, influenced by personal relationships with females who brought women's issues to the men's attention. Sociologist Jon Snodgrass (1977), whose relationship with a woman forced him to question some of his sexist attitudes and beliefs, wrote about such a transition:

> My full introduction to the women's movement came through a personal relationship. . . . I met and fell in love with a woman who was being politicized by women's liberation. As our relationship developed, I began to receive repeated criticism for being sexist. At first I responded, as part of the

male backlash, with anger and denial. In time, however, I began to recognize the validity of the accusation, and eventually even to acknowledge the sexism in my denial of the accusation. . . .

One evening, my lover challenged the male supremacist remarks of a television commentator. I defended the commentator and we argued. I denied that I was being sexist and I denied that my refusal to admit being wrong in an intellectual argument with a woman was also associated with my masculinity. Subsequently, I realized that I had supported the commentator simply because he was a man and *not* because I believed he was correct. Threatened by the challenge to my male dominance, I had identified with him against the person I loved because he and I were genitally males. Thus I dimly recognized patriarchal bonding and faintly perceived my own misogyny. (p. 7)

These initial challenges to some men's sexist beliefs and the entrenched patriarchal values in their lives led small groups of men around the country to form *consciousness-raising groups*, or what are usually called C-R groups, modeled after the women's groups. Many of these early men's C-R groups focused on some of the problems men encountered in trying to fulfill the male gender role. Still other groups of men met to discuss the issue of sexism and its social supports that had oppressed women for centuries. Then in 1974, a small group organized the first Men and Masculinity Conference, which was held in Knoxville, Tennessee. Since then there has been a national conference nearly every year in cities like Los Angeles, California, State College, Pennsylvania, Des Moines, Iowa, and Ann Arbor, Michigan. At these conferences, men, and some women, gather to discuss, hold sessions on various topics, and "play out" some of the questions and concerns of the attending participants. The focus for most of these conferences was and is the overriding issue that men in our society are cut off from their full potential as human beings and that many of the male gender role's prescriptions harm both men and women; there are also discussions of feminist issues like rape, abortion, and the end of patriarchy. But during the late 1970s and into the 1980s, those interested in pursuing the issues of gender roles in society became divided.

The Two Men's Movements

During the late 1970s, many men began to organize "men's rights" and "fathers' rights" groups. The largest and best organized is *Free Men*, which is based in Columbia, Maryland; Free Men has members in over thirty-five states (Haddad, 1979). The focus of the men's rights groups has been primarily on changing the laws that they feel discriminate against men in their roles as husbands and fathers, for example, divorce laws, child custody laws, and visitation rights (Ornstein, 1978). Most of these men support the ERA, however. Psychologist Herb Goldberg (1976, 1979) has become a central figure in this wing of the men's movement, and his writings are a major source for elaborating the concerns and views of the men's rights group. Some men in these groups view themselves as being victimized by women, especially by feminist women. The concern about male oppression is common among many men's rights groups. In an open letter addressed to a national conference, Robert Sides, the director of Free Men/ Boston, wrote:

> It is oppressive to hear of universal female powerlessness while seeing the ubiquity of "Women's" . . . Studies, Book-store Sections, Theatre, Art Shows, Information vans, Health Centers, Radio Shows, etc. . . . It is not a little ironic, too, to hear of women's "second-class" status when they have such privilege in divorce settlements, custody hearing, draft acts, statutory rape laws, sexual harassment hearings, lifeboat seat allocations, etc. . . .
>
> It is bad enough not to meet many assertive women. It is worse to meet so many the feminists never mention: insensitive and rude women who, far from being the "intuitive, feeling" beings we think *all* women are, act like emotional-bank examiners when they deal with the inner lives of men; who ignore or act crudely toward men who *must* approach them if anyone is to get their needs met; who dehumanize male *feeling* by calling them, clinically, "egos"; whose passivity necessarily causes them to respond to the very macho behavior they decry . . . ; who don't care what pressures "privileged" men are under to earn money just so long as they spend it on them . . . ; who are sexual only if prompted by booze-or-bennies to avoid responsibility and blame male sexuality (A.K.A. "lust") for *taking advantage* of them. . . . All women are not like this, but few are truly *acting* like the New Woman they so often *talk* about. (quoted in Interrante, 1981, pp. 58–59)

Overall, the men's rights side of the men's movement tends to focus on areas where they perceive that men are not treated equally or, from their point of view, fairly, by society. The culprit for many of these men is the feminist woman who demands that society rectify its wrongs against her at the expense of men. It seems that the men's rights groups react much like white men and women who feel discriminated against when society enacts laws to give minority groups an edge in employment. Some believe these men to be antifeminist in their views and philosophy (Brannon, 1981, 1982; Pleck, 1980).

The second wing of the men's movement is much more socially and politically conscious and more concerned with bringing down the patriarchal social structures that have oppressed and discriminated against minorities such as women, gay men and lesbians, blacks and Hispanics, and Third World countries. For this group, the men's rights wing of the men's movement is elitist (i.e., white, middle class, and educated) and covertly, if not overtly, antifeminist. In fact, many of those involved with this group disavow totally the title of men's movement, seeing in it further evidence of the not-so-subtle antifemale bias. One such person is Bob Lamm (1977), who writes of the men's movement in rather unflattering terms.

> The men's movement has a line all right. Note the cover statement from the first "national newsletter" of Men's Awareness Network (M.A.N.—get it?) from Knoxville, Tennessee—"A newsletter dedicated to consciously creating awareness between, among, and about men and men's issues and concerns." Read the quote carefully, because *this* is the line of the men's movement. Not because the Knoxville men are a powerful vanguard, but because this has *always* been the line of the men's movement. The Knoxville collective has merely spelled it out.

What are the implications of this line? Does this line express or even imply any commitment to fight male privilege, heterosexual privilege, class privilege, or white skin privilege? Not that I can see. What it does do is reveal the essential *male bonding* of this men's movement, which is awfully similar to the male bonding of all other men's movements.

There is no mention of women in the quote. There is no mention of feminism. There is no mention of male supremacy. There is no mention of woman-hating. There is no mention of rape, abortion, child care, or forced sterilization. Just men "sharing men's issues and concerns with other men." How is *that* different from other men's movements? Women are as invisible and unimportant to this men's movement as they are in any other corner of our male supremacist society. (p. 155)

Thus, the second wing of the men's movement is primarily concerned with social issues that will put to rest the bigotry, oppression, and alienation suffered by all victims of white, male supremacy. For these men, the questions of unfair divorce settlements, child-custody cases, and the like are a ruse used by some men who favor perpetuating their own dominant status in society. It seems that the two factions of the men's movement have little in common except that they support another bid for the Equal Rights Amendment.

A Synthesis of Sorts

In the spring of 1983, a group met in New York City and announced the formation of the National Organization for Men (NOM). Sensing the growing division among the two factions of the men's movement, many men and women have made a concerted effort in recent years to form a national organization that could address the personal issues of concern for men caught up in these changing times, as well as confront head-on the oppression caused by the sexist ideology that permeates our social structures. In his opening remarks, Robert Brannon (1983), the National Council chairperson for NOM, noted the goals of and some of the history behind NOM. He stated:

This afternoon marks the first public appearance of a new national organization. It is one composed primarily of American men, and devoted to a wide range of issues and actions which especially affect the lives of men in this society.

We wish to make clear also that together with our concern for the lives and welfare of men, we are committed to changing other injustices which have since ancient times been associated with a human being's sex. We are committed to full equality and justice for women, and with equal conviction, to full equality and acceptance of those who have been stigmatized because of their sexual preference. We believe, in fact, that all of these issues are far more closely connected than most human beings have recognized in the past.

There have been other, previous groups of men who were concerned about one or another of the many special problems and issues of men. There are today organizations of women who demand equal treatment, and organizations of gay men and Lesbian women who are asking for the simple justice of being treated fairly and equally. Although less well-known, there have also been groups of men in the past who fought valiantly for the rights of women, and there have been heterosexual men who worked for an end to prejudice against gays. But the record will show that there has never before been an organized national movement of men with the breadth of concern, and the determination to bring about social change, as the one that we are launching today. (p. 5)

In April, 1984, the governing council of NOM (after a vote of the membership) changed its name to the National Organization for Changing Men (NOCM). The abrupt organizational name change resulted, at least partly, from the action of Sidney Siller, a New York lawyer and outspoken critic of the women's movement. Siller selected the name National Organization for Men to identify his newly formed group, which feels men have suffered unduly because of the actions of feminist women. Thus to clearly differentiate themselves from Siller's group and his persecuted colleagues, the membership of NOM voted to become the National Organization for Changing Men.

The fledgling men's movement, which began in the 1970s as an outgrowth of the women's movement and has been called "the most significant social movement of the twentieth century" (Boulding, 1976, p. 117), continues to this very day. The men's movement consists of the men's rights groups across the country, the loosely knit, socially conscious, antisexist groups, and the recently introduced National Organization for Changing Men; however, these groups have not succeeded in coalescing. The men's movement has splintered and has been unsuccessful in its attempts to attract large numbers of men and women to its cause. In fact, the membership of NOCM is only approximately 550. We will have to wait to see how successful NOCM is in achieving its goals. Alan Gross, Ronald Smith, and Barbara Wallston (1981) give a less than enthusiastic analysis of the men's movement and its impact on the social and psychological conditions that caused its members to seek change. They write:

> Theoretically at least, the fledgling U.S. men's movement has easy access to money, organizational skills, and other resources traditionally controlled by males, yet in the past decade it has failed to cohere and prosper as a nationally influential movement. In contrast with its frequent comparison, modern feminism, it has not succeeded in significantly altering the fabric of society, in suggesting new legislation, or even in providing an alternative avenue for the personal frustrations of millions of American men. Nonetheless, the men's movement, largely through men's groups, men's conferences, and a few shoestring publications, has directly and indirectly influenced the lives of several thousand men. The men's movement is certainly not a case study of success. . . .

However, the men's movement and its causes are not dead. The founding of NOCM will attest to this, as will the recent books that continue to analyze the male gender role and point out where changes should be made (Doyle, 1983; Grady, Brannon, and Pleck, 1979; Harrison, 1978; *Men's Studies Bibliography*, 1977). Also, instructional materials have been prepared to help high school males become more aware of their adherence to male gender stereotypes and to eliminate such stereotypes (Sadker, 1977). If there is to be a real and significant change in men's lives, however, it will probably not come from anything approaching a bona fide organized social movement rallying for a change in the male gender role. Rather, change is more likely to come from the grass roots where males from every walk of life and educational background begin to change their own attitudes, behavior, and beliefs, which affect not only their own lives but the lives of others around them. Are most males ready to take this step toward their own liberation from their gender role and an end to the patriarchal systems that favor males over females? Some are, but most are not.

Author Jack Nichols anticipates a world in which men and women are free from the limitations and debilitations of their own gender roles. Speaking directly to the issue of male liberation and the need for it, Nichols (1975) writes:

> A saner society will flower when men liberate themselves from contrived, socially fabricated prohibitions, cultural straitjackets, and mental stereotypes that control and inhibit behavior through arbitrary definitions of what it means to be a man. When it is clear that the worship of the intellect is destructive, as are the idolization of competition, admiration for what is big, and the resort to violence as remedy, men will react differently to one another, with different expectations, priorities, purposes, and awareness. Instead of admiring top dogs, domineering masters and bosses, and instead of supporting power coups, they will regard such persons and their activities as anachronistic and counterproductive. (pp. 317–18)

It does seem that most men have little awareness of what Nichols and others are talking about. Moreover, before any real and significant change can come about in the system that oppresses women in so many ways and oppresses men mainly in psychological ways, social institutions will have to change and legislation will have to be passed that will cause the majority of men to evaluate their gender role and decide that self-change is necessary. Thus it remains to be seen whether the men's movement will be successful.

THE GAY RIGHTS MOVEMENT

Most people know little about men-loving men and women-loving women. Why there is so much misunderstanding, myth, and misinformation about gay women and men is a question that has never been fully answered. And yet, gays have grown tired of trying to educate nongays about gays and the gay community. Gays as a group have become more militant in the past several years and have stopped leading a double existence. The *Gay Rights Movement* has broken into the public's consciousness and has influenced society's conceptions of homosexuals (Altman, 1983).

In this section we will examine the gay rights movement and its historical roots. We will first look at the movement as it developed among gay men and then as it unfolded among gay women, or lesbians.

Gay Men: Out of the Closet

As might be expected, the present-day gay rights movement did not just spring into existence in the last decade or so. Its roots extend back at least into the last century (Lauritsen and Thorstad, 1974). One of the first Americans to speak openly about male-male love was the American poet Walt Whitman, who is considered a "founding father" of homosexual emancipation (Katz, 1976). Whitman's writings profoundly influenced two Englishmen, John A. Symonds and Edward Carpenter, who began working for gay emancipation in England during the latter half of the nineteenth century (Grosskurth, 1975; Rowbotham and Weeks, 1980).

The first organization to publicly support gay people was founded in Berlin in 1897 and was called the *Scientific-Humanitarian Committee.* "The committee's goals," according to Jonathan Katz (1976), "were to abolish the German law against male homosexuality, to change the public's generally negative opinion of homosexuals, and to interest homosexuals themselves in the struggle for their rights" (p. 381). In the United States, however, it was more than twenty-five years later that the first gay organization came into existence. In December, 1924, the *Society for Human Rights* was incorporated by the state of Illinois. For a brief time, the Society published a magazine entitled *Friendship and Freedom,* which was to serve as a public forum for the discussion of homosexuality and as a vehicle to educate the populace about the discrimination against and the misunderstandings and lies about gay people. The Society, however, lasted only for about two years before several of its founders were arrested and subsequently lost their jobs.

The next step in the development of gay rights did not take place for almost another quarter of a century. Henry Hay is credited with being the driving force behind what was to become the *Mattachine Society.* Founded in 1950, the Mattachine Society quickly became an organization in Los Angeles where gay men met to share their ideas of what gayness meant for them. The Mattachine Society also provided counseling, education, and other supports for gays. However, organizational disputes soon erupted, and the original Mattachine group splintered into several factions. At the heart of the break were the different philosophies of what the organization should become. One group wished to present a "respectable image" of the gay male to the general public, while another pushed for a more militant stance by openly advocating gay rights. Still, the Mattachine Society allowed the gay male community to come out of its self-imposed seclusion, and the gay rights movement made its first rather discrete rumblings.

Finally, two events that occurred at opposite ends of our country and just about ten years apart radicalized gay men. The first occurred in New York City in June, 1969, and the second in San Francisco in May, 1979. The Stonewall was a bar on Christopher Street in New York City that was frequented by gays. On a hot June night, the police raided the Stonewall and arrested many of its patrons and the manager. The extreme force used by the police caused many to resist and a riot broke out. The "Stonewall rebellion" has since become likened, among gays, to the "Boston Tea Party." On that June night in 1969, a group of gays finally stood up to the authorities and demanded their rights (Weinberg and Williams, 1975).

In November, 1978, Harvey Milk, an outspoken gay and popular elected city official in San Francisco, was shot by Dan White. The next May, White, who had confessed to the killing, received the lightest sentence possible, voluntary manslaughter, on the basis of his defense's argument of "diminished capacity" because White had been eating junk food (the celebrated Twinkie defense). Both the gay community and many members of the nongay community became enraged at such a travesty of justice, and protests broke out in San Francisco. The gay community saw the verdict as another example of just how deeply embedded the antigay sentiment was in many people's minds. Once again the gay community found a need to push even more strongly for its own rights.

The gay male community became politicized in the 1970s and has openly lobbied ever since then for their rights, as citizens first and as gays second (Altman, 1971; Marotta, 1981).

Lesbians' Rights

"So little is known about the Lesbian," write Del Martin and Phyllis Lyon (1972), "that even Lesbians themselves are caught up in the myths and stereotypes so prevalent in our society" (p. 5). Part of the reason for the lack of knowledge about lesbians, their sexuality, and their life-style is that they have lived even more secluded and private lives, throughout history, than most gay men. The move from isolation to openness has taken some time, but more and more lesbians are coming out and proudly proclaiming their sexual preference (Gidlow, 1976; Kennard, 1984). The organized lesbian movement began about eighty years ago.

One of the first modern-day women to speak out against the unjust treatment of the gay person was Emma Goldman. Goldman was a socialist and a feminist and an advocate of many unpopular causes during her day. She lectured widely on the topic of homosexuality, and by her own account she was able to help some women who had never known that other women had lesbian feelings. Recounting one such incident, Goldman wrote:

> One young woman confessed to me that in the twenty-five years of her life she had never known a day when the nearness of a man, her own father and brothers even, did not make her ill. . . . She had hated herself, she said, because she could not love her father and brothers as she loved her mother. . . . She had never met anyone, she told me, who suffered from a similar affliction, nor had she ever read books dealing with the subject. My lecture had set her free; I had given her back her self-respect. (quoted in Katz, 1976, p. 377)

Goldman and other women, like F. W. Stella Browne and Margaret Sanger, did much to enlighten audiences about homosexuality during the early years of the twentieth century. But one of the first breakthroughs for lesbians came with the publication of a novel whose main character was a lesbian. Radclyffe Hall's novel *The Well of Loneliness*, first published in England in 1928, described the pain and misery suffered by a lesbian woman and was written to win the sympathy and understanding of heterosexuals (Trowbridge, 1975). Many gays of that period, however, felt that it pandered to heterosexuals' misconceptions about the loveless lives that gay people supposedly led (Newton, 1984). Nevertheless, *The Well of Loneliness* enjoyed tremendous popularity; it was translated into eleven languages and only fourteen years after its publication enjoyed an "annual sale of one-hundred thousand copies in the United States alone." *The Well of Loneliness* became known as the "lesbian bible" (Martin and Lyon, 1972, p. 17).

Finally, in 1955, Del Martin and Phyllis Lyon founded the *Daughters of Bilitis (DOB)*. The DOB was the first public organization devoted to the needs of lesbians and to promoting a correct image of the lesbian in society. Two years later, Barbara Gittings founded the New York City chapter of the DOB. Gittings was also instrumental in starting the publication *The Ladder*, which during its years in print (1956–1972) was to become one of the most visible manifestations of lesbian liberation.

During the late 1960s many lesbians joined the women's movement. Most, however, kept their sexual preference to themselves. One who did not was Rita Mae Brown, who had joined NOW in 1969 and refused to keep her gayness a secret. In 1970, after considerable pressure, Brown resigned from NOW, stating: "Lesbianism is the one word which gives the New York N.O.W. Executive Committee a collective heart attack" (quoted in Abbott and Love, 1973, p. 112). After leaving NOW, Brown and others formed the group Radicalesbians.

The women's movement struggled with the question of lesbians and their double oppression, first as women and second as lesbians. In September 1971, at the National Convention of NOW, a strongly worded resolution was passed by the membership owning up to its previous rejection of lesbian women. The resolution openly admitted that NOW had treated its lesbian members rather shamefully during its formative years. Although potential members were never questioned about their sexual preference or lifestyle, NOW did admit that its lesbian members had been an embarrassment to the organization and had treated them as if they were "stepsisters" in the movement. The resolution noted as how NOW had accepted its lesbian members' contributions of financial support and work but assiduously avoided taking any public stance on lesbian issues or providing any support when lesbians and their relationships were denounced in public. The resolution made it clear that NOW would from that time onward give its full support to all women regardless of their sexual preference or lifestyle. Moreover, NOW acknowledged that specific lesbian issues and demands were to be considered an integral part of the women's movement in general.

Today, lesbians and gay men are members of various rights movements. Regardless of whether they are part of NOCM, NOW, or some other antisexist liberation movement, gays are beginning to demand the rights and privileges that all citizens of this "free country" are guaranteed in the Constitution.

SUMMARY

The women's movement has been one of the most influential social movements of this century. The beginnings of the women's movement extend back to the middle ages, when female groups like the Beguines challenged the patriarchal economic order of the day. The nineteenth century abolitionist movement gave rise to the suffrage movement, which included many different groups with different goals and tactics but all with the common desire to win for women the right to vote. Today's women's movement has two branches: a more structurally oriented, politically motivated faction and a person-oriented, socially motivated radical group.

During the 1970s, a fledgling men's movement emerged from a small number of men who were influenced by the women's movement. As with the women's movement, the men's movement developed two forces: one concerned with personal issues of those men who feel threatened by the changes in women's roles, and a second one that was more concerned about political and social issues like an end to sexism in our culture. The men's movement as a whole has not had the impact of the women's movement.

During the 1960s and 1970s, gay men and lesbians also became a social force working for their rights. Although only a small minority, the impact of both the gay men's and lesbians' rights movements have changed society's conceptions of these once-closeted persons.

SUGGESTED READINGS

Altman, D. (1983). *The homosexualization of America: The Americanization of the homosexual.* Boston: Beacon Press.

Deckard, B. (1983). *The women's movement* (3d ed.). New York: Harper & Row.

Doyle, J. (1983). *The male experience.* Dubuque, IA: Wm. C. Brown Publishers.

Ehrenreich, B. (1983). *The hearts of men: American dreams and the flight from commitment.* New York: Doubleday.

Fraser, A. (1984). *The weaker vessel.* New York: Knopf.

Kanowitz, L. (1981). *Equal rights: The male stake.* Albuquerque: University of New Mexico.

Lucas, A. (1983). *Women in the Middle Ages.* New York: St. Martin's Press.

Midgley, M., and Hughes, J. (1983). *Women's choices.* New York: St. Martin's Press.

Stuard, S. (Ed.). (1976). *Women in medieval society.* Philadelphia: University of Pennsylvania.

Point/Counterpoint

Men and Feminism

Over the past decade, feminism has been attacked by those who think it is a sinister ideology that will, if successful, undermine the wills and minds of men (Gilder, 1972; Gordon, 1982). John Gordon, for one, thinks ". . . that whatever it may be in principle, for the last ten years or so feminism has in fact been quite possibly the most prolific single fountainhead of fashionably malignant and fraudulent drivel on the national scene. A movement that began as a genuinely liberating call for a radical enlargement of freedom, generosity, and sympathy has increasingly come to be represented by the sour, the mean, and the dumb" (pp. xiii–xiv). The backlash by men like Gordon and Mike Royko (1984) and women like Phyllis Schlafly have caught the attention of the media and much of the public as well. People are concerned that men will be emasculated, that the family will be ruined, and that women will lose their "protected" status if feminist-oriented people take over. In many people's minds, then, feminism ranks right up there with atheism and communism.

However, feminism simply refers to the ideology that advocates the political, social, and economic equality between the sexes. How equality of the sexes gets translated into a godless and totalitarian social system is beyond its adherents. Possibly, many of those who so staunchly oppose feminism are themselves among the most privileged, and thus they fear losing their most favored status; feminism would be one means of making them equals with rather than masters over others. Men have little to fear from feminism if they truly believe in their minds and in their hearts in equality for all regardless of sex.

What do you think?

Reading   *Psychological Frontiers for Men*

In February 1973, at Brandeis University, Joseph Pleck gave the following address. Here we can read about some of the key issues facing men in these times when different facets of the male gender role are being critically examined.

Tonight I'd like to talk about what I call "psychological frontiers" for men, areas where men are beginning to take new perspectives and attitudes toward their experiences as men.

First, men's relationships with women. There's no question that the changes apparent in women today are having great impact on men. Since women and men are so interdependent, women cannot change without causing adjustments and accommodations in men, at the very least, if not more far-reaching and enduring changes in men going beyond simple accommodation. Changes in male styles of relating to women are probably the most obvious and clear frontier of sex role change for men, but one that is leading to or connected with changes in other areas.

Over and above the very concrete issues of sharing scarce job opportunities and all too abundant housework and childcare responsibility, it's helpful to distinquish two deeper and broader aspects of the contemporary changes in women that men are responding to. First, women are showing *increased achievement*, challenging traditional male superiority in high status careers. There are several different theories about why men having superior performance compared to females, or more typically, excluding females from competition in the same areas altogether, has been necessary for the psychological well-being of so many men, and how deep-seated these needs for superiority are. I'd like to believe that male resistance to female achievement, while extremely serious, is ultimately a short-run problem, a temporary cultural lag between men and women, with the more critical long-run

problem being how to restructure and integrate work and family life (and their alternatives) to better meet the needs of both men and women. Although at the moment, many men seem caught between paternalism and backlash, we should also recognize that many men are relating to female achievement quite positively.

A second area of change in women which men are reacting to is *decreased female willingness to serve male emotional* needs. In traditional sex role relationships, men depend on women to facilitate their emotional expression, if not express their emotions for them. A striking illustration comes in a scene from the film *Carnal Knowledge*, where Art Garfunkel tells Jack Nicholson that Candy Bergen, his girlfriend, "tells me thoughts I never even knew I had." Nicholson, who is having an affair with her on the side, then goes to her and whiningly demands, "you tell him his thoughts, *you have to tell me my thoughts!*" For many men, it takes some effort to learn to experience themselves emotionally without a facilitative woman. Women becoming more emotionally independent can be quite threatening for this reason. But many men today are learning to become more emotionally self-sufficient, more secure in their ability to take care of themselves emotionally.

A second psychological frontier for men, after relationships with women, is relationships with other men. When we think of male-male relationships, probably one of the things that comes to mind first is the kind of all-male groups described by Lionel Tiger in *Men in Groups*. For many reasons, this kind of relating among men seems to be on the way out. Although certain kinds of relating were permitted in such groups, and they have been

Source: "Psychological frontiers for men" by J. Pleck, 1973, *Rough Times, 3(6)*, pp. 14–15. Copyright © 1973 by Joseph H. Pleck.

important for men, it's clear that most relationships in them were not very deep, and were based to a large extent on the exclusion of women.

As we know, these institutions have come under widespread attack, by women recently, but also earlier, and by men, as in the military or in college fraternities. A major force in the discrediting of all-male institutions, though, has been men's expectations for earlier and more intense heterosexual relationships. This change in expectations has had liberating as well as oppressive effects for men. The idea that every person should have a significant and all-fulfilling relationship with someone of the other sex, and that naturally any same-sex friendship should give way to it, is so powerful and pervasive in the culture that it is hard to realize how recent an idea it really is. Most men would simply rather be with women than with other men. It's ironic that men have been so thoroughly socialized into putting all their emotional energy into relationships with women and de-emphasizing relationships with other men, only to find that women are now changing and won't accept this the way they used to.

So, today many men are seeking new kinds of relationships with other men. Men vary greatly in how much they put into relationships with other men. Some men say that they have not had an important friendship with a man since they were 15. Others have always had significant relationships with other men, and feel a part of themselves as being "in business" with other men, even during important relationships with women. Both groups are beginning to approach relationships with men in a new way, with uncertainty and shyness, but also with excitement. A man in a group said "I have a pretty good idea of what I can get from a relationship with a woman, but I don't know what I could get from a relationship with a man. I just don't know." Here, as elsewhere, we learn something about what is important to us in ourselves by looking at what we seek from others. Men's groups (or men's consciousness-raising, or men's liberation groups) are one new social form in which these issues are being explored.

An important issue in the development of relationships among men is homosexualilty. Many men consciously report that fears of homosexuality are a major factor keeping them from closer relationships with other men. For other men, developing relationships with other men has consciously and deliberately included gay sexuality. The new men's awareness will be broad enough, I hope, to include both.

A third and final psychological frontier for men is men's changing involvements in work, and changing balance of investments in work and family life. The so-called "executive drop-out" and the "blue collar blues" are signs of these changes in men's involvement with work.

In sociological language, work has always been the main institutional anchorage or support for the adult male role. We can also put this in reverse: the adult male role is the main underpinning for the institution of work in modern society. But today more and more men are experiencing work as oppressive and alienating, on the one hand, or are finding that others value their work less and less, or that their work is simply of no value to the society, on the other hand.

I don't think we have yet a full analysis of the connections between work and masculinity for men. It seems clear that there are autonomous drives in the individual toward satisfaction from competence and accomplishment. But it is also clear that in men these drives become involved with culturally-induced needs for masculine status and standing, through competition and power over others. By adulthood, it can be very hard for men to disentangle their inner and outer motivations for work and productivity.

For many men, re-evaluation of the place of work in their lives has coincided with a reassessment of the importance of family and relationship experiences in their lives. In particular, many men are taking more responsibility for and investing more of themselves in children. For many men, in fact, the realization of how involved they get with their children has been one of the main sources of insight that they have some basic needs that are not being met elsewhere in their lives, and a main starting place for reconsideration of themselves as men. As childcare becomes more equally shared, many more men may have this experience.

To sum up and conclude, relationships with women, relationships with men, and involvements with work and family life are three areas where men have traditionally gotten support for masculine identity. But women aren't the way they used to be, older forms of male relationships have been largely discredited, and work just doesn't mean what it used to. Men are simultaneously reacting to these potentially threatening changes, but are also becoming aware of newer, more inner needs for more flexible and open experiences with women, other men, and work, which these changes are now making possible. Increasingly, men are getting in touch with their needs and are finding in the realignment of the sexes and other social changes new freedom and new liberation for themselves.

Chapter 13

THE FUTURE OF SEX AND GENDER

A new civilization is emerging in our lives, and blind men everywhere are trying to suppress it. This new civilization brings with
it new family styles; changed ways of working, loving, and living; a
new economy; new political conflicts; and beyond all this an altered
consciousness as well. Pieces of this new civilization exist today. Millions are already attuning their lives to the rhythms of tomorrow. Others,
terrified of the future, are engaged in a desperate, futile flight into the
past and are trying to restore the dying world that gave them birth.

Alvin Toffler

We will begin our last chapter by examining some of the issues surrounding the soon-to-be-realized option for parents: selecting the sex of
their children. Scientists are now beginning to unlock the mysteries of
conception and are finding ways to increase the chances of having either
a female or male child. Such a possibility creates problems that most of us
have not even begun to consider and that our society has not begun to deal
with.

Our second topic is androgyny. During the 1970s and early 1980s, androgyny was seen as an ideal personality type, one to which both females
and males should aspire. However, perhaps androgyny's real value is not
that it is an ideal personality pattern but that it is a transitional concept: it
introduces new possibilities for both women and men.

Finally, we will examine the issue of moral reasoning. For some time,
researchers have noted that males and females differ in their values and in
their ways of dealing with moral issues. As expected, male values and moral
reasoning have become the norm, the moral standard, so to speak. However, Carol Gilligan has challenged the male-as-norm approach to moral
reasoning. We will end our discussion of sex and gender by exploring Gilligan's revolutionary ideas on moral reasoning and some of their implications for the future of our world.

THE COMING AGE OF SELECT-A-SEX

The day is fast approaching when a couple will be able to unerringly select the sex of their unborn children. The social and demographic changes such a technological reality holds are overwhelming. Some facts, however, are known about people's preferences for one sex over the other, making the issue even more problematic.

In this section we will first examine which sex is generally preferred by couples. Next, we will look at some of the techniques being studied that will allow parents to select the sex of their infants. And last, we will examine some of the consequences of such a possibility.

Boys over Girls

Some years ago, Nancy Williamson (1976a) expressed her concern about the technologies that will in the future allow parents to select their children's sex. "Sex control," wrote Williamson, "would be a significant development because parents around the world now tend to have preferences about the number and sex of their children. The majority still prefer boys" (p. 847). When expectant parents are asked what they want their future offspring to be, most answer "healthy," but many also wish their newborns to be males—especially those parents who want a single child. The preference for males over females is well documented.

During the 1930s, sociologist Sanford Winston (1932) studied upper-class families and speculated that their preference for male offspring revolved around their desire to have male heirs take over the families' businesses. Winston reasoned that a family who wanted a boy would continue to have children until they had a son. In order to support his thinking, Winston studied birth records and indeed found that the last child born to an upper-class family was more often a male. Thus Winston provided some of the first scientific evidence for male preference, at least among America's elite class.

Since Winston's work, others have found a marked preference among adults for male children. In general, males are unquestionably the favorite among couples who state a preference for their firstborn or who express a desire for a single child (Hoffman, 1977; Rent and Rent, 1977). The magnitude of the preference for male children can be seen in Candida and James Peterson's (1973) research. When the Petersons asked a group of young adults about their plans for children, nearly two-thirds had a sex preference, and of these, over 90 percent wanted a male child. Of those who stated that they wanted only one child, over two-thirds of the females and over 80 percent of the males wanted a male.

Even the interval between a couple's first and second child indicates a preference for males. One study found that the interval between a couple's first and second child was much shorter if the first child was a female (Pohlman, 1969). Thus, considerable research clearly shows a male preference among a large percentage of adults.

Box 13.1

No More Girls

> Dear Abby:
> We have two baby girls. One is 3 and the other is 2. My wife is pregnant and will have the baby in January. We are now thinking that if we should get another girl baby, we should get a sex-change operation for her that people say is now possible.
> How much would it cost?
> No More Girls, British Columbia
>
> Dear No More Girls:
> Sex-change operations were not intended for infants whose parents are disappointed with the sex of a child. If you can't thank God for a healthy, normal, baby girl, why not adopt a boy?

Why are males preferred over females? Several possibilities come to mind: for example, a male child can carry on the family name, give a father someone to share "manly" activities with, or even be a sign of a father's masculinity. However, the ultimate basis for such a sex preference is elusive unless we wish to consider the issue of society's deep-seated misogynous ideology. Setting aside the issue of antiwoman sentiment, there appear to be two general conclusions we can make about the findings related to sex preference. First, males tend to prefer male children more than females do (Coombs et al., 1975; Williamson, 1976b). Second, Catholics and Jews tend to prefer boys over girls more than Protestants do (Markle, 1974). Although women are less likely to prefer sons over daughters, some studies suggest that wives who say they prefer sons may do so to please their husbands (Uddenberg et al., 1971).

There is little doubt that males are preferred over females, but as long as child-bearing was left to chance, there was little to worry about. As we noted earlier, however, science is quickly closing in on the day when parents will be able to decide which sex their offspring shall be. Some parents are already turning to or thinking about newfound technologies that allow them to make a choice (see box 13.1).

Technology over Nature

Presently, three ways have been suggested to tip the scales in favor of a couple's having an infant of a particular sex: the rhythm-and-douche method, selective abortion (after determining the fetus's sex), and artificial insemination with the preferred sex-bearing sperm. We will briefly discuss each of these approaches.

Box 13.2

Dr. Shettles's Ways to Improve Nature's Odds

Male babies

1. Before intercourse, the female should douche with a solution of water and baking soda to create an alkaline environment.
2. The couple should have intercourse during ovulation, having abstained during the previous cycle.
3. The female should have an orgasm, thus increasing a favorable environment for the androsperm.
4. Emission of sperm should occur during deep penetration.

Female babies

1. Before intercourse, the female should douche with a solution of water and vinegar to create an acidic environment.
2. The couple should have intercourse two to three days before ovulation.
3. The female should refrain from having an orgasm.
4. Emission of sperm should occur during shallow penetration.

Source: The male experience (p. 52) by J. Doyle, 1983, Dubuque, IA: Wm. C. Brown Publishers. Reprinted by permission. All rights reserved.

The Proper Timing   In the early 1970s, sex researcher Landrum Shettles revealed his "sure-fire" method for determining the sex of a newborn (Rorvik and Shettles, 1970). Shettles recommended, on the basis of his research, that couples wanting a child of a specific sex should restrict their intercourse to certain times of the monthly menstrual cycle because the timing of intercourse has a bearing on the conception of one or the other sex. For example, he recommends that a couple wanting a male should have intercourse during ovulation, whereas couples wanting a female should have intercourse two to three days prior to ovulation. Furthermore, Shettles says that a woman should use a douche because certain chemicals create different types of environments (see box 13.2). Male-bearing sperm (androsperm) appear to thrive in an alkaline solution, while female-bearing sperm (gynosperm) do better in an acidic environment.

Although Shettles' methods have not been tested with large samples, others have suggested that there is some justification for thinking that the timing of intercourse plays a part in determining the sex of the unborn (Guerrero, 1974).

Selective Abortion   With the advent of *amniocentesis*, we now are able to determine some forms of chromosomal abnormality, as well as the fetus's sex (with a fair degree of certainty). In this process, generally performed during the fourth month of pregnancy, a hollow needle is inserted through the abdominal wall and into the uterus of a pregnant woman, from which a small sample of amniotic fluid is removed and used to determine the chromosomal composition of the fetus. If XY cells are found in the sample, there is a high probability that the fetus is male; if no XY cells are found, the chances are that the fetus is female (Milunsky, 1973). Other techniques are being studied. Fluorescence cell sorting, for instance, is believed to allow identification of the fetus's sex as early as 47 days after conception (Powledge, 1979).

However, the public's acceptance of aborting a fetus simply on the basis of a parent's desire for a girl or a boy is questionable. In fact, one study found that only 7 percent of over 1,600 women who were questioned about abortion as a means of sex selection approved of abortion for such a reason (Sell et al., 1978). However, in a more recent study conducted by Richard Feil and his associates (1984), nearly a quarter of the college males who were questioned (24.5 percent) favored abortion as a means of sex selection, while 15.1 percent of college females approved of such a procedure. Thus, although most people apparently reject abortion as a technique for selecting the sex of the unborn, some see this procedure as an option.

Separating Males from Females   Since X-bearing sperm are heavier than Y-bearing sperm, it is possible to separate the two kinds of sperm through differing techniques—a centrifuge, for example (Lindahl, 1958). It is also possible to apply certain staining substances to the sperm, which would make the separation of the two sperm types easier (Barlow and Bosa, 1970). After separating the two types of sperm, the designated sex-sperm of the parents' choice would be used for artificial insemination.

All of the techniques described thus far are not science-fiction proposals: but rather present-day medical and technological realities. Although the issue of sex preference is debatable, the fact is that some parents do wish to have one sex rather than the other, and now the technology exists that will permit them to fulfill their wish.

Consequences of Select-a-Sex

As with every new scientific advancement, both some good and some ill will result. As the technology that allows us to select the sex of the unborn becomes more commonplace, we need to examine both the positive and the negative consequences.

First, there will be several positive effects stemming from a couple's (or a single parent's) choice to have either a boy or a girl. It is possible that family size would decrease with parents selecting the sex of their child, instead of resorting to the "fifty-fifty" method until they get the desired sex. Having smaller families would allow many women more time for non-family activities. For example, a single woman who may wish to have one child of a specific sex would benefit from the preselection of the sex of her child. Possibly the greatest benefit of such a select-a-sex arrangement would be that women would have greater control over their reproductive functions and ultimately over their own bodies (Williamson, 1976a).

The negative consequences of sex control are much more far-reaching. There are innumerable problems with some of the techniques used for determining the sex of an already-conceived fetus, such as potential complications of amniocentesis (Corea, 1985). Furthermore, there are the moral questions of abortion when the fetus is determined to be the "wrong" sex. We should not minimize the psychological impact that an abortion might have on a woman who feels she was pressured into by her spouse because he wanted a child of another sex, for instance. Another potential negative outcome is that because boys are preferred by many families, boys would be the first or only child in many families. The literature is quite convincing that firstborns are the recipients of better education and other social advantages (Williamson, 1976a). The chances that parents would choose a boy first and then a girl may only further limit a female's future in terms of what her family would provide for her in comparison to her older brother. And what about those families who wish for only a single child and choose a son over a daughter? It is possible that, with such a pronounced preference for males, males could greatly outnumber females in our society.

Although we can only speculate on the possible ramifications of a society that can select the sex of its children, one thing seems certain: by the turn of the century this situation will be a reality. Thus we need to prepare for all consequences and make intelligent and unbiased decisions about how to deal with a world in which choosing the sex of a baby will be as easy as deciding what type of toy to buy for it.

ANDROGYNY: A TRANSITIONAL CONCEPT

Few concepts have generated as much public attention and social psychological research in the past decade as androgyny (*Psychology of Women Quarterly*, 1979; *Sex Roles*, 1979). To a large degree, the increasing interest in androgyny among social scientists and laypeople alike was stimulated by psychologist Sandra Bem's seminal ideas and the introduction of her scale for measuring androgyny (Bem, 1974). Since Bem's approach to measuring androgyny was discussed earlier (chapter 3), we will focus here on the concept of androgyny and its value as a transitional concept.

Initially, androgyny was considered an ideal personality pattern wherein a person combined the socially valued stereotypic characteristics associated with both masculinity and femininity. Rather than simply exhibiting either the masculine or feminine traits, an androgynous person would exhibit both masculine and feminine traits, depending on the situation. Thus, a male could be sensitive and emotionally expressive (both thought to be feminine traits) *as well as* independent and competent (both viewed as typically masculine traits). The androgynous female would be expected to show socially valued feminine and masculine traits when appropriate. According to the concept of androgyny, people, regardless of their gender, were no longer expected or encouraged to restrict their behaviors to traditional gender-specific traits (Kaplan and Sedney, 1980). Carolyn Heilbrun (1973) considered androgyny a way of liberating males and females from the restrictive stereotypes imposed on them by society's definitions of masculinity and femininity. An androgynous person would merge the "masculine" and "feminine" stereotypes into one integrated personality pattern. Heilbrun wrote:

> The ideal toward which I believe we should move is best described by the term "androgyny." This ancient Greek word—from *andro* (male) and *gyn* (female)—defines a condition under which the characteristics of the sexes, and the human impulses expressed by men and women, are not rigidly assigned. Androgyny seeks to liberate the individual from the confines of the appropriate. . . .
>
> Androgyny suggests a spirit of reconciliation between the sexes; it suggests, further, a full range of experience open to individuals who may, as women, be aggressive, as men, tender; it suggests a spectrum upon which human beings choose their places without regard to propriety or custom. (pp. x–xi)

After being introduced into the public's consciousness, androgyny became a buzzword of the seventies. Overnight, it seemed, the media caught onto the idea of androgyny, and articles appeared proclaiming the value of exhibiting an androgynous personality pattern (Bruck, 1977). The message was straightforward: if people were to live fuller lives, they should reject the restricted, mutually exclusive gender roles of old and develop their personalities so as to express both masculine and feminine elements. If education were to be free of gender bias and conventional tracking systems, it needed an androgynous curriculum. If one was to be fully actualized as a whole person, she or he needed to develop an androgynous personality. Even psychological health came to be defined in terms of androgyny. Sandra Bem herself (1977) and others (Marecek, 1979) prescribed androgyny as a liberating force, leading people, especially women, to fuller lives.

However, along with accolades comes criticism, and androgyny was no exception to this. Although androgyny was an improvement over the view that masculinity and femininity were opposite and mutually exclusive ends of an important personality dimension, the androgynous perspective still held that personality comprises masculine and feminine elements (Lott, 1981; Taylor and Hall, 1982). Others criticized androgyny for being little more than the result of the social pressures on people to express their individuality to an extreme degree (Sampson, 1977).

While androgyny has proved to be less of a panacea than many of its early proponents had hoped, its real value may be its potential as a transitional concept. Androgyny set the stage, in a manner of speaking, for the next step in understanding gender. In the mid-seventies, researchers began to question the relevance of merging masculine and feminine characteristics (Hefner et al., 1975). At issue here was the notion that people should go beyond social definitions of masculinity and femininity—even in their combined androgynous form—to yet another stage. Linda Garnets and Joseph Pleck (1979) wrote of a new vision of gender development, calling for people to transcend, rather than simply merge, prescribed gender characteristics. Garnets and Pleck wrote:

> Sex role transcendence theorists suggest that the ideal state in sex role development is not the combination or integration of masculine and feminine traits in the personality, but a stage in which masculinity and femininity are "transcended" as ways of organizing and experiencing psychological traits.
> Further, sex role transcendence is embedded in a stage theory of sex role development. In individual development, transcendence is seen as superseding the androgynous stage in which the individual blends masculinity and femininity, which in turn supersedes the role identity stage of polarized sex roles. For sex role transcendent individuals, there is no relationship between having and not having sex role related traits and psychological adjustment. (pp. 273–74)

This new approach to gender suggests that people could—possibly should—supersede or transcend the traditional stereotypical male and female characteristics altogether. Thus androgyny's real usefulness may come not from replacing a polarized view of gender roles, but in being a stepping-stone toward a new vision of people moving completely beyond gender roles. Possibly, in the future, personality may be viewed in terms other than those related to gender stereotypes. Although research into the transcendence of masculinity and femininity is still in its infancy, *gender role transcendency* may well be the research concept of the eighties and beyond.

A QUESTION OF MORALS

In a world of escalating nuclear arms, on-again, off-again SALT talks, contested Baby Jane Doe cases, courtroom debates about when a person is considered to be clinically dead, emotional debates over capital punishment in our society, and so on, we seem inundated with a variety of moral questions that demand prudent answers. Making the "morally right" decision is becoming a matter of increasing concern and necessity as moral issues become more complex and potentially more life-threatening.

Harvard psychologist Lawrence Kohlberg (1976) pioneered the study of moral decision making and concluded that moral reasoning could be divided into six categories or stages. According to Kohlberg, stage one moral thinking is based on simple rewards and punishment. A young child who displays stage one moral reasoning, for instance, obeys his or her parents and acts "good" simply to avoid punishment or to gain a reward. At the other end of the moral spectrum, stage six moral reasoning finds a person espousing a system of generalized ethical principles, such as living one's life according to universal moral principles, with little or no reference to what others may think.

Kohlberg's research, however, suffers from a major flaw—it was predicated on males' responses *only*. On the basis of his androcentric studies, Kohlberg concluded that his six moral stages adequately described the levels of moral reasoning for all people. Frequently, though, when comparing females to males in terms of moral decision making, we find that females approach questions of morality differently than do males. On the basis of Kohlberg's stages of moral development, it has been argued that female moral reasoning is less developed than that of their male counterparts.

However, the work of another Harvard professor, Carol Gilligan (1982), is especially revealing in terms of the differences between male and female moral decision making. Kohlberg and Gilligan both used the following moral dilemma to test moral development: A man named Heinz has a wife who is dying but who can be saved by a drug invented by a local druggist. Heinz can neither afford the drug nor get the credit to purchase it. What should Heinz do in this situation?

One of the young people to whom Gilligan posed the dilemma was an eleven-year-old boy named Jake, who reasoned that stealing the drug was a logical solution, given Jake's view that life takes precedence over property. When questioned about his reasons for suggesting that Heinz should steal the drug, Jake responded:

> For one thing, a human life is worth more than money, and if the druggist only makes $1,000, he is still going to live, but if Heinz doesn't steal the drug, his wife is going to die. (*Why is life worth more than money?*) Because the druggist can get a thousand dollars later from rich people with cancer, but Heinz can't get his wife again. (Gilligan, 1982, p. 26)

Gilligan also posed the same moral dilemma to eleven-year-old Amy, whose solution was quite different from Jake's. When Amy was asked if Heinz should steal the drug, she was less convinced that stealing is a solution to the problem. Amy responded:

> Well, I don't think so. I think there might be other ways besides stealing it, like if he could borrow the money or make a loan or something, but he really shouldn't steal the drug—but his wife shouldn't die either. (Gilligan, 1982, p. 28)

When questioned further, Amy finally described how Heinz's stealing may have short-term benefits (getting the drug for his dying wife) but may also have long-term negative consequences for the relationship of Heinz and his wife as well.

> If he stole the drug, he might save his wife then, but if he did, he might have to go to jail, and then his wife might get sicker again, and he couldn't get more of the drug, and it might not be good. So, they should really just talk it out and find some other way to make the money. (Gilligan, 1982, p. 28)

Both Jake and Amy desire that Heinz's wife live. But Amy's solution is to "find some other way" besides stealing to get the drug. Jake, on the other hand, opts for stealing it—reasoning that life is more important than the druggist's demand to be paid for the drug. In other words, Amy sees the dilemma in terms of how to gain the drug while preventing any negative consequences that may come from simply stealing the drug; Jake solves the dilemma by suggesting that stealing is morally acceptable given the situation of the money-conscious druggist. Amy's moral reasoning revolves around the "connectedness" (Gilligan's term) between Heinz and his wife. Jake, on the other hand, seems more concerned about the unreasonableness of the druggist's demand to be paid. The druggist is the villain in Jake's mind, and Jake believes that Heinz's moral predicament—how to save his wife's life—permits him to take whatever action necessary, even if it means breaking the law.

Gilligan suggests that a typical male response to moral questions involves the concern with autonomy or control over the situation, while a typical female approach to moral questions focuses on the relationships between those involved in the situation. Thus, Gilligan finds that females and males approach moral dilemmas in different ways.

Few of us will be faced with a moral dilemma like Heinz's in our lifetime. However, all of us are presently faced with a moral dilemma of incalculable proportions—nuclear warfare and the end of the world. Thus, let's focus on the issue of potential nuclear destruction as an example of a moral dilemma and examine, in a general way, how males differ from females in approaching this issue.

The Ultimate Moral Dilemma

Throughout history, the usual method for resolving conflict between nations has been war—simple bloodletting until one or the other side capitulated. Consequently, millions of humans have died over the centuries in senseless carnage when nations—or more accurately the nations' leaders—found themselves in conflict. However, at no time did a single nation or group of nations possess the means to totally destroy its adversaries. That is until now. Today, the world's superpowers could destroy the entire human race with nuclear weapons. (There are approximately 50,000 nuclear weapons in the world today.) The Soviet Union and the United States both have the nuclear weapons and delivery systems to destroy every human being on the face of the planet several times over. How then do we prevent this insane and morally unconscionable event from occurring?

Carol Gilligan believes that the solution to this moral dilemma may rest in the way that females approach moral issues. She states:

Then we have this group here—women—who seem less warlike, and we say that 'they're having a problem with aggression.' What if instead you *took* these seemingly peace-loving souls and before you so readily attribute their

Figure 13.1 Today, we face the growing possibility that humanity will destroy itself in a nuclear conflagration. Bold, new approaches for solving international conflicts are needed. Finding that females value human relationships more than males do, may prove to be the key for a truly lasting peace for all peoples.

behavior to biology you asked in all seriousness, 'What is it about the way women deal with conflict that makes it less likely to erupt in violence?' And what if you said, 'Our notions of winning and losing have been rendered obsolete by nuclear technology, so we need a new set of rules,' and you in fact have this microcosm of little girls who've been saying all along that they don't like to play games where people win and lose and get their feelings hurt and feel bad—I mean, instead of ignoring them or thinking that there's something wrong with them, why aren't we out there *studying* them? (quoted in Van Gelder, 1984, p. 38)

Have the leaders of the superpowers become possessed by a "masculine" approach to the nuclear dilemma, which translates into "nuclear macho-madness"? Helen Caldicott (1984), founder of Women's Action for Nuclear Disarmament, sees the nuclear arms dilemma as caused by the world's leaders acting out a distorted and potentially destructive masculine ethic. Caldicott writes that, "The whole ethic of masculinity is tied up with being tough and courageous, macho and fearless, and they cling to this behavior by building more weapons with almost frantic desperation" (p. 318). Is the morally correct solution to preventing a worldwide nuclear disaster to be found in men's preoccupation with numbers of nuclear weapons? Or should a different type of moral reasoning prevail, one based on female-oriented moral decision making? Should not the relationships among all humans on a constantly shrinking globe be our overriding concern? Should not the survival of humanity and our planet be the superordinate goal by which all leaders approach any question of conflict between their groups? Or are we to continue on a path toward total human destruction because our male leaders are preoccupied with winning at all costs and proving themselves tougher than the other guy? Rather than constantly emphasizing the differences between the superpowers, maybe a more sane and more moral world could develop if similarities and interpersonal connections would be stressed. Possibly, if we were to take a lesson from Amy rather than from Jake, our children and grandchildren would have a better chance of living a full life without the ever-present and growing likelihood of total annihilation.

SUMMARY

The research into sex and gender promises to be one of the more exciting areas in all of the social scientific areas. Three areas are especially important and worthy of further research.

That parents might soon be able to choose the biological sex of their offspring offers several challenges. Given the preference for male children over female children, both the positive and negative consequences of such sex selection must be explored.

Researchers are now beginning to question the relevance of androgyny in studies of gender-related characteristics and behaviors. The future may hold a greater emphasis on gender role transcendency rather than on simply merging masculine and feminine elements in personality development.

Carol Gilligan's work on moral reasoning offers an alternative to the androcentric view of moral reasoning so pervasive in social psychology. Gilligan's findings that females, especially young females, have a very different perspective on moral issues than males have may prove beneficial in solving conflict situations in the future. Because our world teeters on the brink of nuclear disaster, Gilligan's call for a "feminine" approach to moral reasoning may help us find new solutions to ancient problems.

SUGGESTED READINGS

Bennett, N. (Ed.). (1983). *Sex selection of children.* New York: Academic Press.

Caldicott, H. (1984). *Missle envy.* New York: Morrow.

Corea, G. (1985). *The mother machine: Reproductive technologies from artificial insemination to artificial wombs.* New York: Harper & Row.

Fox, G. (Ed.). (1982). *The child bearing decision: Fertility attitudes and behavior.* Beverly Hills, CA: Sage.

Gerzon, M. (1982). *A choice of heroes: The changing faces of America's manhood.* Boston: Houghton-Mifflin.

Gilligan, C. (1982). *In a different voice.* Cambridge: Harvard University Press.

Point/Counterpoint

Feminism—Are We Ready for a Second Stage?

Although the women's movement of the 1960s and 1970s came about through the efforts of many female leaders, few names are more often associated with the movement than Betty Friedan. Her book *The Feminine Mystique* (1963) is considered to be the seminal work responsible for changing millions of lives. Friedan (1981), however, has recently published another work calling for a new social movement. This new movement, feminism's second stage (to use Friedan's term), will supplant feminism's goals with another set of objectives. Friedan describes the second stage in the following way:

> Though the women's movement has changed all our lives and surpassed our dreams in its magnitude, and our daughters take their own personhood for granted, they—and we—are finding that it's not so easy to *live*, with or without men and children, solely on the basis of that first feminist agenda. I think, in fact, that the women's movement has come just about as far as it can in terms of women alone. The very choices, options, aspirations, opportunities that we have won for women—no matter how far from real equality—and the small degree of new power women now enjoy, or hunger for, openly, honestly, as never before, are converging on and into new economic and emotional urgencies. Battles lost or won are being fought in terms that are somehow inadequate, irrelevant to this new personal, and political, reality. I believe it's over, that first stage: the women's movement. And yet the larger revolution, evolution, liberation that the women's movement set off, has barely begun. (pp. 26–27)

Thus Friedan has called for the feminist movement to move into a second stage, a stage where women and men supposedly will move toward greater equality in interpersonal relations and where social institutions will be transformed for the greater good of all. According to Friedan, today's woman—the one who has benefited from the first stage of the women's movement—wants to come "to new terms with the family—new terms with love and with work" (p. 28). Apparently then, the second stage will move beyond the economic sphere of the workplace, the means for legal reform, and greater involvement in the political arena; it will focus on women's re-involvement in the family. In other words, the second stage will move away from the primary concern of women establishing their identities outside of the home (a first-stage issue) and focus on the many features intimately tied to women's and men's relationships.

Friedan's noble-sounding goals for a second stage have not gone un-challenged. Catherine Stimpson (1981), for one, setting aside Friedan's lau-datory goals for feminism's second stage, argues that in reality feminism's original agenda has not been met. Women still do not have equal access to a variety of economic, political, and social institutions. The problem is that many do not think that the "women's movement has come just about as far as it can." There is much work still to be accomplished—the passage of the ERA, for example. Friedan's new analysis, however, does serve to keep those involved in the women's movement from becoming overly dogmatic in their views of what needs to be changed. But a call for a new agenda when the first one has not been completed seems somewhat shortsighted.

What do you think?

Reading   *A Quantum Leap in Feminist Theory*

Feminist author Robin Morgan presents an interesting overview of how feminist theory can reshape our view of our world.

It's been said that three developments, more than any others in history, have shaken Man's sense of himself. *Copernican astronomy* changed Man's cosmocentric vision of himself as being at the center of the universe. Darwin's *On the Origin of Species by Natural Selection* changed Man's biocentric vision of himself as being at the center of life forms. The birth of the science of *anthropology* changed Man's ethnocentric vision of himself as being at the center of only one possible, foreordained culture.

But this list is incomplete if we would have it include the present and reach toward the future. In that case, we would have to add two more developments, in their immediate and especially their potential effects equal to if not greater than the shifts in consciousness listed above: *feminism,* which challenges Man's androcentric vision of himself as being at the center of humanity—and *modern physics,* which challenges Man's vision of reality itself.

Feminism is, at this moment and on this planet, the DNA/RNA call for survival and for the next step in evolution—and even beyond that, feminism is, in its metaphysical and metafeminist dynamic, the helix of hope that we have for communication with whatever lies before us in the vast, witty mystery of the universe. I base my premise—that feminism is the key to our survival and transformation—not on rhetoric but on facts:

The "Otherizing" of women is the oldest oppression known to our species, the model for all other oppressions. Until this division is healed, we put Band-Aids on our most mortal wound.

Women share this suffering across the barriers of age, race, class, nationality, culture, sexual preference, and ethnic background: a Hong Kong prostitute and a Grosse Pointe matron are battered because both are women; a 60-year-old nun in England is raped and a seven-year-old girl in Yemen is sold in marriage because both are female; an Indonesian peasant dies of childbirth and a Brazilian socialite dies of a butchered illegal abortion because both are women; a Kenyan adolescent is physically clitoridectomized and a Swiss nurse is psychologically clitoridectomized because both are female human beings. The tactical potential for unification across such Man-made barriers as race and nationality is limited only by the extent to which all women are willing to recognize the similarity of our condition, develop acute sensitivity to a diversity of priorities, and commit ourselves to exposing and *unmaking* those very barriers.

Women comprise the majority of humanity. This means that a variety of strategic options are open to us that are not available to an oppressed *minority* group which, because of its relative size, often must resort to desperate or violent tactics even to be noticed.

The suffering of women *is* the suffering of the human species, and vice versa. Numerically and geographically, women are the world's poor, the world's refugees, the world's illiterates.

The physiological reality experienced by every woman is one of continual change: change at

Source: The anatomy of freedom: Feminism, physics, and global politics by R. Morgan, 1982, NY: Doubleday/Anchor, pp. 281–285, 291–298, 301. Copyright © 1982 by Robin Morgan. Reprinted by permission of Doubleday & Co., Inc., and Edite Kroll.

menarche, thereafter every 28 days for an average of 40 years, then menopause—and, in between, the possibilities of pregnancy, childbirth, postpartum, and lactation. This experienced reality lends most women a less rigid psychological attitude toward physical existence in all its forms, including the political and strategic.

Women in all cultures have been assigned (stereotypically, as Woman) the positive values of "humanism," pacifism, nurturance, ecoconsciousness, and reverence for life. While these values have been (1) regarded by Man as amusingly irrelevant, and (2) understood by women not to be inherently "womanly," they *are* objectively positive values. This in itself affects our strategical approach to change and might give us, at least for a while, a certain moral imperative which could be useful.

Women in all cultures and times seem to have developed a "spiritual dimension" to our lives—whether as a code for secular rebellion or an escape from our temporal suffering or an ongoing religious strand of connection to cosmic mystery. This tendency has shown itself repeatedly in women's political movements, too, including the present feminist wave. At its most superficial, such a tendency can lead to sophomoric superstition and political evasion, but at its most profound it can lead to political change as deep as those religious and cultural revolutions which affect consciousness itself.

Last: *it will happen because it is happening.*

The physicist Fritjof Capra sees three imminent transitions that will shake the very foundations of lives: "the reluctant but inevitable decline of patriarchy," the decline of the fossil-fuel age, and a "paradigm shift" in our basic way of perception. Of these three, he feels that the end of patriarchy is the first and perhaps the most profound transition, because patriarchy "has influenced our most basic ideas about human nature and about our relation to the universe. . . . It is the one system . . . whose doctrines were so universally accepted that they seemed to be the laws of nature." Consequently, he concludes that "the feminist movement is one of the strongest cultural currents of our time and will have a profound effect on our further evolution." Capra further understands the value of science not only for itself but in this political context:

Physicists can provide the scientific background to the changes in attitudes and values that our society so urgently needs. In a culture dominated by science, it will be much easier to convince our social institutions . . . if we can give our arguments a scientific basis. Modern physics can show the other sciences that scientific thinking does not necessarily have to be reductionist and mechanistic, that holistic and ecological views are also scientifically sound . . . that such a framework is not only scientific but is in agreement with the most advanced scientific theories of physical reality.

I am not a physicist. I am a poet, a feminist writer, a theorist, and an activist. Being a poet, I understand the lifesaving value of audacious and serious play. Being a feminist activist, I understand the urgency of communicating this message in ever newer, more connective, and far-reaching ways. Being a writer, I understand the power of words, their independent life and energy. What, then, if we were to combine the supportive framework some of the new physicists are offering humanity, with this politics, these living words?

Using as our metaphor first classical physics and then quantum physics (less in a strict chronological progression than in an unfolding), we might take a quantum leap and look at political evolution:

The Past

Mechanical (Classical) Physics Theory
"Building Blocks" comprise the stuff of the universe.

Mechanical (Traditional) Political Theory
"Building blocks" are the stuff of society: sexes, races, class, the family, clans, tribes, nations, and so on.

The "ultimate" building block is the atom.

The "ultimate" unit is the individual.

Building blocks can assemble in variable ways but are also reducible.

Comparable variables are social systems: the rule of chiefs, the warrior class, institutional monarchy, feudalism, the rise of the bourqeoisie.

Material and matter are seen as real.

Materialism—and dialectical materialism—are seen as realistic analyses, especially after the "Revolution."

The Present

Quantum Mechanics
Energy seems fluid but is composed of discontinuity.

The Beginning of Quantum Politics
The idea of progress breaks down; the "building blocks" disturb the system's fluidity (socialist and anticolonial revolutions); discontinuity in "norms" begins (family structures shift, sexual options are openly articulated).

Special Theory of Relativity
Mass/energy is seen as one; space/time is also seen as one, and as relative. This is the end of the notion of "matter." The theory is limited in not yet including movement.

Special Theory of Feminism
The majority of humanity (female) is seen as sharing the same condition, relative to the (male) minority of humanity. This is the beginning of the end of materialism. The theory so far is limited to intrafeminist movement impact, not yet including its full constituency.

The Concept of Particles Being Waves and Waves Being Particles

The Feminist Emphasis on "Process"
Means are affirmed as transforming—even becoming—the goals or ends. Freedom is intuited as being both a state and a dynamic.

The Principle of Uncertainty
One can see a "wavicle" (of light, for example) either as a wave or a particle, but not both at once; one can chart its position or velocity, but not both at the same time.

The Principle of Polarity
Either/or thinking emerges in feminist (fundamentalist) theory: radical *or* reformist, activist *or* thinker, lesbian *or* heterosexual, economic analysis *or* cultural/spiritual approach, race *or* sex priority, work within the system *or* outside it, et cetera, *ad nauseam.*

The Theory of Complementarity
One doesn't *need* to see wave and particle at once; one can *imagine* the whole from its fragments or assume their complementarity. The possibility of interpenetration and permeability of particles is explored. It is no longer necessary to impose a system of coherence in order to work with and study disparate parts.

Pragmatic but Fragile Coalitions
Women of color and white women in dialogue, growth of international network, connections sought on environmental, academic, economic, age, cultural, and other "fronts"; a lessening of alienation between lesbian and heterosexual women and the emergence of genuine bisexual affirmation; an attempt to reach out to women in the grip of the Right Wing and other fundamentalisms.

Fission: Splitting of the Atom
The end of the "ultimate building block" notion. Study of subatomic particles and *sub*-subatomic particles begins.

Fragmentation of the Individual
Feminists *and* nonfeminists, women *and* men feel this: chronic anxiety, burn-out, doomsday political tactics and increased terrorism, psychological reductionism combined with a desperate search for "self."

Fusion: Thermonuclear Fusing of the Atom Is Risked
The hydrogen bomb is created with the possibility of nuclear energy through forced fusion, even with its incomprehensibly great dangers.

Fusion of the Old Orders is Risked

An alliance is forced between the "workers" and state capitalism (contemporary "communism"); an alliance is forced between the "consumer" and the megamerchant corporations (contemporary "capitalism"); attempts are made to pass off old ways as new ones, ignoring the great danger this presents.

Reading

The Future

General Theory of Relativity
Discovery that gravitational attraction between massive bodies is also relative.

Concept of the Participatory Observer
The realization by some physicists that the experiment changes what is being observed by the very observing of it; all things interact.

Quantum Field Theory
The theory attempts to merge quantum mechanics and relativity, posits that particles are actually interactions between energy fields "instantaneously and locally": the concept that space itself isn't empty at all.

Ongoing Attempts at a Unified Field Theory
These approaches include the diverse concepts of "hidden variables" and "concealed order"; The Yang-Mills gauge field theory of symmetrical but unstable interactions within an energy field. Böhm's "implicate universe"—that everything exists in a cosmic web of interrelations; Chew's "bootstrapping theory"—particles "involving" one another in self- and other-boosting patterns of "self-consistency." The possibility is explored that there are no fundamental constituents of matter, no fundamental principles or laws, except possibly, those of consciousness.

General Theory of Feminism
The feminist vision begins to make an impact on all human beings, and *relative to their own situations*, they make an impact, in turn, on feminism. The discovery is made that feminism is central to the solving of crises in population growth, hunger, war, illiteracy, disease, nationalism, environmental destruction, and so on; that feminism affects all perceptions of sexuality, age, socioeconomic, cultural/spiritual, and scientific/aesthetic issues. Nationalism and other traditional political systems begin to collapse in the enormous gravitational pull among individuals and groups within them who are making these connections.

The End of the Exception
The inescapable (admitted) recognition among women and the inescapable (not yet admitted) recognition among men of their participation in the situation identified by feminism, and their (admitted *and* nonadmitted) longing for change.

Metafeminist Synchronicities
Metafeminism attempts to synthesize the breakdown of global systems with the feminist vision as a relevant solution toward change; the realization dawns that this synthesis is precisely what has been intuited, longed for, and feared by the species for millennia.

Metafeminism as the Bridge to Metapolitics
All fundamental laws, categories and categorizing, and "norms" of behavior are discovered to be illusory. *Fundamentalism vanishes along with fundamentals.* Consciousness is reinvented. A balance emerges between the individual and the collective/species/sentient life/universal movement. Uniqueness and commonality are seen as *uncontradictory*; differences and similarities are celebrated as self-consistent and mutually involved.

Reading _Continued_

Ongoing Discovery of Sub-subatomic Particles

These discoveries amount so far to almost 300, including protons (and their possible decay), leptons, gluons, baryons, mesons, and hadrons—and then hadron "particles" postulated as quarks (a quark is sized at 10 million times smaller than the atom), or charmed quarks (because they seem to obey only their own erraticism) or red, white, and blue quarks, or "psi-particles," or particles referred to merely as "resonances," which have "a tendency to exist"—postulatable, but traceable only by the trails of light they leave when monitored in bubble chambers.

Micro- and Macrocosmic Revo- and Evolution in a Vertical Curve

All facets of consciousness flower, new forms of intelligence develop and create still newer forms in turn. Eccentric and eclectic agnostic acrostic solutions to old problems fall into place via quarky ingenious strategies. Freedom actually is _traceable_ now as well as _postulatable_; freedom, which has a "tendency to exist" and which can be known to have existed only by the trail of light it leaves behind.

Let's call our framework the F-matrix Theory, equated as $F = et^2$ or: _Feminism equals equality/empowerment/evolution times the squared velocity of transformation._

A full awareness in each of us of the centrality of feminist vision in itself will have a monumental effect on the way each of us carries her/himself, the way we conduct our personal lives and political strategies.

No more begging for "rights": the future of intelligence is itself at stake. _No more single-issue politics:_ since when does the electron not touch everything in its orbit at once? _No more victimization_ (permitting the grief and pain of our situation as women to paralyze us into burn-out, or sell-out): just because you can see the picture only as wave or particle at any given time doesn't mean it isn't both at all times, and dynamic in its movement, too. _No more correct-line politics:_ because one of us focuses on velocity and the other on position doesn't mean that together we can't assemble the whole picture (Principle of Uncertainty). Our diversity makes for an ultimate unity. (Theory of Complementarity).

The courage it required two decades ago for feminists to name the already existing division between men and women—that courage would need to be squared (the velocity of transformation) in order to accomplish this naming of the already existing "implicate" integration which connects, embraces us all. It would have to be a courage equal to the task. It would have to refuse to sacrifice the integrity of self _or_ of feminism for some illusory "second stage," as Betty Friedan has suggested, that leaves sexual politics behind (and still unsolved): forced fusion all over again. No, _this_ approach—of _radical integration_—sacrifices nothing except false categories and burned-out strategies. _This_ approach suggests that the power is already there for the touching by audacious hands. And this approach suggests a way for those hands, once having touched that power, to have the grace to use it well.

When we really comprehend the full meaning of what it is we are fighting for, that in itself will inspire the strategies, and give us the strength and endurance necessary to win.

Carry yourself as one who will save the world. Because you will.

REFERENCES

Abbey, A. (1982). Sex differences in attributions for friendly behavior: Do males misperceive females' friendliness? *Journal of Personality and Social Psychology, 42,* 830–38.

Abbot, S., & Love, B. (1973). *Sappho was a right-on woman.* New York: Stein and Day.

Abel, G., et al. (1978). Differentiating sexual aggressiveness with penile measures. *Criminal Justice and Behavior, 5,* 315–32.

Aberle, D. (1967). *The peyote religion among the Navaho.* Chicago: Wenner-Gren Foundation for Anthropological Research and Aldine Publishing Company.

Abramowitz, C., & Dokecki, P. (1977). The politics of clinical judgment: Early empirical returns. *Psychological Bulletin, 84,* 460–76.

Abu-Lughod, R. (1983). A community of secrets: The separate world of Bedouin women. Paper presented at the Conference on Communities of Women, sponsored by *Signs,* Stanford University.

Abzug, B., & Kelber, M. (1984). How to win with the gender gap: 3 scenarios for the '84 election. *Ms., March,* 39–42, 92–93.

Adams, C., & Laurikietis, R. (1977). *The gender trap.* New York: Academy Press.

Adams, J. (1984). Women at West Point: A three-year perspective. *Sex Roles, 11,* 525–41.

Afonja, S. (1981). Changing modes of production and the sexual division of labor among the Yoruba. *Signs, 7,* 299–313.

Aiello, J. (1972). A test of equilibrium theory: Visual interaction in relation to orientation, distance, and sex of interractants. *Psychonomic Science, 27,* 335–36.

Albee, G. (1984). Reply to Lantz. *American Psychologist, 39,* 82–84.

Albin, R. (1977). Psychological studies of rape. *Signs, 3,* 423–35.

Aldrich, M. (1978). Women in science. *Signs, 4,* 126–35.

Alexander, K., & Cook, M. (1982). Curricula and coursework: A surprise ending to a familiar story. *American Sociological Review, 47,* 626–40.

Al-Issa, I. (1982). Gender and adult psychopathology. In I. Al-Issa (Ed.), *Gender and psychopathology.* New York: Academic Press.

Allen, I. (1984). Male sex roles and epithets for ethnic women in American slang. *Sex Roles, 11,* 43–50.

Allen, S., & Hubbs, J. (1980). Outrunning Atalanta: Feminine destiny in alchemical transmutation. *Signs, 6,* 210–29.

Allgeier, E., & Allgeier, A. (1984). *Sexual interactions.* Lexington, MA: D.C. Heath.

Allport, G. (1958). *The nature of prejudice.* Garden City, NY: Doubleday.

Aloni, S. (1973). The status of women in Israel. *Judaism, 22(Spring),* 248–56.

Aloni, S. (1974). Israeli women need liberation. In *Sisters in exile: Sources on the Jewish woman.* New York: Ichud Habonim Labor Zionist Youth.

Altbach, E. (1984). The new German women's movement. *Signs, 9,* 454–69.

Altman, D. (1971). *Homosexual oppression and liberation.* New York: Avon.

Altman, D. (1983). *The homosexualization of America.* Boston: Beacon Press.

American Psychiatric Association. (1980). *Diagnostic and statistical manual of mental disorders* (3rd ed.). Washington, DC: (Author).

American Psychological Association (APA). (1975). Report of the Task Force on sex bias and sex-role stereotyping in psychotherapeutic practice. *American Psychologist, 30,* 1169–75.

American Psychological Association (APA). (1978). Task force on sex bias and sex-role stereotyping in psychotherapeutic practices: Guidelines for therapy with women. *American Psychologist, 33,* 1122–23.

Anderson, K. (1981). *Wartime women.* Westport, CT: Greenwood Press.

Apple, R. (1984). Church of England moves toward letting women be priests. *The New York Times,* November 6, 7.

Archer, C. (1984). Children's attitudes toward sex-role division in adult occupational roles. *Sex Roles, 10,* 1–10.

Aries, E. (1976). Interaction patterns and themes of males, females, and mixed groups. *Small Group Behavior, 7,* 1–18.

Arrington, T., & Kyle, P. (1978). Equal rights amendment activists in North Carolina. *Signs, 3,* 666–80.

Ashmore, R., & Del Boca, F. (1979). Sex stereotypes and implicit personality theory: Toward a cognitive-social psychological conceptualization. *Sex Roles, 5,* 219–48.

Ashmore, R., & Del Boca, F. (1981). Conceptual approaches to stereotypes and stereotyping. In D. Hamilton (Ed.), *Cognitive processes in stereotyping and intergroup behavior* (pp. 1–35). Hillsdale, NJ: Erlbaum.

Association of American Colleges. (1982). The classroom climate: A chilly one for women? Washington, DC: Project on the Status and Education of Women.

Astin, A. (1977). *Four critical years: Effects of college on beliefs, attitudes and knowledge.* San Francisco: Jossey-Bass.

Axelson, L. (1970). The working wife: Differences in perception among Negro and white males. *Journal of Marriage and the Family, 32,* 457–64.

Babad, E. (1979). Personality correlates of susceptibility to biasing information. *Journal of Personality and Social Psychology, 37,* 195–202.

Bahr, R. (1976). *The virility factor.* New York: Putnam.

Baird, L., Clark, M., & Rodney, T. (1973). *The graduates.* Princeton, NJ: Educational Testing Service.

Baker, P. (1984). Age differences and age changes in the division of labor by sex: Reanalysis of White and Brinkeroff. *Social Forces, 62,* 808–14.

Baker, S. (1980). Biological influences on human sex and gender. *Signs, 6,* 80–96.

Baker, S., & Ehrhardt, A. (1978). Prenatal androgen, intelligence, and cognitive sex differences. In R. Friedman, et al. (Eds.), *Sex differences in behavior* (pp. 53–76). Huntington, NY: Krieger Publishing.

Bales, J. (1984). Dispute over comparable worth places burden on evaluators. *APA Monitor, March,* 17–18.

Bandura, A., Ross, D., & Ross, S. (1963). Vicarious reinforcement and imitative learning. *Journal of Abnormal and Social Psychology, 67,* 601–7.

Bandura, A., & Walters, R. (1963). *Social learning and personality development.* New York: Holt, Rinehart & Winston.

Barfield, A. (1976). Biological influences on sex differences in behavior. In M. Teitelbaum (Ed.), *Sex differences* (pp. 62–121). Garden City, NY: Anchor Books.

Barker-Benfield, B. (1972). The spermatic economy: A nineteenth century view of sexuality. *Feminist Studies, 1,* 45–67.

Barlow, P., & Bosa, C. (1970). The Y chromosome in human spermatozoa. *Nature, 226(June),* 959–62.

Baron, R., & Byrne, D. (1984). *Social psychology* (4th ed.). Boston: Allyn and Bacon.

Barrett, K. (1984). Two-career couples: How they do it. *Ms., June,* 39–42, 111, 114.

Bartlett, J. (1980). *Familiar quotations* (15th ed.). Boston: Little, Brown.

Bar-Yosef, R., & Lieblich, A. (1983). Comments on Brandow's "Ideology, myth, and reality: Sex equality in Israel." *Sex Roles, 9,* 419–26.

Baslow, S. (1980). *Sex-role stereotypes: Traditions and alternatives.* Monterey, CA: Brooks/Cole.

Baude, A. (1979). Public policy and changing family patterns in Sweden, 1930–1977. In J. Lipman-Blumen & J. Bernard (Eds.), *Sex roles and social policy.* Beverly Hills, CA: Sage.

Baxter, S., & Lansing, M. (1980). *Women and politics.* Ann Arbor: University of Michigan Press.

Beck, E., Horan, P., & Tolbert, C. (1980). Industrial segmentation and labor market discrimination. *Social Problems, 28,* 113–30.

Beck, L., & Keddie, N. (Eds.). (1978). *Women in the Muslim world.* Cambridge: Harvard University Press.

Beck-Rex, M. (1979). Academic epidemic: Women lose jobs to men. *In the Running, 2(4),* 1–2.

Beer, W. (1982). *Househusbands: Men and housework in American families.* New York: Praeger.

Bell, D. (1981). Women's business is hard work: Central Australian aboriginal women's love rituals. *Signs, 7,* 314–38.

Bell, S. (1982). Medieval women book owners: Arbiters of lay piety and ambassadors of culture. *Signs, 7,* 742–68.

Bem, S. (1974). The measurement of psychological androgyny. *Journal of Consulting and Clinical Psychology, 42,* 155–62.

Bemis, K. (1978). Current approaches to the etiology and treatment of anorexia nervosa. *Psychological Bulletin, 85,* 593–617.

Benbow, C., & Stanley, J. (1980). Sex differences in mathematical reasoning ability: Fact or artifact? *Science, 210(December 12),* 1262–64.

Benbow, C., & Stanley, J. (1983). Sex differences in mathematical reasoning ability: More facts. *Science, 222(December 2),* 1029–31.

Benderly, B. (1982). Rape-free or rape-prone. *Science 82, 3(8),* 40–43.

Benedict, R. (1961). *Patterns of culture.* Boston: Houghton Mifflin.

Benjamin, H. (1966). *The transsexual phenomenon.* New York: Julian Press.

Benson, D., & Thompson, G. (1982). Sexual harassment on a university campus: The confluence of authority relations, sexual interest and gender stratification. *Social Problems, 29,* 236–51.

Berger, P. (1967). *The sacred canopy.* Garden City, NY: Doubleday.

Bergmann, B. (1974). Occupational segregation, wages and profits when employers discriminate by race and sex. *Eastern Economic Journal, 1,* 103–10.

Bermant, G., & Davidson, J. (1974). *Biological bases of sexual behavior.* New York: Harper and Row.

Bernard, J. (1968). *The sex game.* Englewood Cliffs, NJ: Prentice-Hall.

Bernard, J. (1971). The paradox of the happy marriage. In V. Gornick & B. Moran (Eds.), *Women in sexist society* (pp. 145–62). New York: New American Library.

Bernard, J. (1973). *The future of marriage.* New York: Bantam Books.

Bernard, J. (1974). *The future of motherhood.* New York: Dial Press.

Bernard, J. (1975). *Women, wives and mothers.* Chicago: Aldine.

Bernard, J. (1981a). *The female world.* New York: Free Press.

Bernard, J. (1981b). The good-provider role: Its rise and fall. *American Psychologist, 36,* 1–12.

Bertilson, H., Springer, K., & Fierke, K. (1982). Underrepresentation of female referents as pronouns: Examples and pictures in introductory college textbooks. *Psychological Reports, 51,* 923–31.

Berzins, J., Welling, M., & Wetter, R. (1975). *The PRF Andro scale user's manual.* Unpublished manual, University of Kentucky.

Best, R. (1983). *We've all got scars.* Bloomington: Indiana University Press.

Bianchi, S., & Spain, D. (1983). *Wives who earn more than their husbands.* Washington, DC: U.S. Government Printing Office.

Bierstedt, R. (1950). An analysis of social power. *American Sociological Review, 6,* 7–30.

Biller, H. (1974). *Paternal deprivation.* Reading, MA: Heath Lexington.

Billingsly, D. (1977). Sex bias in psychotherapy: An examination of the effects of client sex, client pathology, and therapist sex on treatment planning. *Journal of Consulting and Clinical Psychology, 45,* 250–56.

Binford, S. (1979). Myth & matriarchies. *Human Nature,* May, 62–66.

Bird, P. (1974). Images of women in the Old Testament. In R. Ruether (Ed.), *Religion and sexism* (pp. 41–88). New York: Simon and Schuster.

Blackstone, T., & Fulton, O. (1975). Sex discrimination among university teachers: A British-American comparison. *British Journal of Sociology, 26,* 261–75.

Blackwood, E. (1984). Sexuality and gender in certain native American tribes: The case of cross-gender females. *Signs, 10,* 27–42.

Blank, R. (1981). The partial transsexual. *American Journal of Psychotherapy, 35,* 107–12.

Blau, F. (1975). Women in the labor force. In J. Freeman (Ed.), *Women* (pp. 211–67). Palo Alto, CA: Mayfield.

Blau, F. (1981). On the role of values in feminist scholarship. *Signs, 6,* 538–40.

Blau, F., & Jusenius, C. (1976). Economists' approaches to sex segregation in the labor market: An appraisal. *Signs, 1,* 181–99.

Block, J. (1976). Issues, problems, and pitfalls in assessing sex differences: A critical review of *The Psychology of Sex Differences. Merrill-Palmer Quarterly, 22,* 283–308.

Blood, R., & Wolfe, D. (1960). *Husbands and wives.* New York: Free Press.

Blumberg, R. (1976). Kibbutz women: From the fields of revolution to the laundries of discontent. In L. Iglitzin & R. Ross (Eds.), *Women in the world* (pp. 319–44). Santa Barbara, CA: ABC Clio.

Blumberg, R. (1978). *Stratification: Socioeconomic and sexual inequality.* Dubuque, IA: Wm. C. Brown Publishers.

Blumenthal, M., et al. (1972). *Justifying violence.* Ann Arbor: Institute for Social Research, The University of Michigan.

Blumer, H. (1961). Collective behavior. In A. Lee (Ed.), *Principles of sociology.* New York: Barnes and Noble.

Blumstein, P., & Schwartz, P. (1983). *American couples.* New York: Morrow.

Bolton, B. (1976). Muliers sanctae. In S. Stuard (Ed.), *Women in medieval society.* Philadelphia: University of Pennsylvania Press.

Boulding, E. (1976). Familial constraints on women's work roles. *Signs, 1,* 95–117.

Bowman, K. (1951). The problem of the sex offender. *American Journal of Psychiatry, 108,* 250–57.

Bram, S. (1984). Voluntarily childless women: Traditional or nontraditional? *Sex Roles, 10,* 195–206.

Brandes, S. (1983). *Metaphors of masculinity.* Philadelphia: University of Pennsylvania Press.

Brandow, S. (1980). Ideology, myth, and reality: Sex equality in Israel. *Sex Roles, 6,* 403–19.

Brannon, R. (1976). The male sex role: Our culture's blueprint of manhood, and what it's done for us lately. In D. David & R. Brannon (Eds.). *The forty-nine percent majority* (pp. 1–45). Reading, MA: Addison-Wesley.

Brannon, R. (1981–82). Are the "Free Men" a faction of our movement? *M. 7(Winter),* 14–15, 30–32.

Brannon, R. (1982). The men's movement. *Ms., October,* 42.

Brannon, R. (1983). Press conference statement. *Brother: The News Quarterly of the National Organization for Men, 1(2),* 5, 23.

Brannon, R., & Creane, J. (1984). How to form a consciousness-raising group. *M., 13(Fall),* 35–37.

Braunthal, H. (1981). Working with transsexuals. *International Journal of Social Psychology, 27,* 3–12.

Brawley, B. (1921). *A social history of the American Negro.* New York: The Macmillan Company.

Brodsky, A. (1977). Countertransference issues and the woman therapist: Sex and the student therapist. *The Clinical Psychologist, 30(2),* 12–14.

Brodsky, A. (1980). A decade of feminist influence on psychotherapy. *Psychology of Women Quarterly, 4,* 331–44.

Broverman, I., et al. (1970). Sex-role stereotypes and clinical judgments of mental health. *Journal of Consulting and Clinical Psychology, 34,* 1–7.

Broverman, I., et al. (1972). Sex-role stereotypes: A current appraisal. *Journal of Social Issues, 28,* 59–78.

Brown, D. (1956). Sex-role preference in young children. *Psychological Monographs, 70(14),* Whole No. 421.

Brown, D. (1957). Masculinity-femininity development in children. *Journal of Consulting Psychology, 21,* 197–202.

Brown, P., & Elliott, R. (1965). Control of aggression in a nursery school class. *Journal of Experimental Child Psychology, 2,* 103–7.

Brownmiller, S. (1975). *Against our will.* New York: Simon and Schuster.

Bruer, J. (1983). Women in science: Lack of full participation. *Science, 221(September),* 1339.

Bryant, A. (1976). *Bless this house.* New York: Bantam Books.

Buck, R. (1976). *Human motivation and emotion.* New York: Wiley.

Buhle, M. (1971). Women and the Socialist Party, 1901–1914. In E. Altback (Ed.), *From feminism to liberation.* Cambridge, MA: Schenkman.

Buhle, M. (1980). *Women and American socialism, 1870–1920.* Urbana: University of Illinois Press.

Buric, O., & Zecevic, A. (1967). Family authority, marital satisfaction, and the social network in Yugoslavia. *Journal of Marriage and the Family, 29,* 325–36.

Burke, C. (1978). Report from Paris: Women's writing and the women's movement. *Signs, 3,* 843–55.

Burt, M. (1980). Cultural myths and supports for rape. *Journal of Personality and Social Psychology, 38,* 217–30.

Busby, L. (1974). Defining the sex-role standards in commercial network television programs directed toward children. *Journalism Quarterly, 51,* 690–96.

Buss, A. (1975). The emergent field of the sociology of psychological knowledge. *American Psychologist, 30,* 988–1002.

Buss, D. (1981). Sex differences in the evaluation and performance of dominant acts. *Journal of Personality and Social Psychology, 40,* 147–54.

Butler, M., & Paisley, W. (1980). *Women and the mass media.* New York: Human Science Press.

Callender, C., & Kochems, L. (1983). The North American berdache. *Current Anthropology, 24,* 443–70.

Cantor, M., & Pingree, S. (1983). *The soap opera.* Beverly Hills, CA: Sage.

Caplan, P. (1984). The myth of women's masochism. *American Psychologist, 39,* 130–39.

Carlsson, M. (1977). Equality between men and women in Sweden. In L. Cater, et al. (Eds.), *Women and men: Changing roles, relationships, and perceptions* (pp. 245–70). New York: Praeger.

Carmen, E., Russo, N., & Miller, J. (1981). Inequality and women's mental health: An overview. *American Journal of Psychiatry, 138,* 1319–30.

Carter, G., & Kinsbourne, M. (1979). The ontology of right cerebral lateralization of spatial mental set. *Developmental Psychology, 15,* 241–45.

Cartwright, D. (Ed.). (1959). *Studies in social power.* Ann Arbor: University of Michigan, Institute for Social Research.

Casper, R., et al. (1980). Bulimia: Its incidence and clinical importance in patients with anorexia nervosa. *Archives of General Psychiatry, 37,* 1030–35.

Cauwels, J. (1983). *Bulimia: The binge-purge compulsion.* Garden City, NY: Doubleday.

Cerullo, M., Stacey, J., & Breines, W. (1977–78). Alice Rossi's sociobiology and antifeminist backlash. *Berkeley Journal of Sociology, 22,* 166–77.

Chafe, W. (1972). *The American woman.* New York: Oxford University Press.

Chafetz, J. (1974). *Masculine/feminine or human?* Itasca, IL: Peacock Publishers.

Chambless, D., & Goldstein, A. (1980). Anxieties: Agoraphobia and hysteria. In A. Brodsky & R. Hare-Mustin (Eds.), *Women and psychotherapy.* New York: Guilford.

Chapman, J., & Gates, M. (Eds.). (1977). *Women into wives.* Beverly Hills, CA: Sage.

Chappell, D., Griss, R., & Geiss, G. (Eds.). (1977). *Forcible rape.* New York: Columbia University Press.

Cherlin, A., & Walters, P. (1981). Trends in United States men's and women's sex-role attitudes: 1972 and 1978. *American Sociological Review, 46,* 453–60.

Cherry, F. (1983). Gender roles and sexual violence. In E. Allgeier & N. McCormick (Eds.), *Changing boundaries* (pp. 245–60). Palo Alto, CA.: Mayfield.

Chesler, P. (1971). Patient and patriarchy: Women in the psychotherapeutic relationship. In V. Gornick & B. Moran (Eds.), *Women in sexist society* (pp. 362–92). New York: New American Library.

Chesler, P. (1972). *Women and madness.* New York: Avon Books.

Chesno, F., & Kilmann, P. (1975). Effects of stimulation on sociopathic avoidance learning. *Journal of Abnormal Psychology, 84,* 144–50.

Chino, A., & Funabiki, D. (1984). A cross-validation of sex differences in the expression of depression. *Sex Roles, 11,* 175–87.

Chodorow, N. (1971). Being and doing: A cross-cultural examination of the socialization of males and females. In V. Gornick & B. Moran (Eds.), *Women in sexist society* (pp. 259–91). New York: New American Library.

Chodorow, N. (1976). Oedipal asymmetries and heterosexual knots. *Social Problems, 23,* 454–68.

Chodorow, N. (1977–78). Considerations on "A bio-social perspective on parenting." *Berkeley Journal of Sociology, 22,* 179–98.

Chodorow, N. (1978). *The reproduction of mothering.* Berkeley: University of California Press.

Christ, C., & Plaskow, J. (1979). *Womanspirit rising.* New York: Harper and Row.

Chronicle of Higher Education. (1982). Fact-file: 9–month faculty salaries for 1981–1982. *July 7,* 10.

Clayton, O., Baird, A., & Levinson, R. (1984). Subjective decision making in medical school admission: Potentials for discrimination. *Sex Roles, 10,* 527–32.

Cole, C., Hill, F., & Dayley, L. (1983). Do masculine pronouns used generically lead to thoughts of men? *Sex Roles, 9,* 737–50.

Coleman, J. (1976). Athletics in high school. In D. David & R. Brannon (Eds.), *The forty-nine percent majority* (pp. 264–69). Reading, MA: Addison-Wesley.

Coleman, J., Butcher, J., & Carson, R. (1984). *Abnormal psychology and modern life* (7th ed.). Glenview, IL: Scott, Foresman.

Collins, R. (1971). A conflict theory of sexual stratification. *Social Problems, 19,* 3–21.

Collins, R. (1975). *Conflict sociology.* New York: Academic Press.

Colwill, N. (1982). *The new partnership.* Palo Alto, CA: Mayfield.

Combs, C., Coombs, L., & McClelland, G. (1975). Preference scales for number and sex of children. *Population Studies, 29,* 273–98.

Condry, J., & Condry, S. (1976). The development of sex differences: A study of the eye of the beholder. *Child Development, 47,* 812–19.

Conn, J., & Kanner, L. (1947). Children's awareness of sex differences. *Journal of Child Psychiatry, 1,* 3–57.

Connell, N., & Wilsen, C. (Eds.). (1974). *Rape.* New York: New American Library.

Constantinople, A. (1973). Masculinity-femininity: An exception to a famous dictum? *Psychological Bulletin, 80,* 389–407.

Constantinople, A. (1979). Sex-role acquisition: In search of the elephant. *Sex Roles, 5,* 121–33.

Contratto, S. (1984). Mother: Social sculptor and trustee of the faith. In M. Lewin (Ed.), *In the shadow of the past* (pp. 226–55). New York: Columbia University Press.

Corea, G. (1985). *The mother machine.* New York: Harper and Row.

Cott, N. (1975). Young women in the Second Great Awakening in New England. *Feminist Studies, 3,* 15–29.

Cott, N. (1977). *The bonds of womanhood.* New Haven, CT: Yale University Press.

The Counseling Psychologist. (1978). *7,* 1–72. (Special issue on men).

The Counseling Psychologist. (1979). *8,* 1–75. (Special issue on women).

Crisp, A. (1977). The prevalence of anorexia nervosa and some of its associations in the general population. In S. Kasl & F. Reichsman (Eds.), *Advances in psychosomatic medicine* (pp. 38–47). Basel, Switzerland: S. Karger.

Croll, E. (1981a). Women in rural production and reproduction in the Soviet Union, China, Cuba, and Tanzania: Socialist development experiences. *Signs, 7,* 361–74.

Croll, E. (1981b). Women in rural production and reproduction in the Soviet Union, China, Cuba, and Tanzania: Case studies. *Signs, 7,* 375–99.

Crosby, F. (1984). The denial of personal discrimination. *American Behavioral Scientist, 27,* 371–86.

Crosby, F., Jose, P., & Wong-McCarthy, W. (1982). Gender, androgyny, and conversational assertiveness. In C. Mayo & N. Henley (Eds.), *Gender and nonverbal behavior.* New York: Springer-Verlag.

Crowley, J., Levitan, T., & Quinn, R. (1973). Seven deadly half-truths about women. *Psychology Today,* March, 94–96.

Cullen, R. (1982). A sexual rite on trial. *Newsweek,* November 1, 55.

Cunningham, S. (1983). Women still do majority of child care, housework. *APA Monitor,* November, 16.

Curtin, K. (1975). *Women in China.* New York: Pathfinder.

Dahlberg, F. (Ed.). (1981). *Woman the gatherer.* New Haven, CT: Yale University Press.

Dahlstrom, E. (Ed.). (1971). *The changing roles of men and women.* Boston: Beacon Press.

Dahrendorf, R. (1959). *Class and class conflict in industrial society.* Stanford: Stanford University Press.

Dalton, K. (1959). Menstruation and acute psychiatric illness. *British Medical Journal,* January 17, 148–49.

Dalton, K. (1964). *The premenstrual syndrome.* Springfield, IL: Thomas.

Dalton, K. (1980). Cyclical criminal acts in premenstrual syndrome. *Lancet, 2,* 1070–71.

Daly, M. (1968). *The church and the second sex.* New York: Harper & Row.

Daly, M. (1973). *Beyond God the father.* Boston: Beacon Press.

Daly, M. (1978). *Gyn/ecology: The metaethics of radical feminism.* Boston: Beacon Press.

Daniels, M., Darcy, R., & Westphal, J. (1982). The ERA won—at least in the opinion polls. *PS, 15,* 578–84.

Daniloff, N. (1982). For Russian women, worst of both worlds. *U.S. News & World Report,* June 28, 53–54.

Darcy, R., & Schramm, S. (1977). When women run against men. *Public Opinion Quarterly, 41,* 1–12.

Darden, E. (1972). Masculinity-femininity body rankings by males and females. *Journal of Psychology, 80,* 205–12.

Darley, J., & Fazio, R. (1980). Expectancy confirmation processes arising in the social interaction sequence. *American Psychologist, 35,* 867–81.

Darwin, C. (1859/1967). *On the origin of species.* New York: Atheneum.

David, D., & Brannon, R. (Eds.). (1976). *The forty-nine percent majority.* Reading, MA: Addison-Wesley.

Davidson, C., & Abramowitz, S. (1980). Sex bias in clinical judgment: Later empirical returns. *Psychology of Women Quarterly, 4,* 377–95.

Davis, A. (1984). Sex differentiated behaviors in nonsexist picture books. *Sex Roles, 11,* 1–16.

Davis, E. (1972). *The first sex.* New York: Penguin.

Davis, J., & Hubbard, C. (1979). On the measurement of discrimination against women. *American Journal of Economics and Sociology, 38,* 287–92.

Dayhoff, S. (1983). Sexist language and person perception: Evaluation of candidates from newspaper articles. *Sex Roles, 9,* 527–39.

Deaux, K. (1984). From individual differences to social categories: Analysis of a decade's research on gender. *American Psychologist, 39,* 105–16.

Deaux, K., & Emswiller, T. (1974). Explanations of successful performance on sex-linked tasks: What is skill for the male is luck for the female. *Journal of Personality and Social Psychology, 29,* 80–85.

Deaux, K., & Lewis, L. (1983). Assessment of gender stereotypes: Methodology and components. *Psychological Documents, 13,* 25. (Ms. No. 2583).

Deaux, K., & Lewis, L. (1984). Structure of gender stereotypes: Interrelationships among components and gender label. *Journal of Personality and Social Psychology, 46,* 991–1004.

Deaux, K., White, L., & Farris, E. (1975). Skill versus luck: Field and laboratory studies of male and female preferences. *Journal of Personality and Social Psychology, 32,* 629–36.

de Beauvoir, S. (1952). *The second sex.* New York: Knopf.

DeBold, J., & Luria, Z. (1983). Gender identity, interactionism, and politics: A reply to Rogers and Walsh. *Sex Roles, 9,* 1101–8.

DeCecco, J. (Ed.). (1984). *Homophobia.* New York: Haworth Press.

Deckard, B. (1983). *The women's movement* (3rd ed.). New York: Harper and Row.

Delaney, J., Lupton, M., & Toth, E. (1977). *The curse.* New York: New American Library.

Department of Labor. (1980). *Perspectives on working women: A datebook.* Washington, DC: U.S. Government Printing Office.

Derlega, V., Winstead, B., & Wong, P. (1984). Self-disclosure in an initial encounter: A case where males disclose more intimately than women in opposite-sex pairs. Paper presented at the meeting of the Southeastern Psychological Association, New Orleans.

Deutsch, H. (1944). *The psychology of women* (Vol. I). New York: Grune & Stratton.

Deutsch, H. (1945). *The psychology of women* (Vol. II). New York: Grune & Stratton.

Dewhurst, J., & Gordon, R. (1984). Fertility following change of sex: A follow up. *Lancet, 2*, 1461–62.

Diamond, M., & Karlen, A. (1980). *Sexual decisions.* Boston: Little, Brown.

Dinnerstein, D. (1976). *The mermaid and the minotaur.* New York: Harper & Row.

Dion, K., Berscheid, E., & Walster, E. (1972). What is beautiful is good. *Journal of Personality and Social Psychology, 24*, 285–90.

Dipboye, R., Fromkin, H., & Wiback, K. (1975). Relative importance of applicant sex, attractiveness, and scholastic standing in evaluation of job applicant resumes. *Journal of Applied Psychology, 60*, 39–45.

Dittes, J. (1984). *The male predicament.* New York: Harper & Row.

Dodge, N. (1966). *Women in the Soviet economy.* Baltimore: Johns Hopkins University Press.

Doering, C., et al. (1975). Negative affect and plasma testosterone: A longitudinal human study. *Psychosomatic Medicine, 37*, 484–91.

Dohrenwend, B., & Dohrenwend, B. (1976). Sex differences and psychiatric disorders. *The American Journal of Sociology, 81*, 1447–54.

Dohrenwend, B., et al. (1980). *Mental illness in the United States.* New York: Praeger.

Dominick, J. (1979). The portrayal of women in prime time, 1953–1977. *Sex Roles, 5*, 405–11.

Dominick, J., & Rauch, G. (1972). The image of women in network TV commercials. *Journal of Broadcasting, 16*, 259–65.

Donahue, T., & Costar, J. (1977). Counselor discrimination against young women in career selection. *Journal of Counseling Psychology, 24*, 481–86.

Donnerstein, E. (1983). Erotica and human aggression. In R. Geen & E. Donnerstein (Eds.), *Aggression.* New York: Academic Press.

Douglas, A. (1977). *The feminization of American culture.* New York: Knopf.

Douglass, J. (1974). Women and the continental reformation. In R. Ruether (Ed.), *Religion and sexism* (pp. 292–318). New York: Simon and Schuster.

Doyle, J. (1983). *The male experience.* Dubuque, IA: Wm. C. Brown Publishers.

Doyle, J., & Moore, R. (1978). Attitudes toward the male's role scale (AMR). JSAS *Catalog of Selected Documents in Psychology, 8*, 35–36. (Ms. No. 1678).

DuBois, E. (1978). *Feminism and suffrage.* Ithaca, NY: Cornell University Press.

Dukes, J. (1984). Women underground come up fighting. *New Directions for Women, 13*(6), 10.

Duncan, B., & Duncan, O. (1978). *Sex typing and social roles.* New York: Academic Press.

Dunham, R., & Brower, H. (1984). The effects of assertiveness training on the nontraditional role assumption of geriatric nurse practitioners. *Sex Roles, 11*, 911–21.

Durkheim, E. (1965/1912). *The elementary forms of the religious life.* New York: Free Press.

Dweck, C. (1975). The role of expectations and attributions in the alleviation of learned helplessness. *Journal of Personality and Social Psychology, 31*, 674–85.

Dweck, C., et al. (1978). Sex differences in learned helplessness: II. The contingencies of evaluative feedback in the classroom and III. An experimental analysis. *Developmental Psychology, 14*, 268–76.

Dweck, C., Goetz, T., & Strauss, N. (1980). Sex differences in learned helplessness: An experimental and naturalistic study of failure generalization and its mediators. *Journal of Personality and Social Psychology, 38*, 441–51.

Dworkin, A. (1974). *Woman hating.* New York: Dutton.

Dworkin, A. (1981). *Pornography.* New York: Perigee Books.

Dworkin, A. (1983). *Right-wing women.* New York: Putnam.

Dye, N. (1980). *As equals and as sisters.* Columbia: University of Missouri Press.

Eagly, A. (1983). Gender and social influence: A social psychological analysis. *American Psychologist, 38*, 971–81.

Eagly, A., & Steffen, V. (1984). Gender stereotypes stem from the distribution of women and men into social roles. *Journal of Personality and Social Psychology, 46*, 735–54.

Eagly, A., & Wood, W. (1982). Inferred sex differences in status as a determinant of gender stereotypes about social influence. *Journal of Personality and Social Psychology, 43*, 915–28.

Eakins, B., & Eakins, R. (1978). *Sex differences in human communication.* Boston: Houghton Mifflin.

Eckholm, E. (1984). Theory on man's origins challenged. *The New York Times, September 4*, C1, C2.

Edelsky, C. (1981). Who's got the floor? *Language in Society, 10*, 383–421.

Ehrenkranz, J., Bliss, E., & Sheard, M. (1974). Plasma testosterone: Correlation with aggressive behavior and social dominance in man. *Psychosomatic Medicine, 36*, 469–75.

Ehrhardt, A., & Baker, S. (1978). Fetal androgens, human central nervous system differentiation, and behavior sex differences. In R. Friedman, et al. (Eds.), *Sex differences in behavior* (pp. 33–51). Huntington, NY: Krieger Publishing.

Eichler, M. (1977). Sociology of feminist research in Canada. *Signs, 3*, 409–22.

Eisenstein, Z. (1982). The sexual politics of the New Right: Understanding the "crisis of liberalism" for the 1980s. *Signs, 7*, 567–88.

Eisenstock, B. (1984). Sex-role differences in children's identification with counterstereotypic televised portrayals. *Sex Roles, 10*, 417–30.

Eisler, R. (1978). *The equal rights handbook.* New York: Avon Books.

Eitzen, S., & Sage, G. (1978). *Sociology of American sport.* Dubuque, IA: Wm. C. Brown Publishers.

El Guindi, F. (1981). Veiling *infitah* with Muslim ethic: Egypt's contemporary Islamic movement. *Social Problems, 28,* 465–85.

Elizondo, V., & Greenacher, N. (Eds.). (1980). *Women in a men's church.* New York: The Seabury Press.

Elshtain, J. (1982). Feminist discourse and its discontents: Language, power, and meaning. *Signs, 7,* 603–21.

Emihovich, C., Gaier, E., & Cronin, N. (1984). Sex-role expectations changes by fathers for their sons. *Sex Roles, 11,* 861–68.

Engels, F. (1942). *The origin of the family, private property, and the state.* New York: International Publishing.

England, P. (1984). Wage appreciation and depreciation: A test of neoclassical economic explanations of occupational sex segregation. *Social Forces, 3,* 726–49.

England, P., Chassie, M., & McCormack, L. (1982). Skill demands and earnings in female and male occupations. *Sociology and Social Research, 66,* 147–68.

England, P., & McLaughlin, S. (1979). Sex segregation of jobs and male-female income differentials. In R. Alvarez & K. Lutterman (Eds.), *Discrimination in organizations.* San Francisco: Jossey-Bass.

Epstein, C. (1981). *Women in law.* New York: Basic Books.

Ericksen, J., Yancey, W., & Ericksen, E. (1979). The division of family roles. *Journal of Marriage and the Family, 41,* 301–12.

Erickson, B., Lind, E. A., Johnson, B. C., and O'Barr, W. M. (1978). Speech style and impression formation in a court setting: The effects of "powerful" and "powerless" speech. *Journal of Experimental Social Psychology, 14,* 266–79.

Estler, S. (1975). Women as leaders in public education. *Signs, 1,* 363–86.

Etheredge, L. (1978). *A world of men.* Cambridge, MA: The MIT Press.

Exline, R. (1971). Visual interaction: The glance of power and preference. In J. Cole (Ed.), *Nebraska Symposium on motivation.* Lincoln: University of Nebraska Press.

Fagot, B. (1978). The influence of sex of child on parental reactions to toddler children. *Child Development, 49,* 459–65.

Fagot, B. (1984a). The child's expectations of differences in adult male and female interactions. *Sex Roles, 11,* 593–600.

Fagot, B. (1984b). Teacher and peer reactions to boys' and girls' play styles. *Sex Roles, 11,* 691–702.

Fairburn, C. (1981). A cognitive behavioral approach to the treatment of bulimia. *Psychological Medicine, 11,* 707–11.

Fairburn, C., & Cooper, P. (1982). Self-induced vomiting and bulimia nervosa: An undetected problem. *British Medical Journal, 284,* 1153–55.

Falbo, T., Hazen, M., & Linimon, D. (1982). The costs of selecting power bases or messages associated with the opposite sex. *Sex Roles, 8,* 147–57.

Faragher, J. (1979). *Women and men on the overland trail.* New Haven, CT: Yale University Press.

Farah, B. (1976). Climbing the political ladder: The aspirations and expectations of partisan elites. In D.

McGuigan (Ed.), *New research on women and sex roles* (pp. 238–50). Ann Arbor: University of Michigan Press.

Farrell, W. (1974). *The liberated man.* New York: Random House.

Fasteau, M. (1974). *The male machine.* New York: McGraw-Hill.

Feather, N., O'Driscoll, M., & Nagel, T. (1979). Conservatism, sex-typing, and the use of titles: Miss, Mrs., or Ms? *European Journal of Social Psychology, 9,* 419–26.

Feather, N., & Simon, J. (1975). Reactions to male and female sucess and failure in sex-linked occupations: Impressions of personality, causal attributions and perceived likelihood of different consequences. *Journal of Personality and Social Psychology, 31,* 20–31.

Feil, R., Largey, G., & Miller, M. (1984). Attitudes toward abortion as a means of sex selection. *The Journal of Psychology, 116,* 269–72.

Feinbloom, D. (1976). *Transvestites and transsexuals.* New York: Delacorte Press.

Feldman, S., & Nash, S. (1984). The transition from expectancy to parenthood: Impact of the firstborn on men and women. *Sex Roles, 11,* 61–78.

Fennema, E., & Sherman, J. (1977). Sex-related differences in mathematics achievement, spatial visualization and affective factors. *American Educational Research Journal, 14,* 51–71.

Fennema, E., & Sherman, J. (1978). Sex-related differences in mathematics achievement and related factors: A further study. *Journal of Research in Mathematics Education, 9,* 189–203.

Fernberger, S. (1948). Persistence of stereotypes concerning sex differences. *Journal of Abnormal and Social Psychology, 43,* 97–101.

Fernea, E., & Fernea, R. (1979). A look behind the veil. *Human Nature, January,* 69–80.

Ferrante, J. (1975). *Woman as image in medieval literature.* New York: Columbia University Press.

Fidell, L. (1980). Sex role stereotypes and the American physician. *Psychology of Women Quarterly, 4,* 313–30.

Field, M., & Flynn, K. (1970). Worker, mother, housewife: Soviet woman today. In G. Seward & R. Williamson (Eds.), *Sex roles in changing society.* New York: Random House.

Fields, M., & Kirchner, R. (1978). Battered women are still in need: A reply to Steinmetz. *Victimology, 3,* 216–22.

Fields, R. (1975). *Psychotherapy.* Pittsburgh: Know.

Filene, P. (1974). *Him/her/self.* New York: Harcourt Brace Jovanovich.

Fillmer, H., & Haswell, L. (1977). Sex-role stereotyping in English usage. *Sex Roles, 3,* 257–63.

Findlay, S. (1984). Active dads see rewards and snags. *USA Today, November 7,* 3D.

Finkelhor, D., et al. (Eds.). (1983). *The dark side of families.* Beverly Hills, CA: Sage.

Finkler, K. (1981). Dissident religious movements in the service of women's power. *Sex Roles, 7,* 481–95.

Fisher, J., Rytling, M., & Heslin, R. (1976). Hands touching hands: Affective and evaluative effects of an interpersonal touch. *Sociometry, 39,* 416–21.

Fisher, W., & Byrne, D. (1978). Individual differences in affective, evaluative, and behavioral responses to an erotic film. *Journal of Applied Social Psychology, 8,* 355–65.

Fishman, P. (1978). Interaction: The work women do. *Social Problems, 25,* 397–406.

Fiske, E. (1982). Computers alter lives of pupils and teachers. *The New York Times, 1,* 42.

Flexner, E. (1971). *Century of struggle.* New York: Atheneum.

Flora, C. (1971). The passive female: Her comparative image by class and culture in women's magazine fiction. *Journal of Marriage and the Family, 33,* 435–44.

Forden, C. (1981). The influence of sex-role expectations on the perception of touch. *Sex Roles, 7,* 889–94.

Forgey, D. (1975). The institution of berdache among the North American Plains Indians. *Journal of Sex Research, 11,* 1–15.

Forisha, B. (1981). The inside and the outsider: Women in organizations. In B. Forisha & B. Goldman (Eds.), *Outsiders on the inside.* Englewood Cliffs, NJ: Prentice-Hall.

Forman, M. (1984). Few wives are outlearning husbands. *The New York Times, October 31,* 24.

Fox, C., et al. (1972). Studies in the relationship between plasma testosterone levels and human sexual activity. *Journal of Endocrinology, 52,* 51–58.

Fox, G. (1983). Sex roles. In R. Hagedorn (Ed.), *Sociology.* (pp. 138–62) Dubuque, IA: Wm. C. Brown Publishers.

Frances, S. (1979). Sex differences in nonverbal behavior. *Sex Roles, 5,* 519–35.

Franck, K., & Rosen, E. (1949). A projective test of masculinity-femininity. *Journal of Consulting Psychology, 13,* 247–56.

Frank, R. (1931). The hormonal causes of premenstrual tension. *Archives of Neurology and Psychiatry, 26,* 1053–57.

Franken, M. (1983). Sex role expectations in children's vocational aspirations and perceptions of occupations. *Psychology of Women Quarterly, 8,* 59–68.

Franzwa, H. (1975). Female roles in women's magazine fiction, 1940–1970. In R. Unger & F. Denmark (Eds.), *Woman* (pp. 42–53). New York: Psychological Dimensions.

Freeman, J. (1975a). How to discriminate against women without really trying. In J. Freeman (Ed.), *Women* (pp. 194–208). Palo Alto, CA: Mayfield.

Freeman, J. (1975b). *The politics of women's liberation.* New York: David McKay.

Freeman, J. (1984). The women's liberation movement: Its origins, structures, impact, and ideas. In J. Freeman (Ed.), *Women* (3rd ed., pp. 543–56). Palo Alto, CA: Mayfield.

Freimuth, M., & Hornstein, G. (1982). A critical examination of the concept of gender. *Sex Roles, 8,* 515–32.

French, J., & Raven, B. (1959). The bases of social power. In D. Cartwright (Ed.), *Studies in social power* (pp. 150–67). Ann Arbor: University of Michigan, Institute for Social Research.

Freud, S. (1927). Some psychical consequences of the anatomical distinction between the sexes. *International Journal of Psychoanalysis, 8,* 133–42.

Freud, S. (1959a). Female sexuality. In J. Strachey (Ed.), *Sigmund Freud: Collected Papers* (Vol. 5, pp. 252–72). New York: Basic Books.

Freud, S. (1959b). "Civilized" sexual morality and modern nervousness. In E. Jones (ed.), *The collected papers of Sigmund Freud* (pp. 76–99). New York: Basic Books.

Freud, S. (1965). *New introductory lectures on psychoanalysis.* New York: Norton.

Freudiger, P., & Almquist, E. (1978). Male and female roles in the lyrics of three genres of contemporary music. *Sex Roles, 4,* 51–65.

Friday, N. (1980). *Men in love.* New York: Dell.

Friedan, B. (1963). *The feminine mystique.* New York: Norton.

Friedan, B. (1981). *The second stage.* New York: Summit Books.

Friedl, E. (1978). Society and sex roles. *Human Nature, April,* 70.

Frieze, I., & Ramsey, S. (1976). Nonverbal maintenance of traditional sex roles. *Journal of Social Issues, 32,* 133–41.

Frodi, A., Macaulay, J., & Thome, P. (1977). Are women always less aggressive than men? *Psychological Bulletin, 84,* 634–60.

Fruch, T., & McGhee, P. (1975). Traditional sex role development and amount of time watching television. *Developmental Psychology, 11,* 109.

Gadlin, H., & Ingle, G. (1975). Through the one-way mirror: The limits of experimental self-reflection. *American Psychologist, 30,* 1003–9.

Gadpaille, W. (1972). Research into the physiology of maleness and femaleness. *Archives of General Psychiatry, 26,* 193–206.

Gadpaille, W. (1980). Biological factors in the development of human sexual identity. *Psychiatric Clinics in North America, 3,* 3–20.

Gaebelein, J. (1977). Sex differences in instigative aggression. *Journal of Research in Personality, 11,* 466–74.

Gagnon, J., & Simon, W. (1973). *Sexual conduct.* Chicago: Aldine.

Galdston, R. (1965). Observations of children who have been physically abused by their parents. *American Journal of Psychiatry, 122,* 440–42.

Gallup Opinion Index. (1976). Worker attitudes. No. 126.

Gardiner, A. (1976). *Women and Catholic priesthood.* New York: Paulist Press.

Gardner, J. (1970). Sesame street and sex role stereotypes. *Women, 1,* 42.

Gardner, J. (1971). Sexist counseling must stop. *Personnel and Guidance Journal, 49,* 705–13.

Garfinkel, H. (1967). *Studies in ethnomethodology.* Englewood Cliffs, NJ: Prentice-Hall.

Garfinkel, P., & Garner, D. (1982). *Anorexia nervosa.* New York: Brunner/Mazel.

Garfinkel, P., Moldofsky, H., & Garner, D. (1980). The heterogeneity of anorexia nervosa. *Archives of General Psychiatry, 37,* 1036–40.

Garnets, L., & Pleck, J. (1979). Sex role identity, androgyny, and sex role transcendence: A sex role strain analysis. *Psychology of Women Quarterly, 3,* 270–83.

Garrett, C. (1977). Women and witches: Patterns of analysis. *Signs, 3,* 461–70.

Garrison, D. (1981). Karen Horney and feminism. *Signs, 6,* 672–91.

Garvey, C. (1977). *Play.* Cambridge: Harvard University Press.

Gayford, J. (1978). Battered wives. In J. Martin (Ed.), *Violence and the family.* New York: Wiley.

Gazzaniga, M. (1983). Rights hemisphere language following brain bisection: A 20 year perspective. *American Psychologist, 38,* 525–37.

Gecas, V., & Nye, I. (1974). Sexual class differences in parent-child interaction: A test of Kohn's hypothesis. *Journal of Marriage and the Family, 36,* 742–49.

Geertz, C. (1968). The impact of the concept of culture on the concept of man. In Y. Cohen (Ed.), *Man and adaptation.* Chicago: Aldine.

Geertz, C. (1973). *The interpretation of cultures.* New York: Basic Books.

Geiger, H. (1968). *The family in Soviet Russia.* Cambridge: Harvard University Press.

Geis, F., Brown, V., Jennings (Walstedt), J., & Porter, N. (1984). TV commercials as achievement scripts for women. *Sex Roles, 10,* 513–25.

Gelles, R. (1979). *Family violence.* Beverly Hills, CA: Sage.

Gelles, R. (1980). Violence in the family: A review of research in the seventies. *Journal of Marriage and the Family, 42,* 873–85.

Gelles, R. (1983). An exchange/social control theory. In D. Finkelhor, et al. (Eds.), *The dark side of families* (pp. 151–65). Beverly Hills, CA: Sage.

Gelpi, B. (1982). Editorial. *Signs, 7,* 739–41.

Geng, V. (1976). Requiem for the women's movement. *Harpers, November,* 49–56, 61–68.

Gerdes, E., Gehling, J., & Rapp, J. (1981). The effects of sex and sex-role concept on self-disclosure. *Sex Roles, 7,* 989–98.

Gerson, M. (1971). Women in the kibbutz. *American Journal of Orthopsychiatry, 41,* 566–73.

Gerson, M. (1983). A scale of motivation for parenthood: The index of parenthood motivation. *Journal of Psychology, 113,* 211–20.

Gerson, M. (1984). Feminism and the wish for a child. *Sex Roles, 11,* 389–99.

Gerson, M., Alpert, J., & Richardson, M. (1984). Mothering: The view from psychological research. *Signs, 9,* 434–53.

Gibson, J. (1978). *Growing up.* Reading, MA: Addison-Wesley.

Gidlow, E. (1976). *Ask no man pardon.* Mill Valley, CA: Druid Heights.

Gilbert, L. (1980). Feminist therapy. In A. Brodsky & R. Hare-Mustin (Eds.), *Women and psychotherapy.* New York: Guilford.

Gilbert, S. (1975). *What's a father for?* New York: Warner Books.

Gilder, G. (1975). *Sexual suicide.* New York: Bantam Books.

Gillespie, D. (1971). Who has the power? The marital struggle. *Journal of Marriage and the Family, 33,* 445–58.

Gilligan, C. (1982). *In a different voice.* Cambridge: Harvard University Press.

Glass, G., McGaw, B., & Smith, M. (1981). *Meta-analysis in social research.* Beverly Hills, CA: Sage.

Glen, E., & Feldberg, R. (1977). Degraded and deskilled: The proletarianization of clerical work. *Social Problems, 25,* 52–64.

Goff, D., Goff, L., & Lehrer, S. (1980). Sex-role portrayals of selected female television characters. *Journal of Broadcasting, 24,* 467–78.

Goffman, E. (1959). *The presentation of self in everyday life.* New York: Doubleday.

Goffman, E. (1979). *Gender advertisements.* Cambridge: Harvard University Press.

Gold, A., & St. Ange, M. (1974). Development of sex role stereotypes in black and white elementary school girls. *Developmental Psychology, 10,* 461.

Goldberg, A., & Shiflett, S. (1981). Goals of male and female college students: Do traditional sex differences still exist? *Sex Roles, 7,* 1213–22.

Goldberg, H. (1976). *The hazards of being male.* New York: Nash.

Goldberg, H. (1979). *The new male.* New York: Signet.

Goldstein, B., & Oldham, J. (1979). *Children and work.* New Brunswick, NJ: Transaction Books.

Gollob, H. (1984). Detecting sex bias in salaries. *American Psychologist, 39,* 448–51.

Golub, S. (1976). The effect of premenstrual anxiety and depression on cognitive function. *Journal of Personality and Social Psychology, 34,* 99–104.

Golub, S. (Ed.). (1983). *Lifting the curse of menstruation.* New York: Haworth Press.

Gonen, J., & Lanksy, L. (1968). Masculinity, femininity, and masculinity-femininity: A phenomenological study of the Mf scale of the MMPI. *Psychological Reports, 23,* 183–94.

Goodall, H., & Roberts, A. (1976). Differences in motility of human X- and Y-bearing spermatozoa. *Journal of Reproduction and Fertility, 48,* 433–36.

Gordon, J. (1982). *The myth of the monstrous male.* New York: Playboy Press.

Gough, H. (1952). Identifying psychological femininity. *Educational and Psychological Measurement, 12,* 427–39.

Gough, K. (1984). The origin of the family. In J. Freeman (Ed.), *Women* (3rd ed., pp. 83–99). Palo Alto: CA: Mayfield.

Gould, M. (1980). The new sociology. *Signs, 5,* 459–67.

Gould, M., & Kern-Daniels, R. (1977). Toward a sociological theory of gender and sex. *American Sociologist, 12,* 182–89.

Gould, R. (1974). Measuring masculinity by the size of a paycheck. In J. Pleck & J. Sawyer (Eds.), *Men and masculinity* (pp. 96–100). Englewood Cliffs, NJ: Prentice-Hall.

Gould, S. (1976). Biological potential vs. biological determinism. *Natural History Magazine, May,* 12–22.

Gove, W. (1979). Sex differences in the epidemiology of mental disorder: Evidence and explanations. In E. Gomberg & V. Franks (Eds.), *Gender and disordered behavior*. New York: Brunner/Mazel.

Gove, W. (1980). Mental illness and psychiatric treatment among women. *Psychology of Women Quarterly, 4,* 345–62.

Gove, W., & Geerken, M. (1977). Response bias in surveys of mental health: An empirical investigation. *American Journal of Sociology, 82,* 1289–1317.

Gove, W., & Herb, T. (1974). Stress and mental illness among the young: A comparison of the sexes. *Social Forces, 54,* 256–65.

Gove, W., & Tudor, J. (1973). Adult sex roles and mental illness. *American Journal of Sociology, 73,* 812–35.

Goy, R. (1978). Development of play and mounting behavior in female rhesus monkeys virilized prenatally with esters of testosterone or dihydrotestosterone. In D. Chivers & J. Herbert (Eds.), *Recent advances in primatology* (Vol. 1). New York: Academic Press.

Grady, K., Brannon, R., & Pleck, J. (1979). *The male sex role: A selected and annotated bibliography*. Rockville, MD: National Institute of Mental Health.

Grant, B. (1980). Five liturgical songs by Hildegard von Bingen (1098–1179). *Signs, 5,* 557–67.

Grant, P., & Holmes, J. (1981). The integration of implicit personality theory schemas and stereotype images. *Social Psychology Quarterly, 44,* 107–15.

Grant, P., & Holmes, J. (1982). The influence of stereotypes in impression formation: A reply to Locksley, Hepburn, and Ortiz. *Social Psychology Quarterly, 45,* 274–76.

Gray-Little, B. (1982). Marital quality and power processes among black couples. *Journal of Marriage and the Family, 44,* 633–46.

Gray-Little, B., & Burks, N. (1983). Power and satisfaction in marriage: A review and critique. *Psychological Bulletin, 93,* 513–38.

Green, R. (1974). *Sexual identity conflict in children and adults*. New York: Basic Books.

Greenberg, M., & Morris, N. (1974). Engrossment: The newborn's impact upon the father. *American Journal of Orthopsychiatry, 44,* 520–31.

Greenberger, E., & Steinberg, L. (1981). The workplace as a context for the socialization of youth. *Journal of Youth and Adolescence, 10,* 185–210.

Greenberger, E., & Steinberg, L. (1983). Sex differences in early labor force experience: Harbinger of things to come. *Social Forces, 62,* 467–86.

Greenwald, A. (1975). Consequences of prejudice against the null hypothesis. *Psychological Bulletin, 82,* 1–20.

Gross, A. (1978). The male role and heterosexual behavior. *Journal of Social Issues, 34,* 87–107.

Gross, A., Smith, R., & Wallston, B. (1981). The men's movement: Personal vs. political. In J. Freeman (Ed.), *Social movements of the sixties and seventies*. New York: Longman.

Gross, H., et al. (1979). Considering "a biosocial perspective on parenting." *Signs, 4,* 695–717.

Gross, L., & Jeffries-Fox, S. (1978). What do you want to be when you grow up, little girl? In G. Tuchman, A. Daniels, & J. Benet (Eds.), *Hearth and home*. New York: Oxford University Press.

Grosskurth, P. (1975). *John Addington Symonds*. New York: Arno.

Groth, A., & Burgess, A. (1980). Male rape: Offenders and victims. *American Journal of Psychiatry, 137,* 806–10.

Gruberg, M. (1968). *Women in American politics*. Oshkosh, WI: Academia Press.

Guerrero, R. (1974). Association of the type and time of insemination within the menstrual cycle with the human sex ratio at birth. *New England Journal of Medicine, 291,* 1056.

Guttentag, M., Salasin, S., & Belle, D. (Eds.). (1980). *The mental health of women*. New York: Academic Press.

Guttentag, M., & Secord, P. (1983). *Too many women? The sex ratio question*. Beverly Hills, CA: Sage.

Haavio-Mannila, E. (1975). Convergences between east and west: Traditional modernity in sex roles in Sweden, Finland, and the Soviet Union. In M. Mednick, S. Tangri, & L. Hoffman (Eds.), *Women and achievement* (pp. 71–84). New York: Halstead.

Hacker, H. (1951). Women as a minority group. *Social Forces, 30,* 60–69.

Hacker, H. (1975). Gender roles from a cross-cultural perspective. In L. Duberman (Ed.), *Gender and sex in society* (pp. 185–215). New York: Praeger.

Haddad, R. (1979). *The men's liberation movement*. Columbia, MD: Free Men.

Hall, C. (1984). "A ubiquitous sex difference in dreams" revisited. *Journal of Personality and Social Psychology, 46,* 1109–17.

Hall, E. (1966). *The hidden dimension*. New York: Doubleday.

Hall, E. (1981). *Beyond culture*. Garden City, NY: Doubleday.

Hall, J. (1978). Gender effects in decoding nonverbal cues. *Psychological Bulletin, 85,* 845–57.

Hall, J. (1979). Gender, gender roles and nonverbal communication skills. In R. Rosenthal (Ed.), *Skill in nonverbal communication*. Cambridge, MA: Harvard University Press.

Halleck, S. (1971). Therapy is the handmaiden of the status quo. *Psychology Today, 4,* 30.

Hamburg, B. (1978). The psychobiology of sex differences: An evolutionary perspective. In R. Friedman, et al. (Eds.), *Sex differences in behavior* (pp. 373–92). Huntington, NY: Krieger Publishing.

Hamerton, J., et al. (1975). A cytogenetic survey of 14,069 newborn infants. *Clinical Genetics, 8,* 223–43.

Haraway, D. (1978a). Animal sociology and a natural economy of the body politic, Part I: A political physiology of dominance. *Signs, 4,* 21–36.

Haraway, D. (1978b). Animal sociology and a natural economy of the body politic, Part II: The past is the contested zone: Human nature and theories of production and reproduction in primate behavior studies. *Signs, 4,* 37–60.

Haraway, D. (1981). In the beginning was the word: The genesis of biological theory. *Signs, 6,* 469–82.

Hardin, G. (1974). *Mandatory motherhood*. Boston: Beacon Press.

Hare, R. (1970). *Psychopathy*. New York: Wiley.

Hare-Mustin, R. (1978). A feminist approach to family therapy. *Family Process, 17,* 181–94.

Hare-Mustin, R. (1983). An appraisal of the relationship between women and psychotherapy: 80 years after the case of Dora. *American Psychologist, 38,* 593–601.

Hare-Mustin, R., & Broderick, P. (1979). The myth of motherhood: A study of attitudes toward motherhood. *Psychology of Women Quarterly, 4,* 114–28.

Haroutunian, J. (1949). *Lust for power*. New York: Scribner's.

Harrigan, R. (1982). The German women's movement and ours. *Jump Cut, 27,* 42–44.

Harris, B. (1979). Careers, conflict, and children. In A. Roland & B. Harris (Eds.), *Career and motherhood*. New York: Human Sciences Press.

Harris, B. (1984). The power of the past: History and the psychology of women. In M. Lewin (Ed.), *In the shadow of the past* (pp. 1–25). New York: Columbia University Press.

Harrison, B. (1983). *Our right to choose*. Boston: Beacon Press.

Harrison, J. (1978). Men's roles and men's lives. *Signs, 4,* 324–36.

Hartmann, H. (1981). The family as the locus of gender, class, and political struggle: The example of housework. *Signs, 6,* 366–94.

Hashell, D. (1979). The depiction of women in leading roles in prime-time television. *Journal of Broadcasting, 23,* 191–96.

Hathaway, S., & McKinley, J. (1943). *The Minnesota Multiphasic Personality Inventory*. New York: Psychological Corporation.

Heckinger, G. (1981). Happy mother's day. *Newsweek, May 11,* 19.

Hefner, R., Rebecca, M., & Oleshansky, B. (1975). Development of sex role transcendence. *Human Development, 18,* 143–56.

Heide, W. (1979). Scholarship/action: In the human interest. *Signs, 5,* 189–91.

Heilbrun, C. (1973). *Toward a recognition of androgyny*. New York: Harper Colophon Books.

Heilman, M. (1975). Miss, Mrs., Ms., or none of the above. *American Psychologist, 30,* 516–18.

Helmreich, R., & Spence, J. (1977). The secret of success. *Discovery, Research and Scholarship at the University of Texas at Austin, 2(2),* 4–7.

Henley, N. (1973). Status and sex: Some touching observations. *Bulletin of the Psychonomic Society, 2,* 91–93.

Henley, N. (1977). *Body politics*. Englewood Cliffs, NJ: Prentice-Hall.

Herberle, R. (1951). *Social movements*. New York: Appleton-Century-Crofts.

Herbert, W., & Greenberg, J. (1983). Fatherhood in transition . . . but sex roles remain. *Science News, 124(11),* 172.

Herlihy, D. (1973). Alienation in medieval culture and society. In *Alienation: Concept, term and meanings*. New York: Seminar Press.

Herlihy, D. (1975). Life expectancies for women in medieval society. In R. Morewedge (Ed.), *The role of woman in the Middle Ages*. Albany: State University of New York Press.

Herzog, D. (1982). Bulimia: The secretive syndrome. *Psychosomatics, 23,* 481–83, 487.

Hilpert, F., Kramer, C., & Clark, R. (1975). Participants' perception of self and partner in mixed-sex dyads. *Central States Speech Journal, 26(Spring),* 52–56.

Hochreich, D. (1975). Sex-role stereotypes for internal-external control and interpersonal trust. *Journal of Consulting and Clinical Psychology, 43,* 273.

Hoferek, M. (1980). At the crossroad: Merger or ———? *Quest, 32,* 95–102.

Hoffman, L. (1975). Early childhood experiences and women's achievement motives. In M. Mednick, S. Tangri, & L. Hoffman (Eds.), *Women and achievement*. New York: Halstead.

Hoffman, L. (1977). Changes in family roles, socialization and sex differences. *American Psychologist, 32,* 644–57.

Hoffnung, M. (1984). Motherhood: Contemporary conflict for women. In J. Freeman (Ed.), *Women* (3rd ed., pp. 124–38). Palo Alto, CA: Mayfield.

Hole, J., & Levine, E. (1984). The first feminists. In J. Freeman (Ed.), *Women* (3rd ed., pp. 533–42). Palo Alto, CA: Mayfield.

Holroyd, J., & Brodsky, A. (1977). Psychologists' attitudes and practices regarding erotic and non-erotic physical contact with patients. *American Psychologist, 32,* 843–49.

Hopson, J., & Rosenfeld, A. (1984). PMS: Puzzling monthly symptoms. *Psychology Today, August,* 30–35.

Horner, M. (1972). Toward an understanding of achievement-related conflicts in women. *Journal of Social Issues, 28,* 157–76.

Horney, K. (1967). *Feminine psychology*. New York: Norton.

Horney, K. (1978). The problem of feminine masochism. In J. Miller (Ed.), *Psychoanalysis and women*. New York: Penguin.

Hornung, C., McCullough, B., & Sugimoto, T. (1981). Status relationships in marriage: Risk factors in spouse abuse. *Journal of Marriage and the Family, 43,* 675–92.

Household and family characteristics. (1983). Current Population Reports. Washington, DC: U.S. Bureau of the Census, author.

Houseknecht, S. (1979). Timing of the decision to remain voluntarily childless: Evidence for continuous socialization. *Psychology of Women Quarterly, 4,* 81–96.

Hoyenga, K., & Hoyenga, K. (1979). *The question of sex differences*. Boston: Little, Brown.

Huber, J. (1976a). Sociology. *Signs, 1,* 685–97.

Huber, J. (1976b). On the generic use of male pronouns. *American Sociologist, 11,* 89.

Hunt, M. (1959). *The natural history of love*. New York: Knopf.

Hunter, J. (1984). *The gospel of gentility*. New Haven, CT: Yale University Press.

Hurwitz, E. (1978). Carrie C. Catt's "suffrage militancy." *Signs, 3,* 739–43.

Huston, T. (1983). Power. In H. Kelley, et al. (Eds.), *Close relationships* (pp. 169–219). New York: W. H. Freeman.

Hyde, J. (1981). How large are cognitive differences? *American Psychologist, 36*, 892–901.

Hyman, H., & Wright, C. (1979). *Education's lasting influence on values.* Chicago: University of Chicago Press.

Ibsen, H. (1958). *Four great plays by Henrik Ibsen* (R. Sharp, Trans.). New York: Bantam Books.

Imperato-McGinley, J., et al. (1974). Steroid 5a-reductase deficiency in man: An inherited form of male pseudohermaphroditism. *Science, 186*, 1213–15.

Imperato-McGinley, J., Peterson, R., & Gautier, T. (1976). Gender identity and hermaphroditism. *Science, 191*, 872.

Imperato-McGinley, J., et al. (1979). Androgens and the evolution of male-gender identity among male pseudohermaphrodites with 5a-reductase deficiency. *New England Journal of Medicine, 300(22)*, 1233–37.

Inglis, J., & Lawson, J. (1981). Sex differences in the effects of unilateral brain damage on intelligence. *Science, 212*, 693–95.

Interrante, J. (1981). Dancing along the precipice: The men's movement in the '80s. *Radical America, 15(5)*, 53–71.

Izraeli, D., Friedman, A., & Shrift, A. (1982). *The double bind.* Tel Aviv: Hakibbutz Hameuchad Publishing House Ltd.

Jackson, M. (1972). Minorities and women in sociology: Are opportunities changing? *The American Sociologist, 7*, 3–5.

Jackson, P. (1968). *Life in the classroom.* New York: Holt, Rinehart and Winston.

Jacobs, P., et al. (1965). Aggressive behavior, mental subnormality and the XYY male. *Nature, 208*, 1351–52.

Jacobs, S. (1968). Berdache: A brief review of the literature. *Colorado Anthropologist, 1*, 25–40.

Jacobson, M. (1983). Attitudes toward the Equal Rights Amendment as a function of knowing what it said. *Sex Roles, 9*, 891–96.

Jacobson, M., & Popovich, P. (1983). Victim attractiveness and perceptions of responsibility in an ambiguous rape case. *Psychology of Women Quarterly, 8*, 100–104.

Jago, A., & Vroom, V. (1982). Sex differences in the incidence and evaluation of participative leader behavior. *Journal of Applied Psychology, 67*, 776–83.

Jakubowski, P. (1977). Assertive behavior and clinical problems of women: Self-assertion training procedures for women. In E. Rawlings & D. Carter (Eds.), *Psychotherapy for women* (pp. 147–90). Springfield, IL: Thomas.

Jakubowski, P. (1978). Facilitating the growth of women through assertive training. In L. Harmon, et al., (Eds.), *Counseling women* (pp. 106–22). Monterey, CA: Brooks/Cole.

Janeway, E. (1971). *Man's world, woman's place.* New York: Delta.

Janowsky, D., Berens, S., & Davis, J. (1973). Correlations between mood, weight, and electrolytes during the menstrual cycle: A renin-angiotensin-aldosterone hypothesis of premenstrual tension. *Psychosomatic Medicine, 35*, 143–54.

Janssen-Jurreit, M. (1982). *Sexism* (V. Moberg, Trans.). New York: Farrar, Straus and Giroux.

Jennings, M., & Farah, B. (1978). Social roles and political resources: An over-time study of men and women in party elites. Paper presented at the Midwest Political Science Association, Chicago.

Jennings (Walstedt), J., Geis, F., & Brown, V. (1980). Influence of television commercials on women's self-confidence and independent judgment. *Journal of Personality and Social Psychology, 38*, 203–10.

Johnson, A. (1980). On the prevalence of rape in the United States. *Signs, 6*, 136–46.

Johnson, M. (1978). Influence of counselor gender on reactivity to clients. *Journal of Counseling Psychology, 25*, 359–65.

Johnson, M. (1980). Mental illness and psychiatric treatment among women: A response. *Psychology of Women Quarterly, 4*, 363–71.

Johnson, P. (1976). Women and power: Toward a theory of effectiveness. *The Journal of Social Issues, 32*, 99–110.

Johnson, P. (1978). Women and interpersonal power. In I. Frieze, et al. (Eds.), *Women and sex roles* (pp. 301–20). New York: Norton.

Johnson, S., & Black, K. (1981). The relationship between sex-role identity and beliefs in personal control. *Sex Roles, 7*, 425–31.

Jones, H., et al. (1979). The role of the H-Y antigen in human sexual development. *The Johns Hopkins Medical Journal, 145*, 33–43.

Jones, J., & Lovejoy, F. (1980). Discrimination against women academics in Australian universities. *Signs, 5*, 518–26.

Jourard, S. (1964). *The transparent self.* Princeton, NJ: Van Nostrand.

Jourard, S. (1971). *Self disclosure.* New York: Wiley.

Jourard, S. (1974). Some lethal aspects of the male role. In J. Pleck & J. Sawyer (Eds.), *Men and masculinity* (pp. 21–29). Englewoods Cliffs, NJ: Prentice-Hall.

Kahn, A. (1984). The power war: Male response to power loss under equality. *Psychology of Women Quarterly, 8*, 234–47.

Kalisch, P., & Kalisch, B. (1984). Sex-role stereotyping of nurses and physicians on prime-time television: A dichotomy of occupational portrayals. *Sex Roles, 10*, 533–53.

Kaminer, W. (1980). Pornography and the First Amendment: Prior restraints and private action. In L. Lederer (Ed.), *Take back the night* (pp. 241–47). New York: Morrow.

Kanowitz, L. (1969). *Women and the law.* Albuquerque: The University of New Mexico.

Kanter, R. (1984). *Men and women of the corporation* (2nd ed.). New York: Basic Books.

Kaplan, M. (1983a). A woman's view of DSM-III. *American Psychologist, 38*, 786–92.

Kaplan, M. (1983b). The issue of sex bias in DSM-III: Comments on the articles by Spitzer, Williams, and Kass. *American Psychologist, 38,* 802–3.

Kass, F., Spitzer, R., & Williams, J. (1983). An empirical study of the issue of sex bias in the diagnostic criteria of DSM-III Axis II personality disorders. *American Psychologist, 38,* 799–801.

Kassell, P. (1984). Ordeal by the press. *New Directions for Women, 13(6),* 2.

Katchadourian, H., & Lunde, D. (1979). *Fundamentals of human sexuality* (3rd ed.). New York: Holt, Rinehart and Winston.

Katz, J. (1976). *Gay American history.* New York: Crowell.

Katz, M. (1975). *Class, bureaucracy and schools.* New York: Praeger.

Kaufman, A., et al. (1980). Male rape victims: Noninstitutionalized assault. *American Journal of Psychiatry, 137,* 221–23.

Kaufman, P. (1984). *Women teachers on the frontier.* New Haven, CT: Yale University Press.

Kaufmann-McCall, D. (1983). Politics of difference: The women's movement in France from May 1968 to Mitterrand. *Signs, 9,* 282–93.

Keller, E. (1978). Gender and science. *Psychoanalysis and Contemporary Thought, 1,* 409–33.

Keller, E. (1982). Feminism and science. *Signs, 7,* 589–602.

Kelly, J. (1983). Sex role stereotypes and mental health: Conceptual models in the 1970's and issues for the 1980's. In V. Franks & E. Rothblum (Eds.), *The stereotyping of women.* New York: Springer.

Kelly, M. (1981). Development and the sexual division of labor: An introduction. *Signs, 7,* 268–78.

Kemper, S. (1984). When to speak like a lady. *Sex Roles, 10,* 435–43.

Kennard, J. (1977). The history of physical education. *Signs, 2,* 835–42.

Kennard, J. (1984). Ourself behind ourself: Theory for lesbian readers. *Signs, 9,* 647–62.

Kerber, L. (1980). *Women of the Republic.* Chapel Hill: University of North Carolina Press.

Kessler, R., & McRae, Jr., J. (1982). The effects of wives' employment on the mental health of married men and women. *American Sociological Review, 47,* 216–26.

Kessler, S., & McKenna, W. (1978). *Gender.* New York: Wiley.

Ketter, P. (1952). *Christ and womankind.* Westminster, MD: Newman Press.

Key, M. (1975a). The role of male and female in children's books—Dispelling all doubt. In R. Unger & F. Denmark (Eds.), *Woman* (pp. 56–70). New York: Psychological Dimensions.

Key, M. (1975b). *Male/female language.* Metuchen, NJ: Scarecrow Press.

Kilson, M. (1976). The status of women in higher education. *Signs, 1,* 935–42.

Kimble, G. (1984). Psychology's two cultures. *American Psychologist, 39,* 833–39.

Kimmel, E. (1974). The status of women in psychology in the southeast: A case study. *American Psychologist, 29,* 519–40.

Kimmel, E. (1984). The status of women in SEPA: A progress report. Paper presented at the meeting of the Southeastern Psychological Association, New Orleans.

King, D., & Buchwald, A. (1982). Sex differences in subclinical depression: Administration of the Beck Depression Inventory in public and private disclosure situations. *Journal of Personality and Social Psychology, 42,* 963–69.

King, M. (1978). The religious retreat of Isotta Nogarola (1418–1466): Sexism and its consequences in the fifteenth century. *Signs, 3,* 807–22.

Kingston, M. (1976). *The woman warrior.* New York: Vintage Books.

Kipnis, D. (1976). *The powerholders.* Chicago: University of Chicago Press.

Kirkpatrick, J. (1974). *Political women.* New York: Basic Books.

Kirkpatrick, J. (1976). *The new presidential elite.* New York: Russell Sage Foundation.

Kirsh, B. (1974). Consciousness-raising groups as a therapy for women. In V. Franks & V. Burtle (Eds.), *Women in therapy* (pp. 326–54). New York: Brunner/Mazel.

Klein, V. (1984). The historical background. In J. Freeman (Ed.), *Women* (3rd ed., pp. 519–32). Palo Alto, CA: Mayfield.

Knoxville News-Sentinel. (1984). Househusbandry down to a science. *June 27,* C1.

Koch, S. (1981). The nature and limits of psychological knowledge: Lessons of a century qua "science." *American Psychologist, 36,* 257–69.

Koeske, R. (1976). Premenstrual emotionality: Is biology destiny? *Women and Health, 1,* 11–14.

Kohlberg, L. (1966). A cognitive-developmental analysis of children's sex role concepts and attitudes. In E. Maccoby (Ed.), *The development of sex differences* (pp. 82–173). Stanford: Stanford University Press.

Kohlberg, L. (1976). Moral stages and moralization: The cognitive-development approach. In T. Lickona (Ed.), *Moral development and behavior.* New York: Holt, Rinehart and Winston.

Kohlstedt, S. (1978). In from the periphery: American women in science, 1830–1880. *Signs, 4,* 81–96.

Kohn, M. (1977). *Class and conformity* (2nd ed.). Chicago: University of Chicago Press.

Kolata, G. (1980). Math and sex: Are girls born with less ability? *Science, 210(December 9),* 1234–35.

Kolbe, R., & LaVoie, J. (1981). Sex-role stereotyping in preschool children's picture books. *Social Psychology Quarterly, December,* 369–74.

Komarovsky, M. (1940). *The unemployed man and his family.* New York: Dryden.

Komarovsky, M. (1964). Cultural contradictions and sex roles. *American Journal of Sociology, 52,* 182–89.

Komarovsky, M. (1976). *Dilemmas of masculinity.* New York: Norton.

Komisar, L. (1971). The image of woman in advertising. In V. Gornick & B. Moran (Eds.), *Woman in sexist society* (pp. 304–17). New York: New American Library.

Koo, H., & Suchindran, C. (1980). Effects of children on women's remarriage prospects. *Journal of Family Issues, 1,* 497–515.

Kraditor, A. (Ed.). (1968). *Up from the pedestal.* Chicago: Quadrangle.

Kraditor, A. (1971). *The ideas of the woman suffrage movement, 1890–1920.* New York: Doubleday.

Kramer, C., Thorne, B., & Henley, N. (1978). Perspectives on language and communication. *Signs, 3,* 638–51.

Kreuz, L., & Rose, R. (1972). Assessment of aggressive behavior and plasma testosterone in a young criminal population. *Psychosomatic Medicine, 34,* 321–32.

Kristeva, J. (1975). On the women of China. *Signs, 1,* 57–82.

Krulewitz, J., & Kahn, A. (1983). Preferences for rape reduction strategies. *Psychology of Women Quarterly, 7,* 301–12.

Krulewitz, J., & Payne, E. (1978). Attribution about rape: Effects of rapist force, observer sex, and sex role attitudes. *Journal of Applied Social Psychology, 8,* 291–305.

Kuhn, D., Nash, S., & Brucken, L. (1978). Sex role concepts of two- and three-year-olds. *Child Development, 49,* 445–51.

Kuhn, T. (1962). *The structure of scientific revolutions.* Chicago: University of Chicago Press.

Kukla, A. (1982). Logical incoherence of value-free science. *Journal of Personality and Social Psychology, 43,* 1014–17.

Kutner, N., & Lacy, W. (1984). Report on women's status: On women's representation on Sociology faculties. *The Southern Sociologist, 15(2),* 20–23.

Kutner, N., & Levinson, R. (1978). The toy salesperson: A voice for change in sex-role stereotypes? *Sex Roles, 4,* 1–7.

LaFrance, M., & Carmen, B. (1980). The nonverbal display of psychological androgyny. *Journal of Personality and Social Psychology, 38,* 36–49.

Lakoff, R. (1973). Language and woman's place. *Language in Society, 2,* 45–79.

Lakoff, R. (1975). *Language and woman's place.* New York: Harper and Row.

Lamb, M. (1981). *The role of the father in child development* (2nd ed.). New York: Wiley.

Lamb, M. (1982). Why Swedish fathers aren't liberated. *Psychology Today, October, 74,* 76–77.

Lamb, M., & Levine, J. (1982). The Swedish parental insurance policy: An experiment in social engineering. In M. Lamb & A. Sagi (Eds.), *Fatherhood and social policy.* Hillsdale, NJ: Lawrence Erlbaum Associates.

Lamb, M., Owen, M., & Chase-Lansdale, L. (1979). The father-daughter relationship: Past, present, and future. In C. Kopp & M. Kirkpatrick (Eds.), *Becoming female* (pp. 113–40). New York: Plenum.

Lamb, M., & Sagi, A. (Eds.). (1982). *Fatherhood and social policy.* Hillsdale, NJ: Lawrence Erlbaum Associates.

Lamm, B. (1977). Men's movement hype. In J. Snodgrass (Ed.), *For men against sexism* (pp. 153–57). Albion, CA: Times Change Press.

Lamson, P. (1968). *Few are chosen.* Boston: Houghton Mifflin.

Lamson, P. (1979). *In the vanguard.* Boston: Houghton Mifflin.

Lapidus, G. (1978). *Women in Soviet society.* Berkeley: University of California Press.

LaPlante, M., McCormick, N., & Brannigan, G. (1980). Living the sexual script: College students' views of influence in sexual encounters. *Journal of Sex Research, 16,* 338–55.

Lauer, R., & Handel, W. (1983). *Social psychology* (2nd ed.). Englewood Cliffs, NJ: Prentice-Hall.

Lauritsen, J., & Thorstad, D. (1974). *The early homosexual rights movement (1864–1935).* San Rafael, CA: Times Change Press.

Laws, J. (1976). Work aspirations of women: False leads and new starts. *Signs, 1,* 33–49.

Lear, M. (1976). You'll probably think I'm stupid. *The New York Times Magazine, April 11.*

Leavitt, R. (1971). Women in other cultures. In V. Gornick & B. Moran (Eds.), *Woman in sexist society* (pp. 393–427). New York: New American Library.

Lederer, L. (Ed.). (1980). *Take back the night.* New York: Morrow.

Lee, M. (1976). Why few women hold public office: Democracy and sexual roles. *Political Science Quarterly, 91,* 297–314.

Lee, R., & Devore, I. (1968). *Man the hunter.* Chicago: Aldine Press.

Lefcourt, H. (1976). *Locus of control.* Hillsdale, NJ: Lawrence Erlbaum Associates.

Leffler, A., Gillespie, D., & Conaty, J. (1982). The effects of status differentiation on nonverbal behavior. *Social Psychology Quarterly, 45,* 153–61.

Lefkowitz, B. (1979). *Breaktime.* New York: Hawthorne Books.

LeGuin, U. (1969). *The left hand of darkness.* New York: Ace Books.

Lehne, G. (1976). Homophobia among men. In D. David & R. Brannon (Eds.), *The forty-nine percent majority* (pp. 66–88). Reading, MA: Addison-Wesley.

Leiss, W. (1974). *The domination of nature.* Boston: Beacon Press.

Lemons, J. (1973). *The woman citizen.* Champaign: University of Illinois Press.

Leo, J. (1984). Big thoughts about small talk. *Time, September 17, 98.*

Lerner, G. (1975). Sarah M. Grimke's "Sister of Charity." *Signs, 1,* 246–56.

Leserman, J. (1981). *Men and women in medical school.* New York: Praeger.

Levin, S., Kamin, L., & Levine, E. (1974). Sexism and psychiatry. *American Journal of Orthopsychiatry, 44,* 327–36.

Levin, W. (1984). *Sociological ideas.* Belmont, CA: Wadsworth.

Levy, J. (1976). Cerebral lateralization and spatial ability. *Behavior Genetics, 6,* 71–78.

Levy, J. (1981). Yes, Virginia, there is a difference: Sex differences in human brain asymmetry and in psychology. *The L.S. Leaky Foundation News, 20(Fall).*

Levy, J., & Reid, M. (1976). Variations in writing posture and cerebral organization. *Science, 194,* 337–39.

Lewin, M. (1984a). "Rather worse than folly?" Psychology measures femininity and masculinity, 1: From Terman and Miles to the Guildfords. In M. Lewin (Ed.), *In the shadow of the past* (pp. 155–78). New York: Columbia University Press.

Lewin, M. (1984b). Psychology measures femininity and masculinity, 2: From "13 gay men" to the instrumental-expressive distinction. In M. Lewin (Ed.), *In the shadows of the past* (pp. 179–204). New York: Columbia University Press.

Lewin-Epstein, N. (1981). *Youth employment during high school.* Washington, DC: National Center for Educational Statistics.

Lewis, E. (1968). *Developing woman's potential.* Ames: Iowa State University Press.

Lewis, M. (1972). State as an infant-environment interaction: An analysis of mother-infant behaviors as a function of sex. *Merrill-Palmer Quarterly, 18,* 95–211.

Lindahl, E. (1958). Separation of bull spermatozoa carrying X and Y chromosomes by counterstreaming centrifugation. *Nature, 181(March),* 784.

Lindholm, C., & Lindholm, C. (1980). Life behind the veil. *Science Digest, Special-Summer, 42,* 44–47, 106.

Lipman-Blumen, J. (1984). *Gender roles and power.* Englewood Cliffs, NJ: Prentice-Hall.

Lipton, J., & Hershaft, A. (1984). "Girl," "woman," "guy," "man": The effects of sexist labeling. *Sex Roles, 10,* 183–94.

Locksley, A., et al. (1980). Sex stereotypes and social judgment. *Journal of Personality and Social Psychology, 39,* 821–31.

Locksley, A., Hepburn, C., & Ortiz, V. (1982). On the effect of social stereotypes on judgments of individuals: A comment on Grant and Holmes's "The integration of implicit personality theory schemas and stereotypic images." *Social Psychology Quarterly, 45,* 270–73.

Lombardo, J., & Lavine, L. (1981). Sex-role stereotyping and patterns of self-disclosure. *Sex Roles, 7,* 403–11.

Lombardo, W., et al. (1983). Fer cryin' out loud—there is a sex difference. *Sex Roles, 9,* 987–95.

Longino, H., & Doell, R. (1983). Body, bias, and behavior: A comparative analysis of reasoning in two areas of biological science. *Signs, 9,* 206–27.

Lopata, H. (1971). *Occupation: Housewife.* New York: Oxford University Press.

Lopata, H. (1976). Sociology. *Signs, 2,* 165–76.

Lopata, H., & Pleck, J. (Eds.). (1983). *Research in the interweave of social roles, Vol. 3: Families and jobs.* Greenwich, CT: JAI Press.

Lopata, H., & Thorne, B. (1978). On the term "sex roles." *Signs, 3,* 718–20.

Lorber, J. (1984). Trust, loyalty and the place of women in the informal organization of work. In J. Freeman (Ed.), *Women* (3rd ed., pp. 370–78). Palo Alto, CA: Mayfield.

Lothstein, L. (1982). Sex reassignment surgery: Historical, bioethical, and theoretical issues. *American Journal of Psychiatry, 139,* 417–26.

Lott, B. (1981). A feminist critique of androgyny: Toward the elimination of gender attributions for learned behavior. In C. Mayo & N. Henley (Eds.), *Gender and nonverbal behavior* (pp. 171–80). New York: Springer.

Lott, B. (1983). *The devaluation of women's competence.* Unpublished manuscript.

Lyles, J. (1979). UMC's women clergy: Sisterhood and survival. *Christian Century, 96,* 117–19.

Lynn, N. (1975). Women in American politics: An overview. In J. Freeman (Ed.), *Women* (pp. 364–85). Palo Alto, CA: Mayfield.

Lynn, N. (1984). Women and politics: The real majority. In J. Freeman (Ed.), *Women* (3rd ed., pp. 402–22). Palo Alto, CA: Mayfield.

Lynn, N., & Flora, C. (1977). Societal punishment and aspects of female political participation: 1972 National Convention delegates. In M. Githens & J. Prestage (Eds.), *A portrait of marginality* (pp. 139–49). New York: Longman.

Lyon, L., et al. (1982). The national longitudinal surveys data for labor market entry: Evaluating the small effects of racial discrimination and the large effects of sexual discrimination. *Social Problems, 29,* 524–39.

McCauley, C., Stitt, C., & Segal, M. (1980). Stereotyping: From prejudice to prediction. *Psychological Bulletin, 87,* 195–208.

McC. Dachowski, M. (1984). DSM-III: Sexism or societal reality? *American Psychologist, 39,* 702–3.

Maccoby, E., & Jacklin, C. (1974). *The psychology of sex differences.* Stanford: Stanford University Press.

McConnell, E. (1969). *The Beguines and beghards in medieval culture.* New York: Octagon Books.

McCormick, N. (1979). Come-ons and put-offs: Unmarried students' strategies for having and avoiding sexual intercourse. *Psychology of Women Quarterly, 4,* 194–211.

McCormick, N., & Jesser, C. (1983). The courtship game: Power in the sexual encounter. In E. Allgeier & N. McCormick (Eds.), *Changing boundaries* (pp. 64–86). Palo Alto, CA: Mayfield.

McGinnies, E., et al. (1974). Sex and cultural differences in perceived locus of control among students in five countries. *Journal of Consulting and Clinical Psychology, 42,* 451–55.

McGrady, M. (1975). *The kitchen sink papers: My life as a househusband.* New York: Doubleday.

McGrath, C. (1979). The crisis of the domestic order. *Socialist Review, 43,* 11–30.

McGuinness, D. (1979). How schools discriminate against boys. *Human Nature, February,* 82–88.

McGuinness, D., & Pribram, K. (1978). The origins of sensory bias in the development of gender differences in perception and cognition. In M. Bortner (Ed.), *Cognitive growth and development* (pp. 3–56). New York: Brunner/Mazel.

McKee, J., & Sherriffs, A. (1957). The differential evaluation of males and females. *Journal of Personality, 25,* 356–71.

McKee, J., & Sherriffs, A. (1959). Men's and women's beliefs, ideals, and self-concepts. *American Journal of Sociology, 64,* 356–63.

McKenna, W., & Kessler, S. (1977). Experimental design as a source of sex bias in social psychology. *Sex Roles, 3,* 117–28.

McLaughlin, E. (1974). Equality of souls, inequality of sexes: Woman in medieval theology. In R. Ruether (Ed.), *Religion and sexism* (pp. 213–66). New York: Simon and Schuster.

McLaughlin, E. (1976). Male and female in Christian tradition: Was there a reformation in the sixteenth century? In R. Barnhouse & U. Holmes, III (Eds.), *Male and female* (pp. 39–52). New York: The Seabury Press.

Macleod, D. (1983). *Building character in the American boy.* Madison: University of Wisconsin.

MacLusky, N., & Naftolin, F. (1981). Sexual differentiation of the central nervous system. *Science, 211,* 1294–1303.

Maimon, A. (1962). *Women build a land.* New York: Herzl Press.

Malamuth, N., & Check, J. (1981a). The effects of mass media exposure on acceptance of violence against women. A field experiment. *Journal of Research in Personality, 15,* 436–46.

Malamuth, N., & Check, J. (1981b). Penile tumescence and perceptual reponses to rape as a function of victim's perceived reactions. *Journal of Applied Social Psychology, 10,* 528–47.

Malamuth, N., & Donnerstein, E. (1982). The effects of aggressive-pornographic mass media stimuli. In L. Berkowitz (Ed.), *Advances in experimental social psychology* (Vol. 15). New York: Academic Press.

Malamuth, N., Haber, S., & Feshbach, S. (1980). Testing hypotheses regarding rape: Exposure to sexual violence, sex differences, and the "normality" of rapists. *Journal of Research in Personality, 14,* 121–37.

Mandelbaum, D. (1978). Women in medicine. *Signs, 4,* 136–45.

Mann, J. (1981). Women. *Washington Post, October 16,* 1.

Mann, J. (1984). Elizabeth Dole: The gender gap from the Reagan camp. *Ms., March,* 74, 76, 99.

Marecek, J. (1978). Psychological disorders in women: Indices of role strain. In I. Frieze, et al. (Eds.), *Women and sex roles* (pp. 255–76). New York: Norton.

Marini, M., & Greenberger, E. (1978). Sex differences in occupational aspirations and expectations. *Sociology of Work and Occupations, 5,* 147–78.

Markle, G. (1974). Sex ratio at birth: Values, variance, and some determinants. *Demography, 11,* 131–42.

Marotta, T. (1981). *The politics of homosexuality.* Boston: Houghton-Mifflin.

Marshall, D. (1971). Sexual behavior on Mangaia. In D. Marshall & R. Suggs (Eds.), *Human sexual behavior* (pp. 103–62). New York: Basic Books.

Marshall, S. (1984). Keep us on the pedestal: Women against feminism in twentieth-century America. In J. Freeman (Ed.), *Women* (3rd ed., pp. 568–82). Palo Alto, CA: Mayfield.

Martin, D., & Lyon, P. (1972). *Lesbian/woman.* New York: Bantam Books.

Martin, K., & Voorhies, B. (1975). *Female of the species.* New York: Columbia University Press.

Martyna, W. (1980). Beyond the "he/man" approach: The case for nonsexist language. *Signs, 5,* 482–93.

Marwell, G. (1975). Why ascription: Parts of a more-or-less formal theory of the functions and dysfunctions of sex roles. *American Sociological Review, 40,* 445–55.

Marx, K. (1964/1844). Contribution to the critique of Hegel's philosophy of right. In K. Marx & F. Engels (Eds.), *On religion* (pp. 41–58). New York: Schocken.

Maslin, A., & Davis, L. (1975). Sex-role stereotyping as a factor in mental health standards among counselors-in-training. *Journal of Counseling Psychology, 2,* 87–91.

Masling, J., & Harris, S. (1969). Sexual aspects of TAT administration. *Journal of Consulting and Clinical Psychology, 33,* 166–69.

Mauss, A. (1975). *Social problems as social movements.* Philadelphia: Lippincott.

Mayes, S. (1979). Women in positions of authority: A case study of changing sex roles. *Signs, 4,* 556–68.

Mayes, S., & Valentine, K. (1979). Sex-role stereotyping in Saturday morning cartoon shows. *Journal of Broadcasting, 23,* 41–50.

Mayo, C., & Henley, N. (Eds.). (1981). *Gender and nonverbal behavior.* Seacaucus, NJ: Springer-Verlag.

Mazumdar, V. (1978). Comment on suttee. *Signs, 4,* 269–73.

Mead, G. (1934). *Mind, self, and society.* Chicago: University of Chicago Press.

Mead, M. (1935/1963). *Sex and temperament in three primitive societies.* New York: Norton.

Mednick, M. (1975). Social change and sex-role inertia: The case of the kibbutz. In M. Mednick, S. Tangri, & L. Hoffman (Eds.), *Women and achievement* (pp. 85–103). New York: Halstead.

Mehrabian, A. (1971). Verbal and nonverbal interaction of strangers in a waiting room. *Journal of Experimental Research in Personality, 5,* 127–38.

Men's studies bibliography (3rd ed.). (1977). Cambridge, MA: Massachusetts Institute of Technology, Human Studies Collection, Humanities Library.

Mernissi, F. (1975). *Beyond the veil.* New York: Schenkman.

Merritt, S. (1982). Sex roles and political ambition. *Sex Roles, 8,* 1025–36.

Merton, R. (1968). *Social theory and social structure.* New York: Free Press.

Messenger, J. (1971). Sex and repression in an Irish folk community. In D. Marshall & R. Suggs (Eds.), *Human sexual behavior* (pp. 3–37) New York: Basic Books.

Meyer, J., & Hoopes, J. (1974). The gender dysphoria syndromes: A position statement on so-called "transsexualism." *Plastic and Reconstructive Surgery, 54,* 444–51.

Meyer, J., & Reter, D. (1979). Sex reassignment. *Archives of General Psychiatry, 36,* 1010–15.

Meyer-Bahlburg, H., et al. (1974). Aggressiveness and testosterone measures in man. *Psychosomatic Medicine, 36,* 269–74.

Miller, D., & Swanson, G. (1960). *Inner conflict and defense.* New York: Holt.

Miller, J. (1982). Psychological recovery in low-income single parents. *American Journal of Orthopsychiatry, 52,* 346–52.

Miller, J., & Garrison, H. (1982). Sex roles: The division of labor at home and in the workplace. In R. Turner & J. Short (Eds.), *Annual review of sociology* (Vol. 8, pp. 237–62). Palo Alto, CA: Annual Reviews.

Millett, K. (1972). *Sexual politics.* London: Abacus.

Minton, C., Kagan, J., & Levine, J. (1971). Maternal control and obedience in the two-year-old child. *Child Development, 42,* 1873–94.

Minuchin, S., Rosman, B., & Baker, L. (1978). *Psychosomatic families.* Cambridge, MA.: Harvard University Press.

Mischel, W. (1966). A social-learning view of sex differences in behavior. In E. Maccoby (Ed.), *The development of sex differences* (pp. 56–81). Stanford: Stanford University Press.

Mischel, W. (1970). Sex-typing and socialization. In P. Mussen (Ed.), *Carmichael's manual of child development.* New York: Wiley.

Mitchell, J. (1974). *Psychoanalysis and feminism.* New York: Pantheon.

Model, S. (1982). Housework by husbands: Determinants and implications. In J. Aldous (Ed.), *Two paychecks* (pp. 193–205). Beverly Hills, CA: Sage.

Modleski, T. (1980). The disappearing act: A study of Harlequin romances. *Signs, 5,* 435–48.

Money, J. (1964). Two cytogenetic syndromes: Psychologic comparisons. 1. Intelligence and specific-factor quotients. *Journal of Psychiatric Research, 2,* 223–31.

Money, J. (1973). Prenatal hormones and postnatal socialization in gender identity differentiation. In J. Cole & R. Dienstbier (Eds.), *Nebraska symposium on motivation 1973* (pp. 221–95). Lincoln: University of Nebraska Press.

Money, J. (1975a). Ablatio penis: Normal male infant sex-reassigned as a girl. *Archives of Sexual Behavior, 4,* 65–72.

Money, J. (1975b). Hormones, gender identity and behavior. In B. Eleftheriou & R. Spratt (Eds.), *Hormonal correlates of behavior.* New York: Plenum.

Money, J. (1980). *Love and lovesickness.* Baltimore: Johns Hopkins University Press.

Money, J., & Ehrhardt, A. (1972). *Man and woman, boy and girl.* Baltimore: Johns Hopkins University Press.

Money, J., & Granoff, D. (1965). IQ and the somatic stigmata of Turner's syndrome. *American Journal of Mental Deficiency, 70,* 69–77.

Money, J., & Tucker, P. (1975). *Sexual signatures.* Boston: Little, Brown.

Money, J., & Wiedeking, C. (1980). Gender identity/role: Normal differentiation and its transpositions. In B. Wolman & J. Money (Eds.), *Handbook of human sexuality* (pp. 269–84). Englewood Cliffs, NJ: Prentice-Hall.

Montagu, A. (1952). *The natural superiority of women.* New York: Collier Books.

Monti, P., Brown, W., & Corriveau, D. (1977). Testosterone and components of aggressive and sexual behavior in man. *American Journal of Psychiatry, 134,* 692–94.

Morgan, M. (1975). *The total woman.* New York: Pocket Books.

Morgan, R., & Steinem, G. (1980). The international crime of genital mutilation. *Ms., March,* 65–68.

Morris, J. (1974). *Conundrum.* New York: Signet Books.

Mowbray, C., Lanir, S., & Hulce, M. (Eds.). (1984). *Women and mental health.* New York: Haworth Press.

Moyer, K. (1978). Sex differences in aggression. In R. Friedman, et al. (Eds.), *Sex differences in behavior* (pp. 335–72). Huntington, NY: Krieger Publishing.

Ms. (1984). Special issue on men. *August.*

Mueller, M. (1977). Women and men, power and powerlessness in Lesotho. *Signs, 3,* 154–66.

Murdock, G. (1937). Comparative data on the division of labor by sex. *Social Forces, May,* 551–53.

Murdock, G. (1945). The common denominator of cultures. In R. Linton (Ed.), *The science of man in the world crisis* (pp. 123–42). New York: Columbia University Press.

Mussen, P., Conger, J., & Kagen, J. (1974). *Child development and personality.* New York: Harper and Row.

Myrdal, A. (1971). Forward. In E. Dahlstrom (Ed.), *The changing roles of men and women* (pp. 9–18). Boston: Beacon Press.

Myrdal, A., & Klein, V. (1956). *Women's two roles: Home and work.* London: Routledge.

Nadelman, L. (1974). Sex identity in American children: Memory, knowledge and preference tests. *Developmental Psychology, 10,* 413–17.

Narus, L., & Fischer, J. (1982). Strong but not silent: A reexamination of expressivity in the relationship of men. *Sex Roles, 8,* 159–68.

Nash, J. (1978). The Aztecs and the ideology of male dominance. *Signs, 4,* 349–62.

Nash, S. (1975). The relationship among sex-role stereotyping, sex-role preference, and the sex difference in spatial visualization. *Sex Roles, 1,* 15–32.

Neal, M. (1979). Women in religious symbolism and organization. *Sociological Inquiry, 49,* 218–50.

Newcombe, N., & Arnkoff, D. (1979). Effects of speech style and sex of speaker on person perception. *Journal of Personality and Social Psychology, 37,* 1293–1303.

Newman, L., & Stoller, R. (1974). Nontranssexual men who seek sex reassignment. *American Journal of Psychiatry, 131,* 437–41.

Newton, E. (1984). The mythic mannish lesbian: Radclyff Hall and the new woman. *Signs, 9,* 557–75.

The New York Times/CBS Poll. (1984). Portrait of the electorate. *The New York Times, November 8,* 11.

Nichols, J. (1975). *Men's liberation.* New York: Penguin.

Nielsen, J., & Christensen, A. (1974). Thirty-five males with double Y chromosome. *Journal of Psychological Medicine, 4,* 37–38.

Nigg, J., & Axelrod, M. (1981). Women and minorities in the PSA region. *Sociological Review, 24,* 107–28.

Nilsen, A., et al. (1977). *Sexism and language.* Urbana, IL: National Council of Teachers of English.

Noel, B., et al. (1974). The XYY syndrome: Reality or myth? *Clinical Genetics, 5,* 387–94.

Norgren, J. (1984). Child care. In J. Freeman (Ed.), *Women* (3rd ed., pp. 139–53). Palo Alto, CA: Mayfield.

Norton, M. (1980). *The revolutionary experience of American women, 1750–1800.* Boston: Little, Brown.

Norton, M., et al. (1982). *A people and a nation* (Vol. I). Boston: Houghton Mifflin.

Oakley, A. (1972). *Sex, gender and society.* New York: Harper and Row.

O'Brient, J. (1971). Violence in divorce-prone families. *Journal of Marriage and the Family, 33,* 692–98.

Olien, M. (1978). *The human myth.* New York: Harper and Row.

O'Neill, W. (1971). *Everyone was brave.* Chicago: Quadrangle.

Orlinsky, D., & Howard, K. (1976). The effects of sex of therapist on the therapeutic experience of women. *Psychotherapy: Theory, Research and Practice, 13,* 82–88.

Orne, M. (1962). On the social psychology of the psychological experiment: With particular reference to demand characteristics and their implications. *American Psychologist, 17,* 776–83.

Owen, D. (1972). The 47,XYY male: A review. *Psychological Bulletin, 78,* 209–33.

Pagelow, M. (1981). Sex roles, power, and woman battering. In L. Bowker (Ed.), *Women and crime in America.* New York: Macmillian.

Pagels, E. (1976). What became of God the mother? Conflicting images of God in early Christianity. *Signs, 2,* 293–303.

Paige, K. (1973). Women learn to sing the menstrual blues. *Psychology Today, April,* 41–46.

Paige, K. (1983). Virginity rituals and chastity control during puberty: Cross-cultural patterns. In S. Golub (Ed.), *Menarche* (pp. 155–74). Lexington, MA: Lexington Books.

Paludi, M., & Bauer, W. (1983). Goldberg revisited: What's in an author's name. *Sex Roles, 9,* 387–90.

Panek, P., Rush, M., & Greenawalt, J. (1977). Current sex stereotypes of 25 occupations. *Psychological Reports, 40,* 212–14.

Papanek, H. (1973). Purdah: Separate worlds and symbolic shelter. *Comparative Studies in Society and History, 15(3),* 289–325.

Parke, R., & O'Leary, S. (1975). Father-mother-infant interaction in the newborn period. In K. Riegel & J. Meacham (Eds.), *The developing individual in a changing world* (Vol. II). The Hague: Mouton.

Parlee, M. (1973). The premenstrual syndrome. *Psychological Bulletin, 80,* 454–65.

Parlee, M. (1975). Psychology. *Signs, 1,* 119–38.

Parlee, M. (1979). Psychology and women. *Signs, 5,* 121–33.

Parlee, M. (1981). Appropriate control groups in feminist research. *Psychology of Women Quarterly, 5,* 637–44.

Parsons, T. (1971). *The system of modern societies.* Englewood Cliffs, NJ: Prentice-Hall.

Parsons, T., & Bales, R. (1955). *Family, socialization and interaction process.* New York: Free Press.

Parvey, C. (1974). The theology and leadership of women in the New Testament. In R. Ruether (Ed.), *Religion and sexism* (pp. 117–49). New York: Simon and Schuster.

Pauly, I. (1968). The current status of the change of sex operation. *Journal of Nervous and Mental Disorders, 147,* 460–71.

Pauly, I. (1974). Female transsexualism: Part I. *Archives of Sexual Behavior, 3,* 487–507.

Payton, I. (1982). Single-parent households: An alternative approach. *Family Economics Review, Winter,* 11–16.

Pearson, J. (1985). *Gender and communication.* Dubuque, IA: Wm. C. Brown Publishers.

Peck, E., & Senderowitz, J. (Eds.). (1974). *Pronatalism.* New York: Crowell.

Pennington, V. (1957). Meprobamate (Miltown) in premenstrual tension. *Journal of the American Medical Association, 164,* 638.

Peplau, L. (1983). Roles and gender. In H. Kelley, et al. (Eds.), *Close relationships* (pp. 220–64). New York: W. H. Freeman.

Peplau, L., Rubin, Z., & Hill, C. (1976). The sexual balance of power. *Psychology Today, 10,* 142–47.

Peplau, L., Rubin, Z., & Hill, C. (1977). Sexual intimacy in dating relationships. *Journal of Social Issues, 33,* 86–109.

Perrucci, C., Potter, H., & Rhoads, D. (1978). Determinants of male family role performance. *Psychology of Women Quarterly, 3,* 53–66.

Perry, L. (1979). "Progress, not pleasure, is our aim": The sexual advice of an antebellum radical. *Journal of Social History, 12,* 354–67.

Persky, H. (1978). Reproductive hormones, moods, and the menstrual cycle. In R. Friedman, et al. (Eds.), *Sex differences in behavior* (pp. 455–66). Huntington, NY: Krieger Publishing.

Persky, H., Smith, K., & Basu, G. (1971). Relation of psychologic measures of aggression and hostility to testosterone production in man. *Psychosomatic Medicine, 33,* 265–77.

Persky, H., et al. (1977). The effect of alcohol and smoking on testosterone function and aggression in chronic alcoholics. *American Journal of Psychiatry, 134,* 621–25.

Peterson, C., & Peterson, J. (1973). Preference for sex of offspring as a measure of change in sex attitudes. *Psychology, 10,* 3–5.

Petty, R., & Mirels, H. (1981). Intimacy and scarcity of self-disclosure: Effects on interpersonal attraction for males and females. *Personality and Social Psychology Bulletin, 7,* 490–503.

Pfeiffer, J. (1969). *The emergence of man.* New York: Harper and Row.

Phares, E. (1976). *Locus of control in personality.* Morristown, NJ: General Learning Press.

Phelps, L. (1979). Female sexual alienation. In J. Freeman (Ed.), *Women* (2nd ed.). Palo Alto, CA: Mayfield.

Pheterson, G., Kiesler, S., & Goldberg, P. (1971). Evaluation of the performance of women as a function of their sex, achievement, and personal history. *Journal of Personality and Social Psychology, 19,* 114–18.

Phillips, C., & Hogan, P. (1984). The wages of history. *History News, 39(8),* 6–10.

Phoenix, C. (1978). Prenatal testosterone in the nonhuman primate and its consequences for behavior. In R. Friedman, et al. (Eds.), *Sex differences in behavior* (pp. 19–32). Huntington, NY: Krieger Publishing.

Piaget, J. (1948). *The moral judgement of the child.* Glencoe, IL: Free Press.

Piliavin, J., & Martin, R. (1978). The effects of the sex composition of groups on style of social interaction. *Sex Roles, 4,* 281–96.

Pines, M. (1978). Is sociobiology all wet? *Psychology Today, May,* 23–24.

Pizzey, E. (1974). *Scream quietly or the neighbors will hear.* Baltimore: Penguin.

Pleck, E. (1976). Two worlds in one: Work and family. *Journal of Social History, 10,* 178–95.

Pleck, E. (1979). Wife beating in the 19th century. *Victimology, 4,* 60–74.

Pleck, E., et al. (1977–78). The battered data syndrome: A comment on Steinmetz article. *Victimology, 2,* 680–83.

Pleck, E., & Pleck, J. (1980). *The American man.* Englewood Cliffs, NJ: Prentice-Hall.

Pleck, J. (1974). My male sex role—and ours. *WIN Magazine, April 11,* 8–12.

Pleck, J. (1975). Masculinity-femininity: Current and alternate paradigms. *Sex Roles, 1,* 161–78.

Pleck, J. (1976). The male sex role: Definitions, problems, and sources of change. *Journal of Social Issues, 32,* 155–64.

Pleck, J. (1981). *The myth of masculinity.* Cambridge: The MIT Press.

Pleck, J. (1983). Husbands' paid work and family roles: Current research issues. In H. Lopata & J. Pleck (Eds.), *Research in the interweave of social roles, Vol. 3: Families and jobs* (pp. 251–333). Greenwich, CT: JAI Press.

Pleck, J. (1984). The theory of male sex role identity: Its rise and fall, 1936 to the present. In M. Lewis (Ed.), *In the shadow of the past* (pp. 205–25). New York: Columbia University Press.

Pleck, J., & Sawyer, J. (1974). *Men and masculinity.* Englewood Cliffs, NJ: Prentice-Hall.

Pleck, J., Staines, G., & Lang, L. (1980). Conflict between work and family life. *Monthly Labor Review, March,* 29–32.

Pohlman, E. (1969). *The psychology of birth planning.* Cambridge, MA: Schenkman.

Polani, P. (1972). Errors of sex determination and sex chromosome anomalies. In C. Ounsted & D. Taylor (Eds.), *Gender differences* (pp. 13–39). London: Churchill Livingstone.

Pomazal, R., & Clore, G. (1973). Helping on the highway: The effects of dependency and sex. *Journal of Applied Social Psychology, 3,* 150–64.

Pope, K., Levenson, H., & Schover, L. (1979). Sexual intimacies in psychology training. *American Psychologist, 34,* 682–89.

Prial, F. (1982). More women work at traditional male jobs. *The New York Times, November 11,* A1, C20.

Psychology of Women Quarterly. (1979). Psychological androgyny: Further considerations. *3,* 221–315.

Ptacek, J. (1980). Herb Goldberg and the politics of "Free Men." *M. 2,* 10–11.

Pyle, R., Mitchell, J., & Eckert, E. (1981). Bulimia: A report of 34 cases. *Journal of Clinical Psychiatry, 42,* 60–64.

Quinn, J. (1984). Comparable pay for women. *Newsweek, January 16,* 66.

Rabin, A. (1970). The sexes: Ideology and reality in the Israeli kibbutz. In G. Seward & R. Williamson (Eds.), *Sex roles in a changing society* (pp. 285–307). New York: Random House.

Rabiner, S. (1976). How the superwoman myth puts women down. *The Village Voice, May 24.*

Radin, N. (1981). The role of the father in cognitive, academic, and intellectual development. In M. Lamb (Ed.), *The role of the father in child development* (Vol. II). New York: Wiley.

Radloff, L. (1975). Sex differences in depression: The effects of occupation and marital status. *Sex Roles, 1,* 249–65.

Raven, B. (1965). Social influence and power. In I. Steiner & M. Fishbein (Eds.), *Current studies in social psychology.* New York: Holt, Rinehart and Winston.

Rawlings, E., & Carter, D. (Eds.). (1977). *Psychotherapy for women.* Springfield, IL: Thomas.

Reed, B., & Garvin, C. (Eds.). (1983). *Groupwork with women/groupwork with men.* New York: Haworth Press.

Regan, M., & Roland, H. (1982). University students: A change in expectations and aspirations over the decade. *Sociology of Education, 55,* 223–28.

Reinartz, K. (1975). The paper doll: Images of American women in popular songs. In J. Freeman (Ed.), *Women* (pp. 293–308). Palo Alto, CA: Mayfield.

Remick, H. (Ed.). (1984). *Comparable worth and wage discrimination.* Philadelphia: Temple University Press.

Rendely, J., Holmstrom, R., & Karp, S. (1984). The relationship of sex-role identity, life style, and mental health in suburban American homemakers: 1. Sex role, employment and adjustment. *Sex Roles, 11,* 839–48.

Rent, C., & Rent, G. (1977). More on offspring-sex preference: A comment on Nancy E. Williamson's "Sex preferences, sex control, and the status of women" (vol.1, no. 4). *Signs, 3,* 505–13.

Rheingold, H., & Cook, K. (1975). The contents of boys' and girls' rooms as an index of parents' behaviors. *Child Development, 46,* 459–63.

Rhodes, A. (1983). Effects of religious denomination on sex differences in occupational expectations. *Sex Roles, 9,* 93–108.

Rideau, W., & Sinclair, B. (1982). Prison: The sexual jungle. In A. Scacco, Jr. (Ed.), *Male rape* (pp. 3–29). New York: AMS Press.

Riger, S., & Gordon, M. (1979). The structure of rape prevention beliefs. *Personality and Social Psychology Bulletin, 5,* 186–90.

Robbins, J., & Siegel, R. (Eds.). (1983). *Women changing therapy.* New York: Haworth Press.

Robbins, P., & Tanck, R. (1984). Sex differences in problems related to depression. *Sex Roles, 11,* 703–7.

Robinson, J. (1980). Housework technology and household work. In S. Berk (Ed.), *Women and household labor.* Beverly Hills, CA: Sage.

Rodman, H., & Safilios-Rothschild, C. (1983). Weak links in men's worker-earner roles: A comparative perspective. In H. Lopata & J. Pleck (Eds.), *Research in the interweave of social roles, Vol. 3: Families and jobs.* Greenwich, CT: JAI Press.

Rogan, A. (1978). The threat of sociobiology. *Quest, 4,* 85–93.

Rogers, L. (1983). Hormonal theories for sex differences—politics disguised as science: A reply to DeBold and Luria. *Sex Roles, 9,* 1109–13.

Rogers, L., & Walsh, J. (1982). Shortcomings of the psychomedical research of John Money and co-workers into sex differences in behavior: Social and political implications. *Sex Roles, 8,* 269–81.

Rohrbaugh, J. (1979). *Women.* New York: Basic Books.

Rorvik, D., & Shettles, L. (1970). *Your baby's sex.* New York: Dodd, Mead and Co.

Rosaldo, M. (1974). Woman, culture, and society: A theoretical overview. In M. Rosaldo & L. Lamphere (Eds.), *Woman, culture, and society* (pp. 17–42). Stanford: Stanford University Press.

Rosaldo, M., & Lamphere, L. (Eds.). (1974). *Woman, culture, and society.* Stanford: Stanford University Press.

Rosenfield, S. (1980). Sex differences in depression: Do women always have higher rates? *Journal of Health and Social Behavior, 21,* 33–42.

Rosenkrantz, P., et al. (1968). Sex-role stereotypes and self-concepts in college students. *Journal of Consulting and Clinical Psychology, 32,* 287–95.

Rosenthal, R. (1976). *Experimenter effects in behavioral research.* New York: Halstead Press.

Rosenthal, R. (1979). The "file drawer problem" and tolerance for null results. *Psychological Bulletin, 86,* 638–41.

Rosenthal, R., & Jacobson, L. (1968). *Pygmalion in the classroom.* New York: Holt, Rinehart and Winston.

Rossi, A. (1964). Equality between the sexes: An immodest proposal. *Daedalus (Spring),* 607–52.

Rossi, A. (1968). Transition to parenthood. *Journal of Marriage and the Family, 30,* 26–39.

Rossi, A. (1977). A biosocial perspective on parenting. *Daedalus, 106(2),* 1–31.

Rossi, A. (1982). *Feminists in politics.* New York: Academic Press.

Rossi, A. (1983a). Beyond the gender gap: Women's bid for political power. *Social Science Quarterly, 64,* 718–33.

Rossi, A. (1983b). *Season's of a woman's life.* Amherst: Social and Demographic Research Institute, University of Massachusetts.

Rossi, A. (1984). Gender and parenthood. *American Sociological Review, 49,* 1–19.

Rossi, A., & Calderwood, A. (Eds.). (1973). *Academic women on the move.* New York: Russell Sage Foundation.

Rossi, A., & Rossi, P. (1977). Body time and social time: Mood patterns by menstrual cycle and day of week. *Social Science Research, 6,* 273–308.

Rotter, J. (1966). Generalized expectancies for internal vs. external control of reinforcement. *Psychological Monographs, 80,* 1–28.

Rounsaville, B. (1978). Theories in marital violence: Evidence from a study of battered women. *Victimology, 3,* 11–31.

Rowbotham, S. (1973). *Woman's consciousness: Man's world.* Baltimore: Penguin Books.

Rowbotham, S., & Weeks, J. (1980). *Socialism and the new life.* New York: Pluto Press.

Royko, M. (1984). U.S. has corned the wimp market. *The Knoxville News-Sentinel, April 21,* A5.

Rubenstein, C. (1982). Real men don't earn less than their wives. *Psychology Today, November,* 36–38, 40–41.

Rubin, J., Provenzano, F., & Luria, Z. (1974). The eye of the beholder: Parents' views on sex of newborns. *American Journal of Orthopsychiatry, 44,* 512–19.

Rubin, Z. (1983). Are working wives hazardous to their husbands' mental health? *Psychology Today, May,* 70–72.

Ruble, T. (1983). Sex stereotypes: Issues of change in the 1970s. *Sex Roles, 9,* 397–402.

Ruether, R. (Ed.). (1974a). *Religion and sexism.* New York: Simon and Schuster.

Ruether, R. (1974b). Misogynism and virginal feminism in the fathers of the church. In R. Ruether (Ed.), *Religion and sexism* (pp. 150–83). New York: Simon and Schuster.

Ruether, R., & Bianchi, E. (1976). *From machismo to mutuality.* New York: Paulist Press.

Ruether, R., & McLaughlin, E. (Eds.). (1979). *Woman of spirit.* New York: Simon and Schuster.

Rush, F. (1980). *The best kept secret.* New York: McGraw-Hill.

Russell, D. (1973). Rape and the masculine mystique. Paper presented at the American Sociological Association, New York.

Russell, D. (1975). *The politics of rape.* New York: Stein & Day.

Russell, D. (1984). *Sexual exploitation.* Beverly Hills, CA: Sage.

Russell, L. (1974). *Human liberation in a feminist perspective.* Philadelphia: Westminster Press.

Russell, L. (Ed.). (1976). *The liberating word.* Philadelphia: Westminster Press.

Russo, N. (1975). Eye contact, interpersonal distance, and the equilibrium theory. *Journal of Personality and Social Psychology, 31,* 497–502.

Russo, N. (1976). The motherhood mandate. *Journal of Social Issues, 32,* 143–53.

Russo, N. (1979). Overview: Sex roles, fertility, and the motherhood mandate. *Psychology of Women Quarterly, 4,* 7–15.

Sabatelli, R., Buck, R., & Dreyer, A. (1980). Communication via facial cues in intimate dyads. *Personality and Social Psychology Bulletin, 6,* 242–48.

Sabatelli, R., Buck, R., & Dreyer, A. (1982). Nonverbal communication accuracy in married couples: Relationship with marital complaints. *Journal of Personality and Social Psychology, 43,* 1088–97.

Sadker, D. (1977). *Being a man.* Washington, DC: U.S. Government Printing Office.

Saeger, S., & Hart, R. (1976). The development of environmental competence in girls and boys. In P. Burnet (Ed.), *Women in society.* Chicago: Maaroufa Press.

Sampson, E. (1977). Psychology and the American ideal. *Journal of Personality and Social Psychology, 35,* 767–82.

Sampson, E. (1978). Scientific paradigms and social values. *Journal of Personality and Social Psychology, 36,* 1332–43.

Sanday, P. (1973). Toward a theory of the status of women. *American Anthropologist, 75,* 1682–1700.

Sandler, B. (1981). Summary of proposed amendments to Title IX: Impact on postsecondary institutions. *Project on the status of women.* Washington, DC: Association of American Colleges.

Sapp, S. (1977). *Sexuality, the Bible and science.* Philadelphia: Fortress Press.

Sawyer, J. (1970). On male liberation. *Liberation, 15,* 32–33.

Scacco, Jr., A. (1982). *Male rape.* New York: AMS Press.

Scanzoni, J. (1972). *Sexual bargaining.* Englewood Cliffs, NJ: Prentice-Hall.

Scanzoni, L., & Scanzoni, J. (1981). *Men, women and change* (2nd ed.). New York: McGraw-Hill.

Scarf, M. (1980). The promiscuous woman. *Psychology Today, July, 78,* 80, 83–84, 87.

Schaef, A. (1981). *Women's reality.* Minneapolis: Winston Press.

Schaffer, K. (1981). *Sex roles and human behavior.* Cambridge, MA: Winthrop Publishers.

Scharf, L. (1980). *To work and to wed.* Westport, CT: Greenwood Press.

Schlafly, P. (1977). *The power of the positive woman.* New York: Harcourt Brace Jovanovich.

Schlafly, P. (1981). Testimony. *Sex discrimination in the work place, 1981* (pp. 400–427). Washington, DC: U.S. Government Printing Office.

Schlesier-Stropp, B. (1984). Bulimia: A review of the literature. *Psychological Bulletin, 95,* 247–57.

Schneider, J., & Hacker, S. (1973). Sex role imagery and the use of the generic "man" in introductory texts. *American Sociologist, 8(8),* 12–18.

Schneider, J., & Schneider-Düker, M. (1984). Sex roles and nonverbal sensitivity. *The Journal of Social Psychology, 122,* 281–82.

Schreiber, E. (1978). Education and change in American opinions on a woman for president. *Public Opinion Quarterly, 42,* 178.

Schuckit, M., et al. (1975). Premenstrual symptoms and depression in a university population. *Diseases of the Nervous System, 36,* 516–17.

Schwabacker, S. (1972). Male vs. female representation in psychological research: An examination of the *Journal of Personality and Social Psychology, 1970, 1971.* JSAS *Catalog of Selected Documents in Psychology, 2,* 20–21.

Schwendinger, J., & Schwendinger, H. (1983). *Rape and inequality.* Beverly Hills, CA: Sage.

Scott, A. (1970). *The southern lady.* Chicago: University of Chicago Press.

Scott, J. (1982). The mechanization of women's work. *Scientific American, 247,* 167–87.

Sears, R., Maccoby, E., & Levin, H. (1957). *Patterns of child rearing.* White Plains, NY: Row, Peterson.

Sears, R., Rau, L., & Alpert, R. (1965). *Identification and child rearing.* Stanford: Stanford University Press.

Seavey, C., Katz, P., & Zalk, S. (1975). Baby X: The effect of gender labels on adult responses to infants. *Sex Roles, 1,* 103–9.

Sedugin, P. (1973). *New Soviet legislation on marriage and the family.* Moscow: Progress Publishers.

Seiden, A. (1976). Overview: Research on the psychology of women. II. Women in families, work, and psychotherapy. *The American Journal of Psychiatry, 133,* 1111–23.

Seligman, M. (1975). *Helplessness.* San Francisco: W. H. Freeman.

Sell, R., Roghmann, K., & Doherty, R. (1978). Attitudes toward abortion and prenatal diagnosis of fetal abnormalities: Implications for educational programs. *Social Biology, 25,* 288–301.

Serbin, L., et al. (1973). A comparison of teacher response to the preacademic and problem behavior of boys and girls. *Child Development, 44,* 796–804.

Sexias, F., & Cadoret, R. (1974). What is the alcoholic man? *New York Academy of Sciences, 223* (April 15), 13–14.

Sex Roles. (1979). Androgyny. *5,* 703–840.

Sexton, P. (1969). *The feminized male.* New York: Random House.

Shaevitz, M. (1984). *The superwoman syndrome.* New York: Warner Books.

Shapiro, J. (1980). The battle of the sexes. *Science, 207(March 14),* 1193–94.

Shapiro, J. (1981). Anthropology and the study of gender. *Soundings, 64,* 446–65.

Sharma, U. (1978). Women and their affairs: The veil as a symbol of separation. *Man, 13,* 218–33.

Shaver, P. (1976). Questions concerning fear of success and its conceptual relatives. *Sex Roles, 2,* 305–20.

Shehan, C. (1984). Wives' work and psychological well-being: An extension of Gove's social role theory of depression. *Sex Roles, 11,* 881–99.

Sheils, M. (1983). A portrait of America. *Newsweek, January 17,* 20–33.

Sherif, C. (1976). *Orientation in social psychology.* New York: Harper & Row.

Sherif, C. (1979). Bias in psychology. In J. Sherman & E. Beck (Eds.), *The prism of sex.* Madison, WI: University of Wisconsin Press.

Sherif, C. (1980). A social psychological perspective on the menstrual cycle. In J. Parson (Ed.), *The psychobiology of sex differences and sex roles* (pp. 245–68). New York: McGraw-Hill, Hemisphere.

Sherif, C. (1982). Needed concepts in the study of gender identity. *Psychology of Women Quarterly, 6*, 375–98.

Sherman, J. (1971). *On the psychology of women.* Springfield, IL: Thomas.

Sherman, J. (1978). *Sex-related cognitive differences.* Springfield, IL: Thomas.

Sherman, J. (1980). Therapist attitudes and sex-role stereotyping. In A. Brodsky & R. Hare-Mustin (Eds.), *Women and psychotherapy.* New York: Guilford.

Sherman, J. (1982a). Mathematics the critical filter: A look at some residues. *Psychology of Women Quarterly, 6*, 428–44.

Sherman, J. (1982b). Continuing in mathematics: A longitudinal study of the attitudes of high school girls. *Psychology of Women Quarterly, 7*, 132–40.

Sherman, J. (1983). Girls talk about mathematics and their future: A partial replication. *Psychology of Women Quarterly, 7*, 338–42.

Sherman, J., Koufacos, C., & Kenworthy, J. (1978). Therapists: Their attitudes and information about women. *Psychology of Women Quarterly, 2*, 299–313.

Shields, S. (1975). Functionalism, Darwinism, and the psychology of women: A study in social myth. *American Psychologist, 30*, 739–54.

Shields, S. (1982). The variability hypothesis: The history of a biological model of sex differences in intelligence. *Signs, 7*, 769–97.

Shinar, E. (1978). Person perception as a function of occupation and sex. *Sex Roles, 4*, 679–93.

Sidorowicz, L., & Lunney, C. (1980). Baby X revisited. *Sex Roles, 6*, 67–73.

Sigalow, S., & Reuter, J. (1975). Sex-role stereotyping and preference for activities in elementary children. Paper presented at the meeting of the Midwestern Psychological Association, Chicago.

Silverman, C. (1968). *The epidemiology of depression.* Baltimore: Johns Hopkins University Press.

Simmel, G. (1955). *Conflict and the web of group affiliations.* New York: Free Press.

Simmons, R., & Rosenberg, F. (1975). Sex, sex roles, and self-image. *Journal of Youth and Adolescence, 4*, 229–58.

Simpson, I., & England, P. (1982). Conjugal work roles and marital solidarity. In J. Aldous (Ed.), *Two paychecks* (pp. 147–71). Beverly Hills, CA: Sage.

Singer, J., Westphal, M., & Niswander, K. (1968). Sex differences in the incidence of neonatal abnormalities and abnormal performances in early childhood. *Child Development, 39*, 103–12.

Skrypnek, B., & Synder, M. (1982). On the self-perpetuating nature of stereotypes about women and men. *Journal of Experimental Social Psychology, 18*, 277–91.

Slocum, W., & Nye, F. (1976). Provider and housekeeper roles. In F. Nye (Ed.), *Role structure and analysis of the family.* Beverly Hills, CA: Sage.

Smeal, E. (1984). *Why and how women will elect the next president.* New York: Harper & Row.

Smith, M. (1980). Sex bias in counseling and psychotherapy. *Psychological Bulletin, 87*, 392–407.

Smith, P. (1979). Sex markers in speech. In K. Scherer & H. Giles (Eds.), *Social markers in speech* (pp. 134–37). Cambridge: Cambridge University Press.

Smith, R. (1978). *The psychopath in society.* New York: Academic Press.

Snell, J., Rosenwald, R., & Robey, A. (1964). The wifebeater's wife: A study of family interaction. *Archives of General Psychiatry, 11*, 107–13.

Snodgrass, J. (1977). *For men against sexism.* Albion, CA: Times Change Press.

Snyder, M., & Swann, W. (1978). Behavioral confirmation in social interaction: From social perception to social reality. *Journal of Experimental Social Psychology, 14*, 148–62.

Snyder, M., Tanke, E., & Berscheid, E. (1977). Social perception and interpersonal behavior: On the self-fulfilling nature of social stereotypes. *Journal of Personality and Social Psychology, 35*, 656–66.

Sokoloff, N. (1980). *Between money and love.* New York: Praeger.

Sommer, B. (1984). PMS in the courts: Are all women on trial? *Psychology Today, August*, 36–38.

Sopchak, A., & Sutherland, A. (1960). Psychological impact of cancer and its treatment, VII: Exogenous sex hormones and their relation to life-long adaptations in women with metastatic cancer of the breast. *Cancer, 5*, 857–72.

Speizer, J. (1981). Role models, mentors, and sponsors: The elusive concepts. *Signs, 6*, 692–712.

Spence, J., & Helmreich, R. (1978). *Masculinity and femininity.* Austin: University of Texas Press.

Spence, J., Helmreich, R., & Stapp, J. (1974). The personal attributes questionnaire. JSAS *Catalog of Selected Documents in Psychology, 4*, 127.

Spender, D. (1980). *Man made language.* London: Routledge and Kegan Paul.

Spiro, M. (1971). *Kibbutz.* New York: Schocken Books.

Stacy, J. (1975). When patriarchy kowtows: The significance of the Chinese family revolution for feminist theory. *Feminist Studies, 2*, 64–112.

Staines, G., & Pleck, J. (1983). *The impact of work schedules on the family.* Ann Arbor, MI: Institute for Social Research, University of Michigan.

Stanley, J. (1977). Paradigmatic woman: The prostitute. In D. Shores (Ed.), *Papers in language variation.* Birmingham: University of Alabama Press.

Starr, P. (1983). *The social transformation of American medicine.* New York: Basic Books.

Stearns, P. (1979). *Be a man! Males in modern society.* New York: Holmes & Meier.

Steiger, J. (1981). The influence of the feminist subculture in changing sex-role attitudes. *Sex Roles, 7*, 627–33.

Steil, J. (1984). Marital relationships and mental health: The psychic costs of inequality. In J. Freeman (Ed.), *Women* (3rd ed., pp. 113–23). Palo Alto, CA: Mayfield.

Stein, D. (1978). Women to burn: Suttee as a normative institution. *Signs, 4*, 253–68.

Steinem, G. (1984). How women live, vote, think. *Ms., July*, 51–54.

Steinmetz, S. (1977). Wife beating, husband beating: A comparison of the use of physical violence between spouses to resolve marital fights. In M. Roy (Ed.), *Battered women.* New York: Van Nostrand Reinhold.

Steinmetz, S. (1977–78). The battered husband syndrome. *Victimology, 2,* 499–509.

Steinmetz, S. (1978). Violence between family members. *Marriage and Family Review, 1,* 3–16.

Stephenson, P., & Walker, G. (1979). The psychiatrist-woman patient relationship. *Canadian Journal of Psychiatry, 24,* 5–16.

Stericker, A. (1981). Does this "he or she" business really make a difference? The effect of masculine pronouns as generics on job attitudes. *Sex Role, 7,* 637–41.

Sterling, J. (1984). Male anorexia nervosa: Issues in diagnosis and treatment. Paper presented at the Southeastern Psychological Association, New Orleans.

Steward, M., Steward, D., & Dary, J. (1983). Women who choose a man's career: A study of women in ministry. *Psychology of Women Quarterly, 8,* 166–73.

Stewart, D. (1980). The women's movement in France. *Signs, 6,* 350–54.

Stier, D., & Hall, J. (1984). Gender differences in touch: An empirical and theoretical review. *Journal of Personality and Social Psychology, 47,* 440–59.

Straus, M. (1980). A sociological perspective on the causes of family violence. In M. Green (Ed.), *Violence in the family.* Boulder, CO: Westview Press.

Straus, M., Gelles, R., & Steinmetz, S. (1980). *Behind closed doors.* New York: Doubleday.

Stricker, G. (1977). Implications of research for psychotherapeutic treatment of women. *American Psychologist, 32,* 14–22.

Strober, M., & Tyack, D. (1980). Why do women teach and men manage? A report on research on schools. *Signs, 5,* 494–503.

Strodtbeck, F. (1951). Husband-wife interaction over revealed differences. *American Sociological Review, 16,* 468–73.

Stroebe, M., & Stroebe, W. (1983). Who suffers more? Sex differences in health risks of the widowed. *Psychological Bulletin, 93,* 279–301.

Strong, B., & DeVault, C. (1983). Inside America's new families. *Family Life Educator, 1(3),* 9–11.

Supplitt, W. (1979). Women in men's professions. Master's thesis, Sociology Department, University of Massachusetts.

Sutherland, H., & Stewart, I. (1965). A critical analysis of the premenstrual syndrome. *Lancet, 1,* 1180–83.

Sutherland, S. (1978). The unambitious female: Women's low professional aspirations. *Signs, 3,* 774–94.

Swacker, M. (1975). The sex of the speaker as a sociolinguistic variable. In B. Thorne & N. Henley (Eds.), *Language and sex.* Rowley, MA: Newbury House.

Swidler, L. (1971). Jesus was a feminist. *Catholic World, January,* 177–83.

Swidler, L. (1976). *Women in Judaism.* Metuchen, NJ: Scarecrow Press.

Swidler, L., & Swidler, A. (1977). *Women priests.* New York: Paulist Press.

Symons, D. (1979). *The evolution of human sexuality.* New York: Oxford University Press.

Szafran, R., & Austin, S. (1984). *Universities and women faculty.* New York: Praeger.

Tabory, E. (1984). Rights and rites: Women's roles in liberal religious movements in Israel. *Sex Roles, 11,* 155–66.

Talmon, Y. (1972). *Family and community in the kibbutz.* Cambridge: Harvard University Press.

Tanner, N. (1981). *Becoming human.* Cambridge: Cambridge University Press.

Tauber, M. (1979). Sex differences in parent-child interaction styles in a free-play session. *Child Development, 50,* 981–88.

Taylor, M., & Hall, J. (1982). Psychological androgyny: Theories, methods, and conclusions. *Psychological Bulletin, 92,* 347–66.

Taylor, R. (1984). Overview and current status of comparable worth. Paper presented at the Southeastern Psychological Association, New Orleans.

Tennes, K., et al. (1975). A developmental study of girls with trisomy X. *American Journal of Human Genetics, 27,* 71–80.

Tennov, D. (1975). *Psychotherapy.* New York: Abelard-Schuman.

Terman, L., & Miles, C. (1936). *Sex and personality.* New York: McGraw-Hill.

Terrien, S. (1976). Toward a biblical theology of womanhood. In R. Barnhouse & U. Holmes, III (Eds.), *Male and female* (pp. 17–27). New York: The Seabury Press.

Thomas, D. (1982). San Francisco's 1979 White Night Riot: Injustice, vengence, and beyond. In W. Paul, et al. (Eds.), *Homosexuality* (pp. 337–50). Beverly Hills, CA: Sage.

Thompson, C. (1964). *Interpersonal psychoanalysis* (M. Green, ed.). New York: Basic Books.

Thompson, Jr., H., & Gongla, P. (1983). Single-parent families. In E. Macklin & R. Rubin (Eds.), *Contemporary families and alternative lifestyles.* Beverly Hills, CA: Sage.

Thompson, S. (1975). Gender labels and early sex role development. *Child Development, 46,* 339–47.

Thorne, B. (1982). Feminist rethinking of the family: An overview. In B. Thorne (Ed.), *Rethinking the family* (pp. 1–24). New York: Longman.

Thurow, L. (1981). Why women are paid less than men. *The New York Times, March 8,* F2.

Tieger, T. (1980). On the biological basis of sex differences in aggression. *Child Development, 51,* 943–63.

Tiger, L. (1969). *Men in groups.* New York: Random House.

Tiger, L., & Fox, R. (1971). *The imperial animal.* New York: Holt, Rinehart & Winston.

Tiger, L., & Shepher, J. (1975). *Women in the kibbutz.* New York: Harcourt.

Tilly, L., & Scott, J. (1978). *Women, work and family.* New York: Holt, Rinehart & Winston.

Tinsley, E., Sullivan-Guest, S., & McGuire, J. (1984). Feminine sex role and depression in middle-aged women. *Sex Roles, 11,* 25–32.

Tobach, E., & Rosoff, B. (Eds.). (1978). *Genes and gender I.* New York: Gordian Press.

Tobias, S. (1978). *Overcoming math anxiety*. New York: Norton.

Tocqueville, A. de. (1840). *Democracy in America (Vol. 2)*. New York: J & H Langley.

Tollison, C., & Adams, H. (1979). *Sexual disorders*. New York: Gardner Press.

Tolmach, R., & Scherr, R. (1984). *Face value*. Boston: Routledge and Kegan Paul.

Tomizuka, C., & Tobias, S. (1981). Mathematical ability: Is sex a factor? *Science, 212(April 10)*, 114.

Toomer, J. (1978). Males in psychotherapy. *The Counseling Psychologist, 7(4)*, 22–25.

Touhey, J. (1974). Effects of additional women professionals on ratings of occupational prestige and desirability. *Journal of Personality and Social Psychology, 29*, 86–89.

Towson, S., & Zanna, M. (1983). Retaliation against sexual assault: Self-defense or public duty? *Psychology of Women Quarterly, 8*, 89–99.

Tresemer, D. (1976). Do women fear success? *Signs, 1*, 863–74.

Trey, J. (1972). Women in the war economy—World War II. *Review of Radical Political Economy, 4*.

Troll, L., & Bengston, V. (1979). Generations in the family. In W. Burr, et al. (Eds.), *Contemporary theories about the family*. New York: The Free Press.

Troubridge, U. (1975). *The life of Radclyffe Hall*. New York: Arno Press.

Tuchman, G. (1978). The symbolic annihilation of women by the mass media. In G. Tuchman, et al. (Eds.), *Hearth and home*. New York: Oxford University Press.

Turner, J., & Beeghley, L. (1981). *The emergence of sociological theory*. Homewood, IL: Dorsey Press.

Tyack, D. (1976). Pilgrim's progress: Toward a social history of the superintendency. *History of Education Quarterly, 32*, 263–67.

Uddenberg, N., Almgren, P., & Nilsson, A. (1971). Preference for sex of the child among pregnant women. *Journal of Biosocial Science, 3*, 267–80.

Unger, R. (1979a). Toward a redefinition of sex and gender. *American Psychologist, 34*, 1085–94.

Unger, R. (1979b). *Female and male*. New York: Harper & Row.

Unger, R. (1981). Sex as a social reality: Field and laboratory research. *Psychology of Women Quarterly, 5*, 645–53.

Unger, R. (1983). Through the looking glass: No wonderland yet! (The reciprocal relationship between methodology and models of reality). *Psychology of Women Quarterly, 8*, 9–32.

United States Bureau of the Census. (1982). *Statistical abstract of the United States: 1982-1983*. Washington, DC: U.S. Government Printing Office.

United States Commission on Civil Rights. (1977). *Window dressing on the set: Women and minorities in television*. Washington, DC: U.S. Government Printing Office.

United States Commission on Civil Rights. (1979). *Window dressing on the set: An update*. Washington, DC: U.S. Government Printing Office.

U.S. News & World Report. (1984). Battle of the sexes over "comparable worth." *February 20*, 73–74.

Valian, V., & Katz, J. (1971). The right to say "he." *Harvard Crimson, November 24*.

van den Berghe, P. (1978). *Man in society* (2nd ed.). New York: Elsevier.

Vickers, J., & Adam, J. (1977). *But can you type? Canadian universities and the status of women*. Ottawa: Clarke Irwin and Company.

Vulliamy, D. (1973). *The newborn child*. Edinburgh: Churchill Livingston.

Waber, D. (1977). Sex differences in mental abilities hemispheric lateralization and rate of physical growth at adolescence. *Developmental Psychology, 13*, 29–38.

Wadley, S. (1977). Women and the Hindu tradition. *Signs, 3*, 113–25.

Wagenvoord, J., & Bailey, J. (1978). *Men*. New York: Avon.

Wagner, S. (1984). The world anti-slavery convention of 1840: Three antisexist men take a stand. *M. 12*, 35, 41.

Walker, B. 1983. *The woman's encyclopedia of myths and secrets*. New York: Harper and Row.

Walker, L. (1977–78). Battered women and learned helplessness. *Victimology, 2*, 525–34.

Walker, L. (1979). *The battered woman*. New York: Harper & Row.

Wallace, J. (1982). Chinese men and women are equal—but men are more equal. *U.S. News & World Report, June 28*, 54.

Wallace, P. (Ed.). (1982). *Women in the workplace*. Boston: Auburn House.

Walstedt, J. (1977). The altruistic other orientation: An exploration of female powerlessness. *Psychology of Women Quarterly, 2*, 162–76.

Walstedt, J. (1978). Reform of women's roles and family structures in the recent history of China. *Journal of Marriage and the Family, 40*, 379–92.

Wardell, L., Gillespie, D., & Leffler, A. (1983). Science and violence against wives. In D. Finkelhor, et al. (Eds.), *The dark side of families* (pp. 69–84). Beverly Hills, CA: Sage.

Ware, S. (1981). *Beyond suffrage*. Cambridge: Harvard University Press.

Warner, R. (1984). Mating behavior and hermaphroditism in coral reef fishes. *American Scientist, 72(2)*, 128–36.

Weathers, D., & Lord, M. (1979). Can a Mormon support ERA? *Newsweek, December 3,* 88.

Weinberg, M., & Williams, C. (1975). *Male homosexuals.* New York: Penguin.

Weissman, M. (1980). Depression. In A. Brodsky & R. Hare-Mustin (Eds.), *Women and psychotherapy.* New York: Guilford.

Weissman, M., & Klermann, G. (1977). Sex differences in the epidemiology of depression. *Archives of General Psychiatry, 34,* 98–111.

Weissman, M. et al. (1977). Symptom pattern in primary and secondary depression. *Archives of General Psychiatry, 34,* 854–62.

Weisstein, N. (1971). Psychology constructs the female. In V. Gornick & B. Moran (Eds.), *Woman in sexist society* (pp. 207–24). New York: New American Library.

Weithorn, C. (1975). Woman's role in cross-cultural perspective. In R. Unger & F. Denmark (Eds.), *Woman* (pp. 276–96). New York: Psychological Dimensions.

Weitzman, L. (1979). *Sex role socialization.* Palo Alto, CA: Mayfield.

Weitzman, L., et al. (1972). Sex-role socialization in picture books for preschool children. *American Journal of Sociology, 77,* 1125–50.

Welch, R., et al. (1979). Subtle sex-role cues in children's commercials. *Journal of Communication, 29,* 202–9.

Welch, S. (1978). Recruitment of women to public office: A discriminant analysis. *Western Political Quarterly, 31,* 372–80.

Welter, B. (1974). The feminization of American religion: 1800–1860. In M. Hartman & L. Banner (Eds.), *Clio's consciousness-raised* (pp. 137–57). New York: Harper & Row.

West, C., & Zimmerman, D. (1977). Women's place in everyday talk: Reflections on parent-child interaction. *Social Problems, 24,* 521–29.

West, S., Whitney, G., & Schnedler, R. (1975). Helping a motorist in distress: The effects of sex, race, and neighborhood. *Journal of Personality and Social Psychology, 31,* 691–98.

Wetzel, R., et al. (1975). Premenstrual affective syndrome and affective disorder. *British Journal of Psychiatry, 127,* 219–21.

Wexler, H. (1980). Research developments: Coed practical arts. *American Education, 16,* 32–33.

White, L., & Brinkerhoff, D. (1981). The sexual division of labor: Evidence from childhood. *Social Forces, 60,* 170–81.

White, M. (1975). Women in the professions: Psychological and social barriers to women in science. In J. Freeman (Ed.), *Women* (pp. 227–37). Palo Alto, CA: Mayfield.

Wiggins, J. (1983). Family violence as a case of interpersonal aggression: A situational analysis. *Social Forces, 62,* 102–23.

Will, J., Self, P., & Datan, N. (1976). Maternal behavior and perceived sex of infant. *American Journal of Orthopsychiatry, 46,* 135–39.

Williams, J., & Miller, D. (1983). Sex-role orientation and athletic administration. *Sex Roles, 9,* 1137–48.

Williams, J., & Spitzer, R. (1983). The issue of sex bias in DSM-III: A critique of "a woman's view of DSM-III" by Marcie Kaplan. *American Psychologist, 38,* 793–98.

Williams, P. (1982). Minorities and women in sociology: An update. *ASA Footnotes, 10(9),* 6–9.

Williams, Jr., R. (1970). *American society* (3rd ed.). New York: Knopf.

Williams, S. (1978). *Riding the nightmare.* New York: Atheneum.

Williamson, N. (1976a). Sex preferences, sex control, and the status of women. *Signs, 1,* 847–62.

Williamson, N. (1976b). *Sons or daughters?* Beverly Hills, CA: Sage.

Wilson, E. (1978). *On human nature.* Cambridge: Harvard University Press.

Wilson, J. (1978). *Religion in American society.* Englewood Cliffs, NJ: Prentice-Hall.

Winslow, D. (1976). Sex and anti-sex in the early church fathers. In R. Barnhouse & U. Holmes, III (Eds.), *Male and female* (pp. 28–38). New York: The Seabury Press.

Winston, S. (1932). Birth control and the sex ratio at birth. *American Journal of Sociology, 38,* 225–31.

Wirtenberg, T., & Nakamura, C. (1976). Education: Barrier or boon to changing occupational roles of women? *Journal of Social Issues, 32,* 165–79.

Wise, E., & Rafferty, J. (1982). Sex bias in language. *Sex Roles, 8,* 1189–96.

Witkin, H., et al. (1976). Criminality in XYY and XXY men. *Science, 193,* 547–55.

Wolf, M. (1980). Uterine families and the women's community. In J. Spradley & D. McCurdy (Eds.), *Conformity and conflict* (4th ed, pp. 177–84). Boston: Little, Brown.

Wolkind, S. (1974). The component of "affectionless psychopathy" in institutionalized children. *Journal of Child Psychology and Psychiatry, 15,* 215–220.

Women voters, winners and losers. (1984). *The New York Times, November 17,* 18.

Wong, A. (1981). Planned development, social stratification, and the sexual division of labor in Singapore. *Signs, 7,* 434–52.

Wong, M. (1978). Males in transition and the self-help group. *The Counseling Psychologist, 7(4),* 46–50.

Wooley, S., & Wooley, O. (1980). Eating disorders: Obesity and anorexia. In A. Brodsky & R. Hare-Mustin (Eds.), *Women and psychotherapy.* New York: Guilford.

Yamamoto, K., & Dizney, H. (1967). Rejection of the mentally ill: A study of attitudes of student teachers. *Journal of Counseling Psychology, 14,* 264–68.

Yankelovich, D. (1974). The meaning of work. In J. Rosow (Ed.), *The worker and the job.* Englewood Cliffs, NJ: Prentice-Hall.

Yinger, M. (1982). *Counterculture.* New York: Free Press.

Yllo, K., & Straus, M. (1980). Interpersonal violence among married and cohabiting couples. *Family Coordinator, 29,* 229–35.

Zellman, G. (1978). Politics and power. In I. Frieze, et al. (Eds.), *Women and sex roles* (pp. 335–56). New York: Norton.

Zelnick, M., & Kanter, J. (1980). Sexual activity, contraceptive use and pregnancy among metropolitan-area teenagers: 1971–79. *Family Planning Perspectives, 12,* 230–37.

Zimet, S., & Zimet, C. (1977). Teachers view people: Sex-role stereotyping. *Psychological Reports, 41,* 583–91.

Zimmerman, D., & West, C. (1975). Sex roles, interruptions and silences in conversations. In B. Thorne & N. Henley (Eds.), *Language and sex.* Rowley, MA: Newbury House.

Zuckerman, M., DePaulo, B., & Rosenthal, R. (1981). Verbal and nonverbal communication of deception. In L. Berkowitz (Ed.), *Advances in experimental social psychology.* New York: Academic Press.

Zuckerman, M., et al. (1982). Masculinity-femininity and encoding of nonverbal cues. *Journal of Personality and Social Psychology, 42,* 548–56.

NAME INDEX

Bliss, E., 379
Block, J., 56, 57
Blood, R., 281
Blumberg, R., 131, 143
Blumenthal, M., 90
Blumer, H., 320
Blumstein, P., 273, 293
Bolton, B., 322
Bosa, C., 355
Boulding, E., 342
Bowker, L., 390
Bowman, K., 165
Bram, S., 284
Brandes, S., 335
Brandow, S., 144
Brannigan, G., 386
Brannon, R., 90, 311, 334, 340, 341, 342
Braunthal, H., 53
Brawley, B., 375
Brehm, S., 293
Breines, W., 376
Broderick, P., 383
Brodsky, A., 310, 313, 315
Brooks-Gunn, J., 93
Broverman, I., 58, 60, 157, 158, 193, 222, 306, 307, 308
Brown, D., 62
Brown, P., 101
Brown, R., 346
Brown, V., 380
Brown, W., 389
Browne, F., 346
Brownmiller, S., 164
Brucken, L., 386
Bruer, J., 15
Bryant, A., 264
Brzoza, M., 297
Buber, M., 162
Buchwald, A., 304
Buck, R., 193
Buhle, M., 328
Bulwer-Lytton, E., 178
Burgess, A., 165, 171
Buric, O., 375
Burke, C., 334
Burks, N., 163, 282
Burr, W., 180
Burt, M., 164
Burtle, V., 385
Busby, L., 99
Busch, W., 271
Buss, A., 13, 19
Buss, D., 162
Butcher, J., 376
Butler, M., 98

Byrne, D., 170, 222
Calderwood, A., 294
Caldicott, 362, 363
Callender, C., 137–38
Calvin, J., 248
Cantor, M., 99
Caplan, P., 69
Capra, F., 367
Carlsson, M., 143
Carmen, B., 193
Carmen, E., 376
Carpenter, E., 344
Carson, R., 376
Carter, D., 312
Carter, G., 36
Carter, J., 190
Carter, R., 264
Cartwright, D., 150
Casper, R., 303
Castrilli, H., 226–27
Cater, L., 375
Cato, 288
Catt, C., 329
Cauwels, J., 303
Cerullo, M., 44
Chafe, W., 329
Chafetz, J., 214
Chambless, D., 301
Chapman, J., 281
Chapman, M. W., 255
Chappell, D., 164
Chase-Lansdale, L., 386
Chassie, M., 379
Check, J., 166
Cherlin, A., 215, 259
Cherry, F., 165
Chesler, P., 179, 298, 300, 301, 306, 307, 308, 314
Chesno, F., 305
Child, L. M., 255
Chino, A., 304
Chodorow, N., 14, 44, 70
Christ, C., 376
Christensen, A., 27
Clark, M., 374
Clark, R., 383
Clore, G., 157
Cohen, Y., 380
Cole, C., 179
Cole, J., 379, 389
Coleman, J., 103, 302, 305
Collins, G., 296
Collins, M. L., 256
Collins, R., 109
Colwill, N., 156
Conaty, J., 386

Condry, J., 188
Condry, S., 188
Conger, J., 389
Conn, J., 72
Connell, N., 169
Constantinople, A., 63, 67, 73–76, 78, 79
Cook, K., 93
Cook, M., 202
Coombs, C., 354
Coombs, L., 377
Cooney, J. G., 173
Cooper, P., 304
Corea, G., 357, 363
Corriveau, D., 389
Costar, J., 307
Cott, N., 276, 323
Crisp, A., 303
Croll, E., 139
Crosby, F., 185, 191
Crowley, J., 221
Cullen, R., 136
Cunningham, S., 275
Curtin, K., 141
Dachowski, M., 301
Dahlberg, F., 130, 277
Dahlstrom, E., 142
Dahrendorf, R., 109
Dalton, K., 42
Daly, M., 211
Daniels, A., 114
Daniels, M., 264
Daniloff, N., 140
Darcy, R., 264
Darden, E., 8
Darley, J., 63
Darwin, C., 24, 123–24
Dary, J., 395
Datan, N., 93
David, D., 334
Davidson, C., 308, 313
Davidson, J., 36
Davis, A., 96
Davis, E., 146
Davis, J., 217
Davis, L., 388
Dayhoff, S., 377
Dayley, L., 376
Deaux, K., 59, 60, 66, 159
DeBold, J., 34
Deborah, 239
De Cecco, J., 311
Deckard, B., 203, 327, 328, 329, 330, 333, 346, 347
Delaney, J., 41

Del Boca, F., 57
Delilah, 239
Denmark, F., 380
DePaulo, B., 397
Derlega, V., 190
Deutsch, H., 69
DeVault, C., 268, 286
Devore, I., 269
Diamond, M., 52
Dienstbier, R., 389
Dinnerstein, D., 14
Dion, K., 302
Dipboye, R., 157
Dittes, J., 170
Dizney, H., 305, 397
Dobash, R., 289, 293
Dodge, N., 139
Doell, R., 15
Doering, C., 37, 41
Dohrenwend, B., 298
Dokecki, P., 308
Dominick, J., 47, 98
Donahue, T., 307
Donnerstein, E., 170
Douglas, A., 378
Douglass, J., 378
Doyle, J., 90, 94, 113, 154, 167, 170,
    192, 213, 222, 290, 306, 320, 334,
    342, 347
Drinkwater, B., 49
Duberman, L., 382
DuBois, E., 326
Duncan, B., 275
Duncan, O., 275
Durkheim, E., 280, 281
Dweck, C., 102, 159
Dworkin, A., 164, 170, 264, 333
Dye, N., 378
Eagly, A., 59, 60
Eakins, B., 188, 191–92, 197
Eakins, R., 188, 191–92, 197
Eckert, E., 391
Eckholm, E., 269
Edelsky, C., 188
Ehrenkranz, J., 379
Ehrenreich, B., 347
Ehrhardt, A., 26, 27, 30
Eichler, M., 17
Eisenstein, Z., 333
Eisenstock, B., 99
Eisler, R., 379
Eitzen, S., 209
Eleftheriow, B., 389
El Guindi, F., 132
Elizabeth I., 252

Elizando, V., 379
Elliot, R., 101
Elshtain, J., 176, 177, 197
Emswiller, T., 159
Engels, F., 108, 138
England, P., 219
Epstein, C., 113, 204, 219, 223, 225
Erhardt, A., 374
Ericksen, E., 379
Ericksen, J., 275
Erickson, B., 185
Ernest, M., 181
Esther, 239
Estler, S., 206
Etheredge, L., 335
Eve, 239, 241, 267
Exline, R., 194
Fagot, B., 93
Fairburn, C., 303, 304
Falbo, T., 154
Faragher, J., 276
Farah, B., 379, 384
Farley, J., 230
Farrel, M., 113, 311
Farrell, W., 90
Farris, E., 377
Fasteau, M., 91, 335
Faux, M., 293
Fazio, R., 63, 377
Feather, N., 178
Feinbloom, D., 53
Feldberg, R., 221
Feldman, S., 81
Fennema, E., 81
Fernberger, S., 58
Fernea, E., 132
Fernea, R., 132
Ferrante, J., 321
Feshback, S., 388
Fidell, L., 309
Field, M., 140
Fields, R., 290, 306
Fierke, K., 375
Filene, P., 335
Fillmer, H., 180
Finkelhor, D., 287
Finkler, K., 379
Fiorenza, E., 263
Fischer, J., 194
Fishbein, M., 151
Fisher, J., 195, 379
Fisher, W., 170
Fishman, P., 177–78
Fiske, E., 203
Flammang, J., 263

Flexner, E., 203
Flora, C., 387
Flynn, K., 140
Ford, B., 264
Forden, C., 195
Forgey, D., 137
Forisha, B., 224, 230
Fox, C., 37
Fox, G., 107, 363
Fox, R., 43–44, 296
Frances, S., 379
Franck, K., 65
Frank, R., 41–42
Franken, M., 111, 202
Franks, V., 313
Franzwa, H., 100
Fraser, A., 347
Frazier, N., 230
Freeman, I., 258
Freeman, J., 223–24, 332
Freimuth, M., 9
French, J., 151–53
Freud, S., 65, 67–70, 73–74, 78, 79, 164
Freudiger, P., 95
Friday, N., 166
Friedan, B., 332, 364–65
Friedl, E., 130
Friedman, A., 384
Friedman, R., 389
Frieze, I., 75, 195, 196
Frodi, A., 15, 57
Fromkin, H., 378
Frost, F., 114
Fruch, T., 99
Fulton, O., 207
Funabiki, D., 304
Gadlin, H., 13
Gadpaille, W., 8, 52
Gaebelein, J., 57
Gagnon, J., 163
Galdston, R., 290
Gardiner, A., 379
Gardner, J., 96, 307
Garfinkel, H., 110
Garfinkel, P., 303
Garfunkel, A., 349
Garner, D., 303
Garnets, L., 359
Garrett, C., 15
Garrison, D., 380
Garrison, H., 219
Garvey, C., 62
Gates, M., 281
Gautier, T., 384
Gayford, J., 271
Gazzaniga, M., 35

Hyde, J., 56, 57
Hyman, H., 202
Ibsen, H., 276, 383
Iglitzin, L., 375
Imperato-McGinley, J., 52
Ingle, G., 13
Inglis, J., 35–36
Interrante, J., 340
Izraeli, D., 144
Jacklin, C., 37, 51, 54, 55–57, 71, 79, 80, 158
Jackson, M., 207
Jackson, P., 202
Jacobs, P., 27
Jacobs, S., 137
Jacobson, L., 101
Jacobson, M., 167
Jago, A., 162
Jakubowski, P., 311
Janeway, E., 51, 320
Janowsky, D., 42
Janssen-Jurreit, M., 334
Jeffries-Fox, S., 99
Jennings, M., 384
Jennings (Walstedt), J., 98, 99
Jesser, C., 163
Jesus, 242–43
Jezebel, 239
Johnson, A., 167
Johnson, M., 161, 312
Johnson, P., 154–56, 196, 308
Johnson, S., 159
Jones, E., 380
Jones, H., 28
Jones, J., 207
Jones, M., 328
Jorgensen, C., 53
Jose, P., 377
Jourard, S., 90, 189
Jusenius, C., 220
Kagen, J., 389
Kahn, A., 150, 170, 172, 186
Kalisch, B., 98
Kalisch, P., 98
Kamin, L., 46
Kaminer, W., 170
Kaneko, J., 328
Kanner, L., 72
Kanowitz, L., 180, 281, 347
Kanter, J., 163
Kanter, R., 161, 222, 230
Kaplan, A., 79
Kaplan, M., 300–301, 358
Karlen, A., 52
Kasl, 377
Kass, F., 301
Kataami, L., 134–35

Katchadourian, H., 53
Katz, J., 198, 344
Katz, M., 206
Katz, P., 393
Kaufman, A., 165
Kaufman, P., 206
Kaufmann-McCall, K., 334
Keddie, N., 132
Kelber, M., 373
Keller, E., 13, 14, 15
Kelley, H., 171, 283
Kelly, J., 305
Kelly, M., 129
Kempe, C., 171
Kempe, R., 171
Kemper, S., 185
Kennard, J., 209, 345
Kennedy, J., 5, 329
Kenworthy, J., 394
Keohane, N., 263
Kerber, L., 385
Kern-Daniels, R., 7
Kessler, R., 285
Kessler, S., 8, 15
Ketter, P., 385
Key, M., 96, 179
Khomeini, R., 134
Kiesler, S., 391
Kilmann, P., 305
Kilson, M., 208
Kimble, G., 66
Kimmel, E., 208
King, D., 304, 321
King, M., 385
Kingston, M., 137
Kinroy, B., 313
Kinsbourne, M., 36
Kipnis, D., 160, 161–62, 171
Kirchner, R., 290
Kirkpatrick, J., 260
Kirkpatrick, M., 386
Kirsh, B., 311
Klein, J. D., 172
Klein, V., 142
Klerman, G., 304
Klinman, D., 293
Knox, J., 249
Koch, S., 10
Kochems, L., 137–38
Koeske, R., 41
Kohl, R., 293
Kohlberg, L., 72–73, 79, 359–60
Kohlstedt, S., 15
Kohn, M., 94
Kolata, G., 81
Kolbe, R., 96
Komarovsky, M., 163, 189, 273

Komisar, L., 98
Koo, H., 286
Koop, C., 386
Koufacos, C., 394
Kraditor, A., 255, 386
Kramer, C., 185, 187
Kreps, J., 261
Kreuz, L., 41
Kristeva, J., 137
Krulewitz, J., 166, 170
Kuhn, D., 14, 19, 60
Kukla, A., 11, 14
Kunin, M., 256
Kutner, N., 92, 207, 208
Kyle, P., 264
Lacy, W., 207, 208
LaFrance, M., 193
Lakoff, R., 185, 191
Lamb, M., 92, 142, 272, 296
Lamm, B., 340
Lamphere, L., 130
Lamson, P., 386
Lang, L., 391
Lanier, S., 313
Lanir, S., 389
Lansing, M., 374
Lansky, L., 381
Lapidus, G., 140
LaPlante, M., 164
La Rose, R., 114
Lauer, R., 386
Laurenzo, N., 173
Laurikietis, R., 201, 202
Lauritsen, J., 344
Lavine, L., 190
LaVoie, J., 96
Laws, J., 214
Lawson, J., 35–36
Lear, M., 386
Leavitt, R., 130, 133
Lederer, L., 170
Lee, A., 376
Lee, R., 269
Lefcourt, H., 158
Leffler, A., 113
Lefkowitz, A., 230
Leghorn, L., 230
LeGuin, U., 6
Lehne, G., 386
Lehne, S., 381
Leiss, W., 386
Lemons, J., 329
Lenin, V., 139
Leo, J., 178, 185
Lerner, G., 386
Leserman, J., 206

Levant, R., 296
Levin, E., 386
Levin, H., 393
Levin, S., 310
Levin, W., 124
Levine, E., 325, 329
Levine, J., 386
Levinson, R., 92
Levitan, T., 377
Levy, J., 387
Levy, N., 313
Lewin-Epstein, N., 212
Lewis, A., 259
Lewis, E., 81
Lewis, L., 59, 60
Lewis, M., 92
Lewontin, R., 46
Lickona, T., 385
Lieblich, A., 144
Lilith, 266–67
Lilly, C., 184
Lindahl, E., 355
Lindholm, C., 387
Linimon, D., 379
Linton, R., 389
Lipman-Blumen, J., 171, 270
Lips, H., 171
Lipton, F., 296
Lipton, J., 185
Locksley, A., 59
Lombardo, J., 190
Lombardo, W., 15
Longin, E., 297
Longin, M., 297
Longino, H., 15
Lopata, H., 7, 85, 89, 272, 276
Lorber, J., 224
Lord, M., 250
Lothstein, L., 54
Lott, B., 114, 157, 358
Love, B., 346
Lovejoy, F., 207
Luckmann, T., 19
Luepton, L., 114
Lumsden, C., 46
Lunde, D., 53
Lunney, C., 92
Lupton, M., 377
Luria, Z., 34
Luther, M., 248
Lutterman, K., 379
Lyles, J., 250
Lynn, N., 258, 259, 260, 261
Lyon, L., 218
Lyon, P., 346
Macaulay, J., 379
McCauley, C., 57

Maccoby, E., 37, 51, 54, 55–57, 71, 79, 80, 158
McConnell, E., 322
McCormack, L., 379
McCormick, N., 163, 164
McCullough, B., 383
McCurdy, D., 199
McGaw, B., 381
McGhee, P., 99
McGinnies, E., 159
McGrady, M., 283
McGrath, C., 289
McGuigan, D., 379
McGuinness, D., 231–32
McGuire, J., 395
McKee, J., 58
McKenna, W., 8
McKinley, J., 65
Macklin, E., 395
McLaughlin, E., 247, 248, 250
McLaughlin, S., 219
Macleod, D., 388
MacLusky, N., 52
McRae, J., 285
Maimon, A., 143
Malamuth, N., 166, 170
Mamonova, T., 145
Mandelbaum, D., 205
Mann, J., 259
Mao, T., 141
Marecek, J., 358
Marini, M., 212
Markle, G., 354
Marotta, T., 345
Marshall, D., 123
Marshall, S., 388
Martha, 243, 245
Martin, D., 345, 346
Martin, J., 380
Martin, K., 130, 145
Martin, R., 188
Martyna, W., 388
Marx, K., 108, 138–39, 238
Mary, 243, 245
Mary I, 252
Maslin, A., 388
Masling, J., 313
Matthews, W., 79
Mauss, A., 320
Mayes, S., 96, 172
Mayo, C., 193
Mazumdar, V., 132
Mead, G., 110
Mead, M., 388
Mednick, M., 143
Mednick, S., 388
Mehrabian, A., 194

Meir, G., 144
Mernissi, F., 133
Merritt, S., 260
Merton, R., 63, 86–87
Messenger, J., 122
Meyer, J., 54
Meyer-Bahlburg, H., 388
Midgley, M., 347
Miles, C., 65
Milk, H., 345
Miller, D., 65, 211
Miller, J., 219, 286
Millett, K., 69
Milunsky, A., 355
Minton, C., 93
Minuchin, S., 303
Mirels, H., 190
Miriam, 239
Mischel, W., 70, 79
Mitchell, J., 70
Moberg, V., 384
Model, S., 275
Modleski, T., 95
Moldofsky, H., 303
Mondale, W., 259
Money, J., 8, 9, 26, 27, 28, 30, 46, 52, 53, 84, 334–35
Montagu, A., 24, 46
Monti, P., 37
Moore, R., 94
Moran, B., 374, 386
Morgan, M., 264
Morgan, R., 136, 366
Morris, J., 53
Morris, N., 45
Morrow, L., 236
Morrs, E., 327
Moses, 239
Mott, L., 325
Mowbray, C., 306, 313
Moyer, K., 37
Mueller, M., 137
Murdock, G., 128–31
Mussen, P., 103
Myrdal, A., 142, 274
Nadelman, L., 94
Naftolin, F., 52
Nagel, T., 379
Nakamura, C., 202
Narus, L., 194
Nash, J., 130
Nash, S., 89
Neal, M., 389
Nelson, E., 171
Nelson, R., 186
Nettleship, P., 174
Newcombe, N., 185

Newman, L., 54
Newton, E., 346
Nichols, J., 343
Nicholson, J., 349
Nielsen, J., 27
Nigg, J., 207
Nightingale, F., 317
Nilsen, A., 179
Nilsson, A., 396
Niswander, K., 394
Noel, B., 27
Nogarola, I., 321, 322
Norgren, J., 390
Norton, M., 253, 254
Nye, F., 272
Nye, I., 94
O'Brient, J., 287, 292
O'Connor, S., 256
O'Driscoll, M., 379
Oldham, J., 93
O'Leary, S., 45
Olein, M., 138
Oleshansky, B., 382
O'Neill, T., 261
O'Neill, W., 303
Orkinsky, D., 315
Orne, M., 12
Ounsted, C., 391
Owen, D., 390
Owen, M., 386
Pagelow, M., 291
Pagels, E., 246
Paige, K., 41, 132
Paine, T., 179
Paisley, W., 98
Paludi, M., 157, 185
Panek, P., 219
Papanek, H., 132
Parke, R., 45
Parker, K., 230
Parlee, M., 15, 16, 42
Parson, J., 75
Parsons, T., 106-7, 181
Parvey, C., 243, 245, 246
Pasteur, L., 317
Paul, W., 395
Pauly, I., 54
Payer, M., 19
Payne, E., 166
Payton, I., 286
Pearson, J., 191, 192, 195, 197
Peck, E., 88
Pennington, V., 390
Peplau, L., 108, 162, 163
Perrucci, C., 390
Perry, L., 278
Persky, H., 37, 41, 42

Perum, P., 230
Peterson, C., 353
Peterson, E., 329
Peterson, J., 353
Peterson, R., 384
Petty, R., 190
Pfeiffer, J., 270
Phares, E., 159
Phelps, L., 90
Pheterson, G., 257, 185
Phoenix, C., 30
Piaget, J., 71-73
Piliavin, J., 188
Pines, M., 45
Pingree, S., 99
Pizzey, E., 286
Plaskow, J., 376
Pleck, E., 272, 273, 274, 278, 287, 290,
    334, 335, 340, 342, 349, 359
Pleck, J., 275, 276, 293, 335
Pohlman, E., 353
Polani, P., 26
Pomazal, R., 157
Pope, A., 181
Pope, K., 224
Popovich, P., 167
Porter, N., 380
Potter, H., 390
Prestage, J., 387
Prial, F., 219
Pribram, K., 231
Priscilla, 245
Ptacek, J., 391
Pyle, R., 391
Pyle, S., 303, 304
Pythagoras, 181
Quinn, J., 228
Quinn, R., 377
Rabin, A., 143
Rabiner, S., 115
Rachel, 241
Radin, N., 95
Radloff, L., 304
Rafferty, J., 307
Ramsey, S., 195
Rapp, J., 380
Raskin, R., 53
Rau, L., 394
Rauch, G., 97
Raven, B., 151-53
Rawlings, E., 312
Ray, D., 256
Read, M., 147-48
Reagan, R., 256, 258, 259, 333
Rebecca, W., 382
Reed, B., 310
Regan, M., 204

Reichsman, F., 377
Reid, M., 36
Reigel, D., 391
Reinartz, K., 100
Remick, H., 227, 230
Rent, C., 353
Rent, G., 353
Reter, D., 54
Reynolds, R., 268
Rheingold, H., 93
Rhoads, A., 251, 391
Rhoads, D., 391
Richards, R., 53
Richardson, M., 380
Rideau, W., 165
Riger, S., 169
Robbins, J., 310
Roberts, A., 26
Roberts, H., 19
Robey, A., 394
Robinson, J., 275
Rodman, H., 272
Rodney, T., 374
Rogan, A., 44
Rogers, L., 34
Rohrbaugh, J., 298
Roland, A., 382
Roland, H., 204
Rorvik, D., 355
Rosaldo, M., 130, 144
Rose, R., 386
Rose, S., 46
Rosen, E., 65
Rosenberg, S., 113
Rosenfeld, A., 42, 305
Rosenkrantz, P., 58-59
Rosenthal, R., 12, 13, 101
Rosenwald, R., 394
Rosman, B., 389
Rosoff, B., 7
Ross, D., 374
Ross, N., 256
Ross, R., 375
Ross, S., 374
Rossi, A., 22, 24, 42, 89, 263, 294-95
Rossi, P., 292
Rothblum, E., 385
Rotter, J., 158, 161
Rounsaville, B., 291
Rowbotham, S., 178-79, 233, 344
Roy, M., 394
Royko, M., 348
Rubenstein, C., 285
Rubin, J., 92, 285
Rubin, R., 395
Rubin, Z., 390

SUBJECT INDEX

Feminism
    from 1830 to 1920, 254–55
    men and, 348
    during Middle Ages, 321–23
Feminism—Are We Ready for a
        Second Stage?, Point/
        Counterpoint, 364–65
Feminist-oriented social science,
        proposal for, 16–18
Feminist therapy, 312
File clerks, percentage women, 220
Fillers, as communication strategy,
        192
Franck Drawing Completion Test, 65
Functionalist perspective, on general
        roles, 106–8
The Game, reading, 199–200
Gatekeepers, and women in
        workplace, 223–24
Gay Rights Movement, 343–47
Gender
    anthropological aspects of, 122–45
    differences
        evidence of, 56–57
        myths of, 55
    and education, 201–11
    and family, 268–97
    identity
        defined, 52
        transsexualism, 52–54
    and language and
            communication, 176–200
    masculinity and femininity
        androgynous conception of,
            66–67
        as muddy concepts, 63–64
        multilevel conception of, 65
        simple conception of, 64–65
    and mental health, 298–313
    and politics, 251–62
    and power, 150–75
    psychological theories on
            development of, 67–78
    and religion, 236–51
    roles in family and, 270–80
    and sex, 9
    and social movements, 320–50
    sociological aspects of, 85–121
    stages of development of, 25
    stereotypes
        behavior according to, 62–63
        learning, 62
        term defined, 58
        "typical" men and women,
            58–61

study of, and bias, 13–18
    and work, 214–35
Gender differences on issues, 258
Gender gap, in politics, 256–59
Genital stage, psychosexual
        development, 68
God as female, 246
Gynosperm, 25–26
Hermaphroditism, 7, 32
He's a Feminist, But . . . , box item,
        336–38
Heterosexual relationships, and
        power, 162–64
Hidden curriculum, 202
Historical Changes Affecting the
        Views of Women's Mental
        Health, reading, 316–17
Hormones
    and abnormal development,
        29–34
    and Adam principle, 28–29
    and emotional expression, 36–37,
        41
    and premenstrual syndrome, 41
HOT DOG (Humanitarians Opposed
        to Degrading Our Girls),
        264
Househusbands, 283–84
Housework and childcare, as female
        responsibility, 273–76
Hunting, and division of labor,
        269–70
Husband and father gender roles,
        271–75
Hwame, among Mohave Indians, 138
H-Y antigen, 28
Identification concept, and theory of
        gender development, 67
Ignoring female, and linguistic
        sexism, 179–80
Imitation, and gender development,
        71
India, male dominance in, 132
Informational power, 151, 153, 155
Inis Berg island, sexual relationship
        on, 122
In Sports, Lions vs. Tigers, reading,
        49–50
Instrumental leader, defined, 106–7
Interdependency, and members of
        groups, 106
International Ladies Garment
        Workers Union, 327
Jewish history, women in, 241–42
Job segregation, by gender, 219–26

Judeo-Christian traditions and
        values, 238–39
Kibbutzim, gender roles in, 143–44
Kinder, Kuche, and Kriche, 277
Klinefelter's syndrome, 26–27
Kuwait Women: The Exception to the
        Rule, box item, 134–35
Labia, 29
Language and communication
    nonverbal
        body position and posture,
            195–97
        emotions and gender, 192–93
        eye contact, 194
        female skill in, 193–94
        touch, 194–95
    verbal
        chatter differences, female-
            male, 188
        conversational differences,
            male-female, 177–78
        defining female, 178, 180–81
        deprecating female, 181, 185
        ignoring female, 179–80
        language strategies, 190–92
        linguistic sexism, 178–85
        male-female language
            patterns, 185–90
        talking about self, female-male
            differences, 189–90
Language-humanness linkage, 269
Latent stage, psychosexual
        development, 68
Lawyers and judges, percentage
        women, 220
Learned helplessness
    defined, 102
    and domestic violence, 291
Left hemisphere, brain, 35
Legitimate power, 151, 153, 154
Lengthening requests, as
        communication strategy,
        191–92
Lesbian rights, 345–47
Libido, 36
Librarians, archivists, and curators,
        percentage women, 220
Life and physical scientists,
        percentage women, 220
Linguistic sexism, 178–85
Locus of control, and power, 158–59
Loss of interest, and depression, 304

during Revolutionary period, 252–54

situational barriers to women, 261–62

women in, 252–59

Polygyny, in Islamic cultures, 132–33

Postal carriers, percentage women, 220

POW (Protect Our Women), 264

Power

coercive, 151, 152, 154

competence versus helplessness, 157

and communication, 177, 178

contempt and, 161–62

continuing debate over, 172

and courtship game, 163–64

defined, 151

dimensions of, 156

direct versus indirect, 155–56

and domestic violence, 292–93

expert, 151, 153, 154–55

gender differences in use of, 154–55

informational, 151, 153, 155

intimate relationships and, 162–64

locus of control, 158–59

metamorphic effects of, 160–62

and morality change, 161

pleasant effects of holding, 159–60

rape and, 164–67, 169–70

and sense of autonomy, 157–58

strategies in use of, 155–57

types of, 151, 152–53

women on, 173–74

Precision machine operatives, percentage women, 220

Prejudice, against women in workplace, 222–23

Premenstrual syndrome (PMS), 41–42

President's Commission on the Status of Women, 330

Print media, as socializing agent, 95–96

Probability judgments, male-female stereotypes, 61

Progesterone, 41

Prostate gland, 29

Protandry and protogyny, 8

Provocative woman, and domestic violence, 291

Psychological Frontiers for Men, reading, 349–51

Psychological theories, gender development

cognitive-developmental, gender roles, 71–73

psychoanalytic-identification, 67–70

sex-role-as-rule model, 73–76

sex role strain model, 70–71

social-learning theory, 70–71

Psychopathic personality, 305

Psychosexual development, stages of, 67–68

Publication bias, 13

Purdah, in Islamic cultures, 132

Qualifiers, as communication strategy, 191

A Quantum Leap in Feminist Theory, reading, 366–71

Radicals, in women's movement, 331–32

Raising a Boy as a Girl, reading, 81–84

Rape

and power, 164–66

problems in reporting, 166–67

as social concern, 167, 169–70

Readings

The Boys' Dormitory, 147–48

The Coming of Lilith, 266–67

The Game, 199–200

Historical Changes Affecting the View of Women's Mental Health, 316–17

The Issue of the 80s, 233–35

Parley Explores the Father's Role, 296–97

Psychological Frontiers for Men, 349–51

A Quantum Leap in Feminist Theory, 366–71

Raising a Boy as a Girl, 81–84

In Sports, Lions vs. Tigers, 49–50

The Story of X, 116–21

What If?, 20–21

Women Speak Out about Having Power, 173–74

Real-estate agents and brokers, percentage women, 220

Redstockings, 332

Referent power, 151, 152, 154

Registered nurses, dietitians, and therapists, percentage women, 220

Religion

contemporary, and women, 249–51

defined, 237

early Christian church, 245–49

functions of, 237–38

women in New Testament, 242–45

women in Old Testament, 238–42

Researcher bias, 11–12

Revolutionary period, women's involvement in, 252–54

Reward power, 151, 152, 154

Right hemisphere, brain, 35

Role conflicts, and women in workplace, 225–26

"Sacralization" of motherhood, 279–80

Sales clerks, retail trade, percentage women, 220

Science, bias in, 14–16

Scientific bias, 10–11

Scrotum, 29

Secondary school teachers, percentage women, 220

Second Great Awakening, 254

Secretaries, percentage women, 220

Selective abortion, 355–56

Self-disclosure, male-female differences, 189–90

Self-esteem, and power, 161

Self-fulfilling prophesy, and gender stereotypes, 63

Self-reliant element, as male gender norm, 91

Seminal vesicles, 29

Senders and receivers, nonverbal communication, 193–94

Seneca Falls Convention, 1848, 325

Sex

defined, 7

dichotomy inference, 7–8

differences and prenatal development, 24–28

unchangeable inference, 8–9

Sex bias, and therapy and counseling, 306–9

Sexism

in classroom, 204–5

in language, 178–85

linguistic, 178, 180–81

Sex reassignment surgery, 53–54